Civil Procedure in Singapore

Civil Procedure in Singapore

Fourth Edition

Chen Siyuan
Eunice Chua Hui Han

This book was originally published as a monograph in the International Encyclopaedia of Laws/Civil Procedure.

Founding Editor: Roger Blanpain
General Editor: Frank Hendrickx
Volume Editor: Wannes Vandenbussche

Wolters Kluwer

Published by:
Kluwer Law International B.V.
PO Box 316
2400 AH Alphen aan den Rijn
The Netherlands
E-mail: international-sales@wolterskluwer.com
Website: lrus.wolterskluwer.com

Sold and distributed by:
Wolters Kluwer Legal & Regulatory U.S.
7201 McKinney Circle
Frederick, MD 21704
United States of America
E-mail: customer.service@wolterskluwer.com

ISBN 978-94-035-3821-1

e-Book: ISBN 978-94-035-3822-8
web-PDF: ISBN 978-94-035-3823-5

The Authors

Chen Siyuan and Eunice Chua are a husband and wife tag-team, and this work represents their latest collaboration in law. They first met in the law faculty of National University of Singapore (NUS), and along the way attended the University of Toronto together on a yearlong exchange programme in 2006. Their first collaboration in law was to participate in the Philip C. Jessup Moot (Jessup Moot) in their final year, and their team reached the international semi-finals in Washington DC and was also a recipient of the Alona E. Evans Award for best-written submissions.

They both graduated from NUS in 2007 with First Class Honours in Law. Eunice was also awarded the NUS Undergraduate Scholarship and won various prizes for top first-year student, the Asia Cup Moot championship, and the prize for best Singapore Law Review Law Symposium article, while Siyuan won the Public Law and Jurisprudence prizes and was awarded the Kwa Geok Choo and Allen & Overy-Shook Lin & Bok Scholarships. They completed the local bar examinations in 2007, with Eunice topping the cohort. Between 2007 and 2009, they worked in the

Supreme Court of Singapore as Justices' Law Clerks for various Court of Appeal and High Court Judges, and also had stints as Assistant Registrars, hearing matters on civil procedure and personal bankruptcy. During that period, Siyuan also taught the Evidence and International Legal Process courses at NUS and the Legal Research & Writing course (LRW) at Singapore Management University (SMU).

In 2009, they attended Harvard University on fully paid scholarships for their LLM. Thereafter, Siyuan joined SMU on a full-time basis as an Assistant Professor of Law, while Eunice resumed duties as an Assistant Registrar of the Supreme Court of Singapore (with a focus on civil procedure, probate, crime, and building and construction, financial, and complex commercial matters) and was also appointed as a Magistrate of the Subordinate Courts of Singapore (as they were then known) and to the Secretariat of the Disciplinary Tribunal. In 2014, Eunice was seconded to the Singapore International Mediation Centre (SIMC), where she assumed the role of Deputy Chief Executive Officer and helped build the organization from ground up. She then joined SMU as an Assistant Professor of Law in 2016.

Siyuan's current teaching and research interests lie in Evidence & Procedure, and he has published in journals such as International Journal of Evidence & Proof, Civil Justice Quarterly, and the International Commentary on Evidence, and is the lead author for the most recent Singapore textbooks on evidence law, civil procedure, and family procedure. As for Eunice, while she has since taken on the role as CEO of the Financial Disputes Resolution Centre, she still maintains a teaching and research role at SMU. As an accredited mediator, she also has various publications, ranging from book chapters for the Singapore Academy of Law to journal pieces in the Singapore Academy of Law Journal and Asian Journal of Mediation.

Siyuan and Eunice are particularly united in their passion in grooming and coaching mooters, and recent achievements of the international moots programme they had initiated in SMU in 2009 include the Philip C. Jessup team reaching back-to-back championship finals of the international rounds in 2013 and 2014 and the Asia Cup, LawAsia, and Monroe E. Price teams winning dozens of championships between them. In 2015, SMU became the first university to reach the championship final of both the Willem C. Vis and Willem C. Vis East moots in the same year, and won the latter; in 2016, the university would reach both championship finals again. With wins in other major competitions such as the International Criminal Court Moot, SMU international mooters recorded the best-ever moot seasons in international mooting history between 2014 and 2021.

This work is dedicated to their families, their two children Timothy and Joy, and God, whose love and patience sustains them. Personal thanks also go to Associate Professor Goh Yihan. Special thanks go to Geraldine Kuah (JD), who provided tremendous assistance in the extensive proofreading, research, and rewriting in our very first update to this monograph, an endeavour which rendered subsequent updates much more manageable. We also thank Nicholas Poon for his help in refreshing the Part on Arbitration for the second update and Chow Zi En and Terence Yeo for their help with the general research and proofreading in subsequent editions. All errors, however, remain the principal authors'.

Table of Contents

List of Abbreviations

A & E	Adolphus & Ellis
AC	Appeal Cases
ADR	Alternative Dispute Resolution
A-G	Attorney-General
AGC	Attorney-General's Chambers
ALR	Australian Law Reports
All ER	All England Law Reports
AMA	Arbitration-Mediation-Arbitration
App Cas	Appeal Cases
ASEAN	Association of Southeast Asian Nations
BLE	Board of Legal Education
C.f./c.f.	*Confer/confer*
CA	Court of Appeal
Cap.	Chapter
CAPS	Counselling and Psychological Services
CDR	Court Dispute Resolution
CEDAW	Convention on the Elimination of all Forms of Discrimination against Women
Ch	Chancery
Ch D	Chancery Division
Civ J Q	Civil Justice Quarterly
CJC	Civil Justice Commission
CLAS	Criminal Legal Aid Scheme
CMC	Community Mediation Centre
CMU	Community Mediation Unit
Co	Company
Const LJ	Construction Law Journal
Corp	Corporation
CP Rep	Civil Procedure Law Reports
d/o	daughter of

List of Abbreviations

D & L	Dowling & Lownde's Bail Court Reports
DAG	Deputy Attorney-General
DART	Digital Audio Recording and Transcription
Dow PR	Dow's House of Lords Cases
DPC	Dowling's Practice Cases
DTS	Digital Transcription System
e-PD	Electronic Practice Directions
E & P	International Journal of Evidence & Proof
EFS	Electronic Filing System
EWCA Civ	England and Wales Court of Appeal (Civil)
Exch	Exchequer
Fam	Law Reports Family Division
FDR Conference	Family Dispute Resolution Conference
FJC	Family Justice Courts
FLR	Family Law Reports
FSR	Fleet Street Reports
GDP	Gross Domestic Product
HKLR	Hong Kong Law Reports
HKLRD	Hong Kong Law Reports & Digest
ICE	International Commentary on Evidence
ICR	Industrial Cases Reports
iELS	Integrated Electronic Litigation System or eLitigation
Intl Comm Evid	International Commentary on Evidence
Intl J Evid & Proof	International Journal of Evidence & Proof
Intl R L	International Review of Law
IP	Intellectual Property
KB	King's Bench
KIR	Knight's Industrial Reports
LAWASIA J	LAWASIA Journal
Law Soc	Law Society
LLC	Limited Liability Company
LLP	Limited Liability Partnership
Lloyd's Rep	Lloyd's Law Reports
LJ Ch	Law Journal Chancery
LR App Cas	Law Report Appeal Cases
LR Ch App	Law Report Chancery Appeal Cases
LR Eq	Law Report Equity Cases
LR P & D	Law Report Probate and Divorce Cases
LSC	Legal Service Commission

LT	Law Times
Ltd	Limited
Mal LR	Malaya Law Review
MC	Malayan Cases
MCST	Management Corporation Strata Title
MinLaw	Ministry of Law
MLJ	Malayan Law Journal
MNC	Multinational Corporation
MOU	Memorandum of Understanding
NLJ	New Law Journal
No	Number
NSWLR	New South Wales Law Reports
NUJSLR	National University of Juridical Sciences Law Review
NUS	National University of Singapore
O	Order
OR	Ontario Reports
OUCLJ	Oxford University Commonwealth Law Journal
PC	Privy Council
PD	Practice Directions
PDRC	Primary Dispute Resolution Centre
PIQR	Personal Injury and Quantum Reports
PPP	Purchasing Power Parity
Pte Ltd	Private Limited
QB	Queen's Bench
QBD	Queen's Bench Division
QC	Queen's Counsel
QFLP	Qualifying Foreign Law Practice
R. or R/r/rr	Rule/rule/rules
Rev. Ed.	Revised Edition
ROC	Rules of Court
RPC	Reports of Patents, Design, and Trademark Cases
S-G	Solicitor-General
s/o or a/l	son of
s./ss	section/sections
SAcLJ	Singapore Academy of Law Journal
SAL	Singapore Academy of Law
SC	Senior Counsel
SCJA	Supreme Court of Judicature Act
SCR	Supreme Court Reports

List of Abbreviations

Sdn Bhd	*Sendirian Berhad*
SG	Singapore
SGCA	Singapore Court of Appeal
SGD	Singapore Dollar
SGDC	Singapore District Court
SGHC	Singapore High Court
SGHCR	Singapore High Court Registrar
SIAC	Singapore International Arbitration Centre
SICC	Singapore International Commercial Court
SILE	Singapore Institute of Legal Education
SIMC	Singapore International Mediation Centre
SIMI	Singapore International Mediation Institute
Sing Law Gaz	The Singapore Law Gazette
Sing LR	Singapore Law Review
SJC	Singapore Judicial College
SJLS	Singapore Journal of Legal Studies
SLB	Singapore Law Blog
SLR	Singapore Law Reports
SLR(R)	Singapore Law Reports (Reissue)
SLS	Singapore Legal Service
SLW	Singapore Law Watch
SLWC	Singapore Law Watch Commentaries
SMC	Singapore Mediation Centre
SMU	Singapore Management University
SSLR	Straits Settlements Law Reports
ST	The Straits Times
Stat LR	Statute Law Review
TLR	The Times Law Reports
UK	United Kingdom
UKHL	United Kingdom House of Lords
UKSC	United Kingdom Supreme Court
UniSIM	SIM University
US	United States
USD	United States Dollar
VR	Victorian Reports
WLR	Weekly Law Reports
WN	Weekly Notes

Preface

In Singapore, the law of civil procedure continuously has a tremendous impact on civil litigation, yet it evolves ever so quickly to meet the demands of both efficiency and justice. In just the last twenty years or so, a sea of change has swept mightily across the civil justice landscape here.

In terms of rules, the procedural rules of the State Courts (previously known as the Subordinate Courts) and the Supreme Court were consolidated for the first time before the turn of the century; the Rules of Court have since undergone extremely frequent review and change with input from the entire spectrum of the legal profession, and together with the Practice Directions have been made online so that any amendments can be reflected as quickly as possible. Changes to the Supreme Court of Judicature Act have also created ripple effects in the appellate process, some of which may not have been anticipated when they were first introduced, and subsequently amended.

In terms of integrating technology into civil litigation, the courts have been at the global forefront in rolling out technological revolutions with regard to modernizing, streamlining, and enhancing the overall litigation process: first with the Electronic Filing System (otherwise known as EFS), and later on with its successor the Integrated Electronic Litigation System (otherwise known as iELS or eLitigation).

In terms of legal education and the legal profession, the relatively recent emergence of two new law schools in the last ten years – will slowly but surely increase the number of legal professionals; many of them would have under the old run of things taken up civil litigation upon graduation, but with the dramatic liberalization of the legal industry in just the last couple of years, the options in practice have widened considerably at all levels even as the number of civil suits filed continue to be on the rise. Separately, with the introduction of mandatory Continuing Professional Development and the possible introduction of mandatory *pro bono* requirements for young lawyers, civil practice may take on new dimensions as well.

In terms of jurisprudential development and direction-setting, the Court of Appeal – the highest court of the land – is now helmed by a third Chief Justice within the span of just slightly over ten years; the Attorney-General's Chambers has seen (amidst a massive expansion of the organization) more than a half-dozen apex leadership changes since 2006; and a new Minister of Law was appointed in 2008. While one obviously cannot predict the future, the indications are that these leaderships are likely to be in place for some time.

In turn, several espoused aims may be materialized for the Singapore legal landscape: the continued push, in tandem with targeted unshackling of the English common law legacy, towards an autochthonous legal system; the continued growth as a jurisdiction that is amenable structurally and intellectually to all things international, especially in relation to dispute resolution; and the continued development of lawyers, legal work, and judgments that are influential and world-class.

But to return to an earlier point about the rules of civil procedure and one that is most pertinent for present purposes: in Singapore, the law of civil procedure seeks to strike a balance between principle and pragmatism, and to look beyond form and into substance where necessitated.

In this regard, it has been observed thus by Professor Jeffrey Pinsler SC and Cavinder Bull SC in a recent conference organized by the Singapore Academy of Law that:

> It may not be an exaggeration to state that judicial developments in Singapore over the last five years [2006–2010] have taken civil procedure to its third and ultimate stage of evolution. In the centuries prior ... procedure frequently controlled access to substantive justice through the rigidity of forms of action and the hyper-technical requirements of processes such as pleadings ... Today, civil procedure is neither a mistress nor a handmaid although her multi-faceted nature includes both capacities. She does not stand as a separate mechanism but as a co-partner with substantive law in their joint endeavour to achieve justice beyond their respective personalities.

Indeed, though largely inspired by English law in its earlier days, Singapore's law of civil procedure has evolved in its own right in various respects.

For instance, in terms of case management techniques, Singapore has eschewed the longstanding English approach of enacting new civil procedure rules with built-in overarching principles, in favour of incremental modification to introduce practical tools, such as pre-trial conferences, the requirement for evidence-in-chief of witnesses in civil trials to be by affidavit rather than led by oral evidence, not permitting parties to agree to extensions of time for setting down a case for trial or for filing notices of appeal, the requirement for parties to submit a bundle of documents, authorities, and an opening statement before a trial and written submissions before an appeal, as well as the regime of automatic discontinuance when no party has for more than one year taken any step or proceedings in the action.

The offer to settle regime is also a unique Singapore innovation, which incentivizes parties to make reasonable settlement offers and to bring litigation to an expeditious end without judgment, thus saving costs and judicial time. At the same time, the courts work closely with mediation agencies so that alternative dispute resolution options can be explored where appropriate.

As mentioned, Singapore has also led the way in terms of the use of technology not only in the courtrooms but also in the entire conduct of civil litigation. Since 1997, with the launch of the first phase of the EFS, documents may be filed and served over an electronic platform, because papers may be extracted electronically from the courts or through a service bureau, and searches of information maintained by the court registries may also be conducted electronically.

More recently in 2012, iELS was launched in the Singapore Supreme Court. The iELS significantly improves on EFS by leveraging on new electronic form technology that enables information to be stored and reused as well as a workflow middleware that automates various processes. In terms of the substantive law on civil procedure, Singapore has also developed its own unique approaches, adopting English principles as well as those in other foreign jurisdictions where appropriate, but departing from or modifying them to suit local conditions where the need has arisen.

One example is Singapore's approach towards setting aside regularly obtained default judgments. In *Mercurine Pte Ltd v. Canberra Development Pte Ltd*, the Singapore Court of Appeal departed from the English Court of Appeal decision of *Alpine Bulk Transport Co Inc v. Saudi Eagle Shipping Co Inc*, preferring the test set out in the older House of Lords decision of *Evans v. Bartlam*. The Court of Appeal reasoned that the test in *Evans v. Bartlam* struck the better balance between efficiency and the substantive rights of the parties, eliminated the ambiguity contained in the phrase 'real prospect of success', and was also consistent with a more restrictive interpretation of *Saudi Eagle*.

Another example relates to the test for the discovery of documents. Pursuant to the classic English decision of *Compagnie Financiere Et Commerciale Du Pacifique v. Peruvian Guano*, a document may be discoverable if it may lead a party to a 'train of inquiry' that may enable him to advance his case or adversely affect the case of his adversary. However, English law has moved away from this rule following the recommendations of Lord Woolf who was concerned that there would be a virtually unlimited range of potentially discoverable documents that would cause inefficiency in the discovery process, particularly in large cases.

Singapore, on the other hand, has taken a more nuanced approach to the 'train of inquiry' test – it has been removed in relation to general discovery but has been retained in O 24 r 5 of the Rules of Court which relates to discovery of specific documents. Any fear of inefficiency is further ameliorated by the application of the overriding principle stated in O 24 r 7 that discovery must be 'necessary either for disposing fairly of the cause or matter or for saving costs' (and this also applies to pre-action discovery). The Singapore Court of Appeal has also in *Tan Chin Seng v. Raffles Town Club Pte Ltd* emphasized that in applying the 'train of inquiry' test, an applicant must still show in what way the requested document may lead to a document relevant to the pleaded case so that discovery is kept under proper control.

There are, of course, many more examples of where Singapore has followed suit or departed from English developments, but they will be duly covered in the rest of this monograph.

Finally, it would be remiss of us not to mention the Singapore International Commercial Court and Singapore International Mediation Centre which were both launched in 2014. In essence, the former is a division of the Singapore High Court and is meant to present itself as a neutral third-party venue for international commercial dispute resolution, a first of its kind. As for the latter, in seeking to provide world-class mediation services for parties in cross-border commercial disputes, it complements the Singapore International Commercial Court, as well as the pre-existing Singapore International Arbitration Centre (via the innovative Arb-Med-Arb Protocol in particular). A fuller summary of changes is provided in the next section.

We are humbled and grateful to have been presented the opportunity to produce this important piece of work, and we have endeavoured to state the law as of April 2021.

Chen Siyuan and Eunice Chua
April 2021

General Introduction

§1. General Background

I. People and Government

1. The Republic of Singapore is a very small tropical island nation state located in Southeast Asia with a total land area of just 700-plus square kilometres. A former British colony founded by Sir Thomas Stamford Raffles in 1819, it achieved independence fairly recently in 1965 not long after a short-lived merger with its much larger neighbour Malaya (which was renamed Malaysia after the merger).

2. Between its founding and independence, it capitalized on its strategic geographical location and relied heavily on entrepôt trade, and many immigrants arrived to work and eventually, many of them started their own families and settled down permanently. Due to its near-complete lack of natural resources and extremely limited land area, Singapore focused most of its nation-building efforts post-independence on industrialization, investing in education, and attracting foreign direct investment to create the core foundations of a modern, free, and market- and knowledge-based economy.

3. Today, the highly urbanized city-state: is one of the four 'Asian Tiger' economies; is the world's fourth leading financial centre;[1] is the world's fourteenth largest trading nation;[2] has one of the busiest (if not the busiest) seaports in the world;[3] has an airport that is consistently ranked as one of the best in the world;[4] is consistently considered the world's easiest place to start and run a business;[5] is consistently

1. *Hong Kong Named Top Financial Centre for Second Year*, http://www.reuters.com/article/2012/10/31/, 30 Sep. 2017; *New York Dethrones London to Become World's Top Financial Centre for the First Time in Seven Years*, http://www.dailymail.co.uk/news/article-2582110, 30 Sep. 2017.
2. *Speech by Minister for Law and Foreign Affairs, K Shanmugam, at the International Bar Association 4th Asia Pacific Regional Forum Conference*, https://www.mlaw.gov.sg/content/minlaw/en.html, 30 Sep. 2017.
3. *Top 10 Busiest Ports in the World*, http://www.marineinsight.com/marine/top-10-busiest-ports-in-the-world/, 30 Sep. 2017; *Top 50 World Container Ports*, http://www.worldshipping.org/, 30 Sep. 2017.
4. *The World's Premier Airport Awards*, http://www.worldairportawards.com/, 30 Sep. 2017; *The World's Best Airports for 2014*, http://www.forbes.com/sites/grantmartin/2014/03/27/worlds-best-airports-for-2014/, 30 Sep. 2017.
5. *Singapore Best Country in which to Run a Business*, http://www.bbc.co.uk/news/business-11671839, 30 Sep. 2017; *Best Countries for Business*, http://www.forbes.com/best-countries-for-business/list/, 30 Sep. 2017.

ranked as one of the least corrupt in the world;[6] and is generally considered a very safe country with one of the world's lowest crime rates[7] and best Global Peace Index scores.[8]

4. Further, with the state-owned Government of Singapore Investment Corporation Pte Ltd managing assets worth over USD 240 billion (the sixth largest sovereign wealth fund in the world) and Temasek Holdings handling a net portfolio of USD 160 billion worth of assets, Singapore has been described as a 'corporatist state'.[9]

5. Singapore's civil service bureaucracy is also widely renowned for being highly efficient and technocratic, thus enhancing its image as a place where everything 'works'.[10]

6. Singapore's Gross Domestic Product is around USD 330 billion;[11] its per capita Gross Domestic Product (based on Purchasing Power Parity) is around USD 61,000,[12] placing it as one of the top five countries in the world by most reputable international rankings.[13] Singapore's per capita Gross Domestic Product was around USD 400 when it achieved independence in 1965. However, Singapore also has a rather high Gini coefficient – one of the more commonly used measurements for income inequality – of around forty-seven.[14] Nonetheless, the country is ranked fourth in the world for life expectancy,[15] and unemployment rates have remained relatively low over the years.[16]

7. Public housing is also widely available (though not necessarily at low-cost), but at the same time, the majority of the citizenry is expected to be self-reliant in a wide array of personal financial matters (including healthcare), as opposed to be

---

6. *Corruption Perceptions Index 2014*, http://www.transparency.org/cpi2014/results, 30 Sep. 2017.
7. *Singapore 2013 Crime and Safety Report*, https://www.osac.gov/pages/ContentReportDetails.aspx?cid=13850, 30 Sep. 2017.
8. *Singapore*, http://www.visionofhumanity.org/#page/indexes/global-peace-index/2013/, 30 Sep. 2017.
9. S. Murugesan, *Judicial Independence in a Corporatist State: Singapore – A Case Study*, 7 LAWASIA J. 99, 101 (2012).
10. *See Facts and Figure*, http://www.edb.gov.sg, 30 Sep. 2017; *Head of the Singapore Public Service Gives Public Services Reform Lecture*, http://www.guardian.co.uk/public-leaders-network/2012/nov/29, 30 Sep. 2017.
11. *Report for Selected Countries and Subjects*, http://www.imf.org/external/pubs/ft/weo/2012/01, 30 Sep. 2017.
12. *Report for Selected Countries and Subjects*, http://www.imf.org/external/pubs/ft/weo/2012/01, 30 Sep. 2017.
13. *See* e.g., *GDP – Per Capita (PPP)*, https://www.cia.gov/library/publications/the-world-factbook/rankorder/2004rank.html, 30 Sep. 2017.
14. *Distribution of Family Income*, https://www.cia.gov/library/publications/the-world-factbook/fields/2172.html, 30 Sep. 2017. Separately, there has been an exponential influx of foreign wealth in recent years: *see Wealth Over the Edge: Singapore*, http://online.wsj.com/, 30 Sep. 2017.
15. *Singapore*, https://www.cia.gov/, 30 Sep. 2017.
16. *Labour Market Report First Quarter 2015*, http://www.mom.gov.sg/newsroom/press-releases/2015/0615-labour-market-q1, 30 Sep. 2017.

overly reliant on the government for programmes that create a generous welfare system and social safety net.[17] In addition, individual and corporate tax rates, as well as the rate on goods and services tax are comparatively low for a developed country. Professional, managerial, and executive (PME) jobs currently constitute one-third of Singapore's workforce, a proportion that is likely to increase in the long term.

8. There are now over 5 million people living in Singapore, of which about 3 million are born locally (the remainder being permanent residents and foreign workers).[18] Dual citizenship is forbidden; if citizenship is acquired in another country, the Singapore citizenship must be renounced by a certain age if the former is to be retained. However, Singaporeans are permitted to be permanent residents in other countries. The population figures cited above give the country a very high population density of around 7,500 persons per square kilometre,[19] with not much unused land to spare.

9. There is conscription in Singapore: all male Singapore citizens and non-first-generation permanent residents who have reached 18 years of age must enrol for what is known as national service; the period of service is between twenty-two and twenty-four months, and conscripts may be drafted into the army, police, or civil defence forces.

10. Singapore's population is fairly diverse, with Chinese forming 75% of the total population and Malays and Indians constituting the most significant minority races.[20] The population is almost evenly split in terms of male-to-female ratio, but there are more males than females in the workforce (around 76% versus 56%) despite increasingly equal ratios in terms of education levels, even at tertiary levels.[21] The population is projected to increase by at least another one to two million over the next twenty years,[22] but due to falling total fertility rates,[23] any increase in population is only likely to be possible with liberal immigration policies.

11. English is the official working language, but the country also has Mandarin, Malay, and Tamil as its official languages. Through the way language is taught in schools, most Singaporeans are at least bilingual (i.e., in English and one Mother

17. *Security with Self-Reliance: The Argument for the Singapore Model*, http://www.cscollege.gov.sg, 30 Sep. 2017.
18. *Latest Data on Population & Land Area*, http://www.singstat.gov.sg/statistics/latest_data.html#12, 30 Sep. 2017.
19. *Country Comparison*, http://www.indexmundi.com/g/r.aspx?v=21000, 30 Sep. 2017.
20. *Singapore*, https://www.cia.gov/library/publications/the-world-factbook/geos/sn.html, 30 Sep. 2017. Most of the Chinese in Singapore are Han Chinese.
21. *Latest Data on Population & Land Area*, http://www.singstat.gov.sg/statistics/latest-data#19, 30 Sep. 2017.
22. *A Sustainable Population for a Dynamic Singapore*, http://population.sg/whitepaper/downloads/population-white-paper.pdf, 30 Sep. 2017.
23. With an increase in affluence an healthcare standards, there is also the problem of a greying population too.

Tongue language).[24] Literacy rate for residents 15 years old and above stands at 96.7%, and more than two-thirds of the population has at least secondary school education and one-quarter has at least a university degree, and this only looks set to increase in the years to come.[25]

12. In terms of religion, approximately one in three people profess to practise Buddhism or Taoism, one in five Christianity (including Catholicism), and one in seven Islam.[26] Christianity and Islam, however, are the fastest-growing religions in Singapore.

13. Due in large part to its colonial history, Singapore adopts a Westminster system of unicameral parliamentary government. Since 1959 (the first-year of self-government), Singapore has been governed by the People's Action Party, which has adopted largely centrist, meritocracy-heavy policies with respect to social and economic issues.

14. Executive power rests with the ministers of the Cabinet (which oversees the ministries), which is headed by the Prime Minister, though more broadly speaking the Executive would include various other departments and agencies as well, such as the Attorney-General's Chambers. Legislative power rests with Parliament (and to a limited extent the elected President),[27] which as of the last General Election (held every five years on average) in 2015 comprises eighty-nine elected Members of Parliament, three Non-constituency Members of Parliament, and nine Nominated Members of Parliament.

15. For most bills to be made into law, it has to pass through three readings (one being a debate) with a simple majority voting in favour and the President granting his assent. For certain bills, they are referred to Select Committees for a report to be generated before they are debated in Parliament; there is also a Presidential Council of Minority Rights that acts as a check against bills that contain elements of racial

24. So-called third languages – ranging such as Japanese, German, and French – are often offered to students who have done well academically. Singapore students are also known to be very proficient in mathematics and science: *US Students Still Lag Globally in Math and Science, Tests Show*, http://www.nytimes.com/2012/12/11/education, 30 Sep. 2017. Some 40% of each cohort of students go on to obtain university degrees.
25. *Latest Data on Population & Land Area*, http://www.singstat.gov.sg/statistics/latest-data#19, 30 Sep. 2017; *Education & Training: Percentage of University Graduates in Singapore*, http://app.msf.gov.sg/ResearchRoom/ResearchStatistics/PercentageofUniversityGraduatesinSingapore.aspx, 30 Sep. 2017. The education landscape has changed dramatically in the last ten years, with the introduction of integrated programmes, the International Baccalaureat, specialist high schools, and specialist universities. An ever-increasing number of students are going abroad for their university studies. In law alone for instance, the number of students who study overseas increased fivefold from 300 to 1500 from 2007 to 2015.
26. *Census of Population 2010 Statistical Release 1: Demographic Characteristics, Education, Language and Religion*, http://www.singstat.gov.sg, 30 Sep. 2017. Religious discourse is occasionally engaged when debating matters of public policy.
27. *See also* Tan, E. *The Legislature of Singapore*, in *The Legal System of Singapore* (G. Chan & J. Lee eds, LexisNexis 2015).

and/or religious prejudice.[28] In addition, Government Parliamentary Committees may be formed to examine the laws and policies of particular ministries. Most parliamentary reports and debates (including Select Committee reports) are accessible for free from the government-run website.[29]

16. Elected Members of Parliament are voted on a first-past-the-post basis and represent either single- or group-representation constituencies (which are composed of four to six members of varying ethnicities). As mentioned, there is also an elected President, but while this role as head of state was historically ceremonial, constitutional amendments in the 1990s gave the President certain limited powers with regard to the use of the country's financial reserves and appointments to key public offices; in addition to this, the President also has a crucial role to play with regard to the prevention of corruption in the public service, the maintenance of racial and religious harmony, and the maintenance of diplomatic relations with other states.[30]

17. For the larger part of its modern history, Singapore has been perceived by some within and without to have been governed by a top-down, internally cohesive government that prioritizes communitarianism or collective welfare over individual rights and liberties. The government, however, considers that the democratic process bestows on it a broad mandate to govern decisively on a broad spectrum of issues, though it has indicated that a consultative relationship with the citizenry is an evolutionary step in democracy.

18. In addition to this, the government has been known to be extremely sensitive about anything that can affect the nation's social fabric, and has, amongst other strategies, promoted a national ideology which comprises several other basic values: upholding the family as the basic building block of society; resolving major issues through consensus instead of contention; and stressing the importance of racial and religious tolerance and harmony. Some of these values have been characterized by the government as distinctively 'Asian' in nature, though some critics challenge the plausibility of such a notion given the many diversities of race, ethnicity, religion, and culture in Asia. National security, both internal and external, is also taken very seriously, manifested in the form of strong penal laws and the maintenance of a strong multipronged defence force.

19. Singapore is a member of the UN and the Commonwealth of Nations and closer to home, one of the founding members of the Association of Southeast Asian States (ASEAN). It is also, inter alia, a member economy of the Asia Pacific Economic Cooperation (APEC), a member of the World Trade Organization (WTO), a

28. *The Singapore Legal System*, www.singaporelaw.sg/content/LegalSyst1.html, 30 Sep. 2017.
29. *Publications – Singapore Parliament Reports*, http://www.parliament.gov.sg/publications-singapore-parliament-reports, 30 Sep. 2017.
30. 30 Sep. 2017. C. Siyuan, *The Executive,* in *The Legal System of Singapore* (G. Chan & J. Lee eds, LexisNexis 2015). In 2016, a Constitutional Commission was set up to review certain aspects of the office, including qualifying criteria, minority representation, and the size and structure of the Council of Presidential Advisers.

member of the Forum of East Asia-Latin America Cooperation, and its current network of Free Trade Agreements includes twenty-one bilateral and regional ones in force with thirty-two trading partners.[31] Singapore's foreign policy is essentially predicated on the idea of maintaining political and economic security in a potentially volatile region, while outside of the region it generally prefers to adopt a stance of neutrality and non-interference – a consequence of which is that it does not appreciate external intrusions into its political matters either, matters which it considers a sovereign prerogative. Singapore has diplomatic relations with more than 180 other states,[32] but it has particularly close ties with the United States and China.

II. Key Facets of the Legal System

20. Singapore's legal system is predominantly[33] based on the English common law (which includes the rules on equity)[34] tradition[35] (which importation began in the 1800s), albeit with substantial modifications via the enactment of the Application of English Law Act[36] and the abolition of the jury trial and appeals to the Privy Council in 1970 and 1994 respectively.[37] These modifications are consistent with Singapore's gradual push over the last few decades to develop an autochthonous legal system,[38] and one of the consequences of this is that increasingly, foreign (including English) case law and/or legal developments are only invoked or relied upon when there is a high degree of necessity and/or legal relevance;[39] at the same time, however, with globalization and increasing cross-border work, there will always be utility in being apprised of the major positive developments in other jurisdictions.

21. As a common law jurisdiction, the legal process in the Singapore courts is, notwithstanding gradual changes to certain practices of the law (such as family law) and the push to facilitate alternative dispute resolution options, largely adversarial, rather than inquisitorial or conciliatory.[40] This, in turn, has many significant trickle-down effects in how the pre-trial and trial applications and rules are conceptualized, as well as how the legal profession is regulated.

31. *FTAs*, http://www.mfa.gov.sg/content/mfa/international_organisation_initiatives/ftas.html, 30 Sep. 2017.
32. *Missions Locater*, http://www.mfa.gov.sg, 30 Sep. 2017.
33. The Syariah Court administers Muslim law in certain areas of the law: *see* Administration of Muslim Law Act (Cap. 3, 2009 Rev. Ed.).
34. *See* Civil Law Act (Cap. 43, 1999 Rev. Ed.), s 3.
35. Hence, doctrines such as *stare decisis* and *ratio decidendi* apply. It is therefore also not uncommon for Singapore courts to cite decisions and/or developments from the rest of the Commonwealth, though much depends on the subject matter in question.
36. (Cap. 7A, 1994 Rev. Ed.).
37. *The Singapore Legal System*', www.singaporelaw.sg/content/LegalSyst1.html, 30 Sep. 2017.
38. *See* A. Phang, *From Foundation to Legacy – The Second Charter of Justice* 52–60 (Sing. Acad. L. 2006).
39. *See* generally *Singapore Law: 50 Years in the Making* (Goh Y.H. & P. Tan eds., Acad. Publg. 2015).
40. *High Litigation Cost 'Most Critical Hurdle' to Justice*, http://www.asiaone.com, 30 Sep. 2017.

22. As for Singapore's reception of international law obligations, its approach may be better described as dualist, rather than monist.[41] This, in turn, has created a tense interface, perhaps most so in the context of reconciling so-called international human rights and norms on the one hand, and domestic prerogatives to enact various penal offences and protect security interests on the other hand.[42]

23. There is a written, amendable constitution – often described as being cut from the same cloth as the Malaysian Constitution – that is fairly comprehensive (it includes a sectional equivalent of a bill of rights that cover the fundamental liberties) and which forms the apex source of law.[43] In other words, laws or actions that violate the Constitution can be struck down or declared unconstitutional by the court. The Constitution is followed by statutory law,[44] and then the common law as one moves down the hierarchy of sources of law. Subsidiary legislation is also being made all the time, and for all intents and purposes has the force of law, but it should be distinguished from the internal guidelines, practices, or policies of government organizations.

24. The apex court is the Court of Appeal,[45] followed by the High Court (collectively they form the Supreme Court) and the various courts in the State Courts (which until 2014 were known as the Subordinate Courts).[46] Most of these courts have jurisdiction to preside over civil and criminal matters, while broadly speaking the High Court and Court of Appeal are the main courts associated with appellate, precedent-creating functions (the High Court also functions as a court of first instance for high-value and/or more complex disputes and cases).

41. *See* generally C. Siyuan, *The Relationship Between International Law and Domestic Law*, 23 Sing. Acad. L.J. 350 (2011). *See also Yong Vui Kong v. Public Prosecutor*, [2015] 2 SLR 1129, [28]–[36].
42. *See Report of the Working Group on the Universal Periodic Review*, http://www.mfa.gov.sg, 30 Sep. 2017. *See also Singapore*, http://travel.state.gov/travel/cis_pa_tw/cis/cis_1017.html, 30 Sep. 2017; C. Siyuan, *A Preliminary Survey of the Right to Presumption of Innocence in Singapore*, 7 LAWASIA J. 79 (2012).
43. *Constitution of the Republic of Singapore* (1985 Rev. Ed., 1999 Reprint).
44. The Interpretation Act (Cap. 1, 2002 Rev. Ed.) also sets out some of the canons of statutory interpretation, chief of which is found in s 9A(1).
45. Apart from Court of Appeal hearings which typically comprises a bench of two to three judges, all other judicial hearings in Singapore are presided by just one judge. A notable exception exists for more complex criminal appeals emanating from the State Courts (which are heard at the High Court level).
46. *The Singapore Legal System*, www.singaporelaw.sg/content/LegalSyst1.html, 30 Sep. 2017. Special -purpose tribunals may also be convened from time to time, and there are also permanent specialized courts (or more specifically, divisions) such as those dealing with family law, juvenile, and coroner matters, as well as small claims. The State Courts take on an overwhelming majority of the case load, dealing with around 350,000 cases a year: *Renaming of State Courts*, https://app.statecourts.gov.sg/Data/Files/file/InforBooklet_Brochures/Newsletter_Jun.2014.pdf, 30 Sep. 2017. There is of course also the Singapore International Commercial Court which was launched in 201 4/15, and this will be covered in greater detail elsewhere in this monograph.

25. Parenthetically, although the President may refer to the Constitutional Tribunal for its opinion any question as to the effect of any provision of the Constitution which has arisen or appears likely to raise,[47] the High Court and Court of Appeal are primarily responsible for adjudicating over constitutional challenges (and most administrative law cases).

26. Because of stare decisis, the majority of decisions that are cited in the Supreme Court are those from the Supreme Court, though of course foreign decisions and/or developments are commonly relied on too.[48]

27. Where (High Court and Court of Appeal) judgments are written, some of them may be reported in the Singapore Law Reports (marked either as SLR or SLR(R)), but all written judgments (including those rendered by the State Courts and High Court Assistant Registrars (marked as SGHCR since 2012)) are available on LawNet (a paid database). Whether written judgments will be rendered depends on various factors, such as whether the matter is being brought on appeal, whether written grounds will advance public interest (broadly conceived), whether there are important findings of fact to be made for the record, and whether there is already enough information furnished to the litigants as to how the decisions were arrived at.

28. Singapore Law Watch, which provides free access to the latest legal developments both in Singapore and various parts of the Commonwealth for a limited period, also houses the latest written judgments before they are archived in LawNet. Singapore Law Watch is complemented by Singapore Law Blog, which contains academic and practitioner input on the latest case law, and academic and professional developments in Singapore and the Commonwealth. The latter is meant to be a more responsive platform for academics and young practitioners to highlight the very latest changes in the law (legislation, cases, comparative developments, and legal education), and also contains a database of academic literature that pertains to developments in Singapore law.

29. The Attorney-General, whose chambers engage in criminal, civil, international, and statutory drafting work, is both advisor to and advocate for the Singapore government at the same time;[49] the Attorney-General's Chambers also runs the website where the public can freely access statutory (including subsidiary legislation) and constitutional documents.

---

47. *Constitution of the Republic of Singapore* Art. 100(1) (1985 Rev. Ed., 1999 Reprint).
48. *See also* Chan, G. 'The Doctrine of Judicial Precedent and Case Method and Analysis', in *The Legal System of Singapore* (G. Chan & J. Lee eds, LexisNexis 2015).
49. *See* generally C. Siyuan, *The Limits on Prosecutorial Discretion in Singapore: Past, Present, and Future*, 2 Intl. Rev. L. 5 (2013). As provided in the Constitution, the Attorney-General may not necessarily have security of tenure but there is security of remuneration during his employment. Following 2014 amendments to the Constitution, the Attorney-General now has deputies in the form of Deputy Attorneys-General, a Solicitor-General, and a Deputy Solicitor-General. The increase in the

30. Singapore's judicial and legal system is consistently ranked as one of the top three in Asia,[50] and the country's rule of law, particularly with respect to commerce (including civil justice), enforcement, and order and security, is traditionally seen to be extremely reliable and robust;[51] the rate of wrongful convictions is also known to be very low.[52] In the 2015 report by the World Justice Project, Singapore was ranked: 9th overall for rule of law (2nd in East Asia and the Pacific); 1st out of 102 countries for regulatory enforcement; and 24th and 26th for open government and human rights respectively out of 31 high-income countries.[53]

31. The legal profession in Singapore is 'fused', in that lawyers who have passed the local bar examinations and have been called to the Bar can act as both advocates and solicitors,[54] though a majority of lawyers in Singapore do not necessarily carve out a career in litigation.[55] As of October 2015, there are about 4,400 practicing lawyers (i.e., those with valid practicing certificates) in Singapore,[56] an almost 17% increase from the figure in 2010.[57]

---

number of near-apex positions for government lawyers is the result of a steady increase in recruitment over the years, and reflects the greater volume and greater complexity in the work that is now handled by the Attorney-General's Chambers.

50. *The Singapore Legal System*, www.singaporelaw.sg/content/LegalSyst1.html, 30 Sep. 2017; N. Khng, *Judicial Independence and the Singapore Judiciary*, 7 LAWASIA J. 53 (2012).
51. *See* e.g., *Rule of Law Index Scores and Rankings*, http://worldjusticeproject.org/rule-of-law-index-data, 30 Sep. 2017. In the Opening of Legal Year 2015, Attorney-General Rajah described the rule of law as comprising four features: effective and incorruptible key institutions; a culture in which rights are respected and effectively enforced; justice that is accessible and legal processes that are easily navigable; and a legal system that is predicated upon fairness, moderation, and proportionality.
52. *See* e.g., C. Siyuan & E. Chua, *Wrongful Convictions in Singapore: A General Survey of Risk Factors*, 28 Singapore L. Rev. 98 (2010). More recent and more comprehensive studies on this matter have not been undertaken, however.
53. Countries were evaluated through 47 indicators across eight categories: constraints on government powers, absence of corruption, open government, fundamental rights, order and security, regulatory enforcement, civil justice, and criminal justice.
54. *The Singapore Legal System*, www.singaporelaw.sg/content/LegalSyst1.html, 30 Sep. 2017. As such, references to 'advocate and solicitor' mean any lawyer who has been called to the Singapore Bar. A fused profession has arguably contributed to the high attrition rates, at least for lawyers who prefer litigation work – in the first 10 to 15 years, first chair experience is hard to come by, and most of the work is that of a solicitor rather than a barrister.
55. Broadly speaking, the profile of the legal workforce in Singapore can be divided into corporate work, litigation, arbitration, in-house work, public service (court, advisory, policy, or judicial work), academia, and international practice. Separately, the attrition rate for lawyer in Singapore remains rather high, though no ready or widely consistent statistics are available for this (but *see* e.g. *Another Look at Opening up of the Legal Profession*, http://www.lawgazette.com.sg/2012-11/586.htm, 30 Mar. 2015; *Report of the 4th Committee on the Supply of Lawyers*, http://www.mlaw.gov.sg, 30 Mar. 2015).
56. *General Statistics*, http://www.lawsociety.org.sg/AboutUs/GeneralStatistics.aspx, 30 Sep. 2017. In comparison, England and Wales – which has about 10 times the population of Singapore – issued 130,000 practicing certificates, 5,000 training contracts, and 16,000 law degrees in 2014.
57. *General Statistics*, http://www.lawsociety.org.sg/AboutUs/GeneralStatistics.aspx, 30 Sep. 2017. More than half of these lawyers have been in practice for more than twelve years, and in terms of size, 704 firms have 1–5 lawyers, 126 firms have 6–30 lawyers, and 18 firms have more than 30 lawyers: *General Statistics*, http://www.lawsociety.org.sg/AboutUs/GeneralStatistics.aspx, 30 Sep.

32. The bar examinations were expected to attract almost a thousand applicants by 2016, which would have been more than a twofold increase as compared to the numbers between 2000 and 2006. The eventual numbers were lower: in 2016, there were 650 fresh law graduates from local and overseas universities, with around 100 not receiving any training contracts. Be that as it may, the passing rate for bar examinations remains rather high, with a minimal rate of failures (but whether fresh graduates can secure a job thereafter is a separate matter). These significant increases (which is likely to remain on an upward trajectory) in just a span of a few short years can be attributed to a number of factors, such as the relatively recent creation of a second law school in Singapore,[58] the opening up of the legal industry to overseas players,[59] the expanding recognition of foreign law degrees,[60] the rise of international transactional work in the region, and a general policy by firms to hire extensively without undue consideration of micro and macro factors that cause high attrition rates in the industry.

33. In 2013, following a government-commissioned study on the supply of lawyers, plans were unveiled for an increased intake of law students, as well as the creation of a third law school (UniSIM) that focuses on family law and criminal law, the two areas of practice that are generally perceived to be less popular with young law graduates because of preconceptions of lower pay and more mundane work. This third law school will be primarily targeted at people who are already involved in community work (such as police officers and family social workers) but are considering a second career in law, and will thus in effect only be a part-time law degree as classes can only be held at night. However, graduates of the third law school would have the requisite professional accreditation to practise in the same way as graduates from the other two local law schools; moreover, they cannot be compelled to practice only community law. This move to open a third law school confirms a trend that is happening not only in Singapore but also worldwide (at least in

---

2017. The so-called Big Four – Allen & Gledhill LLP, Drew & Napier LLC, Rajah & Tan LLP, and WongPartnership LLP – have more than 200 lawyers each. Certain firms also have international joint ventures.

58. The Singapore Management University School of Law, which became a full-fledged law school in 2007, produced its first batch of around 150 law graduates (LLB and JD) in 2011. The National University of Singapore Faculty of Law, which was created in 1961, has been producing around 300 law graduates on average in the last few years. Every year hundreds of students from Singapore also obtain law degrees from other countries such as England and Australia, and many of them do return to practice. It takes four years here to obtain an LLB; a significant minority of the students in both schools go on a one-term or two-term overseas exchange stint. There are also tie-ups with various overseas universities for postgraduate studies. As for the JD, it takes two to three years to obtain it. To practice in Singapore, one would first have to graduate from a recognized law school. Next, one would need to complete the bar examinations. Finally, one would need to complete a training contract with a firm; if a graduate begins work in the government sector, the period of training required is three years.

59. *Analysis of Singapore Market Data: Sing it Loud*, http://www.thelawyer.com/1013598.article, 30 Sep. 2017. As of 2015, 40 of the top 100 law firms globally by revenue have offices in Singapore, hiring some 1200 foreign lawyers. *See also* G. Low, *A Globalised Legal Profession*, in *The Legal System of Singapore* (G. Chan & J. Lee eds, LexisNexis 2015).

60. *The Singapore Legal System*, www.singaporelaw.sg/content/LegalSyst1.html, 30 Sep. 2017.

common law jurisdictions): that young lawyers are still primarily attracted to lucrative and supposedly prestigious commercial law careers, at least as a starting point upon graduation.

34. There is perhaps also a belief that the attrition rate in a non-commercial legal career may be lower, and coupled with the fact that the retention rate for young lawyers is likely to be rather low in the foreseeable future, many young graduates may indeed find a non-commercial legal career a viable option. In addition, in the last four years, there has been a market perception that there is an oversupply of lawyers, with insufficient training contracts being given out to fresh law graduates.[61] But this is a problem that has afflicted law graduates from foreign universities (such as those in England and Australia) much more than the local law graduates. Nonetheless, hiring across the board has reduced, and starting pays and bonuses are lower than before; further, it is inescapable that with a fused profession, working hours and conditions have worsened, as have the quality of supervision and specialized work.

35. In recent times, the government has also made a concerted effort to promote Singapore as a leading international arbitration hub for various types of disputes. In other words, it has tried to create a more pro-arbitration environment in terms of both its written laws and jurisprudence, as well as supporting infrastructures.[62]

36. All of the developments in the preceding paragraphs are consistent with its broader agenda to implement alternative dispute resolution platforms (both domestically and internationally) as part of its holistic legal framework.[63] However, as mentioned, despite these various changes to the legal landscape in Singapore and ever-rising education levels and affluence, most Singaporeans (i.e., those suing in their private capacity and those that are not companies) generally remain non-litigious.

37. Various professional bodies are involved in the development of lawyers in Singapore. The Singapore Academy of Law, which was formed in 1988 and comprise all persons who are called as advocates and solicitors of the Supreme Court or

61. In 2016, the Committee for the Professional Training of Lawyers was established by the government to do a 'root and branch' review of how undergraduates were offered training contracts by local law firms, as well as how they were assessed to be suitable for retention and employment. A suggestion was also made that trainees who did not make the cut to be promoted to associates could be made paralegals instead.
62. *See* Chan, G. 'Mediation and Arbitration. In *The Legal System of Singapore*, edited by G. Chan & J. Lee. Singapore: LexisNexis, 2015.
63. For instance, the Singapore International Arbitration Centre was established in 1991 to meet the demands of the international business community for a reliable arbitration institution in a fast-developing Asia. The Singapore Mediation Centre was established in 1997 to promote and develop various types of mediation processes, particularly domestic disputes. The Singapore International Commercial Court and Singapore International Mediation Centre, both launched in 2014, seek to complete the suite of dispute resolution options for entities involved in cross-border work, particularly in the region. Both of these organizations will be covered in greater detail elsewhere in this monograph.

who are appointed as Legal Service Officers, focuses on three areas: the development of the legal industry; the enhancement of legal knowledge (it runs LawNet and Singapore Law Watch and supports Singapore Law Blog, facilitates continuing legal education seminars, symposiums, and conferences (e-Lex was launched in 2014 to allow online viewing of their recordings), and publishes various important academic works); and the improvement of the efficiency of legal practice through technological advances in the legal sector.[64] The Law Society of Singapore, established in 1967, is essentially the bar association for lawyers called in Singapore and has five broad aims: to give representation to members of the profession; to promote the interests of members; to improve the standards of conduct and learning of members; to assist the public in all matters relating to the law; and criminal legal aid in certain areas of the law. The Law Society is also the starting point for which complaints relating to inadequate service and professional misconduct are made against lawyers.[65] Then there is the Singapore Institute of Legal Education (SILE), which recently succeeded the Board of Legal Education (BLE) and is primarily responsible for the standards of legal education[66] in Singapore and administering the bar examinations. The Legal Service Commission has jurisdiction over all officers in the Singapore Legal Service, and is in charge of staffing the judiciary (in the State Courts),[67] the Attorney-General's Chambers, and other various Legal Service and governmental departments. The Singapore Legal Service accepts applications from both fresh law graduates and people making a mid-career switch. Indeed, with Singapore's legal system being a common law one, the legal industry is considered quite fluid; for instance, it is not unusual for a lawyer's work experience to include

64. 30 Sep. 2017. The Singapore Academy of Law also publishes the Annual Review of Cases for a broad range of subjects and *Singapore Academy of Law Journal*, one of the five law journals published locally. The other four journals are *Singapore Journal of Legal Studies*, *Singapore Law Review*, *Asian Journal of Comparative Law*, and *Asian Journal of International Law*.

65. *Complaints Against a Lawyer*, http://www.lawsociety.org.sg/forPublic/YoutheLawyer/ComplaintsAgainstaLawyer.aspx, 30 Sep. 2015.

66. It should be noted that continuing legal education is compulsory for young Singapore lawyers. The rate of participation in *pro bono* work is also likely to increase.

67. The professional profiles of the judges and registrars in the courts warrant brief mention at this juncture. In the State Courts, the Magistrates and District Judges are deployed by the Legal Service Commission, with the younger ones given the office of the former and the older ones the latter (the State Courts are headed by the Presiding Judge (formerly Chief District Judge), followed by the Deputy Presiding Judge, and Senior District Judges). The District Judges have concurrent registrar duties (registrars being the first in line to hear most civil procedure applications). In the Supreme Court, the High Court and Court of Appeal Judges are recruited from the entire spectrum of the legal profession. They also have security of tenure till the age of 65 and security of remuneration. In 2015, the Singapore Judicial College was established. The college comprises a local wing, an international wing, and an empirical judicial research laboratory. The local wing oversees the needs of the Singapore judiciary and focuses on the training and development of judges and judicial officers in an institutionalized and centralized manner. The aim is to enhance the competence and professionalism of the judiciary in response to the increasing expectations of court users and the growing number of complex legal issues encountered by the courts. The local wing is complemented by the empirical judicial research laboratory, which will research and test innovation in judicial studies and practices. The two local law schools would submit proposals on relevant research projects. The international wing will build on the reputation of Singapore's well-developed legal system, as well as efforts of the local wing and research laboratory, in offering Singapore as a forum of judicial training and to export judicial education. The college will be guided in the development of policies by a Board of Governors comprising judges and academics.

stints in the private sector (which may include stints in different (local and international) firms and secondments to government organizations), public service (which may include stints in different types of departments and secondments to private organizations), and academia. The Singapore Legal Service also offers civil litigation practice, albeit in the public service sector; for instance, the Attorney-General's Chambers has various divisions, with the Civil Division being the second largest with around 40 Legal Service Officers (there are more than 200 Legal Service Officers in the Attorney-General's Chambers and 200 support staff).[68] This division not only provides legal advice to the ministries, statutory boards, and other organs of state and drafts and vets legal documents for the government, but it also represents the government in international initiatives and court proceedings instituted by or against the government (such as judicial review and constitutional challenges). Finally, the Ministry of Law is primarily responsible for formulating and reviewing legal policy for Singapore as a whole, and also comprises various agencies relating to community mediation, insolvency, legal aid, intellectual property, and land.[69]

38. Dispute resolution processes in Singapore are generally considered to be fairly low-cost[70] and extremely expedient. With respect to the court process, a massive backlog clearing exercise spearheaded by the former Chief Justice Yong Pung How in the 1990s set the foundations of effective and efficient case management by both levels of the Singapore courts today. Chief Justice Yong also increased the number of courts, streamlined procedures, introduced the justices' law clerk[71] and senior counsel schemes,[72] and leveraged on technology as part of multipronged strategy to make the legal system more comprehensive. His successor in 2006, Chief Justice Chan Sek Keong, focused his six-year tenure on maintaining the expediency of the process, while improving the substantive quality of justice on various

68. *Civil Division*, http://app.sgdi.gov.sg/listing.asp?agency_subtype=dept&agency_id=0000003004, 30 Sep. 2017. In recent times, there has been a push by the Attorney-General to greatly beef up the numbers in and services of the Civil Division. More broadly, the establishment of the AGC Academy in late-2014 has sought not only to provide greater centralized vocational training of the prosecutors and counsel, but also to generate specialized research on the various areas of law so as to bring about greater balance in perspectives.
69. *What We Do*, http://www.mlaw.gov.sg/about-us/what-we-do.html, 30 Sep. 2017.
70. C.f. *High Litigation Cost 'Most Critical Hurdle' to Justice*, http://www.asiaone.com, 30 Sep. 2017. *See also Law Society of Singapore v. Kurubalan s/o Manickam Rengaraju*, [2013] 4 SLR 91, [86]–[89].
71. Justices' Law Clerks assist High Court and Court of Appeal Judges in research and drafting, and generally only fresh graduates (LLB or JD) with a First Class Honours or equivalent are invited to apply for the position. In the last few years, there have been around 20 to 30 Justices' Law Clerks at any one time serving in the Supreme Court.
72. The Senior Counsel is the equivalent of the Queen's Counsel in Singapore. As of 2015, there have been 74 Senior Counsel appointed since 1989 (59 are still active; eight are women), with the bulk coming from private practice, and public service and academia forming the next two pools. It is also possible to be appointed as Senior Counsel (*honoris causa*), or Honorary Senior Counsel. Traditionally, one of the criteria for an applicant to be appointed Senior Counsel was the maintenance of an active litigation practice (which would not include arbitration). However, this requirement has been modified.

fronts, especially with regard to criminal matters.[73] Having said that, many decisions that are cited in this monograph (i.e., those related to civil procedure and civil process generally) were made during his tenure, and in some way reflect his jurisprudential philosophy on civil matters as well. The current Chief Justice, Sundaresh Menon, meanwhile, has set out as one of his visions to be that 'the law [should not become] the preserve of the rarefied few as a result of systems, processes and outputs that seem obscure or even confounding to the reasonably informed lay person'.[74] Another project that is likely to define the early phase of his tenure is the creation of the Singapore International Commercial Court (SICC) and Singapore International Mediation Centre (SIMC), both of which will be covered in greater detail later on.[75]

39. Suffice to say for now that when the SICC was first conceived, it was envisaged that the court would: be a division of the High Court with its own Registry; comprise existing Supreme Court judges, ad hoc Associate Judges, and Court of Appeal Judges for appeals; be governed by a set of rules and practice directions that follow international best practices for commercial dispute resolution; and decline jurisdiction for non-commercial disputes.[76] It was also recommended the court will deal with cases where: parties have consented to the use of the court post-dispute; disputants are parties to a contract giving the court jurisdiction; and where they are within the High Court's jurisdiction but have been transferred to the court by the Chief Justice.[77] Finally, it was recommended that judgments of the court may be enforced through reciprocal enforcement provisions or through a common law action on the judgment debt.[78]

40. As for the SIMC, in seeking to provide world-class mediation services for parties in cross-border commercial disputes, it complements the SICC, as well as

73. '*Response by Chief Justice Sundaresh Menon: Opening of the Legal Year 2013 and Welcome Reference for the Chief Justice*, http://app.lsc.gov.sg/data/OLY%202013%20-%20CJ%20Speech%20OLY%20Welcome%20Reference.pdf, 30 Sep. 2017. *See also The Law in His Hands – A Tribute to Chief Justice Chan Sek Keong* (H.T. Chao, A. Phang, V.K. Rajah & T.M. Yeo eds., Acad. Publg. 2012).
74. *Response by Chief Justice Sundaresh Menon: Opening of the Legal Year 2013 and Welcome Reference for the Chief Justice*, http://app.lsc.gov.sg/data/OLY%202013%20-%20CJ%20Speech%20OLY%20Welcome%20Reference.pdf, 30 Sep. 2017. Another hallmark of his tenure thus far is specialization – recent appointments for Judicial Commissioner and Judge reveal a preference for practitioners with specialized knowledge. Presumably, these judges will be given more cases that comport with their expertise, and this may occur even at the pre-trial stage as well as part of the new strategy in case management.
75. *Response by Chief Justice Sundaresh Menon: Opening of the Legal Year 2013 and Welcome Reference for the Chief Justice*, http://app.lsc.gov.sg/data/OLY%202013%20-%20CJ%20Speech%20OLY%20Welcome%20Reference.pdf, 30 Sep. 2017.
76. *Report of the Singapore International Commercial Court Committee*, http://www.mlaw.gov.sg, 30 Sep. 2017.
77. *Report of the Singapore International Commercial Court Committee*, http://www.mlaw.gov.sg, 30 Sep. 2017.
78. *Report of the Singapore International Commercial Court Committee*, http://www.mlaw.gov.sg, 30 Sep. 2017.

the pre-existing Singapore International Arbitration Centre (via the innovative Arb-Med-Arb Protocol in particular). Again, both of these institutions will receive full coverage later in this monograph.

§2. Delimitation of the Subject Matter

I. Definition of the Term 'Civil Procedure'

41. In Singapore, civil procedure:

> may be said to consist of a group of rules and regulations which enable the parties to pursue or defend legal claims, and provide the process by which rights are realised and liabilities imposed on the basis of sufficient evidence. Its primary objective is the just determination of a claim through judicial resolution or settlement … a substantial part of civil procedure is concerned with interlocutory proceedings.[79]

42. In other words, the main aim of the civil procedure regime in Singapore is to ensure that as many matters as possible are taken care of even before the trial begins. This ensures a focused and speedy resolution of disputes, which is a very important aspect of the rule of law. To that end, registrars, who have many powers and responsibilities delegated from judges, play an important role by deciding on a broad range of interlocutory applications. While parties can always make the applications that were supposed to have been made at the pre-trial stage during the trial, such applications are less likely to be granted unless there is good reason to, given that the whole point of bifurcating the civil process is to obviate and preclude such applications to be made only during the trial. Registrars also have adjudicative powers which are not just limited to matters such as summary judgments but the likes of personal bankruptcy and mortgage actions as well; it is also not uncommon for registrars to conduct assessment of damages proceedings. In light of these characteristics, civil procedure is very much different from criminal procedure in Singapore, in that criminal procedure is as much about the trial (if not more) as it is about pre-trial proceedings and applications.

II. Distinction with Other Types of Procedure and Relevant Laws

43. No branch of law exists in a vacuum or compartmentalized state, and civil procedure in Singapore is no different. To properly understand an area of law, one must be aware of the surrounding context in which it operates; in this connection, the branches of law that are the most contiguous to, but yet distinct from, civil procedure are evidence law and the rules on the legal profession Less contiguous are

79. J. Pinsler, *Principles of Civil Procedure* 5, 11 (Acad. Publg. 2013).

the realms of (as mentioned) criminal procedure, administrative law, and alternative dispute resolution, but they will be briefly considered as well.[80]

44. Beginning with evidence law, one must necessarily begin with section 2(2) of the Evidence Act,[81] which declares that all rules of evidence 'not contained in any written law, so far as such rules are inconsistent with any of the provisions of this Act, are repealed'. This has proven to be an extremely troublesome provision, and despite many opportunities to repeal it (in that the Evidence Act has been amended several times, with one round as recent as 2012) since its enactment in the late-1800s, it has been left intact, while other jurisdictions which have similar evidence laws have repealed it. The problems arising from section 2(2) of the Evidence Act have been well-documented elsewhere;[82] the effect of the provision is that any common law developments that is inconsistent with the Evidence Act will not form part of the law in Singapore. The upshot of this is that much of what has developed in the common law world for evidence – such as fundamental concepts relating to burden of proof, standard of proof, hearsay, similar fact, character, opinion, corroboration, privilege, and so on – cannot (notwithstanding the 2012 amendments that broadened the admissibility of hearsay and expert opinion evidence in emulation of common law developments elsewhere) be automatically considered as part of evidence law in Singapore unless the provisions and spirit of the provisions in the Evidence Act do not preclude the reception.[83] However, it can also be said that foreclosure of reception of the aforementioned common law developments has had a larger impact on criminal proceedings than civil proceedings, as matters of evidence in civil proceedings are considerably less controversial.

45. Then there is section 2(1), which declares that the statute (with the exception of just a few provisions) 'shall apply to all judicial proceedings in or before any court, but not affidavits presented to any court or officer nor to proceedings before an arbitrator'. It has thus been argued that the Evidence Act only applies to the adducing of evidence at trial and does not apply to any of the pre-trial stages.[84] However, this claim ignores the obvious fact that many matters relating to evidence have to be sorted out at the pre-trial stage (for instance, during the summons for

80. Another possible area, conflict of laws or private international law, will be considered at various points in the chapters of this monograph.
81. (Cap. 97, 1997 Rev. Ed.).
82. *See* generally J. Pinsler, *Approaches to the Evidence Act: The Judicial Development of a Code*, 14 Sing. Acad. L.J. 365 (2002); C. Siyuan, *The Judicial Discretion to Exclude Relevant Evidence: Perspectives from an Indian Evidence Act Jurisdiction*, 16 Intl. J. Evid. & Proof 398 (2012); C. Siyuan, *The 2012 Amendments to Singapore's Evidence Act: More Questions than Answers as Regards Expert Opinion Evidence?*, 34 Statute L. Rev. 262 (2013); C. Siyuan, *The Future of the Similar Fact Rule in an Indian Evidence Act Jurisdiction*, 6 Nat. U. Jur. Sci. L. Rev. 361 (2014); C. Siyuan, *Redefining Relevancy and Exclusionary Discretion in Sir James Fitzjames Stephen's Indian Evidence Act of 1872: The Singapore Experiment and Lessons for Other Indian Evidence Act Jurisdictions*, 10 Intl. Comm. Evid. 1 (2014).
83. *See also* C. Siyuan, *Criminal Evidence and Procedure* in *Singapore Law: 50 Years in the Making* (Goh Y.H. & P. Tan eds., Acad. Publg. 2015).
84. *Singapore Civil Procedure 2015 Volume 1*, at 735 (G.P. Selvam ed., Sweet & Maxwell Asia 2014), citing *Riedel-de Haen AG v. Liew Keng Pang*, [1989] 1 SLR(R) 417. However, it is also clear that the Rules of Court contain various references to evidence law.

directions phase), so that time and money will not be wasted later on. On the topic of relevance, questions still persist as to how the Evidence Act conceptualizes and defines relevance (i.e., whether it refers to legal or logical relevance, and whether relevance leads to automatic admissibility and whether relevant and reliable evidence can be excluded, and on what requirements and justifications), though it may be said that having judges as fact-finders considerably lessens the importance of this concern.[85]

46. All of these preliminary points aside, where evidence law most clearly intersects with civil procedure on a regular basis are where the rules of privilege and hearsay are engaged, and where questions of admissibility of new evidence at appellate proceedings arise (this will be addressed in a subsequent Part) – and the requisite standard and burden of proof. Dealing with the last point first, the Evidence Act actually does not explicitly distinguish between the two most well-established common law standards of proof. The specific language used in the Evidence Act is a 'fact is said to be "proved" when, after considering the matters before it, the court either believes it to exist or considers its existence so probable that a prudent man ought, under the circumstances of the particular case, to act upon the supposition that it exists'.[86] Nonetheless, the established position in Singapore case law is that the Evidence Act conceivably bifurcates between the established common law standards,[87] though there have been suggestions that there should be a third standard established for less serious crimes.[88] Discerning the appropriate burden of proof in the Evidence Act, especially for civil cases, is less problematic.[89] First, section 103(1) states that: 'Whoever desires any court to give judgment as to any legal right or liability, dependent on the existence of facts which he asserts, must prove that those facts exist.' Second, section 104 states that: 'The burden of proof in a suit or proceeding lies on that person who would fail if no evidence at all were given on either side.' Third, section 105 states that: 'The burden of proof as to any particular fact lies on that person who wishes the court to believe in its existence, unless it is provided by any law that the proof of that fact shall lie on any particular person.'

85. *See* generally C. Siyuan, *The Judicial Discretion to Exclude Relevant Evidence: Perspectives from an Indian Evidence Act Jurisdiction*, 16 Intl. J. Evid. & Proof 398 (2012); C. Siyuan & N. Poon, *Reliability and Relevance as the Touchstones for Admissibility of Evidence in Criminal Proceedings*, 24 Sing. Acad. L.J. 535 (2012); C. Siyuan, *The 2012 Amendments to Singapore's Evidence Act: More Questions than Answers as Regards Expert Opinion Evidence?* 34 Stat. L. Rev. 262 (2013); C. Siyuan, *The Future of the Similar Fact Rule in an Indian Evidence Act Jurisdiction*, 6 Nat. U. Jur. Sci. L. Rev. 361 (2014); C. Siyuan, *Redefining Relevancy and Exclusionary Discretion in Sir James Fitzjames Stephen's Indian Evidence Act of 1872: The Singapore Experiment and Lessons for Other Indian Evidence Act Jurisdictions*, 10 Intl. Comm. Evid. 1 (2014).
86. Evidence Act (Cap. 97, 1997 Rev. Ed.), s 3(3).
87. C. Siyuan, *A Preliminary Survey of the Right to Presumption of Innocence in Singapore*, 7 LAWASIA J. 79, 84–85 (2012).
88. *See* C. Siyuan, *The Power of the Court to Change an Order for the Division of Matrimonial Assets*, Sing. L. Watch Commentaries (2012).
89. For criminal cases, *see* C. Siyuan, *A Preliminary Survey of the Right to Presumption of Innocence in Singapore*, 7 LAWASIA J. 79, 84–87 (2012).

47. When these provisions are read together, a plaintiff (including a defendant counterclaiming) has the burden of proof to prove his claim (on a balance of probabilities); once sufficient evidence has been adduced, the evidential burden shifts to the defendant, who can successfully defend his claim by showing that the balance does not lie with the plaintiff. One complication arises, however, when section 108 is considered: 'When any fact is especially within the knowledge of any person, the burden of proving that fact is upon him.' While the language of the provision suggests that the burden of proof may shift in the proving of certain facts that is 'especially within the knowledge' of a party (i.e., defendant), it has been clarified that section 108:

> is an exception to the general rule contained in section 103 of the Evidence Act .... Section 108 of the Evidence Act applies only to those matters which are supposed to be within the knowledge of a defendant. It cannot apply when the fact or facts are such that they are capable of being known also by a person other than the defendant.[90]

48. Moving on to privilege (i.e., legal advice privilege and litigation privilege), section 128 of the Evidence Act states:

> (1) No advocate or solicitor shall at any time be permitted, unless with his client's express consent, to disclose any communication made to him in the course and for the purpose of his employment as such advocate or solicitor by or on behalf of his client, or to state the contents or condition of any document with which he has become acquainted in the course and for the purpose of his professional employment, or to disclose any advice given by him to his client in the course and for the purpose of such employment.
> (2) Nothing in this section shall protect from disclosure:
> (a) any such communication made in furtherance of any illegal purpose;
> (b) any fact observed by any advocate or solicitor in the course of his employment as such showing that any crime or fraud has been committed since the commencement of his employment.
> (3) It is immaterial whether the attention of such advocate or solicitor was or was not directed to such fact by or on behalf of his client.[91]

49. Next, section 131(1) states:

> No one shall be compelled to disclose to the court any confidential communication which has taken place between him and his legal professional adviser unless he offers himself as a witness, in which case he may be compelled to

90. *Surender Singh s/o Jagdish Singh (administrators of the estate of Narindar Kaur d/o Sarwan Singh, deceased) v. Li Man Kay*, [2010] 1 SLR 428 at [217]; cited in *Wong Leong Wei Edward v. Acclaim Insurance Brokers Pte Ltd*, [2010] SGHC 352, [29].
91. Section 128A is one of the new privilege provisions introduced in 2012, and targets communications with in-house legal counsel.

disclose any such communications as may appear to the court necessary to be known in order to explain any evidence which he has given, but no others.

50. The Court of Appeal has clarified that when section 128 is read with section 131:

> it becomes clear that they complement each other and give full effect to the legal advice privilege, as the latter provision protects the client from not having to disclose to any other party any legal advice which he has obtained from his legal adviser, whether he is an advocate or a solicitor ...
>
> ... since s 131 is expressed to operate in the broader context of court proceedings where the client might offer himself as a witness, in which case he may be compelled to disclose any communication the court deems necessary, it also extends the area of legal advice privilege to the domain of litigation privilege. That this is the intention of s 131 is made clear by the reference to the use of the expression 'legal professional adviser' who need not necessarily be an advocate or solicitor. When s 131 was enacted, the legal profession in Singapore did not have any advocates or solicitors .... But litigation privilege was applied to all legal advisers involved in assisting their respective clients in litigation.[92]

51. Privilege, of course, is a fundamental right of litigants in an adversarial system[93] and is particularly crucial in civil disputes and may be invoked at the discovery or interrogatories stage, or even during cross-examination at trial.[94]

52. As for hearsay evidence, as alluded to earlier, the Evidence Act is rather murky on this even after recent amendments were made to the relevant provisions. On one view, section 62 offers a starting point on how hearsay is conceptualized in the Evidence Act; the provision states that oral evidence 'must in all cases whatever be direct'. However, not only is section 62 confined to oral evidence, but also it is not located in the Part of the Evidence Act that defines relevance – and therefore admissibility.[95] Indeed, whereas the common law considers hearsay as an exclusionary rule – thus hearsay evidence may only be admissible if it falls under an exception – the Evidence Act does not conceptualize exclusionary evidence in

92. *Skandinaviska Enskilda Banken AB (Publ), Singapore Branch v. Asia Pacific Breweries (Singapore) Pte Ltd*, [2007] 2 SLR(R) 367, [33]–[34].

93. *See* generally *Skandinaviska Enskilda Banken AB (Publ), Singapore Branch v. Asia Pacific Breweries (Singapore) Pte Ltd*, [2007] 2 SLR(R) 367. *See also id.*, [43]–[44] on the relationship between legal advice privilege and litigation privilege.

94. In *HT SRL v. Wee Shuo Woon*, [2016] 2 SLR 442, [19]–[21] and [26]–[40], the court distinguished between admissibility and privilege, and further discussed how privilege related to the law of confidence (such as how an injunction might be granted to prevent the authorized use of confidential information).

95. *See also* C. Siyuan and L. Leo, *The Law of Evidence in Singapore* 276–277 (Sweet & Maxwell 2016).

exclusionary terms but inclusionary terms.[96] The result of this is that the statute (following the 2012 amendments) sets out a series of circumstances in which hearsay evidence may be admitted as evidence, such as when it relates to cause of death, is made in course of trade, or even by agreement.[97]

53. In limited situations, the court has been statutorily conferred discretion to 'exclude' relevant hearsay evidence if it is not 'in the interests of justice to treat it as relevant'.[98] Ultimately, however, the prohibition against hearsay evidence has always been enforced less stringently in civil matters, and the 2012 amendments to the Evidence Act that increased the number of exceptions to the hearsay rule simply confirm this (and indeed, mirror the trends in many common law jurisdictions where the prohibition of hearsay evidence in civil cases has effectively been abolished). It can also be said that as long as the court – which now only comprises professional judges as fact-finders after the jury system was abolished decades ago – is able to weigh the relevance and reliability of hearsay evidence and accord it the appropriate weight once the evidential record is examined as a whole, any concerns regarding hearsay evidence are largely ameliorated.

54. This is provided, of course, that the court bears in mind that:

> Primarily, a witness cannot verify the truth of facts … which he did not personally perceive. As the witness is not legally obliged to account for such facts by oath or affirmation, the statement lacks a vital safeguard. Furthermore, the witness's lack of personal knowledge of the circumstances referred to by the statement means that scrutiny through cross-examination can be avoided. It is logical to assume that the testimony of a witness, who knows that he may be exposed in cross-examination and prosecuted for perjury if he fabricates evidence, is more likely to be reliable than a statement made in ordinary conversation without fear of exposure (at trial) and punishment. The danger of unreliability is very real. The outsider's statement may be a fabrication or based on a mistake or carelessly made or an exaggeration.[99]

---

96. *See* generally C. Siyuan, *The Judicial Discretion to Exclude Relevant Evidence: Perspectives from an Indian Evidence Act Jurisdiction*, 16 Intl. J. Evid. & Proof 398 (2012); C. Siyuan & N. Poon, *Reliability and Relevance as the Touchstones for Admissibility of Evidence in Criminal Proceedings*, 24 Sing. Acad. L.J. 535 (2012); C. Siyuan, *The 2012 Amendments to Singapore's Evidence Act: More Questions than Answers as Regards Expert Opinion Evidence?*, 34 Statute L. Rev. 262 (2013); C. Siyuan, *The Future of the Similar Fact Rule in an Indian Evidence Act Jurisdiction*, 6 Nat. U. Jur. Sci. L. Rev. 361 (2014); C. Siyuan, *Redefining Relevancy and Exclusionary Discretion in Sir James Fitzjames Stephen's Indian Evidence Act of 1872: The Singapore Experiment and Lessons for Other Indian Evidence Act Jurisdictions*, 10 Intl. Comm. Evid. 1 (2014).
97. *See* Evidence Act (Cap. 97, 1997 Rev. Ed.), s 32.
98. Evidence Act (Cap. 97, 1997 Rev. Ed.), s 32(3). This discretion is similarly extended to the reception of expert opinion evidence: *id.*, s 47(4). *See also* C. Siyuan, *The Future of the Similar Fact Rule in an Indian Evidence Act Jurisdiction*, 6 Nat. U. Jur. Sci. L. Rev. 361 (2014); C. Siyuan, *Redefining Relevancy and Exclusionary Discretion in Sir James Fitzjames Stephen's Indian Evidence Act of 1872: The Singapore Experiment and Lessons for Other Indian Evidence Act Jurisdictions*, 10 Intl. Comm. Evid. 1 (2014); C. Siyuan, *'In the Interests of Justice' as the New Test to Exclude Relevant Evidence in Singapore*, 19 Intl. J. Evid. & Proof 67 (2014).
99. J. Pinsler, *Evidence and the Litigation Process*, 116–117 (4th ed., LexisNexis 2013).

55. Before departing from evidence law, it may be helpful to briefly consider a few other rules in evidence law that emerge from time to time in civil claims. The first pertains to the so-called best evidence rule, which is reflected in sections 63–67 of the Evidence Act; these provisions require 'primary' evidence (in the form of original documents) to be given but provide certain exceptions for 'secondary' evidence.[100] However, the Court of Appeal has noted that in modern-day civil litigation where copious documents are the norm, it may not be entirely realistic (or practical or fair) to apply the best evidence rule with punctilious insistence, and has modified the contours of the rule accordingly.[101]

56. The second pertains to the without prejudice rule, which is reflected in section 23 of the Evidence Act: 'In civil cases, no admission is relevant if it is made … upon an express condition that evidence of it is not to be given; or … upon circumstances from which the court can infer that the parties agreed together that evidence of it should not be given.' The Court of Appeal has observed that:

> Even though a piece of correspondence is not marked 'without prejudice', it may still be excluded if it is made in the course of negotiations to settle a dispute … However, where the correspondence concerned is in fact marked … 'the presence of [these] words would place the burden of persuasion on the party who contended that [these] words should be ignored' …
>
> [However, one] key exception … is where 'without prejudice' communications are admitted to determine whether there was a compromise reached and, if so, what the terms … were.[102]

57. The third pertains to the concept of inherent jurisdiction and inherent powers.[103] These are terms that are frequently encountered but their meanings and limits have proven to be quite elusive;[104] at the most basic level, and on one conception, 'jurisdiction' refers to a court's authority to hear a dispute (bearing in mind that a court is ultimately a creature of statute (and therefore Parliament)), 'inherent jurisdiction' refers to a court's inherent authority to hear a dispute, and 'inherent power' refers to a court's power to make certain orders even if a statute has not provided for such a power. In the context of civil litigation, a court may from time to time claim to tap into its inherent powers to assert control over its process and even purport to override what the rules clearly state so as to ensure justice between parties, but given the necessarily limited nature of these powers, such invocation is only used as a matter of last resort and in fairly extreme circumstances (to be clear, sometimes the rules may actually expressly provide for a court's inherent 'power' or

---

100. *Jet Holding Ltd v. Cooper Cameron (Singapore) Pte Ltd*, [2006] 3 SLR(R) 769, [37]–[38].
101. *Jet Holding Ltd v. Cooper Cameron (Singapore) Pte Ltd*, [2006] 3 SLR(R) 769, [48]–[66].
102. *Quek Kheng Leong Nicky v. Teo Beng Ngoh*, [2009] 4 SLR(R) 181, [22] and [24], citing *Greenline-Onyx Envirotech Phils, Inc v. Otto Systems Singapore Pte Ltd*, [2007] 3 SLR(R) 40.
103. The courts' inherent jurisdiction in relation to procedural rules for civil proceedings will be covered in greater detail elsewhere in this monograph.
104. *See Re Nalpon Zero Geraldo Mario*, [2013] 3 SLR 258; *Arun Kaliamurthy v. Public Prosecutor*, [2014] 3 SLR 1023; *ANB v. ANC*, [2014] 4 SLR 747; *Wan Lai Ting v. Kea Kah Kim*, [2014] 4 SLR 795; *Au Wai Pang v. Attorney-General*, [2014] 3 SLR 357.

'jurisdiction' to do as it sees fit, but it has to be borne in mind that such rules are almost always subsidiary legislation and do not have the proper weight of parliamentary contemplation).[105] However, in recent jurisprudence, there appears to have been a conflation of jurisdiction and power, thus perpetuating the mis-descriptions of 'inherent jurisdiction' when courts actually mean the exercise of 'inherent powers'.[106] Thus, even in the evidence law context, it has been said that the admissibility of certain types of potentially unreliable evidence is only permissible as a matter of exceptional jurisdiction,[107] despite (as mentioned) the fact that the Evidence Act was not conceptualized with the decoupling of relevance and admissibility in mind.[108] Nonetheless, ambiguities are obviated as long as one maintains the distinction between jurisdiction and power – jurisdiction is more appropriately used to where there is a dispute of forum, dispute of competence, or (as mentioned) dispute of authority; further, it should be borne in mind that any invocation of inherent powers in the civil context is done at the pre-trial stage – to be able to invoke them in the criminal context at the trial stage to exclude relevant evidence, presents another set of problems.

58. The law of civil procedure also intersects with the rules of the legal profession in that both sets of laws demonstrate how a lawyer has at least[109] dual duties:[110] a duty not only to his client (for instance, not to overcharge when billing[111] and to be reasonably competent),[112] but also an overriding duty to the court (for instance, to remind the client that important evidence should not be withheld from the court during the various pre-trial and trial processes, such as discovery). Parenthetically, the term 'duty', however, may be broadly conceived and some disambiguation is warranted. On the one hand, it may be perceived to comprise only binding and legal obligations (with the more egregious breaches resulting in serious

---

105. For criminal proceedings, *see Kho Jabing v. Public Prosecutor*, [2016] 3 SLR 135, [18]–[23]; *Roslan bin Bakar v. Public Prosecutor*, [2016] 3 SLR 1023, [34]–[42].

106. *See* C. Siyuan, *Is the Invocation of Inherent Jurisdiction the Same as the Exercise of Inherent Powers?* 17 Intl. J. Evid. & Proof 367 (2013); C. Siyuan, *Jurisdiction, Power, Inherent Jurisdiction, and Inherent Power*, Sing. L. Watch Commentaries (2013).

107. *See Teo Wai Cheong v. Crédit Industriel et Commercial*, [2013] 3 SLR 573.

108. *See* generally C. Siyuan, *The Judicial Discretion to Exclude Relevant Evidence: Perspectives from an Indian Evidence Act Jurisdiction*, 16 Intl. J. Evid. & Proof 398 (2012); C. Siyuan & N. Poon, *Reliability and Relevance as the Touchstones for Admissibility of Evidence in Criminal Proceedings*, 24 Sing. Acad. L.J. 535 (2012); C. Siyuan, *The 2012 Amendments to Singapore's Evidence Act: More Questions than Answers as Regards Expert Opinion Evidence?* 34 Statute L. Rev. 262 (2013); C. Siyuan, *The Future of the Similar Fact Rule in an Indian Evidence Act Jurisdiction*, 6 Nat. U. Jur. Sci. L. Rev. 361 (2014); C. Siyuan, *Redefining Relevancy and Exclusionary Discretion in Sir James Fitzjames Stephen's Indian Evidence Act of 1872: The Singapore Experiment and Lessons for Other Indian Evidence Act Jurisdictions*, 10 Intl. Comm. Evid. 1 (2014); C. Siyuan, '*In the Interests of Justice' as the New Test to Exclude Relevant Evidence in Singapore*, 19 Intl. J. Evid. & Proof 67 (2014).

109. It may even be said that lawyers have duties towards other lawyers, but the connecting factor for all the different types of duties is the expectation to behave honestly and with integrity.

110. *See also* J. Pinsler, *Ethics and Professional Responsibility* 4 (Acad. Publg. 2007).

111. *See also* Legal Profession (Professional Conduct) Rules, (Cap. 161, R 1, 2000 Rev. Ed.), R 38.

112. Legal Profession (Professional Conduct) Rules, (Cap. 161, R 1, 2000 Rev. Ed.), R 16: 'An advocate and solicitor shall not accept instructions in a field of practice in which he possesses insufficient knowledge, skill or experience to provide competent representation to the client.'

disciplinary sanctions). On the other hand, it may be perceived to include ethical (but non-binding) obligations as well. Another potential complication arises when the duty to the client clashes with the duty to the court – theoretically, the latter duty overrides the former duty, but it may not always be easy to distinguish between presenting the client's best possible case and conducting oneself honourably (or even just ethically) before a court.[113]

59. At any rate, the Legal Profession Act[114] and the Legal Profession (Professional Conduct) Rules[115] form the main pieces of legislation that govern the professional conduct of lawyers.[116] These two pieces of legislation capture a broad array of obligations for the lawyer, but it is the latter that is more pertinent for present purposes, particularly with regard to the preparation of a trial. For instance, if 'at any time before judgment is delivered in any case, an advocate and solicitor becomes aware that his client has committed perjury or has otherwise been guilty of fraud upon the Court', the lawyer is expected to discharge from acting further in the case.[117] To cite another example, a lawyer:

> shall cease to act for a client if … the client refuses to authorise him to make some disclosure to the Court which his duty to the Court requires him to make; … the advocate and solicitor having become aware during the course of a case of the existence of a document which should have been but has not been disclosed on discovery, the client fails forthwith to disclose it; or … having come into possession of a document belonging to another party by some means other than the normal and proper channels and having read it, he would thereby be embarrassed in the discharge of his duties by the knowledge of the contents of the document.[118]

60. The rules also regulate proceedings during the trial. For instance, during cross-examination, a lawyer:

> shall not make statements or ask questions which are scandalous or intended to insult or calculated only to vilify insult or annoy either the witness or any other person or are otherwise an abuse of the function of the advocate and solicitor; and … shall exercise his own judgment both as to the substance and the form of the questions put or statements made.[119]

---

113. A classic – but theoretically easily disposable – example of this dilemma arises when the lawyer has to choose between characterizing his client's arguments in the best possible terms and citing authorities to the court in a way that is misleading, selective, and/or out of context. In this regard, *see* Legal Profession (Professional Conduct) Rules, (Cap. 161, R 1, 2000 Rev. Ed.), R 56. *See also id.*, R 60.
114. (Cap. 161, 2009 Rev. Ed.).
115. (Cap. 161, R 1, 2010 Rev. Ed.).
116. J. Pinsler, *Ethics and Professional Responsibility* (Acad. Publg. 2007), 9. The common law has a role to play as well; a notable example is the development of the concept of Chinese walls: *id.*, 282–283.
117. Legal Profession (Professional Conduct) Rules, (Cap. 161, R 1, 2010 Rev. Ed.), R 57.
118. Legal Profession (Professional Conduct) Rules, (Cap. 161, R 1, 2010 Rev. Ed.), R 58.
119. Legal Profession (Professional Conduct) Rules, (Cap. 161, R 1, 2010 Rev. Ed.), R 61.

61. To cite another example, a lawyer:

> representing an interested party shall not initiate communication with the Court about the facts, issues or any other matter in a case that the advocate and solicitor knows is pending or likely to be pending before the Court unless the advocate and solicitor has first informed the persons acting for all other interested parties of the nature of the matters he wishes to communicate with the Court and has given them an opportunity to be present or to reply.[120]

62. In terms of undertakings to the court – breaches of which may lead to committal, contempt, or disciplinary proceedings, it is stated that a lawyer 'shall honour the terms of a professional undertaking given to another advocate and solicitor, a court of law, tribunal, client or any other person'.[121] Finally, the rules also regulate conflicts of interest. For instance, a lawyer 'shall not accept instructions in a case in which the advocate and solicitor has reason to believe that he is likely to be a witness on a material question of fact'[122] and 'shall not appear before a Court in a matter where … by reason of his relationship with the client it would be difficult for the advocate and solicitor to maintain his professional independence'.[123] To cite another example, when:

> an advocate and solicitor or any member of his firm has acted for more than one party in the preparation of a document creating rights and obligations between them and a dispute in relation to the matter has arisen between them … the advocate and solicitor or any member of his firm shall not act for any party to the transaction in relation to that dispute.[124]

63. As a final example, 'advocate and solicitor who has acted for a client in a matter shall not thereafter act against the client (or against persons who were involved in or associated with the client in that matter) in the same or any related matter'.[125]

64. Turning to criminal procedure, in Singapore the criminal process is vastly different from the civil process in many respects, and questions have emerged as to why there is so much divergence rather than convergence.[126] Criminal procedure in Singapore is largely regulated by the Criminal Procedure Code,[127] which had overhauled its decades-old predecessor in 2010 after long-standing calls to reform the

120. Legal Profession (Professional Conduct) Rules, (Cap. 161, R 1, 2010 Rev. Ed.), R 63(1).
121. Legal Profession (Professional Conduct) Rules, (Cap. 161, R 1, 2010 Rev. Ed.), R 51.
122. Legal Profession (Professional Conduct) Rules, (Cap. 161, R 1, 2010 Rev. Ed.), R 64(1).
123. Legal Profession (Professional Conduct) Rules, (Cap. 161, R 1, 2010 Rev. Ed.), R 65.
124. Legal Profession (Professional Conduct) Rules, (Cap. 161, R 1, 2010 Rev. Ed.), R 29(1).
125. Legal Profession (Professional Conduct) Rules, (Cap. 161, R 1, 2010 Rev. Ed.), R 31(1).
126. Part of this may be attributed to the 'crime control' model (as opposed to the 'due process' model) that Singapore has adopted for the larger part of its history as regards its philosophy towards criminal justice: C. Siyuan, *The Prosecution's Duty of Disclosure in Singapore*, 11 Oxford U. Cmmw. L.J. 207 (2012).
127. (Cap. 68, 2012 Rev. Ed.).

criminal justice process to be less state-centric[128] (in comparison, the rules on civil procedure receive far greater attention with regard to possible reform and improvement). Whereas parties in a civil dispute are presupposed to be of equal status and expected to deal with each other at arm's length – and this is reflected in the various rules, such as those governing pleadings and discovery[129] – it has taken a while for the dichotomy between the accused individual and the state in the criminal justice context for the gap to be bridged. For instance:

> Part IX of the Criminal Procedure Code … is an entirely new construct that is intended to give effect to the pre-trial procedures in the Subordinate Courts [now known as State Courts] introduced by the Code. In particular, the provisions introduce a new criminal case disclosure regime that operates on a quid pro quo basis by formalising the framework obliging the prosecution and the defence to exchange relevant information about their respective cases before trial. As stated by the Minister of Law when passing the Code, these new pre-trial procedures are intended to provide transparency and consistency to the pre-trial process.[130]

65. Generally, however, the Criminal Procedure Code is barely a few years old, and it will take some time for the common law to develop the jurisprudential philosophy of the law on criminal procedure in Singapore.

66. Then there is the integral part of administrative law – or judicial review. While the topic warrants a monograph on its own, certain universally important (substantive) elements must necessarily be touched upon. Essentially, judicial review in Singapore may (following traditional English law) be brought under the established grounds of illegality, irrationality, and procedural impropriety.[131] Of these three heads, two of them bear some relevance in civil litigation generally. The first, illegality, is tangential, but useful to understand. For example, its embedded sub-concepts of ultra vires and legitimate expectations are rather related to civil process generally. The second, procedural impropriety, is more apparently relevant. Specifically, its sub-concept of the rules of natural justice and the twin elements therein of a fair hearing (or *audi alteram partem*) and the rule against bias may form the grounds of altering a judgment in some form.[132]

67. It is apposite to conclude this survey with alternative dispute resolution (or ADR) as questions of jurisdiction and powers arise. In Singapore, alternative dispute resolution in the forms of, amongst others, arbitration and mediation, have

---

128. *See also* M. Chng, *Modernising the Criminal Justice Framework – The Criminal Procedure Code 2010*, 23 Sing. Acad. L.J. 23 (2011).
129. *See also* D. Wong, *Discovering the Right to Criminal Disclosure – Lessons from Civil Procedure*, 25 Sing. Acad. L.J. 548 (2013).
130. *The Criminal Procedure Code of Singapore* 233 (J. Marie & M. Faizal eds., Acad. Publg. 2012).
131. *Chng Suan Tze v. Minister for Home Affairs*, [1988] 2 SLR(R) 525, [119].
132. *See also* C. Siyuan & L. Leo, *Natural Justice: A Case for Uniform Rigour*, 20 Sing. Acad. L.J. 820 (2009); C. Siyuan & L. Leo, *Reasonable Suspicion or Real Likelihood: A Question of Semantics*, Sing. J. Leg. Stud. 446 (2008).

become increasingly popular due to strong support from the judiciary and strong ADR institutions. The Singapore Institute of Arbitrators promotes domestic arbitration while the Singapore International Arbitration Centre (SIAC) is an arbitration centre for both domestic and international arbitration. Commercial mediation services are provided by the Singapore Mediation Centre (or the SMC). Various government agencies, such as the Community Mediation Centres,[133] and the State Courts also offer mediation services.[134] Alternative dispute resolution has been utilized to divert suitable disputes from the Singapore courts.[135] Diversion is done during pre-trial hearings when the registrar or judge may suggest to the parties that the dispute should be arbitrated or mediated rather than litigated. It is then for the parties to decide whether or not to act on the court's suggestion.

68. The Rules of Court also state that a matter to be taken into account by the court when exercising its discretion as to costs 'the parties' conduct in relation to any attempt at resolving the cause or matter by mediation or any other means of dispute resolution'.[136] This provision brings the Singapore position quite close to that in England where the Civil Procedure Rules also permit consideration of the conduct of the parties to try to resolve the dispute in arriving at an appropriate determination as to costs.[137] In a recent Court of Appeal decision, although no explicit reference was made to the Rules of Court, both parties were ordered to bear their own costs for the appeal proceedings and those below in the light of their 'questionable conduct' that 'stoked sterile litigation'.[138] The Court of Appeal also observed that the parties' dispute was a matter that 'ought to have been resolved by the application of commercial common sense in good faith through the mediation process, rather than through the adversarial curial process'.[139]

69. The judiciary's attitude towards arbitration has also been extremely supportive. The Court of Appeal has held that the Singapore courts will intervene in arbitrations 'only sparingly and in very narrow circumstances, such as where the arbitral tribunal cannot be constituted expediently enough, where the court's coercive enforcement powers are required or where the arbitral tribunal has no jurisdiction to grant the relief sought in the matter at hand'.[140] Further, the Supreme Court and the State Courts employ other unique techniques to encourage ADR in their separate contexts.

---

133. *See* Community Mediation Centres Act (Cap. 49A, 1998 Rev. Ed.); *Community Mediation Centre Website*, http://www.cmc.gov.sg/, 30 Sep. 2017.
134. *See* generally Teh H.H., *Mediation Practices in ASEAN – the Singapore Experience*, paper presented at the 11th General Assembly of the ASEAN Law Association (2012).
135. *Overcoming Backlogs*, http://app.subcourts.gov.sg/Data/Files/File/Speeches/CJChanSpeech_OvercomingBacklogs.pdf, 30 Sep. 2017.
136. Supreme Court of Judicature Act (Cap. 322, R. 5, 2014 Rev. Ed.) Rules of Court, O 59 r 1.
137. English Civil Procedure Rules 1998, Rule 44.5(3)(a).
138. *HSBC Institutional Trust Services (Singapore) Ltd (trustee of Starhill Global Real Estate Investment Trust) v. Toshin Development Singapore Pte Ltd*, [2012] 4 SLR 738, [72].
139. *HSBC Institutional Trust Services (Singapore) Ltd (trustee of Starhill Global Real Estate Investment Trust) v. Toshin Development Singapore Pte Ltd*, [2012] 4 SLR 738, [68].
140. *NCC International AB v. Alliance Concrete Singapore Pte Ltd*, [2008] 2 SLR(R) 565, [53].

70. The Supreme Court partners with the SMC and provides to it information on cases ready for their first pre-trial conference and cases that have reached their fourteen month mark.[141] The SMC will then issue a letter explaining the benefits of mediation and inviting the parties to consider mediation. This partnership with the SMC has produced favourable results. For example, in 2011, 68 out of 146 or 46.6% of the cases dealt with by the SMC were referred to it by the Supreme Court Registry or by Judges or Registrars of the Supreme Court.[142] In general, the SMC's settlement rate of mediated cases is about 75%.[143] Of the disputants who provided feedback after mediation at the SMC, 84% reported costs savings, 88% reported time savings and 94% would recommend the process to other persons in the same conflict situation.[144]

71. The State Courts, unlike the Supreme Court, offers court dispute resolution services, including mediation and neutral services at its Primary Dispute Resolution Centre (PDRC) for motor vehicle accident cases not involving personal injuries and civil cases where parties consent; the Maintenance Mediation Chambers in the Family Court for maintenance-related complaints; the Magistrates' Courts for Magistrates' complaints concerning interpersonal relationships; and in the Small Claims Tribunals for claims less than SGD 10,000.[145] The effectiveness of court dispute resolution in the State Courts is evident from the following statistics: 'in 2010, there were a total of 20,436 civil, family and criminal cases that were mediated. Of these, 17,913 (or 88%) settled. From January to September 2011, 14,948 cases were mediated, of which 13,051 (or 87%) settled.'[146] For Magistrates' complaints, in 2010, about 90% of the cases were disposed of by mediation; an increase from 83% of the cases disposed by mediation in 2008.[147] In 2009, only three Magistrates' complaints proceeded to trial, and for the first ten months of 2011, only two proceeded to trial.[148]

72. To further enhance the use of court dispute resolution, the Subordinate Courts (as they then were) had in recent years introduced Practice Direction No 2 of 2010 and Practice Directions Amendment No 2 of 2012.[149] The former requires solicitors and the parties to fill up an 'ADR Form' and submit it. When submitted,

---

141. Teh H.H., *Mediation Practices in ASEAN – the Singapore Experience*, paper presented at the 11th General Assembly of the ASEAN Law Association (2012); L. Boulle & Teh H.H., *Mediation – Principles, Process and Practice* 216 (Butterworths Asia 2000).
142. The H.H., *Mediation Practices in ASEAN – the Singapore Experience*, paper presented at the 11th General Assembly of the ASEAN Law Association (2012).
143. *Frequently Asked Questions*, http://www.mediation.com.sg, 30 Sep. 2017.
144. *Frequently Asked Questions*, http://www.mediation.com.sg, 30 Sep. 2017.
145. *Court Dispute Resolution/Mediation*, http://app.subcourts.gov.sg/civil/page.aspx?pageid=54106, 30 Sep. 2017.
146. Teh H.H., *Mediation Practices in ASEAN – the Singapore Experience*, paper presented at the 11th General Assembly of the ASEAN Law Association (2012).
147. K.C. Vijayan, *Fewer Neighbours Take Fight to Court*, The Straits Times (6 Dec. 2011).
148. C. Quek, *Number of Neighbour Disputes Hit Hgh; Neighbours Lack Communication and Increasingly Intolerant: CMC*, Today (Singapore) (8 Aug. 2011).
149. *See* generally J. Low & D. Quek, *Introducing a 'Presumption of ADR' for Civil Matters in the Subordinate Courts*, Sing. L. Gaz. (May 2012).

a judicial officer will recommend that the matter proceed on one of the three tracks: mediation in the PDRC or the SMC; arbitration at the Law Society Arbitration Scheme; or adjudication in the trial courts.[150] The latter introduces a 'presumption of ADR' for civil matters in the State Courts, whereby all civil matters in the State Courts are treated on two tracks: a 'recommended ADR' track; and a 'general' track. The 'recommended ADR' track applies to cases where the claim is SGD 20,000 or less; and the 'general' track to cases where the claim is between SGD 20,000 and SGD 60,000 and will take more than three days of trial.[151] When a case is on a 'recommended ADR' track, a party may opt out for three reasons: ADR has been attempted before; the dispute involves a question of law; or for other good reason. Any deviation may be taken into account by the court for the purposes of costs. Where a case is on a 'general' track, a party may opt out for any reason.[152]

73. In 2014, the Rules of Court were amended, stipulating that in civil claims up to SGD 60,000, parties must file the documents and pleadings first and try to negotiate for a resolution to settle the matter early if possible. In 2015, a new division known as the Community Justice and Tribunals Division was established in the State Courts. This division will comprise the Small Claims Tribunal and Community Disputes Resolution Tribunals. The latter will specialize in resolving simple disputes between neighbours at low costs and without lawyers, as well as provide civil and criminal recourse for victims of harassment. The effect of all these measures, both in the State Courts and in the Supreme Court, is to ensure that cases that may be more cost-effectively and suitably resolved via ADR are diverted to ADR instead of being put through time-consuming and costly adversarial litigation.

III. Other Court Systems and Rules of Procedure

74. The rules of procedure discussed herein only apply to court litigation (of all levels) in Singapore. They do not apply to alternative or parallel proceedings such as mediation and arbitration (whether domestic or international). For those processes, the relevant tribunals are usually given liberty to set the own procedural rules (usually of a more flexible standard).

75. The Singapore International Commercial Court would have its own set of procedural rules, and will be discussed later in this monograph together, while its complementary institutions in the form of the SIAC and Singapore International Mediation Centre will also be considered.

150. J. Low & D. Quek, *The ADR Form in the Subordinate Courts: Finding the Appropriate Mode of Dispute Resolution*, Sing. L. Gaz. 18–20 (April 2010).
151. J. Low & D. Quek, *The ADR Form in the Subordinate Courts: Finding the Appropriate Mode of Dispute Resolution*, Sing. L. Gaz. 18–20 (April 2010).
152. J. Low & D. Quek, *The ADR Form in the Subordinate Courts: Finding the Appropriate Mode of Dispute Resolution*, Sing. L. Gaz. 18–20 (April 2010).

§3. SOURCES OF LAW AND HISTORICAL BACKGROUND

I. Reception and Creation of Law of Civil Procedure

76. Civil justice – and concomitantly, civil procedure – is generally considered the bedrock of litigation in Singapore, permeating every aspect of a civil lawsuit regardless of subject matter.

77. Civil procedure sets the standards and rules that govern how a party may pursue or defend a civil claim from commencement (and at times, pre-commencement) to judgment. It stipulates timelines, the types of documents that must be filed and served, the orders that may be made by the court, the manner court proceedings are conducted, avenues to enforce court orders, and so forth. The primary objective of civil procedure today may be said to be 'the just determination of a claim through judicial resolution or settlement'.[153] To that end, civil procedure ought not to be viewed as a set of rigid rules controlling substantive access to justice. Rather, since the enactment of the English Supreme Court of Judicature Acts of 1873[154] and 1875,[155] 'the relation of rules of practice to the work of justice is intended to be that of handmaid rather than mistress'.[156]

78. As will also be seen in the rest of this monograph,[157] much of Singapore's law on civil procedure can be traced to English law (both in terms of statutory and common law development), though as mentioned there have been many departures since as well;[158] nonetheless, certain landmark English cases highlighted here may be familiar to and still stand as the law in other Commonwealth jurisdictions. Singapore's first civil procedure ordinances in 1878 and 1880 were based on English rules of procedure found in the Schedules to the Imperial Judicature Act of 1875. Subsequent civil procedure codes were introduced in Singapore in 1907 and 1926, and these applied the English Rules of the Supreme Court, 1883.[159] The first Rules of the Supreme Court in Singapore[160] – a consolidation of existing civil procedure – came about in 1934.[161] This remained in force until 1970, where following an overhaul of the rules of civil procedure in England in 1966, an equally new edition of the Rules of the Supreme Court[162] was enacted, and indeed mirrored the structure and content of the new English rules.[163] The next major change occurred in

153. J. Pinsler, *Principles of Civil Procedure* 5 (Acad. Publg. 2013).
154. 36 & 37 Victoria, c. 66.
155. 38 & 39 Victoria, c. 77.
156. *Re Coles and Ravenshear*, [1907] 1 KB 1, 4.
157. A perusal of the List of Cases will reveal that the number of English cases cited are not that greatly outnumbered by local cases.
158. Goh Y.H. & P. Tan, *An Empirical Study of the Development of Singapore Law*, 23 Sing. Acad. L.J., 176, 211 (2011).
159. J. Pinsler, *Civil Justice in Singapore* 10 (Butterworths 2000).
160. S 2941/34.
161. J. Pinsler, *Civil Justice in Singapore* 10 (Butterworths 2000).
162. S 274/70.
163. J. Pinsler, *Civil Justice in Singapore* 10 (Butterworths 2000).

1996, when the Rules of the Supreme Court merged with the Rules of the Subordinate Courts[164] for the very first time, in an attempt harmonize the rules of the different courts and eliminate any prior convolution – notably, Singapore was one of the first countries to take such a reformative step.[165] Revised editions of the Rules of Court have since been published in 1997, 2004, 2006, and 2014, reflecting their rapid rate of evolution.[166] The latest edition of the rules comprises almost 130 Orders and four appendices.

79. Though only accorded the status of subsidiary legislation, there is no doubt that the Rules of Court[167] form the most important and consulted source of law for civil litigation. However, it should also not be forgotten that the power to make Rules of Court are prescribed by the Supreme Court of Judicature Act[168] and the State Courts Act.[169] The Supreme Court of Judicature Act and the State Courts Act are also important sources of civil procedure in that they prescribe the structure, composition, jurisdiction, and powers of the Magistrates' Courts, District Courts, High Court, and the Court of Appeal. Supplementing the Supreme Court of Judicature Act, the State Courts Act, and the Rules of Court are the Practice Directions issued by the State Courts and Supreme Court. In 2010 and 2012 respectively, the Supreme Court Practice Directions and State Courts Practice Directions assumed electronic form (meaning they can be viewed and downloaded online), and consolidated and superseded previously existing practice directions. Though they technically do not have the status of law, sanctions may follow if the Practice Directions are not complied with.[170] Both the State Courts and Supreme Court may also issue circulars, which contain announcements and updates on the latest changes to the registry, its practices, and recommended court practices.

80. Like other areas of law, the body of Singapore civil procedure rules has, despite its English origins, moved towards developing autochthony since Singapore gained independence in 1965.[171] As observed by former Chief Justice Yong Pung How:

164. S 59/86. As mentioned, the Subordinate Courts were renamed the State Courts in 2014.
165. J. Pinsler, *Civil Justice in Singapore* 503–504 (Butterworths 2000).
166. E. Chua & L. Leo, *Civil Procedure* in *Singapore Law: 50 Years in the Making* (Goh Y.H. & P. Tan eds., Acad. Publg. 2015).
167. Supreme Court of Judicature Act (Cap. 322, R. 5, 2014 Rev. Ed.) Rules of Court.
168. Supreme Court of Judicature Act (Cap. 322, 2007 Rev. Ed.), s 80.
169. State Courts Act (Cap. 321, 2007 Rev. Ed.), s 69.
170. *See* Supreme Court of Judicature Act (Cap. 322, R. 5, 2014 Rev. Ed.) Rules of Court, O 34A r 1(1A), O 92 rr 2A and 3(1), and O 59 rr 5, 7, and 8. *See also BNP Paribas v. Polynesia Timber Services Pte Ltd*, [2002] 1 SLR(R) 539, [37]; *Odex Pte Ltd v. Pacific Internet Ltd*, [2008] 3 SLR(R) 18, [30].
171. *See* generally A. Phang, *Of Generality and Specificity – A Suggested Approach Toward the Development of an Autochthonous Singapore Legal System*, 1 Sing. Acad. L.J. 68 (1989).

> autochthony does mean that we have to be willing to part ways with England, whenever necessary … We must continue to evolve our own rules of procedure, suited to our own urban, multiracial, multilinguistic, Asian society … We must be willing to adopt new technologies which will assist in the effectiveness of our legal system … [172]

81. Consistent with this approach of not jettisoning useful aspects of English law, citation by the Singapore courts of English cases has generally continued on an upward trajectory, despite the constant push to develop a self-sufficient body of law in this area.[173] In a study of reported cases on civil procedure between 1965 (the year Singapore gained independence) and 2010, the following conclusions were made:

> there has been a general upward trend in the average number of pages per judgment for reported civil procedure cases in the Singapore Supreme Court, with the Court of Appeal leading the way in most years. What is more interesting is that the rate of increase has itself increased …
>
> From 1965 to 1990, there was a gradual increase in the total number of foreign judgments cited. The bulk of these foreign judgments were from England, reflecting the commonality that persisted between the civil procedure rules in England and Singapore. The other jurisdiction referred to most commonly after England was Malaysia, and this is also to be expected given that the Malaysian civil procedure rules also reflected the English practice … In the 1990s, English judgments continued to comprise the bulk of foreign judgments cited but with other Commonwealth jurisdictions such as Australia, Canada and India being cited as well. This continued into the 2000s …
>
> The increasing diversity of foreign jurisdictions cited bears testament to the maturation and confidence of the Singapore judiciary. It also reflects recent amendments to the rules of Singapore civil procedure … [174]

82. Similarly, it has also been observed that there has been greater reliance on academic materials from the 1990s and more so in recent years. This trend is consistent with 'the development and maturation of Singapore civil procedure jurisprudence [and] the growing body of local literature available on the subject'.[175] Since Jeffrey Pinsler published the first comprehensive local reference book on Civil Procedure in 1994,[176] he has gone on to publish Singapore Court Practice – referred to

---

172. *Speech Delivered at the Singapore Academy of Law Second Annual Lecture – 12 September 1995*, in *Speeches and Judgments of Chief Justice Yong Pung How* 193–194 (FT Law & Tax Asia, 1996).
173. Goh Y.H. & P. Tan, *An Empirical Study of the Development of Singapore Law*, 23 Sing. Acad. L.J. 176, 214–215 (2011).
174. E. Chua & L. Leo, *Civil Procedure* in *Singapore Law: 50 Years in the Making* (Goh Y.H. & P. Tan eds., Acad. Publg. 2015).
175. E. Chua & L. Leo, *Civil Procedure* in *Singapore Law: 50 Years in the Making* (Goh Y.H. & P. Tan eds., Acad. Publg. 2015).
176. J. Pinsler, *Civil Procedure* (Butterworths Asia 1994).

by local practitioners as the 'Black Book'.[177] Singapore then obtained its own version of the English 'White Book' – Singapore Civil Procedure[178] – in 2003. Professor Pinsler has most recently in 2013 published a treatise on civil procedure for the Singapore Academy of Law.[179]

II. The Conduct of Hearings

83. Hearings of originating summonses, summonses, applications, or appeals are conducted in chambers, subject to any provisions in the Rules of Court,[180] written law, directions by the court, and Practice Directions issued by the Registrar.[181] A judge also has the power to direct that any matter be disposed of in chambers.[182] When a matter is heard in chambers, it is regarded generally as private and members of the public are not entitled to attend such hearings; however, the court may, in its discretion, permit interested parties to attend hearings in chambers.[183] In contrast, hearings and trials that take place in open court may be freely attended by the public unless the court otherwise directs.[184]

84. Registrars are empowered to:

> to transact all such business and exercise all such authority and jurisdiction under any written law as may be transacted and exercised by a Judge in Chambers except such business, authority and jurisdiction as the Chief Justice [or the Presiding Judge of the State Courts] may from time to time direct to be transacted or exercised by a Judge in person or as may by any of these Rules be expressly directed to be transacted or exercised by a Judge in person.[185]

85. Accordingly, '[a]ll applications in Chambers … shall be filed without specifying whether the application is to be heard before a Judge in person or the Registrar'.[186] This gives the Registry the flexibility to determine the distribution of the workload of chambers hearings between the registrars and judges, though the general pattern has been to assign the more complex and important hearings to the more

177. J. Pinsler, *Singapore Court Practice* (Butterworths Asia 1999). This book has since undergone three revisions: in, 2006 2009, and 2014.
178. *Singapore Civil Procedure* (G.P. Selvam ed., Sweet & Maxwell Asia 2003). The latest edition of this book was released in 2014.
179. J. Pinsler, *Principles of Civil Procedure* (Acad. Publg. 2013).
180. Supreme Court of Judicature Act (Cap. 322, R. 5, 2014 Rev. Ed.) Rules of Court.
181. Supreme Court of Judicature Act (Cap. 322, R. 5, 2014 Rev. Ed.) Rules of Court, O 32 rr 1 and 11(1); Supreme Court Practice Directions 2013 (Part IV).
182. Supreme Court of Judicature Act (Cap. 322, R. 5, 2014 Rev. Ed.) Rules of Court, O 32 r 14.
183. *Lee Hsien Loong v. Review Publishing Co Ltd*, [2007] 2 SLR(R) 453, [8]; Supreme Court Practice Directions 2013 (Part II); State Courts Practice Directions (Part XV). As to whether public access can be granted to court documents filed and/or used in proceedings heard in chambers, *see Tan Chi Min v. The Royal Bank of Scotland Plc*, [2013] 4 SLR 529.
184. *Singapore Civil Procedure 2015 Volume 1*, at 675 (G.P. Selvam ed., Sweet & Maxwell Asia 2014).
185. Supreme Court of Judicature Act (Cap 322, 2007 Rev Ed) s 62; Supreme Court of Judicature Act (Cap. 322, R. 5, 2014 Rev. Ed.) Rules of Court, O 32 r 9.
186. Supreme Court Practice Directions 2013 (Part II); State Courts Practice Directions (Part XV).

senior-ranking registrars. The Registrar is 'given such powers, authority and jurisdiction for administrative convenience, in a bid to save the time of the judge'.[187] Some examples of applications that have been formally designated to be heard by a judge in person include applications for Mareva injunctions and Anton Piller orders.[188] Most interlocutory applications are heard by registrars in the first instance.[189]

86. The registry of the Supreme Court and the State Courts are under 'the control and supervision of the Registrar'; the registry is divided into departments, and the business performed in the registry is distributed among the departments in such manner, as the Chief Justice or the Presiding Judge, as the case may be, directs.[190] The powers and duties of the Registrar of the Supreme Court may be exercised or performed by the Deputy Registrar or any of the Assistant Registrars of the Supreme Court; and those of the Registrar of the State Courts may be exercised or performed by a deputy Registrar of the State Courts.[191] All of these arrangements confirm the emphasis on pre-trial matters in Singapore civil procedure.

III. Case Management

87. In the 1990s, the Singapore judiciary faced a large backlog of cases. To illustrate, in the beginning of 1990, there were 2,050 outstanding civil cases in the High Court. However, these were whittled down to 129 by the beginning of 1994. Today, the Singapore judiciary is widely regarded as being among the most efficient in the world.[192] For instance, in 2011, while the Supreme Court (the High Court, in particular) received 5,757 new civil originating processes, it cleared 5,609.[193] For civil interlocutory applications, it received 6,032 of them, while clearing 5,876.[194] For

187. *Tan Boon Heng v. Lau Pang Cheng David*, [2013] 4 SLR 718, [13], citing *Ang Leng Hock v. Leo Ee Ah*, [2004] 2 SLR(R) 361, [15].
188. Supreme Court Practice Directions 2013 (Part IV).
189. *Singapore Parliamentary Debates*, *Official Report* (18 Oct. 2010) vol. 87 col 1367 (The Senior Minister of State for Law, Assoc Prof Ho Peng Kee).
190. Supreme Court of Judicature Act (Cap. 322, R. 5, 2014 Rev. Ed.) Rules of Court, O 60 r 1.
191. Supreme Court of Judicature Act (Cap. 322, 2007 Rev. Ed.), s 62(2); State Courts Act (Cap. 321, 2007 Rev. Ed.), s 13.
192. *See Global Competitive Report 2014–2015*, https://www.supremecourt.gov.sg/docs/default-source/default-document-library/annual-report-2012.pdf, 30 Sep. 2017. For other accolades that the courts have received, *see State Courts Annual Report 2014*, https://www.statecourts.gov.sg/Resources/Documents/AnnualReport2014.pdf, 30 Sep. 2017; *Rankings in International Surveys*, https://www.supremecourt.gov.sg/docs/default-source/default-document-library/annual-report-2013.pdf, 30 Sep. 2017.
193. *Workload Statistics*, https://www.supremecourt.gov.sg/docs/default-source/default-document-library/annual-report-2013.pdf, 30 Sep. 2017. As of 2013, the numbers are 6,831 out of 7,038, or a 97% clearance rate: *Workload Statistics*, https://www.supremecourt.gov, 30 Sep. 2017. For criminal cases and criminal motions, the percentages are similar.
194. *Workload Statistics*, https://www.supremecourt.gov.sg/docs/default-source/default-document-library/annual-report-2013.pdf, 30 Sep. 2017. As of 2013, the numbers are 6,111 out of 6,864, or a 89% clearance rate: *Workload Statistics*, https://www.supremecourt.gov, 30 Sep. 2017.

appeals made to the Supreme Court, clearance rates were almost 100%.[195] As for average waiting times, they are (with 90% compliance rate) in the Supreme Court: three weeks for trials in writ action, four weeks for inter partes originating summonses, one week for ex parte originating summonses, and up to four weeks for summonses.[196] In the State Courts, almost 75,000 new civil originating processes were received in 2011; despite the sheer workload, the organization managed to be conferred the rare Singapore Quality Award, cementing its reputation and as a prompt and efficient organization.[197] The clearance of the backlog of cases has often been attributed, amongst others, to the implementation and adoption of case management strategies by the Singapore judiciary.[198] Some of these strategies have been built into the Rules of Court and the Practice Directions of the Supreme Court and the State Courts, including the simplification of the modes of commencement of actions, the use of pre-trial conferences to monitor the progress of cases, and the automatic discontinuance of suits after a year of inaction.[199]

88. With an arsenal of case management tools at its disposal, the Supreme Court has set itself the target of disposing of 85% of all writs filed within eighteen months.[200] More recently, in 2013, Chief Justice Sundaresh Menon has signalled an enhancement to the existing case management framework in the Supreme Court, announcing that it will be shifting to a 'modified docket system of litigation', with judges being more involved in dealing with interlocutory processes along the way.[201] Case management in the Singapore courts has also been enhanced by the use of technology. The Supreme Court and the State Courts utilize and leverage on technology extensively to improve the conduct of litigation as well as facilitate access to justice. In the Supreme Court, there are five 'Technology Courts' equipped with plasma screens and video cameras for video-conferencing, an audiovisual system that may be linked to lawyers' laptops and visualizers to allow projection of objects or documents. There are also portable 'Mobile Info-Tech Trolleys' available for use in other courtrooms and chambers.

89. Hearings may be conducted electronically in the Supreme Court and State Courts. For example, the JusticeOnline System has been in use since January 2003

195. *Workload Statistics*, https://www.supremecourt.gov.sg/docs/default-source/default-document-library/annual-report-2013.pdf, 30 Sep. 2017. As of 2013, the clearance rates have remained roughly the same: *Workload Statistics*, https://www.supremecourt.gov, 30 Sep. 2017.
196. *Waiting Periods*, https://www.supremecourt.gov.sg/docs/default-source/default-document-library/annual-report-2013.pdf, 30 Sep. 2017. As of 2013, the waiting times have remained roughly the same: *Workload Statistics*, https://www.supremecourt.gov.sg, 30 Sep. 2017.
197. *Subordinate Courts Annual Report 2011*, http://app.subcourts.gov.sg, 30 Sep. 2017. For the 2013 statistics, *see*: https://app.statecourts.gov.sg, 30 Sep. 2017.
198. *See* E. Chua & L. Leo, *Civil Procedure*, in *Singapore Law: 50 Years in the Making* (Goh Y.H. & P. Tan eds., Acad. Publg. 2015).
199. E. Chua & L. Leo, *Civil Procedure*, in *Singapore Law: 50 Years in the Making* (Goh Y.H. & P. Tan eds., Acad. Publg. 2015).
200. *Overcoming Backlogs*, http://app.subcourts.gov.sg, 30 Sep. 2017.
201. *Response by Chief Justice Sundaresh Menon: Opening of the Legal Year 2013 and Welcome Reference for the Chief Justice*, http://app.lsc.gov.sg, 30 Sep. 2017.

in the Supreme Court to enable registrars to conduct hearings for bankruptcy applications without the need for lawyers to be physically present in court – the lawyers are able to participate over video-conferencing instead. More recently, Skype has been introduced for lawyers to attend before the Duty Registrar for non-contentious matters in the Supreme Court. In the State Courts, video-conferencing is used extensively in pre-trial conferences. Apart from these innovations, the public areas and courtrooms in the Supreme Court and the State Courts are wireless internet hotspots. Electronic kiosks and signages are available throughout both buildings to provide up-to-date information hearing lists and court schedules. Further, the Supreme Court and State Courts offer a wide variety of services to civil litigation practitioners, including interpretation, translation and digital transcription services.

90. As all hearings in the Singapore courts are conducted in English; interpreters are available, on request, to provide interpretation services to witnesses in court proceedings who do not understand or speak English. Where other foreign language interpretation is required, approved third-party interpreters may be utilized. Similarly, translation services are also available for documents, but at a fee. In respect of transcription services, the Supreme Court implemented a Digital Transcription System (DTS) in 2005 to facilitate the audio recording of court hearings.[202] The DTS is available for all criminal trials and trials in civil actions commenced by writ, but parties may also apply for DTS to be used in certain other hearings, subject to approval, such as appeals in open court and hearings in chambers (such as appeals to a judge in chambers and special date or assessment of damages hearings before registrars).[203] In the State Courts, a Digital Audio Recording and Transcription (DART) pilot project was launched in 2010 to facilitate the recording of court proceedings and optimize the use of scarce judicial resources. The DART facilities have since been rolled out to all of the Divisions of the State Courts.[204]

91. Technology has also been utilized to permit, amongst others, electronic filing and service of court documents and conducting electronic searches for information in the Supreme Court and the State Courts. The first such electronic system was known as the 'Electronic Filing System' (EFS) and was introduced in the Singapore courts in phases from 1997 to 2006.[205] The EFS eliminated the need for manual delivery of documents as files could be electronically routed and accessed by different users at the same time, and also automated certain checks on documents as well as the calculation and collection of court fees.[206] More recently, in 2012, the Supreme Court launched the new iELS. Litigation significantly improves on EFS

---

202. *Supreme Court*, http://app.supremecourt.gov.sg/default.aspx?pgID=1, 30 Sep. 2017.
203. *Supreme Court*, http://app.supremecourt.gov.sg/default.aspx?pgID=1, 30 Sep. 2017.
204. 'Subordinate Courts of Singapore Annual Report 2011', http://app.subcourts.gov.sg, 30 Sep. 2017.
205. *See* Tan B.H., *E-litigation: The Singapore Experience*, Sing. L. Gaz. (Nov. 2001); *Write-up on the Electronic Filing System*, http://info.efs.com.sg/default.htm, 30 Sep. 2017; Thian Y.S., *Singapore*, in *IT Support of the Judiciary* 59–62 (A. Oskamp, A. R. Lodder & M. Apistola eds., TMC Asser Press 2004).
206. *Overcoming Backlogs*, http://app.subcourts.gov.sg/Data/Files/File/Speeches/CJChanSpeech_OvercomingBacklogs.pdf, 30 Sep. 2017.

by using two new technologies to make the conduct of litigation even more efficient. First, 'electronic form technology' that allows information keyed into the electronic forms by users to be stored and reused; and second, 'workflow middleware' that enables the automation of certain formerly manual processes.[207] Second, apart from bringing greater convenience and efficiency in the conduct of litigation, these electronic systems further enable close and careful monitoring of the caseload and clearance rates of the Singapore courts, allowing adjustments to be made to case management policy, where necessary.[208] The Chief Justice described the project in the following terms:

> We have set the standard internationally in this area for some years and I am confident that eLitigation will come to be seen as yet another pivotal point in the use of technology by the Supreme Court. The eLitigation system brings the use of electronic tools in litigation to a higher level, by introducing a suite of changes targeted at reducing inefficiencies … An extensive review of the procedural rules and processes has also been undertaken to do away with many unnecessary procedural steps and to more effectively utilise information that has already been filed in Court.[209]

92. Being a new system, fine tuning (including legislative changes) can be expected to be made to iELS over the next few years or so.

IV. Law Reform Processes

93. In Singapore, perhaps because civil procedure is the lifeblood of civil litigation, which in turn is the lifeblood of general commercial practice, the law of civil procedure receives reform attention like no other branch of law both in terms of regularity of change and involvement of the legal fraternity. The Rules Committee is empowered to make Rules of Court regulating and prescribing the procedure and the practice to be followed in the Singapore courts.[210] The Rules Committee comprises the Chief Justice, the Attorney-General, not more than five Judges of the Supreme Court, the Presiding Judge of the State Courts, a District Judge, and two practicing advocates and solicitors.[211] The Rules Committee is supported by a Rules of Court Working Party that makes recommendations and proposals to the Rules

---

207. *Summary of Amendments to the Rules of Court to Facilitate the Implementation of the Integrated Electronic Litigation System*, http://app.supremecourt.gov.sg/data/doc/ManagePage/3461/Summary%20of%20amendments%20to%20the%20Rules%20of%20Court%20Amendment%20No%205%20Rules%202012.pdf, 30 Sep. 2017.

208. E. Chua & L. Ng, *Civil Case Management in Singapore: of Models, Measures and Justice* (forthcoming in the ASEAN L. Assn. J.).

209. *Response by Chief Justice Sundaresh Menon: Opening of the Legal Year 2013 and Welcome Reference for the Chief Justice*, http://app.lsc.gov.sg/data/OLY%202013%20-%20CJ%20Speech%20OLY%20Welcome%20Reference.pdf, 30 Sep. 2017.

210. Supreme Court of Judicature Act (Cap. 322, 2007 Rev. Ed.), s 80; State Courts Act (Cap. 321, 2007 Rev. Ed.), s 69.

211. Supreme Court of Judicature Act (Cap. 322, 2007 Rev. Ed.), s 80(3).

Committee to amend the Rules of Court. The Rules of Court Working Party conducts regular reviews of different areas of civil procedure and also frequently receives feedback and suggestions from all sectors of the legal profession and, at times, from members of the public.[212]

94. For instance, as a result of a public consultation conducted by the Rules of Court Working Party over October and November 2011 in relation to the conduct of discovery in civil litigation,[213] feedback was received from, amongst others, the Bar, the corporate counsels' association, association of banks, and electronic discovery practitioners.[214] After reviewing the feedback, it was decided that the area requiring intervention related to the practice of discovery rather than the rule governing discovery – this led to the issuance of the Supreme Court Practice Directions Amendment No 1 of 2012.[215] Another example related to amendments to O 53 of the Rules of Court concerning the procedure for judicial review applications. These amendments followed a review undertaken by the Rules of Court Working Party, which, after considering the judicial review models of other leading common law jurisdictions, recommended that: an applicant be allowed to seek declaratory relief in judicial review proceedings in addition to prerogative orders; and a procedure be provided in O 53 to allow an applicant to recover damages or other equitable or restitutionary reliefs, if the applicant can prove that he has a valid cause of action such that the additional reliefs would have been obtainable if they had been claimed in a separate private law action.[216] These recommendations of the Rules of Court Working Party were implemented by the Rules of Court (Amendment No 2) Rules 2011.[217]

95. In 2015, the Civil Justice Commission was also established. Chaired by a High Court Judge, the commission would examine issues such as how to simplify court rules, eliminate time-consuming and cost-wasting processes, and how to facilitate greater judicial control of the litigation process to ensure proportionate conduct. It is envisaged that the commission will undertake a three-year study that is meant to be wide-ranging and detailed, and will seek input from the judiciary, the Attorney-General's Chambers, the bar, as well as academia, and it is projected that the current rules on civil procedure in Singapore would be radically transformed as a result of this study. Law reform committees may also be formed by the Singapore Academy of Law, but such committees when looking into matters of civil procedure focus on very particular doctrines as opposed to general civil procedure, such

212. *See also Singapore Civil Procedure 2015 Volume 1*, at xix–xx (G.P. Selvam ed., Sweet & Maxwell Asia 2014).
213. *Consultation Paper – Review of Discovery in Civil Litigation*, http://app.supremecourt.gov.sg/data/doc/ManageHighlights/3026/Discovery%20Consultation%20Paper.pdf, 30 Sep. 2017.
214. S. Leong & Yeong Z.K., *A Commentary on the Supreme Court Practice Directions Amendment No 1 of 2012*, Sing. L. Gaz. (March 2012).
215. S. Leong & Yeong Z.K., *A Commentary on the Supreme Court Practice Directions Amendment No 1 of 2012*, Sing. L. Gaz. (March 2012).
216. Chung Y.J., D. Wong & Peh A.H., *Recent Amendments to Order 53 of the Rules of Court*, Sing. L. Gaz. (November 2011).
217. Supreme Court of Judicature Act (Cap. 322) Rules of Court (Amendment No. 2) Rules 2011 (S 218/2011).

as limitation periods in private international law (2011), the rationalization of leave to appeal (2008), and the enforcement of foreign judgments (2005). In 2016, a Civil Justice Review Committee was established to ensure that Singaporeans have greater access to justice; the committee is expected to make recommendations to allow judges greater control in managing cases and ensure that legal costs are proportionate to the value of the claims.

V. Judicial Philosophy

96. In difficult cases and/or those that involve difficult facts, it is always important to have a firm grasp of the prevailing judicial sentiment on the area of law in question. Perhaps the modern judicial philosophy as regards civil procedure in Singapore is best encapsulated (but is of course by no means exclusively limited) by the following passages. The first is a 2000 High Court decision, made in the context of unless orders:

> Where the attention in the past was the interest of litigants and litigants alone, the new approach in the administration of justice put into the equation the interest of the administration of justice and the communitarian need that limited resources of the courts' time and resources for adjudication were and are not wasted or extravagantly or lopsidedly hogged by any litigant or set of litigants. Timeliness and specific procedural steps had to be laid down to fix dates for trial and disposal of cases … However, our procedural laws are … not permitted to rule us to such an extent that injustice is done …[218]

97. The second is a 2005 High Court decision, which addresses the question of how to strike a balance between procedural and substantive justice:

> It is axiomatic that every party ought to have its day in court. This is the very embodiment of procedural justice … Procedural justice is just one aspect of the holistic ideal and concept of justice itself. In the final analysis, the achievement of a substantively just result or decision is the desideratum. It is more than that, however. It is not merely an ideal. It must be a practical outcome – at least as far as the court can aid in its attainment.
>
> However, the court must be extremely wary of falling into the flawed approach to the effect that 'the ends justify the means' … The obsession with achieving a substantively fair and just outcome does not justify the utilisation of any and every means to achieve that objective …
>
> On the other hand, a just and fair procedure does NOT, in and of itself, ensure a just outcome. In other words, procedural fairness is a necessary but not sufficient condition for a fair and just result.
>
> The quest for justice, therefore, entails a continuous need to balance the procedural with the substantive. More than that, it is a continuous attempt to

218. *Lea Tool and Moulding Industries Pte Ltd (in liquidation) v. CGU International Insurance plc (formerly known as Commer Union Assurance Co plc)*, [2000] 3 SLR(R) 745, [15]–[16].

> ensure that both are integrated, as far as that is humanly possible … This is especially significant because, in many ways, this is how … laypersons perceive the administration of justice to be.
>
> It is true, however, that in the sphere of practical reality, there is often a TENSION between the need for procedural justice on the one hand and substantive justice on the other. The task of the court is to attempt …. to RESOLVE this tension. There is a FURTHER task: it is to actually attempt, simultaneously, to INTEGRATE these two conceptions of justice in order that justice in its fullest orb may shine forth.[219]

98. The third, a 2004 High Court decision, which (albeit in the narrow context of functus officio) addresses the question of how a court must have a wide range of powers, even if not legislated for, to control its own (civil) process:

> both the High Court and the Court of Appeal retain a residual inherent jurisdiction even after an order is pronounced, to clarify the terms of the order and/or to give consequential directions.
>
> That such inherent jurisdiction exists, has never been doubted … This inherent jurisdiction is a virile and necessary one that a court is invested with to dispense procedural justice as a means of achieving substantive justice between parties in a matter. The power to correct or clarify an order is inherent in every court. This power necessarily extends to ensuring that the spirit of court orders are appropriately embodied and correctly reflected to the letter … the court has an unassailable broad discretion and jurisdiction to give effect to the intent and purport of any relief and/or remedy that may be necessary in a particular matter.[220]

99. Aside from these three passages,[221] it may also be said that generally, the courts will not object to parties coming to mutual agreements as regards adjustments to timelines, provided that such adjustments are fairly reasonable. In terms of exploring alternative dispute resolution mechanisms, the courts will not proactively encourage such exploration (and nor should they if the adversarial system is to remain robust and faithful to its roots). Much of this is left to counsel to consider whether such avenues are in the best interests of their clients, and of course the wishes of clients themselves; at the same time, however, it is impossible to ignore the increasing viability of mediation as a means to settle disputes more expediently and amicably.

---

219. *United Overseas Bank Ltd v. Ng Huat Foundations Pte Ltd*, [2005] 2 SLR(R) 425, [4]–[9] (emphasis in original); cited in *Lee Hsien Loong v. Singapore Democratic Party*, [2008] 1 SLR(R) 757, [36]. *See also United Overseas Bank Ltd v. Ng Huat Foundations Pte Ltd*, [2005] 2 SLR(R) 425, [21].

220. *Godfrey Gerald QC v. UBS AG*, [2004] 4 SLR(R) 411, [18]–[19]. *See also Thu Aung Zaw v. Ku Swee Boon*, [2017] SGHC 265, [19]; *Emilia Shipping Inc v. State Enterprise for Pulp and Paper Industries*, [1991] 1 SLR(R) 411, [23].

221. *See also Tan Sia Boo v. Ong Chiang Kwong*, [2007] 4 SLR(R) 298, [4]–[6].

VI. Unique Domains

100. It is important to note that the scope of this monograph does not go beyond the general aspects of civil procedure in Singapore; there are a number of domains within the rules of civil procedure (i.e., the Rules of Court) that have quite a number of rules specific to them, and it will not be feasible to cover them in any great detail. These include (but are not limited to) admiralty or shipping,[222] building and construction adjudications,[223] judicial review,[224] trademarks and patents,[225] mental capacity,[226] and matters relating to probate and wills.[227]

101. Matrimonial proceedings are also another unique domain not covered by this monograph. Up until 2015, the relevant procedural rules for such proceedings were found in the Women's Charter[228] and its accompanying subsidiary legislation, most notably, the Women's Charter (Matrimonial Proceedings) Rules.[229] Matrimonial proceedings were then mainly heard in the Family Court due to the provisions of the Supreme Court of Judicature (Transfer of Matrimonial, Divorce and Guardianship of Infants Proceedings to District Court) Order 2007.[230] In 2015, the family justice landscape was remodelled both procedurally and substantively. As a result of a report by a 2013 committee,[231] four main changes were implemented: first, the family courts were restructured, and their jurisdictional scopes redefined; second, greater access to family justice was to be ensured via a simplification and streamlining of court processes, differentiated case management, and the appointment of Family Court Friends to help litigants-in-person; third, family disputes would be

---

222. The relevant procedure may be found in Supreme Court of Judicature Act (Cap. 322, R. 5, 2014 Rev. Ed.) Rules of Court. O 70; High Court (Admiralty Jurisdiction) Act (Cap. 123, 2001 Rev. Ed.).
223. The relevant procedure may be found in Supreme Court of Judicature Act (Cap. 322, R. 5, 2014 Rev. Ed.) Rules of Court, O 95; Building and Construction Industry Security of Payment Act (Cap. 30B, 2006 Rev. Ed.). This area of procedure may be subject to further review and amendment: *see Admin Construction Pte Ltd v. Vivaldi (S) Pte Ltd*, [2013] 3 SLR 609. *See also Libra Building Construction Pte Ltd v. Emergent Engineering Pte Ltd*, [2016] 1 SLR 481.
224. The relevant procedure may be found in Supreme Court of Judicature Act (Cap. 322, R. 5, 2014 Rev. Ed.) Rules of Court, O 53.
225. The relevant procedure may be found in Supreme Court of Judicature Act (Cap. 322, R. 5, 2014 Rev. Ed.) Rules of Court, O 87 and O 87A; Trademarks Act (Cap. 322, 2005 Rev. Ed.); Patents Act (Cap. 221, 2005 Rev. Ed.).
226. The relevant procedure may be found in Supreme Court of Judicature Act (Cap. 322, R. 5, 2014 Rev. Ed.) Rules of Court, O 99; Mental Capacity Act (Cap. 177A, 2010 Rev. Ed.). It should be noted that proceedings under the Mental Capacity Act are mainly dealt with in the State Courts pursuant to the Supreme Court of Judicature (Transfer of Mental Capacity Proceedings to District Court) Order 2010 (Cap. 322, S 104/2010).
227. The relevant procedure may be found in Supreme Court of Judicature Act (Cap. 322, R. 5, 2014 Rev. Ed.) Rules of Court, O 71 and O 72; Probate and Administration Act (Cap. 251, 2000 Rev. Ed.).
228. Women's Charter (Cap. 353, 2009 Rev. Ed.).
229. Women's Charter (Matrimonial Proceedings) Rules (Cap. 353, R. 4, 2006 Rev. Ed.).
230. Supreme Court of Judicature (Transfer of Matrimonial, Divorce and Guardianship of Infants Proceedings to District Court) Order 2007 (Cap. 322, S 672/2007).
231. *Recommendations of the Committee for Family Justice on the Framework of the Family Justice System,* https://www.mlaw.gov.sg/content/dam/minlaw/corp/News/Family%20Justice%20Report.pdf, 30 Sep. 2017.

made less acrimonious and traumatic, with judges expected to take a more proactive role at all stages of the proceedings and mediation and counselling to feature more prominently;[232] and fourth, a suite of social solutions outside of the courtroom would be introduced.

102. Thus, the Family Justice Courts, a specialized body of courts dealing with all family-related work, were formed. The Family Justice Courts is a collective body that comprise the Family Division of the High Court, the Family Courts, and the Youth Courts. There will be at least one High Court Judge or Judicial Commissioner presiding over the Family Justice Courts. The Youth Courts would hear cases related to children and young persons, the Family Courts would hear all proceedings except cases heard by the Youth Courts, and the High Court (Family Division) would primarily hear appeals against the decisions of the Family and Youth Courts, though it has jurisdiction to hear cases of first instance as well. The Family Justice Courts now have jurisdiction over virtually any family-related matter, such as adoption, inheritance, child abduction, mental capacity, probate, and sterilization.

103. A separate set of rules of court was created; this is known as the Family Justice Rules, which span 999 rules over 19 parts. A separate set of practice directions was also created; this is known as the Family Justice Practice Directions, which runs almost a thousand pages as it includes appendices, samples, and template forms as well. Registrar's Circulars are also issued from time to time to supplement the rules and practice directions. Some of the general principles of civil procedure are retained in these new rules and practice directions, but there is overall a shift in the philosophy, such as a de-emphasis in adversarial litigation and an emphasis in protecting the child. Where necessary, judges hearing family proceedings may dispense with procedural rules as set out in the rules or practice directions if this would help achieve a fairer and more expedient outcome for the case. In this regard, family law proceedings have taken on a more inquisitorial flavour.

104. Parenthetically, it should be noted that the Rules of Court do not apply to criminal proceedings, which are governed by the Criminal Procedure Code.[233] Only selected provisions of the Rules of Court, largely relating to electronic filing and service,[234] apply to bankruptcy proceedings,[235] companies[236] and limited liability

232. More than ever, the focus would be on the welfare of the child. To that end, Child Representatives may be appointed to ensure that the child's wishes are well-conveyed to the court, and that any needs of the child are met expediently.

233. Supreme Court of Judicature Act (Cap. 322, R. 5, 2014 Rev. Ed.) Rules of Court, O 1 r 2; Criminal Procedure Code (Cap. 68, 2012 Rev. Ed).

234. Supreme Court of Judicature Act (Cap. 322, R. 5, 2014 Rev. Ed.) Rules of Court, O 1 r 2.

235. These are governed largely by the Bankruptcy Act (Cap. 20, 2009 Rev. Ed.); Bankruptcy Act (Cap. 20, R 1, 2009 Rev. Ed.) Bankruptcy Rules.

236. These are governed largely by the Companies Act (Cap. 50, 2006 Rev. Ed.); Companies Act (Cap. 50, R 1, 2006 Rev. Ed.) Companies (Winding Up) Rules.

partnerships winding up proceedings,[237] proceedings under Part IV of the Parliamentary Elections Act,[238] and proceedings under Part X of the Women's Charter.[239]

§4. General Features of the Administration of Justice in Civil Matters

I. An Adversarial System

105. As mentioned, since Singapore inherited its legal system from the English, the style of litigation is adversarial rather than inquisitorial (the obvious exception being family law proceedings alluded to above). This necessarily has trickle-down effects on how parties conduct litigation, as well as how judges treat the parties. That is to say – in many civil matters – parties are presumed to be of equal strength and bargaining powers. Parties are also presumed to be adequately, competently, and ethically represented by their own lawyers. The entire corpus of civil procedure rules reflects these presuppositions, though giving the occasional concession to litigants without representation. But in a legal landscape that is constantly shaped by the perils of globalization which in turn causes the business models of law firms to veer in a particular direction (and thus increasing costs and streamlining work processes and purposes), this may not be a fair assumption to make all the time.

106. As regards judges, there is generally less control and intervention over how proceedings take place, as compared to inquisitorial judges in civil systems. Some control will obviously be exercised, however, over how in court proceedings such as cross-examination is taking shape – for instance, if pointless questions are asked. However, despite the exacting demands of legislation, matters of evidence, particularly in civil proceedings, are seldom regulated with legalistic rigour by the courts, especially if parties themselves are not raising objections. A jurisprudence that is largely in part dependent on the evolution of the common law raises questions about the role of judges in law-making. A subsidiary question that arises is whether a judge should be proactive in finding arguments and authorities in addition to what is being presented by counsel. As Singapore is generally conservative in these regards, much is left to Parliament if there are clear lacunas in the law and to counsel to find the answers (such as researching comparative laws) if the position is unclear. Together with the registrars, judges tend to exert great control in the pre-trial aspects of each suit as compared to the trial stage. This is to ensure that matters are moving along on time so that no party is unduly prejudiced either in terms of costs or time.

---

237. These are governed largely by the Limited Liability Partnerships Act (Cap. 163A, 2006 Rev. Ed.); Limited Liability Partnerships Act (Cap. 163A, R. 2, 2007 Rev. Ed.) Limited Liability Partnerships (Winding Up) Rules.
238. These are governed largely by the Parliamentary Elections Act (Cap. 218, 2011 Rev. Ed.).
239. These are governed by the Women's Charter (Cap. 353, 2009 Rev. Ed.); Women's Charter (Matrimonial Proceedings) Rules (Cap. 353, R. 4, 2006 Rev. Ed.).

107. But while parties often cross swords, they may choose to agree on certain things such as extensions of time and amendments to pleadings. When this happens, judges are unlikely to reject the mutual agreement unless there is very good reason to do so. Indeed, despite the hostilities and tactical manoeuvres that often accompany adversarial litigation, counsel are expected to be able to prioritize between advancing their clients' interests and upholding their paramount duty towards the courts.

II. Fundamental Guarantees

108. As mentioned, Singapore has a constitution. However, in it there are no obvious rights (such as rights to property or fairness in civil trials) relating to commercial litigation, which forms the overwhelming bulk of civil litigation in Singapore. There is a right to counsel, but it is limited to criminal cases only and even so that right itself has certain limitations (in the main, access is only granted after some time (for instance when investigations are complete) and the right can be impliedly waived). The civil rights that are guaranteed, albeit with some qualifications, are that of equal protection, freedom of movement, freedom of speech, assembly, and association, freedom of religion, and right to education. However, apart from constitutional challenges, these rights do not form the basis of any type of civil litigation in Singapore.

109. Singapore has signed many international treaties, but also as mentioned given its dualist approach towards international law, these international obligations do not operate in domestic litigation unless the treaty in question has been ratified and passed into domestic law. In terms of international human rights treaties, Singapore has not signed most of them, but has signed and ratified a number of them such as CEDAW. In terms of international commercial treaties, Singapore has signed and ratified a great number, ranging from those related to trade and particular legal domains to those related to arbitral award enforcement and sale of goods. Generally, however, with the exception of award and foreign judgment enforcement, none of the above have any real impact on how civil procedure is conceived and regulated. The practice of commercial litigation in the Singapore courts is thus largely insular and parochial.

III. Inherent Jurisdiction

110. Most of the procedural rules for civil proceedings are found in primary legislation such as the Supreme Court of Judicature Act[240] and State Courts Act,[241] subsidiary legislation such as the Rules of Court,[242] Practice Directions issued by the courts, as well as case law by the courts. Sometimes, the courts may rely on its

240. Cap. 322 (Cap. 322, 2007 Rev. Ed.).
241. Cap. 321 (2007 Rev. Ed.).
242. Supreme Court of Judicature Act (Cap. 322, R. 5, 2014 Rev. Ed.) Rules of Court.

inherent powers to 'make such orders as may be necessary to prevent injustice or to prevent an abuse of the process of the [c]ourts'.[243] This inherent power, as its terminology suggests, stems from the court's status as the adjudicating organ of the legal system.[244] The inherent jurisdiction of the court has been referred to as:

> being the inherent jurisdiction of the court may be defined as being the reserve or fund of powers, a residual source of powers, which the court may draw upon as necessary whenever it is just or equitable to do so, and in particular to ensure the observance of the due process of law, to prevent improper vexation or oppression, to do justice between the parties and to secure a fair trial between them.[245]

111. Although the exercise of the court's inherent jurisdiction 'should not be circumscribed by rigid criteria or tests', the 'essential touchstone is really that of need'.[246] Therefore, the courts must exercise it judiciously when 'it is just and equitable to do so and in particular to ensure the observance of the due process of law, to prevent improper vexation or oppression and to do justice between the parties'.[247] Inherent jurisdiction may be exercised even though there are rules governing a particular application. Cases in which the court may invoke its inherent jurisdiction in civil proceedings include:

(a) to strike out a pleading or dismiss an action on the grounds that it is frivolous, vexatious, or otherwise an abuse of process of the court can be made pursuant to O 18 r 19 or the inherent jurisdiction of the court;[248]
(b) to try a case and give judgment on the merits in the absence of the defendants;[249]
(c) to refuse to entertain an appeal even if it is not included in section 34 of the Supreme Court of Judicature Act, if there is no 'live' issue to be decided between the parties;[250]
(d) to allow trustees to carry out an act or transaction which is expedient in the interest of the trust, but not to the extent of varying the intention of the settlor or testator as expressed in the trust instrument or will;[251]

---

243. Supreme Court of Judicature Act (Cap. 322, R. 5, 2014 Rev. Ed.) Rules of Court, O 92 r 4.
244. J. Pinsler, *Principles of Civil Procedure* 5 (Acad. Publg. 2013). *See also* Goh Y.H., *Demystifying the Inherent Jurisdiction and Inherent Powers of the Singapore Courts: Rethinking the Limits of their Exercise*, Sing. J. Leg. Stud. 178 (2011).
245. *Wellmix Organics (International) Pte Ltd v. Lau Yu Man*, [2006] 2 SLR(R) 117, [84]. *See also Indian Overseas Bank v. Svil Agro Pte Ltd*, [2014] 3 SLR 892, [28]–[29]; *Roberto Building Material Pte Ltd v. Oversea-Chinese Banking Corp Ltd*, [2003] 2 SLR(R) 353, [17]; *Goh Seng Heng v. Wang Xiaopu*, [2020] SGCA 66.
246. *Lee Siew Ngug v. Lee Brothers (Wee Kee) Pte Ltd*, [2015] SGHC 106, [13], citing *Wee Soon Kim Anthony v. Law Society of Singapore*, [2001] 2 SLR(R) 821, [27].
247. *Lee Siew Ngug v. Lee Brothers (Wee Kee) Pte Ltd*, [2015] SGHC 106, [13], citing *Wee Soon Kim Anthony v. Law Society of Singapore*, [2001] 2 SLR(R) 821, [27].
248. *Lee Siew Ngug v. Lee Brothers (Wee Kee) Pte Ltd*, [2015] SGHC 106.
249. *Indian Overseas Bank v. Svil Agro Pte Ltd*, [2014] 3 SLR 892.
250. *Attorney-General v. Joo Yee Construction Pte Ltd (in liquidation)*, [1992] 2 SLR(R) 165.
251. *Goh Nellie v. Goh Lian Teck*, [2007] 1 SLR(R) 453.

(e) to stay proceedings in favour of arbitration in cases not covered by statutory provisions;[252]
(f) to allow a person to intervene in proceedings;[253] and
(g) to reopen and rehear an issue which it decided in breach of natural justice as well as to set aside (in appropriate cases) the whole or part of its earlier decision founded on that issue.[254]

112. However, this is subject to the important qualification that the exercise of inherent jurisdiction must not be inconsistent with express provisions and/or written rules of the courts.[255]

252. *Star-Trans Far East Pte Ltd v. Norske-Tech Ltd*, [1996] 2 SLR(R) 196.
253. *Wee Soon Kim Anthony v. Law Society of Singapore*, [2001] 2 SLR(R) 821.
254. *Management Corporation Strata Title Plan No 301 v. Lee Tat Development Pte Ltd*, [2011] 1 SLR 998.
255. *Singapore Civil Procedure 2015 Volume 1*, at 1486 (G.P. Selvam ed., Sweet & Maxwell Asia 2014), citing *Samsung Corp v. Chinese Chamber Realty Pte Ltd*, [2004] 1 SLR(R) 382, 12. *See also Lee Siew Ngug v. Lee Brothers (Wee Kee) Pte Ltd*, [2015] SGHC 106, [26]; *Wellmix Organics (International) Pte Ltd v. Lau Yu Man*, [2006] 2 SLR(R) 117, [81].

Part I. Judicial Organization

Chapter 1. The Courts and Their Members

§1. Courts

113. The Singapore court system comprises the Supreme Court and the State Courts. The Supreme Court is made up of the High Court and the Court of Appeal which hear both civil and criminal cases. The Court of Appeal became the highest appellate court in Singapore on 8 April 1994 when appeals to the Privy Council were abolished. The Court of Appeal hears appeals from the High Court and is presided over by the Chief Justice, and in his absence, a Judge of Appeal or Judge of the High Court.[256] The Chief Justice and Judges of Appeal sit on the Court of Appeal although there may be instances where the Chief Justice requests a Judge of the High Court to sit on the Court of Appeal.[257] The Court of Appeal is usually made up of three judges although certain appeals may be heard by fewer judges.[258] If necessary, the Court of Appeal can have five or any greater uneven number of judges sitting on it; this is usually done when an appeal is particularly complex or important.[259]

114. The High Court consists of the Chief Justice and the Judges of the High Court, although a Judge of Appeal may also sit as a judge in the High Court.[260] A single judge usually presides over High Court proceedings unless provided otherwise by legislation.[261] Judicial Commissioners are essentially High Court Judges appointed on a contractual basis, and may be appointed High Court Judges after a period of time and enjoy privileges such as security of tenure. To avoid conflicts of interest, Judicial Commissioners are usually not given cases that involve other arms of the government.

115. In 2015, the Constitution was amended to provide for the appointment of Senior Judges. Senior Judges are former Judges of the Supreme Court, and can be

256. Supreme Court of Judicature Act (Cap. 322, 2007 Rev. Ed.), ss 4 and 29.
257. Supreme Court of Judicature Act (Cap. 322, 2007 Rev. Ed.), s 29.
258. Supreme Court of Judicature Act (Cap. 322, 2007 Rev. Ed.), s 30.
259. Supreme Court of Judicature Act (Cap. 322, 2007 Rev. Ed.), s 30. In recent times, it has become more common for capital criminal cases to be heard by five judges. It has also become more common for dissenting or separate opinions to be rendered.
260. Supreme Court of Judicature Act (Cap. 322, 2007 Rev. Ed.), s 10.
261. Supreme Court of Judicature Act (Cap. 322, 2007 Rev. Ed.), s 10.

called upon by the Chief Justice to hear cases before the High Court, Court of Appeal, or Singapore International Commercial Court. This office was created so that the hearing load of the Supreme Court could be eased and to allow the Supreme Court to tap into the specialist legal expertise of recently retired judges.[262] Senior Judges are expected to work on a part-time basis and will hear the most urgent matters as well as shorter non-docketed matters; they will also help with the training and mentoring of new judges, be it in the State Courts or Supreme Court. Five Senior Judges – Supreme Court Judges who had retired in the preceding two years – were appointed in the first year this scheme was introduced. With these appointments – and adding the Judicial Commissioner appointments as well – the Supreme Court now comprises twenty-seven judges, which is the highest ever number, and an almost twofold increase as compared to just a few years ago.

116. For hearings involving disciplinary proceedings against errant lawyers, a Court of Three Judges is constituted. For constitutional questions referred to by the President of Singapore, a Constitutional Tribunal is constituted – for normal constitutional challenges brought by the public, the High Court has jurisdiction. To deal more effectively with the increasingly complex cases before the courts, the High Court has the following specialized lists: Building and Construction, Shipbuilding and Complex Technical Cases; Finance, Securities, Banking, Complex Commercial Cases; Company, Insolvency and Trusts; Arbitration; Shipping and Insurance; Tort Claims; Intellectual Property/Information Technology; Employment; Revenue Law; as well as Public Law and Judicial Review.

117. The Registrar of the Supreme Court oversees the Supreme Court Registry and is assisted by the Deputy Registrar, Senior Assistant Registrars and Assistant Registrars. The court's first Chief Executive Officer, who is in charge of administration and operations, was appointed in 2013. Justices' Law Clerks assist the High Court and Court of Appeal Judges by carrying out research on the law and work directly under the charge of the Chief Justice.

118. The State Courts are headed by the Presiding Judge who oversees the work of all the District Judges, Magistrates and staff. He is assisted by the Deputy Presiding Judge and a leadership team of Senior District Judges, Group Managers, the Registrar of the State Courts, senior judicial officers and senior court administrators. The State Courts comprise three Justice Divisions – the Criminal Justice Division, the Civil Justice Division, and the Family and Juvenile Justice Division (this was changed in 2015). There is also the Strategic Planning and Technology Division (which is responsible for matters such as knowledge management) and Corporate and Court Services Division (which is responsible for matters such as human resource management) which support the administration of the State Courts. In 2015, the Family and Juvenile Justice Division was reconstituted as the Family Justice Courts.

262. *Singapore Parliamentary Debates, Official Report* (4 Nov. 2014) vol. 92 (The Minister for Law, Mr K Shanmugam).

119. Criminal cases in the State Courts are heard by the Bail Court, Criminal Courts, Coroner's Court, Community Court, Centralised Sentencing Court, District Courts, Filter Court, Mentions Court, Night Courts, Neighbourhood Court, and the Traffic Court. Civil cases in the State Courts are heard by the Civil Courts, Primary Dispute Resolution Centre, and Small Claims Tribunals. Up until 2015, family and juvenile cases were heard by the Family Court and the Juvenile Court respectively; these courts are now known as the Family Courts and Youth Courts. For Muslims, the Syariah court has concurrent jurisdiction with the High Court to determine disputes relating to marriage, divorce, division of property upon divorce, and maintenance under Muslim law. The Syariah court also has jurisdiction over inheritance matters for Muslims. For military matters, there is the Military Court, decisions of which can be appealed to the Military Court of Appeal. The Military Court of Appeal consists of five members and is presided by a person who is qualified to be a Supreme Court Judge, but it remains unclear if the High Court has supervisory jurisdiction over it.

§2. MEMBERS OF THE JUDICIARY

120. Singapore generally subscribes to the notion of separation of powers, with the judiciary forming one of the three branches of government. District Judges and Magistrates are appointed by the President of Singapore on the recommendation of the Chief Justice.[263] The only qualifications District Judges and Magistrates need to possess are five years and one year of legal experience (which are defined statutorily) respectively.[264] District Judges and Magistrates are Legal Service Officers, and therefore come under the (disciplinary) jurisdiction of the Legal Service Commission.

121. For Supreme Court Judges – they are not considered Legal Service Officers – there are safeguards to ensure judicial independence, some of which are enshrined in the Constitution. First, the selection process for these judges involves the President, Prime Minister, and Chief Justice – essentially the three highest constitutional offices in the land. Specifically, the Prime Minister must consult the Chief Justice before submitting a nomination to the President; the President has the formal power of appointment but he also has the discretion to refuse the nomination.[265] Second, there is security for tenure until the age of 65 years; judges appointed after that age will be given contracts stipulating specific periods.[266] A judge may only be removed from office if the Prime Minister or Chief Justice (in consultation with the Prime Minister) represents to the President that he has misbehaved or has become unable from infirmity of body or mind or any other cause, to properly discharge the functions of his office, and a tribunal (comprising at least

263. Supreme Court of Judicature Act (Cap. 322, 2007 Rev. Ed.), ss 9 and 10.
264. Supreme Court of Judicature Act (Cap. 322, 2007 Rev. Ed.), ss 9 and 10.
265. Constitution of the Republic of Singapore (1985 Rev. Ed., 1999 Reprint), art 95.
266. Constitution of the Republic of Singapore (1985 Rev. Ed., 1999 Reprint), art 98.

five judges or ex-judges) appointed by the President also makes the same recommendation.[267] Third, there is security for remuneration.[268] Remuneration may not be altered to the judge's disadvantage after his appointment.[269] Fourth, the conduct of judges or persons designated to sit as judges or Judicial Commissioners shall not be discussed in Parliament except on a substantive motion of which notice given by at least one-quarter of the total number of Members of Parliament.[270] Fifth, judges, both of the Supreme Court and State Courts, are immune from suit; in addition to this, anything that is said by them in court is absolutely privileged and cannot be subject to a suit for defamation. Sixth, contempt of court laws – whether by interference or by disobedience – exist to protect the courts from publications that undermine their authority and impartiality.[271]

267. Constitution of the Republic of Singapore (1985 Rev. Ed., 1999 Reprint), art 98.
268. Constitution of the Republic of Singapore (1985 Rev. Ed., 1999 Reprint), art 98.
269. Constitution of the Republic of Singapore (1985 Rev. Ed., 1999 Reprint), art 98.
270. Constitution of the Republic of Singapore (1985 Rev. Ed., 1999 Reprint), art 99.
271. In 2016, the Administration of Justice (Protection) Act was passed. It codifies various types of contempt (including contempt by disobedience of court orders or undertakings), the jurisdiction and punishment for contempt, and defences to contempt.

Chapter 2. The Bar

§1. Exercise of the Legal Profession

I. Conditions for Admission

122. As the legal profession in Singapore is fused, a person who is called to the bar becomes both advocate and solicitor of the Supreme Court of Singapore.[272] There are several conjunctive conditions for admission as an advocate and solicitor. First, an applicant must have graduated from a statutorily approved law school.[273] Second, an applicant must pass the local bar examinations.[274] Third, an applicant must complete a training contract with a law firm.[275] Fourth, after the above has been done, an applicant must file an affidavit.[276] Fifth, at the time of filing the said affidavit an applicant must be at least 21 years old, and must be endorsed to be of good character.[277] Sixth, when the applicant is being called, he faces no objections by organizations such as the Law Society of Singapore and Attorney-General's Chambers.[278] The whole process, with the start of law school as the starting point, can take anywhere between three years and six years.[279] In recent years, upon admission an advocate and solicitor must fulfil certain obligations under the Continuing Professional Development Scheme for a number of years as a condition for renewing his practicing certificate.

123. An advocate and solicitor cannot successfully apply for a practicing certificate if he is an undischarged bankrupt, has entered into a composition or deed of arrangement with his creditors, owes SGD 100,000 in outstanding judgments, fails to prepare the relevant accountancy documents, or fails to obtain the mandatory professional indemnity insurance.[280] A foreign-qualified lawyer who passes the Foreign Practitioner Examinations can apply for a Foreign Practitioner Certificate to practise in limited areas of Singapore law; such a lawyer would be working for a firm that is approved under the Qualifying Foreign Law Practice (QFLP) or Joint Law Venture/Formal Law Alliance schemes, as opposed to a Licensed Foreign Law Practice scheme.[281] If a lawyer works for a Representative Office – that is, a foreign law practice that does purely liaison or promotional work – he cannot provide any legal services. Queen's Counsel (or the equivalent in other jurisdictions) can be

272. *See also* G. Low, *A Globalised Legal Profession*, in *The Legal System of Singapore* (G. Chan & J. Lee eds, LexisNexis 2015).
273. Legal Profession Act (Cap. 161, 2009 Rev. Ed.), ss 10 and 12.
274. Legal Profession Act (Cap. 161, 2009 Rev. Ed.), s 13.
275. Legal Profession Act (Cap. 161, 2009 Rev. Ed.), s 13.
276. Legal Profession Act (Cap. 161, 2009 Rev. Ed.), ss 10 and 12.
277. Legal Profession Act (Cap. 161, 2009 Rev. Ed.), s 13.
278. Legal Profession Act (Cap. 161, 2009 Rev. Ed.), s 12.
279. It takes at least two years to earn a law degree in Singapore, though most students take four years. Students on double degrees (whether double law degrees or with a different second degree) usually take five years.
280. Legal Profession Act (Cap. 161, 2009 Rev. Ed.), s 26.
281. *See also* G. Low, *A Globalised Legal Profession*, in *The Legal System of Singapore* (G. Chan & J. Lee eds, LexisNexis 2015).

admitted on an ad hoc basis for complex cases if they have particular expertise,[282] but with more Senior Counsel who have expertise in diverse fields, the need to engage them will generally decline.[283]

II. Rights and Duties

124. An advocate and solicitor has the exclusive right to appear and plead in all courts of justice in Singapore.[284] An advocate and solicitor can assume duties of a Commissioner for Oaths or a Notary Public, provided that he has a practicing certificate.[285] An advocate and solicitor can only become a sole proprietor, partner, or director if he has had three continuous years of Singapore law practice;[286] to qualify as a consultant, he must have no less than ten years in aggregate of legal employment.[287]

125. A selection committee comprising the Chief Justice, Attorney-General, and Judges of Appeal may appoint an advocate and solicitor or a Legal Service Officer with at least ten years' experience as Senior Counsel – Singapore's equivalent of Queen's Counsel – if it is of the opinion that by virtue of the applicant's ability, standing, or special knowledge or experience in law, is deserving of such an appointment.[288] Senior Counsel rank in precedence after the Attorney-General, Deputy Attorney-General, and Solicitor-General.[289]

126. An advocate and solicitor also has various primary responsibilities to discharge. First, he must maintain the rule of law and assist in the administration of justice. Second, he must maintain the independence and integrity of the profession. Third, he must act in the best interest of his client and charge fairly for work done. Fourth, he must facilitate access to justice by members of the public. These responsibilities are embodied in the oath any person admitted as an advocate and solicitor of the Supreme Court is required to take, that is, to 'truly and honestly conduct [oneself] in the practice of an advocate and solicitor according to the best of [one's] knowledge and ability and according to law'.[290]

127. Flowing from these primary duties are more detailed requirements specified in subsidiary legislation as well as practice directions and circulars issued by the courts. These include rules relating to the keeping of proper accounts of clients

282. Legal Profession Act (Cap. 161, 2009 Rev. Ed.), s 15.
283. For the analytical framework for assessing ad hoc admissions of Queen's Counsel, *see Re Beloff Michael Jacob QC*, [2014] 3 SLR 424, [54]–[65]; *Re Fordham Michael QC*, [2015] 1 SLR 272, [44]; *Re Rogers, Heather QC*, [2015] 4 SLR 1064, [8]–[21]; *Re Woodsworth, Samuel Sherratt QC*, [2016] SGHC 172, [24]–[29].
284. Legal Profession Act (Cap. 161, 2009 Rev. Ed.), s 29.
285. Legal Profession Act (Cap. 161, 2009 Rev. Ed.), s 76.
286. Legal Profession Act (Cap. 161, 2009 Rev. Ed.), s 75C.
287. Legal Profession Act (Cap. 161, 2009 Rev. Ed.), s 75D.
288. Legal Profession Act (Cap. 161, 2009 Rev. Ed.), s 30.
289. Legal Profession Act (Cap. 161, 2009 Rev. Ed.), s 31.
290. Legal Profession Act (Cap. 161, 2009 Rev. Ed.), s 24(1).

and their money,[291] preparing an accountant's report,[292] practice of the law,[293] conduct in relation to fellow advocates and solicitors and clients[294] (e.g., a solicitor may not enter default judgment against his opponent's client without first giving two days' notice; and he cannot act for his client in situations of conflict), management of a law practice,[295] conduct of legal proceedings,[296] as well as general conduct[297] (e.g., an advocate and solicitor cannot permit his name to be made use of for the profit of unauthorized persons).[298] In addition, advocates and solicitors have general ethical obligations that have been developed and elaborated on in case law.[299] The Law Society of Singapore also publishes practice directions, rulings and advice to practitioners although these are subject to the provisions of legislation.

III. Discipline

128. All advocates and solicitors are subject to the control of the Supreme Court.[300] An advocate and solicitor is liable to be punished if he, inter alia: has been convicted of a criminal offence that implies a defect of character that makes him unfit for the legal profession; has been guilty of fraudulent or grossly improper conduct in the discharge of his professional duty; has been adjudicated bankrupt and guilty of certain bankruptcy acts omissions; has bribed to gain business; accepted employment through a tout; or generally conducted himself in a way unbefitting of an officer of the court.[301] Possible punishments he may face once he has been shown to have been guilty of misconduct include being struck off the rolls, suspension, a fine, and censure.[302] A Senior Counsel will lose his title if he is dismissed from the Singapore Legal Service, either of the two law schools (presumably three once the third is open), convicted of offences past a certain threshold, becomes of unsound mind, is an undischarged bankrupt, enters into a composition or deed of arrangement with his creditors, is suspended from practice or struck off the roll, or as recommended by the Court of Three Judges.[303]

---

291. Legal Profession (Solicitors' Accounts) Rules (Cap. 161, R 8, 1999 Rev. Ed.); Legal Profession (Solicitors' Trust Accounts) Rules (Cap. 161, R 9, 2010 Rev. Ed.); Legal Profession (Deposit Interest) Rules (Cap. 161, R 5, 1999 Rev. Ed.).
292. Legal Profession (Accountant's Report) Rules (Cap. 161, R 10, 1999 Rev. Ed.).
293. Legal Profession (Professional Conduct) Rules (Cap. 161, R 1, 2010 Rev. Ed.), Part II.
294. Legal Profession (Professional Conduct) Rules (Cap. 161, R 1, 2010 Rev. Ed.), Part III.
295. Legal Profession (Publicity) Rules (Cap. 161, R 13, 2000 Rev. Ed.).
296. Legal Profession (Professional Conduct) Rules (Cap. 161, R 1, 2010 Rev. Ed.), Part IV.
297. Legal Profession (Professional Conduct) Rules (Cap. 161, R 1, 2010 Rev. Ed.).
298. Legal Profession Act (Cap. 161, 2009 Rev. Ed.), Part VI.
299. *See*, e.g., *Bachoo Mohan Singh v. Public Prosecutor*, [2010] 1 SLR 966; *Wong Keng Leong Rayney v. Law Society of Singapore*, [2006] 4 SLR(R) 934.
300. Legal Profession Act (Cap. 161, 2009 Rev. Ed.), s 82.
301. Legal Profession Act (Cap. 161, 2009 Rev. Ed.), s 83.
302. Legal Profession Act (Cap. 161, 2009 Rev. Ed.), s 83.
303. Legal Profession Act (Cap. 161, 2009 Rev. Ed.), s 30.

129. Clients[304] can file complaints against their lawyers to the Law Society of Singapore.[305] One possible ground of complaint is inadequate professional service, which has a time bar of three years. The Law Society will then consider if an action is negligence is more appropriate; if it is not, then mediation with a view to settlement is proposed as an option; if this option is rejected or exhausted, then the complaint will be referred to an Investigative Tribunal. This tribunal comprises two practicing lawyers and usually takes two to six months to complete its investigation and report to the Council with a report. If there is a finding of inadequate professional service and the Council accepts the finding, it may direct the errant lawyer to, inter alia, rectify the errors at his own expense. Another possible ground is for professional misconduct. The Law Society will refer the complaint to the Council, which will decide if it should be referred to the Chairman of the Inquiry Panel. The Chairman will then refer the complaint to a panel of persons appointed by the Chief Justice to review the matter. The first panel to review this is a two-person Review Committee and if after investigation deems it necessary to begin an inquiry, the Chairman of the Inquiry Panel may refer the matter to a second panel in the form of the Inquiry Committee.[306] An Inquiry Committee is also appointed by the Chief Justice but comprises four persons, and has up to six months to investigate the complaint. If the Inquiry Committee is satisfied that there has been misconduct, it may recommend that the society prosecute the complaint before the Disciplinary Tribunal or recommend a financial penalty of up to SGD 10,000 to be imposed.[307] If the Disciplinary Tribunal determines that disciplinary action is necessary, the society will apply for the matter to be heard by the Court of Three Judges.[308]

§2. Institutions and Organizations

130. Annual fees are payable by advocates and solicitors to the Law Society of Singapore and Singapore Academy of Law. Advocates and solicitors who possess a practicing certificate are members of the Law Society of Singapore, and can attend general meetings and vote in resolutions.[309] The Law Society of Singapore is responsible for, inter alia, maintaining and improving the standards of conduct of the legal profession, facilitating the acquisition of legal knowledge by members of the legal profession, assisting the government in all matters affecting legislation and the administration and practice of the law, representing the interests of the legal profession, granting assistance to organizations in the interests of the legal profession, promoting relations between members, and establishing and maintaining relations with professional bodies of the legal profession in other countries.[310]

---

304. *See also* Legal Profession Act (Cap. 161, 2009 Rev. Ed.), s 92.
305. Legal Profession Act (Cap. 161, 2009 Rev. Ed.), s 85.
306. Legal Profession Act (Cap. 161, 2009 Rev. Ed.), ss 84 and 85.
307. Legal Profession Act (Cap. 161, 2009 Rev. Ed.), s 88.
308. Legal Profession Act (Cap. 161, 2009 Rev. Ed.), s 89.
309. Legal Profession Act (Cap. 161, 2009 Rev. Ed.), s 43.
310. Legal Profession Act (Cap. 161, 2009 Rev. Ed.), s 38.

131. The Council, which comprises fifteen elected members, makes rules for regulating the professional practice, etiquette, conduct, and discipline of advocates and solicitors. The Council, inter alia, takes cognisance of anything affecting the professional conduct of its members and will bring before any general meeting of the society any matter which it considers material or to the interests of the profession and make any recommendations and take such action as it sees fit, examines and reports on proposed legislation, and is in charge of financial matters relating to the Law Society.[311]

132. Advocates and solicitors are also members of the Singapore Academy of Law. The academy, which is governed by a Senate, is responsible for, inter alia, legal education and training for the legal profession (for instance through seminars), law reform (for instance through law reform committees), promoting legal knowledge (for instance through the publication of journals, monographs, and annual reviews), and implementing technology into legal practice (for instance through the running of LawNet and Singapore Law Watch). Both the Law Society and the Singapore Academy of Law have sub-organizations (for instance, the Pro Bono Services Centre for the society and the Singapore Mediation Centre for the academy) and also committees which are populated by various members of the legal community. There are also professional legal organizations not affiliated to these two that lawyers can join, such as the Association of Criminal Lawyers of Singapore, Singapore Association of Women Lawyers, and Singapore Corporate Counsel Association.

311. Legal Profession Act (Cap. 161, 2009 Rev. Ed.), s 59.

Chapter 3. The Bailiffs

133. Following common law tradition, bailiffs and the Sheriff have overlapping roles. The bailiffs are officers of the State Courts whereas the Sheriff is an officer of the Supreme Court.[312] The Supreme Court of Judicature Act provides that the Registrar shall be the Sheriff and the Deputy Registrar shall be the Deputy Sheriff and the Assistant Registrars shall be the Assistant Sheriffs of the Supreme Court.[313] The Sheriff and his officers have the power to: execute all writs, summonses, rules, orders, warrants, commands and process of the Supreme Court given to him by the Court for that purpose; make a return of the same together with the manner of the execution thereof to the Supreme Court from which the process issued; and receive all such persons as are committed to his custody by the Supreme Court.[314] The Sheriff may not act in a matter if he is an interested party; the court will appoint another person to act in the place of the Sheriff.[315] Bailiffs in the State Courts have similar powers which are provided for by the State Courts Act.[316] In addition, the Sheriff and bailiffs have a common law duty to seize only such quantity of goods as would be reasonably sufficient to pay the judgment debt.[317]

134. An excessive seizure claim may be made against the Sheriff or a bailiff if the execution debtor can show that the Sheriff or bailiff had the opportunity to seize fewer goods or goods of lesser value than he actually seized, and the seizure was obviously excessive or clearly disproportionate to the judgment debt.[318] It is, however, a defence to an excessive seizure claim if the Sheriff, a bailiff, or the execution creditor's representative exercised a reasonable and honest discretion in estimating what the goods would realize at auction when choosing how much of the execution debtor's property to seize.[319] Statutes also confer on the Sheriff and on bailiffs protection from liability unless the Sheriff or bailiff knowingly acted in excess of the authority conferred upon him.[320]

135. When executing any writ of seizure and sale or any other writ of execution or of distress, the Sheriff and his officers may use such force as is reasonably necessary to effect entry into a building.[321] The Registrar of the Supreme Court may

312. *See also* Supreme Court of Judicature Act (Cap. 322, 2007 Rev. Ed.), s 67(1).
313. Supreme Court of Judicature Act (Cap. 322, 2007 Rev. Ed.), s 63.
314. Supreme Court of Judicature Act (Cap. 322, 2007 Rev. Ed.), s 64.
315. Supreme Court of Judicature Act (Cap. 322, 2007 Rev. Ed.), s 65.
316. State Courts Act (Cap. 321, 2007 Rev. Ed.), s 15.
317. *South East Enterprises (Singapore) Pte Ltd v. Hean Nerng Holdings Pte Ltd*, [2013] 2 SLR 908, [22]–[23].
318. *South East Enterprises (Singapore) Pte Ltd v. Hean Nerng Holdings Pte Ltd*, [2013] 2 SLR 908, [28]–[29].
319. *South East Enterprises (Singapore) Pte Ltd v. Hean Nerng Holdings Pte Ltd*, [2013] 2 SLR 908, [26]–[27].
320. Supreme Court of Judicature Act (Cap. 322, 2007 Rev. Ed.), s 79(2); State Courts Act (Cap. 321, 2007 Rev. Ed.), s 68(2); *South East Enterprises (Singapore) Pte Ltd v. Hean Nerng Holdings Pte Ltd*, [2013] 2 SLR 908, [56].
321. Supreme Court of Judicature Act (Cap. 322, 2007 Rev. Ed.), s 64; State Courts Act (Cap. 321, 2007 Rev. Ed.), s 16.

authorize a solicitor or a person employed by a solicitor to exercise the powers and perform the duties of an officer of the Sheriff during such period or on such occasion as the Registrar thinks fit.[322] Similarly, the Registrar of the State Courts may authorize a solicitor or a person employed by a solicitor to exercise the powers and perform the duties of a bailiff.[323]

322. Supreme Court of Judicature Act (Cap. 322, 2007 Rev. Ed.), s 65A.
323. State Courts Act (Cap. 321, 2007 Rev. Ed.), s 15A.

Chapter 4. Singapore International Commercial Court

§1. Introduction

I. Inception of the Singapore International Commercial Court

136. The Singapore International Commercial Court (SICC) was first officially conceived in early 2013 with a launch date of 2015 (it was launched in January 2015).[324] Its purpose was and remains to capitalize on the growth of trade and investment in Asia and the strength and reputation of the country's good governance and judiciary by growing the legal services sector as well as expanding the scope for the internationalization and export of Singapore law.[325] The main idea behind the court's inception was to enhance Singapore's status as a leading forum for legal services and commercial dispute resolution in the region;[326] a 2016 report had stated that Singapore is the world's third most preferred seat of arbitration, with the Singapore International Arbitration Centre (SIAC) hearing 271 disputes (including those in progress) valued at USD 6.23 billion in total in 2015 and 343 disputes (from almost 60 jurisdictions) valued at USD 17.13 billion in 2016. Around 80% of those disputes were international in nature. The court has thus been described as a new breed of international commercial court designed to be distinct from the Courts of the Dubai International Financial Centre and to rival the global influence of the Commercial Court of England and Wales.[327]

137. According to the SICC Committee, the court was to provide 'an internationally accepted dispute resolution framework for the resolution of international commercial disputes in accordance with substantive principles of international commercial law'.[328] At the same time, it was thought that there was no equivalent default court in Asia for parties involved in cross-border disputes that did not want to arbitrate or rely in the courts in London or New York. In that sense, the SICC was meant to integrate into the local judiciary. In addition, despite the prevalence of

324. The Singapore International Mediation Centre was also conceived at the same time (together with the longer-established SIAC) to complete the suite of international dispute resolution services. However, unlike the Singapore International Mediation Centre which uses the arbitration-mediation-arbitration protocol, the Singapore International Commercial Court appears at first blush to be a competing player in international arbitration in Singapore. The court's first judgment, *BCBC Singapore Pte Ltd v. PT Bayan Resources TBK*, [2016] SGHC(I) 1, was released in May 2016. It involved a claim of contract and the main issues were the construction of terms and illegality under foreign law.

325. *Report of the Singapore International Commercial Court Committee*, at 3, https://www.mlaw.gov.sg, 30 Sep. 2017.

326. *Report of the Singapore International Commercial Court Committee*, at 5, https://www.mlaw.gov.sg, 30 Sep. 2017.

327. D. Wong, *The Rise of the International Commercial Court: What is it and Will it Work?*, 33(2) Civ. J. Q. 205, 206–207 (2014).

328. *Report of the Singapore International Commercial Court Committee*, at 11–12, https://www.mlaw.gov.sg, 30 Sep. 2017. This committee was chaired by then Judge of Appeal VK Rajah and Senior Minister of State Indranee Rajah.

arbitration in modern times to resolve commercial disputes, 'the coercive jurisdiction of a court may be necessary in a multiple party dispute; the subject matter of the dispute may not be amenable to arbitration … and the New York Convention, while wide in its reach, may not be fully effective for enforcement in some countries'.[329] The SICC was thus designed to address these deficiencies, and in so doing, was meant to coexist with arbitration and not necessarily to compete with it.[330] As for local commercial cases, those would still be handled primarily by local lawyers, so it was not anticipated that that sector of work would be affected. In that connection, though the SICC is a division of the High Court,[331] and though the High Court and Court of Appeal already possess long-standing jurisdiction to hear international commercial cases, as will be seen below there are meant to be certain advantages in creating a separate court within the current Singapore court structure.[332]

II. Summary of Original Key Recommendations

138. The following were the original key recommendations made by the SICC Committee in late-2013.[333] The SICC would be a division of the High Court, which is part of the Supreme Court.[334] The pool of judges would comprise existing

329. *Report of the Singapore International Commercial Court Committee*, at 12, https://www.mlaw.gov.sg, 30 Sep. 2017. *See also* D. Wong, *The Rise of the International Commercial Court: What is it and Will it Work?*, 33(2) Civ. J. Q. 205, 224 (2014): 'On one hand, there is a strong public interest in preventing conflicting judgments with inconsistent and irreconcilable findings and having the entirety of a complex dispute and all interested parties before a single court at the same time in order for them to be bound by a single decision. As an international court, in contra-distinction to an arbitral tribunal which is a creature of parties' consent … the [court] ought to have a wider duty to ensure due administration of justice for transnational disputes … On the other hand, it is both jurisprudentially sound and commercially astute for the court to have an overriding philosophy of respecting party autonomy as to forum.'

330. It has also been contended that arbitration is no longer as viable as before, given the ever-increasing costs and customer dissatisfaction with arbitrator expertise and impartiality: D. Wong, *The Rise of the International Commercial Court: What is it and Will it Work?*, 33(2) Civ. J. Q. 205, 217 (2014). Moreover, that the decisions of the Singapore International Commercial Court may be appealed and that over time a harmonious corpus of jurisprudence may be generated provide further advantages.

331. Supreme Court of Judicature Act (Cap. 322, 2007 Rev. Ed.), s 18A.

332. *See also* Yeo T.M., *Staying Relevant: Exercise of Jurisdiction in the Age of the SICC*, Eighth Yong Pung How Professorship of Law Lecture (2015), 22, http://law.smu.edu.sg/sites/default/files/law/CEBCLA/YPH-Paper-2015.pdf, 30 Sep. 2017: 'The SICC is a specialist court with narrow grounds for taking jurisdiction, and parties in choosing the SICC would have given particular consideration to its specific rules … On the other hand, the High Court is a court of general civil jurisdiction and has very broad grounds for taking jurisdiction, so its rules on the exercise of jurisdiction must be flexible enough to take into account all the circumstances of the case … International comity can take a back seat in the case of the SICC when it is giving effect to party autonomy … While the High Court predominantly serves the public function, the SICC has a strong flavour of commercial service provision.'

333. Some of these recommendations have since been adopted, while others have made been refined; both will be described here for comparison purposes. At the same time, it should be noted that not all procedural rules have been prescribed at this point.

334. *Report of the Singapore International Commercial Court Committee*, at 5, https://www.mlaw.gov.sg, 30 Sep. 2017. A possible consequence of this is that the court will have court powers such as

Supreme Court Judges and so-called Associate Judges (these could be local or international) who are appointed for a fixed period and assigned to cases on an ad hoc basis.[335] If a case goes on appeal (to the Court of Appeal), the appellate judges would be drawn from the aforementioned pool of judges.[336]

139. The SICC would have jurisdiction over three categories of cases: first, where parties have consented to use the court post-dispute;[337] second, where parties have in a contract given the court jurisdiction over any disputes arising out of that contract;[338] and third, cases within the High Court's jurisdiction that have been transferred to the court by the Chief Justice.[339] A set of rules known as the SICC Rules as well as Practice Directions would be created to govern proceedings in the court; these provisions will be drawn from international best practices for commercial dispute resolution (this was done in 2015).[340] A Registry would also be created

---

the awarding of default judgment, which may not be available in arbitration: K. Poon & P. Tan, *The Development of the Singapore International Commercial Court*, Rajah & Tan Client Update 4 (December 2013). The proposed amendments to the Supreme Court of Judicature Act (Cap. 322, 2007 Rev. Ed.) simply state that the court may exercise such powers as the High Court may exercise in its original civil jurisdiction, except for the power under paragraph 1 of the First Schedule. But what is more certain is that the Singapore International Commercial Court 'cannot have a larger base of jurisdiction than the High Court … For example, the limitation that the court will not adjudicate a case that involves title or possessory rights to foreign immovable property … [or] certain types of questions that are regarded as non-justiciable in a court of law': Yeo T.M., *Staying Relevant: Exercise of Jurisdiction in the Age of the SICC*, Eighth Yong Pung How Professorship of Law Lecture (2015), 6, http://law.smu.edu.sg/sites/default/files/law/CEBCLA/YPH-Paper-2015.pdf, 30 Sep. 2017.

335. *Report of the Singapore International Commercial Court Committee*, at 5, https://www.mlaw.gov.sg, 30 Sep. 2017.
336. *Report of the Singapore International Commercial Court Committee*, at 5, https://www.mlaw.gov.sg, 30 Sep. 2017.
337. *Report of the Singapore International Commercial Court Committee*, at 5, https://www.mlaw.gov.sg, 30 Sep. 2017. Supreme Court of Judicature Act (Cap. 322, R. 5, 2014 Rev. Ed.) Rules of Court, O 110 r 7(1). *See also Singapore Parliamentary Debates, Official Report* (4 Nov. 2014) vol. 92 (The Minister for Law, Mr K Shanmugam): 'parties to an agreement to submit to the jurisdiction of the [Singapore International Commercial Court] shall be considered to have agreed: (i) to submit to the exclusive jurisdiction of the [Singapore International Commercial Court]; (ii) to carry out any [Singapore International Commercial Court] judgment without undue delay; and (iii) to waive any recourse to any court or tribunal outside Singapore against any [Singapore International Commercial Court] judgment and the enforcement of such judgment … unless the parties have expressly provided otherwise.'
338. *Report of the Singapore International Commercial Court Committee*, at 5, https://www.mlaw.gov.sg, 30 Sep. 2017. Supreme Court of Judicature Act (Cap. 322, R. 5, 2014 Rev. Ed.) Rules of Court, O 110 r 2(a). Where cases are inappropriately commenced in the court, they may be referred to the High Court.
339. *Report of the Singapore International Commercial Court Committee*, at 5, https://www.mlaw.gov.sg, 30 Sep. 2017. Supreme Court of Judicature Act (Cap. 322, R. 5, 2014 Rev. Ed.) Rules of Court, O 110 r 2(b). Reference will be taken from, for instance, the procedural rules of the Commercial Court of England and Wales as well as the English Commercial Court Guide – and these rules are markedly different from the civil procedure rules used by the Singapore courts. What is also noteworthy is that this feature of the court is another departure from most cases of arbitration, where the procedural laws are not necessarily fixed ahead of time.
340. *Report of the Singapore International Commercial Court Committee*, at 5, https://www.mlaw.gov.sg, 30 Sep. 2017.

to manage the caseload of the court and to support the judges for hearings.[341] Legal representation for cases heard by the court would be generally governed by the Legal Profession Act.[342]

§2. Basic Features of the Court and Its Processes

I. Tenure and Composition

140. Judges drawn from the Supreme Court would already have security of tenure (up to 65 years of age) and security of remuneration by virtue of the Constitution.[343] Based on the 2013 SICC report, the Associate Judges would not enjoy security of tenure, but their remuneration will be calculated (using an agreed rate) based on the length of the commitment required.[344] The Chief Justice would be the one to appoint persons whom he considers have the appropriate experience and qualifications for each case to be Associate Judges.[345] In accordance with High Court proceedings, proceedings in the SICC would be disposed of by a single judge.[346] However, the Chief Justice may, on the application of a party, appoint three judges to hear a case; regard would be had, for instance, to the subject matter of the dispute.[347] As for interlocutory proceedings, they would be heard by judges in a docket system.[348]

141. Pursuant to the court's Practice Directions, it was clarified that proceedings would generally be presided over by a single judge; proceedings must be heard by three judges where all the parties to the proceedings agree (unless the Chief Justice directs otherwise), or where the Chief Justice determines it is appropriate for three

341. *Report of the Singapore International Commercial Court Committee*, at 5, https://www.mlaw.gov.sg, 30 Sep. 2017.
342. (Cap. 161, 2009 Rev. Ed.).
343. Constitution of the Republic of Singapore (1999 Reprint), art 98.
344. *Report of the Singapore International Commercial Court Committee*, at 13, https://www.mlaw.gov.sg, 30 Sep. 2017.
345. *Report of the Singapore International Commercial Court Committee*, at 13, https://www.mlaw.gov.sg, 30 Sep. 2017. It was initially proposed that a foreign Associate Justice could be accorded the honorific of Associate (International) Justice, but based on proposed amendments to the Constitution of the Republic of Singapore (1999 Reprint), the title will be International Judge. Such judges may resign, but may not be removed from office except in accordance with the procedure for removal as set out in the Constitution. For local Associate Judges, the proposed title was Senior Judge. Such judges may sit in the High Court or Court of Appeal if required by the Chief Justice. They will take the same Oath of Office as Judges and Judicial Commissioners of the Supreme Court of Singapore.
346. *Report of the Singapore International Commercial Court Committee*, at 17, https://www.mlaw.gov.sg, 30 Sep. 2017.
347. *Report of the Singapore International Commercial Court Committee*, at 17, https://www.mlaw.gov.sg, 30 Sep. 2017.
348. *Report of the Singapore International Commercial Court Committee*, at 16, https://www.mlaw.gov.sg, 30 Sep. 2017. This system perhaps mirrors the one that was only recently introduced to the Supreme Court, where in certain cases High Court Judges would hear a case even from the pre-trial stage, particularly if their areas of expertise are engaged.

judges to hear the matter.[349] At both levels of hearings, parties do not have any autonomy over the panel selection, marking yet another departure from most types of arbitration.[350] It has been suggested that this feature of the court would make it attractive to parties who find that party-appointed arbitrators may not necessarily be impartial.[351] Where all parties to the proceedings agree, any party may apply for three judges to be designated to hear the matter. The application shall be made by letter to the Registrar, stating the reasons and the consent of all parties, and shall be made as soon as practicable or by any deadline which the judge may direct at a Case Management Conference.[352] It was also clarified in the Practice Directions that appeals to the Court of Appeal may be presided over by two Judges of Appeal for matters such as extension of time, leave to appeal, and interlocutory judgments.[353]

142. In 2015, former Supreme Court Judges were appointed Senior Judges of the Supreme Court for a period of three years; former Chief Justice Chan was also appointed as a Judge of Appeal and Judge of the SICC. At the same time, eleven International Judges were appointed to the SICC for a period of three years: these included eminent members of the bar and judiciary from jurisdictions such as Australia, France, Hong Kong, Japan, and the United Kingdom.[354] Several other International Judges have since been appointed as well.

II. Registry

143. The Registry of the SICC is headed by the Registrar of the Supreme Court, who is supported by officers with the same jurisdiction and powers of the High Court.[355] The Registry assists the judges by administering cases and appeals. The Registry is meant to provide quality and timely adjudication services for the efficient management of each docket and administer the directions of the judges for the preparation and follow-up of cases, including preliminary applications, pre-hearing conferences, and taxation and enforcement matters.[356]

349. Singapore International Commercial Court Practice Directions (Part III); Supreme Court of Judicature Act (Cap. 322, 2014 Rev. Ed.), ss 18G and 18H. In hearings with three judges, the Chief Justice appoints one of them to preside. It is also possible for a case to be heard by two judges, if one of the three judges is unable to continue hearing the dispute and the parties agree to have the case determined by the remaining two judges.
350. D. Wong, *The Rise of the International Commercial Court: What is it and Will it Work?*, 33(2) Civ. J. Q. 205, 213 (2014).
351. K. Poon & P. Tan, *The Development of the Singapore International Commercial Court*, Rajah & Tan Client Update 4 (December 2013).
352. Singapore International Commercial Court Practice Directions (Part III).
353. Singapore International Commercial Court Practice Directions (Part III).
354. The first dispute heard involved Australian, Indonesian, and Singapore interests and claims arising out of a joint venture agreement to produce and sell upgraded coal. The damages sought were USD 750 million and three judges were appointed: Quentin Loh (Singapore High Court), Vivian Ramsey (UK), and Anselmo Reyes (Hong Kong). The parties were represented by two local law firms.
355. *Report of the Singapore International Commercial Court Committee*, at 23, https://www.mlaw.gov.sg, 30 Sep. 2017.
356. *Report of the Singapore International Commercial Court Committee*, at 22, https://www.mlaw.gov.sg, 30 Sep. 2017.

144. The Registry also maintains and court documents and records, collects fees and other charges, as well as convenes court sittings and provides hearing support.[357] Internally, the Registry edits and disseminates court judgments and other publications, updates the Rules and Practice Directions, and assumes the role of liaison for al court business, affairs, and correspondence.[358] Further, the Registry works with providers of mediation services to refer disputes if parties make a request for mediation or if it is appropriate to do so.[359] If settlement is reached, it can be recorded as a court order to facilitate enforcement of the mediated agreement.[360]

III. Jurisdiction

145. This section only sketches out the basic aspects of jurisdiction of the Singapore International Commercial Court; explication of the nuances is covered below. As the SICC is a division of the High Court, it too is constituted under the Supreme Court of Judicature Act.[361] The court's jurisdictional limits are the same as the High Court (but not including the powers of the Family Division and the power to make prerogative orders).[362]

---

357. *Report of the Singapore International Commercial Court Committee*, at 22–23, https://www.mlaw.gov.sg, 30 Sep. 2017.
358. *Report of the Singapore International Commercial Court Committee*, at 23, https://www.mlaw.gov.sg, 30 Sep. 2017.
359. *Report of the Singapore International Commercial Court Committee*, at 23, https://www.mlaw.gov.sg, 30 Sep. 2017. In Singapore, this would be the Singapore International Mediation Centre and Singapore Mediation Centre.
360. *Report of the Singapore International Commercial Court Committee*, at 23, https://www.mlaw.gov.sg, 30 Sep. 2017.
361. *Report of the Singapore International Commercial Court Committee*, at 14, https://www.mlaw.gov.sg, 30 Sep. 2017. Supreme Court of Judicature (Amendment) Act 2014 (No 42 of 2014). The traditional in personam jurisdictional framework of the High Court is founded on proper service of process and distinguishes between the existence of jurisdiction (whether the court can hear the case) and the exercise of it (whether the court should hear the case). Territorial jurisdiction is based on presence, submission, and service (*see* Supreme Court of Judicature Act (Cap. 322, 2007 Rev. Ed.), s 16), but extraterritorial jurisdiction requires leave of court for service of process on a foreign defendant – this is done by showing there is a good arguable case to establish a nexus of jurisdiction (*see* Supreme Court of Judicature Act (Cap. 322, R. 5, 2014 Rev. Ed.) Rules of Court, O 11 r 1), there is a serious issue to be tried on the merits, and that Singapore is a proper forum to try the case. The exercise of jurisdiction, on the other hand, will be determined by the doctrine of *forum non conveniens*. If there is a jurisdiction agreement, this confers in personam jurisdiction on the Singapore courts if the subject matter of the dispute is capture by the jurisdictional clause. If it is an exclusive jurisdiction agreement, the party who wishes to litigate outside of Singapore must show strong cause amounting to exceptional circumstances to succeed in his stay of proceedings application. If there is a non-exclusive jurisdiction agreement, the jurisdiction agreement becomes one of the factors to be considered by the court as to whether it should exercise its jurisdiction. *See also Man Diesel & Turbo SE v. IM Skaugen SE*, [2020] 1 SLR 327.
362. *Report of the Singapore International Commercial Court Committee*, at 15, https://www.mlaw.gov.sg, 30 Sep. 2017. Singapore Parliamentary Debates, Official Report (4 Nov 2011) vol. 92 (The Minister for Law, Mr K Shanmugam); Supreme Court of Judicature (Amendment) Act 2014 (No 42 of 2014).

146. The court has in personam jurisdiction to hear an action if: the action is international and commercial in nature; the action is one that the High Court may hear and try in its original civil jurisdiction; and the action satisfies such other conditions as the Rules of Court may prescribe.[363] It was mentioned earlier (in the section on overview of key recommendations) that there are three possible categories of cases for which the SICC would hear. As regards the second category (jurisdiction via contract), whether the dispute is pursuant to an international commercial transaction will be determined by the definitions applicable in international arbitration.[364] For cases that have been transferred to the High Court, the pricing will generally follow High Court fees, unless the connection with Singapore is not strong.[365]

147. If a party applies to court to stay the Singapore action citing forum non conveniens, this will not be an issue for consensual cases founded on an exclusive jurisdiction agreement as the Singapore courts would not allow a breach of the agreement.[366] In cases where there is non-consensual jurisdiction, there is a question of whether the traditional common law test remains modern and relevant to the SICC.[367] If there is an issue over whether the dispute can be heard by the court, the court has the jurisdiction to hear and determine the issue.[368] But even if there are no

363. Supreme Court of Judicature Act (Cap. 322, 2007 Rev. Ed.), s 18D.

364. *Report of the Singapore International Commercial Court Committee*, at 15, https://www.mlaw.gov.sg, 30 Sep. 2017. The Court of Appeal has recently reiterated that all Singapore courts are pure creatures of statute, devoid of any ability to inherently confer upon itself jurisdiction: *Re Nalpon Zero Geraldo Mario*, [2013] 3 SLR 258, [34]; *Muhammad Ridzuan bin Md Ali v. Public Prosecutor*, [2014] 3 SLR 721, [96]. *See also* C. Siyuan, *Jurisdiction, Power, Inherent Jurisdiction, and Inherent Power*, Sing. Law Watch Commentaries (4/2013).

365. If the connection to Singapore is tenuous, there will be discretion for the full Singapore International Commercial Court rate to be charged. In this regard, *see* Supreme Court of Judicature Act (Cap. 322, 2007 Rev. Ed.), ss 15–18.

366. *Report of the Singapore International Commercial Court Committee*, at 15, https://www.mlaw.gov.sg, 30 Sep. 2017. Accordingly, the court will dismiss the stay of proceedings application unless a strong cause can be shown.

367. *Report of the Singapore International Commercial Court Committee*, at 15–16, https://www.mlaw.gov.sg, 30 Sep. 2017. The Committee was referring to the House of Lords decision in *Spiliada Maritime Corp v. Cansulex Ltd*, [1987] AC 460, which continues to be adopted by the Court of Appeal: *see* for instance *JIO Minerals FZV v. Mineral Enterprises Ltd*, [2011] 1 SLR 391, [42]; *Orchard Capital I Ltd v. Ravindra Kumar Jhunjhunwala*, [2012] 2 SLR 519, [12] and [34]. Under this traditional test, a stay would only be granted if the court is satisfied that there is some other available and more appropriate forum for the trial of the action and the natural forum is one with which the action has the most real and substantial connection. 30 Sep. 2017.

368. *Report of the Singapore International Commercial Court Committee*, at 16, https://www.mlaw.gov.sg, 30 Sep. 2017. *See also* Singapore International Commercial Court User Guides, 2015 (Note 1): 'The Court will not decline to assume jurisdiction solely on the ground that the dispute between the parties … is connected to a jurisdiction other than Singapore: *see* Order 100, Rule 8(2) … Since the parties have agreed in writing to submit to the jurisdiction of the Court, which is an international court, the Court would not examine the connecting factors to Singapore in deciding whether to decline to assume jurisdiction.'

objections to jurisdiction or competence, the court can decline to admit the case if it is clearly inappropriate, and in appropriate situations, transfer the case to the High Court.[369]

148. Decisions of the SICC are appealable to the Court of Appeal, but this right is subject to any prior agreement between the parties to limit or vary the scope of appeals.[370] It has been suggested that allowing parties to contract out of review caters to parties who see review as necessary to ensure accountability as well as to parties who see review as an incursion on the finality of awards.[371] The number of judges required to hear appeals was originally not prescribed, but the appellate panel was expected to comprise local and international jurists.[372] In the court's Practice Directions that were issued in 2015, it was clarified that an appeal to the Court of Appeal may be heard by three or more Judges of Appeal. An appeal must be heard by five Judges of Appeal where all parties to the appeal so agree (unless the Chief Justice directs otherwise), or where the Chief Justice determines that it is appropriate to convene a panel of five Judges of Appeal.[373] Where all parties to the appeal agree, any party may apply for five Judges of Appeal to be designated to hear the appeal. The application shall be by letter to the Registrar, stating the reasons and the consent of all parties, and shall be made as soon as practicable and no later than seven working days after which the Respondent's Case is due to be filed.[374]

149. The Practice Directions also clarified the court's original jurisdiction. The court may hear and try an action if: the claims between the plaintiffs and defendants named in the originating process when it was first filed are of an international and commercial nature; each plaintiff and defendant named in the originating process when it was first filed has submitted to the court's jurisdiction under a written jurisdiction agreement; and the parties do not seek any relief in the form of, or connected with, a prerogative order.[375]

---

369. *Report of the Singapore International Commercial Court Committee*, at 16, https://www.mlaw.gov.sg, 30 Sep. 2017.

370. *Report of the Singapore International Commercial Court Committee*, at 18, https://www.mlaw.gov.sg, 30 Sep. 2017. For instance, as modelled after international arbitration practices, the scope of appeal may be limited to grounds such as breaches of natural justice.

371. K. Poon & P. Tan, The Development of the Singapore International Commercial Court, Rajah & Tan Client Update 4 (December 2013).

372. D. Wong, *The Rise of the International Commercial Court: What is it and Will it Work?*, 33(2) Civ. J. Q. 205, 210 (2014).

373. Singapore International Commercial Court Practice Directions (Part III); Supreme Court of Judicature (Amendment) Act 2014 (No 42 of 2014).

374. Singapore International Commercial Court Practice Directions (Part III). *See also* Singapore International Commercial Court User Guides, 2015 (Note 1): 'The Court has jurisdiction under Order 110, Rule 7 to hear and try any action that the High Court may hear and try in its original civil jurisdiction if: (a) the claims between the plaintiffs and defendants named in the originating process when it was first filed are of an international and commercial nature; (b) each plaintiff and defendant named in the originating process when it was first filed has submitted to the Court's jurisdiction under a written jurisdiction agreement; and (c) the parties do not seek any relief in the form of, or connected with, a prerogative order.'

375. Singapore International Commercial Court Practice Directions (Part IX); Supreme Court of Judicature (Amendment) Act 2014 (No 42 of 2014). When the Singapore International Commercial

As for challenges to the court's jurisdiction, the court may consider whether it has jurisdiction either on its own motion or on an application by a party.[376]

150. If there is a pre-action certificate certifying that the action is of an international and commercial nature, that pre-action certificate must first be set aside before the court's jurisdiction on the ground that the action is not of an international or commercial nature may be challenged.[377] Where the court decides that it has no jurisdiction or that it should decline jurisdiction, it may dismiss or stay the proceedings, or make any other order it sees fit.[378]

IV. Commencement of Action

151. Proceedings in the SICC may be commenced by a writ of summons or originating summons; proceedings in which substantial disputes of facts are likely to arise should be begun by writ unless there is an application for summary judgment.[379] Writs of summons and originating summonses filed must be accompanied by a plaintiff's declaration (explaining why the action is of an international and commercial nature)[380] signed by the plaintiff or the plaintiff's counsel, and the declaration must exhibit a copy of the written jurisdiction agreement to which the

---

Court was first conceived, it was pointed out that 'clarity as to the applicable conflict of law rules matters, especially for an international court dealing with cross-border disputes. A simple option would be for the court to apply Singapore's conflict of law rules': D. Wong, *The Rise of the International Commercial Court: What is it and Will it Work?*, 33(2) Civ. J. Q. 205, 219 (2014). In the absence of this, there will be great uncertainty over jurisdictional challenges such as whether the dispute is covered by the jurisdiction agreement, whether the jurisdiction clause was properly incorporated into the contract, or whether there was even a validly formed contract in the first place.

376. Singapore International Commercial Court Practice Directions (Part IX); Supreme Court of Judicature (Amendment) Act 2014 (No 42 of 2014). *See also* Supreme Court of Judicature Act (Cap. 322, R. 5, 2014 Rev. Ed.) Rules of Court, O 110 rr 10–11.

377. Singapore International Commercial Court Practice Directions (Part IX); Supreme Court of Judicature (Amendment) Act 2014 (No 42 of 2014). A pre-action certificate allows a party who intends to commence an action in the curt, or who may be a party to an action commenced in the court, to obtain an early indication from the court as to whether: the claims are of an international and commercial nature; the intended action is an offshore case; the intended action should be heard in camera; the proceedings should be confidential; the file of the proceedings should be sealed: Supreme Court of Judicature Act (Cap. 322, R. 5, 2014 Rev. Ed.) Rules of Court, O 110 r 39.

378. Singapore International Commercial Court Practice Directions (Part IX).

379. Supreme Court of Judicature Act (Cap. 322, R. 5, 2014 Rev. Ed.) Rules of Court, O 110 r 4.

380. According to Supreme Court of Judicature Act (Cap. 322, R. 5, 2014 Rev. Ed.) Rules of Court, O 110 r 1(2), a claim is international if: the parties have, by a written jurisdictional agreement, agreed to submit the claim for resolution by the court and at the time the agreement was concluded, the parties have their place of business in different states; none of the parties to the claim have their places of business in Singapore; any place where a substantial part of the obligations of the commercial relationship between the parties is to be performed or the place with which the subject matter of the dispute is most closely connected is situated outside any state in which any of the parties have their places of business; or the parties to the claim have expressly agreed that the subject matter of the claim relates to more than one state. The definition of 'commercial' is broadly set out in Supreme Court of Judicature Act (Cap. 322, R. 5, 2014 Rev. Ed.) Rules of Court, O 110 r 1(2).

plaintiff and defendant are party.[381] The validity period for writs of summons and originating summonses is twelve months beginning with the date of issue; this may be extended.[382] Leave is not required for service of process on an overseas defendant where there is a written jurisdiction agreement.[383]

V. Joinder

152. It was envisaged that the SICC may join third parties to the proceedings regardless of whether consent of the third parties is obtained and regardless of whether they are parties to an agreement conferring jurisdiction on the court.[384] Joinder may be initiated by one or more of the disputants.[385] Third parties who do not consent to the joinder but are present in Singapore can still be served the writ if the court so directs.[386] Third parties who are not present may still be joined if they can be served out of jurisdiction.[387] Regard would be had to the grounds found in the Rules of Court.[388] It has been observed that the power of the court to join third parties even without their consent solves a recurring problem in arbitration, which is that the jurisdiction of a tribunal is limited to those who are parties to the arbitration agreement even though non-signatories may be the real parties to the dispute.[389]

153. In the amendments to the Rules of Court in 2015, it was clarified that where the court has and assumes jurisdiction, a person may be joined as a party to the action if the requirements in the Rules of Court for joining the person are met, and the claims by or against the person do not include a claim for any relief in the form of, or connected with, a prerogative order and are appropriate to be heard in the

381. Supreme Court of Judicature Act (Cap. 322, R. 5, 2014 Rev. Ed.) Rules of Court, O 110 r 4. This is not needed if the plaintiff has already obtained a pre-action certificate.
382. Supreme Court of Judicature Act (Cap. 322, R. 5, 2014 Rev. Ed.) Rules of Court, O 110 r 5.
383. Supreme Court of Judicature Act (Cap. 322, R. 5, 2014 Rev. Ed.) Rules of Court, O 110 r 6.
384. *Report of the Singapore International Commercial Court Committee*, at 15, https://www.mlaw.gov.sg, 30 Sep. 2017.
385. *Report of the Singapore International Commercial Court Committee*, at 15, https://www.mlaw.gov.sg, 30 Sep. 2017.
386. *Report of the Singapore International Commercial Court Committee*, at 15, https://www.mlaw.gov.sg, 30 Sep. 2017. Supreme Court of Judicature Act (Cap. 322, R. 5, 2014 Rev. Ed.) Rules of Court, O 110 r 6(2).
387. *Report of the Singapore International Commercial Court Committee*, at 15, https://www.mlaw.gov.sg, 30 Sep. 2017.
388. Supreme Court of Judicature Act (Cap. 322, R. 5, 2014 Rev. Ed.) Rules of Court, O 11 r 1. *See also* Yeo T.M., *Staying Relevant: Exercise of Jurisdiction in the Age of the SICC*, Eighth Yong Pung How Professorship of Law Lecture (2015), 19, http://law.smu.edu.sg/sites/default/files/law/CEBCLA/YPH-Paper-2015.pdf, 30 Sep. 2017.
389. K. Poon & P. Tan, *The Development of the Singapore International Commercial Court*, Rajah & Tan Client Update 3 (December 2013). Trust disputes (in the sense of wealth management) that involve or affect beneficiaries or classes of beneficiaries are perhaps an example: *Singapore: Rolling out the Red Carpet for Family Offices*, WongPartnership 6 (April 2014).

court.[390] In deciding whether to join a party, the court must have regard to the claim's international and commercial character.[391] A state or the sovereign of a state may not be made party to an action unless it has submitted to the jurisdiction of the court under a written jurisdiction agreement.[392]

VI. Transfer of Proceedings

154. A case may be transferred from the High Court to the SICC if: the action is of an international and commercial nature; the parties are not seeking any relief in the form of or connected with a prerogative order; the SICC will assume jurisdiction in the case; it is more appropriate for the case to be heard in the SICC; and by consent of the parties or if the High Court makes the transfer on its own motion.[393] A case may be transferred from the SICC to the High Court if the court considers that the High Court has and will assume jurisdiction in the case and it is more appropriate for the case to be heard in the High Court, and a party has, with the consent of all other parties, applied for the transfer.[394]

VII. Confidentiality

155. Proceedings in the SICC will generally take place in open court.[395] The main justification for this is twofold: transparency is attractive to some parties and is important for the branding of the court, and confidentiality is antithetical to the development of a internally consistent body of jurisprudence.[396] However, special rules may apply for cases that have no substantial connection to Singapore.[397] For instance, if parties confirm that either Singapore law is not the governing law or the choice of Singapore law is the sole connection to Singapore, and further agree that

390. Supreme Court of Judicature Act (Cap. 322, R. 5, 2014 Rev. Ed.) Rules of Court, O 110 r 9(1). *See also* Supreme Court of Judicature (Amendment) Act 2014 (No 42 of 2014).

391. Supreme Court of Judicature Act (Cap. 322, R. 5, 2014 Rev. Ed.) Rules of Court, O 110 r 9(3). *See also* Singapore International Commercial Court User Guides, 2015 (Note 1).

392. Supreme Court of Judicature Act (Cap. 322, R. 5, 2014 Rev. Ed.) Rules of Court, O 110 r 9(2).

393. Supreme Court of Judicature Act (Cap. 322, R. 5, 2014 Rev. Ed.) Rules of Court, O 110 r 12(4). The ambiguities of these conditions have been noted academically: M. Yip, *Singapore International Commercial Court: The Asian Hub for Commercial Litigation*, paper presented at the 12th Asian Law Institute Conference Paper (2015) at 18–19. 30 Sep. 2017: 'a transfer from the High Court to the SICC would raise only issues of internal allocation of jurisdiction. But since the High Court can initiate the transfer at any time, it is possible that international jurisdiction is still a live issue at the time transfer is being considered … In this scenario, should the High Court apply its own international jurisdiction standards, or the international jurisdiction standards of the SICC?'

394. Supreme Court of Judicature Act (Cap. 322, R. 5, 2014 Rev. Ed.) Rules of Court, O 110 r 12(3).

395. *Report of the Singapore International Commercial Court Committee*, at 17, https://www.mlaw.gov.sg, 30 Sep. 2017.

396. *Report of the Singapore International Commercial Court Committee*, at 17, https://www.mlaw.gov.sg, 30 Sep. 2017.

397. *See also* : *Teras Offshore Pte Ltd v. Teras Cargo Transport (America) LLC*, [2016] SGHC(I) 2, [9]–[13].

they desire confidentiality, the hearing can be conducted in camera.[398] If only one party wishes to have confidentiality, an application can be made to the court, which will then consider all the circumstances of the case, including any public interest considerations.[399]

156. In the court's Practice Directions, it was clarified that the court may, on the application of a party, order: that the case be heard in camera; no person to reveal or publish any information or document relating to the case; and/or the court file to be sealed.[400] The court will generally give due weight to such an application for confidentiality if the subject of the order is an offshore case[401] and parties have an agreement on the orders to be made.[402] This is because where a case has limited connections with Singapore or where it is not governed by Singapore law, the public interest in maintaining open court proceedings and ensuring access to the evidence and documents is not readily engaged.[403]

VIII. Injunctive Powers

157. The SICC will have injunctive powers. All applications for interim relief will be heard in chambers by a judge, unless otherwise directed by the court and as far as possible, the Registry will assign all such applications to the judge who will be hearing the trial or other dispositive hearings.[404] Applications for the grant of injunctions may be made ex parte in cases of urgency, though in most cases the respondent should be invited to attend the hearing, with a default minimum of two hours' notice.[405] All ex parte applications must be supported by an affidavit stating: the reasons for an ex parte application, such as risk of dissipation of assets, destruction of evidence, or any other prejudicial conduct; the urgency of the application; the factual basis of the application; the factual basis for any reasonable defences that may be relied by the respondent; whether the applicant is aware of any issues relating to jurisdiction; an undertaking to pay for losses; and any other material facts the court should be aware of.[406]

---

398. *Report of the Singapore International Commercial Court Committee*, at 17, https://www.mlaw.gov.sg, 30 Sep. 2017.
399. *Report of the Singapore International Commercial Court Committee*, at 17, https://www.mlaw.gov.sg, 30 Sep. 2017.
400. Singapore International Commercial Court Practice Directions (Part XV). *See also* Supreme Court of Judicature Act (Cap. 322, R. 5, 2014 Rev. Ed.) Rules of Court, O 110 r 30. *See also* Supreme Court of Judicature Act (Cap. 322, R. 5, 2014 Rev. Ed.) Rules of Court, O 110 rr 1(1) and 34.
401. An offshore case is an action that has no substantial connection with Singapore: *Teras Offshore Pte Ltd v. Teras Cargo Transport (America) LLC*, [2016] SGHC(I) 2, [8].
402. Singapore International Commercial Court Practice Directions (Part XV); Supreme Court of Judicature Act (Cap. 322, R. 5, 2014 Rev. Ed.) Rules of Court, O 110 r 30. Presumably, however, the court can also order redaction or direct for non-publication to lapse after a period of time.
403. M. Yip, 'Singapore International Commercial Court: The Asian Hub for Commercial Litigation', *12th Asian Law Institute Conference Paper* (2015): 1, 6.
404. Singapore International Commercial Court Practice Directions (Part XVII); Supreme Court of Judicature (Amendment) Act 2014 (No 42 of 2014).
405. Singapore International Commercial Court Practice Directions (Part XVII).
406. Singapore International Commercial Court Practice Directions (Part XVII).

158. At present, the Practice Directions only refer to injunctions generally, Mareva injunctions (including worldwide ones), and search orders. Thus, while anti-suit injunctions can be critical weapons for private international lawyers, it remains to be seen if the SICC can grant such relief and even if it can, whether it would be of any practical effect.[407] Specifically, the party bringing the foreign action in breach of a jurisdiction agreement may do so with impunity, since there would be no question of being in contempt of the SICC.[408] Possible workarounds this problem include legislating that breaching an order of the court is tantamount to contempt of the Singapore courts, or that the judgment in question from the foreign court would not be recognized in Singapore.[409]

IX. Costs

159. The costs of an incidental to any application or proceedings are at the discretion of the SICC, and the court has the full power to determine by whom and to what extent the costs are to be paid.[410] It should be noted that O 59 of the Rules of Court does not apply to proceedings in the SICC, appeals from the SICC to the Court of Appeal or applications to the Court of Appeal in relation to such appeals of to SICC proceedings by virtue of O 110 r 46(6). However, common law principles relating to costs would still be relevant. The general rule for costs in the SICC may be found in O 110 r 46(1) and (2), which provides that: 'The unsuccessful party in any application or proceedings in the Court must pay the reasonable costs of the application or proceedings to the successful party, unless the Court orders otherwise … The unsuccessful party in any appeal from the Court to the Court of Appeal must pay the reasonable costs of the appeal to the successful party, unless the Court of Appeal orders otherwise.'

160. In assessing costs, the court shall have regard to the notion that the reasonable costs of any application or proceeding in the court be borne by the unsuccessful party to that application or proceeding unless the court orders otherwise, and

407. D. Wong, *The Rise of the International Commercial Court: What is it and Will it Work?*, 33(2) Civ. J. Q. 205, 224–225 (2014). *See also* Yeo T.M., *Staying Relevant: Exercise of Jurisdiction in the Age of the SICC*, Eighth Yong Pung How Professorship of Law Lecture (2015), 15–16, http://law.smu.edu.sg/sites/default/files/law/CEBCLA/YPH-Paper-2015.pdf, 30 Sep. 2017: 'Order 110 does not apply to anti-suit injunctions so the common law continues to apply. In the absence of a breach of contract, the anti-suit injunction will be granted on very restrictive grounds. Generally it should not be as difficult to obtain an anti-suit injunction to restrain a breach of contract because international comity plays a reduced role where the objective of the injunction is to enforce a contractual bargain.'

408. D. Wong, *The Rise of the International Commercial Court: What is it and Will it Work?*, 33(2) Civ. J. Q. 205, 225 (2014).

409. D. Wong, *The Rise of the International Commercial Court: What is it and Will it Work?*, 33(2) Civ. J. Q. 205, 225 (2014).

410. Singapore International Commercial Court Practice Directions (Part XXIII). Generally, however, it is expected that 'costs follow the event' would form the starting point in most cases.

may: apportion costs between the parties if the court determines that the apportionment is reasonable in the circumstances of the case; take into account relevant circumstances; order costs to be paid by counsel personally, or by a person who is not a party to the application or proceeding; order interest on costs; or make any ancillary order, including the time and manner of payment.[411] The relevant circumstances which the court may take into account include: the conduct of all parties before and during the application or proceeding; the value of the claim; the complexity or novelty of the claim; the skill, expertise, and specialized knowledge involved; the time and effort expended on the application or proceeding; any payment of money into account; and any offer to settle.[412] The court may require parties to provide a costs schedule to be submitted with closing submissions, or to submit cost estimates in the course of proceedings.[413] The hearing and court fees for SICC proceedings are provided for by O 110 rr 47 and 48. Upon commencement of an SICC case, a party must pay to the Registrar a deposit in accordance with Part VII, paragraph 36 of the SICC Practice Directions. The failure to pay any fee or deposit may lead to the Registrar refusing to administer or continue the proceedings pursuant to O 110 r 50.

§3. International Character and Challenges Ahead

I. Jurisdictional Issues

161. If there is a jurisdiction agreement, the parties shall be considered, if there is no express provision to the contrary, to have agreed to: submit to the exclusive jurisdiction of the SICC; carry out any judgment or order of the court without undue delay; and waive any recourse to any court or tribunal outside Singapore against any order or judgment of the court and against the enforcement of such judgment or order.[414]

162. It has been suggested that there are three ways to interpret a jurisdictional agreement within such a framework: first, if Singapore law is the proper law of contract, the above is implied into the contract as a term; second, if the proper law of the contract is an issue in dispute, the court may apply the law of forum to interpret the jurisdiction agreement and the above would be brought in as a term implied in law; and third, the above is invoked as a mandatory rule of the forum and therefore

411. Singapore International Commercial Court Practice Directions (Part XXIII). *See also* Supreme Court of Judicature Act (Cap. 322, R. 5, 2014 Rev. Ed.) Rules of Court, O 110 r 46.

412. Singapore International Commercial Court Practice Directions (Part XXIII).

413. Singapore International Commercial Court Practice Directions (Part XXIII).

414. Supreme Court of Judicature Act (Cap. 322, 2007 Rev. Ed.), s 18F. Model clauses are available from the Singapore International Commercial Court website. *See also* Supreme Court of Judicature Act (Cap. 322, R. 5, 2014 Rev. Ed.) Rules of Court, O 110 r 1(2).

applies to all jurisdiction agreements in favour of the SICC, regardless of the parties' choice of law or even in the absence of choice.[415] However, the first and second interpretations may be unduly restrictive given the purpose of the SICC, while the third interpretation cannot be readily supported either by the express words of the Supreme Court of Judicature Act or any particular national socioeconomic interest.[416] On another view, the framework creates a rebuttable presumption that a choice of the SICC is an exclusive choice, even if the choice of court agreement is governed by foreign law.[417]

163. As to assumption of jurisdiction, the SICC may decline to assume jurisdiction if it is not appropriate for the action to be heard in the court (regard to the international and commercial character of the action will be had), though the court must not decline jurisdiction solely on the ground that the dispute between the parties is connected to a jurisdiction other than Singapore (if there is a written jurisdiction agreement between the parties).[418] Under the common law, forum non conveniens is determined in two stages: first by examining the connecting factors of the case with the competing fora from the point of view of expense and inconvenience (such personal connections, connections to events and transactions, governing law), and second by asking whether substantial justice can be obtained (factors such as access to practical justice and international comity are considered).[419] Accordingly, it has been suggested that the common law test may not be relevant in determining whether the SICC should assume jurisdiction in any given case; it has also been suggested that the test of appropriateness is not exhausted by the consideration of whether the dispute is of an international and commercial character.[420]

415. M. Yip, *Singapore International Commercial Court: The Asian Hub for Commercial Litigation*, paper presented at the 12th Asian Law Institute Conference Paper (2015) at 12–13.
416. M. Yip, *Singapore International Commercial Court: The Asian Hub for Commercial Litigation*, paper presented at the 12th Asian Law Institute Conference Paper (2015) at 13.
417. Yeo T.M., *Staying Relevant: Exercise of Jurisdiction in the Age of the SICC*, Eighth Yong Pung How Professorship of Law Lecture (2015), 9–10 and 15, http://law.smu.edu.sg/sites/default/files/law/CEBCLA/YPH-Paper-2015.pdf, 30 Sep. 2017.
418. Supreme Court of Judicature Act (Cap. 322, R. 5, 2014 Rev. Ed.) Rules of Court, O 110 r 8.
419. *JIO Minerals FZC v. Mineral Enterprises Ltd*, [2011] 1 SLR 391, [42].
420. M. Yip, *Singapore International Commercial Court: The Asian Hub for Commercial Litigation*, paper presented at the 12th Asian Law Institute Conference Paper (2015) at 16–17. The author further notes that 'if the SICC only has jurisdiction … over a matter that is international and commercial in nature, why is there a need to reconsider this issue at the posterior stage concerning exercise of jurisdiction … the international and commercial character of a case could even be determined preliminarily through the optional procedure of applying for a pre-action certificate'. *See also* Yeo T.M., *Staying Relevant: Exercise of Jurisdiction in the Age of the SICC*, Eighth Yong Pung How Professorship of Law Lecture (2015), 13–14, http://law.smu.edu.sg/sites/default/files/law/CEBCLA/YPH-Paper-2015.pdf, 30 Sep. 2017: 'jurisdiction may be declined if and only if the case is not appropriate to be heard in the SICC … At first blush, [O 110 r 8] looks conceptually similar to the Australian 'clearly inappropriate forum test' that was previously rejected in Singapore. However, to the extent that [O 110 r 8] is read to exclude the most appropriate forum test because of its reliance on foreign connections, it is hard to *see* how the 'clearly inappropriate forum' test, which also analyses foreign connections closely, has survived [O 110 r 8] (emphasis in original).'

164. Pending the growth of jurisprudence by the SICC to inject greater clarity in this realm, the following conclusions have been surmised.[421] If there is an exclusive choice of Singapore court clause, the SICC will only decline jurisdiction if it is not the appropriate forum, and it cannot decide solely on grounds of foreign connections, while under the common law proceedings will only be stayed if there are exceptional circumstances amounting to strong cause to detract from the parties' bargain.[422] If there is an exclusive choice of foreign court clause, the SICC has no jurisdictional basis at all, while under the common law the test of strong cause applies as well.[423] If there is a non-exclusive choice of court agreement, the SICC treats the clause as the same as an exclusive choice of court agreement insofar as the exercise of its international jurisdiction is concerned, while under the common law this will depend on the content of the agreement.[424] If there is no jurisdiction agreement, the SICC has no jurisdiction unless a case is transferred to it (but the High Court would have decided international jurisdiction under common law principles) or there is a joinder of third parties (meaning there is a conflict between the connecting factors or strong cause test and the appropriateness of forum test).[425]

II. Foreign Laws and Rules of Evidence

165. Given its international character, foreign law need not be pleaded and proved as fact in proceedings before the SICC; judges can take judicial notice with the assistance of oral and written submissions that are supported by the relevant authorities.[426] Foreign law can thus be applied to resolve the dispute, especially if parties have agreed in wiring as to the choice of law that applies to the dispute.[427] This approach is very similar to that taken in arbitration.[428] The Evidence Act[429] would be amended accordingly to reflect the changes.[430]

---

421. Yeo T.M., *Staying Relevant: Exercise of Jurisdiction in the Age of the SICC*, Eighth Yong Pung How Professorship of Law Lecture (2015), 26–27, http://law.smu.edu.sg/sites/default/files/law/CEBCLA/YPH-Paper-2015.pdf, 30 Sep. 2017.
422. With respect to the Hague Convention on Choice of Court Agreements, the court can only decline jurisdiction if the exclusive clause is null and void.
423. With respect to the Hague Convention on Choice of Court Agreements, the convention will prevail if the foreign court is in a contracting state, and the Singapore courts will have very limited grounds for assuming jurisdiction.
424. With respect to the Hague Convention on Choice of Court Agreements, it will not apply.
425. With respect to the Hague Convention on Choice of Court Agreements, it will not apply.
426. *Report of the Singapore International Commercial Court Committee*, at 17, https://www.mlaw.gov.sg, 30 Sep. 2017. *See also* Evidence Act (Cap. 97, 1997 Rev. Ed.), s 59.
427. *Report of the Singapore International Commercial Court Committee*, at 17, https://www.mlaw.gov.sg, 30 Sep. 2017.
428. D. Wong, *The Rise of the International Commercial Court: What is it and Will it Work?*, 33(2) Civ. J. Q. 205, 210 (2014). Another feature adopted from arbitral procedure is that of production of documents.
429. (Cap. 97, 1997 Rev. Ed.).
430. The proposed s 59A(1) reads: 'When in any civil proceedings the court has to form an opinion on any aspect of the law of a foreign country, the court may take judicial notice of … the legislation of that foreign country … the decisions of the courts of that foreign country … any judgment of the Court of Appeal or High Court that is relevant … any other material that, in the opinion of the

166. In the court's Practice Directions, it was clarified that the court may upon an application of a party order that any question of foreign law arising in any cause or matter in the court to be determined on the basis of submissions instead of proof.[431] In making such an order, the court must be satisfied that all parties are or will be represented by counsel who is competent to submit on the relevant question of foreign law; it may consider the experience and qualifications of counsel in practicing the foreign law or subject matter in question, as well as the proficiency of counsel in the language in question.[432] It has been noted that there are various shortcomings associated with the process of proving foreign law via expert witnesses (such as nuances of foreign law being mistranslated), and while SICC seemingly overcomes these by dispensing with the need for foreign law to be pleaded and proved as fact, there is still the issue of whether it is able to secure a range of international judges familiar with the laws of different jurisdictions.[433] One potential difficulty in this regard is that a complex international commercial case may take a very long time to be heard; another potential difficulty is that a foreign jurist may not be the best person to resolve any dispute as to the governing law.[434] Nonetheless, at the very least the SICC provides a more than theoretical possibility that in a dispute that has issues of foreign law, the ideal situation of the case being argued by counsel and decided by judges well-versed in that foreign law can be achieved.[435]

167. As regards rules of evidence, parties may apply for certain rules of evidence to apply to their dispute, though the SICC retains discretion to modify this if this achieves a more just, expeditious, and economical disposal of the dispute.[436] It has thus been observed that this flexibility 'is consistent with the trend of limiting the role of the lex fori in determining issues in cases with international elements' and that 'party autonomy is accorded greater prominence' in international commercial disputes.[437]

---

court, is authoritative in determining or interpreting the law of that foreign country.' Further, the proposed s 59B(1) reads: 'When in any civil proceedings to which this section applies the court has to form an opinion on any aspect of the law of a foreign country, the court may, in accordance with Rules of Court, make an order that proof of law of that foreign country shall be dispensed with and that the law of that foreign country shall be determined on the basis of submissions … .'

431. Singapore International Commercial Court Practice Directions (Part XVIII). *See also* Supreme Court of Judicature Act (Cap. 322, R. 5, 2014 Rev. Ed.) Rules of Court, O 110 r 25.
432. Singapore International Commercial Court Practice Directions (Part XVIII).
433. D. Wong, *The Rise of the International Commercial Court: What is it and Will it Work?*, 33(2) Civ. J. Q. 205, 222 (2014).
434. D. Wong, *The Rise of the International Commercial Court: What is it and Will it Work?*, 33(2) Civ. J. Q. 205, 222–223 (2014).
435. M. Yip, *Singapore International Commercial Court: The Asian Hub for Commercial Litigation*, paper presented at the 12th Asian Law Institute Conference Paper (2015) at 5.
436. Supreme Court of Judicature Act (Cap. 322, R. 5, 2014 Rev. Ed.) Rules of Court, O 110 r 23.
437. M. Yip, *Singapore International Commercial Court: The Asian Hub for Commercial Litigation*, paper presented at the 12th Asian Law Institute Conference Paper (2015) at 7.

III. Representation

168. As the SICC is a division of the High Court,[438] proceedings before it (and the Court of Appeal if there is an appeal) are governed by the Legal Profession Act.[439] Consequently, as was originally envisaged, parties can by default only be represented by members of the Singapore Bar, though Queen's Counsel or foreign counsel of equivalent distinction can be admitted on an ad hoc basis.[440] However, similar to the characteristic confidentiality, for cases that do not have a substantial connection to Singapore – such as where Singapore law is not the governing law or where the choice of Singapore law is the sole connection to Singapore – foreign counsel may appear before the SICC if they are registered with the court's Registry.[441] Parties can apply to disallow foreign counsel if it can be shown that there is no absence of substantial connection to Singapore.[442] To be registered with the court, foreign counsel must provide an address representing their place of business, undertake to abide by the ethical rules applicable, and undertake to abide by a code of ethics.[443] If there is a breach of the ethical rules, there may be revocation of registration and blacklisting against future registration.[444]

169. There will be two types of registration: full registration, which allows a foreign lawyer to appear and act in proceedings before the SICC and appeals from it in certain cases; and restricted registration, which allows a foreign lawyer to appear and act solely to make submissions on matters of foreign law in the specific case permitted by the SICC.[445] A foreign lawyer's registration may be cancelled in limited circumstances, if, for instance, he has been subject to disciplinary action in

---

438. *Report of the Singapore International Commercial Court Committee*, at 17, https://www.mlaw.gov.sg, 30 Sep. 2017.
439. (Cap. 161, 2009 Rev. Ed.). This applies to interlocutory and procedural issues as well. *See also* Singapore International Commercial Court User Guides, 2015 (Note 3).
440. *Report of the Singapore International Commercial Court Committee*, at 18, https://www.mlaw.gov.sg, 30 Sep. 2017. This will also apply to cases transferred from the High Court to the Singapore International Commercial Court. *See also Re Lord Goldsmith Peter Henry PC QC*, [2013] 4 SLR 921; *Re Beloff Michael Jacob QC*, [2013] 4 SLR 849; *Re Caplan Jonathan Michael QC*, [2013] 3 SLR 66; *Re Andrews Geraldine Mary QC*, [2013] 1 SLR 872; *Re Joseph David QC*, [2012] 1 SLR 791; *Re Millar Gavin James QC*, [2008] 1 SLR(R) 297.
441. *Report of the Singapore International Commercial Court Committee*, at 19 and 23, https://www.mlaw.gov.sg, 30 Sep. 2017. *Singapore Parliamentary Debates, Official Report* (4 Nov. 2014) vol. 92 (The Minister for Law, Mr K Shanmugam); Supreme Court of Judicature Act (Cap. 322, 2007 Rev. Ed.), s 18M.
442. *Report of the Singapore International Commercial Court Committee*, at 19, https://www.mlaw.gov.sg, 30 Sep. 2017.
443. *Report of the Singapore International Commercial Court Committee*, at 19, https://www.mlaw.gov.sg, 30 Sep. 2017.
444. *Report of the Singapore International Commercial Court Committee*, at 19, https://www.mlaw.gov.sg, 30 Sep. 2017. A report of the breach may also be sent to home jurisdiction of the foreign counsel.
445. *Singapore Parliamentary Debates, Official Report* (4 Nov. 2014) vol. 92 (The Minister for Law, Mr K Shanmugam).

another jurisdiction.[446] The judge hearing this application will give the foreign lawyer a reasonable opportunity to be heard, but the judge's decision will not be appealable.[447] If there is an allegation of professional misconduct and a complaint has been received by the Chief Justice, he will appoint a complaints committee to hear and investigate the complaint.[448] If the committee determines there is a prima facie case for investigation, it will appoint a solicitor to frame the charges and conduct proceedings before it.[449] The foreign lawyer will have a reasonable opportunity to be heard, but if the committee finds cause of sufficient gravity for disciplinary action, there will be a hearing before the Court of Three Judges.[450]

170. In the court's Practice Directions, it was clarified that a party to proceedings commenced in the court and in appeals from such proceedings may be represented by foreign lawyers: in a joint request for a pre-action certificate; where the case is treated as an offshore case; where the court exercises its discretion to allow foreign representation; in an application for leave to commit a person for contempt in respect of any judgment or order made by the court or Court of Appeal in connection with proceedings and foreign representation was allowed in the underlying proceedings; or where the court has made an order that any question of foreign law be determined on the basis of submissions and an order permitting a foreign lawyer to make submissions on the question of foreign law on behalf of a party.[451]

IV. Enforceability

171. Judgments of the SICC may be enforced in other jurisdictions[452] via the Reciprocal Enforcement of Commonwealth Judgments Act,[453] Reciprocal Enforcement of Foreign Judgments Act,[454] or a common law action on the judgment debt – this means the judgments will essentially be enforceable as judgments of the High Court and be of equal force in enforceability.[455] In addition, model SICC dispute resolution clauses should indicate that parties who have submitted or have agreed to submit to the court's jurisdiction may be deemed to waive their rights to defend

446. *Singapore Parliamentary Debates, Official Report* (4 Nov. 2014) vol. 92 (The Minister for Law, Mr K Shanmugam).
447. *Singapore Parliamentary Debates, Official Report* (4 Nov. 2014) vol. 92 (The Minister for Law, Mr K Shanmugam).
448. *Singapore Parliamentary Debates, Official Report* (4 Nov. 2014) vol. 92 (The Minister for Law, Mr K Shanmugam).
449. *Singapore Parliamentary Debates, Official Report* (4 Nov. 2014) vol. 92 (The Minister for Law, Mr K Shanmugam).
450. *Singapore Parliamentary Debates, Official Report* (4 Nov. 2014) vol. 92 (The Minister for Law, Mr K Shanmugam).
451. Singapore International Commercial Court Practice Directions (Part IV). *See also* Singapore International Commercial Court User Guides, 2015 (Note 3).
452. *Report of the Singapore International Commercial Court Committee*, at 17, https://www.mlaw.gov.sg, 30 Sep. 2017.
453. (Cap. 264, 1985 Rev. Ed.).
454. (Cap. 265, 2001 Rev. Ed.).
455. D. Wong, *The Rise of the International Commercial Court: What is it and Will it Work?*, 33(2) Civ. J. Q. 205, 211–212 (2014).

against an action based on a court's judgment in all jurisdictions.[456] On a more macro level, it is expected that the Singapore government will enhance the enforceability of the court's judgments via bilateral and multilateral agreements (such as free trade agreements), appropriate international conventions, and inter-court arrangements (including memoranda of guidance and memoranda of understanding).[457] Further, it has been suggested that since the court's judgments, unlike international arbitral awards, do not have the benefit of ease of enforceability under the New York Convention, it may be ideal for Singapore to sign up and champion the 2005 Hague Convention on Choice of Court Agreements[458] (in 2015, it became the fourth party in the world to do so, after the United States, European Union, and Mexico). This will be but part of a broader vision to create a multipronged legal infrastructure in Singapore to promote and protect cross-border trade.[459]

172. More specifically, because the Hague Convention helps ensure that exclusive choice of court agreements are effective and that judgments by the chosen courts are recognized and enforced in contracting states, it will help enhance the

456. *Report of the Singapore International Commercial Court Committee*, at 20, https://www.mlaw.gov.sg, 30 Sep. 2017. Written consent is required so as to create issue estoppels which will bind parties to the decision of the referred jurisdiction. *See also Singapore Parliamentary Debates, Official Report* (5 Mar. 2014) vol. 91 (The Minister for Law, Mr K Shanmugam); K. Poon & P. Tan, *The Development of the Singapore International Commercial Court*, Rajah & Tan Client Update 5 (December 2013); H. Singh SC, *The Singapore International Commercial Court – A Masterstroke*, Clifford Chance Cavenagh Law LLP Briefing Note 2 (December 2013).

457. *Report of the Singapore International Commercial Court Committee*, at 20–22, https://www.mlaw.gov.sg, 30 Sep. 2017. With respect to inter-court agreements, it was proposed by the Committee that an arrangement could be established with the Commercial Court of England and Wales such that any dispute on whether a dispute falls within the jurisdiction should be decided by the Singapore International Commercial Court. However, this is 'a rather curious position whereby although the [court] will not insist on giving effect to a jurisdiction agreement in its favour regardless of the circumstances, it would expect the English Commercial Court to do that and stay English proceedings in favour [of it] notwithstanding there may be strong compelling reasons why the matter should stay in England': D. Wong, *The Rise of the International Commercial Court: What is it and Will it Work?*, 33(2) Civ. J. Q. 205, 223 (2014). *See also* S. Menon, *Transnational Commercial Law: Realities, Challenges and a Call for Meaningful Convergence*, Sing. J. Leg. Stud. 231, 250 (2013); S. Menon, *The Somewhat Uncommon Law of Commerce*, 26 Sing. Acad. L.J. 23, 47–48 (2014).

458. D. Wong, *The Rise of the International Commercial Court: What is it and Will it Work?*, 33(2) Civ. J. Q. 205, 226 (2014). *See also Singapore Parliamentary Debates, Official Report* (5 Mar. 2014) vol. 91 (The Minister for Law, Mr K Shanmugam).

459. The infrastructure also involves regional harmonization of the rules of enforcement of judgments, regional harmonization of the laws of dispute resolution processes, and regional harmonization of substantive commercial law rules: S. Menon, *Transnational Commercial Law: Realities, Challenges and a Call for Meaningful Convergence*, Sing. J. Leg. Stud. 231, 248–250 (2013); *Singapore International Commercial Court: A New Brand of Litigation?*, http://www.legal500.com/c/singapore/developments/28769, 30 Sep. 2017. However, it has also been posited that such harmonization is likely to take a long time to materialize and will likely not be comprehensive: Yeo T.M., *Staying Relevant: Exercise of Jurisdiction in the Age of the SICC*, Eighth Yong Pung How Professorship of Law Lecture (2015), 21, http://law.smu.edu.sg/sites/default/files/law/CEBCLA/YPH-Paper-2015.pdf, 30 Sep. 2017.

enforceability of judgments of the SICC vis-à-vis other parties to the Hague Convention.[460] However, as has been observed, not every Hague Convention case will be an SICC case, and not every SICC case will be a Hague Convention case since a choice of court agreement may be exclusive under the common law but not under the Hague Convention; moreover, the Hague Convention goes beyond the jurisdictional reach of the SICC in covering civil but non-commercial matters, but is narrower in jurisdiction in certain contracts, such as contracts for the carriage of goods and passengers.[461] In the court's Practice Directions, it was clarified that where a judgment or order of the court is to be enforced in Singapore, that judgment or order may be enforced in accordance with the Rules of Court, and such enforcement proceedings are to be commenced in the High Court.[462]

460. Yeo T.M., *Staying Relevant: Exercise of Jurisdiction in the Age of the SICC*, Eighth Yong Pung How Professorship of Law Lecture (2015), 23–24, http://law.smu.edu.sg/sites/default/files/law/CEBCLA/YPH-Paper-2015.pdf, 30 Sep. 2017. 30 Sep. 2017. However, it has been observed that 'considerable difficulties remain in enforcing judgments against third parties in other countries': Yeo T.M., *Staying Relevant: Exercise of Jurisdiction in the Age of the SICC*, Eighth Yong Pung How Professorship of Law Lecture (2015), 20, http://law.smu.edu.sg/sites/default/files/law/CEBCLA/YPH-Paper-2015.pdf, 30 Sep. 2017.

461. Yeo T.M., *Staying Relevant: Exercise of Jurisdiction in the Age of the SICC*, Eighth Yong Pung How Professorship of Law Lecture (2015), 24, http://law.smu.edu.sg/sites/default/files/law/CEBCLA/YPH-Paper-2015.pdf, 30 Sep. 2017. The author further notes that 'if an action on a dispute subject to an exclusive choice of the Singapore court (inclusive of all its divisions) clause is commenced in the High Court, it can be transferred to the SICC … without contravention of the Convention. However, if the parties have chosen one division to the exclusion of others, a transfer from the chosen division to another may have serious consequences.'

462. Singapore International Commercial Court Practice Directions (Part XXI).

Part II. Jurisdiction

Chapter 1. Domestic Jurisdiction

§1. Subject Matter Jurisdiction

173. The jurisdiction of the High Court and State Courts (which comprise, inter alia, the Magistrates' Courts and the District Courts) is based on service of process in or out of Singapore in accordance with the Rules of Court,[463] a party's submission to the jurisdiction of the court,[464] or the creation of jurisdiction pursuant to a statute.[465] The Magistrate's Court's jurisdiction has a pecuniary limit of SGD 60,000, while the limit for the District Court is SGD 250,000 (SGD 3,000,000 for probate and administration cases and SGD 500,000 for road traffic accident cases as well as personal injury cases arising from industrial accidents).[466]

174. Changes were made in 2014, which led to the introduction of O 108 of the Rules of Court[467] to simplify the process of the Magistrate's Court or District Court when dealing with civil claims involving SGD 60,000 and less. With the aim to facilitate 'the fair, expedient and inexpensive determination of all civil proceedings'[468] that are applicable under O 108, notable aspects of O 108 include the need for parties to produce all relevant documents up front so that both sides can better understand the relative merits of their cases;[469] the flexibility for judges to narrow down the issues and see if the case can be better resolved through mediation;[470] exclusions of certain procedures such as summary judgment and disposal of cases

463. Supreme Court of Judicature Act (Cap. 322, 2007 Rev. Ed.), s 16(1); State Courts Act (Cap. 321, 2007 Rev. Ed.), ss 19(2) and 52(1).
464. Supreme Court of Judicature Act (Cap. 322, 2007 Rev. Ed.), s 16(1); State Courts Act (Cap. 321, 2007 Rev. Ed.), ss 19(2) and 52(1). *See also* C. Bull & J. Pinsler, *Civil Procedure: Annual Review of Singapore Cases* [6.16] (Sing. Acad. L. 2002).
465. Supreme Court of Judicature Act (Cap. 322, 2007 Rev. Ed.), s 17; State Courts Act (Cap. 321, 2007 Rev. Ed.), s 19(5). *See also Ong Pang Wee v. Chiltern Park Development Pte Ltd*, [2003] 2 SLR(R) 267, [14]–[27].
466. State Courts Act (Cap. 321, 2007 Rev. Ed.), s 2.
467. Supreme Court of Judicature Act (Cap. 322, R. 5, 2014 Rev. Ed.) Rules of Court. *See also* K. C. Vijayan, *Simpler State Court Process for Civil Claims,* The Straits Times (2 Jan. 2015).
468. Supreme Court of Judicature Act (Cap. 322, R. 5, 2014 Rev. Ed.) Rules of Court, O 108 r 1(3).
469. Supreme Court of Judicature Act (Cap. 322, R. 5, 2014 Rev. Ed.) Rules of Court, O 108 r 2.
470. Supreme Court of Judicature Act (Cap. 322, R. 5, 2014 Rev. Ed.) Rules of Court, O 108 r 3.

(O 14), discovery and inspection of documents (O 24) as well as interrogatories (O 26);[471] and provision of a simplified trial with a restriction on the number of expert witnesses.[472]

175. Anything above SGD 250,000 should ideally be heard in the High Court.[473] In addition, parties to an action can agree, via a signed memorandum, that a District Court shall have jurisdiction to hear the dispute notwithstanding that the amount claimed exceeds the District Court's pecuniary limit or that any relief sought in the dispute is in respect of a subject matter the value of which exceeds the District Court limit.[474] Further, proceedings normally heard in the High Court may be allocated to the District Court if the Chief Justice 'considers it necessary or expedient to improve efficiency in the administration of justice and to provide for more speedy disposal of proceedings'.[475] Likewise, proceedings normally heard in the District Court may be allocated to the High Court if the Chief Justice 'considers it necessary or expedient to improve efficiency in the administration of justice and to provide for more speedy disposal of proceedings'.[476] However, a party is estopped from subsequently arguing that the monetary value of his claim exceeds SGD 250,000 once he has accepted the pecuniary jurisdiction of the court and the trial has commenced.[477] A party before any court of limited jurisdiction (i.e., any court below the High Court) is also precluded from dividing a single cause of action by suing one part in a court of limited jurisdiction and suing the other part or parts in another court of limited jurisdiction.[478]

176. If the dispute is of a relatively straightforward variety and the claim is for less than SGD 10,000 (SGD 20,000 if parties consent), the Small Claims Tribunal may be considered.[479] However, parties before the Small Claims Tribunal are not permitted to be represented by lawyers[480] and the adjudicatory process operates independently of the rules in the Rules of Court.[481] Moreover, while an appeal may be made from the Small Claims Tribunal to the High Court, the latter may not 'reverse or vary any determination made by a tribunal on questions of fact; or … receive further evidence'.[482]

471. Supreme Court of Judicature Act (Cap. 322, R. 5, 2014 Rev. Ed.) Rules of Court, O 108 r 4.
472. Supreme Court of Judicature Act (Cap. 322, R. 5, 2014 Rev. Ed.) Rules of Court, O 108 r 5.
473. *See also* State Courts Act (Cap. 321, 2007 Rev. Ed.), s 22(1).
474. State Courts Act (Cap. 321, 2007 Rev. Ed.), s 23.
475. Supreme Court of Judicature Act (Cap. 322, 2007 Rev. Ed.), s 28A(1).
476. State Courts Act (Cap. 321, 2007 Rev. Ed.), s 41(1).
477. *Virtual Map (Singapore) Pte Ltd v. Singapore Land Authority*, [2009] 2 SLR(R) 558, [24]; *Nim Minimart v. MCST Title Plan No 1079*, [2014] 1 SLR 108, [24].
478. State Courts Act (Cap. 321, 2007 Rev. Ed.), s 35; *Ng Kong Choon v. Tang Wee Goh*, [2016] SGHC 83, [43]. As to what constitutes a single cause of action, that is a question of fact. In this area of the law the Singapore court has departed from the position adopted in other common law jurisdictions.
479. *Checklist for Small Claims Tribunal*, http://app.subcourts.gov.sg/Data/Files/File/GeneralAsstChecklist.pdf, 30 Sep. 2015 (all figures in Singapore dollars).
480. *Lodging a Claim*, http://app.subcourts.gov.sg/sct/page.aspx?pageid=4515, 30 Sep. 2015.
481. Supreme Court of Judicature Act (Cap. 322, R. 5, 2014 Rev. Ed.) Rules of Court.
482. Small Claims Tribunal Act (Cap. 308, 199 Rev. Ed.), s 39(2). *See also Seino Merchants Singapore Pte Ltd v. Porcupine Pte Ltd*, [1999] 3 SLR(R) 221.

177. In terms of costs implications, if:

> an action is commenced in the High Court which could have been commenced in a state court, then … the plaintiff … if he recovers a sum not exceeding the District Court limit, shall not be entitled to any more costs of the action than those to which he would have been entitled if the action had been brought in a District Court; and … if he recovers a sum not exceeding the Magistrate's Court limit, shall not be entitled to any more costs of the action than those to which he would have been entitled if the action had been brought in a Magistrate's Court.[483]

178. This is important as the costs recoverable in the High Court will almost always be significantly higher than the costs awarded in the State Courts.[484] However, the plaintiff may be able to avoid this if the High Court is satisfied 'that there was sufficient reason for bringing the action in the High Court';[485] if the defendant or one of the defendants 'objected to the transfer of the action to a state court';[486] if the plaintiff is the Government of Singapore;[487] or if 'it appears to the High Court that there was reasonable ground for supposing the amount recoverable in respect of the plaintiff's claim to be in excess of the amount recoverable in an action commenced in a state court'.[488] With respect to the fourth exception, the test is:

> not one of hindsight but of reasonableness refracted through the factual prism existing when the proceedings were initiated. Needless to say, if solicitors realize that the upper limit of recoverability falls within the subordinate [state] courts' jurisdiction prior to the commencement of a hearing, steps ought to be taken to immediately transfer the proceedings to the appropriate forum.[489]

179. Accordingly, if a plaintiff is uncertain if his claim will exceed the pecuniary limit of the Magistrate's Court or District Court, he should commence proceedings in that court first, and apply for a transfer when the quantum of his claim becomes more certain.[490] It should also be noted that if a lawyer acts unreasonably and proceeds in the High Court without due consideration, he may be ordered to pay costs out of his own pocket and further suffer a reduction in the costs payable to him by his client.[491]

483. State Courts Act (Cap. 321, 2007 Rev. Ed.), s 39(1). *See also OTF Aquarium Farm v. Lian Shing Construction Co Pte Ltd (Liberty Insurance Pte Ltd, third party)*, [2010] SGHC 245, [33]–[34].
484. *See also* State Courts Act (Cap. 321, 2007 Rev. Ed.), ss 39(4) and 54G.
485. State Courts Act (Cap. 321, 2007 Rev. Ed.), s 39(4).
486. State Courts Act (Cap. 321, 2007 Rev. Ed.), s 39(4).
487. State Courts Act (Cap. 321, 2007 Rev. Ed.), s 39(5).
488. State Courts Act (Cap. 321, 2007 Rev. Ed.), s 39(6).
489. *Cheong Ghim Fah v. Murugian s/o Rangasamy*, [2004] 3 SLR(R) 193, [14].
490. *Cheong Ghim Fah v. Murugian s/o Rangasamy*, [2004] 3 SLR(R) 193, [12].
491. *Cheong Ghim Fah v. Murugian s/o Rangasamy*, [2004] 3 SLR(R) 193, [12]–[13].

§2. VENUE

I. Procedural Aspects

180. An application to transfer proceedings between the State Courts and the High Court or between a Magistrate's Court and a District Court is either by way of originating summons or summons, based on whether the proceedings have already commenced;[492] if proceedings are pending, the application should be by summons.[493] In hearing an application for transfer of proceedings, the High Court or District Court may order the proceedings to be stayed until the application has been determined.[494] If:

> an order is made by the High Court for the transfer of any proceedings from the State Courts to the High Court, the Registrar of the State Courts must send to the Registrar of the Supreme Court the file of the proceedings, all documents, exhibits and a certified copy of the notes of evidence (if any) of the proceedings ... The Registrar of the Supreme Court must [also] give notice of the transfer to every party to the proceedings.[495]

181. Similarly, if:

> an order is made by the High Court for the transfer of any proceedings from the High Court to the State Courts, the Registrar of the Supreme Court must send to the Registrar of the State Courts the file of the proceedings, all documents, exhibits and a certified copy of the notes of evidence (if any) of the proceedings ... The Registrar of the State Courts must [also] give notice of the transfer to every party to the proceedings.[496]

II. Substantive Aspects

182. A party may apply for a transfer of proceedings between courts, or in certain circumstances a court may initiate such a transfer. In this connection, the High Court has the power 'to transfer any proceedings to any other court or to or from any state court, and in the case of transfer to or from a state court to give any directions as to the further conduct thereof, except that this power shall be exercised in such manner as may be prescribed by Rules of Court'.[497] As for the State Courts, they also have the power over the transfer of proceedings between the High Court

492. Supreme Court of Judicature Act (Cap. 322, R. 5, 2014 Rev. Ed.) Rules of Court, O 89 rr 1(1) and 4(1). *See also* J. Pinsler, *Principles of Civil Procedure* 11 (Acad. Publg. 2013).
493. J. Pinsler, *Principles of Civil Procedure* 27 (Acad. Publg. 2013).
494. Supreme Court of Judicature Act (Cap. 322, R. 5, 2014 Rev. Ed.) Rules of Court, O 89 rr 1(2) and 4(2).
495. Supreme Court of Judicature Act (Cap. 322, R. 5, 2014 Rev. Ed.) Rules of Court, O 89 r 2.
496. Supreme Court of Judicature Act (Cap. 322, R. 5, 2014 Rev. Ed.) Rules of Court, O 89 r 3.
497. Supreme Court of Judicature Act (Cap. 322, R. 5, 2014 Rev. Ed.) Rules of Court, First Schedule, paragraph 10.

and the State Courts,[498] as well as the transfer of proceedings between the District Court and Magistrate's Court.[499] A party has to make an application for proceedings to transfer from the State Courts to the High Court, and convince the High Court that 'the proceedings, by reason of its involving some important question of law, or being a test case, or for any other sufficient reason, should be tried in the High Court'.[500] The court may make an order for the transfer on such terms as it sees fit,[501] and it will also consider if any undue prejudice to the defendant as a result of the transfer.[502]

183. Typical examples of what constitute 'sufficient reason' are when it is anticipated that the plaintiff's damages would exceed the pecuniary limit of the State Courts,[503] and when there is an intention for the judgment to be enforced overseas under an enforcement agreement in force.[504] Further examples of when such a transfer might be appropriate are:

> First, the plaintiff's injuries, especially in personal injury cases, may have worsened or are of a continuing nature ... second, the allowable damages might have been raised by court decisions that dealt with similar cases, after the filing of the action in a lower court; third, the amount [counterclaimed] by the defendant might be higher than what the lower court in which the plaintiff who commenced the action can give; or, fourth, the plaintiff might have inadvertently filed his claim in the wrong court.[505]

184. The entry of an interlocutory judgment (as opposed to a judgment rendered after the trial) does not affirm a state court's jurisdiction over the plaintiff's claim so as to prevent a transfer to the High Court.[506] However, in exercising its discretion whether to order a transfer, the court will take into account all the circumstances of the case.[507] A party can apply (or the court can take the initiative) to transfer proceedings from the High Court to the appropriate court in the State Courts; the test for whether the transfer should take place is identical to the 'sufficient reason' requirement for the transfer from the State Courts to the High Court.[508]

---

498. State Courts Act (Cap. 321, 2007 Rev. Ed.), ss 54B, 54C, and 54E.
499. State Courts Act (Cap. 321, 2007 Rev. Ed.), ss 54D and 54F.
500. State Courts Act (Cap. 321, 2007 Rev. Ed.), s 54B(1).
501. State Courts Act (Cap. 321, 2007 Rev. Ed.), s 54B(2).
502. *Keppel Singmarine Dockyard Pte Ltd v. Ng Chan Teng*, [2010] 2 SLR 1015, [16]–[17].
503. *Keppel Singmarine Dockyard Pte Ltd v. Ng Chan Teng*, [2008] 2 SLR(R) 839, [38], citing *Ricky Charles s/o Gabriel Thanabalan v. Chua Boon Yeow*, [2003] 1 SLR(R) 511, [15]. *See also Ng Djoni v. Miranda Joseph Jude*, [2017] SGHCR 13, [7]–[9].
504. State Courts Act (Cap. 321, 2007 Rev. Ed.), s 54B.
505. *Keppel Singmarine Dockyard Pte Ltd v. Ng Chan Teng*, [2008] 2 SLR(R) 839, [37].
506. *Keppel Singmarine Dockyard Pte Ltd v. Ng Chan Teng*, [2008] 2 SLR(R) 839, [32] and [39]. C.f. *Ricky Charles s/o Gabriel Thanabalan v. Chua Boon Yeow*, [2003] 1 SLR(R) 511, [21]–[24]; C. Bull & J. Pinsler, *Civil Procedure: Annual Review of Singapore Cases* [6.1]–[6.4] (Sing. Acad. L. 2003).
507. J. Pinsler, *Principles of Civil Procedure* 23 (Acad. Publg. 2013). At bottom, the court would *see* if there would be any prejudice caused.
508. State Courts Act (Cap. 321, 2007 Rev. Ed.), s 54C.

185. Two additional things need to be noted, however. First, an order for such a transfer may only be made 'in respect of such proceedings as could have been commenced in the state court to which the application relates, if the value of the claim had been within the District Court limit or the Magistrate's Court limit, as the case may be'.[509] Second, the fact that:

> the proceedings fall within the civil jurisdiction of the state courts would not, by itself, ordinarily constitute sufficient reason for transferring the proceedings to the state courts, if enforcement overseas is intended of any judgment obtained in the High Court under any enforcement arrangements currently in force.[510]

186. If there is a counterclaim or set-off that is beyond the District Court's pecuniary jurisdiction, the High Court may, upon a party's application or on its own motion, order that the whole proceedings be transferred to the High Court, order that the whole proceedings be tried in the State Courts, or order that the proceedings on the counterclaim or set-off be transferred to the High Court, and the remaining proceedings be tried in the State Courts.[511] A party has to make an application for proceedings to transfer from the Magistrate's Court to the District Court, and convince the District Court that 'the proceedings, by reason of its involving some important question of law, or being a test case, or for any other sufficient reason, should be tried in the District Court'.[512] The court may make an order for the transfer on such terms as it sees fit.[513]

187. A party can make an application (or the court can take the initiative) to transfer proceedings from the District Court to Magistrate's Court; the test for whether the transfer should take place is whether there is a 'sufficient reason'.[514] An order for such a transfer may only be made 'in respect of such proceedings as could have been commenced in the Magistrate's Court if the value of the claim had been within the Magistrate's Court limit'.[515] If there is a counterclaim or set-off that is beyond the Magistrate's Court's pecuniary jurisdiction, the District Court may, upon a party's application or on its own motion, order that the whole proceedings be transferred to the District Court or tried in the Magistrate's Court, or order that the proceedings on the counterclaim or set-off be transferred to the District Court and the remaining proceedings be tried in the Magistrate's Court.[516] Finally, in any given transfer that is ordered:

509. State Courts Act (Cap. 321, 2007 Rev. Ed.), s 54C(3).
510. State Courts Act (Cap. 321, 2007 Rev. Ed.), s 54C.
511. State Courts Act (Cap. 321, 2007 Rev. Ed.), s 54E. *See also id.*, s 54E(3).
512. State Courts Act (Cap. 321, 2007 Rev. Ed.), s 54A(1).
513. State Courts Act (Cap. 321, 2007 Rev. Ed.), s 54A(2).
514. State Courts Act (Cap. 321, 2007 Rev. Ed.), s 54D.
515. State Courts Act (Cap. 321, 2007 Rev. Ed.), s 54D(3).
516. State Courts Act (Cap. 321, 2007 Rev. Ed.), s 54F. *See also id.*, s 54F(3).

the costs of the whole proceedings both before and after the transfer shall, subject to any order made by the court which ordered the transfer, be in the discretion of the court to which the proceedings are transferred, and that court shall have power to make orders with respect thereto and as to the scales on which the costs of the several parts of the proceedings are to be paid.[517]

§3. Resolution of Jurisdiction Conflicts

188. Please refer to the next Chapter, Part I, Part III, Part V, and Part X.

517. State Courts Act (Cap. 321, 2007 Rev. Ed.), s 54G(1). *See also* Supreme Court of Judicature Act (Cap. 322, R. 5, 2014 Rev. Ed.) Rules of Court, O 59 r 4(2).

Chapter 2. International Jurisdiction

§1. Rules Applicable in the Absence of a Treaty

189. International jurisdiction arises when a case has an international dimension, and as a result courts of several courts might have jurisdiction in the dispute. Singapore generally follows the common law, pro-comity rules. As mentioned, a Singapore court will have jurisdiction[518] over a defendant who has been served with an originating process in Singapore or who has agreed to submit to the jurisdiction of Singapore either through an agreement or through his conduct. These are also the grounds that Singapore recognizes when determining the international jurisdiction of foreign courts.[519] If service of process on the defendant cannot be done within Singapore, the plaintiff may seek permission from the Singapore courts to serve it on the defendant outside Singapore. In either situation, however, it is open to the defendant to argue that Singapore is not the natural forum to try the dispute, and that there is a more appropriate jurisdiction. In this regard, the court will first determine which jurisdiction:

> has the closest and most real connection with the dispute and thus best placed to try the case at the least cost, expense and inconvenience. Examples of factors considered at this first stage are the location of the evidence and witnesses, the relative costs of transport and translation, and the ease with which the court in question could apply the relevant law to the dispute.[520]

190. The court will then ask:

> whether allowing the case to be tried in that jurisdiction would result in the denial of justice. The most extreme example is where the legal system is corrupt or seriously deficient in some way … The fact that the plaintiff would be deprived of a legitimate advantage of trial in the forum if the court were to send the case to the more appropriate forum is not conclusive.[521]

191. As regards disputes over choice of law, if 'there is a rule of the forum that … peremptorily directs itself to apply to the facts irrespective of the foreign elements in the case, then such a rule must be applied irrespective of any choice of law rule'.[522] However, if the issue lends itself to choice of law analysis:

518. The question of justiciability – for instance, whether a court will hear a dispute involving acts by a foreign sovereign within the sovereign's territory – will not be considered here.
519. *The Conflict of Laws*, http://www.singaporelaw.sg/sglaw/laws-of-singapore/overview/chapter-6, 30 Sep. 2015.
520. *The Conflict of Laws*, http://www.singaporelaw.sg/sglaw/laws-of-singapore/overview/chapter-6, 30 Sep. 2017.
521. *The Conflict of Laws*, http://www.singaporelaw.sg/sglaw/laws-of-singapore/overview/chapter-6, 30 Sep. 2017.
522. *The Conflict of Laws*, http://www.singaporelaw.sg/sglaw/laws-of-singapore/overview/chapter-6, 30 Sep. 2017.

> the first step is to characterise the issue before the court. The objective is to identify the nature of the problem in the private international law sense ... The most basic level of characterisation is that between substance and procedure. Matters of procedure are always governed by the law of the forum ... If the issue is substantive, the next step is to determine which substantive category of choice of law it belongs to.[523]

192. The application of foreign law may be excluded if there is some 'contravention of some essential moral, social or economic value of the forum. Moreover, the forum will not enforce, directly or indirectly, any foreign penal, revenue, or other public laws.'[524] Foreign judgments may be recognized and enforced in Singapore, and may be used as estoppel on a specific aspect of a claim or even the entire claim. Foreign judgments that are final and conclusive by the laws of the country in question can be challenged under various defences, such as breach of natural justice.[525]

§2. International Treaties

193. With respect to the relevant Hague conventions relating to cross-border cooperation in civil and commercial matters, Singapore has acceded only to the 1970 Convention on the Taking of Evidence Abroad in Civil or Commercial Matters and the 1980 Convention on the Civil Aspects of International Child Abduction.[526] However, neither of these treaties have any direct impact on general civil litigation in Singapore.

523. *The Conflict of Laws*, http://www.singaporelaw.sg/sglaw/laws-of-singapore/overview/chapter-6, 30 Sep. 2017.
524. *The Conflict of Laws*, http://www.singaporelaw.sg/sglaw/laws-of-singapore/overview/chapter-6, 30 Sep. 2017.
525. *The Conflict of Laws*, http://www.singaporelaw.sg/sglaw/laws-of-singapore/overview/chapter-6, 30 Sep. 2017.
526. *The Hague Conventions*, http://www.hcch.net/upload/statmtrx_e.pdf, 30 Sep. 2017.

Part III. Actions and Claims

Chapter 1. Limitation Period

§1. Introduction

194. Before a party sues for a civil claim, one of the foremost things he has to be mindful of is whether the Limitation Act[527] is going to operate as a bar to his claim.[528] This is because a claim that is time-barred would very likely lead to its dismissal by the court,[529] and therefore result in a waste of time and money for all parties.[530] But while limitation law seeks to be fair to defendants who should be protected from stale claims, this is balanced against what is fair to claimants who wish to have as long a period as allowed to bring their claims.[531]

195. A claim will be time-barred if the time between the date of commencement of the limitation period and the date the action is brought exceeds the limitation period stipulated by the Limitation Act.[532] As regards the date the action is brought, a person joined to the proceedings is deemed to have become a party to proceedings at the date the writ was filed,[533] not when the writ is served on him.[534] New parties may not be joined and new causes of action may not be added to an existing suit if,

527. (Cap. 163, 1996 Rev. Ed.).
528. A limitation period time-bar should be distinguished from the equitable concept of laches and a writ that has had its validity period expired. With respect to laches, *see Mahidon Nichiar bte Mohd Ali v. Dawood Sultan Kamaldin*, [2015] 5 SLR 62, [42]–[43].
529. Given that statutory law is binding on the court, the court can only justify overruling the limitation period on some basis of discretion that is provided for – but it is not. *See also AXF v. Koh Cheng Huat*, [2015] 5 SLR 819, [39] and *Suresh s/o Suppiah v. Jiang Guoliang*, [2016] SGHC 133, [2], which held that there is no room for judicial discretion to override a time bar unless it is expressly provided for. C.f. *AXF v. Koh Cheng Huat*, [2016] SGCA 22, [14], which held that whether the court has a residual equitable jurisdiction to bar a defendant from raising a limitation defence in the event of fraud or fraudulent concealment is not an obviously unsustainable legal argument for the purposes of striking out.
530. *Lian Kok Hong v. Ow Wah Foong*, [2008] 4 SLR(R) 165, [3].
531. *Suresh s/o Suppiah v. Jiang Guoliang*, [2016] SGHC 133, [67].
532. *Management Corporation Strata Title Plan No 282 v. GBI Realty Pte Ltd*, [2014] 3 SLR 229, [6].
533. *Management Corporation Strata Title Plan No 282 v. GBI Realty Pte Ltd*, [2014] 3 SLR 229, [10].
534. *Management Corporation Strata Title Plan No 282 v. GBI Realty Pte Ltd*, [2014] 3 SLR 229, [9]–[10].

at the time of the application, the relevant period has expired in relation to the claim of the new party or the new cause of action.[535]

196. If an action had previously been dismissed for want of prosecution, the court 'would have no power, in the absence of special circumstances, to prevent the plaintiff starting a fresh action within the limitation period and proceeding it with all proper diligence'.[536] It should be noted, however, that the Limitation Act shall not operate as a bar to a claim unless the Limitation Act 'has been expressly pleaded as a defence'.[537] Accordingly, a defendant should plead the Limitation Act in his defence at the earliest opportunity, lest he be precluded in some way from doing so later. The moment a limitation defence is raised by the defendant in pleadings, the plaintiff's burden is to prove that its claim falls within the limitation period.[538]

197. It should also be noted that the Limitation Act does not apply to all actions. First, it does 'not apply to any action or arbitration for which a period of limitation is prescribed by any other written law'.[539] Second, it does not apply to certain causes of action.[540] Third, it does not apply to actions brought under the Small Claims Tribunals Act.[541]

198. Different causes of action have different limitation periods. According to section 6 of the Limitation Act, actions 'founded on a contract or on tort … to enforce a recognisance … to enforce an award … to recover any sum recoverable by virtue of any written law other than a penalty or forfeiture' shall not be brought 'after the expiration of 6 years from the date on which the cause of action accrued'.[542] In this regard, the point at which the cause of action accrues is the point of the breach (even if the damage may not have been suffered by the claimant at that point), while the point at which the action is initiated (for the purposes of the

535. *Management Corporation Strata Title Plan No 3322 v. Mer Vue Developments Pte Ltd*, [2016] 4 SLR 351, [1].
536. *Mercantile Bank Ltd v. Pereira John Philip*, [1979–1980] SLR(R) 48, [5], citing *Birkett v. James*, [1977] 2 All ER 801. *See also Jeyaretnam Joshua Benjamin v. Lee Kuan Yew*, [2001] 2 SLR(R) 831, [29].
537. Limitation Act (Cap. 163, 1996 Rev. Ed.), s 4. *See also* Supreme Court of Judicature Act (Cap. 322, R. 5, 2014 Rev. Ed.) Rules of Court, O 18 r 8; *Hong Hin Kay Albert v. AAHG, LLC*, [2014] SGHC 206, [61].
538. *IPP Financial Advisers Pte Ltd v. Saimee bin Jumaat*, [2020] SGCA 47.
539. Limitation Act (Cap. 163, 1996 Rev. Ed.), s 3. Limitation periods may be extended under some of these other written laws.
540. *See* e.g. Limitation Act (Cap. 163, 1996 Rev. Ed.), s 22. Section 22 relates to trust property, which may be divided into constructive trustees who hold property and fraudulent acquirers of property; it is only the former which is protected by the provision: *Yong Kheng Leng v. Panweld Trading Pte Ltd*, [2013] 1 SLR 173, [36]–[69]. *See also Mahidon Nichiar bte Mohd Ali v. Dawood Sultan Kamaldin*, [2015] 5 SLR 62.
541. (Cap. 308, 1998 Rev. Ed.), s 5(3).
542. *See also Chip Hup Kee Construction Pte Ltd v. Yeow Chern Lean*, [2010] 3 SLR 213, [22]–[25] on the broadness of the phrase 'contract or on tort'.

Limitation Act) is when the appropriate originating process has been commenced.[543] It should further be noted that in computing limitation periods under the Limitation Act, the date the cause of action accrued should be excluded.[544] Finally, it should also be noted that section 6 of the Limitation Act will also apply to a common law action on a foreign judgment.[545]

199. Section 6 of the Limitation Act, which includes causes of action founded on tort, appears to overlap with section 24A of the Limitation Act that applies to 'to any action for damages for negligence, nuisance or breach of duty (whether the duty exists by virtue of a contract or of a provision made by or under any written law or independently of any contract or any such provision)'. Despite the apparent overlaps, it is settled law that section 24A of the Limitation Act carves out exceptions to section 6 of the Limitation Act and the two provisions do not apply concurrently.[546] It should be noted that a purposive interpretation of section 24A(1) of the Limitation Act entailed reading the phrase 'breach of duty' as encompassing all torts.[547] This is especially so in cases of latent damage because as a matter of policy there is no reason 'why a different limitation period should apply based on whether or not the damage was caused by an intentional or unintentional tort, or … a breach of contract'.[548]

200. A longer limitation period – twelve years, specifically – is afforded to certain situations such as executions of judgments and actions to recover land,[549] and extensions (or suspensions) may also be possible in certain circumstances.[550] For certain causes of action, however, short limitation periods may apply, such as in cases of personal injury (three years)[551] or when contribution is claimed (two years).[552] For causes of actions founded on latent damage, the limitation period is '6 years from the date on which the cause of action accrued'[553] or '3 years from the earliest date on which the plaintiff or any person in whom the cause of action was vested before him first had both the knowledge required for bringing an action for

---

543. *Lim Check Meng v. Orchard Credit Pte Ltd*, [1997] 2 SLR(R) 709, [18]; *MCST Plan No 3322 v. Mer Vue Developments Pte Ltd*, [2016] SGHC 28, [28]. *See also* Supreme Court of Judicature Act (Cap. 322, R. 5, 2014 Rev. Ed.) Rules of Court, O 20 r 5(2).
544. *Suresh s/o Suppiah v. Jiang Guoliang*, [2016] SGHC 133, [4]. The court in this case, however, noted that depending on which interpretive basis was used, different outcomes might be reached.
545. *Poh Soon Kiat v. Desert Palace Inc (trading as Caesars Palace)*, [2010] 1 SLR 1129, [49]–[53].
546. *Lian Kok Hong v. Ow Wah Foong*, [2008] 4 SLR(R) 165, [14], cited in *Management Corporation Strata Title Plan No 282 v. GBI Realty Pte Ltd*, [2014] 3 SLR 229, [22]. *See also*, Limitation Act (Cap. 163, 1996 Rev. Ed.), s 24A(3)(a).
547. *Yan Jun v. Attorney-General*, [2015] 1 SLR 752, [61]. The English Court of Appeal decision of *Letang v. Cooper*, [1965] 1 QB 232 formed part of the backdrop for the 1966 and 1992 amendments.
548. *Yan Jun v. Attorney-General*, [2015] 1 SLR 752, [60].
549. Limitation Act (Cap. 163, 1996 Rev. Ed.), ss 6 and 9.
550. *See* e.g. Limitation Act (Cap. 163, 1996 Rev. Ed.), ss 24 and 25.
551. Limitation Act (Cap. 163, 1996 Rev. Ed.), s 24A(2). However, it should be noted that the period will be '3 years from the earliest date on which the plaintiff has the knowledge required for bringing an action for damages in respect of the relevant injury, if that period expires later'.
552. Limitation Act (Cap. 163, 1996 Rev. Ed.), s 6A.
553. Limitation Act (Cap. 163, 1996 Rev. Ed.), s 24A(3)(a).

damages in respect of the relevant damage and a right to bring such an action, if that period expires later than [6 years from the date on which the cause of action accrued]'.[554]

201. As regards the former, the plaintiff's cause of action accrues when the damage occurs, even if the defect may be undiscovered and undiscoverable.[555] As regards the latter, the key determinant is the 'knowledge required for bringing an action for damages in respect of the relevant damage', and section 24A(4) of the Limitation Act specifies that the requirement of knowledge means knowledge:

(a) that the injury or damage was attributable in whole or in part to the act or omission which is alleged to constitute negligence, nuisance or breach of duty;
(b) of the identity of the defendant;
(c) if it is alleged that the act or omission was that of a person other than the defendant, of the identity of that person and the additional facts supporting the bringing of an action against the defendant; and
(d) of material facts about the injury or damage which would lead a reasonable person who had suffered such injury or damage to consider it sufficiently serious to justify his instituting proceedings for damages against a defendant who did not dispute liability and was able to satisfy a judgment.[556]

202. The Court of Appeal in *Lian Kok Hong v. Ow Wah Foong* has elaborated on the threshold level of knowledge:

> the claimant need not know the details of what went wrong, and it is wholly irrelevant whether he appreciated that what went wrong amounted in law to negligence, as long he knew or might reasonably have known the factual essence of his complaint.[557]

203. Additionally, the plaintiff bears the burden to prove it acquired the relevant knowledge; the plaintiff is not expected to prove a negative.[558] Therefore, if the plaintiff's argument is that the latent damage was due to a systematic problem, reliance on a single isolated incident is insufficient to establish knowledge of the systematic problem when it started.[559] A situation may arise where a suit has multiple causes of action, and some causes of action have a shorter limitation period. For example, a plaintiff may claim damages personal injuries (which has a shorter limitation period of three years) in relation to some of his pleaded causes of action. In such a situation, the court may grant leave to the plaintiff to amend his statement of

554. Limitation Act (Cap. 163, 1996 Rev. Ed.), s 24A(3)(b).
555. *Lian Kok Hong v. Ow Wah Foong*, [2008] 4 SLR(R) 165, [24], cited in *Management Corporation Strata Title Plan No 282 v. GBI Realty Pte Ltd*, [2014] 3 SLR 229, [25]–[26].
556. Section 24A(4) of the Limitation Act also applies to the knowledge requirement in s 24A(2) of the Limitation Act.
557. *Lian Kok Hong v. Ow Wah Foong*, [2008] 4 SLR(R) 165, [36], cited in *Management Corporation Strata Title Plan No 282 v. GBI Realty Pte Ltd*, [2014] 3 SLR 229, [33].
558. *Chia Kok Leong v. Prosperland*, [2005] 2 SLR 484, [67].
559. *Chia Kok Leong v. Prosperland*, [2005] 2 SLR 484, [68].

claim to severe the claims with a shorter limitation period.[560] In so doing, the plaintiff's entire suit would not be struck out just because the shorter limitation period has expired. Therefore, in this example, the limitation period of three years will not apply to the plaintiff's entire suit. Instead, the three-year limitation period will only apply to specific cause of action that the plaintiff is relying on to claim damages for personal injuries.[561] This is despite the fact that the plain wording of section 24A(2) of the Limitation Act states 'where the where the damages claimed consist of or include damages in respect of personal injuries to the plaintiff or any other person'.[562]

204. In determining if amendment to the statement of claim should be granted, the court would also consider if there is any prejudice to the defendant who could possibly be deprived of a technical limitation defence were a fresh writ to be filed but which would not have been available at the time the original writ was filed.[563] Ultimately, this is an issue that depends 'in the final analysis, on the facts and circumstances of each case, and, in particular, whether under the original pleading, the defendant was given fair notice of the claim being brought against him'.[564]

205. There will effectively be a postponement of the limitation period in cases of fraud or mistake, in that 'the period of limitation shall not begin to run until the plaintiff has discovered the fraud or the mistake, as the case may be, or could with reasonable diligence have discovered it'.[565] For fraud, the threshold requirement is concealment by the defendant.[566] This is wider than fraud or deceit at common law[567] as case authority has interpreted the fraudulent concealment requirement to include 'unconscionability in the form of a deliberate act of concealment of a right of action by the wrongdoer'.[568] Whether the limitation period was postponed because of fraud or concealment, pursuant to section 29 of the Limitation Act, was unsuitable for determination as a preliminary threshold question in cases where the question of fraud or concealment turned on the proving of a myriad of facts which were hotly contested.[569] For such cases, it should be borne in mind that even if the court found that the action was time-barred because the limitation period was not postponed, the merits of the main cause of action and the limitation period issues

560. *Yan Jun v. Attorney-General*, [2015] 1 SLR 752, [82].
561. *Yan Jun v. Attorney-General*, [2015] 1 SLR 752, [83].
562. *Yan Jun v. Attorney-General*, [2015] 1 SLR 752, [83]. *See also Shade v. The Compton Partnership*, [2000] PNLR 218.
563. *Yan Jun v. Attorney-General*, [2015] 1 SLR 752, [85].
564. *Yan Jun v. Attorney-General*, [2015] 1 SLR 752, [85].
565. Limitation Act (Cap. 163, 1996 Rev. Ed.), s 29(1). *See also Ching Mun Fong (executrix of the estate of Tan Geok Tee, deceased) v. Liu Cho Chit*, [2001] 1 SLR(R) 856, [32].
566. Limitation Act (Cap. 163, 1996 Rev. Ed.), s 29(1)(b).
567. *Management Corporation Strata Title Plan No 282 v. GBI Realty Pte Ltd*, [2014] 3 SLR 229, [45].
568. *Chua Teck Chew Robert v. Goh Eng Wah*, [2009] 4 SLR(R) 716, [27], citing *Bank of America National Trust and Savings Association v. Herman Iskandar*, [1998] 1 SLR(R) 848, [73]–[75]. *See also Mahidon Nichiar bte Mohd Ali v. Dawood Sultan Kamaldin*, [2014] 4 SLR 1309, [61]; *Management Corporation Strata Title Plan No 282 v. GBI Realty Pte Ltd*, [2014] 3 SLR 229, [45].
569. *Mahidon Nichiar bte Mohd Ali v. Dawood Sultan Kamaldin*, [2014] 4 SLR 1309, [62], citing *Bank of America National Trust and Savings Association v. Herman Iskandar*, [1998] 1 SLR(R) 848.

would have been determined and the main cause of action would be subject to the usual res judicata principles.[570] In addition, if a person who is liable on a claim or debt acknowledges or makes part payment of such claim or debt, then the right to take action on such claim shall be deemed to have accrued on and not before the date of such acknowledgement or part payment.[571]

570. *Mahidon Nichiar bte Mohd Ali v. Dawood Sultan Kamaldin*, [2014] 4 SLR 1309, [63]–[64].
571. Limitation Act (Cap. 163, 1996 Rev. Ed.), s 26. *See also id.*, s 27.

Chapter 2. Actions

§1. Introduction

206. Apart from considering whether an action is time-barred and the appropriate court in which to bring an action, a person seeking to commence civil proceedings ought also to ensure that he possesses the requisite capacity to sue as well as the standing to bring a particular claim. He should further consider whether to act in person. Finally, he should consider the appropriate claims and parties to include in the action. Special rules apply when multiple persons have the same interest in certain proceedings and where a party is the government and these will be canvassed summarily. Separately, another matter for consideration ought to be whether litigation is appropriate or whether some other form of alternative dispute resolution ought to be explored.

§2. Capacity to Sue or Be Sued

207. Sometimes person may not have the legal capacity to sue or be sued. A person cannot be a party to proceedings without such capacity. Under the Rules of Court,[572] 'persons under a disability' are defined to include minors (a person below 18 years).[573] and persons lacking capacity within the meaning of the Mental Capacity Act[574] in relation to matters concerning their property and affairs.[575] A person under a disability 'may not bring, make a claim in, defend, make a counterclaim in, or intervene in any proceedings, or appear in any proceedings … except by his litigation representative'.[576] Accordingly, the litigation representative may do anything that is required or authorized by the Rules of Court to be done by a party to the proceedings.[577]

208. The Rules of Court require that a litigation representative of a person under disability act by a solicitor.[578] An order of court appointing a person litigation representative is only necessary when: the litigation representative is being substituted for an existing litigation representation; a party to the proceedings becomes a person lacking capacity after proceedings have been begun; and where a person under

572. Supreme Court of Judicature Act (Cap. 322, R. 5, 2014 Rev. Ed.) Rules of Court.
573. *See* Supreme Court of Judicature Act (Cap. 322, R. 5, 2014 Rev. Ed.) Rules of Court, O 1 r 4(3). *See also* Civil Law Act (Cap. 43, 1999 Rev. Ed.), s 36(1).
574. *See* Mental Capacity Act (Cap. 177A, 2010 Rev. Ed.), s 4(1): 'a person lacks capacity in relation to a matter if at the material time he is unable to make a decision for himself in relation to the matter because of an impairment of, or a disturbance in the functioning of, the mind or brain'.
575. Supreme Court of Judicature Act (Cap. 322, R. 5, 2014 Rev. Ed.) Rules of Court, O 76 r 1.
576. Supreme Court of Judicature Act (Cap. 322, R. 5, 2014 Rev. Ed.) Rules of Court, O 76 r 2(1).
577. Supreme Court of Judicature Act (Cap. 322, R. 5, 2014 Rev. Ed.) Rules of Court, O 76 r 2(2).
578. Supreme Court of Judicature Act (Cap. 322, R. 5, 2014 Rev. Ed.) Rules of Court, O 76 r 2(3).

disability does not enter an appearance.[579] Otherwise, all the litigation representative has to do is file certain required documents in the Registry[580] before becoming entitled to using his name as litigation representative, entering an appearance for the person under disability, and appearing as litigation representative on the hearing of applications served on the person under disability.[581] Because of the vulnerability and dependence of a person under disability, certain rules of procedure are qualified.[582] For example, an admission may not be implied from the pleading of a person under a disability,[583] where money is claimed by or on behalf of a person under disability, any settlement, compromise or payment and acceptance of money paid into court will only be valid with the approval of the court.[584]

209. Events such as death, bankruptcy and the assignment, transmission, or devolvement of interest may also affect a person's capacity to sue and be sued.[585] When a person who may be sued dies and the cause of action against the deceased survives, proceedings may be brought against the estate of the deceased if no grant of probate or administration has been made.[586] An action brought against 'the personal representatives of a deceased' or against a person who was dead at the action's commencement will be treated as having been brought against that person's estate.[587] In actions against a deceased person's estate, the plaintiff must, during the period of validity for service of the writ or originating process, apply for an order appointing a person to represent the deceased person's estate, or if a grant of probate or administration has been made, an order that the personal representative of the deceased be made a party to the proceedings.[588] In addition, the plaintiff must also apply for an order 'that the proceedings be carried on against the person appointed or, as the case may be, against the personal representative, as if he had been substituted for the estate'.[589] The court may also make any of the above orders on its own motion at any stage of the proceedings and allow amendments to be made as it 'thinks necessary in order to ensure that all matters in dispute in the proceedings may be effectually and completely determined and adjudicated upon'.[590]

210. After proceedings have commenced, a party's death, bankruptcy, or assignment, transmission or devolution of interest or liability to another person will not

579. Supreme Court of Judicature Act (Cap. 322, R. 5, 2014 Rev. Ed.) Rules of Court, O 76 r 3(2), (4), (5); O 76 r 6.
580. These documents are specified in Supreme Court of Judicature Act (Cap. 322, R. 5, 2014 Rev. Ed.) Rules of Court, O 76 r 3(7).
581. Supreme Court of Judicature Act (Cap. 322, R. 5, 2014 Rev. Ed.) Rules of Court, O 76 r 3(6).
582. J. Pinsler, *Principles of Civil Procedure* 239 (Acad. Publg. 2013).
583. Supreme Court of Judicature Act (Cap. 322, R. 5, 2014 Rev. Ed.) Rules of Court, O 76 r 8.
584. Supreme Court of Judicature Act (Cap. 322, R. 5, 2014 Rev. Ed.) Rules of Court, O 76 r 10.
585. *See* generally J. Pinsler, *Principles of Civil Procedure* 241–242 (Acad. Publg. 2013); *Singapore Civil Procedure 2015 Volume 1*, at 227–237 (G.P. Selvam ed., Sweet & Maxwell Asia 2014).
586. Supreme Court of Judicature Act (Cap. 322, R. 5, 2014 Rev. Ed.) Rules of Court, O 15 r 6A(1).
587. Supreme Court of Judicature Act (Cap. 322, R. 5, 2014 Rev. Ed.) Rules of Court, O 15 r 6A(2)–(3).
588. Supreme Court of Judicature Act (Cap. 322, R. 5, 2014 Rev. Ed.) Rules of Court, O 15 r 6A(4).
589. Supreme Court of Judicature Act (Cap. 322, R. 5, 2014 Rev. Ed.) Rules of Court, O 15 r 6A(4).
590. Supreme Court of Judicature Act (Cap. 322, R. 5, 2014 Rev. Ed.) Rules of Court, O 15 r 6A(4).

cause the action to abate where the cause of action survives.[591] However, an ex parte application should be made for an order of court to substitute another person for the original party.[592] The applicant must, unless the court otherwise directs, 'serve the order on every other person who is a party to the cause or matter or who becomes or ceases to be a party by virtue of the order and serve with the order on any person who becomes a defendant a copy of the writ or originating summons by which the cause or matter was begun'.[593] The persons served may then within fourteen days of the service of the order, apply to discharge or vary the order made.[594]

§3. STANDING

211. Standing, or locus standi, refers to '[a] party's right to make a legal claim or seek judicial enforcement of a duty or right'.[595] It is different from the capacity to sue or be sued.[596] A person may have the capacity to sue or be sued, but that person may not have the requisite standing to bring a certain type of claim or to enforce a certain type of right in court. The issue of standing arises most prominently in the context of a claim for prerogative orders, such as prohibiting orders, quashing orders, and mandatory orders. Prior to the Rules of Court (Amendment No 2) Rules 2011[597] coming into operation in 2011, two separate originating processes were prescribed for an application for prerogative orders and an application for a declaration and/or other ordinary private law remedies. The former required an application under O 53 which would require the leave of court, and the latter could be sought by a writ or originating summons which did not require leave.[598] Under those circumstances, the requirements for standing differed according to the remedy sought and have been summarized as follows:

> The threshold was low for a prohibiting order: an applicant had to show only that he was 'adversely affected'. The threshold was also low for a quashing order: … 'It was sufficient that there had been an abuse of power which inconvenienced someone'. It was harder to show standing for a mandatory order. The applicant had to have a 'specific legal right', have a 'direct and substantial interest at stake', or at the very least be 'adversely affected' … The standing

591. Supreme Court of Judicature Act (Cap. 322, R. 5, 2014 Rev. Ed.) Rules of Court, O 15 r 7(1)–(2).
592. Supreme Court of Judicature Act (Cap. 322, R. 5, 2014 Rev. Ed.) Rules of Court, O 15 r 7 (2).
593. Supreme Court of Judicature Act (Cap. 322, R. 5, 2014 Rev. Ed.) Rules of Court, O 15 r 7 (4).
594. Supreme Court of Judicature Act (Cap. 322, R. 5, 2014 Rev. Ed.) Rules of Court, O 15 r 7 (5).
595. *Black's Law Dictionary* (B.A. Garner ed., Thomson Reuters 2009), 'standing'.
596. *Black's Law Dictionary* (B.A. Garner ed., Thomson Reuters 2009), 'capacity'.
597. Supreme Court of Judicature Act (Cap. 322) Rules of Court (Amendment No. 2) Rules 2011 (S 218/2011).
598. Chung Y.J., D. Wong & Peh A.H., *Recent Amendments to Order 53 of the Rules of Court*, Sing. L. Gaz. (November 2011).

requirements for a declaration were stricter than those for the prerogative remedies. The applicant had to show that the declaration he sought related to a right that was personally vested in him and that he had a 'real interest' at stake.[599]

212. However, after the same procedure was prescribed for obtaining the prerogative remedies together with declaratory and other private relief, the Court of Appeal has established a unified test for standing.[600] Although the issue of standing is determined as a preliminary issue, it remains subject to review until the courts arrive at a final determination.[601] For an applicant to have the requisite standing to bring an action or claim, the following three elements must be satisfied: a real interest in bringing the action; a real controversy between the parties concerned; and a violation of a personal right.[602] The element of a real controversy 'goes to the court's discretion and not jurisdiction'.[603] In respect of the 'real interest' requirement, sufficiency of interest is prima facie made out once there is a violation of constitutional rights.[604] In respect of the requirement for a violation of a personal right, 'as every constitutional right is a personal right, demonstrating that a constitutional right has been violated will suffice'.[605] A violation of constitutional rights 'may be brought about by the very existence of an allegedly unconstitutional law in the statute books … and/or by a real and credible threat of prosecution under an allegedly unconstitutional law'.[606] Having said the above, as the focal point of this monograph is general commercial litigation, it will not be necessary further expound on the concept of standing.

§4. Interpleader Relief

213. An interpleader action is appropriate when a party owns property on behalf of another, but does not know to whom the property should be transferred; as a result, such a party initiates an action to compel other parties to litigate a dispute. The objective of interpleader relief is to assist parties who wish to discharge their

599. Tham L.J., *Locus Standi*, in *Judicial Review: Two Roads Diverge in a Singapore Wood*, Sing. L. Gaz. (February 2013), citing S.M. Thio, *Locus Standi and Judicial Review* 84–86, 103, 129–130 (Sing. U. Press 1971); *Chan Hiang Leng Colin v. Minister for Information and the Arts*, [1995] 2 SLR(R) 627, [12]; *Karaha Bodas Co LLC v. Pertamina Energy Trading Ltd*, [2006] 1 SLR(R) 112, [15] and [19].

600. *See Tan Eng Hong v. Attorney-General*, [2012] 4 SLR 476; Tham L.J., *Locus Standi*, in *Judicial Review: Two Roads Diverge in a Singapore Wood*, Sing. L. Gaz. (February 2013). *See also Vellama d/o Marie Muthu v. Attorney-General*, [2013] 4 SLR 1, [53].

601. *Vellama d/o Marie Muthu v. Attorney-General*, [2013] 4 SLR 1, [14].

602. *Tan Eng Hong v. Attorney-General*, [2012] 4 SLR 476, [115], citing *Karaha Bodas Co LLC v. Pertamina Energy Trading Ltd*, [2006] 1 SLR(R) 112, [15]–[16], [19], [25]. *See also Vellama d/o Marie Muthu v. Attorney-General*, [2013] 4 SLR 1, [16].

603. *Tan Eng Hong v. Attorney-General*, [2012] 4 SLR 476, [135].

604. *Tan Eng Hong v. Attorney-General*, [2012] 4 SLR 476, [83].

605. *Tan Eng Hong v. Attorney-General*, [2012] 4 SLR 476, [80].

606. *Tan Eng Hong v. Attorney-General*, [2012] 4 SLR 476, [110] and [114].

legal obligations but do not know to whom to discharge them as well as to prevent a situation where a party discharges his obligation to one claimant only to be faced with a suit from another claimant.[607]

214. O 17 r 1 of the Rules of Court sets out at least three conditions for interpleader relief: first, the applicant has to be under a liability for a debt, money, goods, or chattels; second, the applicant must expect that he would be sued by at least two persons; and third, there has to be adverse claims for the debt, money, goods, or chattels from the persons whom the applicant would sue.[608] For a claim to be 'adverse', it has to be symmetrical in that the competing claims must relate to the same subject matter, mutually exclusive, and there must be actual disagreement in that the applicant must face an actual dilemma as to how to proceed.[609]

§5. Legal Representation

215. Generally, any person (whether or not he sues as a trustee or personal representative or in any other representative capacity) may begin and carry on proceedings in court in person, without being legally represented if that person so desires.[610] However, legal representation is required in certain circumstances, such as where a litigation representative acts on behalf of a person under disability. Other circumstances where legal representation is required are where the party is a body corporate or an unincorporated association (other than a partnership).[611] It is nevertheless possible for the court to, upon application, give leave to an officer of a company, limited liability partnership or unincorporated association to act on behalf of the company, limited liability partnership or unincorporated association if the court is satisfied that the officer has been duly authorized to act and that it is appropriate to give such leave in the circumstances of the case.[612] Procedurally, the steps set out in the relevant rules must be strictly complied with before any application is considered.[613]

216. Substantively, the High Court has clarified that it is not necessary for the company to establish that there are exceptional circumstances justifying the grant

---

607. *Precious Shipping Public Co Ltd v. OW Bunker Far East (Singapore) Pte Ltd*, [2015] 4 SLR 1229, [58]–[60].
608. The High Court is given the power to grant interpleader relief: Supreme Court of Judicature Act (Cap. 322, 2007 Rev. Ed.), s 18(2).
609. *Precious Shipping Public Co Ltd v. OW Bunker Far East (Singapore) Pte Ltd*, [2015] 4 SLR 1229, [60]–[80].
610. Supreme Court of Judicature Act (Cap. 322, R. 5, 2014 Rev. Ed.) Rules of Court, O 5 r 6(1).
611. Supreme Court of Judicature Act (Cap. 322, R. 5, 2014 Rev. Ed.) Rules of Court, O 5 rr 6(2) and (3).
612. Supreme Court of Judicature Act (Cap. 322, R. 5, 2014 Rev. Ed.) Rules of Court, O 1 rr 9(2) and (3); Legal Profession Act (Cap. 161, 2009 Rev. Ed.), ss 34(1) and 34(3). *See also Bulk Trading SA v. Pevensey Pte Ltd*, [2015] 1 SLR 538, [48]; *Allergan, Inc v. Ferlandz Nutra Pte Ltd*, [2015] 2 SLR 94, [22]; *Elbow Holdings Pte Ltd v. Marina Bay Sands Pte Ltd*, [2015] 5 SLR 289, [13].
613. *HG Metal Manufacturing Ltd v. Gayathri Steels Pte Ltd*, [2016] SGHC 176, [6].

of leave.[614] Instead, the test is whether the court is satisfied that it is appropriate to grant leave in the circumstances of the case.[615] In exercising its discretion, the court must look at all circumstances of the case (such as the financial position of the relevant parties, good faith, and the complexity of the issues), not just the reason relied on by the applicant company since it has to consider the perspective of all parties and the public interest in a fair, efficient, and timely administration of justice.[616] The application for leave must be supported by an affidavit fulfilling the requirements of O 1 r 9(4) of the Rules of Court. As part of the requirements under O 1 r 9(4), the affidavit is to be made by 'any other officer of the company'. The reason for this is to serve as a procedural safeguard to ensure that the company has indeed given its authorization to that officer for whom leave is sought to represent it in the proceedings.[617] This exception to the rule requiring legal representation for bodies corporate and unincorporated associations only applies to any matter or proceeding in a District Court or a Magistrate's Court and not to proceedings in the High Court or Court of Appeal.[618]

217. Separately, every solicitor representing any party in any cause or matter has to obtain from that party or his duly authorized agent a warrant to act for that party, either generally or in the particular cause or matter.[619] If a solicitor's authority to act is disputed, the absence of a warrant to act constitutes prima facie evidence that the solicitor has not been authorized to represent the party.[620] A solicitor must be prepared to disclose his warrant to act or any other document establishing his authority if that authority was challenged.[621] A party to a cause or matter may change his solicitor without an order of court, however, until a notice of the change is filed and served in accordance with the Rules of Court, the former solicitor shall, unless another party or the solicitor himself takes step to remove the solicitor from the record,[622] be considered the solicitor of the party until the final conclusion of the cause or matter.[623] Similarly, a party who had initially acted in person may also appoint a solicitor without an order of court as long as he files and serves a notice of appointment of the solicitor,[624] and a party who had initially received legal representation is entitled to act in person without an order of court as long as he files

614. *Allergan, Inc v. Ferlandz Nutra Pte Ltd*, [2015] 2 SLR 94, [34] citing *Bulk Trading SA v. Pevensey Pte Ltd*, [2015] 1 SLR 538, [78]. *See also* C. Bull & C. Voon Jiet, *Civil Procedure: Annual Review of Singapore Cases* [8.2]–[8.5] (Sing. Acad. L. 2015).
615. *Allergan, Inc v. Ferlandz Nutra Pte Ltd*, [2015] 2 SLR 94, [35].
616. *Allergan, Inc v. Ferlandz Nutra Pte Ltd*, [2015] 2 SLR 94, [46]. *See also Allergan, Inc v. Ferlandz Nutra Pte Ltd*, [2015] 2 SLR 94, [52]–[53]; *Elbow Holdings Pte Ltd v. Marina Bay Sands Pte Ltd*, [2015] 5 SLR 289, [7].
617. *Allergan, Inc v. Ferlandz Nutra Pte Ltd*, [2015] 2 SLR 94, [25]. *See also Bulk Trading SA v. Pevensey Pte Ltd*, [2015] 1 SLR 538, [91].
618. Supreme Court of Judicature Act (Cap. 322, R. 5, 2014 Rev. Ed.) Rules of Court, O 1 r 9(5).
619. Supreme Court of Judicature Act (Cap. 322, R. 5, 2014 Rev. Ed.) Rules of Court, O 64 r 7(1). *See also The Agency for Policy Coordination on State Property of Mongolia v. Batbold Sukhbaatar*, [2021] SGHC 50.
620. Supreme Court of Judicature Act (Cap. 322, R. 5, 2014 Rev. Ed.) Rules of Court, O 64 r 7(2).
621. *Tung Hui Mannequin Industries v. Tenet Insurance Co Ltd*, [2005] 3 SLR(R) 18, [43].
622. Supreme Court of Judicature Act (Cap. 322, R. 5, 2014 Rev. Ed.) Rules of Court, O 64 rr 4–5.
623. Supreme Court of Judicature Act (Cap. 322, R. 5, 2014 Rev. Ed.) Rules of Court, O 64 r 1.
624. Supreme Court of Judicature Act (Cap. 322, R. 5, 2014 Rev. Ed.) Rules of Court, O 64 r 2.

and serves a notice of intention to act in person.[625] The same consequence as with the failure to file and serve a notice of change of solicitors will follow if the notice of appointment or notice of intention to act in person is not filed and served in accordance with the Rules of Court.[626]

§6. REPRESENTATIVE ACTION

218. Where 'numerous persons have the same interest in any proceedings … the proceedings may be begun, and, unless the Court otherwise orders, continued, by or against any one or more of them as representing all or as representing all except one or more of them'.[627] The main purpose of such a procedure is to 'facilitate access to and the efficacious administration of justice' and the courts have the discretion to discontinue such a procedure if it 'will not provide an efficient or effective means of dealing with the claims in question, or where it is otherwise inappropriate in the circumstances'.[628] Similarly, the court may also appoint 'any one or more of the defendants or other persons as representing whom the defendants are sued to represent all, or all except one or more, of those persons in the proceedings'.[629]

219. To illustrate, a 'same interest' between plaintiff country club members was found where they received the exact same representation from the defendant country club and raised the same complaints against the country club.[630] It was also found by the Court of Appeal in a situation where although various plaintiffs became members of a club at different times and under different arrangements, the plaintiffs had to rely on the same transfer agreement to found their claims in relation to proving the terms of the transfer agreement, repudiation of the plaintiffs' respective member agreements and misrepresentation.[631] However, the plaintiffs were not found to have the 'same interest' in relation to their claims for breach of contract due to the differing circumstances surrounding the alleged breaches of contract as between the various plaintiffs.[632]

220. The following principles may be discerned from common law jurisprudence on the 'same interest' requirement.[633] First, the class of represented persons must be capable of clear definition; members of the class of represented persons must be identified by an objective criterion which bears a rational relationship to the common issues being asserted. Second, the representative plaintiffs must

---

625. Supreme Court of Judicature Act (Cap. 322, R. 5, 2014 Rev. Ed.) Rules of Court, O 64 r 3.
626. Supreme Court of Judicature Act (Cap. 322, R. 5, 2014 Rev. Ed.) Rules of Court, O 64 rr 2–3.
627. Supreme Court of Judicature Act (Cap. 322, R. 5, 2014 Rev. Ed.) Rules of Court, O 15 r 12(1).
628. *Koh Chong Chiah v. Treasure Resort Pte Ltd*, [2013] 4 SLR 1204[2013] 4 SLR 1204, [36] and [86]. *See also Syed Nomani v. Chong Yeow Peh*, [2017] SGHC 117, [7]–[12].
629. Supreme Court of Judicature Act (Cap. 322, R. 5, 2014 Rev. Ed.) Rules of Court, O 15 r 12(2).
630. *Tan Chin Seng v. Raffles Town Club Pte Ltd*, [2002] SGHC 278.
631. *Koh Chong Chiah v. Treasure Resort Pte Ltd*, [2013] 4 SLR 1204.
632. *Koh Chong Chiah v. Treasure Resort Pte Ltd*, [2013] 4 SLR 1204, [112].
633. *Koh Chong Chiah v. Treasure Resort Pte Ltd*, [2013] 4 SLR 1204, [78].

adequately represent the interests of the class of represented persons, and must vigorously and capably prosecute the interests of the entire class. Third, there must be significant issues of fact or law common to all the claimants, and the courts must compare the significance of the common issues between the claimants with the significance of the issues which differ between them. Fourth, all the claimants must benefit from the relief granted by the court and must have the same interest in the relief granted by the court.

221. A judgment or order given in representative actions binds 'all the persons as representing whom the plaintiffs sue or, as the case may be, the defendants are sued' and may also be enforced against any other person not a party to the proceedings with leave of court.[634] The representative action is the only general process in Singapore which enables a large number of persons to be directly involved in the litigation; this is unlike other jurisdictions which recognize class actions or other forms of case-managed group litigation.[635]

§7. Action Against the Government

222. The Government Proceedings Act[636] stipulates the circumstances in which the government may sue and be sued as well as the various rules relating to procedure. The Government Proceedings Act also permits legal officers to appear as advocate(s) on behalf of the government or a public officer.[637] The statute should be read together with O 73 of the Rules of Court.[638] Where an originating process is to be served on the government, and the proceedings are by or against an authorized government department, the originating process is to be served on the solicitor authorized by the government department, or the person acting as solicitor for that department.[639] If there is no such solicitor or person acting as solicitor, or if the proceedings are brought by or against the Attorney-General, the originating process should be served on the Attorney-General.[640] The manner of service may be by way of leaving the document at the office of the person to be served or of an agent nominated by the person to be served, or by posting it to such persons.[641] Personal service is not required.

223. Discovery and interrogatories are available against the government, but that this is without prejudice to any other written law or rule of law 'which authorises or requires the withholding of any document or the refusal to answer any question on

634. Supreme Court of Judicature Act (Cap. 322, R. 5, 2014 Rev. Ed.) Rules of Court, O 15 r 12(3).
635. J. Pinsler, *Principles of Civil Procedure* 248 (Acad. Publg. 2013). *See also Koh Chong Chiah v. Treasure Resort Pte Ltd*, [2013] 4 SLR 1204, [36].
636. Government Proceedings Act (Cap. 121, 1985 Rev. Ed.).
637. Government Proceedings Act (Cap. 121, 1985 Rev. Ed.), s 24.
638. Supreme Court of Judicature Act (Cap. 322, R. 5, 2014 Rev. Ed.) Rules of Court, O 73.
639. Government Proceedings Act (Cap. 121, 1985 Rev. Ed.), s 20.
640. Government Proceedings Act (Cap. 121, 1985 Rev. Ed.), s 20.
641. Supreme Court of Judicature Act (Cap. 322, R. 5, 2014 Rev. Ed.) Rules of Court, O 73 r 3.

the ground that the disclosure of the document or the answering of the question would be injurious to the public interest'.[642]

224. The methods of enforcement provided by O 45 to O 52 of the Rules of Court do not apply against the government.[643] Instead, an application may be made for the purpose of restraining any person from receiving money payable to him by the government and directing that the money be paid to the applicant or any other person.[644] Such an application must be made by way of summons supported by affidavit setting out the facts giving rise to the application and identifying the particular debt from the government in respect of which the application is made; the application must be served at least four days before the return day on the government and, unless the court otherwise orders, on the person to be restrained or his solicitor.[645]

225. Costs may be awarded against the government or a public officer in civil proceedings, including judicial review proceedings, in the same manner and upon the same principles as in proceedings between private persons.[646] However, in exercising its discretion as to costs in such situations, the court will take into account the public interest, for example, where the court proceedings raised public law issues of general importance, and where the applicant in the proceedings was not seeking to protect some private interest.[647]

§8. CONSOLIDATION AND JOINDER

226. The provision in the Rules of Court dealing with consolidation is O 4 r 1. An order of consolidation essentially involves two or more pending causes or matters being combined into one set of proceedings. Upon an order of consolidation being made, 'the file of the cause or matter in which the application is made shall be transferred to and added to the file of such other cause or matter, and the copy of the order shall be left in place of the file so transferred'.[648] It should be noted, however, that O 4 r 1 does not apply to appeals but to causes or matters that have yet to be tried.[649] For two or more pending causes or matters to be consolidated, the court must be satisfied of one of the three things. First, that 'some common question of law or fact arises in both or all of them'; second, that 'the rights to relief claimed therein are in respect of or arise out of the same transaction or series of transactions'; or third, that 'for some other reason it is desirable to make an order

642. Government Proceedings Act (Cap. 121, 1985 Rev. Ed.), s 34; Supreme Court of Judicature Act (Cap. 322, R. 5, 2014 Rev. Ed.) Rules of Court, O 73 r 10.
643. Government Proceedings Act (Cap. 121, 1985 Rev. Ed.), s 31; Supreme Court of Judicature Act (Cap. 322, R. 5, 2014 Rev. Ed.) Rules of Court, O 73 r 12.
644. Government Proceedings Act (Cap. 121, 1985 Rev. Ed.), s 33(1).
645. Supreme Court of Judicature Act (Cap. 322, R. 5, 2014 Rev. Ed.) Rules of Court, O 73 r 13.
646. Government Proceedings Act (Cap. 121, 1985 Rev. Ed.), ss 2(2) and 29.
647. *Vellama d/o Marie Muthu v. Attorney-General*, [2013] 1 SLR 797, [39]–[42] and [44].
648. Supreme Court of Judicature Act (Cap. 322, R. 5, 2014 Rev. Ed.) Rules of Court, O 4 r 1(3).
649. *Lai Swee Lin Linda v. Attorney-General*, [2006] 2 SLR(R) 565, [19].

[of consolidation]'.[650] If so, the court 'may order those causes or matters to be consolidated on such terms as it thinks just or may order them to be tried at the same time or one immediately after another or may order any of them to be stayed until after the determination of any other of them'.[651]

227. The main purpose of O 4 r 1 is 'to save costs, time and effort and for reasons of convenience in the handling of the hearing of several actions which are linked by one of the common threads provided in the rules'.[652] However, it is not always clear when consolidation is desirable. For instance, the court may, instead of consolidation, order that various defamation actions against the same defendant in respect of the same defamatory words be tried one after the other before the same judge because there are a large number of plaintiffs all of whom are separately represented, and there appears to be no justification to direct the plaintiffs to seek common representation by a single counsel.[653] However, in the same situation, it may also be said that consolidation may be appropriate and is likely to result in a saving of costs; accordingly, the plaintiffs will not be awarded full costs if such a sentiment prevails.[654]

228. It has also been said that two actions cannot be consolidated where 'the plaintiff in one action is the same person as the defendant in another action, unless one action can be ordered to stand as a counterclaim or third party proceedings in another action'.[655] The circumstances in which actions may be consolidated are generally similar to those in which parties may be joined in one action.[656] The requirements for joinder of parties are that two or more persons may be joined together in one action as plaintiffs or defendants with the leave of court or where: 'if separate actions were brought by or against each of them, as the case may be, some common question of law or fact would arise in all the actions'; and 'all rights to relief claimed in the action … are in respect of or arise out of the same transaction or series of transactions'.[657] The rationale for this rule is to ensure that 'as far as possible all necessary parties should be before the court that all the issues can be determined by the court'.[658]

229. Generally, where a plaintiff in any action claims relief to which any other person is entitled jointly with him, all such entitled persons must be parties to the

---

650. Supreme Court of Judicature Act (Cap. 322, R. 5, 2014 Rev. Ed.) Rules of Court, O 4 r 1(1).
651. Supreme Court of Judicature Act (Cap. 322, R. 5, 2014 Rev. Ed.) Rules of Court, O 4 r 1(1).
652. *Lee Kuan Yew v. Tang Liang Hong*, [1997] 2 SLR(R) 141, [4].
653. *Goh Chok Tong v. Jeyaretnam Joshua Benjamin*, [1997] 1 SLR(R) 606, [6]–[8].
654. *Goh Chok Tong v. Jeyaretnam Joshua Benjamin*, [1997] 3 SLR(R) 46, [211]–[212].
655. *Singapore Civil Procedure 2015 Volume 1*,at 54 (G.P. Selvam ed., Sweet & Maxwell Asia 2014).
656. *Singapore Civil Procedure 2015 Volume 1*, at 53–54 (G.P. Selvam ed., Sweet & Maxwell Asia 2014).
657. Supreme Court of Judicature Act (Cap. 322, R. 5, 2014 Rev. Ed.) Rules of Court, O 15 r 4(1). *See also Lee Bee Eng (formerly trading as AFCO East Development) v. Cheng William*, [2020] SGHC 207.
658. *Singapore Civil Procedure 2015 Volume 1*, at 204 (G.P. Selvam ed., Sweet & Maxwell Asia 2014).

action and if they do not consent to being joined as a plaintiff must be made a defendant.[659] Where persons are jointly, but not severally, liable under a contract and relief is claimed against some but not all of them, the court may, on the application of any defendant to the action, stay proceedings in the action until the other persons liable are added.[660] Joinder of causes of action is also permissible 'if the plaintiff claims, and the defendant is alleged to be liable, in the same capacity in respect of all the causes of action'; 'if the plaintiff claims or the defendant is alleged to be liable in the capacity of executor or administrator of an estate in respect of one or more of the causes of action and in his personal capacity'; or with leave of court.[661] The right to apply for joinder is still subject to the law of limitation.[662]

230. If it appears to the court that the joinder of causes of action or of parties 'may embarrass or delay the trial or is otherwise inconvenient' the court may order separate trials.[663] The non-joinder or misjoinder of parties, however, will not defeat a cause or matter, and the court may determine the issues in dispute so far as they affect the rights and interests of the persons who are parties in the cause or matter.[664] Even if a person who has an interest in the proceedings decides not to be a party, he is bound by the court's decision in those proceedings and cannot seek to reopen the case.[665]

231. It should be noted that the court has the power to order joinder (under O 15 r 6(2)) regardless of whether the relevant parties have effected joinder (under O 15 r 4); the two grounds it can do so are if it is 'necessary to ensure that all matters in the cause or matter may be effectually and completely determined and adjudicated upon' or if there may be a 'a question or issue arising out of or relating to or connected with any relief or remedy claimed in the cause or matter which in the opinion of the Court it would be just and convenient to determine as between him and that party as well as between the parties to the cause or matter'.[666] The purpose of O 15 r 6(2) is 'to bring all parties to disputes relating to one subject matter before the court at the same time so that the dispute may be determined without the delay,

659. Supreme Court of Judicature Act (Cap. 322, R. 5, 2014 Rev. Ed.) Rules of Court, O 15 r 4(2).
660. Supreme Court of Judicature Act (Cap. 322, R. 5, 2014 Rev. Ed.) Rules of Court, O 15 r 4(3).
661. Supreme Court of Judicature Act (Cap. 322, R. 5, 2014 Rev. Ed.) Rules of Court, O 15 r 1(1).
662. *Abdul Gaffer bin Fathil v. Chua Kwang Yong*, [1994] 3 SLR(R) 1056, [16]; *MCST Plan No 3322 v. Mer Vue Developments Pte Ltd*, [2016] SGHC 28, [16].
663. Supreme Court of Judicature Act (Cap. 322, R. 5, 2014 Rev. Ed.) Rules of Court, O 15 r 5(1). *See also Suresh Agarwal v. Naseer Ahmad Akhtar*, [2019] SGCA 55.
664. Supreme Court of Judicature Act (Cap. 322, R. 5, 2014 Rev. Ed.) Rules of Court, O 15 r 6(1). *See also Lee Bee Eng (formerly trading as AFCO East Development) v. Cheng William*, [2020] SGHC 207.
665. *Family Food Court (a firm) v. Seah Boon Lock (trading as Boon Lock Duck and Noodle House)*, [2008] 4 SLR(R) 272, [65], citing *Wytcherley v. Andrews*, (1871) LR 2 P & D 327, 328–329.
666. *See also Family Food Court (a firm) v. Seah Boon Lock (trading as Boon Lock Duck and Noodle House)*, [2008] 4 SLR(R) 272, [63]; *Attorney-General v. Aljunied-Hougang-Punggol East Town Council*, [2016] 1 SLR 915, [38]–[39]; *Oh Bernard v. Six Capital Investments Ltd (in liquidation)*, [2020] SGHC 42.

inconvenience and expense of separate actions and trials'.[667] It may even be possible for the court to exercise the power of joinder pursuant to its so-called inherent jurisdiction, subject to the strict criterion of need.[668] However, the leave to intervene will generally be granted only if it is filed during the pendency of the cause or matter in which intervention is sought.[669]

§9. Appropriate Dispute Resolution

232. The available alternative dispute resolution avenues in Singapore have earlier been set out and include arbitration as well as mediation.[670] The importance of evaluating one's case before commencing civil proceedings has been highlighted by the Court of Appeal, particularly in cases involving paltry monetary claims.[671] The Court of Appeal has stated that although 'an advocate and solicitor has a duty to pursue his client's interest vigorously, he should only do so with the informed consent of the client, especially when pursuing the client's interest is counterproductive'.[672] It should be noted that the Legal Profession (Professional Conduct) Rules require an advocate and solicitor to evaluate with his client in an appropriate case 'whether the consequence of a matter justifies the expense or the risk involved' in going to court.[673] There may be costs consequences for not only the party but also the solicitor if litigation is inappropriately and unreasonably pursued.

233. The Rules of Court also provide that one of the special matters the court will consider in exercising its discretion on costs is 'the parties' conduct in relation to any attempt at resolving the cause or matter by mediation or any other means of dispute resolution'.[674] Some instances of adverse costs orders that have been made include ordering that each of the parties bear their own costs in the proceedings in the Court of Appeal as well as those below due to both parties' 'questionable conduct … that has in turn stoked sterile litigation';[675] and ordering that until the conduct of a solicitor had been properly investigated by the Law Society of Singapore

---

667. *Abdul Gaffar bin Fathil v. Chua Kwang Yong* [1994] 2 SLR(R) 99, [48]; cited in *Family Food Court (a firm) v. Seah Boon Lock (trading as Boon Lock Duck and Noodle House)*, [2008] 4 SLR(R) 272, [64]. In the context of representative and derivative actions, *see Actis Excalibiur Ltd v. KS Distribution Pte Ltd*, [2016] SGHCR 11. *See also Syed Ahmad Jamal Alsagoff v. Harun bin Sayed Hussain Aljunied*, [2017] SGHC 85, [23].
668. *Family Food Court (a firm) v. Seah Boon Lock (trading as Boon Lock Duck and Noodle House)*, [2008] 4 SLR(R) 272, [63], citing *Wee Soon Kim Anthony v. Law Society of Singapore*, [2001] 2 SLR(R) 821, [27]. C.f. *Attorney-General v. Aljunied-Hougang-Punggol East Town Council*, [2016] 1 SLR 915, [39].
669. *Syed Ahmad Jamal Alsagoff v. Harun bin Sayed Hussain Aljunied*, [2017] SGHC 85, [26]–[30].
670. *See* the General Introduction.
671. *Lock Han Chng Jonathan (Jonathan Luo Hancheng) v. Goh Jessiline*, [2008] 2 SLR(R) 455.
672. *Lock Han Chng Jonathan (Jonathan Luo Hancheng) v. Goh Jessiline*, [2008] 2 SLR(R) 455, [46].
673. Legal Profession (Professional Conduct) Rules (Cap. 161, R 1, 2010 Rev. Ed.), R 40.
674. Supreme Court of Judicature Act (Cap. 322, R. 5, 2014 Rev. Ed.) Rules of Court, O 59 r 5.
675. *HSBC Institutional Trust Services (Singapore) Ltd (trustee of Starhill Global Real Estate Investment Trust) v. Toshin Development Singapore Pte Ltd*, [2012] 4 SLR 738.

as to whether he had acted in his own interests rather than in those of his client in taking all the steps that he did to enforce payment of a small settlement sum and the disbursements claimed, he should not be allowed to tax his solicitor and client costs.[676]

676. *Lock Han Chng Jonathan (Jonathan Luo Hancheng) v. Goh Jessiline*, [2008] 2 SLR(R) 455.

Chapter 3. Originating Process

§1. Introduction

234. In Singapore, proceedings may be commenced by writ or originating summons.[677] This has been the case since 2006, when the other originating processes of originating motion and petition were statutorily abolished.[678] Generally, leave of the court is not required for the commencement of an action.[679] A principal exception to this is when the Attorney-General files an application to restrain a person commencing legal proceedings on the basis that such proceedings are an abuse of the process of the court; for instance, if the litigant has habitually and persistently without any reasonable ground instituted vexatious legal proceedings.[680] A writ is the appropriate originating process if 'a substantial dispute of fact is likely to arise'.[681] An originating summons will be more appropriate when there is no dispute of fact and only where there are 'issues of law such as the construction of legislation or legal instrument or an application pursuant to statute'.[682] If a plaintiff merely uses an improper originating process, this does not necessarily mean that the proceedings must be terminated; the court retains discretion to allow the action to continue subject to the appropriate amendments.[683]

235. Proceedings commenced by originating summons may be ordered by the court (or on application by a party) to be continued as if the action had been commenced by writ if a dispute of fact subsequently arises.[684] This is otherwise known

677. Supreme Court of Judicature Act (Cap. 322, R. 5, 2014 Rev. Ed.) Rules of Court, O 5 r 1.
678. *Singapore Civil Procedure 2015 Volume 1*, at 56 (G.P. Selvam ed., Sweet & Maxwell Asia 2014).
679. J. Pinsler, *Principles of Civil Procedure* 97 (Acad. Publg. 2013), citing *Dresser UK v. Falcongate Freight Management, The Duke of Yare*, [1992] 2 All ER 450, 463.
680. Supreme Court of Judicature Act (Cap. 322, 2007 Rev. Ed.), s 74(1). *See also Chua Choon Lim Robert v. MN Swami*, [2000] 2 SLR(R) 589, [18]; *Lai Swee Lin Linda v. Attorney-General*, [2016] 5 SLR 476, [7]–[10]; *Attorney-General v. Tham Yim Siong and others*, [2017] SGHC 267, [34]. Other exceptions include Supreme Court of Judicature Act (Cap. 322, R. 5, 2014 Rev. Ed.) Rules of Court, O 5 r 6 (when disabled and mentally ill persons sue) and O 76 (when unincorporated associations sue).
681. Supreme Court of Judicature Act (Cap. 322, R. 5, 2014 Rev. Ed.) Rules of Court, O 5 r 2. It should be noted that there is also the expedited writ track for claims up to SGD 20,000 (and thus is only available in the State Courts). This track is meant to minimize costs for such (small) claims, and apart from the application of the Rules of Court, there are certain Practice Directions that apply to govern this track too: *see* State Courts Practice Directions.
682. J. Pinsler, *Principles of Civil Procedure* 83 (Acad. Publg. 2013). Accordingly, there are generally no pleadings and discovery processes for originating summonses, though evidence may be set out in affidavits: *id.*, 113. Another consequence is that unlike a writ, which will eventually be heard in open court, an originating summons is normally heard in chambers: *id.*, 113. *See also* Supreme Court of Judicature Act (Cap. 322, R. 5, 2014 Rev. Ed.) Rules of Court, O 5 r 4(2).
683. *Suhaidah bte Mohd Noor (trustees and executors of the estate of Haji Hassan bin Haji Ismail, deceased) v. Syed Ahmad Jamal Alsagoff*, [2014] SGHC 116, [54]. *See also* Supreme Court of Judicature Act (Cap. 322, R. 5, 2014 Rev. Ed.) Rules of Court, O 2 r 1(3); *In re Deadman, deceased; Smith v. Garland and others*, [1971] 1 WLR 426, 429.
684. Supreme Court of Judicature Act (Cap. 322, R. 5, 2014 Rev. Ed.) Rules of Court, O 28 r 8. *See also Tan Yeow Khoon v. Tan Yeow Tat*, [1998] 2 SLR(R) 19, [18]; *Woon Brothers Investments Pte Ltd v. MCST Plan No 461*, [2011] 4 SLR 777, [29]; *Suresh Agarwal v. Naseer Ahmad Akhtar*, [2019]

as converting an originating summons to a writ, and may be done even if there is a statute stating that a claim has to be by originating summons.[685] Nonetheless, it is possible that some costs be incurred when there is such a change and in extreme cases, the use of an improper originating process may result in the termination of proceedings:[686] for instance, 'where a writ or originating summons is used in contravention of a statutory provision or rule of court, it may be set aside for a lack of legal basis and, where the procedure was intentionally or recklessly used, for abuse of process'.[687] In addition, the mere dispute of facts may not be sufficient to warrant converting an originating summons to a writ, regardless of the cause of action; allegations must be accompanied by the existence of at least a credible matrix of facts.[688] A wider range and greater number of rules govern writs than originating summonses. This is mainly because the writ 'sets up, and connects to, subsequent processes such as pleadings, summons for directions, interim reliefs, discovery, exchange of affidavits, setting down, and trial, which cumulatively constitute the action'.[689] It is possible for a party to lose the ability to ask the court to order a conversion of an originating summons to a writ, particularly if its conduct is consistent with that of foregoing the right of cross-examination.[690]

§2. Writ

I. Formalities and Contents

236. There is a prescribed form for writs.[691] The identities of the parties (plaintiff(s) and defendant(s)) must be accurately stated,[692] or this may result in setting

---

SGCA 55. If the court is of the view that the dispute will be better resolved by going through the pleading and (eventual) cross-examination process, a conversion will be appropriate.

685. *Woon Brothers Investments Pte Ltd v. MCST Plan No 461*, [2011] 4 SLR 777, [14]–[22].
686. C.f. Supreme Court of Judicature Act (Cap. 322, R. 5, 2014 Rev. Ed.) Rules of Court, O 2 r 1(3).
687. J. Pinsler, *Principles of Civil Procedure* 85 (Acad. Publg. 2013). *See also Independent State of Papua New Guinea v. PNG Sustainable Development Program Ltd*, [2016] 2 SLR 366, [33]: 'an originating summons is appropriate where no substantial dispute of fact exists … If disputes of fact arise, the court still has the discretion to allow the originating summons to continue as such rather than converting it to a writ action. In that event, if the summons cannot be decided on the undisputed facts, it will have to be dismissed.'
688. *Rainforest Trading Ltd v. State Bank of India Singapore*, [2012] 2 SLR 713, [41]–[42]. In cases of fraud, it is usually more appropriate to proceed by writ as cogent evidence is required to prove it: *Woon Brothers Investment Pte Ltd v. MCST Plan No 461*, [2011] 4 SLR 777, [30]; *TDA v. TCZ*, [2016] SGHC 63, [28]. C.f. *Cheong Kim Hock v. Lin Securities (Pte) (in liquidation)* [1992] 1 SLR(R) 497, [11].
689. J. Pinsler, *Principles of Civil Procedure* 82 (Acad. Publg. 2013). These various processes are canvassed in greater detail in other Parts and Chapters.
690. *LS Investment Pte Ltd v. Majlis Ugama Islam Singapura*, [1998] 3 SLR(R) 369, [55]; *Haco Far East Pte Ltd v. Ong Heh Lai Francis*, [1999] 3 SLR(R) 959, [17]; *TDA v. TCZ*, [2016] SGHC 63, [35].
691. Supreme Court of Judicature Act (Cap. 322, R. 5, 2014 Rev. Ed.) Rules of Court, O 6 r 1.
692. This would include the identity numbers of the parties (*see* Supreme Court Practice Directions 2013 (Part III); State Courts Practice Directions (Part II)), addresses of the parties and/or their lawyers (*see* Supreme Court of Judicature Act (Cap. 322, R. 5, 2014 Rev. Ed.) Rules of Court, O 6 r 2), and signatures by the parties or their lawyers (*see* Supreme Court of Judicature Act (Cap. 322, R. 5,

aside proceedings and/or compromise default judgments.[693] Particular complications arise such as when the party is a disabled person,[694] when parties are partners,[695] and when the proceedings are for admiralty claims.[696] If a party is suing or being sued in a representative capacity, there must be an endorsement with a statement of the said capacity.[697] Though non-compliance with this requirement is curable[698] and unlikely to be unduly detrimental in terms of prejudice, representative proceedings which are improperly brought may be set aside.[699] This is because clarifying the capacities in which parties are suing and being sued forms a crucial backdrop to the claims and has significant substantive implications with respect to the rights and obligations.[700]

237. In terms of pleadings, there must either be a concise statement of the nature of the claim or statement of claim endorsed with the writ.[701] Specifically, the former 'is simply a generally worded claim, the purpose of which is to communicate to the defendant the nature of the suit and the reasons why legal action is taken against him … it must contain sufficient information to enable the defendant to identify the circumstances which are alleged by the plaintiff to have resulted in the wrong'.[702] The latter, on the other hand, while also identifying the issues, 'consists of a much more comprehensive account of the material facts'.[703] The main advantage of endorsing the writ with a statement of claim instead of a concise statement of the nature of the claim is that the need to subsequently file and serve the statement of claim after the defendant has entered an appearance is obviated. This in turn expedites later proceedings, such as summary judgment (which may only be applied for after the defence is served subsequent to the entering of appearance) and default judgment (whether in default of appearance or defence). Thus, a concise statement of the nature of the claim is usually only resorted to when the writ needs to be filed urgently (for reasons such as impending limitation period).[704]

238. If the claim made by the plaintiff is for a debt or liquidated demand only, the writ must be endorsed with 'a statement of the amount claimed in respect of the

---

2014 Rev. Ed.), s 2; Supreme Court of Judicature Act (Cap. 322, R. 5, 2014 Rev. Ed.) Rules of Court, O 1 r 7)) and Registrar of the Supreme Court or Registrar of the State Courts (*see* Supreme Court of Judicature Act (Cap. 322, R. 5, 2014 Rev. Ed.) Rules of Court, O 6 r 3(2)).

693. *See* Supreme Court of Judicature Act (Cap. 322, R. 5, 2014 Rev. Ed.) Rules of Court, O 2 r 1(1). *See also id.*, O 2 rr 1(2) and 1(3).
694. Supreme Court of Judicature Act (Cap. 322, R. 5, 2014 Rev. Ed.) Rules of Court, O 76 r 2.
695. Supreme Court of Judicature Act (Cap. 322, R. 5, 2014 Rev. Ed.) Rules of Court, O 77 r 1.
696. Supreme Court of Judicature Act (Cap. 322, R. 5, 2014 Rev. Ed.) Rules of Court, O 70 r 2.
697. Supreme Court of Judicature Act (Cap. 322, R. 5, 2014 Rev. Ed.) Rules of Court, O 6 r 2(1).
698. Supreme Court of Judicature Act (Cap. 322, R. 5, 2014 Rev. Ed.) Rules of Court, O 20 r 5(4).
699. *See also Ong Kay Eng v. Ng Chiow Tong*, [2001] 1 SLR(R) 422, [10].
700. *Foo Jee Boo v. Foo Jhee Tuang*, [2015] SGHC 176, [32]. *See also* C. Bull & C. Voon Jiet, *Civil Procedure: Annual Review of Singapore Cases* [8.7] (Sing. Acad. L. 2015).
701. Supreme Court of Judicature Act (Cap. 322, R. 5, 2014 Rev. Ed.) Rules of Court, O 6 r 2(1).
702. J. Pinsler, *Principles of Civil Procedure* 89–90 (Acad. Publg. 2013), citing *Marshall v. London Passenger Transport Board*, [1936] 3 All ER 83.
703. J. Pinsler, *Principles of Civil Procedure* 91 (Acad. Publg. 2013). *See also Singapore Civil Procedure 2015 Volume 1*, at 62–63 (G.P. Selvam ed., Sweet & Maxwell Asia 2014).
704. J. Pinsler, *Principles of Civil Procedure* 92 (Acad. Publg. 2013).

debt or demand and for costs and also with a statement that further proceedings will be stayed if, within the time limited for appearing, the defendant pays the amount so claimed'.[705] This requirement is to 'expedite dispute resolution by giving the defendant the opportunity to settle the claim'.[706] However, such an endorsement will not be appropriate if the amount in question is incapable of precise ascertainment at the point in time when the writ is issued.[707]

239. The writ must be endorsed 'with the number of days within which an appearance is required to be entered'[708] as well as an indication of the person who served the writ, the manner in which it was served, and any other relevant details.[709] The writ is deemed to be issued when the court assigns a serial number to, signs, seals, and dates the writ.[710] If the court has made an administrative error in the assignment of the date of issue of the writ, it would probably exercise its inherent power to prevent any prejudice that may be suffered by the plaintiff as a result of the error.[711] Finally, the writ may be amended, though depending on the circumstance, leave of the court may be required.

II. Validity Period and Renewal

240. If a writ is to be served within jurisdiction (i.e., Singapore), it will be valid for six months from the date of its issue.[712] An exception to this is if the writ is for admiralty proceedings; such a writ will be valid for twelve months from the date of its issue.[713] If a writ is to be served out of jurisdiction, it will be valid for twelve months from the date of its issue.[714]

241. The period of validity runs from the date of its issue, including such date, and if renewed for the period of the renewal. Validity of the writ for the appropriate period begins with the actual day on which it is issued – for example, a writ issued

705. Supreme Court of Judicature Act (Cap. 322, R. 5, 2014 Rev. Ed.) Rules of Court, O 6 r 2(1).
706. J. Pinsler, *Principles of Civil Procedure* 92 (Acad. Publg. 2013).
707. J. Pinsler, *Principles of Civil Procedure* 92–93 (Acad. Publg. 2013).
708. Supreme Court of Judicature Act (Cap. 322, R. 5, 2014 Rev. Ed.) Rules of Court, O 6 r 2(1). The usual periods to be stated would be eight and twenty-one days after service of the writ for service of the writ within and without the jurisdiction respectively: *id.*, O 12 r 4 and O 10 r 2(5).
709. J. Pinsler, *Principles of Civil Procedure* 95–96 (Acad. Publg. 2013).
710. Supreme Court of Judicature Act (Cap. 322, R. 5, 2014 Rev. Ed.) Rules of Court, O 6 r 3(1). Generally, leave of court is not required for the writ to be issued. For a list of scenarios in which leave is required, *see Singapore Civil Procedure 2015 Volume 1*, at 68 (G.P. Selvam ed., Sweet & Maxwell Asia 2014).
711. J. Pinsler, *Principles of Civil Procedure* 98–99 (Acad. Publg. 2013), citing *Kok Song Kong v. BSP Co Sdn Bhd*, [1998] 2 MLJ 440.
712. Supreme Court of Judicature Act (Cap. 322, R. 5, 2014 Rev. Ed.) Rules of Court, O 6 r 4(1). For instance, if a writ is issued on 3 Jan. 2013, its validity will expire on 2 Jun. 2013. *See Trow v. Ind Coope (West Midlands) Ltd*, [1967] 2 QB 899.
713. Supreme Court of Judicature Act (Cap. 322, R. 5, 2014 Rev. Ed.) Rules of Court, O 70 r 2(4).
714. Supreme Court of Judicature Act (Cap. 322, R. 5, 2014 Rev. Ed.) Rules of Court, O 6 r 4(1).

on 1 January 2012 is not valid for service on 1 July 2012.[715] The entering of appearance by the defendant after becoming aware that service is out of time does not amount to a waiver of objection to the service since O 12 r 7 requires an appearance to be entered before an application to set aside service can be made.[716] It also does not amount to waiver of the right to object to an order renewing the writ or otherwise extending the time for service.[717]

242. While the plaintiff is expected to pursue his claim in a timely manner in the interests of justice to all involved, and while the default six (or twelve, as the case may be) months is presumed to be a reasonable period for service of the writ to be effected, the plaintiff may be permitted to seek a renewal of the writ under certain circumstances.[718]

243. O 6 r 4 that concerns the validity of the writ provides a comprehensive code for the renewal of a writ. Therefore an irregularity in procedure caused by the failure to renew a writ under this rule is such a fundamental defect in the proceedings that the court's wide powers under O 2 rr 1 and 2 to cure non-compliance with the Rules ought not to be exercised by treating a writ has become invalid for service as though it had been renewed and is therefore valid for service.[719] In this regard:

> where a writ has not been served on a defendant, the Court may by order extend the validity of the writ from time to time for such period, not exceeding six months at any one time, beginning with the day next following that on which it would otherwise expire, as may be specified in the order, if an application for extension is made to the Court before that day or such later day (if any), as the Court may allow.[720]

244. Further, if the court is 'satisfied … that, despite the making of reasonable efforts, it may not be possible to serve a writ within six months, the Court may, if it thinks fit, extend the validity of the writ for such period, not exceeding twelve months at any one time, as the Court may specify'.[721] To establish 'the making of reasonable efforts', the plaintiff will have to provide a supporting affidavit and set

715. *Trow v. Ind Coope Ltd*, [1967] 2 All ER 900.
716. *See also First Property Holdings Pte Ltd v. U Myo Nyunt (alias Michael Nyut)*, [2020] SGHC 276.
717. *Singapore Civil Procedure 2015 Volume 1*, at 70 (G.P. Selvam ed., Sweet & Maxwell Asia 2014).
718. *See also* Supreme Court of Judicature Act (Cap. 322, R. 5, 2014 Rev. Ed.) Rules of Court, O 12 r 8(1); J. Pinsler, *Principles of Civil Procedure* 217 (Acad. Publg. 2013).
719. *Singapore Civil Procedure 2015 Volume 1*, at 69 (G.P. Selvam ed., Sweet & Maxwell Asia 2014), citing *Jason Textile Industries Pte Ltd (in liquidation) v. QBE Insurance (International) Ltd*, [1988] 2 SLR(R) 491; *Bernstein v. Jackson*, [1982] 2 All ER 806. *See also Singapore Civil Procedure 2015 Volume 1*, at 70–73 (G.P. Selvam ed., Sweet & Maxwell Asia 2014).
720. Supreme Court of Judicature Act (Cap. 322, R. 5, 2014 Rev. Ed.) Rules of Court, O 6 r 4(2).
721. Supreme Court of Judicature Act (Cap. 322, R. 5, 2014 Rev. Ed.) Rules of Court, O 6 r 4(2A).

out the difficulties he had faced.[722] However, unless there are very compelling reasons to do, the court is unlikely to provide the maximum extension possible.[723] Indeed, more broadly speaking, the court will:

> consider all relevant matters for the purpose of an application for renewal ... [The plaintiff] will have to explain why the writ was not served during the original six-month period and refer to the efforts he made to do so. The fact that the parties are involved in negotiations is not normally an excuse ... The court will also consider the defendant's conduct, such as his representation that he would not object to any application to renew ... the critical factor is whether it is just to permit the renewal.[724]

245. Examples of a sufficiently good reason to ask for renewal include: where the plaintiff reasonably postponed his litigation until another set of legal proceedings was over;[725] where an error was made by the court registry;[726] where there was a clear agreement between the parties that the service would be deferred;[727] and where there was a delay emanating from the operation of the legal aid system.[728] Examples of an insufficiently good reason to ask for renewal include: where the delay was due to bad advice from the lawyers;[729] where the delay was due to insufficient funds to begin litigation;[730] where there was difficulty tracing witnesses and/or obtaining evidence;[731] and where the delay was due to mistakes made by the lawyers.[732] Although a plaintiff is technically allowed to apply for renewal even after the writ has expired, the 'underlying assumption ... is that an application would be made during the initial period of validity of the writ'.[733] Indeed, there is a question of whether there is any limit to the court's power to keep renewing the validity of a writ. The prevailing view appears to be that:

> the court's power [under the Rules of Court] is limited to extending the validity of the writ for a maximum of twelve months at any one time. This means that any application for renewal must be made at the latest within twelve

722. J. Pinsler, *Principles of Civil Procedure* 102 (Acad. Publg. 2013). *See also The 'Antares v'*, [2001] 2 SLR(R) 616, [20]; C. Bull & J. Pinsler, *Civil Procedure: Annual Review of Singapore Cases* [6.4] (Sing. Acad. L. 2002).
723. J. Pinsler, *Principles of Civil Procedure* 102 (Acad. Publg. 2013), citing *Baly v. Harret*, [1988] NI 369, The Times (19 May 1989).
724. J. Pinsler, *Principles of Civil Procedure* 102–103 (Acad. Publg. 2013), citing *Kleinwort Benson Ltd v. Barbrak Ltd; The Myrto (No 3)*, [1987] AC 597, 622; *The Mouna*, [1991] 2 Lloyd's Rep 221, 229.
725. *Lim Hong Kan v. Mohd Sainudin bin Ahmad*, [1992] 1 SLR(R) 108.
726. *Ward-Lee v. Linehan*, [1993] 1 WLR 754.
727. *Kun Kay Hong v. Tan Teo Huat*, [1983–1984] SLR(R) 762.
728. *Waddon v. Whitecroft Scovill Ltd*, [1988] 1 WLR 309, 316.
729. *Jason Textile Industries Pte Ltd v. QBE Insurance (International) Ltd*, [1988] 2 SLR(R) 491, [28].
730. *Baly v. Harret*, [1988] NI 369, The Times (19 May 1989).
731. *Portico Housing Association v. Brian Moorehead and Partners*, (1985) 1 Const LJ 226.
732. *Singh v. Duport Harper Foundries Ltd*, [1994] 1 WLR 769.
733. J. Pinsler, *Principles of Civil Procedure* 104 (Acad. Publg. 2013). *See also Singapore Civil Procedure 2015 Volume 1*, at 71 (G.P. Selvam ed., Sweet & Maxwell Asia 2014).

months of the expiry of the writ. There is no power to grant two or more successive renewals to bring the writ up to date.[734]

246. Related to this question of limited renewals is the issue of limitation period. The following passage from an influential House of Lords decision has been adopted in Singapore:

> Category (1) cases are where the application for extension is made at a time when the writ is still valid and before the relevant period of limitation has expired. Category (2) cases are where the application for extension is made at a time when the writ is still valid but the relevant period of limitation has expired. Category (3) cases are where the application for extension is made at a time when the writ ceased to be valid and the relevant period of limitation has expired. In both category (1) cases and category (2) cases, it is still possible for the plaintiff (subject to any difficulties of services which there may be) to serve the writ before its validity expires, and, if he does so, the defendant will not be able to rely on a defence of limitation. In category (1) cases, but not category (2) cases, it is also possible for the plaintiff, before the original writ ceases to be valid, to issue a fresh writ which will remain valid for a further 12 months. In neither category (1) cases and category (2) cases, therefore, can it properly be said that, at the time when the application for extension is made, a defendant who has not been served has an accrued right of limitation. In category (3) cases, however, it is not possible for the plaintiff to serve the writ effectively unless its validity is first retrospectively extended. In category (3) cases, therefore, it can properly be said that, at the time when the application for extension is made, a defendant in whom the writ has not been served has an accrued right of limitation.[735]

247. Accordingly, it may be said, for instance, that a 'defendant's loss of a limitation defence might be regarded as less compelling if the plaintiff's inaction was induced by the defendant's consent to the extension of the writ. The court must decide for itself the cumulative effect of all the factors which support or are against renewal.'[736]

---

734. *Official Receiver, Liquidator of Jason Textiles Industries Pte Ltd v. QBE Insurance (International) Ltd*, [1988] 2 SLR(R) 491, [11]. However, the court also said (*id.*, [21]; cited in *ITC Global Holdings Pte Ltd (under judicial management) v. ITC Limited*, [2007] SGHC, [53]) that even if the non-renewal of a writ is an irregularity, it can be cured by the court's inherent powers. *See also Singapore Civil Procedure 2015 Volume 1*, at 71 (G.P. Selvam ed., Sweet & Maxwell Asia 2014).

735. *Kleinwort Benson Ltd v. Barbrak Ltd; The Myrto (No 3)*, [1987] AC 597, 615–616; cited in *Lim Hong Kan v. Mohd Sainudin bin Ahmad*, [1992] 1 SLR(R) 108, [14]; *The Lircay*, [1997] 1 SLR(R) 699, [19]; *The 'Ching Ho'*, [2001] 3 SLR(R) 84, [20].

736. J. Pinsler, *Principles of Civil Procedure* 105 (Acad. Publg. 2013). For a discussion on the extent to which it a defendant may consent to an extension of the validity of a writ, *see id.*, 105–106.

248. In terms of formal requirements for renewal, the application is by an ex parte summons which is supported by an affidavit.[737] As this is an ex parte application, there is a duty of full and frank disclosure (in the affidavit) on the part of the applicant.[738] The original writ must accompany the affidavit. If the writ's validity is extended, it must, before it is served, be marked with an official stamp in the prescribed form showing the period from which the validity has been so extended.[739]

§3. ORIGINATING SUMMONS

249. There are two prescribed forms for originating summonses,[740] depending on whether the summons is ex parte or inter partes.[741] Each originating summons should bear a title that states 'with sufficient particularity either in its heading or in its body, the statute or rule of court under which the court is being moved'.[742] If the application is inter partes, the originating summons should also refer to the parties in the title.[743] In terms of contents, the originating summons:

> must include a statement of the questions on which the plaintiff seeks the determination or direction of the Court or, as the case may be, a concise statement of the relief or remedy claimed in the proceedings begun by the originating summons with sufficient particulars to identify the cause or causes of action in respect of which the plaintiff claims that relief or remedy.[744]

250. In this regard, most of the rules that apply to writs also apply here.[745] The rules that apply to writs for issuance also apply to originating summonses.[746] The rules that apply to writs vis-à-vis duration and renewal of their validity also apply to originating summonses.[747] Finally, an originating summons may be amended, but in certain situations leave of the court may be required.

---

737. *Singapore Civil Procedure 2015 Volume 1*, at 74 (G.P. Selvam ed., Sweet & Maxwell Asia 2014).
738. *See The 'Vasiliy Golovnin'*, [2008] 4 SLR(R) 994, [83] and [85]–[87].
739. Supreme Court of Judicature Act (Cap. 322, R. 5, 2014 Rev. Ed.) Rules of Court, O 6 r 4(3).
740. Supreme Court of Judicature Act (Cap. 322, R. 5, 2014 Rev. Ed.) Rules of Court, O 7 r 2. *See also* Supreme Court Practice Directions 2013 (Parts III and XII); State Courts Practice Directions (Parts II and IX).
741. *Singapore Civil Procedure 2015 Volume 1*, at 76–77 (G.P. Selvam ed., Sweet & Maxwell Asia 2014).
742. *Singapore Civil Procedure 2015 Volume 1*, at 77–78 (G.P. Selvam ed., Sweet & Maxwell Asia 2014).
743. *Singapore Civil Procedure 2015 Volume 1*, at 78 (G.P. Selvam ed., Sweet & Maxwell Asia 2014).
744. Supreme Court of Judicature Act (Cap. 322, R. 5, 2014 Rev. Ed.) Rules of Court, O 7 r 3(1). *See also Punton v. Ministry of Pensions*, [1963] 1 WLR 186, 192; *Engineering Construction Pte Ltd v. Attorney-General*, [1992] 2 SLR(R) 905, [10]–[14].
745. Supreme Court of Judicature Act (Cap. 322, R. 5, 2014 Rev. Ed.) Rules of Court, O 7 r 3(2). If there is a counterclaim, the defendant must inform the court of this at as early a stage as is practicable (*id.*, O 28 r 7(2)); it is possible that the court may prefer to hear the counterclaim separately (*id.*, O 28 r 7(3)). *See also Suresh Agarwal v. Naseer Ahmad Akhtar*, [2019] SGCA 55.
746. Supreme Court of Judicature Act (Cap. 322, R. 5, 2014 Rev. Ed.) Rules of Court, O 7 r 4.
747. Supreme Court of Judicature Act (Cap. 322, R. 5, 2014 Rev. Ed.) Rules of Court, O 7 r 5.

§4. Possibility of Appeal

251. Section 34 of the Supreme Court of Judicature Act,[748] read together with the Fourth and Fifth Schedules of the statute, determines whether any given order of civil procedure is appealable to the Court of Appeal[749] or not.[750] However, applications relating to originating processes are not explicitly covered by either the Fourth (orders made by a judge that are non-appealable) or Fifth (orders made by a judge that are only appealable with leave) Schedules. Accordingly, it would seem that an appeal against a decision that say, refuses to renew the validity of a writ is either as of right or requires leave from the court, since the Fourth Schedule does not declare it to be non-appealable and the Fifth Schedule does not require leave to be sought.

252. Due to recent amendments to the Supreme Court of Judicature Act, the law on this is currently in flux and while it has been suggested that the 'default' position is that all interlocutory applications, unless provided for statutorily, are appealable with leave,[751] it may also be possible to argue that for interlocutory applications not expressly addressed by the Fourth and Fifth Schedules, 'an appeal to the Court of Appeal will remain as of right for orders made at interlocutory applications which will finally dispose of the substantive rights of the parties'.[752]

748. (Cap. 322, 2007 Rev. Ed.).
749. The Court of Appeal is the apex court in Singapore. Below it is the High Court, followed by the District and Magistrates' Courts. For appeals arising from the lower courts, *see* Supreme Court of Judicature Act (Cap. 322, R. 5, 2014 Rev. Ed.) Rules of Court, O 55B, 55C, and 55D. It should be noted that generally, for interlocutory applications, there is a right of appeal from first instance. Thus, there is a right of appeal from a registrar in chambers to a judge in chambers (District Judge if it is the State Courts), but not necessarily after that stage.
750. The statute was amended in 2010 and 2014.
751. *See* E. Chua, *Defining an 'Interlocutory Application'*, Sing. L. Watch Commentaries (4/2013); D. Chi, *Clarification on Leave to Appeal Regime in Respect of Interlocutory Matters: OpenNet Pte Ltd v. Info-Communications Development Authority of Singapore* [2013] 2 SLR 880, Sing. L. Watch Commentaries (4/2013); C. Siyuan & E. Chua, *The Right to Appeal Against a Decision Made on an Interlocutory Application: The Immediate Aftermath of the 2010 Amendments*, 25 Sing. Acad. L.J. 424 (2013).
752. *OpenNet Pte Ltd v. Info-Communications Development Authority of Singapore*, [2013] 2 SLR 880, [29]. *See also Dorsey James Michael v. World Sport Group Pte Ltd*, [2013] 3 SLR 354, [98]. On the other hand, where the statute has made it clear that there is no appeal as of right, one is precluded from arguing that substantive rights have been engaged: *Kosui Singapore Pte Ltd v. Thangavelu*, [2016] 2 SLR 105, [28]–[29].

Chapter 4. Service

§1. Introduction

253. Service essentially 'enables one party to establish a legal act and notify the other party and the court of a document or process which is significant to the case'.[753] In the service of an originating process, it also establishes the jurisdiction of the court.[754] There are various methods of and formalities for service, depending on the document and party being served in question.[755] The rules and procedures for service are primarily found in O 10 (service of originating process), O 11 (service of process out of Singapore), and O 62 (service of documents) of the Rules of Court.[756]

§2. Service in Singapore

I. Personal Service

254. By default, both types of originating processes – writs and originating summonses – require personal service,[757] as opposed to just ordinary[758] or substituted service. For most other documents, however, personal service is usually not required, unless there is a rule that states otherwise.[759] Personal service may be effected in either of two ways. First, it is effected by 'leaving with the person to be served … in the case of an originating process, a sealed copy … in any other case, a copy of the document'.[760] Second, it may also be effected 'in such other manner as may be agreed between the party serving and the party to be served'.[761] These two types of personal service vary the traditional common law requirement of physical delivery, in that 'the document does not have to be actually "delivered". It

753. J. Pinsler, *Principles of Civil Procedure* 126 (Acad. Publg. 2013). C.f. Supreme Court of Judicature Act (Cap. 322, R. 5, 2014 Rev. Ed.) Rules of Court, O 62 r 11.
754. J. Pinsler, *Principles of Civil Procedure* 126 (Acad. Publg. 2013).
755. J. Pinsler, *Principles of Civil Procedure* 126–127 (Acad. Publg. 2013).
756. Supreme Court of Judicature Act (Cap. 322, R. 5, 2014 Rev. Ed.) Rules of Court.
757. Supreme Court of Judicature Act (Cap. 322, R. 5, 2014 Rev. Ed.) Rules of Court, O 10 r 1(1) and O 10 r 5.
758. As for how ordinary service can be effected, *see* Supreme Court of Judicature Act (Cap. 322, R. 5, 2014 Rev. Ed.) Rules of Court, O 62 r 6(1). Substituted service is addressed below.
759. Supreme Court of Judicature Act (Cap. 322, R. 5, 2014 Rev. Ed.) Rules of Court, O 62 r 1. *See also id.*, O 62 r 10. C.f. Supreme Court of Judicature Act (Cap. 322, R. 5, 2014 Rev. Ed.) Rules of Court, O 15 (commencement and enforcement against person not party to the action); O 16 r 3(3) (third-party notice to person not party to the action); O 20 r 1(2) (amended writ of summons without leave and before service); O 24 r 16 (failure to comply with discovery and the like); O 26 r 6 (failure to comply with order for interrogatories); O 38 r 18 (subpoena); O 45 r 7(2) (enforcement by committal); O 48 r 1(2) (order for examination of judgment debtor); O 49 r 3 (provisional garnishee order); O 52 r 3 (application for committal); O 54 r 6 (application for order for review of detention); O 65 (certain foreign legal processes); O 67 r 7(1) (notice of registration of foreign judgment); O 77 r 5 (execution against a partner).
760. Supreme Court of Judicature Act (Cap. 322, R. 5, 2014 Rev. Ed.) Rules of Court, O 62 r 3(1).
761. Supreme Court of Judicature Act (Cap. 322, R. 5, 2014 Rev. Ed.) Rules of Court, O 62 r 3(2).

is sufficient if it is left with the defendant. As for the alternative method ... the plaintiff and defendant can agree to any method even if it does not involve "personal" service in the literal sense'.[762]

255. In specific relation to the first type of service, the person[763] serving the sealed copy of the originating process (or any other document for the matter, so long as personal service is required) should first ensure that he has correctly identified the defendant before handing over the document. If the defendant declines to accept the document, the server should inform the defendant of the nature of the document and then leave it in a place where the defendant can later retrieve it.[764] In specific relation to the second type of service, party autonomy is usually respected even if personal service is effectively waived.[765]

256. A common type of agreement is where parties agree in a contract that if a dispute arises, service is to be sent by registered post, and that personal service is effected even if the defendant is not personally aware of such service.[766] A problem may emerge, however, if the contract does not provide for ad hoc arrangements and 'the defendant proposes an alternative proposes an alternative arrangement on the spot, and the process server obliges without obtaining the plaintiff's authority'.[767] In such a situation, the process server would want to obtain the plaintiff's authority before proceeding. Once the originating process has been duly served on a defendant,[768] the plaintiff has eight days to sign and file a memorandum of service (using the prescribed form):

> containing the following particulars, that is to say, the day of the week, date and time on which it was served, where it was served, how it was served, the

762. J. Pinsler, *Principles of Civil Procedure* 128 (Acad. Publg. 2013). *See also Pacific Assets Management v. Chen Lip Keong*, [2006] 1 SLR(R) 658, [8].
763. *See* Supreme Court of Judicature Act (Cap. 322, R. 5, 2014 Rev. Ed.) Rules of Court, O 62 rr 2(1) and 2(2).
764. J. Pinsler, *Principles of Civil Procedure* 129 (Acad. Publg. 2013); *Singapore Civil Procedure 2015 Volume 1*, at 1102 (G.P. Selvam ed., Sweet & Maxwell Asia 2014). Fairly ancient authorities are often cited to illustrate what constitutes good personal service, such as *Thomson v. Pheney*, (1832) 1 DPC 441, 443 (server is permitted to thrown the document down in defendant's presence instead of handing it to him); *Frith v. Lord Donegal*, (1834) 2 Dow PR 527 (it is not sufficient to serve on the wife of the defendant); *Heath v. White*, (1844) 2 D & L 40 (server is not permitted to thrown the document down in the wife's presence (in lieu of the defendant's presence)); *Christmas v. Eicke*, (1848) 6 D & L 156 (it is not sufficient to put the document through the door crevice and inform the defendant of the nature of the document); *Banque Russe v. Clarke*, [1894] WN 203 (it is not sufficient to enclose the document in an envelope without explaining the contents of the envelope).
765. *Pacific Assets Management v. Chen Lip Keong*, [2006] 1 SLR(R) 658, [8].
766. *See also* Supreme Court of Judicature Act (Cap. 322, R. 5, 2014 Rev. Ed.) Rules of Court, O 10 r 3; *Kenneth Allision Ltd v. AE Limehouse & Co*, [1992] 2 AC 105 at 116–117; *Oversea-Chinese Banking Corp Ltd v. Measurex Corp Bhd*, [2002] 2 SLR(R) 684, [14]; *Singapore Civil Procedure 2015 Volume 1*, at 1102 (G.P. Selvam ed., Sweet & Maxwell Asia 2014).
767. J. Pinsler, *Principles of Civil Procedure* 131 (Acad. Publg. 2013).
768. *See also* Supreme Court of Judicature Act (Cap. 322, R. 5, 2014 Rev. Ed.) Rules of Court, O 62 r 9.

person on whom it was served, and, where he is not the defendant, the capacity in which he was served, the plaintiff in the action begun by the writ shall not be entitled to enter final or interlocutory judgment against that defendant in default of appearance or in default of defence, unless the Court otherwise orders.[769]

257. In addition, a:

> writ is deemed to have been discontinued against a defendant if the memorandum of service … is not filed in respect of the service of the writ on that defendant within 12 months after the validity of the writ for the purpose of service has expired, and, within that time … a memorandum of appearance has not been filed in the action by that defendant; and … judgment has not been obtained in the action against that defendant in respect of the whole or any part of the relief claimed against that defendant in the action.[770]

258. There are, however, various scenarios in which the rules on personal service of the originating process on the defendant may be waived, considered impractical, or modified in some way. Two have already been mentioned: when the parties agree, and when there is appearance gratis.[771] Broadly speaking, the other scenarios are: when service is accepted by the defendant's lawyer;[772] when service is accepted by an agent or manager of the defendant's business;[773] where a defendant is a minor, lacks capacity, or is under a disability such that service should instead be effected on a representative;[774] where the defendant is running a sole proprietorship using a business name or is part of a partnership;[775] where the defendant is an unincorporated association,[776] corporation which is not a registered company,[777] local company,[778] or foreign company;[779] where the action is for possession of immovable

769. Supreme Court of Judicature Act (Cap. 322, R. 5, 2014 Rev. Ed.) Rules of Court, O 10 r 1(4). *See also id.*, O 10 r 1(3); O 11 r 3(4).
770. Supreme Court of Judicature Act (Cap. 322, R. 5, 2014 Rev. Ed.) Rules of Court, O 21 r 2(5).
771. *See also Lehman Brothers Special Financing Inc v. Hartadi Angkosubroto*, [1998] 3 SLR(R) 664, [24].
772. Supreme Court of Judicature Act (Cap. 322, R. 5, 2014 Rev. Ed.) Rules of Court, O 10 r 1(2). *See also Lee Lian Choo v. Lee Kar Choo*, [1964] 1 MLJ 363, 364; *NM Rothschild & Sons (S) Pte Ltd v. Plaza Rakyat Sdn Bhd*, [1995] 2 SLR(R) 565, [8]–[10].
773. Supreme Court of Judicature Act (Cap. 322, R. 5, 2014 Rev. Ed.) Rules of Court, O 10 r 2(1). *See also Bank Central Asia v. Harry Rosenberg*, [1994] 3 SLR(R) 981, [24] and [26].
774. Supreme Court of Judicature Act (Cap. 322, R. 5, 2014 Rev. Ed.) Rules of Court, O 76 rr 1 and 14(1)–(2). *See also id.*, O 76 r 14(4).
775. Supreme Court of Judicature Act (Cap. 322, R. 5, 2014 Rev. Ed.) Rules of Court, O 77.
776. Societies Act (Cap. 311, 1985 Rev. Ed.), s 35(c).
777. Supreme Court of Judicature Act (Cap. 322, R. 5, 2014 Rev. Ed.) Rules of Court, O 62 r 4. *See also Summit Company (M) Sdn Bhd v. Nikko Products (M) Sdn Bhd*, [1985] 1 MLJ 68.
778. Companies Act (Cap. 50, 2006 Rev. Ed.), s 387. *See also Nanyang Law LLC v. Alphomega Research Group Ltd*, [2010] 3 SLR 914, [10].
779. Companies Act (Cap. 50, 2006 Rev. Ed.), s 376(a). *See* Companies Act (Cap. 50, 2006 Rev. Ed.), s 365 for definition of 'foreign company'. *See also Singapore Civil Procedure 2015 Volume 1*, at 1104 (G.P. Selvam ed., Sweet & Maxwell Asia 2014).

property;[780] where the proceedings are in rem;[781] and where the government is being sued.[782] Then there is substituted service – which is actually another exception to personal service – but warrants separate discussion below.

II. Substituted Service

259. Substituted service, which if properly effected is equivalent to actual service,[783] can be resorted to when 'it appears to the Court that it is impracticable for any reason to serve that document personally on that person, the Court may make an order in [the prescribed form] for substituted service of that document'.[784] The order for substituted service must be served with the writ and should also describe clearly the place where the document should be posted.[785] Specifically, the applicant must show to the court that he 'is in fact unable to effect personal service of the writ; and … the writ is likely to reach the defendant or come to his knowledge if the method of substituted which is asked for is adopted'.[786]

260. With respect to the first requirement, typical scenarios include when the whereabouts of the defendant being unknown, when the defendant is constantly travelling abroad, or when the defendant clearly trying to constantly evade personal service.[787] In this connection, the plaintiff must show, by way of affidavit, that two 'reasonable attempts at personal service' have been made.[788] As to what constitutes reasonable attempts at personal service, one helpful yardstick may be to ascertain if

780. Supreme Court of Judicature Act (Cap. 322, R. 5, 2014 Rev. Ed.) Rules of Court, O 10 r 4.
781. Supreme Court of Judicature Act (Cap. 322, R. 5, 2014 Rev. Ed.) Rules of Court, O 70 r 7.
782. Supreme Court of Judicature Act (Cap. 322, R. 5, 2014 Rev. Ed.) Rules of Court, O 73 r 3; Government Proceedings Act (Cap. 121, 1985 Rev. Ed.), s 19(2).
783. *Watt v. Barnett*, (1878) 3 QBD 363, 366.
784. Supreme Court of Judicature Act (Cap. 322, R. 5, 2014 Rev. Ed.) Rules of Court, O 62 r 5(1). *See also Consistel Pte Ltd v. Nasir Farooq*, [2009] 3 SLR(R) 665, [27], citing *Fry v. Moore*, (1889) 23 QBD 395, 397–398.
785. *Singapore Civil Procedure 2015 Volume 1*, at 1106 (G.P. Selvam ed., Sweet & Maxwell Asia 2014).
786. *Lim Quee Choo (suing as co-administratrix of the estate of Koh Jit Meng) v. David Rasif*, [2008] SGHC 36, [17], citing *Porter v. Freudenberg*, [1915] 1 KB 857, 888. Indeed, an order for substituted service (which is an *ex parte* order) may be set aside if the other party raises the necessary evidence and arguments to do so: *Lim Quee Choo (suing as co-administratrix of the estate of Koh Jit Meng) v. David Rasif*, [2008] SGHC 36, [17], citing *WEA Records Ltd v. Visions Channel 4 Ltd*, [1983] 1 WLR 721.
787. J. Pinsler, *Principles of Civil Procedure* 149 (Acad. Publg. 2013). A complication may arise, however, when a defendant is out of jurisdiction (thereby requiring service out of jurisdiction instead) but frequently keeps in contact with relatives and/or friends in jurisdiction. There is case law to suggest that this may actually present a real prospect that the defendant would be duly notified by substituted service: *Ng Swee Hong v. Singmarine Shipyard Pte Ltd*, [1991] 1 SLR(R) 980. C.f. *PT Garuda Indonesia v. Birgen Air*, [2001] SGHC 262, [107]–[113]; *Consistel Pte Ltd v. Nasir Farooq*, [2009] 3 SLR(R) 665, [30]–[45].
788. Supreme Court Practice Directions 2015, paragraph 33(2); State Courts Practice Directions, paragraph 11(2). *See also Singapore Civil Procedure 2013 Volume 1*, at 971 (G.P. Selvam ed., Sweet & Maxwell Asia 2012); Supreme Court of Judicature Act (Cap. 322, R. 5, 2014 Rev. Ed.) Rules of Court, O 62 rr 6A and 8.

there were methods of communication which were reasonably obvious and could have been used but which were not.[789] With respect to the second requirement, 'the court has the discretion to endorse any method of substituted service which is likely to be effective in bringing notice of the document to the person to be served'.[790] Typical methods proposed, and which may be used in any combination and in conjunction with posting a copy of the document on the notice board of the court that issued the originating process,[791] are: posting the document on the front door of the last known[792] residential address or business address of the defendant;[793] leaving the document with a person who is likely to come into contact with the defendant;[794] and placing advertisements in the appropriate newspapers based on the language(s) that the defendant would understand.[795]

261. In recent times, with the advent of technology, the allowance of substituted service via electronic means (such as email and various social media platforms) has already taken place in certain foreign jurisdictions.[796] Thus, it is now provided even in the Rules of Court that 'the steps which the Court may direct to be taken for substituted service of a document to be effected include the use of such electronic means (including electronic mail or Internet transmission) as the Court may specify'.[797] So far, however, there has only been one case that has granted an application for substituted service through social media – Facebook and an internet message board specifically (Skype and email were also used).[798] The court granted the application for the following reasons: first, the language of O 62 r 5 is wide enough (the term 'electronic means' in particular) to encompass service through such means; second, O 62 r 5 was conceived with a broad range of electronic means in mind; third, the proposed method of substituted service was effective in bringing the document to the notice of the person to be served; fourth, such substituted service is common in other common law jurisdictions; and finally, the Supreme Court itself had issued a consultation paper which concluded that substituted service through social media should be considered permissible.[799] The court also noted that the risk

---

789. *Singapore Civil Procedure 2015 Volume 1*, at 1106 (G.P. Selvam ed., Sweet & Maxwell Asia 2014), citing *Lim Quee Choo (suing as co-administratrix of the estate of Koh Jit Meng) v. David Rasif*, [2008] SGHC 36.
790. J. Pinsler, *Principles of Civil Procedure* 149 (Acad. Publg. 2013). *See also* Supreme Court of Judicature Act (Cap. 322, R. 5, 2014 Rev. Ed.) Rules of Court, O 62 r 5(3).
791. J. Pinsler, *Principles of Civil Procedure* 151 (Acad. Publg. 2013).
792. The plaintiff has to provide evidence that the defendant to be served is either the owner of or resident at the said property: Supreme Court Practice Directions 2013; State Courts Practice Directions.
793. Where there is more than one (confirmed) residential address to choose from, the plaintiff is free to elect the place: *TR Networks Ltd v. Elixir Health Holdings Pte Ltd*, [2005] SGHC 106, [28]. *See also Oversea-Chinese Banking Corp Ltd v. Frankel Motor Pte Ltd*, [2009] 3 SLR(R) 623, [10].
794. J. Pinsler, *Principles of Civil Procedure* 150 (Acad. Publg. 2013), citing *Bank of Whitehaven v. Thompson*, [1877] WN 45; *Montgomery, Jones & Co v. Liebenthal & Co*, [1898] 1 QB 487.
795. *Teo Ah Bin v. Tan Kheng Guan*, [1981] 2 MLJ 146.
796. *Singapore Civil Procedure 2015 Volume 1*, at 1108 (G.P. Selvam ed., Sweet & Maxwell Asia 2014).
797. Supreme Court of Judicature Act (Cap. 322, R. 5, 2014 Rev. Ed.) Rules of Court, O 62 r 5(4).
798. *Storey, David Ian Andrew v. Planet Arkadia Pte Ltd*, [2016] SGHCR 7.
799. *Storey, David Ian Andrew v. Planet Arkadia Pte Ltd*, [2016] SGHCR 7, [7]–[11].

of electronic means of substituted service being ineffective at bringing notice can be curtailed by a court imposing requirements such as ordering electronic service to be accompanied by either posting on the front door or AR registered post, proof that the electronic platform in question is used by the person to be served, and proof that such platform was recently used by the person to be served.[800]

262. It should be noted that where a defendant has left Singapore before a writ was issued against him, the plaintiff has to seek leave of court to serve the writ out of jurisdiction before resorting to substituted service, as substituted service can only be employed when personal service is impracticable.[801] However, there are two possible exceptions to this. First, where the defendant has left the country in anticipation that legal proceedings would be initiated against him and hence, is trying to evade service.[802] Second, where the defendant is constantly moving from country to country such that it is impossible to serve the writ personally on him.[803]

§3. Service Out of Singapore

I. Options for the Parties

263. If a defendant is not based in Singapore, the Singapore court may establish jurisdiction if 'the defendant is served with a writ of summons or any other originating process … outside Singapore in the circumstances authorised by and in the manner prescribed by Rules of Court'.[804] In other words, jurisdiction of the Singapore courts over foreign defendants is expressly conferred by statute and service in accordance with O 11 of the Rules of Court is a 'statutory condition precedent to the exercise of jurisdiction' under section 16(1)(a)(ii) of the Supreme Court of Judicature Act.[805] Consequently, the question of jurisdiction must be decided by the lex fori[806] and the plaintiff bears the burden of proof to establish that the method of service employed complies with O 11.[807]

---

800. *Storey, David Ian Andrew v. Planet Arkadia Pte Ltd*, [2016] SGHCR 7, [14].
801. *Consistel Pte Ltd v. Nasir Farooq*, [2009] 3 SLR(R) 665, [30]–[31]. *See also Storey, David Ian Andrew v. Planet Arkadia Pte Ltd*, [2016] SGHCR 7, [15].
802. *Consistel Pte Ltd v. Nasir Farooq*, [2009] 3 SLR(R) 665, [32] and [35], citing *In re Urquhart; Ex parte Urquhart*, [1890] 24 QBD 723.
803. *Consistel Pte Ltd v. Nasir Farooq*, [2009] 3 SLR(R) 665, [35] and [45], citing *Ng Swee Hong v. Singmarine Shipyard Pte Ltd*, [1991] 1 SLR(R) 980, [11].
804. Supreme Court of Judicature Act (Cap. 322, 2007 Rev. Ed.) s 16(1).
805. *Humpuss Sea Transport Pte Ltd (in compulsory liquidation) v. PT Humpuss Intermoda Transportasi TBK*, [2015] SGHC 144, [100].
806. *Humpuss Sea Transport Pte Ltd (in compulsory liquidation) v. PT Humpuss Intermoda Transportasi TBK*, [2015] SGHC 144, [101], citing *Pacific Assets Management Ltd v. Chen Lip Keong*, [2006] 1 SLR(R) 658, [14].
807. *Humpuss Sea Transport Pte Ltd (in compulsory liquidation) v. PT Humpuss Intermoda Transportasi TBK*, [2015] SGHC 144, [102], citing *Pacific Assets Management Ltd v. Chen Lip Keong*, [2006] 1 SLR(R) 658, [12]; *Reemtsma Cigarettenfabriken GmbH v. Hugo Boss AG*, [2003] 3 SLR(R) 469, [10].

264. Jurisdiction is not a monolithic concept[808] – there is a distinction between personal and subject-matter jurisdiction. The former refers to the question of whether a person is amenable to the jurisdiction of the court in the sense that he is or can be brought before the court. The latter, also known as 'substantive jurisdiction', refers to what a court is permitted to do in terms of regulating the conduct in another country of someone over whom it has personal jurisdiction.[809] The Court of Appeal has recently departed from the traditional common law position of conceiving jurisdiction as being monolithically rooted in presence, and recognized the notion of subject-matter jurisdiction.[810] The issues of personal and subject matter jurisdiction arose because the court, in deciding if personal jurisdiction should be exercised over the foreign officer, had to have regard to the anterior question of subject matter jurisdiction in relation to the enforcement of judgment debtor order on the foreign officer. Ultimately, the Court of Appeal held that O 11 r 8(1) did not allow a party to serve enforcement of judgment debtor orders out of jurisdiction without first obtaining leave.[811]

265. Related to the concept of jurisdiction, it is also important to distinguish between service of a writ, which is a command to the defendant from service of a notice of a writ which is simply a notification to the defendant that an action has been commenced against him.[812] The former is an exercise of judicial power of a state outside Singapore's territorial limits, while the latter is not.

266. O 11 r 1 of the Rules of Court establishes no less than nineteen grounds on when service of an originating process out of Singapore is permissible with the leave of the court,[813] all of which use some form of connecting factors to justify extraterritorial reach.[814] It may be said that these nineteen grounds can be roughly classified into five groups:[815] the defendant's connection to Singapore;[816] specific claims such as injunctions and remedies arising from contracts, restitution, and torts;[817] claims concerning property, estates, and trusts;[818] claims arising from or made pursuant to legislation;[819] and where an appropriate party is to be involved.[820]

---

808. *Burgundy Global Exploration Corp v. Transocean Offshore International*, [2014] 3 SLR 381, [79].
809. *Burgundy Global Exploration Corp v. Transocean Offshore International*, [2014] 3 SLR 381, [80]–[82], citing *Mackinnon v. Donaldson, Lufkin and Jenrette Securities Corporation*, [1986] Ch 482; *Masri v. Consolidated Contractors International (UK) Ltd (No 4)* [2010] 1 AC 90.
810. *Burgundy Global Exploration Corp v. Transocean Offshore International*, [2014] 3 SLR 381.
811. *Burgundy Global Exploration Corp v. Transocean Offshore International*, [2014] 3 SLR 381, [104]–[107].
812. *Humpuss Sea Transport Pte Ltd (in compulsory liquidation) v. PT Humpuss Intermoda Transportasi TBK*, [2015] SGHC 144, [2] and [45], citing S. Menon, *Effecting Service of Process Out of the Jurisdiction,* 2 Sing. Acad. L.J. 111 (1990).
813. *See Singapore Civil Procedure 2015 Volume 1*, at 92 (G.P. Selvam ed., Sweet & Maxwell Asia 2014).
814. J. Pinsler, *Principles of Civil Procedure* 160 (Acad. Publg. 2013). *See also id*., 160.
815. J. Pinsler, *Principles of Civil Procedure* 161–166 (Acad. Publg. 2013).
816. Supreme Court of Judicature Act (Cap. 322, R. 5, 2014 Rev. Ed.) Rules of Court, O 11 rr 1(a) (domicile, business, or property in Singapore); 1(p) (cause of action arises in Singapore); and 1(r) (defendant has submitted to jurisdiction of the court).
817. Supreme Court of Judicature Act (Cap. 322, R. 5, 2014 Rev. Ed.) Rules of Court, O 11 rr 1(b) (injunction to be carried out in Singapore); 1(e) (some significant aspect of a contract dispute

267. The application for leave to serve outside of Singapore is made ex parte.[821] The applicant has a heavy duty to make full and frank disclosure of material facts in its ex parte application for leave for service out of Singapore.[822] Specifically, the applicant is required to disclose all material facts that may potentially have an impact of the court's decision.[823] Such disclosure of facts must also be set out in the body of the affidavit, especially so for more important facts and if the background circumstances are more complicated.[824] Failure to make full and frank disclosure of material facts may result in the leave being set aside, even if the non-disclosure is innocent.[825] Thus, there must be a supporting affidavit using the prescribed form that sets out: the grounds of the application; the belief that there is a good cause of action; the place where the defendant is likely to be found; and whether it is necessary to extend the validity of the writ.[826] No leave will be granted, however, until it is 'made sufficiently clear to appear to the Court that the case is a proper one for service out of Singapore'.[827]

268. If leave is granted, the defendant has twenty-one days to enter an appearance unless the court otherwise orders or any written law provides.[828] The defendant can apply to set aside the service by invoking O 12 r 7(1) (dispute of jurisdiction) or to stay proceedings by invoking O 12 r 7(2) (dispute of proper forum).[829] If leave has not yet been granted for service of the originating process (to be served out of Singapore), leave is required for the service out of Singapore of

---

related to Singapore); 1(f) (some significant aspect of a tort dispute related to Singapore); and 1(o) (some aspect of a restitution dispute related to Singapore). *See also Karaha Bodas Co LLC v. Pertamina Energy Trading Ltd*, [2006] 1 SLR(R) 112, [35]–[44].

818. Supreme Court of Judicature Act (Cap. 322, R. 5, 2014 Rev. Ed.) Rules of Court, O 11 rr 1(g)–(l).
819. Supreme Court of Judicature Act (Cap. 322, R. 5, 2014 Rev. Ed.) Rules of Court, O 11 rr 1(m) (enforcement of construction awards); 1(n) (claims concerning corruption, drug trafficking, terrorism and serious offences); and 1(s) (claims concerning the construction, effect, or enforcement of any written law).
820. Supreme Court of Judicature Act (Cap. 322, R. 5, 2014 Rev. Ed.) Rules of Court, O 11 rr 1(c) (claims against a person duly served and a person out of Singapore is a necessary of proper party thereto) and 1(q) (claims concerning contributions or indemnities that are enforceable in Singapore). *See also* Supreme Court of Judicature Act (Cap. 322, R. 5, 2014 Rev. Ed.) Rules of Court, O 11 r 2(1)(d).
821. Supreme Court of Judicature Act (Cap. 322, R. 5, 2014 Rev. Ed.) Rules of Court, O 11 r 2(1). *See also Transniko Pte Ltd v. Communication Technology Sdn Bhd*, [1995] 3 SLR(R) 941, [11]–[12].
822. *Manharlal Trikamdas Mody v. Sumikin Bussan International (HK) Ltd*, [2014] 3 SLR 1161, [79].
823. *Manharlal Trikamdas Mody v. Sumikin Bussan International (HK) Ltd*, [2014] 3 SLR 1161, [91].
824. *Manharlal Trikamdas Mody v. Sumikin Bussan International (HK) Ltd*, [2014] 3 SLR 1161, [90].
825. *Lazard Brothers and Company v. Midland Bank, Limited*, [1933] AC 289, 306–307.
826. Supreme Court of Judicature Act (Cap. 322, R. 5, 2014 Rev. Ed.) Rules of Court, O 11 r 2(1). *See also Bradley Lomas Electrolok Ltd v. Colt Ventilation East Asia Pte Ltd*, [1999] 3 SLR(R) 1156, [16], citing *Seaconsar Far East Ltd v. Bank Markazi Jomhouri Islami Iran*, [1994] 1 AC 438, 454; *Lee Hsien Loong v. Review Publishing Co Ltd*, [2007] 2 SLR(R) 453, [25]–[29].
827. Supreme Court of Judicature Act (Cap. 322, R. 5, 2014 Rev. Ed.) Rules of Court, O 11 r 2(2). *See also* C. Bull & J. Pinsler, *Civil Procedure: Annual Review of Singapore Cases* [6.20] (Sing. Acad. L. 2003); *Siemens AG v. Holdrich Investment Ltd*, [2010] 3 SLR 1007, [4] and [8].
828. Supreme Court of Judicature Act (Cap. 322, R. 5, 2014 Rev. Ed.) Rules of Court, O 11 r 2(3).
829. *NM Rothschild & Sons (S) Pte Ltd v. Plaza Rakyat Sdn Bhd*, [1995] 2 SLR(R) 565, [10]. *See also Civelli, Carlo Giuseppe v. Mulacek, Philippe Emanuel*, [2019] SGHC 182.

any summons, notice, or order issued given or made in any proceedings.[830] In addition, the rules on the various modes of service apply to the service of such documents too.[831]

269. Since the plaintiffs always bear the burden of proving that the service has been validly effected, the plaintiffs must establish the following:

a. First, they have to identify exactly which method of service they are relying on … If they had effected service by a method specifically provided for by that jurisdiction for foreign process (r 3(3)) or by that jurisdiction for the service of domestic process (r 4(2)(c)), they will necessarily have to lead evidence on the content of the supporting foreign law.
b. Second, they have to prove that service had been validly effected via the identified method. For example, if they had effected substituted service, they must demonstrate compliance with the terms of the order granting leave for substituted service. In order to prove that service had been validly effected, the plaintiffs must tender either a memorandum of service under O 10 r 1(4) or an official certificate under O 11 r 3(4), as the case may be. Whatever the method of service employed, it cannot be in contravention of the law of the foreign jurisdiction in question (r 3(2)).
c. Third, if the service were proven to be invalid, they have to show that the non-compliance with the Rules can and should be cured under O 2 r (1). Sufficient evidence must be placed before the court to justify the exercise of its discretion to cure the defect in service.[832]

270. Defendants who want to challenge the validity of service may go through three principal routes:

a. First, they can demonstrate that service had not, despite the attempt, been effected. For example, in the case of personal service, they may show that the attempt at service had not been successful in giving the defendant notice of the claim … In the case of substituted service, the defendants may show that service had been effected in a manner not provided for in the order granting leave.
b. Second, they can demonstrate that the method of service employed was not one that is provided for under the law of the foreign jurisdiction. This only applies to service purportedly carried out under rr 3(3) or 4(2)(c) …
c. Third, the defendants can demonstrate that service was contrary to the law of the jurisdiction in question, thus violating r 3(2).

830. Supreme Court of Judicature Act (Cap. 322, R. 5, 2014 Rev. Ed.) Rules of Court, O 11 r 8(1).
831. Supreme Court of Judicature Act (Cap. 322, R. 5, 2014 Rev. Ed.) Rules of Court, O 11 r 8(3).
832. *Humpuss Sea Transport Pte Ltd (in compulsory liquidation) v. PT Humpuss Intermoda Transportasi TBK*, [2015] SGHC 144, [109].

d. Finally, in response to the plaintiff's attempt to cure an invalid service, the defendants can show that the invalid service is one which is either not curable under O 2 r (1) of the Rules or that, even if curable, the court's discretion should not be exercised.[833]

271. Where the (Singapore) court is asked to cure the irregularity in service out of jurisdiction,[834] two particular factors are relevant: 'If the defendant was in fact apprised of and took steps to contest the proceedings, he would have suffered no prejudice. Another factor which was considered is whether the plaintiff had properly done all that he could to effect service.'[835] The rationale for this is that O 11 r 4(2) is not designed as a technical obstacle but as a rule to protect foreign parties from orders against their knowledge.[836] The High Court recently held that the court will not exercise its discretion to cure irregularity in service out of jurisdiction in cases held to be invalid because the attempted service was unsuccessful in bringing notice of the claim to the defendant[837] and also in cases where service was held to be invalid because the method of service employed (though successful in bringing notice) was contrary to the law of the foreign jurisdiction.[838] However, a plaintiff may rely on a cause of action and/or a O 11 head of jurisdiction in an inter partes application by the defendant to set aside service, even if the cause of action or O 11 head of jurisdiction was not relied upon in the initial ex parte application for service.[839]

II. Different Process Servers for Different Jurisdictions

272. If the defendant is in Malaysia or Brunei (which are two neighbouring states of Singapore with common historical and legal foundations), the originating process must be served through its government or Singapore consular authority in that country, or by a method of service authorized by the law of that country, or

833. *Humpuss Sea Transport Pte Ltd (in compulsory liquidation) v. PT Humpuss Intermoda Transportasi TBK*, [2015] SGHC 144, [110].
834. *Humpuss Sea Transport Pte Ltd (in compulsory liquidation) v. PT Humpuss Intermoda Transportasi TBK*, [2015] SGHC 144, [81]: Court will exercise its discretion to cure the irregularity pursuant to O 2 r 1.
835. *Omae Capital Management Pte Ltd v. Tetsuya Motomura*, [2015] SGHCR 8, [16] and *SRS Commerce Ltd v. YujiImabeppu*, [2015] 1 SLR 1, [9], citing *ITC Global Holdings Pte Ltd (in liquidation) v. ITC Ltd*, [2011] SGHC 150, [49]. *See also Humpuss Sea Transport Pte Ltd (in compulsory liquidation) v. PT Humpuss Intermoda Transportasi TBK*, [2015] SGHC 144, [92].
836. *SRS Commerce Ltd v. YujiImabeppu*, [2015] 1 SLR 1, [9], citing *ITC Global Holdings Pte Ltd (in liquidation) v. ITC Ltd*, [2011] SGHC 150, [49].
837. *Humpuss Sea Transport Pte Ltd (in compulsory liquidation) v. PT Humpuss Intermoda Transportasi TBK*, [2015] SGHC 144, [78]–[84].
838. *Humpuss Sea Transport Pte Ltd (in compulsory liquidation) v. PT Humpuss Intermoda Transportasi TBK*, [2015] SGHC 144, [85]–[91].
839. *William Jacks & Co (Singapore) Pte Ltd v. Nelson Honey & Marketing (NZ) Ltd* [2015] SGHCR 21, [19].

through its judicial authority.[840] The most commonly used method, however, is to serve through a law practice in that country.[841] The High Court has recently clarified that provisions on service via official channels listed in O 11 rr 4(1) and 4(2) are not intended to be mandatory.[842]

273. If the defendant is in a country where a civil procedure convention – that is, 'any convention, treaty or agreement of any description or any provision thereof between different States relating to civil procedure in the court'[843]– applies, the originating process may be served through the judicial authorities of that country or through a Singapore consular authority in that country.[844] If the defendant is in a country where a civil procedure convention does not apply, the originating process must be served through the government of that country,[845] or through a Singapore consular authority in that country (unless such service is contrary to the law of that country),[846] or by a method of service authorized by the law of that country.[847] The High Court has recently clarified that the interpretation of O 11 r 4(2)(c) should refer to the law of the foreign jurisdiction with respect to the service of domestic process, not its foreign process.[848] Finally, it should be noted that if the plaintiff intends to use substituted service instead of personal service, he must ensure that such service: would in all reasonable probability notify the defendant of the action;[849] is legal in the foreign jurisdiction in question;[850] and is not sought as an abuse.[851]

---

840. Supreme Court of Judicature Act (Cap. 322, R. 5, 2014 Rev. Ed.) Rules of Court, O 11 rr 3(8) and 4(2).
841. J. Pinsler, *Principles of Civil Procedure* 179 (Acad. Publg. 2013). *See also United Overseas Bank Ltd v. Wong Hai Hong*, [1999] 1 MLJ 474, which rendered invalid the service of a Singapore writ by a private agent in Malaysia; *Fortune Hong Kong Trading Ltd v. Cosco Feoso (Singapore) Pte Ltd*, [2000] 1 SLR(R) 962, [34]–[37]. C.f. *Malayan Banking Berhad v. Ng Man Heng*, [2005] 1 MLJ 470.
842. *Humpuss Sea Transport Pte Ltd (in compulsory liquidation) v. PT Humpuss Intermoda Transportasi TBK*, [2015] SGHC 144, [42]. C.f. *Ong & Co Pte Ltd v. Chow YL Carl*, [1987] SLR(R) 281.
843. Supreme Court of Judicature Act (Cap. 322, R. 5, 2014 Rev. Ed.) Rules of Court, O 1 r 4.
844. Supreme Court of Judicature Act (Cap. 322, R. 5, 2014 Rev. Ed.) Rules of Court, O 11 r 4(1).
845. Supreme Court of Judicature Act (Cap. 322, R. 5, 2014 Rev. Ed.) Rules of Court, O 11 r 4(2)(a).
846. Supreme Court of Judicature Act (Cap. 322, R. 5, 2014 Rev. Ed.) Rules of Court, O 11 r 4(2)(b). *See also* J. Pinsler, *Principles of Civil Procedure* 182–187 (Acad. Publg. 2013).
847. Supreme Court of Judicature Act (Cap. 322, R. 5, 2014 Rev. Ed.) Rules of Court, O 11 r 4(2)(c).
848. *Humpuss Sea Transport Pte Ltd (in compulsory liquidation) v. PT Humpuss Intermoda Transportasi TBK*, [2015] SGHC 144, [38], citing B. Tan, *Curing Non-Compliance with Foreign Laws in the Context of Service out of Jurisdiction*, 27 Sing. Acad. L.J. 91, 98–99 (2015). C.f. *SRS Commerce Ltd v. Yujilmabeppu*, [2015] 1 SLR 1.
849. J. Pinsler, *Principles of Civil Procedure* 188 (Acad. Publg. 2013), citing *Porter v. Freudenberg*, [1915] 1 KB 857, 889. *See also Aw Chen v. Johannes Koplan*, [1969] 2 MLJ 190, 191.
850. Supreme Court of Judicature Act (Cap. 322, R. 5, 2014 Rev. Ed.) Rules of Court, O 11 rr 3(2) and 3(3).
851. J. Pinsler, *Principles of Civil Procedure* 188 (Acad. Publg. 2013).

§4. Possibility of Appeal

274. Section 34 of the Supreme Court of Judicature Act,[852] read together with the Fourth and Fifth Schedules of the statute, determines whether any given order of civil procedure is appealable to the Court of Appeal[853] or not.[854] However, applications relating to service are not explicitly covered by either the Fourth (orders made by a judge that are non-appealable) or Fifth (orders made by a judge that are only appealable with leave) Schedules. Accordingly, it would seem that an appeal against a decision that say, substituted service is either as of right or requires leave from the court, since the Fourth Schedule does not declare it to be non-appealable and the Fifth Schedule does not require leave to be sought.

275. Due to recent amendments to the Supreme Court of Judicature Act, the law on this is currently in flux and while it has been suggested that the 'default' position is that all interlocutory applications, unless provided for statutorily, are appealable with leave,[855] it may also be possible to argue that for interlocutory applications not expressly addressed by the Fourth and Fifth Schedules, 'an appeal to the Court of Appeal will remain as of right for orders made at interlocutory applications which will finally dispose of the substantive rights of the parties'.[856]

852. (Cap. 322, 2007 Rev. Ed.).

853. The Court of Appeal is the apex court in Singapore. Below it is the High Court, followed by the District and Magistrates' Courts. For appeals arising from the lower courts, *see* Supreme Court of Judicature Act (Cap. 322, R. 5, 2014 Rev. Ed.) Rules of Court, O 55B, 55C, and 55D. It should be noted that generally, for interlocutory applications, there is a right of appeal from first instance. Thus, there is a right of appeal from a registrar in chambers to a judge in chambers (District Judge if it is the State Courts), but not necessarily after that stage.

854. The statute was amended in 2010 and 2014.

855. *See* E. Chua, *Defining an 'Interlocutory Application* Sing. L. Watch Commentaries (4/2013); D. Chi, *Clarification on Leave to Appeal Regime in Respect of Interlocutory Matters: OpenNet Pte Ltd v. Info-Communications Development Authority of Singapore* [2013] 2 SLR 880, Sing. L. Watch Commentaries (4/2013); C. Siyuan & E. Chua, *The Right to Appeal Against a Decision Made on an Interlocutory Application: The Immediate Aftermath of the 2010 Amendments*, 25 Sing. Acad. L.J. 424 (2013).

856. *OpenNet Pte Ltd v. Info-Communications Development Authority of Singapore*, [2013] 2 SLR 880, [29]. *See also Dorsey James Michael v. World Sport Group Pte Ltd*, [2013] 3 SLR 354, [98]. On the other hand, where the statute has made it clear that there is no appeal as of right, one is precluded from arguing that substantive rights have been engaged: *Kosui Singapore Pte Ltd v. Thangavelu*, [2016] 2 SLR 105, [28]–[29].

Chapter 5. Appearance

§1. Introduction

276. Appearance is the process by which a defendant shows his intention to defend the suit brought against him and submits himself to the jurisdiction of the court.[857] Until an appearance is properly entered, the defendant 'is generally not entitled to take any step in the action or proceedings'.[858] The rules and procedures for appearance are primarily found in O 12 of the Rules of Court,[859] which are essentially based on the old English rules on this order.[860]

§2. Procedural Aspects

277. A 'defendant to an action begun by writ[861] may … enter an appearance in the action and defend it by a solicitor or in person'.[862] This is done via a memorandum of appearance, which is 'a request to the Registry to enter an appearance for the defendant or defendants specified in the memorandum'.[863] There is a prescribed form for a memorandum of appearance.[864] If the defendant is appearing in person,[865] he must sign the memorandum and a copy of it,[866] and also specify his residential address in them[867] before handing them in at the Registry for the appearance to be entered properly.[868] If the defendant has no place of residence, then he should state the address of a place within the jurisdiction (Singapore) where documents for him may be sent.[869]

857. *Singapore Civil Procedure 2015 Volume 1*, at 116 (G.P. Selvam ed., Sweet & Maxwell Asia 2014).
858. *Singapore Civil Procedure 2015 Volume 1*, at 116 (G.P. Selvam ed., Sweet & Maxwell Asia 2014). A 'step in the proceedings' is explained later in this chapter.
859. Supreme Court of Judicature Act (Cap. 322, R. 5, 2014 Rev. Ed.) Rules of Court. Examples of other rules which concern appearance are O 15 (counterclaims), O 16 (third parties), O 20 (amendments), O 21 (withdrawals), O 70 (admiralty actions), and O 77 (partnerships).
860. *Singapore Civil Procedure 2015 Volume 1*, at 115–126 (G.P. Selvam ed., Sweet & Maxwell Asia 2014).
861. No appearance need be entered for originating summonses: Supreme Court of Judicature Act (Cap. 322, R. 5, 2014 Rev. Ed.) Rules of Court, O 12 r 9. *See* Chapter on originating process for further details on originating summonses.
862. Supreme Court of Judicature Act (Cap. 322, R. 5, 2014 Rev. Ed.) Rules of Court, O 12 r 1(1). *See also id.*, O 12 r 1(4). A lawyer who enters an appearance for a defendant must have authority to do so (that is, possess a warrant to act): *Tung Hui Mannequin Industries v. Tenet Insurance Co Ltd*, [2005] 3 SLR(R) 184, [40]–[41]. Otherwise, the defendant has a right to vacate the appearance (*Newland Enterprises Pte Ltd v. Owners of Santa Arona*, [1988] 2 MLJ 246) or the plaintiff may strike out the appearance (*Tan Lian Hong v. Min Ngai Knitting Factory (M) Ltd*, [1974] 1 MLJ 76).
863. Supreme Court of Judicature Act (Cap. 322, R. 5, 2014 Rev. Ed.) Rules of Court, O 12 r 2(1).
864. Supreme Court of Judicature Act (Cap. 322, R. 5, 2014 Rev. Ed.) Rules of Court, O 12 r 2(2).
865. An appearance in person cannot be entered if the defendant is a corporation or if he is a person under disability: Supreme Court of Judicature Act (Cap. 322, R. 5, 2014 Rev. Ed.) Rules of Court, O 12 r 1(2) and O 76 r 2(1).
866. Supreme Court of Judicature Act (Cap. 322, R. 5, 2014 Rev. Ed.) Rules of Court, O 12 r 2(2).
867. Supreme Court of Judicature Act (Cap. 322, R. 5, 2014 Rev. Ed.) Rules of Court, O 12 r 2(3).
868. Supreme Court of Judicature Act (Cap. 322, R. 5, 2014 Rev. Ed.) Rules of Court, O 12 r 1(3).
869. Supreme Court of Judicature Act (Cap. 322, R. 5, 2014 Rev. Ed.) Rules of Court, O 12 r 2(3).

278. If the defendant is represented by a solicitor,[870] his solicitor must sign the memorandum and a copy of it,[871] and also specify his business address in them[872] before handing them in at the Registry for the appearance to be entered properly.[873] Unless there has been an application to extend time, if the writ was served within the jurisdiction, the defendant has eight days after service of the writ to enter an appearance.[874] If, however, the writ was served out of the jurisdiction, the defendant has twenty-one days to enter an appearance.[875] Once the memorandum of appearance and a copy of it are received, 'an officer of the Registry must in all cases affix to the copy of the memorandum of appearance an official stamp showing the date on which he received those documents and hand back that copy of the memorandum'.[876]

§3. Substantive Aspects

279. If a defendant duly enters an appearance, one of the main legal effects is that the plaintiff is precluded from entering judgment in default of appearance under O 13. Another main legal effect is that the defendant is now entitled to issue a third-party notice.[877] If a defendant does not state the correct address (his residence, the office of his solicitor, or a place within jurisdiction as the case may be) in the memorandum of appearance,[878] 'the Court may on application by the plaintiff set aside the appearance or order the defendant to give an address'.[879] If a defendant does not enter an appearance in time, judgment in default of appearance may be awarded against him,[880] though he can subsequently apply to try to set aside such a judgment[881] (but even if he succeeds there may be costs implications for him if there was unjustified protraction of the proceedings). Furthermore, if judgment has been entered, the defendant may not enter an appearance except with the leave of the court,[882] and such an application cannot be ex parte either.[883] If judgment has not

870. *See also Tan Lian Hong v. Min Ngai Knitting Factory (M) Ltd*, [1974] 1 MLJ 76.
871. Supreme Court of Judicature Act (Cap. 322, R. 5, 2014 Rev. Ed.) Rules of Court, O 12 r 2(2).
872. Supreme Court of Judicature Act (Cap. 322, R. 5, 2014 Rev. Ed.) Rules of Court, O 12 r 2(3).
873. Supreme Court of Judicature Act (Cap. 322, R. 5, 2014 Rev. Ed.) Rules of Court, O 12 r 1(3).
874. Supreme Court of Judicature Act (Cap. 322, R. 5, 2014 Rev. Ed.) Rules of Court, O 12 r 4.
875. Supreme Court of Judicature Act (Cap. 322, R. 5, 2014 Rev. Ed.) Rules of Court, O 12 r 4.
876. Supreme Court of Judicature Act (Cap. 322, R. 5, 2014 Rev. Ed.) Rules of Court, O 12 r 3(1).
877. Supreme Court of Judicature Act (Cap. 322, R. 5, 2014 Rev. Ed.) Rules of Court, O 16 r 1.
878. The defendant may amend the memorandum of appearance, but leave of court is required: Supreme Court of Judicature Act (Cap. 322, R. 5, 2014 Rev. Ed.) Rules of Court, O 20 r 2. Such an amendment is also likely to entail some costs.
879. Supreme Court of Judicature Act (Cap. 322, R. 5, 2014 Rev. Ed.) Rules of Court, O 12 r 2(4). *See also id.*, O 10 r 1(3).
880. This is so even if the plaintiff has served the writ but not the statement of claim: *Singapore Civil Procedure 2015 Volume 1*, at 297 (G.P. Selvam ed., Sweet & Maxwell Asia 2014).
881. Supreme Court of Judicature Act (Cap. 322, R. 5, 2014 Rev. Ed.) Rules of Court, O 13. *See also Singapore Telecommunications Ltd v. APM Infotech Pte Ltd*, [2011] SGHC 147, [20]–[21].
882. Supreme Court of Judicature Act (Cap. 322, R. 5, 2014 Rev. Ed.) Rules of Court, O 12 r 5(1).
883. *Singapore Civil Procedure 2015 Volume 1*, at 123 (G.P. Selvam ed., Sweet & Maxwell Asia 2014), citing *Stern v. Friedman*, [1953] 1 WLR 969.

been entered but the time limited for appearing is over, the defendant still has to comply with the timeframes set out in the Rules of Court as if he had entered an appearance in time.[884]

280. An exception to the requirement for entering an appearance is where the claim 'made by the plaintiff is for a debt or liquidated demand only, with a statement of the amount claimed in respect of the debt or demand and for costs and also with a statement that further proceedings will be stayed if, within the time limited for appearing, the defendant pays the amount so claimed'.[885] In such a situation, the need to enter an appearance is, by operation, obviated. Separately, it should be noted that an appearance by a defendant 'shall not be treated as a waiver by him of any irregularity in the writ or service thereof or in any order giving leave to serve the writ out of the jurisdiction or extending the validity of the writ for the purpose of service'.[886]

281. In other words, the defendant can still resist the action against him, and this may be done in various ways. First, the defendant may choose to defend the claim and therefore file and serve his defence on the plaintiff 'before the expiration of 14 days after the time limited for appearing or after the statement of claim is served on him, whichever is the later'.[887] Second, the defendant may within the time limited for serving a defence contest that the court has no jurisdiction to hear the dispute because of some legal impediment or irregularity, and seek the appropriate relief.[888] The burden of proof is on the defendant to establish any such impediment or irregularity.[889] It should be noted, however, that while entering an appearance would not prejudice the defendant's position in relation to contesting jurisdiction, the defendant should not undertake any act that involves the merits of the claim (such as filing a defence), as that would contradict his own argument that the court has no jurisdiction.[890] At the same time, the plaintiff should not be applying for judgment

884. Supreme Court of Judicature Act (Cap. 322, R. 5, 2014 Rev. Ed.) Rules of Court, O 12 r 5(2).

885. Supreme Court of Judicature Act (Cap. 322, R. 5, 2014 Rev. Ed.) Rules of Court, O 6 r 2(1).

886. Supreme Court of Judicature Act (Cap. 322, R. 5, 2014 Rev. Ed.) Rules of Court, O 12 r 6. C.f. *id.*, O 12 r 8(1).

887. Supreme Court of Judicature Act (Cap. 322, R. 5, 2014 Rev. Ed.) Rules of Court, O 18 r 2(1).

888. Supreme Court of Judicature Act (Cap. 322, R. 5, 2014 Rev. Ed.) Rules of Court, O 12 r 7(1). Possible relief include: an order setting aside the writ or service of the writ; an order declaring that the writ was not duly served; the discharge of any order giving leave to serve the writ on him out of jurisdiction; the discharge of any order extending the validity of the writ; the protection or release of any property of the defendant seized or threatened with seizure in the proceedings; the discharge of any order made to prevent any dealing with any property of the defendant; a declaration that the court has no jurisdiction over the defendant in respect of the subject matter or relief sought of the claim. *See also id.*, O 12 r 7(6).

889. J. Pinsler, *Principles of Civil Procedure* 201 (Acad. Publg. 2013). The only exception is he relies on the limb that the method of service is irregular: *Lee Hsien Loong v. Review Publishing Co Ltd*, [2007] 2 SLR(R) 453, [19]–[21]. C.f. *Pacific Assets Management Ltd v. Chen Lip Keong*, [2006] 1 SLR(R) 658, [12].

890. *Chan Chin Cheung v. Chan Fatt Cheung*, [2010] 1 SLR 1192, [22]. C.f. *Wing Hak Man v. Bio-Treat Technology Ltd*, [2009] 1 SLR(R) 446, [59]–[65].

in default of defence or summary judgment either.[891] Third, the defendant may within the time limited for serving a defence contest that while the court has jurisdiction, Singapore is not the proper forum for the dispute and therefore ask that a stay of proceedings to be ordered.[892]

282. The test for proper forum is whether the jurisdiction in question has 'the most real and substantial connection with the dispute'.[893] Because the defendant is not disputing that the court has jurisdiction, it is possible that he may still take a step in the proceedings and apply for a stay of proceedings without self-contradicting his position or waiving his right to challenge the forum.[894] In this regard, it should also be noted that if there is an arbitration agreement involved, the International Arbitration Act[895] or Arbitration Act[896] may apply, depending on the nature of the dispute. Specifically, section 6(1) of both Acts provide that if a party to such an agreement commences court proceedings, the other party may apply to stay the proceedings after he has entered an appearance, but before delivering any

891. *Singapore Civil Procedure 2015 Volume 1*, at 124–125 (G.P. Selvam ed., Sweet & Maxwell Asia 2014).
892. Supreme Court of Judicature Act (Cap. 322, R. 5, 2014 Rev. Ed.) Rules of Court, O 12 r 7(2).
893. *Sun Jin Engineering Pte Ltd v. Hwang Jae Woo*, [2011] 2 SLR 196, [47], citing *Spiliada Maritime v. Cansulex Ltd*, [1987] 1 AC 460. There are two stages to this test (*JIO Minerals FZC v. Mineral Enterprises Ltd*, [2011] 1 SLR 391, [41] and [43], citing Yeo T.M., *Halsbury's Laws of Singapore*, vol. 6(2) (Singapore: LexisNexis, 2009), [75.090] and [75.096]): 'General connecting factors are considered at [the first] stage. These include the locations of the parties, relevant witnesses, facts, and evidence, and the applicable law to the issues in dispute. As the search is for the forum that is *prima facie* clearly more appropriate to try the case, it is important to *see* what the case is about, and connections which have no or little bearing on adjudication of the issues in dispute between the parties will carry little weight. While there is a natural emphasis on the minimisation of expense and inconvenience of trial at this stage, it should be borne in mind that the true test is appropriateness. … In Stage Two, the court is primarily concerned with the question whether there are circumstances by reason of justice why it should exercise its jurisdiction even if it is not the prima facie natural forum. The ultimate question of where the case should be heard for the interests of the parties and the ends of justice must not be lost sight of. This part of the test requires all circumstances to be taken into consideration, including factors already taken into consideration in Stage One. The main consideration in Stage Two is whether substantial justice can be obtained in the foreign *prima facie* natural forum. The court of the forum needs to tread a fine balance between justice to the parties and international comity. In considering this question, the court will not pass judgment on the competence or independence of the judiciary of another country, all the more so of a friendly foreign country, and will assiduously avoid comparing the quality of justice obtainable under its own legal system and the foreign legal system. It is not true that the quality of foreign judiciary will never be questioned, but the court of the forum will take a very cautious approach. The mere fact that the plaintiff has a legitimate or juridical advantage in proceedings in Singapore will not be decisive. The plaintiff must establish with cogent evidence that he will be denied substantial justice if the case is not heard in the forum.'

   This two-staged test is 'essentially a factors-based test; the weight to be placed on the various factors varies with the specific factual matrix of the case': *AZS v. AZR*, [2013] 3 SLR 700, [12], citing *BDA v. BDB*, [2013] 1 SLR 607, [24].
894. *Chan Chin Cheung v. Chan Fatt Cheung*, [2010] 1 SLR 1192, [22]. C.f. *International SOS Pte Ltd v. Overton Mark Harold George*, [2001] 2 SLR(R) 777, [6]; C. Bull & J. Pinsler, *Civil Procedure: Annual Review of Singapore Cases* [6.80]–[6.81] (Sing. Acad. L. 2001).
895. (Cap. 143A, 2002 Rev. Ed.).
896. (Cap. 10, 2002 Rev. Ed.).

pleading or taking any other step in the proceedings.[897] This means the party seeking to rely on the arbitration agreement should avoid affirming the correctness of the proceedings and his willingness to go along with a determination by the courts instead of the arbitration tribunal.[898] Ostensibly, an application by that latter party to strike out the action on the basis that it is unmeritorious will be regarded as an act that signifies a submission to the Court's jurisdiction.[899] The Court may even, in exceptional circumstances, find a co-defendant in the action to have taken a step in proceedings by reason of a striking out application filed by another defendant.[900]

283. For the two preceding applications (contesting jurisdiction and forum), they must each be made by summons supported with affidavit,[901] and exhibits if any.[902] The summons should state the grounds on which the application is made.[903] In addition, for the hearing of either of these two applications, 'the Court may make such order as it thinks fit and may give such directions for its disposal as may be appropriate, including directions for the trial thereof as a preliminary issue'.[904] The court also has the general power to extend time even though neither application expressly provides for an extension of time (but merely sets out the timeframes for the applications to be made).[905] Factors that would be considered include the length of the delay; the reasons for the delay; the extent, if any, of the prejudice that will be suffered by the plaintiff; the merits of the application for a stay; and any other factor that should be considered to ensure justice.[906] Costs may be awarded accordingly against any party which has been particularly blameworthy in causing any undue delay.

§4. Possibility of Appeal

284. Section 34 of the Supreme Court of Judicature Act,[907] read together with the Fourth and Fifth Schedules of the statute, determines whether any given order

897. *See also Carona Holdings Pte Ltd v. Go Go Delicacy Pte Ltd*, [2008] 4 SLR(R) 460, [93].
898. *Star-Trans Far East Pte Ltd v. Norske-Tech Ltd*, [1995] 2 SLR(R) 720, [24].
899. *L Capital Jones Ltd and another v. Maniach Pte Ltd* [2017] SGCA 3, [78]. The Court further noted at [83] that the fact that a striking out application is withdrawn prior to or was not pursued at the hearing does not negate submission to the Court's jurisdiction.
900. *See L Capital Jones Ltd and another v. Maniach Pte Ltd* [2017] SGCA 3, [86]–[91].
901. Supreme Court of Judicature Act (Cap. 322, R. 5, 2014 Rev. Ed.) Rules of Court, O 12 r 7(3).
902. *Singapore Civil Procedure 2015 Volume 1*, at 125 (G.P. Selvam ed., Sweet & Maxwell Asia 2014).
903. J. Pinsler, *Principles of Civil Procedure* 200 (Acad. Publg. 2013), citing *Carmel Exporters (Sales) Ltd v. Sea-Land Services Inc*, [1981] 1 WLR 1068, 1074.
904. Supreme Court of Judicature Act (Cap. 322, R. 5, 2014 Rev. Ed.) Rules of Court, O 12 r 7(4). *See also Williams & Glyn's Bank plc v. Astro Dinamico Compania Naviera SA*, [1984] 1 WLR 438, 442.
905. Supreme Court of Judicature Act (Cap. 322, R. 5, 2014 Rev. Ed.) Rules of Court, O 3 r 4(1).*See also Carona Holdings Pte Ltd v. Go Go Delicacy Pte Ltd*, [2008] 4 SLR(R) 460, [38].
906. J. Pinsler, *Principles of Civil Procedure* 211–212 (Acad. Publg. 2013), citing *Sun Jin Engineering Pte Ltd v. Hwang Jae Woo*, [2011] 2 SLR 196, [31]–[42]. C.f. *Sun Jin Engineering Pte Ltd v. Hwang Jae Woo*, [2010] 3 SLR 684, [11]–[19]. *See also The 'Tokai Maru'*, [1998] 2 SLR(R) 646, [16]–[23].
907. (Cap. 322, 2007 Rev. Ed.).

of civil procedure is appealable to the Court of Appeal[908] or not.[909] However, applications relating to appearance do not feature in either the Fourth (orders made by a judge that are non-appealable) or Fifth (orders made by a judge that are only appealable with leave) Schedules. Of course, this can be explained by the fact that first, there is no conceivable basis to appeal against a party entering an appearance, as no decision by the court is actually rendered in specific respect of a party properly entering an appearance, nor is it plausible that a party will be prevented either by the court or by the other party from entering an appearance. Second, the only point in which an appeal might arise is when a defendant fails to enter an appearance, and default judgment is entered against him. Default judgment and setting aside, including the possibility of appeal for those applications, however, will be addressed in greater detail under the Part of early termination of proceedings.

---

908. The Court of Appeal is the apex court in Singapore. Below it is the High Court, followed by the District and Magistrates' Courts. For appeals arising from the lower courts, *see* Supreme Court of Judicature Act (Cap. 322, R. 5, 2014 Rev. Ed.) Rules of Court, O 55B, 55C, and 55D. It should be noted that generally, for interlocutory applications, there is a right of appeal from first instance. Thus, there is a right of appeal from a registrar in chambers to a judge in chambers (District Judge if it is the State Courts), but not necessarily after that stage.

909. The statute was amended in 2010 and 2014.

Chapter 6. Claims and Defences

§1. Introduction

285. Pleadings are of paramount importance as a poorly pleaded case may make the difference between victory and defeat for a litigant. Pleadings are also instrumental in determining the occurrence of the burden of proof because the pleadings state the material facts establishing the legal elements of a claim or defence.[910] Pleadings serve to uphold the rules of natural justice by preventing a trial by ambush.[911] Pleadings can be:

> broadly described as the parties' respective statements of primary or material facts on which they rely … They provide the framework of civil litigation by isolating the issues in dispute and thereby determine the scope of the adjudication and the evidence to be presented at trial … [They] are the record of the matters to be decided by the court and, subject to any amendments which may be permitted, will generally bind the parties in the interest of certainty and due process.[912]

286. Indeed, well-drafted pleadings will:

> ensure that the plaintiffs have a legally sustainable claim and thereby eliminate frivolous and baseless actions; and … inform the opponent in advance of the case he has to meet when the case comes on for trial so that justice can be done

---

910. *SCT Technologies Pte Ltd v. Western Copper Co Ltd*, [2015] SGHC 135, [13], citing *Cooperatieve Centrale Raiffeisen-Boerenleenbank BA (trading as Rabobank International), Singapore Branch v. Motorola Electronics Pte Ltd*, [2011] 2 SLR 63, [31].

911. *Sheagar s/o TM Veloo v. Belfield International (Hong Kong) Ltd*, [2014] 3 SLR 524, [90]; *V Nithia (co-administrix of the estate of Ponnusamy Sivapakiam, deceased) v. Buthmanaban s/o Vaithilingam*, [2015] 5 SLR 1422, [37]; *Royal Melbourne Institute of Technology v. Stansfield College Pte Ltd* [2018] SGHC 232 at [123]. *See also SIC College of Business and Technology Pte Ltd v. Yeo Poh Siah*, [2016] 2 SLR 118, [40]–[46].

912. J. Pinsler, *Principles of Civil Procedure* 532–533 (Acad. Publg. 2013), citing *Thorp v. Holdsworth*, (1876) 3 Ch D 637, 639; *Multi-Pak Singapore Pte Ltd (in receivership) v. Intraco Ltd*, [1992] 2 SLR(R) 382, [24]; *Hadmor Productions Ltd v. Hamilton*, [1983] 1 AC 191, 233. *See also Ang Sin Hock v. Khoo Eng Lian*, [2010] 3 SLR 179, [56]; *The 'Ohm Mariana' ex Peony*, [1993] 2 SLR(R) 113, [51], citing *Farrell v. Secretary of State for Defence*, [1980] 1 WLR 172, 180. Exceptions to when courts have permitted parties to depart from their pleadings are when the evidence discloses an unpleaded cause of action (*Thai Kenaf Co Ltd v. Keck Seng (S) Pte Ltd*, [1992] 3 SLR(R) 194); when the opposing party was aware of an unpleaded cause of action to begin with (*Boustead Trading (1985) Sdn Bhd v. Arab-Malaysian Merchant Bank Bhd*, [1995] 3 MLJ 331); when the matter was clearly implied by the original pleadings or has been adopted by the opposing party (*Lee Kuan Yew v. Vinocur John*, [1995] 3 SLR(R) 38); when there is illegality (*Re Robinson's Settlement, Gant v. Hobbs*, [1912] 1 Ch 717, 725); or when otherwise justice dictates that it should be put before the court (*OMG Holdings Pte Ltd v. Pos Ad Sdn Bhd*, [2012] 4 SLR 231, [18]–[21]): J. Pinsler, *Principles of Civil Procedure* 533–534 (Acad. Publg. 2013).

to both sides expeditiously and smoothly. It is a requirement of essential justice that an opponent is given adequate opportunity to prepare and present his view of the cause.[913]

287. The rules and procedures for pleadings are primarily found in O 18 of the Rules of Court,[914] many of which were adopted and adapted from the English civil procedure rules on pleadings. Pleadings comprise the statement of claim, defence, reply, rejoinder, surrejoinder, and further and better particulars.[915] Depending on how the claim unfolds between the parties, not all of these pleadings may be filed or necessitated.

§2. Procedural Aspects

I. Timelines

288. Much more often than not, the plaintiff initiates the pleading process by preparing his statement of claim.[916] This and the writ are then served on the defendant(s) either at the point when the writ is served or at any time after service, but before the expiration of fourteen days after the defendant enters an appearance.[917] If the plaintiff does not serve the statement of claim in time, 'the defendant may, after the expiration of the period fixed under these Rules for service of the statement of claim, apply to the Court for an order to dismiss the action, and the Court may by order dismiss the action or make such other order on such terms as it thinks just'.[918] Assuming, however, that the statement of claim is served in time and the defendant intends to defend the action (as opposed to contest jurisdiction or forum or seek to strike out), he will enter an appearance and then file and serve a defence within fourteen days after the time limited for appearing, or after the service on him of the statement of claim, whichever is later.[919] The failure to do either of the following in a timely fashion may lead to the plaintiff seeking default judgment.

913. *Multi-Pak Singapore Pte Ltd (in receivership) v. Intraco Ltd*, [1992] 2 SLR(R) 382, [22]. *See also Palmer v. Guadagni*, [1906] 2 Ch 494, 497; *The Why Not*, (1868) 2 A & E 265, 266.

914. Supreme Court of Judicature Act (Cap. 322, R. 5, 2014 Rev. Ed.) Rules of Court.

915. *See also* Supreme Court of Judicature Act (Cap. 322, R. 5, 2014 Rev. Ed.) Rules of Court, O 1 r 4(1): '"pleading" does not include an originating summons, a summons or a preliminary act'. If there is a counterclaim, the plaintiff will assume the role of the defendant: *id.*, O 18 r 18. In addition, the rules governing pleadings pertain only to actions begun by writ and not originating summons. *See also Bachoo Mohan Singh v. Public Prosecutor*, [2010] 4 SLR 137, where the court considered what would constitute a 'claim' in the context of (but presumably not only in the context of) an offence of dishonestly making a claim before a court of justice which a person knows to be false at the point of filing the statement of claim or defence.

916. The statement of claim may have been endorsed on the writ, or first filed as a concise statement of the nature of the claim (which will then be followed up with a full statement of claim after the defendant has entered an appearance).

917. Supreme Court of Judicature Act (Cap. 322, R. 5, 2014 Rev. Ed.) Rules of Court, O 18 r 1.

918. Supreme Court of Judicature Act (Cap. 322, R. 5, 2014 Rev. Ed.) Rules of Court, O 19 r 1. It should also be noted that if the writ is not served, the defendant cannot enter an appearance either: *Singapore Civil Procedure 2015 Volume 1*, at 298 (G.P. Selvam ed., Sweet & Maxwell Asia 2014).

919. Supreme Court of Judicature Act (Cap. 322, R. 5, 2014 Rev. Ed.) Rules of Court, O 18 r 2(1).

Assuming, however, that there is no such failure and the plaintiff serves a reply,[920] the plaintiff has fourteen days to do so after the date on which he was served the defence.[921]

289. A reply is only necessary if 'the defendant has raised a matter for the first time in his defence, which matter requires a response from the plaintiff. It is unnecessary to serve a reply if the plaintiff only wishes to traverse the allegations contained in the defence, since if no reply is served, all material facts alleged in the defence are put in issue'.[922] If the defendant raises a counterclaim against the plaintiff,[923] he has up to fourteen days after the time limited for appearing or after the statement of claim is served (whichever is later) to serve the counterclaim, while the plaintiff has fourteen days after the service of the counterclaim to serve his defence to the counterclaim.[924] A plaintiff's failure to file a reply and defence to the counterclaim precludes him from raising at trial any positive case that he should have pleaded in reply to the defence or as defence to the counterclaim.[925] A counterclaim may or may not include a set-off,[926] and may also be made against either a person other than the plaintiff if he is a party to the action or a non-party.[927] Any pleadings subsequent to the statement of claim, defence, and reply – that is, the rejoinder by the defendant and the surrejoinder by the plaintiff – can only be served when the leave of the court has been granted.[928] Leave to serve a rejoinder would only be granted if it is 'really required to raise matters which must be specifically pleaded', and thus a rejoinder cannot be a mere repetition of what has already been pleaded but must be necessary to a reply.[929]

290. The pleadings are deemed to be closed in any of the following scenarios that may apply: fourteen days after the service of the defence if there is no reply or the defence to counterclaim; fourteen days after the service of the reply; or fourteen days after service of the defence to counterclaim if there is no reply but only a defence to counterclaim.[930] This is important to note because the close of pleadings

920. The plaintiff is only required to reply if he intends to raise matters that are required to be specifically pleaded; mere disagreement with the defendant's arguments in the defence does not necessitate a reply: Supreme Court of Judicature Act (Cap. 322, R. 5, 2014 Rev. Ed.) Rules of Court, O 18 rr 3(1) and 8.

921. Supreme Court of Judicature Act (Cap. 322, R. 5, 2014 Rev. Ed.) Rules of Court, O 18 r 3(4).

922. *Singapore Civil Procedure 2015 Volume 1*, at 300 (G.P. Selvam ed., Sweet & Maxwell Asia 2014).

923. *See* Supreme Court of Judicature Act (Cap. 322, R. 5, 2014 Rev. Ed.) Rules of Court, O 15 r 2. *See also Suresh Agarwal v. Naseer Ahmad Akhtar*, [2019] SGCA 55.

924. Supreme Court of Judicature Act (Cap. 322, R. 5, 2014 Rev. Ed.) Rules of Court, O 18 r 3(4). If the reply and defence to the counterclaim are both served by the plaintiff, they must be combined in a single document: *id.*, O 18 r 3(3).

925. *Panwell Investments Pte Ltd v. Lau Ee Theow*, [1996] 3 SLR(R) 73, [19]–[20]. However, it does not imply that the plaintiff admits to the allegations in the counterclaim: *Singapore Civil Procedure 2015 Volume 1*, at 301 (G.P. Selvam ed., Sweet & Maxwell Asia 2014).

926. Supreme Court of Judicature Act (Cap. 322, R. 5, 2014 Rev. Ed.) Rules of Court, O 18 r 17.

927. Supreme Court of Judicature Act (Cap. 322, R. 5, 2014 Rev. Ed.) Rules of Court, O 15 r 3(1).

928. Supreme Court of Judicature Act (Cap. 322, R. 5, 2014 Rev. Ed.) Rules of Court, O 18 r 4.

929. *Champion Management Pte Ltd v. Kee Onn Engineering Pte Ltd*, [2017] SGHC 116, [5] and [8]. *See also Yeow Chern Lean v. Neo Kok Eng*, [2009] 3 SLR(R) 1131, [34].

930. Supreme Court of Judicature Act (Cap. 322, R. 5, 2014 Rev. Ed.) Rules of Court, O 18 r 20.

may preclude parties from taking out certain interlocutory applications, such as summary judgment. Indeed, the importance of the close of pleadings has been described in the following terms:

> The close of pleadings is an important juncture in a writ action. It indicates that the issues in dispute have been sufficiently crystallised by the process of allegation, denial, admission and deemed denial in that order. There is thus at the close of pleadings an implied joinder of issue on the pleading last served (see O 18 r 14(2)(a) of the Rules). The close of pleadings also serves as the cut-off point for one-time amendments to the writ or other pleadings made without the leave of the court under O 20 r 1 and O 20 r 3 respectively of the Rules. Further, it signifies the commencement of the timeline under O 25 r 1 of the Rules for taking out a summons for directions as well as triggers in appropriate cases the operation of the automatic directions under O 25 r 8 of the Rules.[931]

291. That having been said, generally, the court has the power to vary the timeframe for the service and filing of the statement of claim and/or defence, but this is likely to result in costs being awarded against any blameworthy party (if there is any).[932] In addition, the fact that the defendant has filed a stay application (perhaps because of say, the existence of an arbitration agreement) does not automatically bring all the timelines in the Rules of Court to a standstill.[933] Thus, unless the court has directed otherwise, a defendant who has filed a stay must assume that the timelines in the Rules of Court continue to run. Finally, it ought to be noted that in exceptional scenarios, the court may dispense with the requirement of pleadings.[934] However, such dispensation is extremely rare, and there must be irrefutably exceptional reasons furnished, given that the absence of pleadings will by definition mean that the issues are completely undefined in writing.

II. Form Requirements

292. As for form requirements, there are five main requirements. First, every pleading 'must bear on its face … the year in which the writ in the action was issued and the number of the action; … the title of the action; and … the description of the pleading'.[935] Second, if necessary, every pleading must also 'be divided into paragraphs numbered consecutively, each allegation being so far as convenient contained in a separate paragraph'.[936] Third, where dates, sums, and other numbers are used, they must be expressed in figures rather than words.[937] Fourth, every pleading must be endorsed 'where the party sues or defends in person, with his name and address; … in any other case, with the name or firm and business address

931. *Obegi Melissa v. Vestwin Trading Pte Ltd*, [2008] 2 SLR(R) 540, [13].
932. Supreme Court of Judicature Act (Cap. 322, R. 5, 2014 Rev. Ed.) Rules of Court, O 18 rr 1 and 2.
933. *Carona Holdings Pte Ltd v. Go Go Delicacy Pte Ltd*, [2008] 4 SLR(R) 460, [25].
934. Supreme Court of Judicature Act (Cap. 322, R. 5, 2014 Rev. Ed.) Rules of Court, O 18 r 22.
935. Supreme Court of Judicature Act (Cap. 322, R. 5, 2014 Rev. Ed.) Rules of Court, O 18 r 6(1).
936. Supreme Court of Judicature Act (Cap. 322, R. 5, 2014 Rev. Ed.) Rules of Court, O 18 r 6(2).
937. Supreme Court of Judicature Act (Cap. 322, R. 5, 2014 Rev. Ed.) Rules of Court, O 18 r 6(3).

of the solicitor by whom it was served'.[938] Fifth, every pleading 'must be signed by the party's solicitor or by the party, if he sues or defends in person'.[939] These requirements demonstrate the need for clarity and reliability.

§3. Substantive Aspects

293. In terms of substantive content, there are a number of key parameters, some general and some specific, that parties' pleadings have to conform to.

I. Material Facts and Brevity

294. One of the most fundamental principles governing pleadings is that 'every pleading must contain, and contain only, a statement in a summary form of the material facts on which the party pleading relies for his claim or defence, as the case may be ... and the statement must be as brief as the nature of the case admits'.[940] This in turn allows for the clear, precise, and efficient identification of the issues for the parties to argue and for the court to consider and resolve in a timely fashion.[941] Brevity, however, is not always easily gauged, especially in seemingly complex cases, for the lawyer 'must exercise his judgment to ensure that his pleading is not unnecessarily detailed so as to be prolix; nor too short so that the issues are not sufficiently defined'.[942] This is especially so since facts that are not pleaded may not be allowed to be proved at trial[943] and also cannot be relied on at trial.[944] The proper use of paragraphing, headings, unambiguous language, proper signposting, and a well-thought out structure[945] would also be helpful in keeping the pleadings manageable.[946]

---

938. Supreme Court of Judicature Act (Cap. 322, R. 5, 2014 Rev. Ed.) Rules of Court, O 18 r 6(4).
939. Supreme Court of Judicature Act (Cap. 322, R. 5, 2014 Rev. Ed.) Rules of Court, O 18 r 6(5).
940. Supreme Court of Judicature Act (Cap. 322, R. 5, 2014 Rev. Ed.) Rules of Court, O 18 r 7(1). *See also Koh Kim Teck v. Credit Suisse AG, Singapore Branchi*, [2015] SGHC 52, [42], citing J. Pinsler, *Principles of Civil Procedure* 545 (Acad. Publg. 2013). The pleadings should also be set out in strict chronological order: *Singapore Civil Procedure 2013 Volume 1*, at 272 (G.P. Selvam ed., Sweet & Maxwell Asia 2012).
941. *See also Lipkin Gorman v. Karpnale Ltd*, [1989] 1 WLR 1340, 1352. It should be noted that a 'pleader should never allege any fact which is not material at the present stage of the action, even though he may reasonably suppose that it may become material' at a later point: *Singapore Civil Procedure 2015 Volume 1*, at 307 (G.P. Selvam ed., Sweet & Maxwell Asia 2014).
942. J. Pinsler, *Principles of Civil Procedure* 549 (Acad. Publg. 2013).
943. *Yap Chwee Khim v. American Home Assurance Co*, [2001] 1 SLR(R) 638, [27]; *Ong Seow Pheng v. Lotus Development Corp*, [1997] 3 SLR 137, [41]; *Multi-Pak Singapore Pte Ltd (in receivership) v. Intraco Ltd*, [1992] 2 SLR(R) 382, [24].
944. *Nava Bharat (Singapore) Pte Ltd v. Straits Law Practice LLC*, [2015] SGHC 146, [183], citing *PT Jaya Sumpiles Indonesia v. Kristle Trading Ltd*, [2009] 3 SLR(R) 689, [30]; *The 'Ohm Mariana' ex Peony*, [1993] 2 SLR(R) 113, [49]–[54].
945. *See* J. Pinsler, *Principles of Civil Procedure* 579–584 (Acad. Publg. 2013).
946. J. Pinsler, *Principles of Civil Procedure* 549–550 (Acad. Publg. 2013).

295. As for the test of materiality (and indeed, the rules on pleadings generally), it has largely been driven by English case law (which has since been adopted locally).[947] The test that has been distilled is twofold: whether a fact is necessary to establish a cause of action or defence, and whether a party is entitled to prove a fact at trial.[948] In other words, the question is whether a fact is relevant (in a strict and narrow sense)[949] to the dispute,[950] bearing in mind of course whether a fact is relevant would have to also depend on the cause of action and circumstances of the case.[951] However, if there is any doubt surrounding the materiality of a fact, the party should err on the side of caution and plead it lest the court does not permit it to be proved later on.[952] Indeed, 'unless statements are ambiguous or otherwise embarrassing, the court as a rule will not inquire very closely into their materiality'.[953]

296. If a statement of claim does not disclose a cause of action, it may be struck out under O 18 r 19, but probably not before the plaintiff is given reasonable time and opportunity to make the necessary amendments (though this is likely to entail some cost penalties).[954] This applies to a defendant's defence as well. On the other

947. *See* e.g., *Banner Investments Pte Ltd v. Hoe Seng Metal Fabrication & Engineers (S) Pte Ltd*, [1996] 3 SLR(R) 244, [8].

948. J. Pinsler, *Principles of Civil Procedure* 542 (Acad. Publg. 2013), citing *Millington v. Loring*, (1880) 6 QBD 190, 194–196; *Phillips v. Phillips*, (1878) 4 QBD 127, 138–139; *Esso Petroleum Co Ltd v. Southport Corp*, [1956] AC 218, 238. *See also Bruce v. Odhams Press, Limited*, [1936] 1 KB 697, 712, cited in *Multi-Pak Singapore Pte Ltd (in receivership) v. Intraco Ltd*, [1992] 2 SLR(R) 382, [23]. C.f. *Ali bin Jais v. Linton Albert*, [1999] 6 MLJ 304.

949. The Evidence Act (Cap. 97, 1997 Rev. Ed.), which applies to civil and criminal proceedings, defines relevance, but due to its antiquity is mostly ignored by the Singapore courts: *see* generally C. Siyuan, *The Judicial Discretion to Exclude Relevant Evidence: Perspectives from an Indian Evidence Act Jurisdiction*, 16 Intl. J. Evid. & Proof 398 (2012); C. Siyuan & N. Poon, *Reliability and Relevance as the Touchstones for Admissibility of Evidence in Criminal Proceedings*, 24 Sing. Acad. L.J. 535 (2012); C. Siyuan, *The 2012 Amendments to Singapore's Evidence Act: More Questions than Answers as Regards Expert Opinion Evidence?* 34 Stat. L. Rev. 262 (2013); C. Siyuan, *The Future of the Similar Fact Rule in an Indian Evidence Act Jurisdiction*, 6 Nat. U. Jur. Sci. L. Rev. 361 (2014); C. Siyuan, *Redefining Relevancy and Exclusionary Discretion in Sir James Fitzjames Stephen's Indian Evidence Act of 1872: The Singapore Experiment and Lessons for Other Indian Evidence Act Jurisdictions*, 10 Intl. Comm. Evid. 1 (2014).

950. It should be noted that for certain types of claims, specific particulars (such as for claims relating to fraud) and documents (such as for claims relating to personal injuries) need to be provided: Supreme Court of Judicature Act (Cap. 322, R. 5, 2014 Rev. Ed.) Rules of Court, O 18 r 12. Other prominent examples (*See also id.*, O 18 r 8) include confidence and copyright, contributory negligence, defamation, estoppel, duress, illegality, misrepresentation, and special damages: *Singapore Civil Procedure 2015 Volume 1*, at 310–316 (G.P. Selvam ed., Sweet & Maxwell Asia 2014). *See also Tat Seng Machine Movers Pte Ltd v. Orix Leasing Singapore Ltd*, [2009] 4 SLR(R) 1101, [76], which states that the more serious an allegation made, the more adequate the notice should be given to the other party in terms of express pleadings.

951. *See also* J. Pinsler, *Principles of Civil Procedure* 542–543 (Acad. Publg. 2013).

952. J. Pinsler, *Principles of Civil Procedure* 543 (Acad. Publg. 2013). *See also Multi-Pak Singapore Pte Ltd v. Intraco Ltd*, [1992] 2 SLR(R) 382: *Yap Chwee Khim v. American Home Assurance Co*, [2001] 1 SLR(R) 638.

953. *Singapore Civil Procedure 2015 Volume 1*, at 305 (G.P. Selvam ed., Sweet & Maxwell Asia 2014), citing *Knowles v. Roberts*, (1888) 38 Ch D 263, 271.

954. However, the judge has the discretion to refuse any amendments to the pleadings: *Ohm Pacific Sdn Bhd v. Ng Hwee Cheng Doreen*, [1994] 2 SLR(R) 633, [6].

hand, if a statement of claim or defence contains any immaterial facts, the other party may apply to have them struck out.[955] The stating of material facts should not be confused and conflated with the making of an argument. Indeed, a consequence of stating 'material facts' is the avoidance of factual and legal arguments,[956] to which we now turn to.

II. Factual and Evidential Arguments to Be Avoided

297. The pleadings phase is not the appropriate juncture to bring in questions or arguments pertaining to evidence,[957] which includes any subordinate facts to support allegations,[958] as well as admissions (whether express or implied).[959] Indeed, there is a 'critical distinction between material facts and the subordinate facts which constitute the evidence intended to establish the material facts',[960] since '[n]ot all facts which tend to prove a fact in issue and are therefore relevant at the trial are "material facts" for pleading purposes'.[961] The rationale for this distinction is that the overarching objective of the pleading process is simply to define the issues clearly for both the parties and the court so that a fair hearing can be ensured. This 'is sufficiently achieved by stating the material facts. The role of evidence is to prove these facts, not to identify them'; therefore, 'it is unnecessary to include evidence in a pleading'.[962]

298. Moreover, in the same vein, the inclusion of evidence in the pleading stage 'may involve additional material thereby obscuring the material facts and causing confusion – the very circumstances which the pleading process is intended to avoid'.[963] However, sometimes the material facts can overlap with the evidence. This tends to occur in disputes concerning written contracts, where reference to the relevant parts of the relevant documents is almost impossible to avoid in the pleading. Such a pleading will be deemed acceptable.[964] In the premises, a pleading or parts of it which consist merely of evidence and are divorceable from the material fact may be struck out by the court.[965]

955. *Singapore Civil Procedure 2015 Volume 1*, at 306 (G.P. Selvam ed., Sweet & Maxwell Asia 2014), citing *Murray v. Epsom Local Board*, [1897] 1 Ch 35.
956. J. Pinsler, *Principles of Civil Procedure* 541 (Acad. Publg. 2013).
957. Supreme Court of Judicature Act (Cap. 322, R. 5, 2014 Rev. Ed.) Rules of Court, O 18 r 7(1). *See also Hoo Su Hen v. Sim Mao Sheng Desmond*, [2019] SGHC 189.
958. *Williams v. Wilcox*, (1838) 8 A & E 314.
959. *Davy v. Garrett*, (1877) 7 Ch D 473, 483–485; *Jusoh v. Ng Ah Sooi*, [1963] MLJ 92, 94.
960. J. Pinsler, *Principles of Civil Procedure* 543 (Acad. Publg. 2013). *See also id.*, 543–544.
961. *Jusoh v. Ng Ah Sooi*, [1963] MLJ 92, 93.
962. J. Pinsler, *Principles of Civil Procedure* 543 (Acad. Publg. 2013). *See also North Western Salt Co Ltd v. Electrolytic Alkali Co Ltd*, [1913] 3 KB 422, 425; *Williams v. Wilcox*, (1838) 8 A & E 314, 331.
963. J. Pinsler, *Principles of Civil Procedure* 543 (Acad. Publg. 2013).
964. *See* e.g. *Bruce v. Odhams Press Ltd*, [1936] 1 KB 697, 714. C.f. *Singapore Civil Procedure 2015 Volume 1*, at 305 (G.P. Selvam ed., Sweet & Maxwell Asia 2014).
965. *See also Ohm Pacific Sdn Bhd v. Ng Hwee Cheng Doreen*, [1994] 2 SLR(R) 633, [6].

III. Legal Arguments to Be Avoided

299. The pleadings phase is also not the appropriate juncture to make legal arguments[966] or to state legal results.[967] The rationale that prohibits the inclusion of factual and evidential arguments in pleadings equally applies here.[968] Accordingly, it is neither necessary for a party to plead the specific legal elements or statutory criteria of a cause of action or defence nor to plead the legal consequences that should follow.[969] Instead, all the party has to do is set out the circumstances and facts in a way that would meet the elements and justify the desired legal conclusion.[970] This means that the (material) facts that form the basis for the legal result sought must still be pleaded.[971] Likewise, if a party wishes to raise a point that involves mixed issues of law and fact, it is necessary to plead it.[972]

300. However, while legal argument is avoided at this stage, parties are at liberty to 'raise any point of law'.[973] This may give rise to some confusion in that as stated above, as long as material facts are properly pleaded, the legal rule and/or principle that is being relied on would be apparent, and the need to raise points of law would be unnecessary and therefore detract from the principle to keep pleadings brief and to the point. This ostensible contradiction is resolvable in the sense that the Rules of Court simply permit the party to raise any point of law 'where necessary'. Such necessity may arise, for instance, 'where a more specific statute or a convention or other legal source is involved, it is good practice to refer to it to ensure that the legal issues in dispute are clearly identified and to avoid any surprise at trial'.[974] Another example may be when foreign law is used; since if 'the parties do not plead foreign law, Singapore law applies … In general, the wrong has to be one that would be actionable if committed in Singapore, and not justifiable by the place where it was done. Where either party seeks to rely on foreign law, it ought

966. *North Western Salt Company Ltd v. Electrolytic Alkali Company Ltd*, [1914] 1 AC 461.
967. *In re Vandervell's Trusts (No 2)*, [1974] 1 Ch 269, 321.
968. *Development Bank of Singapore Ltd v. Bok Chee Seng Construction Pte Ltd*, [2002] 2 SLR(R) 693, [19].
969. J. Pinsler, *Principles of Civil Procedure* 545 (Acad. Publg. 2013). An exception to this may be found in Supreme Court of Judicature Act (Cap. 322, R. 5, 2014 Rev. Ed.) Rules of Court, O 11 r 1, which governs service of process out of jurisdiction.
970. J. Pinsler, *Principles of Civil Procedure* 545–546 (Acad. Publg. 2013), citing *MK (Project Management) Ltd v. Baker Marine Energy Pte Ltd*, [1994] 3 SLR(R) 823, [26]; *Middlesex County Council v. Nathan*, [1937] 2 KB 272, 274.
971. J. Pinsler, *Principles of Civil Procedure* 546–547 (Acad. Publg. 2013). *See also Seagate Technology International v. Changi International Airport Services Pte Ltd*, [1996] 3 SLR(R) 345, [28].
972. J. Pinsler, *Principles of Civil Procedure* 548 (Acad. Publg. 2013). An example would be if a defendant contends that a clause in the contract is a penalty provision rather than a liquidated damages clause: *Banner Investments Pte Ltd v. Hoe Seng Metal Fabrication & Engineers (S) Pte Ltd*, [1996] 3 SLR(R) 244, [14]–[16].
973. Supreme Court of Judicature Act (Cap. 322, R. 5, 2014 Rev. Ed.) Rules of Court, O 18 r 11. *See also Singapore Civil Procedure 2015 Volume 1*, at 304 (G.P. Selvam ed., Sweet & Maxwell Asia 2014): O 18 r 7 is to be read subject to O 18 r 10 (departure), O 18 r 11 (points of law may be pleaded) and O 18 r 12 (particulars of pleadings).
974. J. Pinsler, *Principles of Civil Procedure* 548 (Acad. Publg. 2013). *See also Singapore Civil Procedure 2015 Volume 1*, at 319 (G.P. Selvam ed., Sweet & Maxwell Asia 2014).

to be raised in their pleadings.'[975] The default position of pleading only material facts thus remains unaffected by the option given to parties to raise points of law.

IV. Reference to Certain Documents and Conversations

301. The 'effect of any document or the purport of any conversation referred to in the pleading must, if material, be briefly stated, and the precise words of the document or conversation shall not be stated, except in so far as those words are themselves material'.[976] This means that reference to certain (material) documents and conversations is permitted, provided that such reference is kept as brief as possible.[977] For instance, in a breach of contract dispute, it suffices for the plaintiff to set out the substance of the term without setting out the words of the contract in full, though of course in certain situations it may be necessary to include the actual words for clarity or the precise terminology of a term is dispositive.[978]

V. Presumptions and Burdens

302. A plaintiff has the burden of 'pleading, particularizing and proving of each cause of action' he pursues against the defendant.[979] This burden of proof requires the plaintiff to positively assert the essential elements of his cause of action, and not invite the court to draw inferences from the surrounding circumstances.[980] Additionally, the proof that the plaintiff relies on to prove his claim 'can be nothing more than his own uncorroborated and self-serving testimony as to facts with his personal knowledge'.[981] A plaintiff who fails to discharge this burden is at risk of having his suit struck out under O 18 r 19 of the Rules of Court, possibly on the ground that this amounts to an abuse of process.[982] While the rules of pleadings set a high bar for the plaintiff, they are necessary to: (a) deter speculative litigation and suppress litigiousness; (b) prevent a plaintiff from circumventing the allocation of the burden of proof by alleging allegations which cannot be falsified; and (c) ensure plaintiff has an incentive to take the necessary care to be accurate in his assertions.[983]

---

975. *Singapore Civil Procedure 2015 Volume 1*, at 320 (G.P. Selvam ed., Sweet & Maxwell Asia 2014), citing *Goh Chok Tong v. Tang Liang Hong*, [1997] 1 SLR(R) 811.
976. Supreme Court of Judicature Act (Cap. 322, R. 5, 2014 Rev. Ed.) Rules of Court, O 18 r 7(2).
977. *Singapore Civil Procedure 2015 Volume 1*, at 307 (G.P. Selvam ed., Sweet & Maxwell Asia 2014).
978. C.f. *Darbishire v. Leigh*, [1896] 1 QB 554, 559. *See also* Supreme Court of Judicature Act (Cap. 322, R. 5, 2014 Rev. Ed.) Rules of Court, O 18 r 12, which sets out instances where precise wording is highly material in certain causes of action.
979. *Chandra Winata Lie v. Citibank NA*, [2015] 1 SLR 875, [34].
980. *Chandra Winata Lie v. Citibank NA*, [2015] 1 SLR 875, [22], [35], [56]. This rule also applies to the plaintiff's claim in the alternative: *Chandra Winata Lie v. Citibank NA*, [2015] 1 SLR 875, [74].
981. *Chandra Winata Lie v. Citibank NA*, [2015] 1 SLR 875, [35].
982. *Chandra Winata Lie v. Citibank NA*, [2015] 1 SLR 875, [34] and [45].
983. *Chandra Winata Lie v. Citibank NA*, [2015] 1 SLR 875, [78]–[81].

303. A 'party need not plead any fact if it is presumed by law to be true or the burden of disproving it lies on the other party, unless the other party has specifically denied it in his pleading'.[984] To cite an example of the former, there is a presumption of value and good faith for bills under the Bills of Exchange Act.[985] When such a presumption is relied on by the plaintiff, he need not specifically plead the presumption but he must plead the material facts that give rise to this presumption; it is then for the defendant to plead the facts showing the absence of consideration. To cite an example of the latter, if the plaintiff is relying on the principle of res ipsa loquitur, the burden of proof is imposed on the defendant. It will be sufficient for the plaintiff to allege the material facts which give rise to the principle without pleading the principle itself.[986] Finally, if a fact is sufficiently well-known, it is judicially noticed and it need not be proved.[987] Some examples of facts which the court ought to take judicial notice are found in the Evidence Act.[988]

VI. Conditions Precedent

304. A 'statement that a thing has been done or that an event has occurred, being a thing or even the doing or occurrence of which, as the case may be, constitutes a condition precedent necessary for the case of a party is to be implied in his pleading'.[989] Such a condition precedent may be imposed by law or by agreement between the parties. An example of the former is a statutory requirement for the plaintiff to perform a certain act before he can proceed; an example of the latter is a dispute resolution clause.[990] Typically, if a defendant believes that a condition precedent has not been fulfilled, he will plead that as well as the plaintiff's failure to perform the condition precedent (otherwise it will be assumed that there was due performance);[991] the plaintiff would then plead in his reply that the condition precedent has either been satisfied or that the defendant has waived its performance.[992]

---

984. Supreme Court of Judicature Act (Cap. 322, R. 5, 2014 Rev. Ed.) Rules of Court, O 18 r 7(3). *See also* Evidence Act (Cap. 97, 1997 Rev. Ed.), ss 103–116 for provisions on burdens and presumptions of proof.
985. (Cap. 23, 2004 Rev. Ed.), s 30.
986. *See also Ong Ee Lim v. Government of the Federated Malay States*, [1937] MLJ 40, 42–47; *Amara Hotel Properties Pte Ltd v. Sie Choon Poh*, [2004] 3 SLR(R) 157, [13].
987. Evidence Act (Cap. 97, 1997 Rev. Ed.), s 58.
988. Evidence Act (Cap. 97, 1997 Rev. Ed.), s 59.
989. Supreme Court of Judicature Act (Cap. 322, R. 5, 2014 Rev. Ed.) Rules of Court, O 18 r 7(4).
990. J. Pinsler, *Principles of Civil Procedure* 553 (Acad. Publg. 2013).
991. *Singapore Civil Procedure 2015 Volume 1*, at 308 (G.P. Selvam ed., Sweet & Maxwell Asia 2014), citing *Amixco Asia Pte Ltd v. Bank Bumiputra Malaysia Bhd*, [1992] 2 SLR(R) 65, [36].
992. J. Pinsler, *Principles of Civil Procedure* 553–554 (Acad. Publg. 2013).

VII. Pleadings that Subsequently Arise and Internal Consistency

305. Generally, 'a party may in any pleading plead any matter which has arisen at any time, whether before or since the issue of the writ'.[993] However, this principle is subject to the general rule of factuality, materiality, and brevity (O 18 r 7(1)) and the preclusion of the plaintiff from raising in the statement of claim any cause of action not mentioned in the writ (O 18 r 15(2)).[994] In addition, a 'party shall not in any pleading make an allegation of fact, or raise any new ground or claim, inconsistent with a previous pleading of his'.[995] This principle, however, is also subject to 'the right of a party to amend, or apply for leave to amend, his previous pleading so as to plead the allegations or claims in the alternative'.[996] Taking these principles together, should, for instance, a plaintiff choose to reply with claims that were not clearly raised in the statement of claim, the correct approach would be to amend to amend the statement of claim,[997] and in a timely fashion.[998]

306. Nonetheless, if a party pleads an internally inconsistent case, it 'can be detrimental to the party's cause if it is indicative of a weak substantive claim or laxity in pleading. Moreover, inconsistent pleadings may amount to an abuse of the procedure if the inconsistency involves false or substantiated matters, or evinces a lack of seriousness.'[999] In addition, pleading a case that does not square with the eventual evidential record at trial will foreclose any possibility of late amendment and subsequently can lead to a dismissal of the case; to do otherwise would be unduly prejudicial to the other party.[1000]

307. If judgment is given despite the plaintiff's failure to plead properly, such judgment can be set aside and if necessary a new trial ordered.[1001] Accordingly, any amendment made to the pleadings should be done as early as possible[1002] and

993. Supreme Court of Judicature Act (Cap. 322, R. 5, 2014 Rev. Ed.) Rules of Court, O 18 r 9. *See also id.*, O 20 and the Chapter on amendments for further details on amendments.

994. *Singapore Civil Procedure 2015 Volume 1*, at 316 (G.P. Selvam ed., Sweet & Maxwell Asia 2014). *See also id.*, 283: '[O 18 r 9] preserves the right to plead any matter of defence such as a release, bankruptcy … although it has arisen since the commencement of the action'.

995. Supreme Court of Judicature Act (Cap. 322, R. 5, 2014 Rev. Ed.) Rules of Court, O 18 r 10(1). *See also Waghorn v. George Wimpey & Co Ltd*, [1969] 1 WLR 1764, 1770–1771; *Tian Kong Buddhist Temple v. Tuan Kong Beo (Teochew) Temple*, [2020] SGHC 273.

996. Supreme Court of Judicature Act (Cap. 322, R. 5, 2014 Rev. Ed.) Rules of Court, O 18 r 10(2).

997. *Williamson v. London and Northwestern Railway Co*, (1879) 12 Ch D 787, 793; *Nirumalan K Pillay v. A Balakrishnan*, [1996] 2 SLR(R) 650.

998. *See Chua Kwee Chen, Lim Kah Nee and Lim Chah In v. Koh Choon Chin*, [2006] 3 SLR(R) 469, [76].

999. J. Pinsler, *Principles of Civil Procedure* 555 (Acad. Publg. 2013), citing *Herbert v. Vaughan*, [1972] 1 WLR 1128, 1131.

1000. *John G Stein & Co Ltd v. O Hanlon*, [1965] AC 890. C.f. *New Civilbuild Pte Ltd v. Guobena Sdn Bhd*, [2000] 1 SLR(R) 368. *See also OMG Holdings Pte Ltd v. Pos Ad Sdn Bhd*, [2012] 4 SLR 231, [18]; *V Nithia (co-administrix of the estate of Ponnusamy Sivapakiam, deceased) v. Buthmanaban s/o Vaithilingam*, [2015] 5 SLR 1422, [38].

1001. *The Chartered Bank v. Yong Chan*, [1974] 1 MLJ 157. *See also Singapore Civil Procedure 2015 Volume 1*, at 306 (G.P. Selvam ed., Sweet & Maxwell Asia 2014).

1002. *Deans Property Pte Ltd v. Land Estates Apartments Pte Ltd*, [1994] 3 SLR(R) 804.

should result in a harmonious set of arguments and case theory. In the latter regard, this can be done by either removing any contradiction, or framing contradictory arguments as alternatives with the facts being set out separately if necessary.[1003] However, where any alternative causes of action are being pleaded, they should not offend common sense.[1004] Finally, while a party is bound by the four corners of his pleadings at trial, he may not necessarily be so bound in summary judgment proceedings.[1005]

§4. Further and Better Particulars

308. Once the statement of claim and defence have been perused by both parties, it is quite common for parties to seek further and better particulars from each other if the pleadings are not deemed clear enough,[1006] though of course parties can volunteer, if there are no objections from the other side, to serve particulars on each other.[1007] The functions of further and better particulars is but a natural extension of what is already required of pleadings (i.e., all material facts to be pleaded):

(a) to inform the other side of the nature of the case that they have to meet as distinct from the mode in which that case is to be proved;
(b) to prevent the other side from being taken by surprise at the trial;
(c) to enable the other side to know with what evidence they ought to be prepared and to prepare for trial;
(d) to limit the generality of the pleadings or of the claim or the evidence;
(e) to limit and define the issues to be tried, and as to which discovery is required;
(f) to tie the hands of the party so that he cannot without leave go into any matters not included. But if the opponent omits to ask for particulars, evidence may be given which supports any material allegation in the pleadings.[1008]

309. While the 'Court may order a party to serve on any other party particulars of any claim, defence or other matter stated in his pleading, or in any affidavit of his

1003. *Singapore Civil Procedure 2013 Volume 1*, at 284 (G.P. Selvam ed., Sweet & Maxwell Asia 2012).
1004. *Chandra Winata Lie v. Citibank NA*, [2015] 1 SLR 875, [69], citing *Ng Chee Weng v. Lim Jit Ming Bryan*, [2012] 1 SLR 457, [37].
1005. *Poh Soon Kiat v. Desert Palace Inc*, [2010] 1 SLR 1129, [15]. C.f. *Lim Leong Huat v. Chip Hup Kee Construction Pte Ltd*, [2008] 2 SLR(R) 786, [22]–[25].
1006. It is simply more practical to wait for the statement of claim and defence (and any counterclaim or reply) to be served and filed before further and better particulars are sought: *Singapore Civil Procedure 2015 Volume 1*, at 335 (G.P. Selvam ed., Sweet & Maxwell Asia 2014); J. Pinsler, *Principles of Civil Procedure* 559 (Acad. Publg. 2013). C.f. *Gwee Kim Bock v. Singapore Glass Manufacturers Co Ltd*, [1966] 2 MLJ 292, 294.
1007. *Singapore Civil Procedure 2015 Volume 1*, at 338 (G.P. Selvam ed., Sweet & Maxwell Asia 2014). *See also Multi-Pak Singapore Pte Ltd (in receivership) v. Intraco Ltd*, [1992] 2 SLR(R) 382, [15]–[20] on whether a failure to object to voluntary particulars being added to the pleadings can constitute a waiver of any objection to their inclusion.
1008. *Johnson Pacific Pte Ltd v. Hogbert Fred Rickard Robin William*, [2004] 4 SLR(R) 200, [11]. *See also Singapore Civil Procedure 2015 Volume 1*, at 321–322 (G.P. Selvam ed., Sweet & Maxwell Asia 2014) for examples of the particulars needed for various causes of action.

ordered to stand as a pleading, or a statement of the nature of the case on which he relies, and the order may be made on such terms as the Court thinks just',[1009] as a starting point, the party seeking further and better particulars should first request them by way of a letter to the other party.[1010] The other party should then try to furnish the requested particulars within a reasonable period of time, using the prescribed form.[1011] Reference to the paragraphs and phrases or words in which the particulars are being sought is usually made.[1012] At the same time, the other party is also at liberty to resist furnishing all that has been requested, or make its own request for further and better particulars (also by letter at this stage). Once this phase is exhausted and there are still some particulars not forthcoming (or it could be the case that no particulars were forthcoming at all), the requesting party can apply to the court for an order for further and better particulars to be made. A supporting affidavit is usually needed for such an application.[1013] This application will then be heard, and the court:

> may refuse to order particulars of a pleading to which a party would otherwise be entitled, where there has been inexcusable delay in making the application, or where the particular is not relevant to any issue raised in the case ... or if the 'particulars sought are in reality in the nature of interrogatories'.[1014]

310. In other words, if the further and better particulars sought are truly relevant in crystallizing the issues and material facts of the dispute,[1015] the court will probably order that such particulars be served on the requesting party, unless the application was made too late in the day for no good reason. The use of the procedure should also not be used to obtain evidence or to achieve an ulterior motive, as this would constitute an abuse of the court's process.[1016] A party whom particulars are sought may take the position 'that he cannot give any further information, or that he

1009. Supreme Court of Judicature Act (Cap. 322, R. 5, 2014 Rev. Ed.) Rules of Court, O 18 r 12(3).
1010. *Tan Hoe Kock v. Ali Akarbara bin Mangudin*, [1997] 4 MLJ 311, 320–321; J. Pinsler, *Principles of Civil Procedure* 559 (Acad. Publg. 2013). *See also* Supreme Court of Judicature Act (Cap. 322, R. 5, 2014 Rev. Ed.) Rules of Court, O 18 r 12(6).
1011. Supreme Court of Judicature Act (Cap. 322, R. 5, 2014 Rev. Ed.) Rules of Court, O 18 r 12(7).
1012. J. Pinsler, *Principles of Civil Procedure* 560 (Acad. Publg. 2013).
1013. *Singapore Civil Procedure 2015 Volume 1*, at 335 (G.P. Selvam ed., Sweet & Maxwell Asia 2014), citing *MBF Capital Bhd v. Tommy Thomas (No 4)*, [1998] 3 MLJ 216.
1014. *Singapore Civil Procedure 2015 Volume 1*, at 335 (G.P. Selvam ed., Sweet & Maxwell Asia 2014), citing *Ransome/Tempil Inc v. Romar Positioning Equipment Pte Ltd*, [1991] 2 CLJ 1642, 1647; *Wright Norman v. Times Business Publications*, [1991] 1 SLR(R) 196, [64]. Indeed, if the particulars are sought so late in the day such that the trial may risk being vacated, the application, however meritorious, may be dismissed: *Astrovlanis Compania Naviera SA v. Linard*, [1972] 2 QB 611.
1015. *Element Six Technologies Ltd v. Ila Technologies Pte Ltd*, [2017] SGHCR 16, [12]. *See also Singapore Civil Procedure 2015 Volume 1*, at 322 (G.P. Selvam ed., Sweet & Maxwell Asia 2014): requests for further and better particulars should not be used purely to harass the opposing party or as a fishing expedition.
1016. J. Pinsler, *Principles of Civil Procedure* 559–560 (Acad. Publg. 2013).

cannot do so without laborious research or exhaustive inquiry. Such objections, if genuine, are often met by an order that he shall deliver forthwith the best particulars which he can at present give.'[1017]

311. It is also possible that a court order for further and better particulars to be served on the other party is accompanied with an unless order. For instance, the court may order that if the requested further and better particulars that have been granted are not furnished to the other party within a certain period of time, the other party's statement of claim or defence may be struck out, or the action is dismissed.[1018] Where appropriate, the court may grant extensions of time to the timeline for the pleading process to accommodate the exchange of further of particulars.[1019] The party which has unnecessarily withheld particulars or unnecessarily sought more particulars will usually be penalized with costs for delaying the proceedings.

§5. Responding to Pleadings

312. It is particularly important, for the defendant, to respond properly to the plaintiff's statement of claim (this applies to the plaintiff responding to counterclaims as well).[1020] The defendant's response to any given alleged fact must take either of these three forms: an admission, or a non-admission or denial.[1021] With regard to admission, 'any allegation of fact made by a party in his pleading is deemed to be admitted by the opposite party unless it is traversed by that party in his pleading or a joinder of issue under [O 18 r 14] operates as a denial of it'.[1022] Indeed, 'a party to a cause or matter may give notice, by his pleading or otherwise in writing, that he admits the truth of the whole or any part of the case of any other party'.[1023] Particulars are not required for admissions.[1024] To refuse to admit to something unjustifiably may lead to cost penalties, as the plaintiff is likely required

1017. *Singapore Civil Procedure 2015 Volume 1*, at 337 (G.P. Selvam ed., Sweet & Maxwell Asia 2014).

1018. *Singapore Civil Procedure 2015 Volume 1*, at 388 (G.P. Selvam ed., Sweet & Maxwell Asia 2014), citing *Pertuobohan Berita Nasional Malaysia v. Stephen Kalong Ningkan*, [1982] 2 MLJ 13.

1019. *Singapore Civil Procedure 2015 Volume 1*, at 336 (G.P. Selvam ed., Sweet & Maxwell Asia 2014), citing *Chiam Heng Chow (executors of the estate of Chim Toh Say deceased) v. Mitre Hotel (Proprietor) (a firm)*, [1996] 1 SLR(R) 899, [9]–[10].

1020. *Singapore Civil Procedure 2015 Volume 1*, at 338 (G.P. Selvam ed., Sweet & Maxwell Asia 2014), citing *Thorp v. Holdsworth*, (1876) 3 Ch D 637.

1021. J. Pinsler, *Principles of Civil Procedure* 590 (Acad. Publg. 2013).

1022. Supreme Court of Judicature Act (Cap. 322, R. 5, 2014 Rev. Ed.) Rules of Court, O 18 r 13(1). This is subject to *id.*, O 18 r 13(4). C.f. *Emjay Enterprises Pte Ltd v. Skylift Consolidator (Pte) Ltd*, [2006] 2 SLR(R) 268, [31].

1023. Supreme Court of Judicature Act (Cap. 322, R. 5, 2014 Rev. Ed.) Rules of Court, O 27 r 1. *See also id.*, O 27 r 2 on notice to admit facts.

1024. *Singapore Civil Procedure 2015 Volume 1*, at 340 (G.P. Selvam ed., Sweet & Maxwell Asia 2014), citing *Fox v. Wood (Harrow) Ltd*, [1963] 2 QB 601.

to incur costs in proving more facts.[1025] If, however, the admission is made by honest mistake, he will probably be allowed to amend his defence and not be bound by the admission.[1026]

313. With regard to denial, while it has the same effect as a non-admission,[1027] a non-admission may be more appropriate when the defendant is not so certain that the allegation is untrue and therefore requires the plaintiff to prove it (a denial on the other hand out rightly rejects the alleged fact in question).[1028] But both denial and non-admission would operate as a traverse. This is because a traverse 'may be made either by a denial or by a statement of non-admission and either expressly or by necessary implication'.[1029] However, it should be noted that:

> every allegation of fact made in a statement of claim or counterclaim which the party on whom it is served does not intend to admit must be specifically traversed by him in his defence or defence to counterclaim, as the case may be; and a general denial of such allegations, or a general statement of non-admission of them, is not a sufficient traverse of them.[1030]

314. In practice, while a 'denial of the paragraph by an appropriate reference to it … is sufficient to constitute a traverse', it is not sufficient to generally deny an allegation by merely asserting that the plaintiff is put to strict proof.[1031] Instead, the traverse must be specific as possible and answer the point of substance, and not be vague or evasive.[1032] Otherwise, in the more extreme cases, the defence may be considered a sham and struck off and the defendant stands to lose the claim.[1033] Finally, there is the concept of joinder of issue, which is to say that both parties accept that a particular allegation is an issue but take diametrically opposed positions as to its veracity. A joiner of issue may be express or implied. As a starting point, if 'there is no reply to a defence, there is an implied joinder of issue on that defence'.[1034] In addition, a joinder of issue:

1025. J. Pinsler, *Principles of Civil Procedure* 592 (Acad. Publg. 2013).
1026. *Singapore Civil Procedure 2015 Volume 1*, at 340 (G.P. Selvam ed., Sweet & Maxwell Asia 2014), citing *Hollis v. Burton*, [1892] 3 Ch 226.
1027. J. Pinsler, *Principles of Civil Procedure* 591 (Acad. Publg. 2013), citing *Warner v. Sampson*, [1959] 1 QB 297, 319.
1028. J. Pinsler, *Principles of Civil Procedure* 591 (Acad. Publg. 2013).
1029. Supreme Court of Judicature Act (Cap. 322, R. 5, 2014 Rev. Ed.) Rules of Court, O 18 r 13(2).
1030. Supreme Court of Judicature Act (Cap. 322, R. 5, 2014 Rev. Ed.) Rules of Court, O 18 r 13(3). *See also WBG Network (Singapore) Pte Ltd v. Meridian Life International Pte Ltd*, [2008] 4 SLR(R) 727, [34]–[35].
1031. J. Pinsler, *Principles of Civil Procedure* 593–594 (Acad. Publg. 2013). *See also Nagase Singapore Pte Ltd v. Ching Kai Huat*, [2007] 3 SLR(R) 265, [172]–[177].
1032. J. Pinsler, *Principles of Civil Procedure* 594 (Acad. Publg. 2013). C.f. *Nagase Singapore Pte Ltd v. Ching Kai Huat*, [2007] 3 SLR(R) 265, [166]–[177].
1033. *Singapore Civil Procedure 2015 Volume 1*, at 341 (G.P. Selvam ed., Sweet & Maxwell Asia 2014), citing *The Jarguh Sawit*, [1997] 1 SLR(R) 213.
1034. Supreme Court of Judicature Act (Cap. 322, R. 5, 2014 Rev. Ed.) Rules of Court, O 18 r 14(1). *See also Williamson v. London and Northwestern Railway Co*, (1879) 12 Ch D 787, 794.

operates as a denial of every material allegation of fact made in the pleading on which there is an implied or express joinder of issue unless, in the case of an express joinder of issue, any such allegation is excepted from the joinder and is stated to be admitted, in which case the express joinder of issue operates as a denial of every other such allegation.[1035]

315. However, there 'can be no joinder of issue, implied or express, on a statement of claim or counterclaim'.[1036] The restriction on the former is a logical necessity as the legal burden is on the plaintiff to establish the issues; the restriction on the latter presupposes that the defendant – qua plaintiff in a counterclaim – is mirrored in that duty as well. If no defence is served, the allegations in the statement of claim or counterclaim would be deemed admitted and judgment may be obtained as a result.

§6. Possibility of Appeal

316. Section 34 of the Supreme Court of Judicature Act,[1037] read together with the Fourth and Fifth Schedules of the statute, determines whether any given order of civil procedure is appealable to the Court of Appeal[1038] or not.[1039] The Fourth Schedule states that no appeal 'shall be brought to the Court of Appeal … where a Judge makes an order giving or refusing further and better particulars'. As for the Fifth Schedule, it states that '[e]xcept with the leave of a Judge, no appeal shall be brought to the Court of Appeal … where a Judge makes an order at the hearing of an interlocutory application other than an application … for further and better particulars'. Read together, this means that if an application (or any part thereof) for further and better particulars is dismissed, the losing party cannot appeal against the decision. If an application (or any part thereof) for further and better particulars succeeds, the losing party also cannot appeal against the decision. The Fourth[1040] and Fifth[1041] Schedules also address various questions whether amendments to

---

1035. Supreme Court of Judicature Act (Cap. 322, R. 5, 2014 Rev. Ed.) Rules of Court, O 18 r 14(4).

1036. Supreme Court of Judicature Act (Cap. 322, R. 5, 2014 Rev. Ed.) Rules of Court, O 18 r 14(3).

1037. (Cap. 322, 2007 Rev. Ed.).

1038. The Court of Appeal is the apex court in Singapore. Below it is the High Court, followed by the District and Magistrates' Courts. For appeals arising from the lower courts, *see* Supreme Court of Judicature Act (Cap. 322, R. 5, 2014 Rev. Ed.) Rules of Court, O 55B, 55C, and 55D. It should be noted that generally, for interlocutory applications, there is a right of appeal from first instance. Thus, there is a right of appeal from a registrar in chambers to a judge in chambers (District Judge if it is the State Courts), but not necessarily after that stage.

1039. The statute was amended in 2010 and 2014.

1040. Supreme Court of Judicature Act (Cap. 322, 2007 Rev. Ed.), Fourth Schedule: 'No appeal shall be brought to the Court of Appeal … where a Judge makes an order giving leave to amend a pleading, except if … the application for such leave is made after the expiry of any relevant period of limitation current at the date of issue of the writ of summons; and … the amendment is an amendment to correct the name of a party or to alter the capacity in which a party sues, or the effect of the amendment will be to add or substitute a new cause of action.'

1041. Supreme Court of Judicature Act (Cap. 322, 2007 Rev. Ed.), Fifth Schedule: 'Except with the leave of a Judge, no appeal shall be brought to the Court of Appeal … where a Judge makes an order refusing leave to amend a pleading, except if … the application for such leave is made

pleadings may be appealable, non-appealable, or appealable only as of right. However, they will be more appropriately canvassed in the (next) Chapter on amendments.

after the expiry of any relevant period of limitation current at the date of issue of the writ of summons; and … the amendment is an amendment to correct the name of a party or to alter the capacity in which a party sues, or the effect of the amendment will be to add or substitute a new cause of action.' *See also id.*: 'Except with the leave of a Judge, no appeal shall be brought to the Court of Appeal … where a Judge makes an order at the hearing of any interlocutory application other than an application … for leave to amend a pleading.'

Chapter 7. Amendments

§1. Introduction

317. It is not uncommon for parties to make amendments to the various pre-trial documents, such as the pleadings and the originating processes. Depending on the nature and timing of the amendment(s), leave of court may be required. In addition, even assuming the amendment is permitted (or assuming, separately, that an unreasonable amendment application is brought to hearing), costs may be incurred by the party (usually the one seeking the amendment) that has caused undue inconvenience, provided costs constitute adequate compensation in the circumstances to begin with.[1042] Any amendment made takes effect 'not from the date when the amendment is made, but from the date of the original document which it amends; and this rule applies to every successive amendment of whatever nature and whatever stage the amendment is made'.[1043]

318. The rules and procedures for amendments are primarily found in O 20 of the Rules of Court,[1044] part of which was adopted from English rules and case law.[1045] The general powers of amendment under O 20 are supplemented by O 2 r 1 (power to amend any proceedings) and O 15 rr 6, 7, and 8 (powers to amend, to add, substitute or strike out a party or to order proceedings to carry on.[1046]

§2. Leave of Court Unnecessary

319. There are essentially three situations in which leave of court is not necessary for an amendment to be made. First, the plaintiff 'may, without the leave of the Court, amend the writ once at any time before the pleadings in the action begun by the writ are deemed to be closed'.[1047] However, this does not apply to amendments which consists of 'the addition, omission or substitution of a party to the action or an alteration of the capacity in which a party to the action sues or is sued', 'the addition or substitution of a new cause of action', or 'an amendment of the statement of claim', unless the amendment is made before service of the writ on any party to the

1042. *Tang Chay Seng v. Tung Yang Wee Arthur*, [2010] 4 SLR 1020, [10]–[11]; cited in *Ng Chee Weng v. Lim Jit Ming Bryan*, [2012] 1 SLR 457, [25]–[26]. *See also Singapore Civil Procedure 2015 Volume 1*, at 388 (G.P. Selvam ed., Sweet & Maxwell Asia 2014).

1043. *Singapore Civil Procedure 2013 Volume 1*, at 356 (G.P. Selvam ed., Sweet & Maxwell Asia 2012).

1044. Supreme Court of Judicature Act (Cap. 322, R. 5, 2014 Rev. Ed.) Rules of Court.

1045. *Singapore Civil Procedure 2015 Volume 1*, at 388–431 (G.P. Selvam ed., Sweet & Maxwell Asia 2014).

1046. *Singapore Civil Procedure 2015 Volume 1*, at 389 (G.P. Selvam ed., Sweet & Maxwell Asia 2014).

1047. Supreme Court of Judicature Act (Cap. 322, R. 5, 2014 Rev. Ed.) Rules of Court, O 20 r 1(1). *See also id.*, O 18 r 20(1). It should be noted that court orders granting leave to amend pleadings do not affect close of pleadings: *United Engineers (Singapore) Pte Ltd v. Lee Lip Hiong*, [2004] 4 SLR(R) 305, [42].

action.[1048] It should further be noted that where 'a writ is amended under [O 20 r 1] after service thereof, then, unless the Court otherwise directs on an application made ex parte, the amended writ must be served on each defendant to the action'.[1049] Second, a party 'may, without the leave of the Court, amend any pleading of his once at any time before the pleadings are deemed to be closed and, where he does so, he must serve the amended pleading on the opposite party'.[1050]

320. In terms of timelines, if an amended statement of claim is served on a defendant, 'the defendant, if he has already served a defence on the plaintiff, may amend his defence', and 'the period for service of his defence or amended defence, as the case may be, shall be either the period fixed under these Rules for service of his defence or a period of 14 days after the amended statement of claim is served on him, whichever expires later'.[1051] If an amended defence is served on a plaintiff, 'the plaintiff, if he has already served a reply on that defendant, may amend his reply' and 'the period for service of his reply or amended reply, as the case may be, shall be 14 days after the amended defence is served on him'.[1052] Within fourteen days after the service on a party of a writ amended under O 20 r 1 or of a pleading amended under O 20 r 3, that party may apply to court to disallow the amendment.[1053] In such a hearing, if the court:

> is satisfied that if an application for leave to make the amendment in question had been made under [O 20 r 5, which pertains to amendments of writs and pleadings with leave of court] at the date when the amendment was made under [O 20 r 1(1)] or [O 20 r 3(1)] leave to make the amendment or part of the amendment would have been refused, it shall order the amendment or that part to be struck out.[1054]

321. Third, 'any pleading in any cause or matter may, by written agreement between the parties, be amended at any stage of the proceedings'.[1055] However, this does not apply 'to an amendment to a counterclaim which consists of the addition, omission or substitution of a party'.[1056]

1048. Supreme Court of Judicature Act (Cap. 322, R. 5, 2014 Rev. Ed.) Rules of Court, O 20 r 1(3).
1049. Supreme Court of Judicature Act (Cap. 322, R. 5, 2014 Rev. Ed.) Rules of Court, O 20 r 1(2).
1050. Supreme Court of Judicature Act (Cap. 322, R. 5, 2014 Rev. Ed.) Rules of Court, O 20 r 3(1). *See also id.*, O 20 r 3(6).
1051. Supreme Court of Judicature Act (Cap. 322, R. 5, 2014 Rev. Ed.) Rules of Court, O 20 r 3(2). *See also id.*, O 20 r 3(4): 'references to a defence and a reply include references to a counterclaim and a defence to counterclaim respectively'.
1052. Supreme Court of Judicature Act (Cap. 322, R. 5, 2014 Rev. Ed.) Rules of Court, O 20 r 3(3). *See also id.*, O 20 r 3(4): 'references to a defence and a reply include references to a counterclaim and a defence to counterclaim respectively'.
1053. Supreme Court of Judicature Act (Cap. 322, R. 5, 2014 Rev. Ed.) Rules of Court, O 20 r 4(1).
1054. Supreme Court of Judicature Act (Cap. 322, R. 5, 2014 Rev. Ed.) Rules of Court, O 20 r 4(2).
1055. Supreme Court of Judicature Act (Cap. 322, R. 5, 2014 Rev. Ed.) Rules of Court, O 20 r 12(1).
1056. Supreme Court of Judicature Act (Cap. 322, R. 5, 2014 Rev. Ed.) Rules of Court, O 20 r 12(2).

§3. Leave of Court Required

322. There are essentially four situations in which leave of court is required (applied for by way of summons)[1057] for an amendment to be made. The first situation is where a defendant wishes to amend his memorandum of appearance.[1058] The second situation is where an amendment – be it to a writ or originating summons – is sought to correct the name of a party, to alter the capacity in which a party sues, or to add or substitute a new cause of action.[1059] In this regard, the court will consider the limitation period, the timing of the amendment, the bona fides of the amendment, and the justice of the case.[1060] Thus, an application by a plaintiff company to change its identification number after having obtained summary judgment was granted, because it was determined that first, the amendment sought to correct a bona fide error rather than to substitute one party for another and second, the defendant would not suffer injustice or undue prejudice arising from the amendment.[1061]

323. In a situation where the proposed amendment to pleadings concerns claims that were not time-barred when the writ was issued but became time-barred after it has been issued (where O 20 rr 5(2) and 5(5) are engaged), the High Court had held that a court needs to determine the following questions: (a) does the plaintiff's proposed amendment add or substitute a new cause of action; (b) has the period of limitation applicable to that new cause of action expired; (c) if so, does that new cause of action arise out of the same facts or substantially the same facts as a cause of action in respect of which the plaintiff has already claimed relief in the action; and (d) if so, is it just to grant the plaintiff leave to make the proposed amendment.[1062] On the first question, the court clarified that the meaning of 'cause of action' is the relief or remedy which the plaintiff seeks, and not the factual basis underpinning it.[1063] In addition, a holistic approach should be taken.[1064] Therefore, a new cause of action is added when an amendment seeks a relief or remedy which carries a different label from the unamended pleading, even if the new relief or remedy is claimed based on the same underlying facts.[1065] An amendment of pleadings would

1057. *Singapore Civil Procedure 2015 Volume 1*, at 400 (G.P. Selvam ed., Sweet & Maxwell Asia 2014).

1058. Supreme Court of Judicature Act (Cap. 322, R. 5, 2014 Rev. Ed.) Rules of Court, O 20 r 2.

1059. Supreme Court of Judicature Act (Cap. 322, R. 5, 2014 Rev. Ed.) Rules of Court, O 20 rr 5 and 7. *See also id.*, O 15 rr 6(2) and 7 on the misjoinder and non-joinder of parties and change of parties respectively.

1060. Supreme Court of Judicature Act (Cap. 322, R. 5, 2014 Rev. Ed.) Rules of Court, O 20 r 5.

1061. *Sunny Daisy Ltd v. WBG Network (Singapore) Pte Ltd*, [2008] 4 SLR(R) 769, [32]–[35]. *See also Thu Aung Zaw v. Ku Swee Boon*, [2017] SGHC 265, [30]; *Lim Yong Swan v. Lim Jee Tee*, [1992] 3 SLR(R) 940, [16]–[19].

1062. *Geocon Piling & Engineering Pte Ltd (in compulsory liquidation) v. Multistar Holdings Ltd (formerly known as Multi-Con Systems Ltd)*, [2015] 3 SLR 1213, [115]. *See also Lim Yong Swan v. Lim Jee Tee*, [1992] 3 SLR(R) 940, [28]; *Ballinger v. Mercer Ltd*, [2014] 1 WLR 3597, [15].

1063. *Multi-Pak Singapore Pte Ltd (in receivership) v. Intraco Ltd*, [1992] 2 SLR(R) 382, [29]–[30].

1064. *Geocon Piling & Engineering Pte Ltd (in compulsory liquidation) v. Multistar Holdings Ltd (formerly known as Multi-Con Systems Ltd)*, [2015] 3 SLR 1213, [126].

1065. *Geocon Piling & Engineering Pte Ltd (in compulsory liquidation) v. Multistar Holdings Ltd (formerly known as Multi-Con Systems Ltd)*, [2015] 3 SLR 1213, [121].

also be regarded as adding a new cause of action under the meaning of O 20 r 5(5) even if the amendment seeks a relief or remedy which carries the same label as an existing relief or remedy.[1066] On the second question, the defendant needs to show it has a prima facie limitation defence; thereafter, the burden of persuasion rests on the plaintiff to persuade the court the defence of limitation is not reasonably arguable.[1067] On the third question, this is substantially a matter of impression.[1068] Ultimately, the court will bear in mind that the purpose of O 20 r 5(5) is to ensure that any new claim allowed by amendment does not have the effect of requiring the defendant to investigate after the limitation has expired, a substantially a new set of underlying facts.[1069] On the fourth and final question, the lateness of the application in itself is not determinative and the court will also have regard to the fact whether the defendant will be adequately compensated by an award of costs.[1070]

324. On appeal, however, the Court of Appeal found two aspects of the High Court's approach erroneous. It first held that 'cause of action' refers to the essential factual material that supports a claim rather than the relief sought, and that in deciding whether an amendment introduces such material, the material pleaded in the original is not to be construed in an overly technical or strict manner.[1071] It then held that where the limitation period has arguably set in, the court would not have a residual discretion under O 20 r 5 to allow an amendment that did not fit within the four corners of O 20 r 5.[1072]

325. In another Court of Appeal decision, it has further been clarified that it is possible for an application to amend pleadings (under O 20 r 5) to engage the issue of joinder of new parties (under O 15 r 6) at the same time.[1073] When this happens, the requirements under both O 15 r 6 and O 20 r 5 have to be met for the application to succeed. The court also made the following clarifications on the legislative framework of O 20 r 5: first, O 20 r 5(1) sets out the court's general power to grant parties leave to amend their pleadings at any stage of the proceedings; second, O 20 rr 5(2)–5(5) address the specific types of amendments that may be made (amendment to correct the name of a party, to alter the capacity in which a party

---

1066. *Geocon Piling & Engineering Pte Ltd (in compulsory liquidation) v. Multistar Holdings Ltd (formerly known as Multi-Con Systems Ltd)*, [2015] 3 SLR 1213, [122]. *See also Steamship Mutual Underwriting Association Ltd v. Trollope & Colls (City) Ltd*, [1986] 33 BLR 77, 98.
1067. *Ballinger v. Mercer Ltd*, [2014] 1 WLR 3597, [27]–[28], cited in *Geocon Piling & Engineering Pte Ltd (in compulsory liquidation) v. Multistar Holdings Ltd (formerly known as Multi-Con Systems Ltd)*, [2015] 3 SLR 1213, [134].
1068. *Ballinger v. Mercer Ltd*, [2014] 1 WLR 3597, [34], cited in *Geocon Piling & Engineering Pte Ltd (in compulsory liquidation) v. Multistar Holdings Ltd (formerly known as Multi-Con Systems Ltd)*, [2015] 3 SLR 1213, [143].
1069. *Geocon Piling & Engineering Pte Ltd (in compulsory liquidation) v. Multistar Holdings Ltd (formerly known as Multi-Con Systems Ltd)*, [2015] 3 SLR 1213, [142].
1070. *Geocon Piling & Engineering Pte Ltd (in compulsory liquidation) v. Multistar Holdings Ltd (formerly known as Multi-Con Systems Ltd)*, [2015] 3 SLR 1213, [150].
1071. *Multistar Holdings Ltd v. Geocon Piling & Engineering Pte Ltd*, [2016] 2 SLR 1, [33]–[48].
1072. *Multistar Holdings Ltd v. Geocon Piling & Engineering Pte Ltd*, [2016] 2 SLR 1, [58]–[62]. *See also MCST Plan No 3322 v. Mer Vue Developments Pte Ltd*, [2016] SGHC 28, [44].
1073. *Management Corporation Strata Title Plan No 3322 v. Mer Vue Developments Pte Ltd*, [2016] 4 SLR 351, [12]–[15].

sues, or to add or substitute a new cause of action) after the expiry of the relevant period of limitation; third, if an amendment is applied for after the expiry of the relevant limitation period and if the defendant has an accrued right of limitation which would be prejudiced by allowing the amendment, O 20 r 5(1) would be of no application and the amendment can only be allowed under O 20 rr 5(2)–(5) (for which the requirements must be met for the amendment to succeed).[1074]

326. Returning to the four situations in which leave of court is required for an amendment to be made, the third situation is for the purpose of:

> determining the real question in controversy between the parties to any proceedings, or of correcting any defect or error in any proceedings, the Court may at any stage of the proceedings and either of its own motion or on the application of any party to the proceedings order any document in the proceedings to be amended on such terms as to costs or otherwise as may be just and in such manner (if any) as it may direct.[1075]

327. The fourth situation is when pleadings are deemed to be closed and a party seeks to amend the pleadings[1076] or the writ.[1077] Generally, amendments to pleadings ought to be allowed if they have the effect of enabling the real questions and issues in controversy between the parties to be resolved, and it is also just to grant leave to amend having regard to all the circumstances of the case;[1078] delay per se may not be a valid enough objection[1079] and certainly honest mistakes are unlikely to form an impediment to leave being granted.[1080] However, there is a difference between an amendment to a pleading that seeks to make an important clarification to the issue(s) and an amendment that attempts to raise a totally new issue at too late a stage,[1081] in that the latter is less likely to be permitted, unless it can be shown that there will not be undue prejudice (in terms of both procedure and substance) to

1074. *Management Corporation Strata Title Plan No 3322 v. Mer Vue Developments Pte Ltd*, [2016] 4 SLR 351, [31]–[48].

1075. Supreme Court of Judicature Act (Cap. 322, R. 5, 2014 Rev. Ed.) Rules of Court, O 20 r 8. *See also Ivanishvili, Bidzina v. Credit Suisse Trust Ltd*, [2020] SGCA 62.

1076. Supreme Court of Judicature Act (Cap. 322, R. 5, 2014 Rev. Ed.) Rules of Court, O 20 r 3(1).

1077. Supreme Court of Judicature Act (Cap. 322, R. 5, 2014 Rev. Ed.) Rules of Court, O 20 r 1(1).

1078. *Review Publishing Co Ltd v. Lee Hsien Loong*, [2010] 1 SLR 52, [113]; *Hwa Lai Heng Ricky v. DBS Bank Ltd*, [2010] 2 SLR 710, [12]; *Geocon Piling & Engineering Pte Ltd (in compulsory liquidation) v. Multistar Holdings Ltd (formerly known as Multi-Con Systems Ltd)*, [2015] 3 SLR 1213, [45]; *TMT Asia Ltd v. BHP Billiton Marketing AG (Singapore Branch)*, [2015] 2 SLR 54, [30]–[31].

1079. C.f. C. Bull & J. Pinsler, *Civil Procedure: Annual Review of Singapore Cases* [6.106] (Sing. Acad. L. 2004); *Chwee Kin Keong v. Digilandmall.com Pte Ltd*, [2004] 2 SLR(R) 594, [87].

1080. *Ketteman v. Hansel Properties Ltd*, [1987] AC 189, 212; cited in *Susilawati v. American Express Bank Ltd*, [2009] 2 SLR(R) 737, [57]. *See also Singapore Civil Procedure 2015 Volume 1*, at 401–404 (G.P. Selvam ed., Sweet & Maxwell Asia 2014); *Abhilash s/o Kunchian Krishnan v. Yeo Hock Huat*, [2019] 1 SLR 873; *JWR Pte Ltd v. Edmond Pereira Law Corp*, [2020] SGCA 68.

1081. *Tang Chay Seng v. Tung Yang Wee Arthur*, [2010] 4 SLR 1020, [11]. A further distinction can be drawn with amendments that go to the relief sought – in which case, the court is more amenable to granting leave to amend: *Singapore Civil Procedure 2015 Volume 1*, at 403 (G.P. Selvam ed., Sweet & Maxwell Asia 2014).

the other party and that a cost penalty can sufficiently compensate the other party.[1082] Thus, for appeals in particular, it has been said that while the court has the power to grant leave to a party to amend his pleadings at any stage,[1083] 'to allow an amendment before a trial begins is quite different from allowing it at the end of the trial to give an apparently unsuccessful defendant an opportunity to renew the fight on an entirely different defence'.[1084] Accordingly, 'the later an application is made, the stronger would be the grounds required to justify it', and the more vigilant the court would be in ensuring that the amendments do not give rise to a situation whereby the appellant is effectively asking for a second bite at the cherry.[1085]

328. However, it is still possible for a court to grant applications at a very late stage – after trial has started and both parties have adduced extensive factual and expert evidence,[1086] or even after both parties have made their closing submissions.[1087] In deciding whether to grant such an application, the Court of Appeal has held that the lateness of the application was not determinative in itself, and the 'overarching consideration was whether, in all circumstances, the amendment operated unfairly to the opposing party'.[1088] Related factors of consideration that the court takes in account, bearing in mind that the rules of court are to facilitate procedural fair play in the context of an adversarial system, are: (a) ensuring that the parties apprise each other and the court of the essential facts that they intend to rely on in addressing the issues in controversy or dispute; (b) requiring that an amendment should be attended to in the usual course of events, at an early stage of the proceedings, to ensure that no surprise or prejudice is inflicted on or caused to opposing parties; (c) requiring careful consideration whether any amendments sought at a late stage of the proceedings will cause any prejudice to the opposing party. Prejudice is to be viewed broadly to encompass any injustice and embraces both procedural and substantive notions; (d) recognizing that while a costs award

---

1082. *Chwee Kin Keong v. Digilandmall.com Pte Ltd*, [2004] 2 SLR(R) 594, [85]. *See also Ketteman v. Hansel Properties Ltd*, [1987] AC 189, 220; cited in *Susilawati v. American Express Bank Ltd*, [2009] 2 SLR(R) 737, [57].

1083. Supreme Court of Judicature Act (Cap. 322, R. 5, 2014 Rev. Ed.) Rules of Court, O 57 r 13(1); *Asia Business Forum Pte Ltd v. Long Ai Sin*, [2004] 2 SLR(R) 173, [9].

1084. *Ketteman v. Hansel Properties Ltd*, [1987] AC 189, 220; cited in *Susilawati v. American Express Bank Ltd*, [2009] 2 SLR(R) 737, [57].

1085. *Asia Business Forum Pte Ltd v. Long Ai Sin*, [2004] 2 SLR(R) 173, [12] and [18]; *Susilawati v. American Express Bank Ltd*, [2009] 2 SLR(R) 737, [58]; *Parakou Shipping Pte Ltd v. Liu Cheng Chan*, [2016] SGHC 48, [13]. In *Lipkin International Ltd v. Swiber Holdings Ltd*, [2015] 5 SLR 962, [48], the court held that where a claim is a complete non-starter to begin with, no amendment to the pleadings can cure the defects.

1086. *Geocon Piling & Engineering Pte Ltd (in compulsory liquidation) v. Multistar Holdings Ltd (formerly known as Multi-Con Systems Ltd)*, [2015] 3 SLR 1213. C.f. *Sin Leng Industries Pte Ltd v. Ong Chai Teck*, [2006] 2 SLR(R) 235, [23]; *Parakou Shipping Pte Ltd v. Liu Cheng Chan*, [2016] SGHC 48, [13].

1087. *Singapore Civil Procedure 2015 Volume 1*, at 407–414 (G.P. Selvam ed., Sweet & Maxwell Asia 2014). *See also Sunbreeze Group Investments Ltd v. Sim Chye Hock Ron*, [2018] SGCA 64.

1088. *Geocon Piling & Engineering Pte Ltd (in compulsory liquidation) v. Multistar Holdings Ltd (formerly known as Multi-Con Systems Ltd)*, [2015] 3 SLR 1213, [49]. *See also Chwee Kin Keong v. Digilandmall.com Pte Ltd*, [2004] 2 SLR(R) 594, [84]–[88].

against the party seeking late amendments can frequently alleviate any inconvenience caused, this may not always be appropriate; and (e) taking into account policy considerations that require finality in proceedings and proper time management of the courts' resources and scheduling. From time to time there will be cases where this is an overriding consideration.[1089] Therefore, the court will likely grant an application for amendment of pleadings if the facts raised in the amendment 'merely formalize what is already before the court', and the amendment is not an opportunity to adduce further evidence in support.[1090]

329. Where there are repeated amendments to pleadings that involve the deletion of large portions of what was originally pleaded and the addition of completely new content, they may be considered to interfere with the progress of the matter and be disallowed, even if the opposing party is not prejudiced by it.[1091] Separately, it should be noted that if:

> the Court makes an order under [O 20] giving any party leave to amend a writ, pleading or other document, then, if that party does not amend the document in accordance with the order before the expiration of the period specified for that purpose in the order or, if no period is so specified, of a period of 14 days after the order was made, the order shall cease to have effect, without prejudice, however, to the power of the Court to extend the period.[1092]

330. As a matter of form, where amendments authorized under O 20:

> are so numerous or of such a nature or length that to make written alterations of the document so as to give effect to them would make it difficult or inconvenient to read, a fresh document, amended as so authorised, must be prepared and, in the case of a writ or originating summons, reissued, but, except as aforesaid and subject to any direction given under [O 20 r 5 or O 20 r 8], the amendments so authorised may be effected by making in writing the necessary alterations of the document and, in the case of a writ or originating summons, causing it to be re-sealed and filing a copy thereof.[1093]

331. In addition, any document which had been amended under O 20 'must be endorsed with a statement that it has been amended, specifying the date on which it was amended and by whom the order (if any) authorising the amendment was

1089. *Chwee Kin Keong v. Digilandmall.com Pte Ltd*, [2004] 2 SLR(R) 594, [85], cited in *Geocon Piling & Engineering Pte Ltd (in compulsory liquidation) v. Multistar Holdings Ltd (formerly known as Multi-Con Systems Ltd)*, [2015] 3 SLR 1213, [49]. *See also Review Publishing Co Ltd v. Lee Hsien Loong*, [2010] 1 SLR 52, [113]; *Sheagar s/o T M Veloo v. Belfield International (Hong Kong) Ltd*, [2014] 3 SLR 524, [122]; *Foo Jee Boo v. Foo Jhee Tuang*, [2015] SGHC 176, [54]; *Parakou Shipping Pte Ltd v. Liu Cheng Chan*, [2016] SGHC 48, [22].

1090. *Geocon Piling & Engineering Pte Ltd (in compulsory liquidation) v. Multistar Holdings Ltd (formerly known as Multi-Con Systems Ltd)*, [2015] 3 SLR 1213, [77], [102]. *See also Chwee Kin Keong v. Digilandmall.com Pte Ltd*, [2004] 2 SLR(R) 594, [86].

1091. *Wee Soon Kim Anthony v. UBS AG (No 2)*, [2003] SGHC 125, [14]–[19].

1092. Supreme Court of Judicature Act (Cap. 322, R. 5, 2014 Rev. Ed.) Rules of Court, O 20 r 9.

1093. Supreme Court of Judicature Act (Cap. 322, R. 5, 2014 Rev. Ed.) Rules of Court, O 20 r 10(1).

made and the date thereof, or, if no such order was made, the number of the Rule of this Order in pursuance of which the amendment was made'.[1094]

§4. Possibility of Appeal

332. Section 34 of the Supreme Court of Judicature Act,[1095] read together with the Fourth and Fifth Schedules of the statute, determines whether any given order of civil procedure is appealable to the Court of Appeal[1096] or not.[1097] The Fourth Schedule states that:

> No appeal shall be brought to the Court of Appeal … where a Judge makes an order giving leave to amend a pleading, except if … the application for such leave is made after the expiry of any relevant period of limitation current at the date of issue of the writ of summons; and … the amendment is an amendment to correct the name of a party or to alter the capacity in which a party sues, or the effect of the amendment will be to add or substitute a new cause of action.

333. The Fifth Schedule then states that:

> Except with the leave of a Judge, no appeal shall be brought to the Court of Appeal … where a Judge makes an order refusing leave to amend a pleading, except if … the application for such leave is made after the expiry of any relevant period of limitation current at the date of issue of the writ of summons; and … the amendment is an amendment to correct the name of a party or to alter the capacity in which a party sues, or the effect of the amendment will be to add or substitute a new cause of action.

334. The Fifth Schedule also states that: 'Except with the leave of a Judge, no appeal shall be brought to the Court of Appeal … where a Judge makes an order at the hearing of any interlocutory application other than an application … for leave to amend a pleading.' In other words, apart from the three aforementioned circumstances, there can be no appeal against a decision to give leave to amend a pleading, but there can be an appeal (leave must be sought, however) against a decision not to give leave to amend a pleading. Finally, it should be noted that clerical

1094. Supreme Court of Judicature Act (Cap. 322, R. 5, 2014 Rev. Ed.) Rules of Court, O 20 r 10(2).
1095. (Cap. 322, 2007 Rev. Ed.).
1096. The Court of Appeal is the apex court in Singapore. Below it is the High Court, followed by the District and Magistrates' Courts. For appeals arising from the lower courts, *see* Supreme Court of Judicature Act (Cap. 322, R. 5, 2014 Rev. Ed.) Rules of Court, O 55B, 55C, and 55D. It should be noted that generally, for interlocutory applications, there is a right of appeal from first instance. Thus, there is a right of appeal from a registrar in chambers to a judge in chambers (District Judge if it is the State Courts), but not necessarily after that stage. It should also be noted that for such appeals from first instance, the cases are heard de novo and the judge may therefore choose to admit fresh evidence if appropriate.
1097. The statute was amended in 2010 and 2014.

mistakes 'in judgments or orders, or errors arising therein from any accidental slip or omission, may at any time be corrected by the Court by summons without an appeal'.[1098]

1098. Supreme Court of Judicature Act (Cap. 322, R. 5, 2014 Rev. Ed.) Rules of Court, O 20 r 11. *See also Ng Kiam Bee v. Ng Bee Eng*, [2013] 2 SLR 442, [16]–[17].

Part IV. Proceedings

Chapter 1. Discovery Proceedings

§1. Introduction

335. Discovery is often described as one of the most fundamental rules in an adversarial system of litigation.[1099] The purpose of the discovery process is to facilitate the parties' disclosure of each other's documents[1100] within their control, provided that such documents are sufficiently linked to the potential or actual issues of the dispute; such a process would, under the normal run of things, result in a fairer resolution of the case and the minimization of costs.[1101] So imperative is the discovery process that the lawyer (including in-house counsel) is duty-bound[1102] to let his client know, at as early a stage as possible of the multi-faceted responsibilities that accompany the process,[1103] so as to insure against the possibility that documents may not be preserved and/or disclosed;[1104] in extreme scenarios, the lawyer may even be ordered to personally pay the costs of the proceedings for dereliction

1099. *See* e.g., *Teo Wai Cheong v. Crédit Industriel et Commercial*, [2013] 3 SLR 573, [41]. However, it is not necessarily available in all types of civil litigation, for instance judicial review: C. Bull & J. Pinsler, *Civil Procedure: Annual Review of Singapore Cases* [8.30] (Sing. Acad. L. 2011), citing *Lim Mey Lee Susan v. Singapore Medical Council*, [2011] 4 SLR 147, [7]. *See also* C. Siyuan & N. Poon, *Recent Developments in Discovery in Singapore*, 33 Civ. J. Q. 21 (2013).

1100. *See also* Evidence Act (Cap. 97, 1997 Rev. Ed.), s 3 for the various definitions for 'document'. Essentially, a document 'is not restricted to paper writings, but extends to anything upon which evidence or information is recorded in a manner intelligible to the senses or capable of being intelligible by the use of equipment: *Singapore Civil Procedure 2015 Volume 1*, at 513 (G.P. Selvam ed., Sweet & Maxwell Asia 2014).

1101. J. Pinsler, *Principles of Civil Procedure* 615–616 (Acad. Publg. 2013). *See also Lee Shieh-Peen Clement v. Ho Chin Nguang*, [2010] 3 SLR 807, [11]. C.f. *Lim May See Susan v. Singapore Medical Council*, [2011] 4 SLR 147, [7], citing *Tweed v. Parades Commission for Northern Ireland*, [2007] 1 AC 650, [2].

1102. *See also* Legal Profession (Professional Conduct) Rules (Cap. 161, R 1, 2010 Rev. Ed.), r 58.

1103. *See also Woods v. Martins Bank*, [1959] 1 QB 55, 60 *Koh Teck Hee (trading as Mui Teck Heng Garments & Trading Co) v. Leow Swee Lim (trading as Meyoung Trading)*, [1991] 2 SLR(R) 328, [23]; *Teo Wai Cheong v. Crédit Industriel et Commercial*, [2013] 3 SLR 573, [47]; *Von Roll Asia Pte Ltd v. Goh Boon Gay*, [2015] SGHC 115, [55].

1104. *Susilawati v. American Express Bank Ltd*, [2009] 2 SLR(R) 737, [36]. *See also Myers v. Elman*, [1940] AC 282, 293–294; *Rockwell Machine Tool Co Ltd v. EP Barrus (Concessionaries) Ltd*, [1968] 1 WLR 693, 694; J. Pinsler, *Destruction of Evidence Prior to the Commencement of Civil Proceedings: How is a Court to Respond*, Sing. J. Leg. Stud. 20 (2004).

of duty in relation to his client's discovery, especially if the client lacks resources or sophistication.[1105] Indeed, the lawyer's duty also includes:

> having a sufficient understanding of the case to know which documents to look for and to appreciate which documents are relevant.[1106] There is also a positive duty to review thoroughly an opponent's list, to consider whether there might be other relevant documents that have not been disclosed, and to make an inquiry about any such documents. The failure to fulfil these obligations might be such a dereliction of duty as to justify a costs order.[1107]

336. There are two types of discovery: general discovery and particular or specific discovery. General discovery between the parties applies to all documents in a party's power, custody, or power on which any party intends to rely or could rely on at trial.[1108] Particular discovery – which is usually made supplemental to and after general discovery in response to any perceived omission in the documents disclosed for general discovery – essentially extends to documents that may not seem directly relevant to the issues, but may lead to the disclosure of relevant documents.[1109] It should be noted that the discovery process is closely linked with the inspection process.[1110] The latter takes place when a party has served a list of documents on another party in compliance with a discovery order, and the other party is allowed to examine and inspect the said documents and take copies thereof at a certain time and place.[1111]

337. The rules and procedures for summons for discovery and inspection are primarily found in O 24 of the Rules of Court.[1112] Electronic discovery (or e-discovery as it is sometimes known), which was implemented in full only recently, will also be discussed.

1105. *Teo Wai Cheong v. Crédit Industriel et Commercial*, [2013] 3 SLR 573, [93].
1106. The exact meaning of relevance in Singapore evidence law, however, remains completely elusive: *see* generally C. Siyuan, *The Judicial Discretion to Exclude Relevant Evidence: Perspectives from an Indian Evidence Act Jurisdiction*, 16 Intl. J. Evid. & Proof 398 (2012); C. Siyuan, *The Future of the Similar Fact Rule in an Indian Evidence Act Jurisdiction*, 6 Nat. U. Jur. Sci. L. Rev. 361 (2014); C. Siyuan, *Redefining Relevancy and Exclusionary Discretion in Sir James Fitzjames Stephen's Indian Evidence Act of 1872: The Singapore Experiment and Lessons for Other Indian Evidence Act Jurisdictions*, 10 Intl. Comm. Evid. 1 (2014).
1107. *Singapore Civil Procedure 2015 Volume 1*, at 515 (G.P. Selvam ed., Sweet & Maxwell Asia 2014).
1108. J. Pinsler, *Principles of Civil Procedure* 616 (Acad. Publg. 2013).
1109. J. Pinsler, *Principles of Civil Procedure* 616 (Acad. Publg. 2013).
1110. Discovery is also linked to various other civil procedure processes; another example being Mareva injunctions, in that an order for discovery may be made in aid of a Mareva injunction.
1111. Supreme Court of Judicature Act (Cap. 322, R. 5, 2014 Rev. Ed.) Rules of Court, O 24 rr 9–10. *See also Singapore Civil Procedure 2015 Volume 1*, at 514 (G.P. Selvam ed., Sweet & Maxwell Asia 2014).
1112. Supreme Court of Judicature Act (Cap. 322, R. 5, 2014 Rev. Ed.) Rules of Court.

§2. PROCEDURAL ASPECTS

338. An application for discovery is made by summons,[1113] though in theory for general discovery (but not particular discovery) the court can make an order regardless of whether a party has taken out an application.[1114] In exceptional circumstances, an oral application for discovery may be permitted by the court.[1115]

339. There is a prescribed form for the list of documents that are made in compliance with a court order for discovery, and the list 'must enumerate the documents in a convenient order and as shortly as possible but describing each of them or, in the case of bundles of documents of the same nature, each bundle, sufficiently to enable it to be identified'.[1116] In the prescribed form, there are two schedules. In Schedule 1, Part 1 requires the party to enumerate in a convenient order the documents or bundles of documents in his possession, custody, or power which he does not object to produce, with a short description of each document or bundle sufficient to identify it.[1117] Before proceeding, it may be helpful to clarify some of the terminology: 'custody' refers to just physical possession of the document, whether or not the holder has legal rights over the document;[1118] 'possession' entails both a physical holding of and possessory right over the document;[1119] while 'power' has been defined as 'a presently enforceable legal right to obtain from whoever actually holds the document inspection of it without the need to obtain the consent of anyone else'.[1120] Returning to the prescribed form, Part 2 of Schedule 1 requires the party to enumerate the aforesaid documents which he objects to produce.[1121] The most likely objection[1122] will be that of legal professional privilege.[1123]

1113. Supreme Court of Judicature Act (Cap. 322, R. 5, 2014 Rev. Ed.) Rules of Court, O 32 r 1. *See also id.*, O 24 r 6(2). However, an appeal against a decision made pursuant to this order may only be available to the non-party in question: *VisionHealthOne Corp Pte Ltd v. HD Holdings Pte Ltd*, [2010] 3 SLR 97, [19] and [46]; C. Bull & J. Pinsler, *Civil Procedure: Annual Review of Singapore Cases* [8.52] (Sing. Acad. L. 2010).

1114. Supreme Court of Judicature Act (Cap. 322, R. 5, 2014 Rev. Ed.) Rules of Court, O 24 r 1(1).

1115. *See* e.g., *Alliance Management SA v. Pendleton Lane P*, [2007] 4 SLR(R) 343, [14]–[16].

1116. Supreme Court of Judicature Act (Cap. 322, R. 5, 2014 Rev. Ed.) Rules of Court, O 24 r 3(1). *See also Singapore Civil Procedure 2015 Volume 1*, at 524 (G.P. Selvam ed., Sweet & Maxwell Asia 2014).

1117. Supreme Court of Judicature Act (Cap. 322, R. 5, 2014 Rev. Ed.) Rules of Court, Annex A.

1118. J. Pinsler, *Principles of Civil Procedure* 620 (Acad. Publg. 2013). If the holder objects to production because he has no legal rights over the document, the court will consider if the person who has legal rights over the document will be unduly prejudiced: *Alfred Crompton Amusement Machines Ltd v. Customs and Excise Commissioners (No 2)*, [1974] AC 405, 429.

1119. J. Pinsler, *Principles of Civil Procedure* 620 (Acad. Publg. 2013). *See also Singapore Civil Procedure 2015 Volume 1*, at 533 (G.P. Selvam ed., Sweet & Maxwell Asia 2014), citing *Dubai Bank Ltd v. Galadari (No 6)*, (1992) The Times, October 14.

1120. *Lonrho Ltd v. Shell Petroleum Co Ltd*, [1980] 1 WLR 627, 635. That is to say, a document is not within the 'power' of a party if he has to take steps to acquire a right he does not yet have.

1121. Supreme Court of Judicature Act (Cap. 322, R. 5, 2014 Rev. Ed.) Rules of Court, Annex A.

1122. It is also possible to claim that certain communications are without prejudice, such as those related to negotiations pursuant to a possibility of settlement. As for confidentiality clauses and their import (as well as the inapplicability of the 'newspaper rule', which exempts newspapers from disclosing sources of information in pre-trial discovery), *see* e.g. *KLW Holdings Ltd v. Singapore Press Holdings Ltd*, [2002] 2 SLR(R) 477, [10].

340. In this regard, if there is any claim that any of the said documents are privileged from production, 'the claim must be made in the list of documents with a sufficient statement of the grounds of the privilege'.[1124] If this is not done (i.e., a party discloses a document in his list and did not mark it as privileged), the other party would have the right to inspect it.[1125] But before inspection happens, the party can of course amend his list of documents by moving any privileged documents wrongly listed in Part 1 of Schedule 1 to Part 2 of Schedule 1 of the prescribed form.[1126] If a privileged document is inadvertently disclosed, the party is likely only able to maintain privilege if, before the time of inspection, he informs the other party of the error and his intention to claim the privilege.[1127] However, if the document has already been inspected by the other party, the claiming party can only rely on privilege with the leave of the court,[1128] but will not be able to go as far as to demand the court to have the documents deleted from the list of documents.[1129] Be that as it may, 'even after inspection, if there has been fraud or it is clear that inspection of a privileged document was given by mistake, the party who saw it may be injuncted from making use of the knowledge gained from that document'.[1130] As for Schedule 2 of the prescribed form, it requires the party to enumerate the aforesaid documents which have been, but at the date of service of the list of documents are not, in his possession, custody, or power.[1131]

341. For general discovery:

> the Court may at any time order any party to a cause or matter (whether begun by writ, originating summons or otherwise) to give discovery by making and serving on any other party a list of the documents which are or have been in his possession, custody or power, and may at the same time or subsequently also order him to make and file an affidavit[1132] verifying such a list and to serve a copy thereof on the other party.[1133]

1123. Under the Evidence Act (Cap. 97, 1997 Rev. Ed.), there is s 128(1), s 128A(1), and s 131(1). Under the common law, privilege is bifurcated into legal advice privilege and litigation privilege: *see* generally *Skandinaviska Enskilda Banken AB (Publ), Singapore Branch v. Asia Pacific Breweries (Singapore) Pte Ltd*, [2007] 2 SLR(R) 367, [32]–[74].
1124. Supreme Court of Judicature Act (Cap. 322, R. 5, 2014 Rev. Ed.) Rules of Court, O 24 r 3(2).
1125. J. Pinsler, *Principles of Civil Procedure* 618 (Acad. Publg. 2013). *See also Gelatissimo Ventures (S) Pte Ltd v. Singapore Flyer Pte Ltd*, [2010] 1 SLR 833, [20]–[26].
1126. *Ser Kim Koi v. Fulton William Merrell*, [2008] 2 SLR(R) 1063, [13].
1127. J. Pinsler, *Principles of Civil Procedure* 618 (Acad. Publg. 2013).
1128. Supreme Court of Judicature Act (Cap. 322, R. 5, 2014 Rev. Ed.) Rules of Court, O 24 r 19.
1129. *Ser Kim Koi v. Fulton William Merrell*, [2008] 2 SLR(R) 1063, [13].
1130. *Ser Kim Koi v. Fulton William Merrell*, [2008] 2 SLR(R) 1063, [13], citing *Guinness Peat Properties Ltd v. Fitzroy Robinson Partnership*, [1987] 1 WLR 1027, 1045.
1131. Supreme Court of Judicature Act (Cap. 322, R. 5, 2014 Rev. Ed.) Rules of Court, Annex A.
1132. There is a prescribed form for this: Supreme Court of Judicature Act (Cap. 322, R. 5, 2014 Rev. Ed.) Rules of Court, O 24 r 3(3).
1133. Supreme Court of Judicature Act (Cap. 322, R. 5, 2014 Rev. Ed.) Rules of Court, O 24 r 1(1). Such an order may apply to co-defendants *inter se*: *id.*, O 24 r 4(1).

342. Nonetheless, any application for discovery is usually made only after pleadings have closed[1134] as the issues in the dispute would probably be properly defined by then.[1135] Therefore, if 'it appears to the Court that any issue or question in the cause or matter should be determined before any discovery of documents is made by the parties, the Court may order that that issue or question be determined first'.[1136] However, this rule is seldom invoked in practice.[1137]

343. It is also possible, but also rare, to apply for an order of discovery before the commencement of proceedings.[1138] This is known as pre-action discovery, the purpose of which is to accommodate the situation where a potential plaintiff does not have sufficient facts to commence proceedings – for instance, when an identity of a person liable to be sued needs to be ascertained.[1139] In other words, pre-action discovery is concerned on whether the plaintiff has sufficient facts that would enable it to formulate a claim, and therefore be in a position to commence proceedings.[1140] Pre-action discovery should not be used to assist a plaintiff in 'developing and finessing his causes of action' or in 'obtaining evidence to boost his case'.[1141] There must be, inter alia, a supporting affidavit that sets out the grounds for the application, issues, and the material facts of the action.[1142] Ultimately, the test is that of justness and necessity.[1143] If a plaintiff is able to commence proceedings without the

---

1134. *See* Supreme Court of Judicature Act (Cap. 322, R. 5, 2014 Rev. Ed.) Rules of Court, O 18 r 20(1). It should be noted that court orders granting leave to amend pleadings do not affect close of pleadings: *United Engineers (Singapore) Pte Ltd v. Lee Lip Hiong*, [2004] 4 SLR(R) 305, [42].

1135. *See also Singapore Civil Procedure 2015 Volume 1*, at 521 (G.P. Selvam ed., Sweet & Maxwell Asia 2014).

1136. Supreme Court of Judicature Act (Cap. 322, R. 5, 2014 Rev. Ed.) Rules of Court, O 24 r 2(1).

1137. *Singapore Civil Procedure 2015 Volume 1*, at 523 (G.P. Selvam ed., Sweet & Maxwell Asia 2014).

1138. Supreme Court of Judicature Act (Cap. 322, R. 5, 2014 Rev. Ed.) Rules of Court, O 24 rr 6–7. In this regard *see Bayerische Hypo-und Vereinsbank AG v. Asia Pacific Breweries (Singapore) Pte Ltd*, [2004] 4 SLR(R) 39, [4]–[5]; *Ching Mun Fong v. Standard Chartered Bank*, [2012] 4 SLR 185, [21]–[23]; *Toyota Tsusho (Malaysia) Sdn Bhd v. United Overseas Bank*, [2016] SGHC 74, [13]; *Aquariva Pte Ltd v. Gezel Group Pte Ltd*, [2017] SGHCR 14, [13]–[15]. *See also id.*, O 24 rr 6(2)–6(6); *Xing Rong Pte Ltd v. Visionhealthhome Corp Pte Ltd*, [2010] 4 SLR 607, [19] on the possibility of applying for discovery against a person who is not a party to the proceedings; C. Bull & J. Pinsler, *Civil Procedure: Annual Review of Singapore Cases* [8.30]–[8.31] (Sing. Acad. L. 2012).

1139. Supreme Court of Judicature Act (Cap. 322, R. 5, 2014 Rev. Ed.) Rules of Court, O 24 r 6(5). *See also La Dolce Vita Fine Dining Co Ltd v. Deutsche Bank AG*, [2016] SGHCR 3, [22]–[23]; *China Merchants Bank Co Ltd v. Sinfeng Marine Services Pte Ltd*, [2019] SGHC 238.

1140. *Manuchar Steel Hong Kong Ltd v. Star Pacific Line Pte Ltd*, [2014] 4 SLR 832, [36]–[39].

1141. *Manuchar Steel Hong Kong Ltd v. Star Pacific Line Pte Ltd*, [2014] 4 SLR 832, [62]–[64], citing *Ching Mun Fong v. Standard Chartered Bank,* [2012] 4 SLR 185, [21], [28].

1142. Supreme Court of Judicature Act (Cap. 322, R. 5, 2014 Rev. Ed.) Rules of Court, O 24 r 6(3). C.f. *Tsusho (Malaysia) Sdn Bhd v. United Overseas Bank*, [2016] SGHC 74, [13]: 'An application for pre-action discovery must be supported by an affidavit setting out the grounds for the application, the material facts pertaining to the intended cause of action and whether the person against whom the order is sought is likely to be a party to subsequent proceedings.' *See also Kuah Kok Kim v. Ernst & Young*, [1996] 3 SLR(R) 485, [37]; *Hau Tau Khang v. Sanur Indonesian Restaurant Pte Ltd*, [2011] 3 SLR 1128, [49].

1143. *Intas Pharmaceuticals Ltd v. DealStreetAsia Pte Ltd*, [2017] SGHC 74, [27]; *Dorsey James Michael v. World Sport Group Pte Ltd*, [2014] 2 SLR 208, [27]; *La Dolce Vita Fine Dining Co*

information he seeks, his application for pre-action discovery would be unnecessary – this is broader than the English position which permits access to documents for the purpose of assessing the strength of the claim.[1144] This is so even though the court's power to order pre-action discovery is concurrently founded under the Rules of Court and its inherent powers.[1145] Relatedly, if there is no prospect of subsequent proceedings being held in Singapore, the application is unlikely to be granted.[1146]

344. As for particular discovery:

> the Court may at any time, on the application of any party to a cause or matter, make an order requiring any other party to make an affidavit stating whether any document specified or described in the application or any class of document so specified or described is, or has at any time been, in his possession, custody or power, and if not then in his possession, custody or power, when he parted with it and what has become of it.[1147]

345. An application for particular discovery would usually not be allowed to precede an application for general discovery, unless such an order is 'necessary or desirable'.[1148] In other words, the applicant must show 'exceptional' circumstances to justify any such application for particular discovery.[1149] Finally, it should be noted that once the list of documents has been finalized, certain admissions may begin to operate. For instance:

> a party on whom a list of documents is served in pursuance of any provision of [O 24] or any order made thereunder shall, unless the Court otherwise orders, be deemed to admit … that any document described in the list as an original document is such a document and was printed, written, signed or executed as it purports respectively to have been; and … that any document described therein as a copy is a true copy.[1150]

Ltd v. Deutsche Bank AG, [2016] SGHCR 3, [26]. *See also Success Elegant Trading Limited v. La Dolce Fine Dining Company*, [2016] SGHC 159, [54]–[57].

1144. C. Bull & J. Pinsler, *Civil Procedure: Annual Review of Singapore Cases* [8.30]–[8.31] (Sing. Acad. L. 2012). *See also Manuchar Steel Hong Kong Ltd v. Star Pacific Line Pte Ltd*, [2014] 4 SLR 832, [37], citing *Ching Mun Fong v. Standard Chartered Bank*, [2012] 4 SLR 185, [23]; *Dorsey James Michael v. World Sport Group Pte Ltd*, [2014] 2 SLR 208, [48].

1145. *See La Dolce Vita Fine Dining Co Ltd v. Deutsche Bank AG*, [2016] SGHCR 3, [22]–[27]; *Liberty Sky Investments Ltd v. Oversea-Chinese Banking Corp Ltd*, [2007] SGHC 20, [16]. *See also UCMI Ltd v. Tokio Marine & Fire Insurance Co (Singapore) Pte Ltd*, [2006] 4 SLR(R) 95, [91].

1146. *La Dolce Vita Fine Dining Co Ltd v. Deutsche Bank AG*, [2016] SGHCR 3, [73].

1147. Supreme Court of Judicature Act (Cap. 322, R. 5, 2014 Rev. Ed.) Rules of Court, O 24 r 5(1).

1148. Supreme Court of Judicature Act (Cap. 322, R. 5, 2014 Rev. Ed.) Rules of Court, O 24 r 5(4).

1149. *Hau Tau Khang v. Sanur Indonesian Restaurant Pte Ltd*, [2011] 3 SLR 1128, [49].

1150. Supreme Court of Judicature Act (Cap. 322, R. 5, 2014 Rev. Ed.) Rules of Court, O 27 r 4(1). *See also id.*, O 27 r 4(2).

346. To cite another example, a:

> party to a cause or matter by whom a list of documents is served on any other party in pursuance of any provision of [O 24] or any order made thereunder shall be deemed to have been served by that other party with a notice requiring him to produce at the trial of the cause or matter such of the documents specified in the list as are in his possession, custody or power.[1151]

§3. Substantive Aspects

I. Touchstones for Discoverability

347. The documents which a party may be ordered to discover for (general) discovery are: 'the documents on which the party relies or will rely; and … the documents which could … adversely affect his own case; … adversely affect another party's case; or … support another party's case'.[1152] This is essentially a test of relevance:[1153]

> Under [O 24], the court may order discovery of any document which is relevant to the matters in dispute insofar as the document could adversely affect a party's own case, adversely affect another party's case or support another party's case. The question of relevance is, quite naturally, determined by reference to the issues raised by the parties' pleadings … At this interlocutory stage, the court should not enter into an in-depth analysis as to the document's exact degree of relevance. Instead, what is required is to determine only whether the document in question may reasonably be expected to assist in proving or disproving the fact in issue.[1154]

348. In this connection, it is important to note that the lawyer has an obligation to look at his client's documents to determine relevance; he cannot simply rely on his client's description of the documents.[1155] Further, where a claim is made for a class of documents, the class must not be defined so widely such that documents

1151. Supreme Court of Judicature Act (Cap. 322, R. 5, 2014 Rev. Ed.) Rules of Court, O 27 r 4(3).

1152. Supreme Court of Judicature Act (Cap. 322, R. 5, 2014 Rev. Ed.) Rules of Court, O 24 r 1(2). *See also Singapore Civil Procedure 2015 Volume 1*, at 519 (G.P. Selvam ed., Sweet & Maxwell Asia 2014).

1153. *See also DBS Bank Ltd v. Yamazaki Mazak Singapore Pte Ltd*, [2010] SGHC 204; *Chiang Sing Jeong v. Treasure Resort Pte Ltd*, [2010] SGHC 65.

1154. *Alliance Concrete Singapore Pte Ltd v. Sato Kogyo (S) Pte Ltd*, [2010] SGHC 338, [7], citing *Tan Chin Seng v. Raffles Town Club Pte Ltd*, [2002] 2 SLR(R) 465, [18]; *MCST Plan No 2297 v. Seasons Park Ltd* [2004] SGHC 142, [15]. *See also* Evidence Act (Cap. 97, 1997 Rev. Ed.), Part I for the provisions and definitions for relevance (c.f. C. Bull & J. Pinsler, *Civil Procedure: Annual Review of Singapore Cases* [6.38] (Sing. Acad. L, 2003)); *Thyssen Hunnebeck Singapore Pte Ltd v. TTJ Civil Engineering Pte Ltd*, [2003] 1 SLR(R) 75, [6].

1155. *TCL Industries (Malaysia) Sdn Bhd v. ICC Chemical Corp*, [2009] 2 SLR(R) 218, [11].

which are barely relevant to the issue are included.[1156] However, relevance is only one of the two touchstones for the court's consideration as to whether to make the order for discovery (including pre-action discovery).

349. The other touchstone is necessity,[1157] since 'the Court may, if satisfied that discovery is not necessary, or not necessary at that stage of the cause or matter, dismiss or, as the case may be, adjourn the application and shall in any case refuse to make such an order if and so far as it is of opinion that discovery is not necessary either for disposing fairly of the cause or matter or for saving costs'.[1158] It should be noted that even if discovery is not considered necessary at a particular stage and the application is adjourned or dismissed, this does not preclude a subsequent application of discovery if this is justified by changed circumstances.[1159] On the other hand, repeatedly or incessantly taking out discovery applications would likely be seen as an attempt to hamper the adjudication of the merits of a case, especially if the applicant has already been given the opportunity to inspect the documents and been given copies thereof.[1160]

350. For particular discovery, the main difference with general discovery is that the nature and/or class of documents contemplated are broader than general discovery.[1161] This is because the documents that can fall under particular discovery are:

> a document on which the party relies or will rely; … a document which could … adversely affect his own case; … adversely affect another party's case; or … support another party's case; and … a document which may lead the party seeking discovery of it to a train of inquiry resulting in his obtaining information which may … adversely affect his own case; … adversely affect another party's case; or … support another party's case.[1162]

1156. *Singapore Civil Procedure 2015 Volume 1*, at 545 (G.P. Selvam ed., Sweet & Maxwell Asia 2014), citing *Fuji Photo Film Co Ltd v. Carr's Paper Ltd*, [1989] RPC 713. In *Lai Swee Lin Linda v. Attorney-General* [2015] SGHC 268, [23], the court refused an application for discovery on the basis that it was related to issues and matters that were raised in a separate suit, and held that it was not open for the party to seek discovery outside that separate suit. In *CIFG Special Assets Capital I Ltd (formerly known as Diamond Kendall Ltd) v. Polimet Pte Ltd*, [2016] 1 SLR 1382, [24]–[25], the court held that seeking an overly broad category of documents gave the impression of a fishing expedition. However, it should be noted that any fishing would not be a bar to discovery if the requirements of discovery (relevance and necessity) are otherwise made out: *Comptroller of Income Tax v. ARW*, [2017] SGHC 16, [22].

1157. There are arguably other considerations as well in certain unique contexts. For instance, in judicial review, discovery may be in favour of the applicant if there is a strong need to establish a case against the state (*see AXY v. Comptroller of Income Tax*, [2016] 1 SLR 616), or where international comity may be implicated (*see Ram Parshotam Mittal v. Portcullis Trustnet (Singapore) Pte Ltd*, [2015] SGHCR 12.

1158. Supreme Court of Judicature Act (Cap. 322, R. 5, 2014 Rev. Ed.) Rules of Court, O 24 r 7. *See also Comptroller of Income Tax v. ARW*, [2017] SGHC 16, [21].

1159. *Banque Cantonale Vaudoise v. Fujitrans (Singapore) Pte Ltd*, [2007] 1 SLR(R) 570, [25]–[32].

1160. *Ting Kang Chung John v. Teo Hee Lai Building Construction Pte Ltd*, [2008] 3 SLR(R) 377, [18].

1161. J. Pinsler, *Principles of Civil Procedure* 617 (Acad. Publg. 2013).

1162. Supreme Court of Judicature Act (Cap. 322, R. 5, 2014 Rev. Ed.) Rules of Court, O 24 r 5(3).

351. As regards the concept of 'train of inquiry', it is ultimately a question of fact.[1163] 'Train of inquiry' documents have been defined as documents that contain 'information which may enable the party (applying for discovery) either to advance his own case or to damage that if his adversary, if it is a document which may fairly lead him to a train of inquiry which may have either of these two consequences.'[1164] Even though specific by definition, particular discovery permits discovery of a class of documents regardless of its size.[1165] However, it will not suffice for a party to simply declare that a document or a class of documents is relevant and necessary. Instead, he must 'offer a real probability of evidential materiality to the pleaded claim and defence'.[1166]

II. Obligations and Consequences of Breach

352. If a party is required to disclose documents pursuant to a court order for discovery, he cannot refuse to perform this obligation based on the fact that the opposing party had failed to comply with his own duty to disclose documents.[1167] At the same time, he also has a continuing duty until the end of the trial to disclose any emerging documents that come within the scope of any order for discovery (be it general or particular).[1168] Deliberate suppression of documents even if pre-action and/or destruction of documents post-action, particularly if they are relevant to the dispute, can lead to a court striking out the entirety of a party's statement of claim (or defence or defence to counterclaim as the case may be).[1169] Such a consequence is most likely where there is both deliberateness in the actions and where fair trial is no longer possible.[1170] The court is unlikely to strike out the party's claims if the documents or correspondence that were requested for discovery were 'thrown away in the ordinary course of business well before any request was made by the plaintiff and if it could be established that it was not done deliberately to frustrate the discovery process'.[1171]

1163. *Thyssen Hunnebeck Singapore Pte Ltd v. TTJ Civil Engineering Pte Ltd*, [2003] 1 SLR(R) 75, [7].
1164. *Compagnie Financiere et Commerciale du Pacifique v. Peruvian Guano Co*, (1882) 11 QBD 55, 63.
1165. *Thyssen Hunnebeck Singapore Pte Ltd v. TTJ Civil Engineering Pte Ltd*, [2003] 1 SLR(R) 75, [6]–[7].
1166. *O Co v. M Co*, [1996] 2 Lloyd's Rep 347. *See also Wright Norman v. Oversea- Chinese Banking Corp Ltd*, [1992] 2 SLR(R) 452, [17]–[20]; *Tan Ching Seng v. Raffles Town Club Pte Ltd*, [2002] 2 SLR(R) 465, [35].
1167. *Rajaratnam Kumar v. Estate of Rajaratnam Saravanamuthu (deceased)*, [2010] 1 SLR 864, [8]. For discovery in the context of confidential arbitral awards, *see AAY v. AAZ*, [2011] 1 SLR 1093, [53]; *Long Well Group Ltd v. Commerzbank AG*, [2016] SGHC 158, [10].
1168. Supreme Court of Judicature Act (Cap. 322, R. 5, 2014 Rev. Ed.) Rules of Court, O 24 r 8. *See also Singapore Civil Procedure 2015 Volume 1*, at 554 (G.P. Selvam ed., Sweet & Maxwell Asia 2014).
1169. *Alliance Management SA v. Pendleton Lane P*, [2008] 4 SLR(R) 1, [14]; *K Solutions Pte Ltd v. National University of Singapore*, [2009] 4 SLR(R) 254, [107]–[109], [125], and [134]–[138]; *Lee Chang-Rung v. Standard Chartered Bank*, [2011] 1 SLR 337, [31]–[35]. C.f. *SMS Pte Ltd v. Power & Energy Pte Ltd*, [1996] 1 SLR(R) 121, [17].
1170. *K Solutions Pte Ltd v. National University of Singapore*, [2009] 4 SLR(R) 254, [126]–[127].
1171. *Von Roll Asia Pte Ltd v. Goh Boon Gay*, [2015] SGHC 115, [13].

353. In rare instances, a new trial may be ordered by an appellate court if it is found that the winning party (thus, it may either a plaintiff or defendant) had not disclosed material documents that would have been discoverable. This is but part of a wider principle that an egregious lack of honesty by a party, even at the pre-trial process, can have exceptionally adverse consequences.[1172] In deciding if a new trial is warranted, the court will consider various factors, such as: the general considerations relating to the administration of justice; the degree of culpability of the winning party; any lack of diligence on the part of the losing party; and the extent of any likelihood that the result would have been different if the discovery order (if any) had been complied with and the non-disclosed material had been made available.[1173] Apart from striking out and the ordering of a retrial, the court may also order that the defaulting party's evidential record obtained at the trial to be excluded.[1174]

354. Once a party has been given access to the documents of another party via the discovery process, there is at the very least an implied undertaking that the party will act in good faith, in that the documents will not be used for any collateral purpose, will not be disclosed to third parties, and will only be used for the immediate litigation; this is because the public interest in privacy and confidence requires the compulsion of the discovery process not to press further than what the court of justice demands (i.e., full and frank disclosure in the interests of justice).[1175] The nature of the Riddick principle is that of 'an implied undertaking owed to the court, and a breach of such an undertaking is a contempt of court, and punishable accordingly'.[1176] This is why a breach of the Riddick principle may justify an injunction taken out against the discloser, or lead to contempt of court proceedings.[1177] The High Court has clarified that the Riddick principle ceases to apply once a document

1172. *Susilawati v. American Express Bank Ltd*, [2009] 2 SLR(R) 737, [36]; *Teo Wai Cheong v. Crédit Industriel et Commercial*, [2013] 3 SLR 573, [1].

1173. *Susilawati v. American Express Bank Ltd*, [2009] 2 SLR(R) 737, [35]–[36].

1174. *Teo Wai Cheong v. Crédit Industriel et Commercial*, [2013] 3 SLR 573, [55].

1175. *Riddick v. Thames Board Mills Ltd*, [1977] QB 881, 886; cited in *Soon Kok Tiang v. DBS Bank Ltd*, [2012] 1 SLR 397, [55]; *Foo Jong Long Dennis v. Ang Yee Lim*, [2015] 2 SLR 578, [20]. One consequence of this prohibition is that a party should not commence a new action against the same party on the disclosed documents: *Miller v. Scorey*, [1996] 1 WLR 1122, 1132. If it is a criminal action and documents have been seized pursuant to a search warrant that is later quashed, the documents have to be returned to the owner and there is similarly a prohibition that the other party cannot use the documents for any collateral purposes: *Microsoft Corp v. SM Summit Holdings Ltd*, [1999] 3 SLR(R) 465, [20]. The prohibition also applies to documents disclosed in arbitration proceedings, though the owner of the documents may consent to disclosure and the opposing party may apply for leave from the court to grant disclosure on the basis that it is either reasonably necessary or in the interests of justice: *Myanma Yaung Chi Oo Co Ltd v. Win Wu Nu*, [2003] 2 SLR(R) 547, [17]–[20].

1176. *Pertamina Energy Trading Ltd v. Karaha Bodas Co LLC*, [2007] 2 SLR(R) 518, [38]–[39], citing *Prudential Assurance Co Ltd v. Fountain Page Ltd*, [1991] 1WLR 756, 764–765. *See also Foo Jong Long Dennis v. Ang Yee Lim*, [2015] 2 SLR 578, [22]. The *Riddick* principle is also relevant for the purposes of criminal investigations: *Amber Compounding Pharmacy Pte Ltd v. Lim Suk Ling Priscilla*, [2019] SGHC 269.

1177. *Singapore Civil Procedure 2015 Volume 1*, at 516 (G.P. Selvam ed., Sweet & Maxwell Asia 2014), citing *Pertamina Energy Trading Ltd v. Karaha Bodas Co LLC*, [2007] 2 SLR(R) 518, [66]–[78] and [93].

has been used in open court, but a party may apply to the court for the undertaking to continue.[1178] However, even if an express undertaking has been given, the court has the discretion (which it naturally will exercise cautiously) to release or modify the undertaking.[1179] It may exercise its discretion if a party seeking release can demonstrate that there are cogent and persuasive reasons for the release, and that there will be no injustice or undue prejudice caused to the person giving discovery.[1180] An example of a good reason may be an overriding public policy (and therefore not just a mere furtherance of a private interest) that justifies the release.[1181] Another example of a good reason is that the party seeking release may have a legal obligation to produce the documents in another jurisdiction,[1182] especially if it is for a claim that is in substance the same as the one at hand.[1183] However, leave of the court is probably required in any event.[1184]

355. Finally, any order made regarding discovery 'may, on sufficient cause being shown, be revoked or varied by a subsequent order or direction of the Court made or given at or before the trial of the cause or matter in connection with which the original order was made'.[1185]

§4. Electronic Discovery

356. With the digitization of documents over the years, it was a matter of time before court systems responded vis-à-vis the discoverability of such documents.[1186] One of the more prominent recent attempts to do so would be the 2009 Supreme Court Practice Directions on 'e-discovery'.[1187] These Practice Directions were introduced:

1178. *Foo Jong Long Dennis v. Ang Yee Lim*, [2015] 2 SLR 578, [54]–[60], citing *Harman v. Secretary of State for the Home Department*, [1983] 1 AC 280.30 Sep. 2017.
1179. *See* generally *Ser Kim Koi v. William Merrell Fulton*, [2009] SGHC 5, [12]–[20]. *See also I-Admin (Singapore) Pte Ltd v. Hong Ying Ting* [2015] SGHC 153, [7]–[11].
1180. *Reebok International Ltd v. Royal Corp*, [1991] 2 SLR(R) 688, [16], citing *Crest Homes plc v. Marks*, [1987] AC 829, 859–860; *GIB Automation Pte Ltd v. Deluge Fire Protection (SEA) Pte Ltd*, [2007] 2 SLR(R) 918, [104].
1181. *Halcon International Inc v. The Shell Transport & Trading Co*, [1979] RPC 97, 122.
1182. *Bank of Crete SA v. Koskotas (No 2)*, [1992] 1 WLR 919, 927.
1183. *Anex Electrical Co Ltd v. Kingsland International Ltd*, [1998] 1 HKLRD 947; cited in *Ser Kim Koi v. William Merrell Fulton*, [2009] SGHC 5, [27]. C.f. the rule in *Harman v. Secretary of State for the Home Department*, [1983] 1 AC 280 that another exception to the *Riddick* principle is that a document may be used if it has been read to or by the court or referred to at a public hearing.
1184. C. Bull & J. Pinsler, *Civil Procedure: Annual Review of Singapore Cases* (Sing. Acad. Law 2000), citing *Armco v. Donahue*, [1999] 2 SLR(R) 481.
1185. Supreme Court of Judicature Act (Cap. 322, R. 5, 2014 Rev. Ed.) Rules of Court, O 24 r 17. An example would be if a defence has been struck out and the defendant applies to have it restored on the ground that a list of documents has since been provided to the plaintiff.
1186. *See* Yeong Z.K., *Recent Developments in Electronic Discovery: Discovering Electronic Documents and Discovering Documents Electronically*, 19 Sing. Acad. L.J. 101, 101 (2007).*See also Singapore Civil Procedure 2015 Volume 1*, at 508–511 (G.P. Selvam ed., Sweet & Maxwell Asia 2014).
1187. *See* generally Yeong Z.K., *Discovery and Inspection of Electronically Stored Documents: A Commentary on Practice Direction No 3 of 2009 (Part 1)*, Sing. L. Gaz. (October 2009); Yeong Z.K.,

> with the aim of providing guidance on how existing legal principles pertaining to the discovery process could be applied in respect of electronically stored documents ... to promote the exchange of electronically stored documents in a text searchable electronic form (in lieu of printed copies) so that parties may capitalise on the twin benefits of, viz., the ability to run keyword searches on the documents in question as well as easy management of the same. This also has the added benefit of avoiding unnecessary photocopying or printing of electronically stored documents ... [the Practice Directions on e-discovery] also [prefer] the inspection and supply of copies of electronic documents in their native formats without any interference with the documents' 'metadata information'.[1188]

357. Following public consultation, a subsequent amendment to the Supreme Court Practice Directions in 2012[1189] further refined the existing regime for e-discovery in the following ways: stipulating the circumstances where parties should consider e-discovery;[1190] providing a checklist of questions to facilitate the conduct of good faith discussions on e-discovery;[1191] emphasizing proportionate and economical use of e-discovery;[1192] and permitting a party to provide discovery and inspection by way of supplying electronic copies.[1193] Other miscellaneous amendments were made to clarify the meanings and definitions of technical terms, such as 'forensic inspection' and 'not reasonably accessible documents',[1194] as well as to improve on the existing e-discovery plans and protocols.[1195] The Practice Directions on e-discovery will apply either by mutual agreement of the parties or when the court orders (either on its own motion or on application).[1196] It is possible for parties to mutually agree not to apply the Practice Directions on e-discovery for the purposes of general discovery, but it is for the court to order compliance with a

---

Discovery and Inspection of Electronically Stored Documents: A Commentary on Practice Direction 3 of 2009 (Part II), Sing. L. Gaz. (November 2009).

1188. *Sanae Achar v. Sci-Gen Ltd*, [2011] 3 SLR 967, [11].

1189. *See* generally *Supreme Court Practice Directions Amendment No. 1 of 2012*, http://app.supremecourt.gov.sg/default.aspx?pgID=4122, 30 Sep. 2017; S. Leong & Yeong Z.K., *A Commentary on the Supreme Court Practice Directions Amendment No 1 of 2012*, Sing. L. Gaz. (March 2012).

1190. Namely, where: the claim or the counterclaim exceeds SGD 1 million; documents discoverable by a party exceeds 2,000 pages in aggregate; or documents discoverable in the case or matter comprise substantially of electronic mail and/or electronic documents: *Supreme Court Practice Directions Amendment No. 1 of 2012*, http://app.supremecourt.gov.sg/default.aspx?pgID=4122, 30 Sep. 2017.

1191. *Supreme Court Practice Directions Amendment No. 1 of 2012*, http://app.supremecourt.gov.sg/default.aspx?pgID=4122, 30 Sep. 2017.

1192. *Supreme Court Practice Directions Amendment No. 1 of 2012*, http://app.supremecourt.gov.sg/default.aspx?pgID=4122, 30 Sep. 2017.

1193. *Supreme Court Practice Directions Amendment No. 1 of 2012*, http://app.supremecourt.gov.sg/default.aspx?pgID=412, 30 Sep. 2017.

1194. *Supreme Court Practice Directions Amendment No. 1 of 2012*, http://app.supremecourt.gov.sg/default.aspx?pgID=4122, 30 Sep. 2017.

1195. *Supreme Court Practice Directions Amendment No. 1 of 2012*, http://app.supremecourt.gov.sg/default.aspx?pgID=4122, 30 Sep. 2017.

1196. Supreme Court Practice Directions 2013 (Part V).

specific protocol for e-discovery or inspection.[1197] Where this is the case, the protocols set out in the Practice Directions on e-discovery will be a default starting point that can be customized to suit the precise needs of the case at hand.[1198]

358. It has been observed by the Singapore High Court that the Practice Directions on e-discovery:

> [supplement] the traditional tests of relevancy and necessity by articulating a non-exhaustive list of matters which the court will consider while applying these existing legal principles of discovery. These matters include … the number of electronic documents involved; … the nature of the case and complexity of the issues; … the value of the claim and the financial position of each party; … the ease and expense of retrieval of any particular electronically stored document or class of electronically stored documents … the significance of any particular electronically stored document or class of electronically stored documents which are likely to be located to the issues in dispute.[1199]

359. The 'train of inquiry' analysis has likewise been applied in the e-discovery context to the discovery and inspection of compound documents (electronic storage media such as computer databases and hard disks containing discrete documents).[1200] Though electronically stored documents are not defined in the Practice Directions, case law has included within the scope of such documents e-mails, databases, backup copies, certain types of sound recordings, video recordings, storage media, and recording devices.[1201] The most common method of conducting e-discovery in respect of electronically stored documents is by way of keyword searches. The Singapore High Court has decided in favour of an iterative process for conducting keyword searches in which litigants and their counsel develop keyword search terms and Boolean operators together through negotiation, conduct a preliminary search or data sampling using those search terms and thereafter further narrow or clarify the search terms.[1202] The court will then eventually sanction a final set of search criteria for the purposes of e-discovery.[1203] In deciding whether a particular keyword or set of keywords should be used, the court will consider whether

1197. *Deutsche Bank AG v. Chang Tse Wen*, [2010] SGHC 125, [15]–[16]; *Surface Stone Pte Ltd v. Tay Seng Leon*, [2011] SGHC 223, [60]–[62].
1198. *Surface Stone Pte Ltd v. Tay Seng Leon*, [2011] SGHC 223, [92]–[93].
1199. *Sanae Achar v. Sci-Gen Ltd*, [2011] 3 SLR 967, [10]. *See also Mondial Assistance (Asia) Pte Ltd v. Eric Jean Raymond Morazin*, [2015] SGHC 160, [6].
1200. *Surface Stone Pte Ltd v. Tay Seng Leon*, [2011] SGHC 223, [8]–[26].
1201. *Sanae Achar v. Sci-Gen Ltd*, [2011] 3 SLR 967, [10], citing *Fermin Aldabe v. Standard Chartered Bank*, [2009] SGHC 194; *RecordTV Pte Ltd v. MediaCorp TV Singapore Pte Ltd*, [2010] 2 SLR 152; *Megastar Entertainment Pte Ltd v. Odex Pte Ltd*, [2005] 3 SLR(R) 91.
1202. *Global Yellow Pages Limited v. Promedia Directories Pte Ltd*, [2013] 3 SLR 758, [44]–[49]; *Breezeway Overseas Ltd v. UBS AG*, [2012] 4 SLR 1035, [26]; *Robin Duane Littau v. Astrata (Asia Pacific) Pte Ltd*, [2011] SGHC 61, [19]–[20]; *Mondial Assistance (Asia) Pte Ltd v. Eric Jean Raymond Morazin*, [2015] SGHC 160, [12].
1203. *Breezeway Overseas Ltd v. UBS AG*, [2012] 4 SLR 1035, [26].

it has 'high accuracy',[1204] 'the subset which is produced by the relevant search, i.e., the number of hits which are produced in proportion to the universal set',[1205] and 'other proportionality and economy considerations such as the importance of the documents sought through these keywords to the issues in dispute, the value and importance of the dispute, and the relative financial resources of the parties to the discovery application'.[1206]

360. The court has also repeatedly emphasized the importance and benefits of collaboration and cooperation between the parties in conducting e-discovery,[1207] as well as doing away with 'costly and time-consuming ocular review' of the documents produced by the keyword searches as far as possible.[1208] These exhortations are consistent with the Supreme Court Practice Directions, which provide that within:

> two weeks after the close of pleadings, parties are encouraged to collaborate in good faith and agree on issues relating to the discovery and inspection of electronically stored documents. Such issues may include the scope and/or any limits on documents to be given in discovery, whether parties are prepared to make voluntary disclosures, whether specific documents or class of documents ought to be specifically preserved, search terms to be used in reasonable searches, whether preliminary searches and/or data sampling are to be conducted and the giving of discovery in stages according to an agreed schedule, as well as the format and manner in which copies of discoverable documents shall be supplied. Parties are encouraged to have regard to the list of issues at Appendix E Part 1 (Check list of issues for good faith collaboration) in their discussions. Parties should exchange their checklists prior to commencing good faith discussions.[1209]

361. The Supreme Court Practice Directions further emphasize proportionality and economy, and the matters the court will have regard to in determining whether an application relating to e-discovery is proportionate and economical shall include:[1210]

1204. *Global Yellow Pages Limited v. Promedia Directories Pte Ltd*, [2013] 3 SLR 758, [54]; citing *Breezeway Overseas Ltd v. UBS AG*, [2012] 4 SLR 1035, [28]–[31].
1205. *Global Yellow Pages Limited v. Promedia Directories Pte Ltd*, [2013] 3 SLR 758, [57].
1206. *Global Yellow Pages Limited v. Promedia Directories Pte Ltd*, [2013] 3 SLR 758, [58].
1207. *Global Yellow Pages Limited v. Promedia Directories Pte Ltd*, [2013] 3 SLR 758, [59]–[60], citing G. L. Paul & J. R. Baron, *Information Inflation: Can the Legal System Adapt?*, 13 Richmond J. L. & Tech. 10 (2007); *Fermin Aldabe v. Standard Chartered Bank*, [2009] SGHC 194, [35].
1208. *Global Yellow Pages Limited v. Promedia Directories Pte Ltd*, [2013] 3 SLR 758, [62]–[68], citing *Breezeway Overseas Ltd v. UBS AG*, [2012] 4 SLR 1035, [30]–[34]; *Sanae Achar v. Sci-Gen Ltd*, [2011] 3 SLR 967, [23].
1209. Supreme Court Practice Directions 2013 (Part V). Appendix E Part 1 sets out various questions.
1210. Supreme Court Practice Directions 2013 (Part V). *See also Response by Chief Justice Sundaresh Menon: Opening of the Legal Year 2013 and Welcome Reference for the Chief Justice*, http://app.lsc.gov.sg/data/OLY%202013%20-%20CJ%20Speech%20OLY%20Welcome%20Reference.pdf, 30 Sep. 2017.

(a) the number of electronic documents involved;
(b) the nature of the case and complexity of the issues;
(c) the value of the claim and the financial position of each party;
(d) the ease and expense of retrieval of any particular electronically stored document or class of electronically stored documents, including:
  (1) the accessibility, location and likelihood of locating any relevant documents;
  (2) the costs of recovering and giving discovery and inspection, including the supply of copies, of any relevant documents;
  (3) the likelihood that any relevant documents will be materially altered in the course of recovery, or the giving of discovery or inspection; and
(e) the availability of electronically stored documents or class of electronically stored documents sought from other sources; and
(f) the relevance and materiality of any particular electronically stored document or class of electronically stored documents which are likely to be located to the issues in dispute.

362. These factors are not intended to be exhaustive but clearly signal to the parties the importance of ensuring that the e-discovery process does not lead to more rather than less time and costs being expended and incurred.

§5. POSSIBILITY OF APPEAL

363. Section 34 of the Supreme Court of Judicature Act,[1211] read together with the Fourth and Fifth Schedules of the statute, determines whether any given order of civil procedure is appealable to the Court of Appeal[1212] or not.[1213] The Fourth Schedule does not mention anything about discovery and/or inspection. However, the Fifth Schedule states that: 'Except with the leave of a Judge, no appeal shall be brought to the Court of Appeal … where a Judge makes an order giving or refusing discovery or inspection of documents.' The Fifth Schedule also states that: 'Except with the leave of a Judge, no appeal shall be brought to the Court of Appeal … where a Judge makes an order at the hearing of any interlocutory application other than an application for … discovery or inspection of documents.' In other words, the losing party must obtain leave from the court to appeal against any decision that either results in discovery being awarded against him or a denial of discovery that was being sought.

364. However, a judge's order giving or refusing discovery in a pre-action discovery application is probably appealable as of right. In two recent cases, the Court

1211. (Cap. 322, 2007 Rev. Ed.).
1212. Below it is the High Court, followed by the District and Magistrates' Courts. For appeals arising from the lower courts, *see* Supreme Court of Judicature Act (Cap. 322, R. 5, 2014 Rev. Ed.) Rules of Court, O 55B, 55C, and 55D. There is a right of appeal from a registrar in chambers to a judge in chambers (District Judge if it is the State Courts), but not necessarily after that stage.
1213. The statute was amended in 2010 and 2014.

of Appeal has clarified that the Fourth and Fifth Schedules apply only to interlocutory orders made upon interlocutory applications.[1214] It is likely that an application for pre-action discovery will not be construed as an interlocutory application within the meaning of the Supreme Court of Judicature Act because it is not an application made between the time a party files a civil case in court and when that case is finally heard for disposal; rather, it is an application made by way of originating summons and its only end is the particular relief sought in the originating summons.[1215]

1214. *OpenNet Pte Ltd v. Info-Communications Development Authority of Singapore*, [2013] 2 SLR 880, [21]; *Dorsey James Michael v. World Sport Group Pte Ltd*, [2013] 3 SLR 354, [98].

1215. An analogy may be drawn with *Dorsey James Michael v. World Sport Group Pte Ltd*, [2013] 3 SLR 354, [60], in which the Court of Appeal applied this reasoning to find that an application for pre-action interrogatories was not an interlocutory application within the meaning of the Supreme Court of Judicature Act.

Chapter 2. Interrogatory Proceedings

§1. Introduction

365. To aid in the elimination and clarification of the issues of a dispute, a person may be required to answer as to the existence of some fact or facts within his knowledge and relevant to the dispute. This is a process known as interrogatories, a form of discovery and method of proof that evolved from the English courts of equity and have since been adopted locally.[1216] While interrogatories are 'relatively rare in practice as the pleadings … and the exchange of affidavits of the evidence-in-chief of the witnesses for both parties before trial, often provide sufficient information', they can be useful in focusing on very specific facts which have not been properly addressed in the other court documents.[1217] Indeed, interrogatories may in certain circumstances also be more appropriate than a particular discovery application, especially if the latter constitutes a 'fishing' expedition of sorts and may harass or embarrass the other party,[1218] and interrogatories may also be helpful in identifying possible parties to any proceedings.[1219] Answers to interrogatories 'form part of the general body of the evidence in the case; the party who puts them in is not bound to accept their truthfulness but may call other evidence which contradicts them'.[1220] The rules and procedures for interrogatories are primarily found in O 26 of the Rules of Court,[1221] while rules and procedures for pre-action interrogatories are found in O 26A.

§2. Procedural Aspects

366. There are two types of interrogatories: those without order (can be administered without the leave of court) and those that are ordered (leave of court is required).[1222] Both types of interrogatories have prescribed forms for service and

1216. *Singapore Civil Procedure 2015 Volume 1*, at 583 (G.P. Selvam ed., Sweet & Maxwell Asia 2014); J. Pinsler, *Principles of Civil Procedure* 671 (Acad. Publg. 2013). *See also Dorsey James Michael v. World Sport Group Pte Ltd*, [2014] 2 SLR 208, [23]–[24]; *Prudential Assurance Co Singapore Pte Ltd v. Tan Shou Yi Peter*, [2018] SGHCR 4.
1217. J. Pinsler, *Principles of Civil Procedure* 671 (Acad. Publg. 2013). *See also Trek Technology (Singapore) Pte Ltd v. Ritronics Components (S'pore) Pte Ltd*, [2007] 1 SLR(R) 846, [6].
1218. *Oversea-Chinese Banking Corp Ltd v. Wright Norman*, [1989] 1 SLR(R) 551, [14]; *XACCT Technologies Ltd v. Orient Telecommunications Networks Pte Ltd formerly known as Orient Telecommunications Networks (Singapore) Pte Ltd and formerly known as XA Alliance Pte Ltd*, [2004] SGHC 144, [3]; C. Bull & J. Pinsler, *Civil Procedure: Annual Review of Singapore Cases* [6.82] (Sing. Acad. L. 2004). *See also* J. Pinsler, *Principles of Civil Procedure* 673 (Acad. Publg. 2013).
1219. *World Sport Group Pte Ltd v. Dorsey James Michael*, [2013] 3 SLR 180, [15]–[16], citing *Norwich Pharmacal Co v. Customs and Excise Commissioners*, [1974] AC 133, 174.
1220. *Singapore Civil Procedure 2013 Volume 1*, at 533 (G.P. Selvam ed., Sweet & Maxwell Asia 2012).
1221. Supreme Court of Judicature Act (Cap. 322, R. 5, 2014 Rev. Ed.) Rules of Court.
1222. It is possible for parties to agree to exclude the operation of interrogatories: *Berry & Stewart v. Tottenham Hotspur Football and Athletic Co Ltd*, [1935] Ch 718, 727.

answers.[1223] A party who wishes to administer interrogatories should first approach the other party and make the request. If this is refused or if the answers are incomplete, the party may then apply to the court (by way of summons).[1224]

367. For interrogatories without order, they may be served on a party not more than twice (anything more would require the leave of court).[1225] In addition, a party on whom interrogatories without order are served 'may, within 14 days of the service of the interrogatories, apply to the Court for the interrogatories to be varied or withdrawn and, on any such application, the Court may make such order as it thinks fit (including an order that the party who served the interrogatories shall not serve further interrogatories without order)'.[1226]

368. As is the case with discovery, it is possible for interrogatories to be served before the commencement of the action and also to be served on non-parties to the action.[1227] However, while 'the Rules of Court do not expressly prohibit the use of interrogatories at trial, this restriction is implied by the nature of the process'.[1228]

§3. Substantive Aspects

369. A party to any cause or matter may 'serve on any other party interrogatories relating to any matter in question between the applicant and that other party in the cause or matter which are necessary either … for disposing fairly of the cause or matter; or … for saving costs'.[1229] This is essentially a test of necessity, and a 'stringent test' applies in its determination.[1230] At least five consequences arise from this stringent requirement of necessity. First, interrogatories should not be used to acquire information on matters not related to the dispute (such as asking the defendant about potential defences that have yet to be pleaded); second, interrogatories should be confined to facts which the interrogator has some basis for believing are true; third, interrogatories should not be preferred over other processes in the civil

1223. Supreme Court of Judicature Act (Cap. 322, R. 5, 2014 Rev. Ed.) Rules of Court, O 26 rr 2 and 4.
1224. Supreme Court of Judicature Act (Cap. 322, R. 5, 2014 Rev. Ed.) Rules of Court, O 26 r 2; *Singapore Civil Procedure 2015 Volume 1*, at 586 (G.P. Selvam ed., Sweet & Maxwell Asia 2014).
1225. Supreme Court of Judicature Act (Cap. 322, R. 5, 2014 Rev. Ed.) Rules of Court, O 26 r 3(1).
1226. Supreme Court of Judicature Act (Cap. 322, R. 5, 2014 Rev. Ed.) Rules of Court, O 26 r 3(2).
1227. Supreme Court of Judicature Act (Cap. 322, R. 5, 2014 Rev. Ed.) Rules of Court, O 26A r 1(2); C. Bull & J. Pinsler, *Civil Procedure: Annual Review of Singapore Cases* [7.52] (Sing. Acad. L. 2007), citing *Tullet Prebon (S) Ltd v. Spring Mark Geoffrey*, [2007] 3 SLR(R) 187. *See also Dorsey James Michael v. World Sport Group Pte Ltd*, [2014] 2 SLR 208, [25]–[27].
1228. C. Bull & J. Pinsler, *Civil Procedure: Annual Review of Singapore Cases* [7.50] (Sing. Acad. L. 2007), citing *Trek Technology (Singapore) Pte Ltd v. Ritronics Components (S'pore) Pte Ltd*, [2007] 1 SLR(R) 846, [4].
1229. Supreme Court of Judicature Act (Cap. 322, R. 5, 2014 Rev. Ed.) Rules of Court, O 26 r 1(1). *See also Richland Logistics Services Pte Ltd v. Biforst Singapore Pte Ltd*, [2006] SGHC 137, [38]; cited in *World Sport Group Pte Ltd v. Dorsey James Michael*, [2013] 3 SLR 180, [18].
1230. J. Pinsler, *Principles of Civil Procedure* 673 (Acad. Publg. 2013), citing *Hall v. Sevalco*, [1996] 1 PIQR 344, 349.

justice process if the latter are more appropriate; fourth, interrogatories should not be prolix or oppressive in nature; and fifth, interrogatories that relate solely to the credit of witnesses are not allowed.[1231]

370. For ordered interrogatories, 'the Court shall take into account any offer made by the party to be interrogated to give particulars, make admissions or produce documents relating to any matter in question and whether or not interrogatories without order have been administered'.[1232]

371. A party on whom interrogatories are sought may challenge the interrogatories on the ground of privilege by objecting in his answer.[1233] Though not provided for in the Rules of Court, a party on whom interrogatories are sought may also object if the questions are illegitimate, unclear, or difficult to answer.[1234] Either type of objection may be raised at the hearing for leave to administer interrogatories.[1235]

372. A party on whom interrogatories are sought should 'answer them to the best of his knowledge and belief … [and] may have to provide information known by another person where the party is responsible for that person acquiring that knowledge'.[1236] This means that he 'must, if necessary, seek the information he is required to give from documents in his possession or power … [and] is bound to give all the information of which he is personally possessed at the time he is interrogated, from whatever sources or persons it has been derived'.[1237] If responses to ordered interrogatories are insufficient, 'the Court may make an order requiring him to make a further answer, either by affidavit or on oral examination as the Court may direct'.[1238] If responses to interrogatories without order are insufficient, 'the party serving the interrogatories may ask for further and better particulars of the answer given and any such request shall not be treated as service of further interrogatories'.[1239] If further and better particulars are not forthcoming, the party making the request should apply to court for an appropriate order to be made, such as dismissal of action, striking out of defence, entering of judgment, making an unless order, or even committal.[1240] Finally, any order for interrogatories 'may, on sufficient cause

1231. J. Pinsler, *Principles of Civil Procedure* 673–675 (Acad. Publg. 2013); Supreme Court of Judicature Act (Cap. 322, R. 5, 2014 Rev. Ed.) Rules of Court, O 26 r 1(3).
1232. Supreme Court of Judicature Act (Cap. 322, R. 5, 2014 Rev. Ed.) Rules of Court, O 26 r 4(2).
1233. Supreme Court of Judicature Act (Cap. 322, R. 5, 2014 Rev. Ed.) Rules of Court, O 26 r 5(1).
1234. J. Pinsler, *Principles of Civil Procedure* 678 (Acad. Publg. 2013).
1235. J. Pinsler, *Principles of Civil Procedure* 678 (Acad. Publg. 2013).
1236. J. Pinsler, *Principles of Civil Procedure* 679–680 (Acad. Publg. 2013) citing *Douglas v. Morning Post*, (1923) 39 TLR 402; *Anderson v. Bank of British Columbia*, (1876) 2 Ch D 644, 657–659.
1237. *Singapore Civil Procedure 2013 Volume 1*, at 532 (G.P. Selvam ed., Sweet & Maxwell Asia 2012).
1238. Supreme Court of Judicature Act (Cap. 322, R. 5, 2014 Rev. Ed.) Rules of Court, O 26 r 5(2).
1239. Supreme Court of Judicature Act (Cap. 322, R. 5, 2014 Rev. Ed.) Rules of Court, O 26 r 5(3).
1240. Supreme Court of Judicature Act (Cap. 322, R. 5, 2014 Rev. Ed.) Rules of Court, O 26 r 6(1); J. Pinsler, *Principles of Civil Procedure* 679, 688 (Acad. Publg. 2013). These various measures are considered at different parts of the book.

being shown, be revoked or varied by a subsequent order or direction of the Court made or given at or before the trial of the cause or matter in connection with which the original order was made'.[1241]

373. As regards pre-action interrogatories, the Court of Appeal has stated on numerous occasions that it is not usual to grant an application for pre-action interrogatories because of its intrusive nature – especially when it involves individuals who may ultimately not (or cannot) be parties to the litigation.[1242] Although the requirements of necessity and relevance remain the main cornerstone, the court also has to be satisfied 'that it would be just in all the circumstances to make an order for a non-party to the potential causes of action … to answer pre-action interrogatories'.[1243] Therefore, a significant consideration against making an order for pre-action interrogatories is if the applicant can, at the time of making of application, immediately commence proceedings against an identified party without the disclosure sought.[1244]

§4. Possibility of Appeal

374. Section 34 of the Supreme Court of Judicature Act,[1245] read together with the Fourth and Fifth Schedules of the statute, determines whether any given order of civil procedure is appealable to the Court of Appeal[1246] or not.[1247] The Fourth Schedule states that: 'No appeal shall be brought to the Court of Appeal … where a Judge makes an order giving or refusing interrogatories.' The Fifth Schedule states that: 'Except with the leave of a Judge, no appeal shall be brought to the Court of Appeal … where a Judge makes an order at the hearing of any interlocutory application other than an application for … interrogatories to be varied or withdrawn, or for leave to serve interrogatories.' In other words, if a party fails to obtain an order for interrogatories, he cannot appeal. Likewise, if a party is ordered to provide responses to interrogatories, he cannot appeal.[1248] However, as regards applications to vary or withdraw interrogatories or for leave to serve them, parties may appeal with leave from the court.

1241. Supreme Court of Judicature Act (Cap. 322, R. 5, 2014 Rev. Ed.) Rules of Court, O 26 r 8.
1242. *Dorsey James Michael v. World Sport Group Pte Ltd*, [2014] 2 SLR 208, [49]–[50]; *Navigator Investment Services Ltd v. Acclaim Insurance Brokers Pte Ltd*, [2010] 1 SLR 25, [63].
1243. *Dorsey James Michael v. World Sport Group Pte Ltd*, [2014] 2 SLR 208, [55]. *See also* id., [47].
1244. *Dorsey James Michael v. World Sport Group Pte Ltd*, [2014] 2 SLR 208, [48], [78].
1245. (Cap. 322, 2007 Rev. Ed.).
1246. Below it is the High Court, followed by the District and Magistrates' Courts. For appeals arising from the lower courts, *see* Supreme Court of Judicature Act (Cap. 322, R. 5, 2014 Rev. Ed.) Rules of Court, O 55B, 55C, and 55D. There is a right of appeal from a registrar in chambers to a judge in chambers (District Judge if it is the State Courts), but not necessarily after that stage.
1247. The statute was amended in 2010 and 2014.
1248. If the order is for pre-action interrogatories to be given, the party so ordered has a right of appeal to the Court of Appeal: *Dorsey James Michael v. World Sport Group Pte Ltd*, [2013] 3 SLR 354, [74].

Chapter 3. Third-Party Proceedings

§1. Introduction

375. If a defendant intends to claim against another party or an existing party so as to be, for instance, indemnified or receive contribution in some way, he may institute third-party proceedings against such a party.[1249] The main purpose of instituting third-party proceedings is twofold: to prevent multiplicity of actions and to enable the court to adjudicate on disputes between all parties in a single action; and to prevent the same question from being tried twice with possibly different results.[1250] In the same vein, because the introduction of third-party proceedings will protract litigation and likely incur greater expenses for all parties, it will only be considered as justified in fairly limited circumstances.[1251] The rules and procedures for third-party proceedings are primarily found in O 16 of the Rules of Court,[1252] and are based almost entirely on (fairly ancient) English law.[1253]

§2. Procedural Aspects

376. As a starting point, third-party proceedings must commence before the termination of the main proceedings.[1254] A 'defendant to an action may not issue a third-party notice without the leave of the Court unless the action was begun by writ and he issues the notice before serving his defence on the plaintiff'.[1255] However, in the alternative, a:

> defendant may, after having entered an appearance if required to do so … issue a notice in [either of the prescribed forms], whichever is appropriate

---

1249. J. Pinsler, *Principles of Civil Procedure* 232 (Acad. Publg. 2013). Third-party proceedings should be differentiated from joinder of parties, which refers to the court's power to add parties to proceedings as plaintiffs or defendants if their presence is necessary for the purpose of adjudication: *id.*, 230. Third-party proceedings should also be differentiated from consolidation. Consolidation is appropriate 'where separate actions have been initiated but ought to be joined because the actions are linked to an extent which would secure the advantages (such as costs, time, effort and convenience of a global adjudication in a single suit': *id.*, 222–223. *See also* Supreme Court of Judicature Act (Cap. 322, R. 5, 2014 Rev. Ed.) Rules of Court, O 4.

1250. *Chancery Law Corp v. Management Corporation Strata Title Plan No 1024 (Mok Wai Hoe, third parties)*, [2015] SGHC 66, [47]; *Firststate Pte Ltd v. Raviland Pte Ltd (trading as Challenge Reticulation)*, [1994] 3 SLR(R) 523, [8], citing *Barclays Bank v. Tom*, [1923] 1 KB 221, 223 and 225; *Benecke v. Frost*, (1876) 1 QBD 419, 422. *See also Ng Kit Har v. Yii Chee Ming*, [2008] 2 SLR(R) 587, [22]–[23].

1251. J. Pinsler, *Principles of Civil Procedure* 233 (Acad. Publg. 2013).

1252. Supreme Court of Judicature Act (Cap. 322, R. 5, 2014 Rev. Ed.) Rules of Court.

1253. *Singapore Civil Procedure 2015 Volume 1*, at 265 – 266 (G.P. Selvam ed., Sweet & Maxwell Asia 2014).

1254. *Ng Kit Har v. Yii Chee Ming*, [2008] 2 SLR(R) 587, [15]–[17]; C. Bull & J. Pinsler, *Civil Procedure: Annual Review of Singapore Cases* [7.55] (Sing. Acad. Law 2008).

1255. Supreme Court of Judicature Act (Cap. 322, R. 5, 2014 Rev. Ed.) Rules of Court, O 16 r 1(2). For notices beyond third parties, *see id.*, O 16 r 9. *See also id.* O 16 r 8 where there are claims between a defendant and some other party.

(referred to in this Order as a third party notice), containing a statement of the nature of the claim made against him and, as the case may be, either of the nature and grounds of the claim made by him or of the question or issue required to be determined.[1256]

377. If leave is required, the application 'may be made by ex parte summons in [the prescribed form] but the Court may direct the summons to be served'.[1257] Such an application must be supported by an affidavit stating:

> the nature of the claim made by the plaintiff in the action; … the stage which proceedings in the action have reached; … the nature of the claim made by the applicant or particulars of the question or issue required to be determined, as the case may be, and the facts on which the proposed third party notice is based; and … the name and address of the person against whom the third party notice is to be issued.[1258]

378. The practice is that 'if a prima facie case is made out which would bring the matter within [O 16 r 1] leave will be granted to issue the notice … and the court will not, in granting leave, consider the merits of the claim'.[1259] However, the court will not grant leave 'where the result will be to embarrass or delay the plaintiff … nor where the questions at issue cannot be completely disposed of in the action'.[1260]

379. In an action begun by writ, the third-party notice is to be treated as a writ, and the proceedings begun thereby an action in which the defendant issuing the notice is a plaintiff and the third party a defendant in that action.[1261] Indeed, 'third party proceedings [have] a life of their own independent from the main action between the plaintiff and the defendant and that even if the main action was settled, the third party proceedings could still proceed as if they were a separate action'.[1262] Once a third-party notice is granted, it will be assigned a serial number by the registry, and it has to be signed, sealed, and dated before it is issued.[1263] When the third-party notice is served, it must be served with 'a copy of the writ or originating summons by which the action was begun and of the pleadings (if any) served in the

1256. Supreme Court of Judicature Act (Cap. 322, R. 5, 2014 Rev. Ed.) Rules of Court, O 16 r 1(1).
1257. Supreme Court of Judicature Act (Cap. 322, R. 5, 2014 Rev. Ed.) Rules of Court, O 16 r 2(1). *See also Furness, Withy & Co v. Pickering*, [1908] 2 Ch 224.
1258. Supreme Court of Judicature Act (Cap. 322, R. 5, 2014 Rev. Ed.) Rules of Court, O 16 r 2(2).
1259. *Singapore Civil Procedure 2015 Volume 1*, at 269 (G.P. Selvam ed., Sweet & Maxwell Asia 2014), citing *Carshore v. North Eastern Rly Co*, (1885) 29 Ch D 344, 347.
1260. *Singapore Civil Procedure 2015 Volume 1*, at 269 (G.P. Selvam ed., Sweet & Maxwell Asia 2014), citing *Bower v. Hartley*, (1876) 1 QBD 652; *Baxter v. France (No 2)*, [1895] 1 QB 591.
1261. Supreme Court of Judicature Act (Cap. 322, R. 5, 2014 Rev. Ed.) Rules of Court, O 16 r 3(3); *Johnson v. Ribbins*, [1977] 1 WLR 1458, 1464. If the action is begun by originating summons, *see id.*, O 16 r 4. *See also id.*, O 16 r 11.
1262. *Kimly Construction Pte Ltd v. Lee Tong Boon (trading as Rango Machinery Services) (Tan Juay Pah, third party; Feng Tianming, fourth parties)*, [2011] SGHC 26, [47], citing *Stott v. West Yorkshire Road Car Co Ltd*, [1971] 2 QB 651, 657.
1263. Supreme Court of Judicature Act (Cap. 322, R. 5, 2014 Rev. Ed.) Rules of Court, O 16 r 3(3).

action'.[1264] By default, personal service of the third-party notice (if it assumes the form of a writ) is required.[1265] If the third party is out of jurisdiction (i.e., out of Singapore), the rules governing service out of jurisdiction will apply.[1266] Once a third-party notice has been properly issued and served, the third party 'shall as from the time of service be a party to the action … with the same rights in respect of his defence against any claim made against him in the notice and otherwise as if he had been duly sued in the ordinary way by the defendant by whom the notice is issued'.[1267]

380. The rules on appearance will also apply to the third-party notice (if it assumes the form of a writ).[1268] Thus, if the third party defaults on appearance, he is deemed to have admitted to any claim stated in the third-party notice and will be bound by any judgment rendered against him.[1269] Furthermore, if the:

> third party or the defendant by whom a third party notice was issued makes default in serving any pleading which he is ordered to serve, the Court may, on the application by summons of that defendant or the third party, as the case may be, order such judgment to be entered for the applicant as he is entitled to on the pleadings or may make such other order as may appear to the Court necessary to do justice between the parties.[1270]

381. The court, however, has the discretion to set aside or vary a judgment entered pursuant to a default of appearance or pleading on the part of the third party 'as it thinks just'.[1271] Once appearance has been entered by the third party, the defendant must by summons (using the prescribed form) to be served on all the other parties to the action, apply to the court for directions.[1272] Where possible, 'the summons for third party directions should be made returnable at the same time as the plaintiff's summons for directions, for this will provide a convenient occasion for the court and all the parties to consider the directions best suited to the future course of action'.[1273] If the defendant fails to apply for directions, the third party may 'in an action begun by writ, not earlier than seven days after entering an appearance; or … in an action begun by originating summons, not earlier than 14

1264. Supreme Court of Judicature Act (Cap. 322, R. 5, 2014 Rev. Ed.) Rules of Court, O 16 r 3(2).
1265. Supreme Court of Judicature Act (Cap. 322, R. 5, 2014 Rev. Ed.) Rules of Court, O 16 r 3(3).
1266. Supreme Court of Judicature Act (Cap. 322, R. 5, 2014 Rev. Ed.) Rules of Court, O 16 r 3(3).
1267. Supreme Court of Judicature Act (Cap. 322, R. 5, 2014 Rev. Ed.) Rules of Court, O 16 r 1(3). *See also Lee Kuan Yew v. Nair Devan (Straits Times Press (1975) Ltd)*, [1992] 3 SLR(R) 757, [14], citing *Barcalys Bank v. Tom*, [1923] 1 KB 221.
1268. Supreme Court of Judicature Act (Cap. 322, R. 5, 2014 Rev. Ed.) Rules of Court, O 16 r 3(3).
1269. Supreme Court of Judicature Act (Cap. 322, R. 5, 2014 Rev. Ed.) Rules of Court, O 16 r 5(1).
1270. Supreme Court of Judicature Act (Cap. 322, R. 5, 2014 Rev. Ed.) Rules of Court, O 16 r 5(2).
1271. Supreme Court of Judicature Act (Cap. 322, R. 5, 2014 Rev. Ed.) Rules of Court, O 16 r 5(3).
1272. Supreme Court of Judicature Act (Cap. 322, R. 5, 2014 Rev. Ed.) Rules of Court, O 16 r 4(1); *Tritton v. Bankhart*, (1887) 56 LJ Ch 629. If the defendant does not apply for directions, the court at the trial will not entertain the claim raised by the notice: *Singapore Civil Procedure 2015 Volume 1*, at 271 (G.P. Selvam ed., Sweet & Maxwell Asia 2014).
1273. *Singapore Civil Procedure 2015 Volume 1*, at 272 (G.P. Selvam ed., Sweet & Maxwell Asia 2014).

days after service of the notice on him, by summons in [the prescribed form] to be served on all the other parties to the action, apply to the Court for directions or for an order to set aside the third party notice'.[1274] Finally, 'the Court may at or after the trial of the action, or, if the action is decided otherwise than by trial, on an application by summons, order such judgment as the nature of the case may require to be entered for the defendant against the third party or for the third party against the defendant'.[1275]

§3. Substantive Aspects

382. A third-party notice can only be justified if it meets one of the three prescribed grounds.[1276] First, the defendant is claiming 'against a person not already a party to the action any contribution or indemnity'.[1277] A 'claim to contribution is a claim to a partial indemnity ... A right to contribution usually arises as between joint debtors, or joint contractors, or joint trustees, or joint sureties, or joint wrongdoers, and it may be created by statute'.[1278] An indemnity, on the other hand, may arise from express contract, some statute, or implied from some principle of law.[1279] Second, the defendant is claiming 'against such a person any relief or remedy relating to or connected with the original subject matter of the action and substantially the same as some relief or remedy claimed by the plaintiff'.[1280] This normally arises 'when the damages or other remedy claimed against the defendant may be claimed by the defendant against a third party'.[1281] Third, the defendant 'requires that any question or issue relating to or connected with the original subject matter of the action should be determined not only as between the plaintiff and the defendant but also as between either or both of them and a person not already

1274. Supreme Court of Judicature Act (Cap. 322, R. 5, 2014 Rev. Ed.) Rules of Court, O 16 r 4(2).
1275. Supreme Court of Judicature Act (Cap. 322, R. 5, 2014 Rev. Ed.) Rules of Court, O 16 r 7(1).
1276. *See also Chancery Law Corp v. Management Corporation Strata Title Plan No 1024 (Mok Wai Hoe, third parties)*, [2015] SGHC 66, [45].
1277. Supreme Court of Judicature Act (Cap. 322, R. 5, 2014 Rev. Ed.) Rules of Court, O 16 r 1(1). There is a prescribed form to be used. *See also* Civil Law Act (Cap. 43, 1999 Rev. Ed.), s 15(1).
1278. *Singapore Civil Procedure 2015 Volume 1*, at 266 (G.P. Selvam ed., Sweet & Maxwell Asia 2014); *Hygeian Medical Supplies Pte Ltd v. Tri-Star Rotary Screen Engraving Works Pte Ltd*, [1993] 2 SLR(R) 411; *Ling Mang Khong Stanley v. Teo Chee Siong (Yeo Boon Hwa, third party)*, [2013] SGHC 58. *See also* Limitation Act (Cap. 163, 1996 Rev. Ed.), s 6A on special rules on limitation for contributions and the Civil Law Act (Cap. 43, 1999 Rev. Ed.) on particular provisions as to entitlement to contribution (and cases such as *Sakae Holdings Ltd v. Gryphon Real Estate Investment Corp Pte Ltd*, [2017] SGHC 100 interpreting those provisions).
1279. *EQ Capital Investments Ltd v. Sunbreeze Group Investments Ltd*, [2017] SGHC 271, [64]; *Singapore Civil Procedure 2015 Volume 1*, at 267 (G.P. Selvam ed., Sweet & Maxwell Asia 2014), citing *Goh Sin Huat Electrical Pte Ltd v. Ho See Jui (t/a Xuanhua Art Gallery)*, [2012] 3 SLR 1038 and *Eastern Shipping Co v. Quah Beng Kee*, [1924] AC 177.
1280. Supreme Court of Judicature Act (Cap. 322, R. 5, 2014 Rev. Ed.) Rules of Court, O 16 r 1(1). There is a prescribed form to be used.
1281. J. Pinsler, *Principles of Civil Procedure* 236 (Acad. Publg. 2013), citing *Myers v. N & J Sherick Ltd*, [1974] 1 WLR 31.

a party to the action'.[1282] Under this ground, 'the issues on which it is sought to have a determination between the defendant and the proposed third party must already be issues in the action between the plaintiff and the defendant. If they are not, then the third party cannot be joined for the purpose of determining those issues.'[1283] If either the plaintiff or the third party wishes to object to the defendant's application for third-party proceedings, he should adduce evidence by affidavit to support such an objection.[1284] The standard to be met is whether there are any 'special circumstances' as to why the third-party proceedings should not be allowed to continue or should be terminated.[1285]

383. From the three prescribed grounds above, the real test in determining if a third-party action should be heard together with the main action is 'not that of connection alone but whether they are inextricably linked and the third party is an integral and inseparable part of the main action'.[1286] In all these cases, the court enjoys a general discretion in deciding whether or not to allow the issuance of a third-party notice.[1287] The court also has discretion to set aside, or to refuse to grant leave to issue a third-party notice, if there may be nothing to gain from determining all matters at once[1288] or where the plaintiff would be embarrassed by the desire of the defendants to have the whole question of the third party's liability decided at once.[1289]

384. During the application for directions, the court can make a number of orders. First, 'if the liability of the third party to the defendant who issued the third party notice is established on the hearing, [the court may] order such judgment as the nature of the case may require to be entered against the third party in favour of the defendant'.[1290] Second, the court may 'order any claim, question or issue stated in the third party notice to be tried in such manner as the Court may direct'.[1291] Third, the court may 'dismiss the application and terminate the proceedings on the

1282. Supreme Court of Judicature Act (Cap. 322, R. 5, 2014 Rev. Ed.) Rules of Court, O 16 r 1(1). There is a prescribed form to be used.
1283. *Nganthavee Teriya v. Ang Yee Lim Lawrence*, [2003] 2 SLR(R) 361, [37]; cited in *Ling Mang Khong Stanley v. Tan Chee Siong (Yeo Boon Hwa, third party)*, [2013] SGHC 58, [33].
1284. *Singapore Civil Procedure 2015 Volume 1*, at 272 (G.P. Selvam ed., Sweet & Maxwell Asia 2014).
1285. *Lee Kuan Yew v. Nair Devan (Straits Times Press (1975) Ltd)*, [1992] 3 SLR(R) 757, [15]–[16].
1286. *CIMB Bank Bhd v. Dresdner Kleinwort Ltd*, [2008] 4 SLR(R) 543, [82], cited in *Chancery Law Corp v. Management Corporation Strata Title Plan No 1024 (Mok Wai Hoe, third parties)*, [2015] SGHC 66, [61]–[62].
1287. *Chancery Law Corp v. Management Corporation Strata Title Plan No 1024 (Mok Wai Hoe, third parties)*, [2015] SGHC 66, [46].
1288. *Chancery Law Corp v. Management Corporation Strata Title Plan No 1024 (Mok Wai Hoe, third parties)*, [2015] SGHC 66, [51].
1289. *Chancery Law Corp v. Management Corporation Strata Title Plan No 1024 (Mok Wai Hoe, third parties)*, [2015] SGHC 66, [51], citing *Carshore v. North Eastern Railway Company*, (1885) 29 Ch D 344, 346. *See also Bower v. Hartley*, (1876) 1 QB 652, 656.
1290. Supreme Court of Judicature Act (Cap. 322, R. 5, 2014 Rev. Ed.) Rules of Court, O 16 r 4(3). There is a prescribed form to be used.
1291. Supreme Court of Judicature Act (Cap. 322, R. 5, 2014 Rev. Ed.) Rules of Court, O 16 r 4(3). There is a prescribed form to be used.

third-party notice; and may do so either before or after any judgment in the action has been signed by the plaintiff against the defendant'.[1292] Fourth, the court:

> may give the third party leave to defend the action, either alone or jointly with any defendant, upon such terms as may be just, or to appear at the trial or hearing and to take such part therein as may be just, and generally may make such orders and give such directions as appear to the Court proper for having the rights and liabilities of the parties most conveniently determined and enforced and as to the extent to which the third party is to be bound by any judgment or decision in the action.[1293]

385. If third-party proceedings are improperly brought, the likely outcome is that the responsible party will be penalized in costs.[1294] Finally, it should be noted that the third-party proceedings 'may, at any stage … be set aside by the Court'.[1295] This discretion is supplementary to the court's powers (as discussed above) to dismiss the summons for third-party directions; set aside the third-party notice on the application of the third party; and to set aside or vary a judgment entered in default.[1296] An application for this is to be made by summons.[1297]

§4. Possibility of Appeal

386. Section 34 of the Supreme Court of Judicature Act,[1298] read together with the Fourth and Fifth Schedules of the statute, determines whether any given order of civil procedure is appealable to the Court of Appeal[1299] or not.[1300] However, applications relating to third-party proceedings are not explicitly covered by either the Fourth (orders made by a judge that are non-appealable) or Fifth (orders made by a judge that are only appealable with leave) Schedules. Accordingly, it would seem that an appeal against a decision that say, a refusal to grant an order for third-party notice requires leave from the court, since the Fourth Schedule does not declare it to be non-appealable and the Fifth Schedule does not require leave to be sought.

1292. Supreme Court of Judicature Act (Cap. 322, R. 5, 2014 Rev. Ed.) Rules of Court, O 16 r 4(3). There is a prescribed form to be used.
1293. Supreme Court of Judicature Act (Cap. 322, R. 5, 2014 Rev. Ed.) Rules of Court, O 16 r 4(4). There is a prescribed form to be used.
1294. *Chan Kern Miang v. Kea Resources Pte Ltd*, [1998] 2 SLR(R) 85, [30].
1295. Supreme Court of Judicature Act (Cap. 322, R. 5, 2014 Rev. Ed.) Rules of Court, O 16 r 6.
1296. *Singapore Civil Procedure 2015 Volume 1*, at 276 (G.P. Selvam ed., Sweet & Maxwell Asia 2014).
1297. *Singapore Civil Procedure 2015 Volume 1*, at 276 (G.P. Selvam ed., Sweet & Maxwell Asia 2014).
1298. (Cap. 322, 2007 Rev. Ed.).
1299. Below it is the High Court, followed by the District and Magistrates' Courts. For appeals arising from the lower courts, *see* Supreme Court of Judicature Act (Cap. 322, R. 5, 2014 Rev. Ed.) Rules of Court, O 55B, 55C, and 55D. There is a right of appeal from a registrar in chambers to a judge in chambers (District Judge if it is the State Courts), but not necessarily after that stage.
1300. The statute was amended in 2010 and 2014.

387. Due to recent amendments to the Supreme Court of Judicature Act, the law on this is currently in flux and while it has been suggested that the 'default' position is that all interlocutory applications, unless provided for statutorily, are appealable with leave,[1301] it may also be possible to argue that for interlocutory applications not expressly addressed by the Fourth and Fifth Schedules, 'an appeal to the Court of Appeal will remain as of right for orders made at interlocutory applications which will finally dispose of the substantive rights of the parties'.[1302]

1301. *See* E. Chua, *Defining an 'Interlocutory Application*, Sing. L. Watch Commentaries (4/2013); D. Chi, *Clarification on Leave to Appeal Regime in Respect of Interlocutory Matters: OpenNet Pte Ltd v. Info-Communications Development Authority of Singapore [2013] SGCA 24*, Sing. L. Watch Commentaries (4/2013); C. Siyuan & E. Chua, '*The Right to Appeal Against a Decision Made on an Interlocutory Application: The Immediate Aftermath of the 2010 Amendments*, 25 Sing. Acad. L.J. 424 (2013).

1302. *OpenNet Pte Ltd v. Info-Communications Development Authority of Singapore*, [2013] 2 SLR 880, [29]. *See also Dorsey James Michael v. World Sport Group Pte Ltd*, [2013] 3 SLR 354, [98]. On the other hand, where the statute has made it clear that there is no appeal as of right, one is precluded from arguing that substantive rights have been engaged: *Kosui Singapore Pte Ltd v. Thangavelu*, [2016] 2 SLR 105, [28]–[29].

Chapter 4. Default Proceedings

§1. Introduction

388. This chapter concerns two closely related applications. The first is default judgment, which allows a plaintiff to obtain expedited justice (i.e., without going through a full trial). The second is setting aside, which allows a defendant to set aside a default judgment awarded against him.[1303] The leading local case on default judgments and setting aside is a recent Court of Appeal decision, which not only made important clarifications on some of the long-standing (local and English) jurisprudence on the applicable law and principles, but also provided a neat summary of the doctrine:[1304]

> A default judgment is usually entered because the defendant has breached procedural rules.[1305] However, there may also be cases where, quite apart from the defendant's non-compliance with procedural rules, the plaintiff itself breaches procedural rules and enters a default judgment when it is not in fact entitled to do so. Case law, quite logically, draws a distinction between regular and irregular default judgments. This approach reflects the court's concern with the reasons for the defendant's setting-aside application, and rightly so since a default judgment, properly entered, confers property rights on the plaintiff. Before exercising its discretion to set aside a default judgment, the court is entitled to inquire into the parties' conduct and assess where the balance of the equities lie. If the default judgment is regular, there is a presumption that the plaintiff acted correctly and should not be lightly deprived of the fruits of its judgment;[1306] conversely, if the default judgment is irregular, there is a presumption that the plaintiff breached the proper procedure and, thus, should not be allowed to take advantage of its own default. (It should, however, be noted that a judgment may be irregular not only because of the plaintiff's intentional failure to comply with procedural rules, but also because of clerical or accidental mistakes made by the plaintiff.) Not surprisingly, the defendant has a heavier burden to discharge when it seeks to set aside a regular default judgment.[1307]

1303. It is also possible for a plaintiff to set aside a default judgment entered in his favour: C. Bull & J. Pinsler, *Civil Procedure: Annual Review of Singapore Cases* [8.47] (Sing. Acad. L. 2010), citing *Panin International Credit (S) Pte Ltd v. Ngan Ching Wen*, [2010] SGHC 332, [9].

1304. *See also* J. Pinsler, *Last Flight of the Eagle: New Principles Governing the Setting Aside of Judgments in Default*, 21 Sing. Acad. L.J. 161, 162 (2009); Goh Y.H., *Setting Aside a Default Judgment: New Developments in Singapore*, 28 Civ. J. Q. 200 (2009).

1305. The breach in question is usually with regard to the defendant's failure to enter an appearance or file a defence.

1306. *See also* J. Pinsler, *Principles of Civil Procedure* 332–333 (Acad. Publg. 2013).

1307. *Mercurine Pte Ltd v. Canberra Development Pte Ltd*, [2008] 4 SLR(R) 907, [43] (emphasis in original); cited in *Oversea-Chinese Banking Corp Ltd v. Frankel Motor Pte Ltd*, [2009] 3 SLR(R) 623, [16]–[20].

389. However, the Rules of Court[1308] only contain rather threadbare provisions on default judgment and setting aside. O 13 r 8 (which concerns default of appearance) and O 19 r 9 (which concerns default of pleadings) each simply states that: the 'Court may, on such terms as it thinks just, set aside or vary any judgment entered in pursuance of this Order.'[1309] These rules should be compared and, if necessary, read with other rules conferring power on the court to set aside or vary any judgment or proceedings.[1310] Examples of such power-conferring rules are rules that: set aside proceedings generally under O 2; set aside judgment under O 14 r 11; set aside judgment in default of discovery or inspection of documents under O 24 r 16; set aside judgment in default of answering interrogatories under O 26 r 6; and set aside default judgment at trial under O 35 r 2.

390. Notably, the provisions do not even distinguish between regular and irregular judgments. As a result, the (substantive) development of this area of the law has virtually been left entirely to the common law.[1311] However, the procedural aspects on default judgment and setting aside are largely addressed by the Rules of Court.

§2. Procedural Aspects

391. If the defendant does not enter an appearance within the prescribed period and thus defaults on entering an appearance, the plaintiff has to make a request to the court in accordance with the prescribed form if default judgment is sought (leave is not required).[1312] If the action was by writ,[1313] 'the Court may require to be satisfied in such manner as it thinks fit that the party is in default of appearance'.[1314] If the defendant does not file a defence within the prescribed period and thus defaults on filing a defence, the plaintiff has to apply to the court if default judgment is sought.[1315] If the defendant is represented, the plaintiff's lawyer must give

1308. Supreme Court of Judicature Act (Cap. 322, R. 5, 2014 Rev. Ed.) Rules of Court.
1309. *See also* Supreme Court of Judicature Act (Cap. 322, R. 5, 2014 Rev. Ed.) Rules of Court, O 14 r 11 (setting aside summary judgment); O 24 r 16 (judgment due to failure to comply with requirement(s) for discovery); O 26 r 16 (judgment due to failure to comply with requirement(s) for interrogatories; O 35 r 2 (judgment due to absence of party at trial). For judgment due to absence of party at trial, *see Wee Yue Chew v. Su Sh-Hsyu*, [2007] 1 SLR(R) 1092; *Su Sh-Hsyu v. Wee Yue Chew*, [2007] 3 SLR(R) 673, [44], which state the factors as whether the successful party would be immediately prejudiced, whether there has been any undue delay in the application, whether there would be a resultant complete retrial on the facts, whether the applicant has a real prospect of success, whether the public interest in finality in litigation would be compromised, and whether there is a likelihood that a real miscarriage of justice had occurred.
1310. *Singapore Civil Procedure 2015 Volume 1*, at 139 (G.P. Selvam ed., Sweet & Maxwell Asia 2014).
1311. J. Pinsler, *Principles of Civil Procedure* 333 (Acad. Publg. 2013).
1312. Supreme Court of Judicature Act (Cap. 322, R. 5, 2014 Rev. Ed.) Rules of Court, O 13 r 7(1). *See also id.*, O 13 rr 1–6 and O 2 rr 1(1)–(3).
1313. As opposed to an originating summons, where there is no dispute of fact.
1314. Supreme Court of Judicature Act (Cap. 322, R. 5, 2014 Rev. Ed.) Rules of Court, O 19 r 7(2).
1315. Supreme Court of Judicature Act (Cap. 322, R. 5, 2014 Rev. Ed.) Rules of Court, O 19 r 7(1). It should be noted that the fact that the defendant has filed a stay application (perhaps because of

2 working days' notice before entering default judgment.[1316] If leave is not sought, the default judgment would be considered irregular and the defendant would be entitled to set it aside.[1317]

392. Though the Rules of Court do not state the form, an application to enter judgment must be made (as is consistent with the practice for many other applications) by way of summons.[1318] If a defendant wishes to set aside a default judgment against him, O 2 r 2(2) states that an application to set aside for irregularity 'may be made by summons and the grounds of objection must be stated in the summons or supporting affidavit'. In addition, the application 'shall not be allowed unless it is made within a reasonable time and before the party applying has taken any fresh step after becoming aware of the irregularity'.[1319]

393. Finally, there are two avenues open to a party against whom default judgment has been entered, subsequent to substituted service. First, he may apply to set aside the order for substituted service, and proceed to have the default judgment set aside on the basis that it is an irregular judgment.[1320] Second, he may apply to set aside the judgment on the basis that it is a regular judgment, and proceed to have it set aside on the merits.[1321]

§3. Substantive Aspects

I. Setting Aside Regular Default Judgments

394. As mentioned above, judgments may be regular or irregular. The main difference between the two is that a regular judgment is free of any procedural lapses. For example, a judgment may be irregular if a plaintiff asks for judgment to be entered on the basis of default of appearance when it is a claim that is not[1322] for liquidated demand,[1323] unliquidated damages,[1324] detinue,[1325] possession of immovable property,[1326] or mixed claims.[1327]

---

say, the existence of an arbitration agreement) does not automatically bring all the timelines in the Rules of Court to a standstill: *Carona Holdings Pte Ltd v. Go Go Delicacy Pte Ltd*, [2008] 4 SLR(R) 460, [25].

1316. Legal Profession Act (Cap. 161, R 1, 2010 Rev. Ed.) Legal Profession (Professional Conduct) Rules, Rule 70.

1317. *Singapore Civil Procedure 2015 Volume 1*, at 142 (G.P. Selvam ed., Sweet & Maxwell Asia 2014).

1318. *Singapore Civil Procedure 2015 Volume 1*, at 140 (G.P. Selvam ed., Sweet & Maxwell Asia 2014).

1319. Supreme Court of Judicature Act (Cap. 322, R. 5, 2014 Rev. Ed.) Rules of Court, O 2 r 2(1). *See also Singapore Civil Procedure 2015 Volume 1*, at 40 (G.P. Selvam ed., Sweet & Maxwell Asia 2014).

1320. *Oversea-Chinese Banking Corp Ltd v. Frankel Motor Pte Ltd*, [2009] 3 SLR(R) 623, [14].

1321. *Oversea-Chinese Banking Corp Ltd v. Frankel Motor Pte Ltd*, [2009] 3 SLR(R) 623, [14].

1322. Supreme Court of Judicature Act (Cap. 322, R. 5, 2014 Rev. Ed.) Rules of Court, O 13 r 6. Another example can be found in O 10 r 1(4). *See also Singapore Civil Procedure 2015 Volume 1*, at 83–84 (G.P. Selvam ed., Sweet & Maxwell Asia 2014).

1323. Supreme Court of Judicature Act (Cap. 322, R. 5, 2014 Rev. Ed.) Rules of Court, O 13 r 1.

395. For setting aside regular default judgments, the latest test is 'whether the defendant can establish a prima facie defence in the sense of showing that there are triable or arguable issues',[1328] since 'there is no point in setting aside a judgment if the defendant has no defence, and because, if the defendant can show merits, the court will not prima facie desire to let a judgment pass on which there has been no proper adjudication'.[1329] This test should not be any stricter than that for obtaining leave to defend summary judgment applications.[1330] In addition, it would appear that the court will 'take into account the merits of the applicant's defence and his defaults or misconduct in a general balance of "equities" or "justice" between the parties'.[1331] The court will also take into account the explanation of the defendant as to how the default came about.[1332] Finally, the court may decide that a default judgment will only be allowed to be set aside if certain (reasonable) conditions are complied with, such as the provision of security (by the defendant).[1333]

II. Setting Aside Irregular Default Judgments

396. As for setting aside irregular default judgments, notwithstanding the courts' wide discretion to uphold or vary irregular default judgments, setting aside an irregular default judgment ex debito justitiae (as of right) should form the starting point, particularly where there has been egregious procedural injustice to the defendant, since all litigants are expected to observe the rules of procedure.[1334] In this regard, the court will consider a number of factors (which cannot be exhaustively listed, and by definition do not amount to criteria or requirements). These factors include: whether the defendant had unduly delayed in making its setting aside application;[1335] whether the defendant took a fresh step in the proceedings after becoming aware of the default judgment; whether the defendant had admitted liability under the default judgment; whether the defendant would be unduly prejudiced if the irregular default judgment is allowed to stand;[1336] whether the judgment had been entered prematurely; and whether the plaintiff's breach of procedural rules was

---

1324. Supreme Court of Judicature Act (Cap. 322, R. 5, 2014 Rev. Ed.) Rules of Court, O 13 r 2.
1325. Supreme Court of Judicature Act (Cap. 322, R. 5, 2014 Rev. Ed.) Rules of Court, O 13 r 3.
1326. Supreme Court of Judicature Act (Cap. 322, R. 5, 2014 Rev. Ed.) Rules of Court, O 13 r 4.
1327. Supreme Court of Judicature Act (Cap. 322, R. 5, 2014 Rev. Ed.) Rules of Court, O 13 r 5.
1328. *Mercurine Pte Ltd v. Canberra Development Pte Ltd*, [2008] 4 SLR(R) 907, [60].
1329. *Singapore Civil Procedure 2015 Volume 1*, at 140 (G.P. Selvam ed., Sweet & Maxwell Asia 2014).
1330. *City Harvest Church v. AMAC Capital Partners*, [2015] SGHC 299, [29].
1331. J. Pinsler, *Principles of Civil Procedure* 343 (Acad. Publg. 2013), citing *Lee Theng Wee v. Tay Chor Teng*, [2003] SGHC 173, [17]; *Ang Kim Soon v. Sunray Marine Pte Ltd*, [1997] 1 SLR(R) 714, [21]–[22].
1332. *Singapore Civil Procedure 2015 Volume 1*, at 140 (G.P. Selvam ed., Sweet & Maxwell Asia 2014).
1333. *Awyong Shi Peng v. Lim Siu Lay*, [2007] 2 SLR(R) 225, [7]. *See also* C. Bull & J. Pinsler, *Civil Procedure: Annual Review of Singapore Cases* [6.50] (Sing. Acad. L. 2005).
1334. *Mercurine Pte Ltd v. Canberra Development Pte Ltd*, [2008] 4 SLR(R) 907, [96], citing *White v. Weston*, [1968] 2 QB 647.
1335. This would depend in part on whether proper notice was given.
1336. Thus, mere prejudice may not suffice.

committed in bad faith.[1337] Ultimately, however, 'in deciding whether there are proper grounds for departing from the ex debito justitiae rule, the overriding principle [is] the court must be guided by the (procedural) justice of the case in hand'.[1338]

397. If an irregular default judgment is not set aside as of right, the court will still have to consider whether to nonetheless set aside the judgment on some other basis. In this regard:

> it is crucial for the court to take into account the merits of the defence. Should the court find that the defendant is 'bound to lose' … if the default judgment is set aside and the matter re-litigated, the court should ordinarily uphold the default judgment, subject to any variation which the court deems fit to make and/or any terms which it deems fit to impose.[1339]

398. To be clear, for regular default judgments, the legal burden is on the defendant to show that his defence raises triable issues.[1340] However, for irregular default judgments, the defendant only needs to establish the (factual or legal) irregularity. Once that has been established, the legal burden is on the plaintiff to show that the judgment should not only not be set aside as of right, but also that the defence is bound to fail.[1341] In terms of costs implications, the party which has been significantly more blameworthy will likely have to incur some costs, though under the normal run of things, the winner of the application gets costs in his favour.

§4. Possibility of Appeal

399. Section 34 of the Supreme Court of Judicature Act,[1342] read together with the Fourth and Fifth Schedules of the statute, determines whether any given order of civil procedure is appealable to the Court of Appeal[1343] or not.[1344] The Fourth Schedule states that:

1337. *Mercurine Pte Ltd v. Canberra Development Pte Ltd*, [2008] 4 SLR(R) 907, [76], [96], and [99].
1338. *Mercurine Pte Ltd v. Canberra Development Pte Ltd*, [2008] 4 SLR(R) 907, [76]. *See also United Overseas Bank v. Ng Huat Foundations*, [2005] 2 SLR(R) 425, [8]; *Lee Chee Wei v. Tan Hor Peow Victor*, [2007] 3 SLR(R) 537, [82].
1339. *Mercurine Pte Ltd v. Canberra Development Pte Ltd*, [2008] 4 SLR(R) 907, [96]. On this point the court considered, at some length, the controversial English decision of *Faircharm Investments Ltd v. Citibank International plc*, [1998] EWCA Civ 171.
1340. *Mercurine Pte Ltd v. Canberra Development Pte Ltd*, [2008] 4 SLR(R) 907, [98].
1341. *Mercurine Pte Ltd v. Canberra Development Pte Ltd*, [2008] 4 SLR(R) 907, [98].
1342. (Cap. 322, 2007 Rev. Ed.).
1343. Below it is the High Court, followed by the District and Magistrates' Courts. For appeals arising from the lower courts, *see* Supreme Court of Judicature Act (Cap. 322, R. 5, 2014 Rev. Ed.) Rules of Court, O 55B, 55C, and 55D. There is a right of appeal from a registrar in chambers to a judge in chambers (District Judge if it is the State Courts), but not necessarily after that stage.
1344. The statute was amended in 2010 and 2014.

> No appeal shall be brought to the Court of Appeal … where a Judge makes an order setting aside unconditionally a default judgment, regardless of how the default judgment was obtained (including whether by reason of a breach of an order of court or otherwise … [or] where a Judge makes an order setting aside a default judgment on condition that the party against whom the judgment had been entered pays into court or gives security for the sum claimed, regardless of how the default judgment was obtained (including whether by reason of a breach of an order of court or otherwise), except if the appellant is that party.

400. The Fifth Schedule then states that: 'Except with the leave of a Judge, no appeal shall be brought to the Court of Appeal … where a Judge makes an order at the hearing of any interlocutory application other than an application for … [setting] aside a default judgment.' In other words, if a default judgment is set aside unconditionally, the plaintiff cannot appeal. If a default judgment is set aside on condition (such as payment into court or the furnishing of security), the plaintiff cannot appeal but the defendant can appeal as of right. Finally, if a default judgment is not set aside, the defendant can appeal as of right. Whether or not a stay of execution would be granted while an appeal (against the outcome of the setting aside application) is pending is entirely within the discretion of the court. The applicant must show special circumstances before such a stay would be granted.[1345] An appeal does not automatically operate as a stay of execution.[1346]

1345. *Lee Sian Hee (trading as Lee Sian Hee Pork Trader) v. Oh Kheng Soon (trading as Ban Hon Trading Enterprise)*, [1991] 2 SLR(R) 869, [5]; cited in *Swiss Singapore Overseas Enterprises Pte Ltd v. Navalmar UK Ltd*, [2003] 1 SLR(R) 688, [7].

1346. Supreme Court of Judicature Act (Cap. 322, 2007 Rev. Ed.), s 41; *Lian Soon Construction Pte Ltd v. Guan Qian Realty Pte Ltd*, [1999] 1 SLR(R) 1053, [13].

Chapter 5. Summary Proceedings

§1. Introduction

401. In certain narrowly defined circumstances, it may be unnecessary – and even unjust – to subject a plaintiff to the full range of interlocutory proceedings and a full trial, which can be rather lengthy and costly, not to mention stressful.[1347] The law thus provides for various avenues in which justice may be expedited and full trial adjudication of the merits avoided, and summary judgment is one of them. The rules and procedures for summary judgment are primarily found in O 14 of the Rules of Court.[1348] The crux of O 14 traces its historical origins to the English rules of civil procedure,[1349] though it can be said that the English position has since developed differently in several respects.[1350] Older, rather than modern English cases are still cited as a result.

402. In the main, O 14 r 1 states that where the 'defendant has served a defence to the statement of claim, the plaintiff may, on the ground that the defendant has no defence to a claim included in the writ, or to a particular part of such a claim, or has no defence to such a claim or part except as to the amount of any damages claimed, apply to the Court for judgment against that defendant'. O 14 r 3(1) further states that if there is no 'issue or question in dispute which ought to be tried or that there ought for some other reason to be a trial of that claim or part, the Court may give such judgment for the plaintiff against the defendant on that claim or part as may be just having regard to the nature of the remedy or relief claimed'. The general principle underlying O 14 is that while by default a defendant should not be denied his day in court, a plaintiff should not be prevented from harvesting the fruit of his litigation either if there is no good reason to do so in the circumstances.[1351]

403. In this regard, the policy underlying summary judgment is twofold and comprises both a private and public element. The private element relates to how summary judgment enables a plaintiff with a strong claim to secure a judgment in a period of time and at an expense which is proportionate to the dispute; the public element pertains to how summary judgment proceedings enable the court to conserve scarce public resources where there is no reasonable or fair probability that deploying those resources in a full trial would make a difference to the just determination of the dispute.[1352]

1347. J. Pinsler, *Principles of Civil Procedure* 255–257 (Acad. Publg. 2013). *See also Republic Airconditioning (S) Pte Ltd v. Shinsung Eng Co Ltd (Singapore Branch)*, [2012] 2 SLR 601, [11].
1348. Supreme Court of Judicature Act (Cap. 322, R. 5, 2014 Rev. Ed.) Rules of Court.
1349. *Singapore Civil Procedure 2015 Volume 1*, at 146 (G.P. Selvam ed., Sweet & Maxwell Asia 2014).
1350. *See* e.g., the language used in Part 24.2 of the English Civil Procedure Rules as compared to the language used in O 14 rr 1 and 3.
1351. *See also Singapore Civil Procedure 2015 Volume 1*, at 146 (G.P. Selvam ed., Sweet & Maxwell Asia 2014).
1352. *Ritzland Investment Pte Ltd v. Grace Management & Consultancy Services Pte Ltd*, [2014] 2 SLR 1342, [46].

404. It should be noted that there are no particular causes of action that cannot be subject to an O 14 application,[1353] given that trial-by-jury in Singapore was abolished shortly after its independence in 1965.[1354] Provisional remedies, such as injunctions, may also be sought in O 14 applications.[1355] Finally, it should be noted that while most summary judgment applications pertain to general liability, O 14 r 12(1) allows the court, when the facts are not in dispute, to determine a point of law or construction, provided that the point is suitable for determination without a full trial and the determination would fully dispose of the entire cause or matter.[1356]

§2. Procedural Aspects

405. Assuming the statement of claim and defence have been served[1357] and no application for a stay of proceedings has been made,[1358] the plaintiff has – unless the court otherwise orders – up to twenty-eight days after the pleadings in the action are deemed to be closed[1359] to file an application for summary judgment.[1360] However, the plaintiff should attempt to invoke O 14 at a relatively early stage of the

1353. *Blue Nile Co Ltd v. Emery Customs Brokers (S) Pte Ltd*, [1990] 1 SLR(R) 396, [11]–[14]; cited in *Blue Nile Co Ltd v. Emery Customs Brokers (S) Pte Ltd*, [1991] 2 SLR(R) 926, [6]. However, if the dispute is only as to amount claimed, summary judgment would not be appropriate: *Ngai Heng Book Binder Pte Ltd v. Syntax Computer Pte Ltd* [1988] 1 SLR(R) 209, [10].

1354. *See* generally *see* generally A. Phang, *Jury Trial in Singapore and Malaysia: The Unmaking of a Legal Institution*, 25 Malaya L. Rev. 50 (1983). However, an O 14 application cannot be taken out against the government: Supreme Court of Judicature Act (Cap. 322, R. 5, 2014 Rev. Ed.) Rules of Court, O 73 r 5.

1355. *Creative Technology Ltd v. Cosmos Trade-Nology Pte Ltd*, [2003] 3 SLR(R) 697, [5].

1356. *See also Basil Anthony v. Premier Security Co-operative Ltd*, [2010] 3 SLR 110, [69]–[70]; *ANB v. ANF*, [2011] 2 SLR 1, [1]; *TMT Asia Ltd v. BHP Billiton Marketing AG (Singapore Branch)*, [2015] 2 SLR 540, [32]; *United Overseas Bank Ltd v. Lippo Marina Collection Pte Ltd*, [2016] 2 SLR 597, [13]–[20]. The court also has the discretion to decide whether, notwithstanding these requirements not being fulfilled, it is nonetheless appropriate to proceed with a summary determination so as to save time and costs for the parties: *Samsonite IP Holdings Sarl v. An Sheng Trading Pte Ltd*, [2017] SGHC 18, [41].

1357. In the past, the defendant needed only to enter an appearance and not file a defence for the O 14 timeline to start. This was changed in 2002 to minimize disruptions to the timeline: *Singapore Civil Procedure 2015 Volume 1*, at 150 (G.P. Selvam ed., Sweet & Maxwell Asia 2014). If the defendant does not enter an appearance or file a defence, the plaintiff may proceed via O 13 r 19 instead for default judgment.

1358. Such an application made may be pursuant to an arbitration agreement, for instance: *Samsung Corp v. Chinese Chamber Realty Pte Ltd*, [2004] 1 SLR(R) 382. Nonetheless, it should be noted that a stay application does not automatically stop time running for the service of the defence: *Australian Timber Products Pte Ltd v. Koh Brothers Building & Civil Engineering Contractor (Pte) Ltd*, [2005] 1 SLR(R) 168, [16]; cited in *Carona Holdings Pte Ltd v. Go G Delicacy Pte Ltd*, [2008] 4 SLR(R) 460, [25]–[32].

1359. *See* Supreme Court of Judicature Act (Cap. 322, R. 5, 2014 Rev. Ed.) Rules of Court, O 18 r 20(1). If there are multiple defendants and pleadings are closed with respect to one but the other(s), the court has the discretion to make any order which is just in the circumstances of the case: *Obegi Melissa v. Vestwin Trading Pte Ltd*, [2008] 2 SLR(R) 540, [37]–[38]. Further, any amendments to pleadings after they have closed do not automatically reopen the pleadings so as to revive a plaintiff's right to file for summary judgment: *id.*, [39]. Apart from the statement of claim and defence, further and better particulars are also an integral element of the parties' pleadings. The hearing of

proceedings, 'given the need to maintain litigation discipline and to ensure efficient implementation of the court's case management processes'.[1361] Furthermore, any amendments to the statement of claim should be completed before an O 14 application is made.[1362] If the application is out of time, the plaintiff 'must satisfactorily explain its delay so as to show persuasively why it should be allowed to potentially hold back the trial further' and 'demonstrate that it has proceeded diligently in its conduct of the action'.[1363]

406. An application for summary judgment is made by summons together with supporting affidavit(s).[1364] The summons and supporting affidavit(s) 'must be filed at the same time, and must be served on the defendant within three days from the date of filing'.[1365] The affidavit(s) 'must contain all necessary evidence in support' of the claim and 'may contain statements of information or belief with the sources and grounds thereof'.[1366] Thus, documents that are necessary to support the claim must be exhibited in the affidavit(s).[1367] The actual amount claimed should also be made clear.

407. Once the summons and supporting affidavit(s) have been served, the defendant has fourteen days to 'show cause against the plaintiff's application'; this is

---

any summary judgment application should thus only take place after the necessary further and better particulars have been exchanged between the parties and both the statement of claim and defence finalized, since parties may not be allowed to depart from their pleadings during the summary judgment hearing: *United States Trading Co Pte v. Ting Boon Aun*, [2008] 2 SLR(R) 981, [24]–[26]; *Lee Hsien Loong v. Review Publishing Co*, [2009] 1 SLR(R) 177, [26].

1360. Supreme Court of Judicature Act (Cap. 322, R. 5, 2014 Rev. Ed.) Rules of Court, O 14 r 14. *See also Obegi Melissa v. Vestwin Trading Pte Ltd*, [2008] 2 SLR(R) 540, [29]–[34]. It should be noted that it is possible to combine a summary judgment application with a striking out application: *Lim Eng Hock Peter v. Lin Jian Wei*, [2008] 4 SLR(R) 444, [2]; *Lee Hsien Loong v. Review Publishing Co*, [2009] 1 SLR(R) 177, [5]–[16].

1361. *Obegi Melissa v. Vestwin Trading Pte Ltd*, [2008] 2 SLR(R) 540, [36]–[37]. However, the plaintiff should also ensure that his case is finalized before applying for summary judgment: C. Bull & J. Pinsler, *Civil Procedure: Annual Review of Singapore Cases* [6.24] (Sing. Acad. L. 2003) citing *Chun Thong Ping v. Soh Kok Hong*, [2003] 3 SLR(R) 204.

1362. *Singapore Civil Procedure 2015 Volume 1*, at 150 (G.P. Selvam ed., Sweet & Maxwell Asia 2014). However, the court has the discretion to grant leave to amend a pleading at any stage of the proceedings: Supreme Court of Judicature Act (Cap. 322, R. 5, 2014 Rev. Ed.) Rules of Court, O 20 r 5(1).

1363. *Obegi Melissa v. Vestwin Trading Pte Ltd*, [2008] 2 SLR(R) 540, [37]. *See also id.*, [38].

1364. Supreme Court of Judicature Act (Cap. 322, R. 5, 2014 Rev. Ed.) Rules of Court, O 14 r 2(1).

1365. Supreme Court of Judicature Act (Cap. 322, R. 5, 2014 Rev. Ed.) Rules of Court, O 14 r 2(2). In *Mohamed Ismail v. Sadique Marican Bin Ibrahim Marican*, [2008] SGHC 189, [10]–[16], the court held that it has the power to extend time under this rule, notwithstanding the use of the word 'must' in the rule.

1366. Supreme Court of Judicature Act (Cap. 322, R. 5, 2014 Rev. Ed.) Rules of Court, O 14 r 2(8). Nonetheless, 'a defective supporting affidavit can be cured by a subsequent or supplement affidavit, and the court looks at the whole of the evidence at the end of the day': *Singapore Civil Procedure 2015 Volume 1*, at 150 (G.P. Selvam ed., Sweet & Maxwell Asia 2014).

1367. *Singapore Civil Procedure 2015 Volume 1*, at 152 (G.P. Selvam ed., Sweet & Maxwell Asia 2014).

done primarily by filing and serving his affidavit(s) on the plaintiff.[1368] Any reply affidavit(s) by the plaintiff must be filed and served within fourteen days after service of the defendant's affidavit(s).[1369] No further affidavit shall be received in evidence after this point without the leave of the court.[1370] As with most other interlocutory applications, parties are at liberty to request for extensions of time with regard to the filing and serving of the relevant documents. However, this is usually subject to possible cost penalties against parties responsible for the delays. Once all of the aforementioned documents have been duly filed and served, parties will be ready for a hearing of the application, which is usually heard by a registrar in chambers.[1371] If, however, the plaintiff is unable to meet all the procedural requirements, his claim may be dismissed (usually with costs).[1372]

408. During the hearing, parties typically present their claims in turn with reference to their pleadings, affidavits, and exhibits,[1373] while the registrar will occasionally seek clarifications from the parties on their submissions; cross-examination of witnesses is rather uncommon.[1374] The fact that 'the papers are voluminous, the facts are many and the arguments are vigorous' does not mean that 'it was not appropriate for the court, at the summary judgment stage, to engage in a precise evaluation of the merits of the rival contentions or to assess the relative probabilities'.[1375] There is also a question of whether a defendant can raise a defence that was not originally pleaded during the hearing for summary judgment.

409. Although the local authorities appear to be divided on this question,[1376] the Court of Appeal in *Olivine Capital Pte Ltd v. Chia Chin Yan* held that in a situation where the plaintiff is seeking to amend its pleadings to introduce a new issue, it is possible for a defendant to introduce new arguments in an appeal from a summary judgment determination.[1377] However, since parties are bound by the four corners of their pleadings, a defendant wishing to raise a fresh defence must first amend its

1368. Supreme Court of Judicature Act (Cap. 322, R. 5, 2014 Rev. Ed.) Rules of Court, O 14 rr 2(3) and 2(4).
1369. Supreme Court of Judicature Act (Cap. 322, R. 5, 2014 Rev. Ed.) Rules of Court, O 14 r 2(5).
1370. Supreme Court of Judicature Act (Cap. 322, R. 5, 2014 Rev. Ed.) Rules of Court, O 14 r 2(6).
1371. A hearing in open court is possible if the court so orders: Supreme Court of Judicature Act (Cap. 322, R. 5, 2014 Rev. Ed.) Rules of Court, O 32 r 11.
1372. *Singapore Civil Procedure 2015 Volume 1*, at 149 (G.P. Selvam ed., Sweet & Maxwell Asia 2014). *See also* Supreme Court of Judicature Act (Cap. 322, R. 5, 2014 Rev. Ed.) Rules of Court, O 2 rr 1(1)–(3).
1373. *See also Abdul Salam Asanaru Pilla (trading as South Kerala Cashew Exporters) v. Nomanbhoy & Sons Pte Ltd*, [2007] 2 SLR(R) 856, [38]–[39], citing *Goh Chok Tong v. Chee Soon Juan*, [2003] 3 SLR(R) 32, [25]; *Lee Kuan Yew v. Chee Soon Juan*, [2003] 3 SLR(R) 8, [24].
1374. J. Pinsler, *Principles of Civil Procedure* 261–262 (Acad. Publg. 2013).
1375. *Abdul Salam Asanaru Pilla (trading as South Kerala Cashew Exporters) v. Nomanbhoy & Sons Pte Ltd*, [2007] 2 SLR(R) 856, [36]–[37].
1376. *See Rankine Bernadette Adeline v. Chenet Finance Ltd*, [2011] 3 SLR 756, [18]–[23]; *PMA Credit Opportunities Fund v. Tantono Tiny (representative of the estate of Lim Susanto, deceased)*, [2011] 3 SLR 1021, [31]–[33].
1377. *Olivine Capital Pte Ltd v. Chia Chin Yan*, [2014] 2 SLR 1371, [21]–[22].

defence.[1378] The guiding principle is that amendments to pleadings ought to be allowed if they would enable the real question and/or issue in controversy between the parties to be determined.[1379] If the defendant does not appear at the hearing, summary judgment can still be entered, but the defendant is at liberty to set aside the judgment.[1380]

§3. Substantive Aspects

I. Prima Facie Case

410. To obtain summary judgment, the 'plaintiff has first to show that he has a prima facie case for judgment'.[1381] Once he has done that, 'the burden shifts to the defendant who, in order to obtain leave to defend, must establish that there is a fair or reasonable probability that he has a real or bona fide defence'.[1382] It should be noted, however, that it is the so-called tactical burden, and not the evidential or legal burden, which shifts to the defendant.[1383] The defendant establishes this – or shows cause – by either showing that there is a triable issue, or there is some other reason for a full trial.[1384] In this regard, it is important that the defendant raises points that correspond to the issues raised by the plaintiff at the initial stage in satisfying that there is prima facie case for summary judgment.[1385] If the defendant is unable to establish either ground, the plaintiff will be granted summary judgment and

1378. *Olivine Capital Pte Ltd v. Chia Chin Yan*, [2014] 2 SLR 1371, [43], cited in *TMT Asia Ltd v. BHP Billiton Marketing AG (Singapore Branch)*, [2015] 2 SLR 540, [29].

1379. *Olivine Capital Pte Ltd v. Chia Chin Yan*, [2014] 2 SLR 1371, [44], citing *Review Publishing Co Ltd v. Lee Hsien Loong*, [2010] 1 SLR 52, [113].

1380. Supreme Court of Judicature Act (Cap. 322, R. 5, 2014 Rev. Ed.) Rules of Court, O 14 r 11.

1381. *Neville, Guy v. Andrla, Dominic* [2017] SGHC 295, [4]; *B2C2 Ltd v. Quoine Pte Ltd*, [2017] SGHC(I) 11, [5].

1382. *Ebony Ritz Sdn Bhd v. Sumatec Resources Bhd*, [2017] SGHC 282, [69]; *Ritzland Investment Pte Ltd v. Grace Management & Consultancy Services Pte Ltd*, [2014] 2 SLR 1342, [43]–[44]; *M2B World Asia Pacific Pte Ltd v. Matsumura Akihiko*, [2014] SGHC 225, [17]; *Wiseway Global Co Ltd v. Qian Feng Group Ltd*, [2015] SGHC 85, [19]; *Australia and New Zealand Banking Group Ltd v. Bombay Talkies (S) Pte Ltd*, [2015] SGHC 112, [13]; *Associated Development Pte Ltd v. Loong Sie Kiong Gerald*, [2009] 4 SLR(R) 389, [22], cited in *Republic Airconditioning (S) Pte Ltd v. Shinsung Eng Co Ltd (Singapore Branch)*, [2012] 2 SLR 601, [9]. *See also Capital Springboard Ltd v. Vanguard Project Management Pte Ltd*, [2018] SGHC 29; *Habibullah Mohamed Yousuff v. Indian Bank*, [1999] 2 SLR(R) 880, [21], citing *James v. Stone*, [1894] AC 122, 124; *KLW Holdings Ltd v. Straitsworld Advisory Ltd*, [2017] SGHC 35, [16]; *Wayne Burt Commodities Pte Ltd v. Singapore DSS Pte Ltd*, [2017] SGHC 70, [5].

1383. *Wee Cheng Swee Henry v. Jo Baby Kartika Polim*, [2015] 4 SLR 250, [36]–[37]; *Ritzland Investment Pte Ltd v. Grace Management & Consultancy Services Pte Ltd*, [2014] 2 SLR 1342, [45]. *See also Singapore Civil Procedure 2015 Volume 1*, at 149 (G.P. Selvam ed., Sweet & Maxwell Asia 2014).

1384. Supreme Court of Judicature Act (Cap. 322, R. 5, 2014 Rev. Ed.) Rules of Court, O 14 rr 2(3) and 3(1).

1385. *Wee Cheng Swee Henry v. Jo Baby Kartika Polim*, [2015] 4 SLR 250, [48].

costs.[1386] This is the case even where liability is clear and only damages have to be assessed, as the only question at this stage is whether the plaintiff is entitled to the relief sought.

411. At the conclusion of the application for summary judgment, having considered all the evidence from opposing parties, the court will enter judgment against the defendant only if the plaintiff has satisfied the court that there is no reasonable probability that the defendant has a real or bona fide defence in relation to the issues in dispute which ought to be tried and (only if the defendant raises this point) that there is no other reason why there ought to be a trial.[1387]

412. A stay of execution of the summary judgment until after the trial may be ordered if the defendant has a counterclaim (but which does not give rise to a right of set-off).[1388] If, however, the plaintiff is unable to show a prima facie case to begin with,[1389] his summary judgment application will be dismissed (usually with costs awarded against him).[1390] Moreover, 'if the plaintiff knew that the defendant relied on a contention which would entitle him to unconditional leave to defend, then, the Court may dismiss the application with costs'.[1391]

II. Whether There Is a Triable Issue

413. As mentioned above, this is the first ground in which the defendant may successfully be given leave to defend his action at a full trial. This ground does not present a very high threshold, because the moment 'a triable issue has been raised, it is not for the court to consider whether the defendant is likely to succeed or fail on it'.[1392] That said, the court in granting a summary judgment application, must

1386. Supreme Court of Judicature Act (Cap. 322, R. 5, 2014 Rev. Ed.) Rules of Court, O 14 r 3(1) and O 59, Appendix 2.

1387. *Wee Cheng Swee Henry v. Jo Baby Kartika Polim*, [2015] 4 SLR 250, [38], citing *Ritzland Investment Pte Ltd v. Grace Management & Consultancy Services Pte Ltd*, [2014] 2 SLR 1342, [43]–[47]. *See also JP Choon Pte Ltd v. Lal Offshore Marine Pte Ltd*, [2016] SGHC 115, [14].

1388. Supreme Court of Judicature Act (Cap. 322, R. 5, 2014 Rev. Ed.) Rules of Court, O 14 r 3(2); *Invar Realty Pte Ltd v. Kenzo Tange Urtec Inc*, [1990] 3 MLJ 388; *Cheng Poh Building Construction Pte Ltd v. First City Builders Pte Ltd*, [2003] 2 SLR(R) 170, [18]–[25]. If a successful counterclaim will result in a direct set-off, the defendant will likely be given unconditional leave to defend if he has furnished sufficient evidence (*see* below): J. Pinsler, *Principles of Civil Procedure* 272, 283 (Acad. Publg. 2013).

1389. For instance, if his statement of claim and/or affidavit(s) are too bare: *Chong Yeo and Partners v. Guan Ming Hardware and Engineering Pte Ltd*, [1997] 2 SLR(R) 30, [66].

1390. Supreme Court of Judicature Act (Cap. 322, R. 5, 2014 Rev. Ed.) Rules of Court, O 14 rr 3(1) and 7. Exceptionally, if the application is dismissed only because too many amendments are required for the pleadings, the plaintiff may recommence the action later on: *Alliance (Malaya) Engineering Co Sdn Bhd v. San Development Sdn Bhd*, [1974] 2 MLJ 94.

1391. Supreme Court of Judicature Act (Cap. 322, R. 5, 2014 Rev. Ed.) Rules of Court, O 14 r 7(1).

1392. *Jacobs v. Booth's Distillery Co*, (1901) 85 LT 262, 263. *See also Ang Eng Thong v. Lee Kiam Hong*, [1998] SGHC 64, [31].

also 'be wary of defendants who seek to evade summary judgment by throwing out spurious allegations, assertions and afterthoughts as convenient smoke screens'.[1393]

414. As the merits of the defence are not being considered, it follows that the defendant is not required to raise a complete defence at this stage.[1394] Indeed, it is entirely possible to succeed in raising a triable issue just by casting sufficient doubt on the plaintiff's evidence.[1395] This is consistent with the notion that since 'the ultimate concern of any court hearing an application for summary judgment must be whether it is just that the plaintiff should be entitled to an expedited judgment as an exception to the ordinary process leading to trial'.[1396] Nonetheless, leave to defend 'will not be granted upon "mere assertions" by defendants; instead, the court will look at the whole situation critically to examine whether the defence is credible'.[1397] The defendant must satisfy the court that he has a fair or reasonable probability of showing a real or bona fide defence, i.e., that his evidence is reasonably capable of belief.[1398] In this regard, the defendant should provide some evidence to show why there is a triable issue, instead of making plain denials without more[1399] or drawing upon adverse inferences from the plaintiff's explanations without finding independent or supporting evidence to support the defendant's account of events.[1400] The rationale for this is that even if the defendant is able to come up with a version of events that is logically possible, mere logical possibility, without any evidence (direct or indirect) to support the defendant's bare assertions of what he claims to be true, is insufficient for summary determination.[1401] In the same vein, the defendant should also not be raising new defences in the affidavit(s) that were not found in his defence, unless there are good reasons to do so.[1402]

1393. *Australia and New Zealand Banking Group Ltd v. Bombay Talkies (S) Pte Ltd*, [2015] SGHC 112, [14]; *Oversea-Chinese Banking Corp Ltd v. Ravichandran s/o Suppiah*, [2015] SGHC 1, [23], citing *Republic Airconditioning (S) Pte Ltd v. Shinsung Eng Co Ltd (Singapore Branch)*, [2012] 2 SLR 601, [11]. *See also Goh Chok Tong v. Chee Soon Juan*, [2003] 3 SLR(R) 32, [25], citing *Microsoft Corporation v. Electro-Wide Limited*, [1997] FSR 580, 593–594; *KLW Holdings Ltd v. Straitsworld Advisory Ltd*, [2017] SGHC 35, [16]; *Wayne Burt Commodities Pte Ltd v. Singapore DSS Pte Ltd*, [2017] SGHC 70, [6].

1394. *Jaya Kumar v. Subramaniam*, [1987] SLR(R) 309.

1395. J. Pinsler, *Principles of Civil Procedure* 264–265 (Acad. Publg. 2013). *See also PT Selecta Bestama v. Sin Huat Huat Marine Transportation Pte Ltd*, [2015] SGHCR 16, [20].

1396. J. Pinsler, *Principles of Civil Procedure* 265 (Acad. Publg. 2013).

1397. *Prosperous Credit Pte Ltd v. Gen Hwa Franchise International Pte Ltd*, [1998] 1 SLR(R) 53, [14]; *Republic Airconditioning (S) Pte Ltd v. Shinsung Eng Co Ltd (Singapore Branch)*, [2012] 2 SLR 601, [10]; *M2B World Asia Pacific Pte Ltd v. Matsumura Akihiko*, [2014] SGHC 225, [19]; *Sim Kim Seng v. New West Coast Shipyard Pte Ltd*, [2016] SGHCR 2, [10]; *Ma Hongjin v. SCP Holdings Pte Ltd*, [2017] SGHC 319, [32]. *See also IBM Singapore Pte Ltd v. Beans Group Pte Ltd*, [2012] 1 SLR 910, [16].

1398. *Singapore Civil Procedure 2015 Volume 1*, at 162 (G.P. Selvam ed., Sweet & Maxwell Asia 2014), citing *Banque de Paris et des Pays-Bas (Suisse) SA v. Costa de Naray*, [1984] 1 Lloyd's Rep 21, [28].

1399. *Thomson Rubbers (India) Pte Ltd v. Tan Ai Hock*, [2012] 1 SLR 772, [10]; *Jaya Kumar v. Subramaniam Mohana Krishnan*, [1987] SLR(R) 309, [3].

1400. *Wiseway Global Co Ltd v. Qian Feng Group Ltd*, [2015] SGHC 85, [27].

1401. *Wiseway Global Co Ltd v. Qian Feng Group Ltd*, [2015] SGHC 85, [33].

1402. *Olivine Capital Pte Ltd v. Chia Chin Yan*, [2014] 2 SLR 1371, [21]–[22]. *See also Singapore Civil Procedure 2015 Volume 1*, at 157 (G.P. Selvam ed., Sweet & Maxwell Asia 2014), citing *United*

415. As a general rule, the defendant should not be permitted to rely on any defence that has not been pleaded, unless the defence is amended or in an exceptional circumstance, where the unpleaded defence struck at the heart of the court's powers.[1403] If the defendant succeeds in raising a triable issue, he will usually be given unconditional leave to defend[1404] (though the converse is not necessarily true all the time).[1405] In order to obtain unconditional leave to defend, the defendant needs to bring forward all evidence necessary to support the grounds which he or she argues that unconditional leave to defend should be granted. This includes documentary evidence as well as the defendant's own evidence given on oath or affirmation in his or her affidavits.[1406] However, if the defendant is unable to 'raise a clear triable issue or the triable issue may not appear to be completely genuine or there may be a concern that the defendant is not acting in good faith',[1407] the court, instead of granting unconditional leave to defend, may grant conditional leave to defend.[1408] In other words, the defence is regarded to be shadowy.[1409] One shortcoming of this approach is that characterization of a defence as shadowy is 'as much as matter of impression as it is of analysis'.[1410] It has been suggested that the words of O 14 r 4(1) and the very wide discretion it confers are wide enough to accommodate the modern English approach (i.e. to make a conditional order where it appears to the court that a defence may succeed but improbable that it will do

---

States Trading Co Pte Ltd v. Ting Boon Aun, [2008] 2 SLR(R) 981, [25]–[26]. The main rationale for this is that the pleadings phase is designed to allow both parties to properly assess the merits of each other's arguments before they decide on their next course of action. C.f. *Lin Securities (Pte Ltd) v. Noone,* [1989] 1 MLJ 321.

1403. *Singapore Civil Procedure 2015 Volume 1*, at 157 (G.P. Selvam ed., Sweet & Maxwell Asia 2014), citing *Olivine Capital Pte Ltd v. Chia Chin Yan*, [2014] 2 SLR 1371, [43] that distinguished *Poh Soon Kiat v. Desert Palace Inc (trading as Caesars Palace)*, [2010] 1 SLR 1129.

1404. Supreme Court of Judicature Act (Cap. 322, R. 5, 2014 Rev. Ed.) Rules of Court, O 14 r 4(1); *Associated Development Pte Ltd v. Loong Sie Kiong Gerald*, [2009] 4 SLR(R) 389. The test for obtaining leave to defend has also been compared with the test for setting aside a regular default judgment: *Mercurine Pte Ltd v. Canberra Development*, [2008] 4 SLR(R) 907, [50]–[60].

1405. Supreme Court of Judicature Act (Cap. 322, R. 5, 2014 Rev. Ed.) Rules of Court, O 14 r 3(1). For instance, in situations of conflicting affidavit evidence, a defendant is not immediately entitled to unconditional leave to defend: *Wiseway Global Co Ltd v. Qian Feng Group Ltd*, [2015] SGHC 85, [20], citing *Bank Negara Malaysia v. Mohd Ismail & Ors*, [1992] 1 MLJ 400. *See also Prosperous Credit Pte Ltd v. Gen Hwa Franchise International Pte Ltd*, [1998] 1 SLR(R) 53, [14].

1406. *Wee Cheng Swee Henry v. Jo Baby Kartika Polim,* [2015] 4 SLR 250, [103].

1407. J. Pinsler, *Principles of Civil Procedure* 268 (Acad. Publg. 2013). *See also Abdul Salam Asanaru Pilla (trading as South Kerala Cashew Exporters) v. Nomanbhoy & Sons Pte Ltd*, [2007] 2 SLR(R) 856, [43]–[44]; cited in *IBM Singapore Pte Ltd v. Beans Group Pte Ltd*, [2012] 1 SLR 910, [15].

C.f. *Lee Hsien Loong v. Singapore Democratic Party*, [2007] 1 SLR(R) 675, [19].

1408. Supreme Court of Judicature Act (Cap. 322, R. 5, 2014 Rev. Ed.) Rules of Court, O 14 r 4(1).

1409. *Wee Cheng Swee Henry v. Jo Baby Kartika Polim,* [2015] 4 SLR 250, [81]; *City Harvest Church v. AMAC Capital Partners*, [2015] SGHC 299, [30].

1410. *Wee Cheng Swee Henry v. Jo Baby Kartika Polim,* [2015] 4 SLR 250, [81].

so)[1411] 'as a useful alternative to the more conventional 'shadowy defence' formulation'.[1412] This may come in the form of providing a sum of money (e.g., via payment into court or a banker's guarantee) as security for the plaintiff's claim.[1413] It must be noted that the court has wide discretion in determining the quantum of money required from the defendant under O 14 r 4(1).[1414] In exercising its discretion, the court will have regard to two factors of consideration. First, doing justice to the plaintiff in light of the strength of the plaintiff's case and the uncertainties attached to the defendant's defences; second, doing justice to the defendant in light of his or her financial means.[1415] As regards the second factor, the High Court has clarified the defendant bears a high burden in satisfying the court that the condition imposed is impossible, as opposed to being merely difficult.[1416] The High Court has further distilled several principles:

(a) Having decided to grant a defendant leave to defend, it is wrong in principle to impose a condition on that leave which the defendant would find impossible – as opposed to merely difficult – to comply with.
(b) The defendant bears the burden, in every sense of the word, of showing that it would be impossible – as opposed to merely difficult – to comply with a condition which the court proposes to impose on the leave to defend.
(c) In discharging that burden, the defendant has a duty fully and frankly to disclose her financial position to the court.
(d) In considering whether it is impossible – as opposed to merely difficult – for the defendant to comply with the condition, it is legitimate to have regard not just to the defendant's own financial resources, but also to the financial resources of those who might reasonably be expected to extend financial assistance to her in her hour of need.[1417]

416. The provision of security is a demonstration of the defendant's earnestness and commitment to defend his claim, though if an amount is clearly out of the defendant's financial means, a lower amount may be ordered instead.[1418] Where the

1411. Paragraph 4 of Practice Direction 24 read together with Part 24 of the Civil Procedure Rules 1998 (SI 1998 No 3132) (UK).
1412. *Wee Cheng Swee Henry v. Jo Baby Kartika Polim,* [2015] 4 SLR 250, [81]–[83].
1413. J. Pinsler, *Principles of Civil Procedure* 264 (Acad. Publg. 2013). Where money has been paid into court (whether voluntarily or by order of court) with the intention of preserving money for the benefit of the other party's claim, the other party is considered a secured creditor to the extent of the sum paid into court, and he is allowed to retain the benefit of that security despite the payee's subsequent bankruptcy; moneys paid to a stakeholder, as a convenient alternative to payment into court, has by and large the same effect: *Ang Tin Gee v. Pang Teck Guan*, [2015] 5 SLR 836, [27]–[38].
1414. *Wee Cheng Swee Henry v. Jo Baby Kartika Polim,* [2015] 4 SLR 250, [109], citing *Mohd Zain bin Abdullah v. Chimbusco International Petroleum (Singapore) Pte Ltd*, [2014] 2 SLR 446, [39].
1415. *Wee Cheng Swee Henry v. Jo Baby Kartika Polim,* [2015] 4 SLR 250, [112].
1416. *Wee Cheng Swee Henry v. Jo Baby Kartika Polim,* [2015] 4 SLR 250, [112]–[119], citing *MV Yorke Motors (a firm) v. Edwards*, [1982] 1 WLR 444. *See also Mohd Zain bin Abdullah v. Chimbusco International Petroleum (Singapore) Pte Ltd*, [2014] 2 SLR 446, [20]; *Citibank NA v. Lim Soo Peng*, [2004] SGHC 266; *International Bank of Singapore Ltd v. Bader*, [1989] 1 MLJ 214.
1417. *Wee Cheng Swee Henry v. Jo Baby Kartika Polim,* [2015] 4 SLR 250, [118].
1418. J. Pinsler, *Principles of Civil Procedure* 268–270 (Acad. Publg. 2013).

defendant's defence is shadowy or improbable to succeed at trial, the provision of security has an added purpose of preserving the claimant's position, to the extent possible to do so, pending trial.[1419]

III. Whether There Is Some Other Reason

417. This is the second ground in which the defendant may successfully be given leave to defend his action at a full trial. It operates in a way such that 'even if the plaintiff appears to have an incontestable claim, he will not automatically be granted summary judgment if the circumstances suggest the absence of critical information or a lack of bona fides going to the root of the claim, so that its final determination would not be just in the absence of further investigation'.[1420] On the other hand, a 'vague allegation that a case needs to be investigated in the absence of good reason would not constitute "some other reason" for trial. The court is particularly circumspect about any ulterior motive'.[1421] Indeed, the mere fact that a claim is extremely complex does not automatically lead to the operation of this ground.[1422]

418. It may be helpful to elaborate on the locus classicus that is often cited to illustrate this broader limb of O 14 r 3(1), i.e., the English decision of *Miles v. Bull*.[1423] There, after the defendant and her husband had separated, the latter sold their matrimonial home to the plaintiff. The plaintiff then sued for possession of the property via summary judgment. The court gave unconditional leave to defend notwithstanding the lack of a triable issue, as it took the view that the circumstances in which the house was so quickly sold and the fact that the defendant was not aware of the sale made this case not sufficiently straightforward for summary judgment.[1424] This principle in *Miles v. Bull* has since been approved in a number of local cases.[1425]

1419. *Wee Cheng Swee Henry v. Jo Baby Kartika Polim*, [2015] 4 SLR 250, [110]–[111]. *See also Mohd Zain bin Abdullah v. Chimbusco International Petroleum (Singapore) Pte Ltd*, [2014] 2 SLR 446, [20].
1420. J. Pinsler, *Principles of Civil Procedure* 266 (Acad. Publg. 2013).
1421. J. Pinsler, *Principles of Civil Procedure* 267 (Acad. Publg. 2013).
1422. *Ma Hongjin v, SCP Holdings Pte Ltd*, [2017] SGHC 319, [33], citing J. Pinsler, *Principles of Civil Procedure* 267 (Acad. Publg. 2013). For situations where counterclaims are involved, *see* J. Pinsler, *The Court's Response to Counterclaims in Proceedings for Summary Judgment*, 23 Sing. Acad. L.J. 517 (2011).
1423. [1969] 1 QB 258, 265.
1424. *Miles v. Bull*, [1969] 1 QB 258, 266.
1425. *Concentrate Engineering Pte Ltd v. United Malayan Banking Corp Bhd* [1990] 1 SLR(R) 465, [12]–[19]; *Habibullah Mohamed Yousuff v. Indian Bank*, [1999] 2 SLR(R) 880, [20]–[21] and [44]; *Citibank NA v. Lim Soo Peng*, [2004] SGHC 266, [56]–[58]. *See also Bakery Mart Pte Ltd v. Sincere Watch Ltd*, [2003] 3 SLR(R) 462, [24].

IV. Issues Suitable for Summary Determination

419. Pursuant to O 14 r 12, there are three requirements for a question to be summarily determined.[1426] First, the question or issue for determination must involve a question of law or construction of any document.[1427] Second, the question must be suitable for determination without a full trial of the action.[1428] Third, the determination must fully determine (subject only to any possible appeal) the entire cause or matter or any claim or issue therein.[1429] Even if all three requirements are satisfied, the court retains the discretion to decide whether it should proceed with the summary determination.[1430] The mere fact that the question raises a complex question of law is not a bar to summary determination.[1431] However, questions that raise factual issues requiring findings of fact[1432] or involve novel questions of considerable public importance are not suitable for summary determination.[1433]

§4. Possibility of Appeal

420. Section 34 of the Supreme Court of Judicature Act,[1434] read together with the Fourth and Fifth Schedules of the statute, determines whether any given order of civil procedure is appealable to the Court of Appeal[1435] or not.[1436] For summary judgments, the Fourth Schedule states that: 'No appeal shall be brought to the Court of Appeal … where a Judge makes an order giving unconditional leave to defend any proceedings … where a Judge makes an order giving leave to defend any proceedings on condition.' The Fifth Schedule then states that: 'Except with the leave of a Judge, no appeal shall be brought to the Court of Appeal … where a Judge

1426. *See also Olivine Capital Pte Ltd v. Chia Chin Yan*, [2014] 2 SLR 1371, [49], citing *Payna Chettiar v. Maimoon bte Ismail*, [1997] 1 SLR(R) 738, [35].
1427. Supreme Court of Judicature Act (Cap. 322, R. 5, 2014 Rev. Ed.) Rules of Court, O 14 r 12(1).
1428. Supreme Court of Judicature Act (Cap. 322, R. 5, 2014 Rev. Ed.) Rules of Court, O 14 r 12(1)(a).
1429. Supreme Court of Judicature Act (Cap. 322, R. 5, 2014 Rev. Ed.) Rules of Court, O 14 r 12(1)(b).
1430. *TMT Asia Ltd v. BHP Billiton Marketing AG (Singapore Branch)*, [2015] 2 SLR 540, [32]–[33], citing *ANB v. ANF*, [2011] 2 SLR 1, [54]. The overriding consideration in deciding when the discretion should be exercised appears to be whether summary determination would fulfil the underlying purpose of O 14 r 12 (i.e., to save time and cost for the parties) given the facts of the case: *ANB v. ANF*, [2011] 2 SLR 1, [61].
1431. *TMT Asia Ltd v. BHP Billiton Marketing AG (Singapore Branch)*, [2015] 2 SLR 540, [33], citing *ANB v. ANF*, [2011] 2 SLR 1, [20]–[28] and *Payna Chettiar v. Maimoon bte Ismail*, [1997] 1 SLR(R) 738, [36].
1432. *TMT Asia Ltd v. BHP Billiton Marketing AG (Singapore Branch)*, [2015] 2 SLR 540, [34], [38]; *Olivine Capital Pte Ltd v. Chia Chin Yan*, [2014] 2 SLR 1371, [51]; *Obegi Melissa v. Vestwin Trading Pte Ltd*, [2008] 2 SLR(R) 540, [42].
1433. *TMT Asia Ltd v. BHP Billiton Marketing AG (Singapore Branch)*, [2015] 2 SLR 540, [35]–[37]; *Obegi Melissa v. Vestwin Trading Pte Ltd*, [2008] 2 SLR(R) 540, [42].
1434. (Cap. 322, 2007 Rev. Ed.).
1435. Below it is the High Court, followed by the District and Magistrates' Courts. For appeals arising from the lower courts, *see* Supreme Court of Judicature Act (Cap. 322, R. 5, 2014 Rev. Ed.) Rules of Court, O 55B, 55C, and 55D. There is a right of appeal from a registrar in chambers to a judge in chambers (District Judge if it is the State Courts), but not necessarily after that stage.
1436. The statute was amended in 2010 and 2014.

makes an order at the hearing of any interlocutory application other than an application for … summary judgment.' In other words, if unconditional leave to defend is given, the plaintiff cannot appeal the decision. If conditional leave to defend is given, the defendant can appeal the decision as of right but the plaintiff cannot (including asking for leave to appeal). And if summary judgment is awarded, the defendant can appeal the decision as of right.

421. It is also possible for a court hearing a summary judgment application to make 'no order' on the application since O 14 r 3 does not purport to lay down an exhaustive list of the possible outcomes of a summary judgment application.[1437] Notably, the Fourth and Fifth Schedules do not provide for 'no order' orders. However, this does not mean that 'no order' orders are appealable as of right. Adopting a purposive approach, it was held in *Sinwa SS (HK) Co Ltd v. Nordic International Ltd* that para (a) of the Fourth Schedule encompasses an order of 'no order' made in respect of a summary judgment application. In other words, such an order is non-appealable.[1438]

422. The asymmetry in appeal rights is consistent with the notion that a litigant should have the right with a full trial, unless there are plainly good reasons not to do so. Whether or not a stay of execution of summary judgment would be granted while an appeal (against the summary judgment) is pending is entirely within the discretion of the court. The applicant must show special circumstances before such a stay would be granted.[1439] An appeal does not automatically operate as a stay of execution.[1440]

1437. *Sinwa SS (HK) Co Ltd v. Nordic International Ltd*, [2015] 2 SLR 54, [27].

1438. *Sinwa SS (HK) Co Ltd v. Nordic International Ltd*, [2015] 2 SLR 54, [37]–[39].

1439. *Lee Sian Hee (trading as Lee Sian Hee Pork Trader) v. Oh Kheng Soon (trading as Ban Hon Trading Enterprise)*, [1991] 2 SLR(R) 869, [5]; cited in *Swiss Singapore Overseas Enterprises Pte Ltd v. Navalmar UK Ltd*, [2003] 1 SLR(R) 688, [7].

1440. Supreme Court of Judicature Act (Cap. 322, 2007 Rev. Ed.), s 41; *Lian Soon Construction Pte Ltd v. Guan Qian Realty Pte Ltd*, [1999] 1 SLR(R) 1053, [13]. *See also HSBC Institutional Trust Services (Singapore) Ltd v. Picket & Rail Asia Pacific Pte Ltd*, [2010] 4 SLR 326, [7].

Chapter 6. Striking Out Proceedings

§1. INTRODUCTION

423. Striking out is another possible avenue in which justice may be expedited, though much depends on what is being sought to be struck out, which has to be specified. It is broadly similar to a summary judgment application insofar as a party is alleging that the other party has no basis to defend or bring a claim or part(s) of a claim, but different in that resolution of the matter may not necessarily be sought in the application. The grounds for succeeding in this application are also markedly different as there could be elements of some kind of bad faith involved. Finally, striking out is more likely to be availed by a defendant than a plaintiff.[1441]

424. The rules for striking out are primarily found in O 18 of the Rules of Court,[1442] which also govern pleadings (including amendments) in general. As is the case with the rules on summary judgment, the crux of striking out traces its historical origins to the English rules of civil procedure,[1443] though it can be said that the English position has since developed differently in several respects[1444] (it is still not uncommon for both old and new English cases to be cited as authority). In the main, O 18 r 19(1) states that the court 'may at any stage of the proceedings order to be struck out or amended any pleading or the endorsement of any writ in the action, or anything in any pleading or in the endorsement' if: '(a) it discloses no reasonable cause of action or defence, as the case may be; (b) it is scandalous, frivolous or vexatious; (c) it may prejudice, embarrass or delay the fair trial of the action; (d) it is otherwise an abuse of the process of the Court'.

425. Parenthetically, it should be noted at this juncture that striking out brought under O 18 r 19 only applies to pleadings (including an originating summons seeking relief), any endorsement of a writ, but not to a summons in a pending cause or matter.[1445] It should further be noted that this specific power to strike out under O 18 r 19 has to be differentiated from the broader and inherent judicial prerogative to strike out, which is usually exercised when a party has committed serious procedural breaches.[1446] Some examples of when the latter discretion would be exercised (sometimes in tandem with the inherent power) include O 19 r 1 (default in service

1441. *See also The 'Melati'*, [2004] 2 SLR(R) 555, [20]–[21].
1442. Supreme Court of Judicature Act (Cap. 322, R. 5, 2014 Rev. Ed.) Rules of Court.
1443. *Singapore Civil Procedure 2015 Volume 1*, at 351–352 (G.P. Selvam ed., Sweet & Maxwell Asia 2014).
1444. *See* e.g., the language used in Part 3.4 of the English Civil Procedure Rules as compared to the language used in O 14 rr 1 and 3.
1445. *Attorney-General v. Aljunied-Hougang-Punggol East Town Council*, [2016] 1 SLR 915, [32]–[33]. In that case, the court looked at the plain words of O 18 r 19 and denied an application to strike out a joinder application.
1446. *See also Singapore Civil Procedure 2015 Volume 1*, at 351 (G.P. Selvam ed., Sweet & Maxwell Asia 2014); *Toh Wee Ping Benjamin v. Grande Corp Pte Ltd*, [2020] SGCA 48.

of statement of claim), O 24 r 16(1) (failure to comply with requirements for discovery, such as suppression and/or destruction of documents for pre- and post action discovery), O 25 r 1(4) (failure by plaintiff to apply for summons for directions), O 34 r 2(2) (failure by plaintiff to set down for trial), and O 34A r 1(2) (failure by party to comply with orders or directions given during pre-trial conferences).[1447] Though this broader judicial prerogative to strike out almost always has the same effect as the O 18 r 19 power to strike out (i.e., pleadings or part of the pleadings may be struck out as a result),[1448] the considerations, motivations, and justifications behind the two powers do not always coincide. To illuminate this point, the passages from the leading local case on this point bear extracting in extenso:

> there are four instances in which the court may in the exercise of its discretion strike out the pleadings for non-compliance with the Rules of Court or orders of court. They are:
>
> a. The defaulting party has deliberately or wilfully failed to comply with an 'unless order' …
> b. The defaulting party has failed to comply with successive non-peremptory orders for discovery so that the default is clearly contumacious …
> c. The consequences of the failure to comply with a rule of court or order requiring discovery is such that there is a serious or real risk that a fair trial may no longer be possible.
> d. The failure to comply with a rule of court or order requiring discovery is due to the deliberate suppression of evidence which justifies a striking out of the pleadings even where a fair trial was still possible.
>
> [T]hese instances of striking out were in circumstances involving (a) procedural abuse or questionable tactics; (b) peremptory orders where the basis of the failure to comply with a peremptory order was contumacious; and (c) repeated and persistent defaults of the rules of court or non-peremptory orders amounting to contumacious conduct. At the opposite end of the spectrum of seriousness are cases of ordinary procedural defaults of a technical complexion that are unlikely to give rise to the exercise of this discretionary power to strike out. As one would expect, the circumstances in which a court may be asked to strike out the pleadings under the Rules of Court are infinitely varied and distinctly fact-sensitive …

1447. *Alliance Management SA v. Pendleton Lane P*, [2008] 4 SLR(R) 1, [6]. These various processes are canvassed in greater detail in other Parts and Chapters. *See also Grande Corp Pte Ltd v. Cubix International Pte Ltd*, [2018] SGHC 13; *K Solutions Pte Ltd v. National University of Singapore*, [2009] 4 SLR(R) 254, [107]–[109] and [134]–[138].

1448. It should be noted that striking out is not confined to pleadings – it is possible, for instance, to strike out notices of appeal as well: *Riduan bin Yusof v. Khng Thian Huat*, [2005] 2 SLR(R) 188, [17]–[21]. It is also possible to strike out affidavits if they do not contain material evidence but collateral evidence that is scandalous, irrelevant or otherwise oppressive: Supreme Court of Judicature Act (Cap. 322, R. 5, 2014 Rev. Ed.) Rules of Court, O 41 r 6; *Lee Hsien Loong v. Singapore Democratic Party*, [2009] 1 SLR(R) 642, [14]–[17]. *See also Cytec Industries Pte Ltd v. APP Chemicals International (Mau) Ltd*, [2009] 4 SLR(R) 769, [17]–[26] on how the mere disclosure of 'with our prejudice' correspondence in an affidavit may not warrant the other party taking out a striking out application.

> Undoubtedly, the power to strike out … is a powerful tool in the court's case management armoury. The effect of the striking out for procedural defaults is to preclude a trial on the merits of either the claim or defence, as the case may be. This notion of access to the court leads me to the second principle that a party should not in the ordinary way be denied adjudication of his claim or defence on its merits because of procedural defaults such as non-compliance with the Rules of Court or orders of court as to the time by which a particular step or matter is to be taken or done unless the default causes prejudice to his opponents for which an award of costs cannot compensate. The second principle is reflected in the general discretion to extend time under O 3 r 4 in accordance with the dictates of justice in the particular case … The interplay of the two principles is usually resolved in favour of one principle over the other in accordance with the dictates of justice based on the facts and merits of the particular case.[1449]

426. On the other hand, the general principle behind the exercise of the O 18 r 19 powers been described in the following terms:

> In general, it is only in plain and obvious cases that the power of striking out should be invoked … It should not be exercised by a minute and protracted examination of the documents and facts of the case in order to see if the plaintiff really has a cause of action. The practice of the courts has been that, where an application for striking out involves a lengthy and serious argument, the court should decline to proceed with the argument unless, not only does it have doubts as to the soundness of the pleading but, in addition, it is satisfied that striking out will obviate the necessity for a trial or reduce the burden of preparing for a trial.[1450]

427. In other words, with respect to the broader power of striking out, it appears that first, there must have been a certain pattern of belligerent and/or dishonest behaviour on the part of one party that causes undue prejudice to the other party.

1449. *Alliance Management SA v. Pendleton Lane P*, [2008] 4 SLR(R) 1, [5]–[7]. *See also* Supreme Court of Judicature Act (Cap. 322, R. 5, 2014 Rev. Ed.) Rules of Court, O 92 r 4(1). This power, however, is usually cited with reference to *id.*, O 18 r 19: *see* e.g., *The 'Bunga Melati 5'*, [2012] 4 SLR 546, [33]. C.f. *K Solutions Pte Ltd v. National University of Singapore*, [2009] 4 SLR(R) 254, [103]–[104].

1450. *Gabriel Peter & Partners (suing as a firm) v. Wee Chong Jin*, [1997] 3 SLR(R) 649, [18], citing *Hubbuck & Sons, Limited v. Wilkinson, Heywood & Clark, Limited*, [1899] 1 QB 86, 91. *See also Qroi Ltd v. Pascoe, Ian* [2019] SGHC 36 at [4]–[6]; *Ebony Ritz Sdn Bhd v. Sumatec Resources Bhd*, [2017] SGHC 282, [73]; *Antariksa Logistics Pte Ltd v. Nurdian Cuaca* [2016] SGHCR 10, [26]; *Koh Kim Teck v. Credit Suisse AG, Singapore Branchi*, [2015] SGHC 52, [20]; *Low Heng Leon Andy v. Low Kian Beng Lawrence (administrator of the estate of Tan Ah Kng, deceased)*, [2013] 3 SLR 710, [10]; *Her Majesty's Revenue & Customs v. Hashu Dhalomal Shahdadpuri*, [2011] 3 SLR 1186, [35]; *Woon Tek Seng v. V. Jayaraman a/l v. A Vellasamy*, [2008] 3 SLR(R) 43, [37]–[38], citing *Kwa Ban Cheong v. Kuah Book Sek*, [2003] 3 SLR(R) 644, [29]; *Tan Eng Khiam v. Ultra Realty Pte Ltd*, [1991] 3 MLJ 234.

Second, such a pattern must be identifiable via specific reference to a particular non-compliance (or more) of a rule of court and/or court order before the court will exercise its power to strike out outside of the grounds provided for in O 18 r 19.[1451] Applying for striking out via O 18 r 19 would be the more appropriate course of action when it is still temporally proximate to the point where the scope of pleadings have more or less been established.[1452] Proceeding via O 18 r 19 will also be the logically prior thing to do in most instances if any of the four grounds therein are engaged, simply as a matter of common sensical statutory approach. In any event, because striking out is such a draconian power, the court will always be slow to exercise it unless there are very good reasons to do so,[1453] regardless of which order it exercises its power under.

§2. Procedural Aspects

428. Although O 18 r 19 does not prescribe a procedure for a striking out application to be taken out, the usual procedure (presumably, this is the case for the broader sort of striking out applications as well) is to apply by way of summons, supported by affidavit(s).[1454] The exception is if the application is based on ground (a) of O 18 r 19.[1455] This exception exists because 'the merits of the application may be determined on the context of the pleading alone'.[1456] However, recent case law suggests that extraneous materials may be referred to in limited circumstances; this is particularly the case where the party's capacity to sue is in issue and can be easily and unequivocally demonstrated by reference to an affidavit or other court document.[1457]

429. In terms of timelines, while the language of O 18 r 19 makes it clear that a court 'may at any state of the proceedings' order striking out, 'it is good practice that striking out applications should always be made promptly, and as a rule preferably before the close of pleadings … Whether a striking out application should be entertained after close of pleadings is a matter of discretion to be decided on a variety of factors such as proximity of the trial dates, alteration of position by the

1451. *See also Alliance Management SA v. Pendleton Lane P*, [2008] 4 SLR(R) 1, [14].

1452. *Singapore Civil Procedure 2013 Volume 1*, at 317 (G.P. Selvam ed., Sweet & Maxwell Asia 2012).

1453. *Lakshmi Anil Salgaocar v. Vivek Sudarshan Khabya*, [2017] SGHC, [38]. *See also Huang Meizhe v. Attorney-General*, [2011] 2 SLR 1149, [21], citing *Bandung Shipping Pte Ltd v. Keppel TatLee Bank*, [2003] 1 SLR(R) 295, [34].

1454. *See* Supreme Court of Judicature Act (Cap. 322, R. 5, 2014 Rev. Ed.) Rules of Court, O 2 r 1(1). *See also id.*, O 2 rr 1(2)–(3).

1455. *Yusen Air & Sea Service (S) Pte Ltd v. KLM Royal Dutch Airlines*, [1999] 2 SLR(R) 955, [46]. *See also* Supreme Court of Judicature Act (Cap. 322, R. 5, 2014 Rev. Ed.) Rules of Court, O 18 r 19(2).

1456. J. Pinsler, *Principles of Civil Procedure* 307 (Acad. Publg. 2013).

1457. J. Pinsler, *Principles of Civil Procedure* 307 (Acad. Publg. 2013), citing *Hong Alvin v. Chia Quee Khee*, [2011] SGHC 249.

parties and the merits of the application.'[1458] Where appropriate,[1459] a party may choose to combine an O 18 r 19 application with an O 14 application (summary judgment) so that they can be heard together in one hearing.[1460] If this is done, it follows that a party should comply with the O 14 timelines as well. As with most other interlocutory applications, parties are at liberty to request for extensions of time with regard to the filing and serving of the relevant documents, but this is subject to possible costs penalties against parties responsible for the delays. However, all necessary amendments to the statement of claim must be made before summary judgment is applied for.[1461]

§3. Substantive Aspects

430. An applicant may rely on more than one of the four grounds in O 18 r 19, and indeed it is actually quite a common practice for applicants to do so.[1462] In addition, total disregard of court orders[1463] and/or failure to comply with terms of an unless order may result in the striking out of the offending party's claim (or defence or counterclaim as the case may be). The legal basis for striking out is anchored on public interest – upholding the authority of the court and ensuring its processes are not used in an unjust way.[1464] The applicant should 'precisely correlate the arguments it advances to the exact limb under O 18 r 19(1) … which it seeks to rely on … [even though] there is some similarity and overlap amongst the four limbs of O 18 r 19(1)'.[1465] The four grounds will now be considered in seriatim.

I. No Reasonable Cause of Action or Defence

431. A 'reasonable cause of action' is 'a claim which has a chance of success on the basis of the allegations in the pleadings'; thus, 'the court will only strike out the

1458. *TTJ Design and Engineering Pte Ltd v. Chip Eng Seng Contractors (1988) Pte Ltd*, [2011] 2 SLR 877, [11]–[12]. *See also Tapematic SpA v. Wirana Pte Ltd*, [2002] 1 SLR(R) 44, [66]; *Orient Centre Investments Ltd v. Société Générale*, [2007] 3 SLR(R) 566, [61].

1459. A combination of summary judgment and striking out parts of a defence or its entirety may be justified on the basis of alternative remedies; It may not be justified where the intention is to challenge the entire defence (not just specific defences): *Lee Hsien Loong v. Review Publishing Co*, [2009] 1 SLR(R) 177, [5]–[16]. If the defence includes several parts, the court may find it more appropriate to strike out a part or parts rather than award summary judgment.

1460. *Lim Eng Hock Peter v. Lin Jian Wei*, [2008] 4 SLR(R) 444, [2]; *Lee Hsien Loong v. Review Publishing Co*, [2009] 1 SLR(R) 177, [5]–[16].

1461. *Lee Hsien Loong v. Review Publishing Co*, [2009] 1 SLR(R) 177, [26].

1462. J. Pinsler, *Principles of Civil Procedure* 305 (Acad. Publg. 2013).

1463. *Ramindo Sukses Perkasa Pte Ltd v. Sim Kwang Oo*, [2015] 3 SLR 403.

1464. *Ramindo Sukses Perkasa Pte Ltd v. Sim Kwang Oo*, [2015] 3 SLR 403, [84], citing *Mitora Pte Ltd v. Agritrade International (Pte) Ltd*, [2013] 3 SLR 1179, [48]; *Alliance Management SA v. Pendleton Lane P*, [2008] 4 SLR(R) 1, [9].

1465. *The 'Bunga Melati 5'*, [2012] 4 SLR 546, [31]. *See also Lim Kok Lian (executor and trustee of the estate of Lee Biau Luan, deceased) v. Lee Patricia (executor and trustee of the estate of Lee Biau Luan, deceased)*, [2015] 1 SLR 1184, [10]; *TTJ Design and Engineering Pte Ltd v. Chip Eng Seng Contractors (1988) Pte Ltd*, [2011] 2 SLR 877, [13].

claim if it is bound to fail'.[1466] It follows then that 'the mere fact that the case is weak and is not likely to succeed is no ground for striking it out.[1467] Since the application is essentially a question of law, the pleaded facts are presumed to be true in favour of the claimant, and no affidavit evidence is involved.[1468] Where a statement of claim is defective only in not containing particulars to which the defendant is entitled, the application should be made for particulars.'[1469] Likewise, if a claim or defence is uncertain in law – for instance, if authority is cited from another jurisdiction with the aim of filling a contentious lacuna in the local jurisprudence – it is unlikely that the court will resort to striking out.[1470] The court will also not resort to striking out if the purported cause of action involves complex facts (such as emerging technologies) and/or complex legal concepts.[1471] Instead, the court will avoid considering the merits of the assertions sought to be struck out, unless the assertions are truly hopelessly devoid of merit and a trial, in part or full, ought to be obviated in the interests of justice.[1472] However, a cause of action that has been pleaded without the support of material facts is defective and should be struck out as either disclosing no reasonable cause of action, or as being frivolous and vexatious, or an abuse of the court's process.[1473] Likewise, if the facts pleaded simply do not justify the legal remedy prayed for on any reasonable resolution of the novel questions of law said to have been raised by the pleadings, the action may still be

---

1466. *Gabriel Peter & Partners (suing as a firm) v. Ween Chong Jin*, [1997] 3 SLR(R) 649, [21]; *Tan Swee Wan v. Lian Tian Yong Johnny*, [2016] SGHC 206, [39]; *Harun bin Syed Hussain Aljunied v. Abdul Samad bin O K Mohamed Haniffa*, [2017] SGHC 248, [29]. A clear example under this ground will be 'where an aggrieved party is unable to establish *locus standi*': *Tan Eng Hong v. Attorney-General*, [2011] 3 SLR 320, [5], citing *Abdul Razak Ahmad v. Majlis Bandaraya Johor Bahru*, [1995] 2 MLJ 287. Another example will be where a party pleads for relief without articulating the cause of action: *Tan Gek Suan Constance v. Lau Kean Wah*, [2017] SGHC 152, [1]. *See also VisionHealthOne Corp Pte Ltd v. HD Holdings Pte Ltd*, [2010] 3 SLR 97, [46]; *Standard Chartered Bank v. Loh Chong Yong Thomas*, [2010] 2 SLR 569, [12]–[14].

1467. *Lim Kok Lian (executor and trustee of the estate of Lee Biau Luan, deceased) v. Lee Patricia (executor and trustee of the estate of Lee Biau Luan, deceased)*, [2015] 1 SLR 1184, [30]. *See also Lee Seng Eder v. Wee Kim Chwee*, [2015] SGHCR 2, [18]; *Chan Boon Siang v. Jasmin Nisban* [2017] SGHC 249 at [5]–[7].

1468. *Koh Kim Teck v. Credit Suisse AG, Singapore Branchi*, [2015] SGHC 52, [22], citing *Tan Eng Khiam v. Ultra Realty Pte Ltd*, [1991] 1 SLR(R) 844, [29]. *See also Millennium Pharmaceuticals, Inc v. Drug Houses of Australia Pte Ltd* [2018] SGHC 149 at [27].

1469. *Gabriel Peter & Partners (suing as a firm) v. Wee Chong Jin*, [1997] 3 SLR(R) 649, [21]; *Ng Chee Weng v. Lim Jit Ming Bryan*, [2012] 1 SLR 457, [112]; *Harwindar Singh s/o Geja Singh v. Michael Wong Lok Yung*, [2015] SGHC 132, [10]; *EA Apartments Pte Ltd v. Tan Bek*, [2016] SGHC 268, [25]. *See also TTJ Design and Engineering Pte Ltd v. Chip Eng Seng Contractors (1988) Pte Ltd*, [2011] 2 SLR 877, [13].

1470. *Pacific Internet Ltd v. Catcha.com Pte Ltd*, [2000] 1 SLR(R) 980, [12]–[14], citing *Hunt v. Carey Canada Inc*, 2 SCR 959, 977. *See also Singapore Civil Procedure 2013 Volume 1*, at 316 (G.P. Selvam ed., Sweet & Maxwell Asia 2012); *Lim Kok Lian (executor and trustee of the estate of Lee Biau Luan, deceased) v. Lee Patricia (executor and trustee of the estate of Lee Biau Luan, deceased)*, [2015] 1 SLR 1184, [13], [16] and [26]; *AYW v. AYX*, [2016] 1 SLR 1183, [36].

1471. C. Bull & J. Pinsler, *Civil Procedure: Annual Review of Singapore Cases* (Sing. Acad. L. 2000), citing *Pacific Internet Ltd v. Catcha.com Pte Ltd*, [2000] 1 SLR(R) 980, [31].

1472. *Lim Eng Hock Peter v. Lin Jian Wei*, [2008] 4 SLR(R) 444, [34].

1473. *RecordTV Pte Ltd v. MediaCorp TV Singapore Pte Ltd*, [2009] 4 SLR(R) 43, [18]–[19], citing *OCM Opportunities Fund II, LP v. Burhan Uray*, [2004] SGHC 115.

struck out.[1474] Further, when a party has been forced out to take out an undue number of interlocutory applications for discovery and further and better particulars, this may indicate that the other party simply has a claim that is too vague and general and one that should be struck out.[1475]

432. Separately, it should be noted that O 18 r 19(1)(a) would not normally apply as a limitation defence. Where the issue concerns expiry of the limitation period or an arguable point of law relating to limitation period, the appropriate strategy would be to make an application either pursuant to O 14 r 12 (determination of a point of law) or O 33 r 2 (preliminary issue before trial).[1476]

433. A question may arise as to whether the cause of action or defence is to be sustainable as a matter of law or as a matter of fact to succeed in defending against this ground. Insofar as O 18 r 19(2) bars the admission of any evidence with respect to this ground, it must be the case that the cause of action or defence is to be sustainable as a matter of law only,[1477] since facts need to be established by evidence. Nonetheless, it has been pointed out that while:

> the effect of the pleaded facts (whether they constitute a reasonable cause of action or defence) is addressed by ground (a), the existence of a cause of action (which is not pleaded) may need to be determined by a consideration of affidavit evidence and other documents. Perhaps it may be more appropriate in this latter situation for the court to rely on its inherent power to make the appropriate order after taking all relevant facts into account.[1478]

II. Scandalous, Frivolous, or Vexatious

434. The term 'frivolous or vexatious' has often been equated with 'plainly unsustainable' and 'obviously unsustainable'.[1479] Unlike the ground of whether a reasonable cause of action or defence is disclosed, this aspect of this ground has

1474. *AYW v. AYX*, [2016] 1 SLR 1183, [40].
1475. *Orient Centre Investments Ltd v. Société Générale*, [2007] 3 SLR 566, [62]–[64].
1476. J. Pinsler, *Principles of Civil Procedure* 310 (Acad. Publg. 2013).
1477. C.f. *Phillip Morris Products Inc v. Power Circle Sdn Bhd*, [1999] 1 SLR(R) 964, [5].
1478. J. Pinsler, *Principles of Civil Procedure* 307 (Acad. Publg. 2013) citing *Hong Alvin v. Chia Quee Khee*, [2011] SGHC 249, [23]. It should also be noted that if an argument on limitation is made, the appropriate procedure would be to make an application under O 14 r 12 (determination of a point of law) or O 33 r 2 (preliminary issue before trial): J. Pinsler, *Principles of Civil Procedure* 310 (Acad. Publg. 2013).
1479. *Chee Siok Chin v. Minister for Home Affairs*, [2006] 1 SLR(R) 582, [37], citing *Attorney-General of the Duchy of Lancaster v. London and North Western Railway Company*, [1892] 3 Ch 274, 277; *The 'Bunga Melati 5'*, [2012] 4 SLR 546, [32]–[33]; *The STX Mumbai*, [2015] 5 SLR 1, [4]–[5]. *See also* J. Pinsler, *Principles of Civil Procedure* 308 (Acad. Publg. 2013) citing *Lehman Brothers Special Financing Inc v. Hartadi Angkosubroto*, [1998] 3 SLR(R) 664; *Chia Kok Kee v. Tan Wah*, [2012] 2 SLR 352. A clear example under this ground would be a person who is unjustifiably made a party to an action: J. Pinsler, *Principles of Civil Procedure* 309 (Acad. Publg. 2013).

both a legal and factual dimension to it. Specifically, an action is legally unsustainable if 'it may be clear as a matter of law at the outset that even if a party were to succeed in proving all the facts that he offers to prove he will not be entitled to the remedy that he seeks'.[1480] Therefore, if it is not clear beyond question that the legal elements of a claim cannot be satisfied, it cannot be said to be legally unsustainable.[1481] On the other hand, an action is factually unsustainable if it is 'possible to say with confidence before trial that the factual basis for the claim is fanciful because it is entirely without substance, [for example, if it is] clear beyond question that the statement of facts is contradicted by all the documents or other material on which it is based'.[1482] Therefore, a claim cannot be said to be factually unsustainable if a court has to choose between conflicting accounts of crucial facts.[1483]

435. To prove that an action is 'frivolous or vexatious', a party need only show that it is either legally or factually unsustainable; he is not required to demonstrate both aspects.[1484] A common example of a vexatious action is when a party attempts to bring a duplicate action, though such a move may conceivably overlap with the other ground of abuse of process of the court (see below).[1485] That said, care must be taken to examine any allegation of duplication of claims.[1486] Another example of a vexatious action is when a party keeps making multiple applications on issues that have already been determined.[1487] As for the term 'scandalous' – which can also be

1480. *The 'Bunga Melati 5'*, [2012] 4 SLR 546, [39], citing *Three Rivers District Council v. Governor and Company of the Bank of England*, [2001] UKHL 16, 95. *See also Chee Siok Chin v. Minister for Home Affairs*, [2006] 1 SLR(R) 582, [33]; *Wee Kim San Lawrence Bernard v. Robinson & Co (Singapore) Pte Ltd*, [2014] 4 SLR 357, [21]; *Koh Kim Teck v. Credit Suisse AG, Singapore Branchi*, [2015] SGHC 52, [23]; *Lee Seng Eder v. Wee Kim Chwee*, [2015] SGHCR 2, [29]; *Lipkin International Ltd v. Swiber Holdings Ltd*, [2015] 5 SLR 962, [46]; *Liew Soon Fook Michael v. Yi Kai Development*, [2017] SGHC 88, [17].

1481. *The 'Bunga Melati 5'*, [2012] 4 SLR 546, [57]–[67]; *Liew Soon Fook Michael v. Yi Kai Development*, [2017] SGHC 88, [17]. *See also Fauziyah bte Mohd Ahbidin (executrix of the estate of Mohamed Ahbideen bin Mohamed Kassim (alias Ahna Mohamed Zainal Abidin bin Kassim), deceased) v. Singapore Land Authority*, [2020] SGHC 123.

1482. *The 'Bunga Melati 5'*, [2012] 4 SLR 546, [39], citing *Three Rivers District Council v. Governor and Company of the Bank of England*, [2001] UKHL 16, 95. *See also Invest-Ho Properties Pte Ltd v. Karuppiah Tanapalan*, [2017] SGHCR 20, [33]; *Koh Kim Teck v. Credit Suisse AG, Singapore Branchi*, [2015] SGHC 52, [23]; *Lee Seng Eder v. Wee Kim Chwee*, [2015] SGHCR 2, [29].

1483. *The 'Bunga Melati 5'*, [2012] 4 SLR 546, [45]–[51].

1484. *The 'Bunga Melati 5'*, [2012] 4 SLR 546, [39]; *Tan Swee Wan v. Lian Tian Yong Johnny*, [2016] SGHC 206, [39].

1485. *Bank of Canton Ltd v. Dart Sum Timber (Pte) Ltd*, [1977–1978] SLR(R) 367, [23], citing *McHenry v. Lewis*, (1883) 22 Ch 397, 400. *See also Syed Ahmad Jamal Alsagoff (administrator of the estate of Noor bte Abdulgader Harharah, deceased) v. Harun bin Syed Hussain Aljunied (alias Harud Aljunied)*, [2011] 2 SLR 661, [42].

1486. *Terrestrial Pte Ltd v. Allgo Marine Pte Ltd*, [2013] 3 SLR 527, [15].

1487. C. Bull & J. Pinsler, *Civil Procedure: Annual Review of Singapore Cases* (Sing. Acad. L. 2000), citing *Chua Choon Lim Robert v. M N Swami*, 2 SLR(R) 589; *Grepe v. Loam*, (1887) 37 Ch D 168. Supreme Court of Judicature Act (Cap. 322, 2007 Rev. Ed.), s 74(1), also allows the Attorney-General to restrain a party from commencing or continuing legal proceedings. In this regard, *see Attorney-General v. Lai Swee Lin Linda*, [2015] 5 SLR 1447, [24]: 'The mere institution of vexatious proceedings does not in itself bring s 74(1) into play. The respondent must have

proven independently of the requirement of 'frivolous or vexatious' for an application under this ground to succeed – it 'describes a needlessly offensive allegation which has no relevance to the issues'.[1488] Put another way, to determine if a pleading is 'scandalous', the 'sole question' to be asked is whether 'the matter alleged to be scandalous had a tendency to show the truth of any allegation material to the relief sought'.[1489] Pleadings can also be scandalous if any unnecessary matter in a pleading contains any imputation on the opponent, or makes any charge of misconduct or bad faith against him or anyone else.[1490] In addition, an allegation that is 'scandalous' ought to be distinguished from allegations of dishonest and/or outrageous conduct that are relevant to the issue(s).[1491]

III. Prejudice, Embarrass, or Delay Fair Trial of the Action

436. This ground usually pertains to 'the impact of an improperly drafted pleading or endorsement',[1492] for instance if there is 'an utterly confused mix of indiscriminatory allegations',[1493] if there are no 'ample and clear allegations',[1494] if 'the pleading is no more than a bare accusation',[1495] or the pleadings are unnecessary, irrelevant, or solely intended to embarrass or vex the opposing party.[1496] However, it should be noted that if the pleadings are simply deficient rather than defective, the better course of action may be to seek further and better particulars first, before resorting to a striking out application under this ground. But if the pleadings are clearly designed to humiliate an opponent such that amendments would be impractical – and therefore raise matters irrelevant to the issues and cause delay and prejudice to the other party – then such pleadings can be expected to be struck out.[1497]

"habitually and persistently and without any reasonable ground instituted vexatious legal proceedings" … The term "habitually" suggests that the institution of legal proceedings occurs as a matter of course, or almost automatically when the appropriate conditions, whatever they may be, exist. The term "persistently" suggests determination, and continuing in the face of difficulty or opposition, with a degree of stubbornness … proceedings are regarded as "vexatious" if, irrespective of the motive of the litigant, they are so obviously untenable as to be utterly hopeless and only serve to tax the resources of the court. They can also be vexatious if they are brought for collateral purposes and not for the purpose of having the court adjudicate on legitimate issues.'

1488. J. Pinsler, *Principles of Civil Procedure* 309 (Acad. Publg. 2013).

1489. *Lai Swee Lin Linda v. Attorney-General*, [2006] 2 SLR(R) 565, [67], citing *Christie v. Christie*, (1872–1873) LR 8 Ch App 499, 503. *See also Jaya Sudhir a/l Jayaram v. Tong Seak Kan*, [2016] SGHC 204, [29]; *Tan Swee Wan v. Lian Tian Yong Johnny*, [2016] SGHC 206, [39].

1490. *Jaya Sudhir a/l Jayaram v. Tong Seak Kan*, [2016] SGHC 204, [29].

1491. *Singapore Civil Procedure 2015 Volume 1*, at 354 (G.P. Selvam ed., Sweet & Maxwell Asia 2014).

1492. J. Pinsler, *Principles of Civil Procedure* 310 (Acad. Publg. 2013). *See also Singapore Civil Procedure 2015 Volume 1*, at 355–356 (G.P. Selvam ed., Sweet & Maxwell Asia 2014), citing *Knowles v. Roberts* (1888) 38 Ch D 263, 270.

1493. *Nirumalan K Pillay v. A Balakrishnan*, [1996] 2 SLR(R) 650, [18].

1494. *Philip Morris Products Inc v. Power Circle Sdn Bhd*, [1999] 1 SLR(R) 964, [6].

1495. *Kim Hok Yung v. Cooperatieve Centrale Raiffeisen-Boerenleenbank BA (trading as Rabobank) (Lee Mon Sun, third party)*, [2000] 2 SLR(R) 455, [6].

1496. *Tan Swee Wan v. Lian Tian Yong Johnny*, [2016] SGHC 206, [39].

1497. *See* e.g., *Lee Kuan Yew v. Nair Devan*, [1990] 2 SLR(R) 51, [16]–[18].

IV. Abuse of Process of the Court

437. This ground has been described as 'the widest general ground for striking out'.[1498] It 'includes considerations of public policy and the interests of justice … [and] signifies that the process of the court must be used bona fide and properly and must not be abused'.[1499] This is because the court 'will prevent the improper use of its machinery … [and] prevent the judicial process from being used as a means of vexation and oppression in the process of litigation. The categories of conduct rendering a claim frivolous, vexatious or an abuse of process are not closed and will depend on all the relevant circumstances of the case.'[1500] There are at least four categories of abuse of process, some of which overlap with the three preceding grounds:

> (a) proceedings which involve a deception on the court … (b) proceedings where the process of the court is not being fairly or honestly used but is employed but for some ulterior or improper purpose or in an improper way … (c) proceedings which are manifestly groundless or without foundation or which serve no useful purpose … (d) multiple or successive proceedings which cause or are likely to cause improper vexation or oppression.[1501]

438. Two clear and oft-cited examples[1502] of abuse of process of the court are litigating despite res judicata (or cause of action estoppel) and issue estoppel.[1503] As

---

1498. *Chee Siok Chin v. Minister for Home Affairs*, [2006] 1 SLR(R) 582, [38]. *See also Chia Kok Kee v. Tan Wah*, [2012] 2 SLR 352, [28]; *Bosch Corp (Japan) v. Wiedson International (S) Pte Ltd*, [2013] 2 SLR 700, [31]. It should be noted, however, that in *Lee Tat Development Pte Ltd v. Management Corporation Strata Title Plan No 301* [2018] 2 SLR 866 and *Leong Sze Hian v. Lee Hsien Loong* [2019] SGCA 53, the Court of Appeal confirmed that there is no distinct tort of the abuse of process in Singapore. Also, abuse of process can also be invoked in the context of continued prosecution of claim despite of a reasonable offer to settle made: *TMT Asia Ltd v. BHP Billiton Marketing AG (Singapore Branch)*, [2019] 2 SLR 710.

1499. *Gabriel Peter & Partners (suing as a firm) v. Wee Chong Jin*, [1997] 3 SLR(R) 649, [22]; cited in *Chee Siok Chin v. Minister for Home Affairs*, [2006] 1 SLR(R) 582, [38]; *Lim Eng Hock Peter v. Lin Jian Wei*, [2008] 4 SLR(R) 444, [37].

1500. *Gabriel Peter & Partners (suing as a firm) v. Wee Chong Jin*, [1997] 3 SLR(R) 649, [22]; cited in *Chee Siok Chin v. Minister for Home Affairs*, [2006] 1 SLR(R) 582, [38]; *Lim Eng Hock Peter v. Lin Jian Wei*, [2008] 4 SLR(R) 444, [37]. *See also Goh Koon Suan v. Heng Gek Kiau*, [1990] 2 SLR(R) 705, [15]; *Goh Nellie v. Goh Lian Teck*, [2007] 1 SLR(R) 453, [53].

1501. *Chee Siok Chin v. Minister for Home Affairs*, [2006] 1 SLR(R) 582, [34]; cited in *Tan Eng Hong v.* SLR 895, [36]. C.f. *Sum Lye Heng (also known as Lim Jessie) v. MCST Plan No 2285*, [2003] 4 SLR(R) 553, [80]. *See also Tey Tsun Hang v. Attorney-General*, [2015] 1 SLR 856, [37]; *Low Heng Leon Andy v. Low Kian Beng Lawrence (administrator of the estate of Tan Ah Kng, deceased)*, [2013] 3 SLR 710, [57]–[58].

1502. *See Zhang Run Zi v. Koh Kim Seng*, [2015] SGHC 175, [35]: 'The doctrine of *res judicata* has often been described as an 'umbrella doctrine' encompassing three conceptually distinct though interrelated principles, namely, cause of action estoppel, issue estoppel, and … abuse of process.' *See also AKN v. ALC*, [2016] 1 SLR 966, [56].

1503. *Wing Joo Loong Ginseng Hong (Singapore) Co Pte Ltd v. Qinghai Xinyuan Foreign Trade Co Ltd*, [2009] 2 SLR(R) 814, [165], citing *Lee Tat Development Pte Ltd v. MCST Plan No 301*, [2005] 3 SLR(R) 157, [14]–[15]. *See also Burgundy Global exploration Corp v. Transocean Offshore International Ventures Ltd*, [2014] 3 SLR 381, [36]; *ADP v. ADQ*, [2012] 2 SLR 143, [21]; *Ching Mun Fong (executrix of the estate of Tan Geok Tee, deceased) v. Liu Cho Chit*, [2000] 1

regards the former, it has been explained that it is 'based on the important principle of public policy that a cause of action … which has been finally and conclusively adjudicated on the merits by a court of competent jurisdiction may not be re-litigated by the same parties'.[1504] It requires there to be a final and conclusive judgment on the merits, and for the judgment to have been made by a court of competent jurisdiction.[1505] The mere fact that the court might have made a legal error in the decision, unless reversed on appeal, makes the decision unimpeachable (and therefore cannot be set aside or reopened), unless fraud or collusion taints the decision.[1506] As regards the latter (issue estoppel), there are two further conditions, that of 'identity between the parties to the two actions that are being compared; and … an identity of subject matter[1507] in the two proceedings'.[1508] The court can consider

---

SLR(R) 53, [22]–[28]; J. Pinsler, *Principles of Civil Procedure* 312–314 (Acad. Publg. 2013). C.f. *The Royal Bank of Scotland NV (formerly known as ABN Amro Bank NV) v. TT International Ltd (nTan Corporate Advisory Pte Ltd)*, [2015] 5 SLR 1104, [98]: '*res judicata* [comprises] (a) cause of action estoppel; (b) issue estoppel; and (c) what is known as either the "extended" doctrine of *res judicata* or the defence of "abuse of process"'. For an elaboration of the 'extended doctrine of *res judicata*', *see Antariksa Logistics Pte Ltd and others v. Nurdian Cuaca and others* [2016] SGHCR 10; *Cost Engineers (SEA) Pte Ltd v. Chan Siew Lun*, [2016] 1 SLR 137, [26]–[28]; *Venkatraman Kalyanaraman v. Nithya Kalyani*, [2016] SGHC 157, [25]; *Lim Cheng Soon David v. Global Maritime Holdings Ltd*, [2016] SGHC 163, [11]. As to whether issue estoppel applies to criminal proceedings, *see Yong Vui Kong v. Attorney-General*, [2015] SGHC 178, [30]–[32].

1504. *Lee Tat Development Pte Ltd v. MCST Plan No 301*, [2009] 1 SLR(R) 875, [13]. However, it is also possible for a party to be estopped even before final adjudication, such as 'where a party commences a new action in respect of a claim or issue which is the subject of matter of current proceedings … by reason of a judgment by consent pursuant to a settlement, or summary judgment or other final decision on an interlocutory application, or where a party puts forward a positive case and then abandons it': J. Pinsler, *Principles of Civil Procedure* 316 (Acad. Publg. 2013). C.f. *Woon Tek Seng v. v. Jayaraman a/l v. A Vellasamy*, [2008] 3 SLR(R) 43, [39], which held that there is no *res judicata* and an abuse of the process of the court if the plaintiff chose not to proceed with a reinstatement application but started immediately with a fresh action, and the rules do not expressly preclude him from starting a fresh action after a deemed discontinuance without first applying for reinstatement.

1505. *Lee Tat Development Pte Ltd v. MCST Plan No 301*, [2009] 1 SLR(R) 875, [4]; *Soh Lay Lian Cherlyn v. Kok Mui Eng*, [2015] 5 SLR 53, [10]–[12].

1506. *The Royal Bank of Scotland NV (formerly known as ABN Amro Bank NV) v. TT International Ltd (nTan Corporate Advisory Pte Ltd)*, [2015] 5 SLR 1104, [68]–[72]. *See also Turf Club Auto Emporium Pte Ltd v. Yeo Boong Hua*, [2017] SGCA 21, [83]; *Petroships Investment Pte Ltd v. Wealthplus Pte Ltd*, [2017] SGHC 122, [77].

1507. *See also Zhang Run Zi v. Koh Kim Seng*, [2015] SGHC 175, [49]: 'the requirement of an identity of cause of action is satisfied as long as the plaintiff seeks the rely on the *same matrix of facts* which were the subject of previous proceedings. It does not matter that legally speaking, the claims are characterised differently. Parties cannot, normally, reopen proceedings over the *same set of facts*' (emphasis in original).

1508. *Cheong Wei Chang v. Lee Hsien Loong*. [2018] SGHC 217; *Turf Club Auto Emporium Pte Ltd v. Yeo Boong Hua*, [2017] SGCA 21, [87]; *Wing Joo Loong Ginseng Hong (Singapore) Co Pte Ltd v. Qinghai Xinyuan Foreign Trade Co Ltd*, [2009] 2 SLR(R) 814, [165], citing *Lee Tat Development Pte Ltd v. MCST Plan No 301*, [2005] 3 SLR(R) 157, [14]–[15]. *See also Woon Tek Seng v. v. Jayaraman a/l v. A Vellasamy*, [2008] 3 SLR(R) 43, [56], citing *Xiamen International Bank v. Sing Eng (Pte) Ltd*, [1993] 2 SLR(R) 176, [28]; *Low Heng Leon Andy v. Low Kian Beng Lawrence (administrator of the estate of Tan Ah Kng, deceased)*, [2013] 3 SLR 710, [49]; *Soh Lay Lian Cherlyn v. Kok Mui Eng*, [2015] 5 SLR 53, [10]–[12]; *Petroships Investment Pte Ltd v. Wealthplus Pte Ltd*, [2017] SGHC 122, [77]. As to whether a litigant should be prevented from taking a point that could have been raised in earlier proceedings, the court would consider factors such as

all relevant material in determining the identity of cause of action, and is not restricted to the pleadings.[1509] Exceptions also exist for res judicata and issue estoppel – the most prominent one being 'where the court itself has made such an egregious mistake that grave injustice … would result if the court's erroneous decision were to form the basis of an estoppel against the aggrieved party'.[1510]

439. The Court of Appeal has also since clarified that only a narrow exception can be made to issue estoppel if the following cumulative requirements can be met.[1511] First, the decision said to give rise to issue estoppel has to directly affect the future determination of the rights of the litigants. Second, the decision has to be clearly wrong. Third, the error in the decision has to stem from the fact that some point of fact or law relevant to the decision was not taken or argued before the court which made that decision, and could not reasonably have been taken or argued on that occasion. Fourth, there has to not be any attempt to claw back rights that had accrued pursuant to the erroneous decision or otherwise to undo the effects of that decision. Fifth, it has to be shown that great injustice would result if the litigant in question were estopped from putting forward the particular point which was said to be the subject of issue estoppel; thus, if the litigant failed to take advantage of an avenue of appeal that was available to him, it would not usually be possible to show that the requisite injustice nevertheless existed. The court reasoned that in the civil sphere at least, the public interest in the finality of litigation must be safeguarded closely; carving a wide exception carried the real risk of encouraging disgruntled litigants to try their luck repeatedly, while allowing exceptions to issue estoppel only in rigidly demarcated categories of case would better achieve the objective of minimising wastage of the court's time and resources, which was in the interests of the court, the public and the litigants themselves, while at the same time allowing some room for intervention in truly exceptional cases.[1512]

440. Quite apart from the two above-mentioned examples of abuse of process, the High Court was asked to determine if a second action should be struck out as an abuse of process given that the cause of action is the same as the first action and is

---

whether the later proceedings in substance is nothing more than a collateral attack upon the previous decision, whether there is fresh evidence warranting relitigation, and whether there are special circumstances: *Goh Nellie v. Goh Lian Teck*, [2007] 1 SLR(R) 453, [52]; *Venkatraman Kalyanaraman v. Nithya Kalyani*, [2016] SGHC 157, [34].

1509. *Zhang Run Zi v. Koh Kim Seng*, [2015] SGHC 175, [52].

1510. *Lee Tat Development Pte Ltd v. MCST Plan No 301*, [2009] 1 SLR(R) 875, [73]. *See also Zhang Run Zi v. Koh Kim Seng*, [2015] SGHC 175, [39]: 'Unless fraud or collision is alleged to set aside the earlier judgment, a cause of action estoppel operates absolutely, with no exception even for special circumstances … Moreover, even if there are new factual or legal points which might have been but were not raised and decided in the earlier proceedings, cause of action estoppel still applies to bar re-litigation'; *The Royal Bank of Scotland NV (formerly known as ABN Amro Bank NV) v. TT International Ltd (nTan Corporate Advisory Pte Ltd)*, [2015] 5 SLR 1104, [103].

1511. *The Royal Bank of Scotland NV (formerly known as ABN Amro Bank NV) v. TT International Ltd (nTan Corporate Advisory Pte Ltd)*, [2015] 5 SLR 1104, [188]–[190]. C.f. *Lee Tat Development Pte Ltd v. MCST Plan No 301*, [2009] 1 SLR(R) 875, [90].

1512. *The Royal Bank of Scotland NV (formerly known as ABN Amro Bank NV) v. TT International Ltd (nTan Corporate Advisory Pte Ltd)*, [2015] 5 SLR 1104, [181]–[187].

brought against the same parties. In that case, the first action was struck out for failure to comply with a peremptory order; the High Court clarified that the case did not concern issues of res judicata or the limitation period, rather an abuse of process under O 18 r 19(6) and the court's inherent jurisdiction.[1513] The propositions of law summarized by the High Court are listed in extenso:

(a) Where a litigant, whose first action has been struck out for failure to comply with a peremptory order, brings a second action based on the same cause of action, that the second action may be struck out as being an abuse of process of the court unless the litigant can give a proper explanation to establish that his failure to comply with the peremptory order was not contumelious. What amounts to a proper explanation depends on each case, but in general, this will involve showing that some extraneous circumstance prevented or at least hindered compliance.
(b) If the litigant can give a proper explanation, the litigant must further show that no further disobedience of court orders will take place before the court will exercise any discretion not to strike out the second action.
(c) Without any proper explanation, disobedience to a peremptory order would generally amount to contumelious conduct.
(d) Even without a proper explanation, the court retains the residual discretion not to strike out the Second Action for an abuse of process … that just because there had been an intentional and contumelious breach of an 'unless order', it did not necessarily follow that the only sanction must be a striking out because there are degrees of contumelious behaviour. Similarly … there are degrees of contumelious conduct and that the court retains a discretion as to whether to strike out.
(e) An evaluation as to how serious the contumelious behaviour was will depend on all relevant considerations including the procedural history of the suit. In cases where the contumelious conduct of the litigant lies at the bottom of the scale (such as where the plaintiff is able to demonstrate that whilst he was not prevented by extraneous circumstances from complying, there were substantial problems which made it objectively hard for him to promptly comply) the court may in its discretion, taking into account other relevant factors such as the apparent strength of the litigant's case and the degree of confidence it has that breaches will not occur.[1514]

1513. *Kraze Entertainment (S) Pte Ltd v. Marina Bay Sands Pte Ltd*, [2014] 1 SLR 78, [27]. *See also Changhe International Investments Pte Ltd (formerly known as Druidstone Pte Ltd) v. Dexia BIL Asia Singapore Ltd (formerly known as Banque Internationale A Luxembourg BIL (Asia) Ltd)*, [2005] 3 SLR(R) 344, [11]–[12]; *Zhang Run Zi v. Koh Kim Seng*, [2015] SGHC 175, [36]: 'It is important to note that whilst cause of action estoppel and issue estoppel operate as an absolute bar to rel-litigation save in special circumstances, the defence of abuse of process is not subject to the same test. In the latter, the court is asked to balance the competing claims of one party to put his case before the court, and the other not to be unjustly hounded given the history of the matter'; *The Royal Bank of Scotland NV (formerly known as ABN Amro Bank NV) v. TT International Ltd (nTan Corporate Advisory Pte Ltd)*, [2015] 5 SLR 1104, [104].

1514. *Kraze Entertainment (S) Pte Ltd v. Marina Bay Sands Pte Ltd*, [2014] 1 SLR 78, [55], citing *Mitora Pte Ltd v. Agritrade International (Pte) Ltd*, [2013] 3 SLR 1179; *Changhe International*

441. Some other illustrations of where abuse of process will be found are: where a defendant who has counterclaimed in an action subsequently initiates new proceedings based on the same or essentially the same claim;[1515] where a plaintiff has sued a prospective buyer of his property who chose not to proceed with the purchase and not to pay the deposit, but brings two separate suits on two different bases;[1516] where a plaintiff, suing for breach of her employment contract, failed to obtain orders for certiorari and mandamus, and brings another suit based on, inter alia, a constitutional challenge;[1517] where a plaintiff has brought about an action for the collateral purpose of removing property from division of matrimonial proceedings;[1518] where a plaintiff has deliberately joined defendants to an action just so as to inconvenience and embarrass them;[1519] where a plaintiff firm (which was dissolved) has filed a proof of debt against another party without the approval of the receiver;[1520] where a plaintiff has sued on a contract despite the defendant acting on the contract in accordance with its express terms;[1521] where a plaintiff, being sued for copyright infringement, has alleged a conspiracy against them by a media company but provides no factual support whatsoever;[1522] where a plaintiff's tortious claim discloses no real and substantial tort;[1523] where a plaintiff has repackaged a fraud claim that was dismissed without the emergence of new evidence and has at the same time alleged that the trial judge who first dismissed his claim was misled by fraud;[1524] and where a settlement agreement had already been concluded with respect to the issues sought to be litigated.[1525]

442. However, where a party has, at different points, merely taken internally inconsistent positions as regards his evidence, this only affects the fact-finding exercise at trial and does not in and of itself satisfy the ground of abuse of the process of the court.[1526] Indeed, on the flipside, strong evidence on the part of the applicant

---

Investments Pte Ltd (formerly known as Druidstone Pte Ltd) v. Dexia BIL Asia Singapore Ltd (formerly known as Banque Internationale A Luxembourg BIL (Asia) Ltd), [2005] 3 SLR(R) 344. *See also Grande Corp Pte Ltd v. Cubix International Pte Ltd*, [2018] SGHC 13.

1515. C. Bull & J. Pinsler, *Civil Procedure: Annual Review of Singapore Cases* [8.75] (Sing. Acad. L. 2013) citing *Terrestrial Pte Ltd v. Allgo Marine Pte Ltd*, [2013] 3 SLR 527.

1516. *Toh Kouw v. Ng Chee Chong*, [1998] SGHC 407, [23]–[29]. This is otherwise known as an application of the rule in *Henderson v. Henderson*, (1843) 3 Hare 100, 115–116. However, on appeal, the appellants succeeded in disputing that this was *res judicata* in any extended or wider sense: *Ng Chee Chong v. Toh Kouw*, [1999] 2 SLR(R) 909, [16]–[18]. *See also Ram Thayalan Raman Siv v. Liew Yap Tong*, [2002] 2 SLR(R) 706, [38]–[54].

1517. *Lai Swee Lin Linda v. Attorney-General*, [2006] 2 SLR(R) 565, [50]–[63].

1518. *Ho Kiang Fah v. Toh Buan*, [2009] 3 SLR(R) 398, [22]–[24].

1519. *Goh Koon Suan v. Heng Gek Kiau*, [1990] 2 SLR(R) 705, [15].

1520. *Re Singapore Souvenir Industry (Pte) Ltd*, [1985–1986] SLR(R) 161, [6].

1521. *Chok Boon Hock v. Great Eastern Life Assurance Co Ltd*, [1998] 2 SLR(R) 878, [26].

1522. *RecordTV Pte Ltd v. MediaCorp TV Singapore Pte Ltd*, [2009] 4 SLR(R) 43, [18].

1523. *Yan Jun v. Attorney-General*, [2015] 1 SLR 752, [120]–[121], citing *Jameel (Yousef) v. Dow Jones & Co Inc*, [2005] QB 946.

1524. *Chia Kok Kee v. Tan Wah*, [2012] 2 SLR 352, [34]–[39].

1525. *Ng Kong Choon v. Tang Wee Goh*, [2016] SGHC 83, [31].

1526. *Ng Chee Weng v. Lim Jit Ming Bryan*, [2012] 1 SLR 457, [118]–[120].

is often required to succeed in a striking out application under this ground.[1527] Similarly, if there is a legal argument that seems to be dispositive by binding authority but may no longer be the case if recharacterized, it should not be resolved at the interlocutory, striking out stage, not least on the ground of abuse of process of the court.[1528] Finally, it is important to distinguish between finality for the purposes of res judicata and finality for the purposes of an appeal. The former 'simply refers to a declaration or determination of a party's liability and/or his rights or obligations leaving nothing else to be judicially determined'.[1529]

443. Just as finality is of significance to the courts, so too is it important to arbitration. As a result, a court would in certain circumstances decline to rehear matters that have already been determined in arbitration.[1530] The court may also disallow a party to raise certain points in court which it could and should have raised in arbitration.[1531]

V. Possible Outcomes

444. It is not necessarily the case that the entirety of the pleadings will be struck out upon a successful application under O 18 r 19. In other words, it is possible for portions of a party's statement of claim or defence to be struck out by the court. However, if a plaintiff's entire statement of claim is struck out, the matter is essentially resolved (pending any counterclaims and/or appeals). If a defendant's entire defence is struck out, it is possible that the plaintiff is awarded judgment, especially if it had been combined with an O 14 application (summary judgment). In the extremely unlikely event that both the statement of claim and defence are struck out, then the matter is essentially resolved as well (again, pending any counterclaims and/or appeals). Much more often than not, any unsuccessful application to strike out will incur some costs for the applicant; conversely, a successful applicant will probably be awarded costs in his favour.

§4. Possibility of Appeal

445. Section 34 of the Supreme Court of Judicature Act,[1532] read together with the Fourth and Fifth Schedules of the statute, determines whether any given order

1527. *Lim Eng Hock Peter v. Lin Jian Wei*, [2008] 4 SLR(R) 444, [37].
1528. *Her Majesty's Revenue & Customs v. Hashu Dhalomal Shahdadpuri*, [2011] 3 SLR 1186, [35]–[40].
1529. *Goh Nellie v. Goh Lian Teck*, [2007] 1 SLR(R) 453, [28].
1530. *Econ Piling Pte Ltd v. Shanghai Tunnel Engineering Co Ltd*, [2011] 1 SLR 246, [37]; *AKN v. ALC*, [2016] 1 SLR 966, [57].
1531. *Denmark Skibstekniske Konsulenter A/S I Likvidation v. Ultrapolis 3000 Investments Ltd*, [2011] 4 SLR 997, [30]–[46]; *AKN v. ALC*, [2016] 1 SLR 966, [57]–[58].
1532. (Cap. 322, 2007 Rev. Ed.).

of civil procedure is appealable to the Court of Appeal[1533] or not.[1534] For striking out applications, the Fourth Schedule states that: 'No appeal shall be brought to the Court of Appeal … where a Judge makes an order refusing to strike out … an action or a matter commenced by writ of summons or by another originating process; or … a pleading or a part of a pleading.' The Fifth Schedule then states that: 'Except with the leave of a Judge, no appeal shall be brought to the Court of Appeal … where a Judge makes an order at the hearing of any interlocutory application other than an application … to strike out an action or a matter commenced by a writ of summons or by any other originating process, a pleading or a part of a pleading.'

446. In other words, if an order is made to strike out an action, a pleading or a part of a pleading, the losing party can appeal as of right. However, if the application to strike out an action, a pleading or a part of a pleading is denied, the losing party cannot appeal the decision. The asymmetry in appeal rights is consistent with the notion that a litigant should have the right with a full trial, unless there are plainly good reasons not to do so. Whether or not a stay of execution of any judgment awarded pursuant to a striking out application would be granted while an appeal is pending is entirely within the discretion of the court. The applicant must show special circumstances before such a stay would be granted.[1535] An appeal does not automatically operate as a stay of execution.[1536]

1533. Below it is the High Court, followed by the District and Magistrates' Courts. For appeals arising from the lower courts, *see* Supreme Court of Judicature Act (Cap. 322, R. 5, 2014 Rev. Ed.) Rules of Court, O 55B, 55C, and 55D. There is a right of appeal from a registrar in chambers to a judge in chambers (District Judge if it is the State Courts), but not necessarily after that stage.

1534. The statute was amended in 2010 and 2014.

1535. *Lee Sian Hee (trading as Lee Sian Hee Pork Trader) v. Oh Kheng Soon (trading as Ban Hon Trading Enterprise)*, [1991] 2 SLR(R) 869, [5]; cited in *Swiss Singapore Overseas Enterprises Pte Ltd v. Navalmar UK Ltd*, [2003] 1 SLR(R) 688, [7].

1536. Supreme Court of Judicature Act (Cap. 322, 2007 Rev. Ed.), s 41; *Lian Soon Construction Pte Ltd v. Guan Qian Realty Pte Ltd*, [1999] 1 SLR(R) 1053, [13].

Chapter 7. Proceedings in First Instance

§1. Introduction

447. After the interlocutory matters (including any attempt to terminate the proceedings early) have been taken care of, the parties will proceed to trial.[1537] This is the phase where the parties will make their most substantial written and oral submissions as well as present and test the witnesses and evidence so that the judge can determine where the truth lies and properly adjudicate over the dispute. As the main purpose of this monograph is to focus on the preliminary or interlocutory civil process, this chapter will only describe the trial process in very general terms, with a particular focus on the speeches rather than attempt to address the entirety of the reception of all types of evidence.[1538]

§2. Opening Statement

448. The trial proceedings usually begin with the plaintiff delivering the opening address (including the usual preliminary formalities such as introduction of counsel); where required, he will present his opening statement too.[1539] The opening statement presents the court with an overview of the issues of the case and an introduction to the evidence that will be adduced, setting the stage for what is to follow in terms of the legal arguments.[1540] Seen in this light, skilful advocates will invariably want to craft a fair but persuasive case theory and narrative when recounting the facts in the opening statement, subject of course to certain constraints.[1541] The opening statement should be brief and therefore long and elaborate arguments, as well as copious citations to numerous authorities (already found in the bundle of authorities), should be avoided.[1542] Instead, the opening statement should (and must) include:

> the nature of the case generally and the background facts insofar as they are relevant to the matter before the Court and indicating which facts, if any, are agreed; … the precise legal and factual issues involved are to be identified with cross-references as appropriate to the pleadings … the principal authorities in support of each legal proposition should be listed, while the key documents and witnesses supporting each factual proposition should be identified … where there is a counterclaim or third party action, the opening statement

1537. Parties may of course still take out various applications throughout the course of trial.
1538. It should be noted that the criminal trial (and indeed, pre-trial) process is vastly different and governed by vastly different rules.
1539. If the trial is in the High Court, the opening statements must be filed no less than 5 days before the trial: Supreme Court of Judicature Act (Cap. 322, R. 5, 2014 Rev. Ed.) Rules of Court, O 34 r 3A.
1540. J. Pinsler, *Evidence and the Litigation Process* 687 (4th ed., LexisNexis 2013).
1541. J. Pinsler, *Evidence and the Litigation Process* 688 (4th ed., LexisNexis 2013). Visual aids may also be used if appropriate.
1542. Supreme Court Practice Directions 2013 (Part VIII).

must similarly address all issues raised therein; and ... an explanation of the reliefs claimed (if these are unusual or complicated).[1543]

449. The Supreme Court Practice Directions also set out various formatting requirements and impose a page limit (including annexes and appendices).[1544] The opening statement may be amended at trial, but counsel will be expected to explain any amendments made.[1545] Because the opening statement is deemed to have been read once filed and submitted, counsel may not be required to deliver it orally. As far as the defendant is concerned,[1546] his main job is to neutralize whatever advantage the plaintiff has obtained up till the point where he has to present his own opening statement, offering, among others, a case theory that is antithetical to the plaintiff's. But be it for the plaintiff or the defendant, the key is to communicate effectively and to present the arguments fairly, and if there are questions, to answer them directly by addressing the underlying concerns.[1547]

§3. Examination-in-Chief

450. The examination-in-chief is the process in which a witness is questioned in court by the party who calls him (usually the party's lawyer) so that his oral responses to certain questions may be adduced as further evidence in court.[1548] The examination-in-chief, while the norm in criminal proceedings, may be required in civil proceedings, particularly 'where the affidavit process is impractical or inappropriate or where it is sought to adduce additional evidence concerning matters which arose after the filing of the affidavit'.[1549] The standard practice, particularly where it is imperative to establish a certain sequence of events, is to examine in a chronological fashion, so that the court and the witness(es) will be able to follow

1543. Supreme Court Practice Directions 2013 (Part VIII). It should be noted that the State Courts Practice Directions differ in some respects: *see* Part VII.
1544. Supreme Court Practice Directions 2013 (Part VIII).
1545. State Courts Practice Directions (Part VII); Supreme Court Practice Directions 2013 (Part VIII).
1546. The defendant will only be called upon after the plaintiff has delivered his opening statement, gone through the evidence-in-chief, and allowed his witnesses to be cross-examined (by the defendant). Theoretically, the defendant can submit 'no case to answer' if the plaintiff has failed to adduce the requisite evidence to prove his claim, but this is not always done and in any event is seldom accepted by the trial judge. What normally happens is that the defendant will proceed to deliver his opening his statements and examine the witnesses (and elect to adduce his own evidence) after the plaintiff is done, before both parties deliver their closing addresses and replies (if any). *See also* C. Bull & J. Pinsler, *Civil Procedure: Annual Review of Singapore Cases* [7.82] (Sing. Acad. L. 2006); *Ho Yew Kong v. Sakae Holdings Ltd*, [2018] 2 SLR 333.
1547. *See* generally C. Siyuan, *Advanced Fundamentals of Oral Appellate Advocacy in a Moot Court*, 30 Sing. L. Rev. 45 (2012).
1548. *See also* Evidence Act (Cap. 97, 1997 Rev. Ed.), s 139(1); *Singapore Civil Procedure 2015 Volume 1*, at 785 (G.P. Selvam ed., Sweet & Maxwell Asia 2014).
1549. J. Pinsler, *Evidence and the Litigation Process* 709 (4th ed., LexisNexis 2013). *See also* Supreme Court of Judicature Act (Cap. 322, R. 5, 2014 Rev. Ed.) Rules of Court, O 38 r 2(3).

the series of facts more easily.[1550] Where appropriate, asking a series of introductory questions that also pertain to the witness's personal circumstances and characteristics may be helpful in easing the witness into the proceedings as well as humanizing him.[1551]

451. After this phase, questions should be asked to establish the background facts leading up to the main facts that constitute the dispute (and if necessary, facts subsequent to the dispute as well).[1552] Where appropriate, references should be made to specific parts of documents found in the agreed bundle of documents.[1553] In terms of how the questions should be framed, leading questions (otherwise known as yes/no questions) cannot be asked during an examination-in-chief,[1554] unless the court has given permission[1555] or they pertain to 'matters which are introductory or undisputed, or which have in its opinion been already sufficiently proved'.[1556] The main reason for this restriction is that 'a witness who is excessively controlled in the course of examination-in-chief … would be inclined to provide the desired responses suggested by the advocate'.[1557] If leading questions are asked, three possible things may happen: the opposing lawyer may object;[1558] the court may ask the lawyer to withdraw the leading question; or the court can disregard the answer or place less evidential weight on it.[1559] Apart from the prohibition of leading questions, questions should be asked in a way such that the witness is able to help the court clearly and comprehensively visualize the material circumstances of the case (i.e., circumstances that pertain to the material facts of the dispute).[1560] In this regard:

> it is not sufficient merely to prepare a list of perfectly crafted questions … the questions should be prepared in a way that will develop the testimony as it progresses. This is effected, not by isolating the questions, but by linking them so that the answer to one question will logically lead to the next question … The effect of this linkage may be enhanced by reference to previous answers

1550. J. Pinsler, *Evidence and the Litigation Process* 710 (4th ed., LexisNexis 2013).
1551. J. Pinsler, *Evidence and the Litigation Process* 711–712 (4th ed., LexisNexis 2013). If the witness is an expert, it will be necessary to establish his qualifications before he sets out the grounds for his opinion evidence (*see* Evidence Act (Cap. 97, 1997 Rev. Ed.), s 47(2).
1552. J. Pinsler, *Evidence and the Litigation Process* 713–718 (4th ed., LexisNexis 2013). *See also* Evidence Act (Cap. 97, 1997 Rev. Ed.), s 5.
1553. *See also* Supreme Court of Judicature Act (Cap. 322, R. 5, 2014 Rev. Ed.) Rules of Court, O 27 r 5(1).
1554. Evidence Act (Cap. 97, 1997 Rev. Ed.), s 144(1). *See also id.*, s 143.
1555. Evidence Act (Cap. 97, 1997 Rev. Ed.), s 144(1).
1556. Evidence Act (Cap. 97, 1997 Rev. Ed.), s 144(2).
1557. J. Pinsler, *Evidence and the Litigation Process* 720 (4th ed., LexisNexis 2013).
1558. The opposing lawyer can also object for other reasons, such as when irrelevant or improper questions are asked.
1559. J. Pinsler, *Evidence and the Litigation Process* 720 (4th ed., LexisNexis 2013).
1560. J. Pinsler, *Evidence and the Litigation Process* 719 (4th ed., LexisNexis 2013).

as a preface to a new question. Different parts of the testimony may require varying emphasis … at crucial stages of the testimony the advocate will want to slow down.[1561]

452. In addition, it is important to ask enough subsidiary questions so that the witness's testimony is internally consistent, justifiable, and coherent.[1562] On the part of the witness, he should recount the facts within his knowledge in an effective manner and show through his demeanour that he is a truthful and reliable witness.[1563] If a witness somehow turns adverse or hostile, the party who has called him may wish to obtain permission from the court to cross-examine him (leading questions are allowed in cross-examination) to perform damage control.[1564] In more extreme scenarios, the witness's credit may even be impeached.[1565]

§4. CROSS-EXAMINATION

453. After the affidavit of evidence-in-chief and/or examination-in-chief comes cross-examination.[1566] The cross-examination process, where one party tests and challenges the testimony of an opposing party,[1567] is one of the key features of the adversarial legal system as lawyers attempt to defend or build their clients' case and destroy their opponents' case through strategic deployment of questions to the witnesses.[1568] As an important device to ascertain the true facts of the dispute, questions in 'cross-examination must relate to relevant facts, but the cross-examination need not be confined to the facts to which the witness testified on his examination-in-chief'.[1569] Indeed, when a witness is being cross-examined, he may be asked any questions which tend 'to test his accuracy, veracity or credibility; … to discover who he is and what is his position in life; or … to shake his credit by injuring his character, although the answer to such questions might tend, directly or indirectly, to criminate him, or might expose or tend, directly or indirectly, to expose him to a penalty or forfeiture'.[1570] However, the court retains discretion in deciding whether the witness should be compelled to answer questions that are not immediately relevant to the dispute.[1571] Specifically, the court:

1561. J. Pinsler, *Evidence and the Litigation Process* 725 (4th ed., LexisNexis 2013).
1562. J. Pinsler, *Evidence and the Litigation Process* 728–729 (4th ed., LexisNexis 2013). *See also* Evidence Act (Cap. 97, 1997 Rev. Ed.), s 161(1).
1563. J. Pinsler, *Evidence and the Litigation Process* 719 (4th ed., LexisNexis 2013).
1564. *Yuen Chun Yii v. Public Prosecutor*, [1997] 2 SLR(R) 209, [28]–[29]. *See also* Evidence Act (Cap. 97, 1997 Rev. Ed.), s 156.
1565. Evidence Act (Cap. 97, 1997 Rev. Ed.), s 157.
1566. Evidence Act (Cap. 97, 1997 Rev. Ed.), s 140(1).
1567. *See* Evidence Act (Cap. 97, 1997 Rev. Ed.), s 139(2).
1568. J. Pinsler, *Evidence and the Litigation Process* 775 (4th ed., LexisNexis 2013). *See also Teo Wai Cheong v. Crédit Industriel et Commercial*, [2013] 3 SLR 573, [25]; *Brown v. Dunne*, (1893) 6 R 67, 70; cited in *Seet Melvin v. Law Society of Singapore*, [1995] 2 SLR(R) 186, [29].
1569. Evidence Act (Cap. 97, 1997 Rev. Ed.), s 140(2).
1570. Evidence Act (Cap. 97, 1997 Rev. Ed.), s 148. *See also Singapore Civil Procedure 2015 Volume 1*, at 737 (G.P. Selvam ed., Sweet & Maxwell Asia 2014).
1571. *See also* Evidence Act (Cap. 97, 1997 Rev. Ed.), s 167(1).

shall have regard to the following considerations: … such questions are proper if they are of such a nature that the truth of the imputation conveyed by them would seriously affect the opinion of the court as to the credibility of the witness on the matter to which he testifies; … such questions are improper if the imputation which they convey relates to matters so remote in time or of such character that the truth of the imputation would not affect or would affect in a slight degree the opinion of the court as to the credibility of the witness on the matter to which he testifies; … such questions are improper if there is a great disproportion between the importance of the imputation made against the witness's character and the importance of his evidence; … the court may, if it sees fit, draw from the witness's refusal to answer, the inference that the answer, if given, would be unfavourable.[1572]

454. Further, the court may 'forbid any questions or inquiries which it regards as indecent or scandalous, although such questions or inquiries may have some bearing on the questions before the court, unless they relate to facts in issue or to matters necessary to be known in order to determine whether or not the facts in issue existed';[1573] the court shall also 'forbid any question which appears to it to be intended to insult or annoy, or which though proper in itself, appears to the court needlessly offensive in form'.[1574] Ultimately, the extent to which a party has to attack an opposing witness's testimony depends largely on the extent to which the opposing party has discharged his burden of proof as well as standard of proof (in civil cases, the burden of proof almost always starts with the plaintiff, while the standard of proof is the balance of probabilities, as opposed to beyond a reasonable doubt).[1575]

455. Techniques that may be used to bolster one's case and/or to weaken the opponent's case include encouraging the witness to concede certain facts, raising facts not brought up in the evidence-in-chief but which are consistent with one's case theory, developing certain aspects of the evidence-in-chief to support one's case, suggesting to the witness that the facts are consistent with an interpretation different from his own but which nevertheless is just as reasonable, asking questions for the purpose of setting a foundation, casting doubt as to whether the witness had accurately perceived the facts, casting doubt as to whether the witness had accurately recalled the facts, pointing out gaps and flaws in the evidence, pointing out the incredulity of the evidence, and pointing out inconsistent conduct and/or statements.[1576]

456. Leading questions – one of the key tools in controlling an adverse witness – are often used, but they 'must not put into the mouth of the witness the very words which he is to echo back again; and … must not assume that facts have been

1572. Evidence Act (Cap. 97, 1997 Rev. Ed.), s 150(2). *See also id.*, s 151.
1573. Evidence Act (Cap. 97, 1997 Rev. Ed.), s 153.
1574. Evidence Act (Cap. 97, 1997 Rev. Ed.), s 154.
1575. J. Pinsler, *Evidence and the Litigation Process* 779 (4th ed., LexisNexis 2013).
1576. J. Pinsler, *Evidence and the Litigation Process* 780–810 (4th ed., LexisNexis 2013).

proved which have not been proved, or that particular answers have been given contrary to the fact'.[1577] While most lawyers would prepare a set of questions that will develop based on their anticipation on how the testimony would unfold, it is important to be flexible and to know when to stop; as regards the former, the case theories on both sides may evolve as the trial progresses, and as regards the latter, once the point that is desired has been made and put on the record, there is little value in asking it to be restated or repeated, not least because the witness may be able to clarify or correct himself. It is also important for the lawyer to plan when to 'put' questions to the witness as it is also a useful way of signposting to the court; this is usually done after a series of questions designed to force the witness to accept (or more likely, (unreasonably) deny) the logical conclusion of his series of responses has been asked.[1578]

§5. RE-EXAMINATION

457. After cross-examination comes re-examination.[1579] The re-examination 'shall be directed to the explanation of matters referred to in cross-examination; and if new matter is, by permission of the court, introduced in re-examination, the adverse party may further cross-examine upon that matter'.[1580] In other words, by default, the re-examination process is not meant to present an opportunity to raise matters not raised in cross-examination, to repeat matters already raised in the examination-in-chief, or to introduce new evidence.[1581] Instead, the main purpose of re-examination is to clarify ambiguous answers given in cross-examination, to 'allow a party to allay the adverse effect of cross-examination on particular [matters] by eliciting additional or peripheral facts so that the [matters] may be viewed in a wider context than that provided in the cross-examination'.[1582] This requires the lawyer to be alert while his witnesses were being cross-examined by the opponent. Leading questions are generally not allowed in re-examination.[1583] If the court permits a witness to be recalled either for further examination-in-chief or for further cross-examination, 'the parties have the right of further cross-examination and re-examination respectively'.[1584] While it is impossible to predict with great certainty how the cross-examination will go, it is still important to prepare the witness for the possibility of re-examination and the purpose that it serves. However, as is the case with cross-examination, witnesses should not be coached to give rehearsed and (in particular) untruthful answers to anticipated questions.

1577. Evidence Act (Cap. 97, 1997 Rev. Ed.), s 145(1).

1578. *See also* C. Bull & J. Pinsler, *Civil Procedure: Annual Review of Singapore Cases* [6.87] (Sing. Acad. L. 2005) citing *Lin Tsang Kit v. Chng Thiam Kwee*, [2005] SGHC 10, [28].

1579. Evidence Act (Cap. 97, 1997 Rev. Ed.), s 140(1). *See also id.*, s 139(3).

1580. Evidence Act (Cap. 97, 1997 Rev. Ed.), s 140(3). *See also* Supreme Court of Judicature Act (Cap. 322, R. 5, 2014 Rev. Ed.) Rules of Court, O 38 rr 2(3) and 2(4).

1581. J. Pinsler, *Evidence and the Litigation Process* 867 (4th ed., LexisNexis 2013) citing *Prince v. Samo*, (1838) 7 A & E 627.

1582. J. Pinsler, *Evidence and the Litigation Process* 869 (4th ed., LexisNexis 2013).

1583. J. Pinsler, *Evidence and the Litigation Process* 873 (4th ed., LexisNexis 2013) citing *Ireland v. Taylor*, [1949] 1 KB 300, 313.

1584. Evidence Act (Cap. 97, 1997 Rev. Ed.), s 140(4).

§6. Closing Address

458. After all the witnesses have been examined, the lawyers would have the opportunity to address the court on the legal arguments and the legal conclusions that arise when applied to the evidence (i.e., the facts) that have been adduced. This is known as the closing address, which offers each party:

> the opportunity of crystallizing his theory of the case ... which should have been evident from his opening address, the evidence-in-chief of his own witnesses and his cross-examination of the opposing witnesses. This is achieved by scanning the whole case for the facts which support his theory and weaken the position of his opponent ... He must organise this material so that the theory is developed logically and convincingly ... As the address progresses, the facts should tie up with and fortify each other.[1585]

459. A closing speech usually takes place after the defendant has examined the witnesses; more precisely, the defendant will make his closing speech and at the close of the defendant's case, the plaintiff may make his closing speech in reply.[1586] However, depending on what the court requires, the closing address may be in the form of written submissions or delivered orally.[1587] The key elements of the closing address are the introduction, the re-identification of the issues in dispute, the highlighting of the facts that concern those issues, the analysis of the legal principles applicable to the facts, and the conclusion.[1588] Even in a closely fought contest, lawyers should strive to be concise (and of course, clear) in their closing addresses; it is also important to appear fair and reasonable, and weaknesses in the case should be neutralized, or at least acknowledged in some way. As with any other phase of the trial, if the judge has questions, they should be answered sincerely, directly, and truthfully, especially in a way that properly addresses the concerns behind the questions. The lawyer should also bear in mind that as Singapore's legal system is based on the common law and the jury system has been abolished for decades, the trial judge acts as fact-finder and decider of the law at the same time – it is therefore of paramount importance to accord the judge the appropriate amount of respect and deference.

§7. Judgments

460. Every judgment, upon the hearing in an open court, shall be pronounced in open court either on the conclusion of the hearing or on a subsequent day of which

1585. J. Pinsler, *Evidence and the Litigation Process* 877 (4th ed., LexisNexis 2013).
1586. Supreme Court of Judicature Act (Cap. 322, R. 5, 2014 Rev. Ed.) Rules of Court, O 35 r 4(4). For multiple defendants, *see* J. Pinsler, *Evidence and the Litigation Process* 894–895 (4th ed., LexisNexis 2013).
1587. It is also important to distinguish between a speech in reply and a right of reply and right of rebuttal.
1588. J. Pinsler, *Evidence and the Litigation Process* 878–886 (4th ed., LexisNexis 2013).

notice shall be given to the parties.[1589] If the hearing was in chambers, the judge may pronounce the judgment in chambers or in open court.[1590] Either type of judgment takes effect from the day of its date.[1591] When a written judgment is delivered, the court may deliver it by directing copies of it to be handed to the parties upon payment of the appropriate charges.[1592] A copy of every judgment delivered in any hearing in open court shall be available for public inspection upon payment of the prescribed fee.[1593] However, if proceedings are heard in camera, any judgment pronounced or delivered shall not be available for public inspection, but the court may on such terms as it may impose, allow an inspection.[1594]

461. A judgment that requires a person to do an act must specify the time after service of the judgment within which that act is to be done, unless the act is to pay money, give possession of any immovable property, or deliver any movable property.[1595] There are prescribed forms for judgments.[1596] Judgments are generally differentiated from orders in that orders are normally made at the end of interlocutory hearings (but sometimes at the end of the trial) directing parties to take particular steps, while judgments usually elaborate on the court's deliberations and reasoning at the end of substantive hearings or trials.[1597] The terms of a judgment or order must be set out in the clearest possible terms to avoid disputes between the parties as to their interpretation.[1598] Judgments and orders may be amended at any time before they are registered and filed.

1589. Supreme Court of Judicature Act (Cap. 322, R. 5, 2014 Rev. Ed.) Rules of Court, O 42 r 1(1).
1590. Supreme Court of Judicature Act (Cap. 322, R. 5, 2014 Rev. Ed.) Rules of Court, O 42 r 1(2).
1591. Supreme Court of Judicature Act (Cap. 322, R. 5, 2014 Rev. Ed.) Rules of Court, O 42 r 7.
1592. Supreme Court of Judicature Act (Cap. 322, R. 5, 2014 Rev. Ed.) Rules of Court, O 42 r 1(3).
1593. Supreme Court of Judicature Act (Cap. 322, R. 5, 2014 Rev. Ed.) Rules of Court, O 42 r 3.
1594. Supreme Court of Judicature Act (Cap. 322, R. 5, 2014 Rev. Ed.) Rules of Court, O 42 r 2.
1595. Supreme Court of Judicature Act (Cap. 322, R. 5, 2014 Rev. Ed.) Rules of Court, O 42 r 6.
1596. Supreme Court of Judicature Act (Cap. 322, R. 5, 2014 Rev. Ed.) Rules of Court, O 42 r 5.
1597. J. Pinsler, *Principles of Civil Procedure* 789 (Acad. Publg. 2013).
1598. J. Pinsler, *Principles of Civil Procedure* 793 (Acad. Publg. 2013).

Chapter 8. Appeal Proceedings

§1. Introduction

462. It may be said that in a common law system, the appellate process serves four main purposes: first, to ensure the integrity and correctness of judicial decision-making; second, to preserve the certainty of the law through judicial precedent; third, to develop the jurisprudence; and fourth, to maintain public confidence in the administration of justice.[1599] On the other hand, it may be argued that:

> the parties should accept the decision given by a first instance court and that the availability of an appeal is an unnecessary luxury. The grounds for such a view could include: the rigorous and comprehensive nature of civil litigation which produces correct first instance decisions most of the time … the unnecessary extension of litigation, as when a party is intent on achieving the result he wants irrespective of the merits, or when his motivation is to delay the enforcement of judgment which has been given against him or to simply protract the dispute; the costs which would have to be incurred in the course of the appeal and the related point that often only parties who are financially well-positioned can their cases to the Court of Appeal … the real possibility that the original dispute may be adapted by new issues, evidence and amendments so that there is a shift in the scope of the adjudication; and the public's perception of inconsistencies within the court system when a higher court agrees with a lower court.[1600]

463. Whether something is appealable or not depends on two questions.[1601] The first is to ask whether the decision appealed against is made in an interlocutory matter or after a trial proper.[1602] The second is to ask where the appeal lies from; that is, the judicial officer from which the decision is appealed. Whether a court has the jurisdiction (usually defined as the authority to hear a dispute)[1603] to hear an appeal is first and foremost dependent on whether statute has provided for appellate recourse, in that an appellate court 'is a creature of statute and, hence, is only seised of the jurisdiction that has been conferred upon it by the relevant provisions in the legislation creating it … A jurisdiction-conferring provision, whether derived from the Act or elsewhere, is a crucial prerequisite that a would-be appellant must satisfy so as to have … a legal basis upon which to canvass the substantive merits of his

1599. J. Pinsler, *Evidence and the Litigation Process* 916, 918 (3rd ed., LexisNexis 2010).
1600. J. Pinsler, *Evidence and the Litigation Process* 917–918 (3rd ed., LexisNexis 2010).
1601. J. Pinsler, *Evidence and the Litigation Process* 918–919 (3rd ed., LexisNexis 2010).
1602. It should be noted that interlocutory appeals during the trial have been described as 'highly undesirable' by the Court of Appeal because trials should not be repeatedly interrupted, the Court of Appeal should not be encumbered with multiple unnecessary appeals, and the appellate court may not be in as good a position to rule on the issue if the decision of the trial judge was based on his direct perception of oral evidence and/or the parties' arguments are not complete. *See also Bank Austria Creditanstalt AG v. Go Dante Yap*, [2007] 4 SLR(R) 667.
1603. *See* e.g., *Re Nalpon Zero Geraldo Mario*, [2013] 3 SLR 258, [13].

or her application.'[1604] If a statute does not confer appellate jurisdiction (as in it is silent), a question may arise as to whether the court can rely on its inherent jurisdiction instead. To that, a Court of Appeal decision has ruled that a court's authority can only be derived from statute; inherent jurisdiction is a misnomer as it supposedly refers to a court's exercise of inherent powers (such as the making of an order to correct a procedural defect even though the legislation does not provide for such a power).[1605] However, as argued in an earlier Part,[1606] this conclusion may not necessarily be true and may require future judicial clarification.[1607]

464. Additional principles exist to ensure the 'integrity and purposefulness of the appeal process', including that an appellate court will not hear an appeal unless there is a real issue between the parties which needs to be determined; and that an appellate court will be more reluctant to disturb findings of fact as opposed to remedying errors of law.[1608] However, where the appeal court is determining whether the court below has properly evaluated or drew the proper inferences from the facts, it is in as good a position as the court below to evaluate the evidence and draw its own inferences.[1609] The Court of Appeal has further observed that with improvements to the record, such as electronically recorded verbatim transcripts, closer

---

1604. *Blenwel Agencies Pte Ltd v. Tan Lee King*, [2008] 2 SLR(R) 529, [23]; cited in *Law Society of Singapore v. Top Ten Entertainment Pte Ltd*, [2011] 2 SLR 1279. *See also Li Li v. Ho Hung Kwong*, [2017] SGCA 57, [15]; *Nim Minimart v. MCST Title Plan No 1079*, [2014] 1 SLR 108, [27]; *Au Wai Pang v. Attorney-General*, [2014] 3 SLR 357, [27]; *Muhammad Ridzuan bin Md Ali v. Public Prosecutor*, [2014] 3 SLR 721, [96]–[97].

1605. *Re Nalpon Zero Geraldo Mario*, [2013] 3 SLR 258, [33]–[41]. C.f. C. Siyuan, *Jurisdiction, Power, Inherent Jurisdiction, and Inherent Power*, Sing. Law Watch Commentaries (4/2013); C. Siyuan, *Is the Invocation of Inherent Jurisdiction the Same as the Exercise of Inherent Powers?*, 17 Intl. J. Evid. & Proof 367 (2013); Goh Y.H., *Demystifying the Inherent Jurisdiction and Inherent Powers of the Singapore Courts: Rethinking the Limits of their Exercise*, Sing. J. Leg. Stud. 178 (2011).

1606. *See* the General Introduction.

1607. This is especially so since a more recent Court of Appeal decision in *Citiwall Safety Glass Pte Ltd v. Mansource Interior Pte Ltd*, [2015] 1 SLR 797, relied on the High Court's inherent supervisory jurisdiction to address a lacuna in O 95 of the Rules of Court and s 27 of the Building and Construction Industry Security of Payment Act (Cap. 30B, 2006 Rev. Ed.). However, in *The Royal Bank of Scotland NV (formerly known as ABN Amro Bank NV) v. TT International Ltd (nTan Corporate Advisory Pte Ltd)*, [2015] 5 SLR 1104, [106], the Court of Appeal reiterated that 'inherent jurisdiction' and 'inherent power' are completely the same and both refer to 'inherent power'.

1608. J. Pinsler, *Principles of Civil Procedure* 952–953 (Acad. Publg. 2013) citing *Attorney-General v. Joo Yee Construction Pte Ltd*, [1992] 2 SLR(R) 165; *Ainsbury v. Millington*, [1987] 1 WLR 379, 380–381; *Lo Sook Ling Adela v. Au Mei Yin Christina*, [2002] 1 SLR(R) 326, [37]; *Lim Hwee Meng v. Citadel Investment Pte Ltd*, [1998] 3 SLR(R) 101, [26]. However, where the findings of fact are plainly wrong or go against the weight of the evidence the appellate court may intervene: *Arts Niche Cyber Distribution Pte Ltd v. Public Prosecutor*, [1999] 2 SLR(R) 936, [30]; cited in *Hin Hup Bus Service (a firm) v. Tay Chwee Hiang*, [2006] 4 SLR(R) 723, [49].

1609. *See* Supreme Court of Judicature Act (Cap. 322, R. 5, 2014 Rev. Ed.) Rules of Court, O 57 r 13(3) and O 55D r 11(2). *See also Benmax v. Austin Motor Co Ltd*, [1955] 1 All ER 326; *MCST Plan No 586 v. Menezes Ignatius Augustine*, [1992] 1 SLR(R) 201, [40]; *Computer Supermarkets (S) Pte Ltd v. Goh Chin Soon Ricky*, [1997] 2 SLR(R) 772, [3].

appellate review of findings of fact by trial courts may now be permitted.[1610] Nevertheless, when it comes to an exercise of discretion, the appellate court will not interfere unless it is clear that the discretion was improperly exercised.[1611]

465. Sometimes, parties may seek to adduce fresh evidence when making appeal applications. Generally, the court may decline to permit the introduction of fresh evidence if such evidence were available at the time of the hearing, that they would not have any influence on the outcome of the trial as they could not help determine the common intention of parties, and if they have no probative value.[1612] However, a broader approach in terms of allowing the introduction of fresh evidence is adopted in hearings from district judges in chambers.[1613]

§2. Appeals to the Court of Appeal

466. This section discusses the key procedural and substantive aspects relating to civil appeals before the Court of Appeal. At this juncture, it is important to note that the Court of Appeal may also hear an application under O 57 r 16(3) even though such an application is not an appeal.[1614] O 57 r 16(3) provides that 'an ex parte application has been refused by the Court below, an application for a similar purpose may be made to the Court of Appeal ex parte within 7 days after the date of the refusal'. However, this does not mean that O 57 r 16(3) is ultra vires vis-à-vis the Supreme Court of Judicature Act. This is because section 29A(3) confers on the Court of Appeal the jurisdiction and powers of the court below if this is incidental to the hearing and determination of an appeal, even though the line between a free-standing and incidental application is potentially difficult to draw.[1615]

I. The Right to Appeal

467. Generally, the civil jurisdiction of the Court of Appeal consists of 'appeals from any judgment or order of the High Court in any civil cause or matter whether made in the exercise of its original or of its appellate jurisdiction', subject to the provisions of the Supreme Court of Judicature Act or any other written law regulating the terms and conditions upon which such appeals may be brought.[1616] There is no difference between a judgment and an order in terms of legal consequences,

1610. *Goh Sin Huat Electrical Pte Ltd v. Ho See Jui*, [2012] 3 SLR 1038, [56].
1611. J. Pinsler, *Principles of Civil Procedure* 954 (Acad. Publg. 2013) citing *Ward v. James*, [1966] 1 QB 273, 293. *See also Tay Beng Chuan v. Official Receiver and Liquidator of Kie Hock Shipping (1971) Pte Ltd*, [1987] SLR(R) 123, [16]; *TDA v. TCZ*, [2016] SGHC 63, [23].
1612. *Seah Kim Seng v. Yick Sui Ping*, [2015] SGHC 150, [13], citing *Ladd v. Marshall*, [1954] 1 WLR 1489.
1613. *Seah Kim Seng v. Yick Sui Ping*, [2015] SGHC 150, [20]–[21].
1614. *Au Wai Pang v. Attorney-General*, [2014] 3 SLR 357, [68]. *See also Dorsey James Michael v. World Sport Group Pte Ltd*,[2013] 3 SLR 354, [95]–[96].
1615. *Au Wai Pang v. Attorney-General*, [2014] 3 SLR 357, [69].
1616. Supreme Court of Judicature Act (Cap. 322, 2007 Rev. Ed.), s 29A(1).

and the two terms can be used interchangeably.[1617] Section 34 of the Supreme Court of Judicature Act[1618] is one such provision that limits the right to appeal to the Court of Appeal and states as follows:[1619]

(1) No appeal shall be brought to the Court of Appeal in any of the following cases:
  (a) where a judge makes an order specified in the Fourth Schedule, except in such circumstances as may be specified in that Schedule;
  (b) where the judgment or order is made by consent of the parties; or;
  (c) where, by any written law for the time being in force, the judgment or order of the High Court is expressly declared to be final.

(2) Except with the leave of a judge, no appeal shall be brought to the Court of Appeal in any of the following cases:
  (a) where the amount in dispute, or the value of the subject matter, at the hearing before the High Court (excluding interest and costs) does not exceed SGD 250,000 or such other amount as may be specified by an order made under subsection (3);
  (b) where the only issue in the appeal relates to costs or fees for hearing dates;
  (c) where a judge in chambers makes a decision in a summary way on an interpleader summons where the facts are not in dispute;
  (d) where a judge makes an order specified in the Fifth Schedule, except in such circumstances as may be specified in that Schedule; or
  (e) where the High Court makes an order in the exercise of its appellate jurisdiction with respect to any proceedings under the Adoption of Children Act (Cap. 4) or under Part VII, VIII or IX of the Women's Charter (Cap. 353).

468. Accordingly, cases that are not appealable to the Court of Appeal are stipulated in section 34(1) of the Supreme Court of Judicature Act read with the Fourth Schedule. The Fourth Schedule has been held to relate only to interlocutory orders made in interlocutory applications[1620] and states that no appeals may be brought to the Court of Appeal in the following cases:

(a) where a judge makes an order giving unconditional leave to defend any proceedings;

1617. *Woo Koon Chee v. Scandinavian Boiler Service (Asia) Pte Ltd*, [2010] 4 SLR 1213, [26].

1618. (Cap. 322, 2007 Rev. Ed.). The statute was amended in 2010 and 2014.

1619. Below it is the High Court, followed by the District and Magistrates' Courts. For appeals arising from the lower courts, *see* Supreme Court of Judicature Act (Cap. 322, R. 5, 2014 Rev. Ed.) Rules of Court, O 55B, 55C, and 55D (unless otherwise stated, all references herein to the Rules of Court are to the Singapore Rules of Court). There is a right of appeal from a registrar in chambers to a judge in chambers (District Judge if it is the State Courts), but not necessarily after that stage.

1620. *Dorsey James Michael v. World Sport Group Pte Ltd*, [2013] 3 SLR 354, [51]–[52], citing *OpenNet Pte Ltd v. Info-Communications Development Authority of Singapore*, [2013] 2 SLR 880, [21].

(b) where a judge makes an order giving leave to defend any proceedings on condition that the party defending those proceedings pays into court or gives security for the sum claimed, except if the appellant is that party;
(c) where a judge makes an order setting aside unconditionally a default judgment, regardless of how the default judgment was obtained (including whether by reason of a breach of an order of court or otherwise);
(d) where a judge makes an order setting aside a default judgment on condition that the party against whom the judgment had been entered pays into court or gives security for the sum claimed, regardless of how the default judgment was obtained (including whether by reason of a breach of an order of court or otherwise), except if the appellant is that party;
(e) where a judge makes an order refusing to strike out:
  (1) an action or a matter commenced by a writ of summons or by any other originating process; or
  (2) a pleading or a part of a pleading.
(f) where a judge makes an order giving or refusing further and better particulars;
(g) where a judge makes an order giving leave to amend a pleading, except if:
  (1) the application for such leave is made after the expiry of any relevant period of limitation current at the date of issue of the writ of summons; and
  (2) the amendment is an amendment to correct the name of a party or to alter the capacity in which a party sues, or the effect of the amendment will be to add or substitute a new cause of action.
(h) where a judge makes an order refusing security for costs;
(i) where a judge makes an order giving or refusing interrogatories.

469. Cases that are appealable to the Court of Appeal with leave of court are stated in section 34(2) of the Supreme Court of Judicature Act read with the Fifth Schedule. With respect to section 34(2)(a), the phrase 'the amount or value of the subject matter' refers to the entire claim of the plaintiff at the trial, regardless of the actual amount awarded by the trial judge or the part(s) of the trial judge's decision appealed against by the appellant, and does not include non-contractual interest and costs as these are consequential matters.[1621] In addition, section 34(2)(a) is meant to be a process to screen appeals to the Court of Appeal, as the legislative intention was to allow only one tier of appeal as of right for civil claims up a certain value.[1622] Therefore, when a claim originated in the High Court, the relevant amount should be quantified by reference to the initial claim before the High Court, whether or not that claim was made at a trial or hearing.[1623] This same approach would also

1621. *Virtual Map (Singapore) Pte Ltd v. Singapore Land Authority*, [2009] 2 SLR(R) 558, [16]–[18].
1622. *Fong Khim Ling (administrator of the estate of Fong Ching Pau Lloyd, deceased) v. Tan Teck Ann*, [2014] 2 SLR 659, [14]; *Citiwall Safety Glass Pte Ltd v. Mansource Interior Pte Ltd*, [2015] 1 SLR 797, [22]; *Virtual Map (Singapore) Pte Ltd v. Singapore Land Authority*, [2009] 2 SLR(R) 558, [19].
1623. *Fong Khim Ling (administrator of the estate of Fong Ching Pau Lloyd, deceased) v. Tan Teck Ann*, [2014] 2 SLR 659, [29].

apply if the appeal to the Court of Appeal is against a High Court Judge's decision in an appeal against a registrar's decision at first instance.[1624]

470. In a situation where a claim originated in the State Courts and is subsequently heard by the High Court in its appellate capacity, the relevant amount should be quantified by reference to the amount of value of the subject matters of the appeal when it is heard by the High Court.[1625] Monetary thresholds for appeals are not restricted only to appeals to the Court of Appeal. For example, there is also a monetary threshold for appeals to the High Court, which is governed by section 21(1)(a). Notably, both sections 21(1)(a) and 34(2)(a) were amended in 2010 to create a unified regime in so far as the determination of the threshold amounts was concerned for appeals to both the High Court and Court of Appeal. The operative phrase in both sections 21(1)(a) and 34(2)(a) is now 'the amount in dispute, or the value of the subject-matter, at the hearing before [the lower court]'.[1626]

471. Section 34(2)(a) does not apply to cases heard and determined by the High Court in the exercise of its original jurisdiction in relation to: proceedings for the maintenance of any wife or child, custody of any child, and disposition or division of property on divorce; summary proceedings for the determination of questions between husband and wife as to property; and 'any written law which requires that case to be heard an determined by the High Court in the exercise of its original jurisdiction'.[1627] The Fifth Schedule, like the Fourth Schedule, has been held to apply only to interlocutory orders in interlocutory applications.[1628] The Fifth Schedule provides for the following orders to be appealable to the Court of Appeal only with leave of court:

(a) where a judge makes an order refusing leave to amend a pleading, except if:
    (1) the application for such leave is made after the expiry of any relevant period of limitation current at the date of issue of the writ of summons; and
    (2) the amendment is an amendment to correct the name of a party or to alter the capacity in which a party sues, or the effect of the amendment will be to add or substitute a new cause of action.
(b) where a judge makes an order giving security for costs;
(c) where a judge makes an order giving or refusing discovery or inspection of documents;

1624. The rationale being that the two-step hearing (before the registrar and High Court Judge) is effectively one hearing, with the High Court Judge exercising confirmatory jurisdiction, and the relevant amount would be the sum claimed before the registrar: *Fong Khim Ling (administrator of the estate of Fong Ching Pau Lloyd, deceased) v. Tan Teck Ann*, [2014] 2 SLR 659, [29], citing *Teo Eng Chuan v. Nirumalan v. Kanapathi Pillay*, [2003] 4 SLR(R) 442, [14].

1625. *Fong Khim Ling (administrator of the estate of Fong Ching Pau Lloyd, deceased) v. Tan Teck Ann*, [2014] 2 SLR 659, [30].

1626. *Fong Khim Ling (administrator of the estate of Fong Ching Pau Lloyd, deceased) v. Tan Teck Ann*, [2014] 2 SLR 659, [21].

1627. Supreme Court of Judicature Act (Cap. 322, 2007 Rev. Ed.), s 34(2A).

1628. *Dorsey James Michael v. World Sport Group Pte Ltd*, [2013] 3 SLR 354, [51]–[52], citing *Open-Net Pte Ltd v. Info-Communications Development Authority of Singapore*, [2013] 2 SLR 880, [21].

(d) where a judge makes an order refusing a stay of proceedings;
(e) where a judge makes an order at the hearing of any interlocutory application other than an application for any of the following matters:
   (1) for summary judgment;
   (2) to set aside a default judgment;
   (3) to strike out an action or a matter commenced by a writ of summons or by any other originating process, a pleading or a part of a pleading;
   (4) to dismiss an action or a matter commenced by a writ of summons or by any other originating process;
   (5) for further and better particulars;
   (6) for leave to amend a pleading;
   (7) for security for costs;
   (8) for discovery or inspection of documents;
   (9) for interrogatories to be varied or withdrawn, or for leave to serve interrogatories;
   (10) for a stay of proceedings.

472. It should be noted that paragraph (e) of the Fifth Schedule makes interlocutory orders by judges at the hearing of interlocutory applications generally appealable to the Court of Appeal only with leave of court save for the exceptions stated.[1629] Both the Fourth Schedule and the Fifth Schedule contain exceptions and to determine if these exceptions are appealable to the Court of Appealable as of right, non-appealable or only with leave of court, one would have to go through the process of determining if they are dealt with explicitly by the other Schedule and whether they are interlocutory orders made at interlocutory applications. Where an order is not stipulated as being non-appealable or appealable only with leave, an appeal to the Court of Appeal will lie as of right.[1630] There are two Court of Appeal decisions dealing with when an application may be regarded as 'interlocutory' in nature for the purposes of the Supreme Court of Judicature Act.[1631]

473. In *OpenNet Pte Ltd v. Info-Communications Development Authority of Singapore*,[1632] the Court of Appeal stated that 'interlocutory applications' are those that do not 'have the effect of finally disposing of the substantive rights of the parties'.[1633] It then held that an appeal to the Court of Appeal is 'as of right for orders made at interlocutory applications which will finally dispose of the substantive rights of the parties'.[1634] In the latter case of *Dorsey James Michael v. World Sport Group Pte Ltd*,[1635] the Court of Appeal endorsed various legal dictionary definitions of the phrase 'interlocutory applications', which described such applications as

1629. *See also The "Chem Orchid"*, [2016] 2 SLR 50, [54]–[55].
1630. *Dorsey James Michael v. World Sport Group Pte Ltd*, [2013] 3 SLR 354, [98].
1631. *See also Nim Minimart v. MCST Title Plan No 1079*, [2014] 1 SLR 108, [27].
1632. [2013] 2 SLR 880.
1633. *OpenNet Pte Ltd v. Info-Communications Development Authority of Singapore*, [2013] 2 SLR 880, [18].
1634. *OpenNet Pte Ltd v. Info-Communications Development Authority of Singapore*, [2013] 2 SLR 880, [29].
1635. [2013] 3 SLR 354.

'peripheral to the main hearing determining the outcome of the case', and 'occurring between the initiation of the action and the final determination'.[1636] It has been suggested that the various definitions referred to may be regarded as factors or indicia to be considered by the court in deciding whether or not an application is 'interlocutory' in nature and should be considered alongside the question of whether the application disposes of the substantive rights of the parties.[1637] Where leave to appeal is required under section 34(2) of the Supreme Court of Judicature Act, the order of a judge giving or refusing leave is final.[1638]

474. There are at least three limbs which can be relied upon to obtain leave to appeal: prima facie case of error; question of general principle decided for the first time; and question of importance upon which further argument and a decision of a higher tribunal would be to the public advantage.[1639] While it was for unclear for a while that the (2010) amendments to the Supreme Court of Judicature Act would have any impact on these limbs, the cases thus far subsequent to the amendments have retained the same test.

II. The Process of Appealing

475. Where leave to appeal is required under section 34 of the Supreme Court of Judicature Act, the application for leave must be filed to the judge within seven days from the date of the order or judgment.[1640] As part of the 2014 amendments to the Supreme Court of Judicature Act, a new section 34A was introduced to enable the Court of Appeal to hear applications for leave to the Court of Appeal under section 34 without compromising its case management capabilities. The new section 34A reads: 'The Court of Appeal may, without hearing oral arguments, decide any application for leave to appeal to that Court, whether under this Act or any other written law.'

476. An appeal to the Court of Appeal must be brought by notice using the prescribed form.[1641] A party who requires leave to appeal under section 34 of the Supreme Court of Judicature Act and has obtained such must file and serve the

1636. *Dorsey James Michael v. World Sport Group Pte Ltd*, [2013] 3 SLR 354, [58].

1637. *See* D. Chi, *Clarification on Leave to Appeal Regime in Respect of Interlocutory Matters: Open-Net Pte Ltd v. Info-Communications Development Authority of Singapore [2013] SGCA 24*, Sing. L. Watch Commentaries (4/2013); C. Siyuan & E. Chua, *The Right to Appeal Against a Decision Made on an Interlocutory Application: The Immediate Aftermath of the 2010 Amendments*, 25 Sing. Acad. L.J. 424 (2013).

1638. Supreme Court of Judicature Act (Cap. 322, 2007 Rev. Ed.), s 29A(1). However, it is noted that legislative change has been hinted at in *Dorsey James Michael v. World Sport Group Pte Ltd*, [2013] 3 SLR 354, [97].

1639. *Lee Kuan Yew v. Tang Liang Hong*, [1997] 2 SLR(R) 862, [16]; cited in *IW v. IX*, [2006] 1 SLR(R) 135. *See also The "Xin Chang Shu"*, [2016] SGHC 93, [46]; *Shi Ka Yee v. Nasrat Lucas Muzayyin*, [2016] SGHC 138, [11].

1640. Supreme Court of Judicature Act (Cap. 322, R. 5, 2014 Rev. Ed.) Rules of Court, O 56 r 3(1).

1641. Supreme Court of Judicature Act (Cap. 322, R. 5, 2014 Rev. Ed.) Rules of Court, O 57 r 3(1).

notice of appeal within one month from the date that leave was given.[1642] The notice of appeal 'may be given either in respect of the whole or in respect of any specified part of the judgment or order of the Court below; and every such notice must state whether the whole or part only, and what part, of the judgment or order is complained of, contain an address for service, and be signed by the appellant or his solicitor'.[1643] When filing the notice of appeal, the appellant must also:

> provide security for the respondent's costs of the appeal in the sum of SGD 10,000 or such other sum as may be fixed from time to time by the Chief Justice by ... depositing the sum in the Registry or with the Accountant-General and obtaining a certificate in [the prescribed form]; or ... procuring an undertaking in [the prescribed form] from his solicitor and filing and certificate in [the prescribed form].[1644]

477. The Chief Justice has fixed the sum to be provided by the appellant by way of security for the respondent's costs of an appeal to the Court of Appeal at SGD 15,000 for appeals against interlocutory orders and SGD 20,000 for all other appeals.[1645] The security deposit is mandatory and cannot be waived by the court.[1646] The notice of appeal must be filed and served within one month from: in the case of an appeal from an order in chambers, from the date when the order was pronounced or when the appellant first had notice of the order; in the case of an appeal against the refusal of an application, from the date of the refusal; and in all other cases, from the date on which the judgment or order appealed against was pronounced.[1647] The court does, however, have discretion to extend the time for filing a notice of appeal.[1648] There are essentially four factors to be considered when the court is deciding whether to exercise its discretion to extend time to file a notice of appeal or to serve a notice of appeal out of time: first, the length of the delay; second, the reasons for the delay; third, the chances of the appeal succeeding if the extension is granted; and fourth, the degree of prejudice to the would-be respondent if the extension is granted.[1649] These four factors are of equal importance and must

1642. Supreme Court of Judicature Act (Cap. 322, R. 5, 2014 Rev. Ed.) Rules of Court, O 56 r 3(2).
1643. Supreme Court of Judicature Act (Cap. 322, R. 5, 2014 Rev. Ed.) Rules of Court, O 57 r 3(2).
1644. Supreme Court of Judicature Act (Cap. 322, R. 5, 2014 Rev. Ed.) Rules of Court, O 57 r 3(3). Where money has been paid into court (whether voluntarily or by order of court) with the intention of preserving money for the benefit of the other party's claim, the other party is considered a secured creditor to the extent of the sum paid into court, and he is allowed to retain the benefit of that security despite the payee's subsequent bankruptcy; moneys paid to a stakeholder, as a convenient alternative to payment into court, has by and large the same effect: *Ang Tin Gee v. Pang Teck Guan*, [2015] 5 SLR 836, [27]–[38].
1645. Supreme Court Practice Directions 2013 (Part XI).
1646. *Lee Hsien Loong v. Singapore Democratic Party*, [2008] 1 SLR(R) 757, [116]–[119].
1647. Supreme Court of Judicature Act (Cap. 322, R. 5, 2014 Rev. Ed.) Rules of Court, O 57 r 4.
1648. Supreme Court of Judicature Act (Cap. 322, R. 5, 2014 Rev. Ed.) Rules of Court, O 3 r 4.
1649. *Werner Samuel Vuillemin v. Overseas Chinese Banking Corp Ltd* [2016] SGHC 265, [15]; *Falmac Ltd v. Cheng Ji Lai Charlie*, [2014] 4 SLR 202, [12]–[13]; *Lee Hsien Loong v. Singapore Democratic Party*, [2008] 1 SLR(R) 757, [18], citing *Lai Swee Lin Linda v. Attorney-General*, [2006] 2 SLR(R) 565; C. Bull & J. Pinsler, *Civil Procedure: Annual Review of Singapore Cases* [8.12] (Sing. Acad. L. 2010). C.f. *MCST Plan No 2911 v. Tham Keng Mun*, [2010] SGHC 326, [29]–[35].

be balanced amongst one another, having regard to all the facts and circumstances of the case.[1650] These four factors must also be considered in tandem with two overarching considerations: whether the Rules of Court have been prima facie obeyed with due diligence, and the need for finality, which is a paramount consideration in the context of appeals.[1651]

478. There may be exceptional cases in which 'the conduct of the plaintiff is so deplorable that the court simply cannot countenance granting an application for an extension of time to file an appeal. For such exceptional cases, a consideration of the other factors, including the merits of an appeal, might be academic, precisely because a holistic approach demands the strictest of responses to the most egregious instances of an abuse of process.'[1652] A recent Court of Appeal decision addressed the issue of whether a Duty Judge had the power to grant an extension of appeal for an appeal application to the Court of Appeal. The Court of Appeal held that section 36(1) of the Supreme Court of Judicature Act, the governing provision on this issue that refers to 'proceeding pending before the Court of Appeal', did not envisage a single judge having the power to sit as the Court of Appeal if an appeal had not been validly commenced.[1653]

479. After a notice of appeal is filed, the judge who gave the judgment or made the order must, unless the judgment was written, certify in writing the grounds of the judgment or order.[1654] However, if no certified grounds of the judgment or order have been given by the judge within six months from the date of the notice of appeal, 'the appellant shall nonetheless proceed with the appeal and apply in writing to the Registrar for a copy of the record of proceedings'.[1655] The Court of Appeal has held that a judge has a duty to ordinarily give adequate reasons for any decision made, however:

> the standard of explanation corresponds to the requirements of the case. The duty should not be equated with a duty to issue a written judgment or provide oral grounds of decision in every case. There were also exceptions to the duty – in very clear cases and in relation to specific and straightforward factual or legal issues, the mere statement of the judge's conclusion might sufficiently indicate the basis of a decision.[1656]

1650. *Lee Hsien Loong v. Singapore Democratic Party*, [2008] 1 SLR(R) 757, [18].

1651. *Falmac Ltd v. Cheng Ji Lai Charlie*, [2014] 4 SLR 202, [13]. *Anwar Siraj v. Ting Kang Chung John*, [2010] 1 SLR 1026, [29]–[30], citing *Pearson v. Chen Chien Wen Edwin*, [1991] 2 SLR(R) 260, [15]–[17]; *Thamboo Ratnam v. Thamboo Cumarasamy and Curamasamy Ariamany d/o Kumarasa*, [1965] 1 WLR 8, 12; *The Melati*, [2004] 4 SLR(R) 7, [37].

1652. *Falmac Ltd v. Cheng Ji Lai Charlie*, [2014] 4 SLR 202, [42].

1653. *Au Wai Pang v. Attorney-General*, [2014] 3 SLR 357, [13], [15], and [23]–[24].

1654. Supreme Court of Judicature Act (Cap. 322, R. 5, 2014 Rev. Ed.) Rules of Court, O 57 r 5(1).

1655. Supreme Court of Judicature Act (Cap. 322, R. 5, 2014 Rev. Ed.) Rules of Court, O 57 r 5(1).

1656. *Thong Ah Fat v. Public Prosecutor*, [2012] 1 SLR 676, [15], [28]–[33]. Although the case is a criminal case, the Court of Appeal had stated its views in a broad manner, citing civil cases in the course of its reasoning. In *Teh Leu Jiun Jeanne-Marie v. National University of Singapore*, [2015] 5 SLR 438, [45]–[47], it was also held that there is no fixed format as to how the court's notes of

480. The record of proceedings consists of a certified copy of the judgment or grounds of judgment or order (if any), and a copy of the certified transcript of the official record of hearing taken at the hearing of the cause or matter.[1657] The Registrar will serve on the appellant or his solicitor a notice that a copy of the record of the proceedings is available.[1658] Within two months after service of this notice, the appellant must file and serve on every respondent to the appeal or his solicitor: one copy of the record of appeal; the appellant's case; and a core bundle of documents.[1659] However, where the appeal is to be heard by a Court of Appeal comprising two Judges of appeal, these documents must be filed and served within one month.[1660] The respondent must file a respondent's case within one month after service on him of the record of appeal, appellant's case, and core bundle.[1661] The contents and form of the record of appeal, appellant's and respondent's case, and the core bundle of documents is provided for in the Rules of Court and the Supreme Court Practice Directions.[1662] The Rules of Court were recently amended to require an appellant to file an appellant's reply within two weeks after service on him of the respondent's case where:

(a) the respondent states in the Respondent's Case that the decision of the Court below should be varied in the event of an appeal being allowed in whole or in part, or that the decision of that Court should be affirmed on grounds other than those relied upon by that Court; and
(b) the appellant disagrees with any of the grounds of contention of the respondent referred to in subparagraph (a) as stated in the Respondent's Case.[1663]

481. The appellant's reply is limited to addressing the issues in the paragraph above raised by the respondent in the respondent's case[1664] and the same requirements as to content and form that apply to the appellant's case and respondent's case apply to the appellant's reply.[1665] Another recent innovation in the appeals process before the Court of Appeal[1666] is that the appellant and respondent must file an 'Appeals Information Sheet' at the same time that their respective cases are filed and

hearing are to be recorded; further, for routine interlocutory applications, there is no duty on the court to provide reasons or written judgments in all cases.

1657. Supreme Court of Judicature Act (Cap. 322, R. 5, 2014 Rev. Ed.) Rules of Court, O 57 r 5(3).
1658. Supreme Court of Judicature Act (Cap. 322, R. 5, 2014 Rev. Ed.) Rules of Court, O 57 r 5(2).
1659. Supreme Court of Judicature Act (Cap. 322, R. 5, 2014 Rev. Ed.) Rules of Court, O 57 r 9(1).
1660. Supreme Court of Judicature Act (Cap. 322, R. 5, 2014 Rev. Ed.) Rules of Court, O 57 r 9(1).
1661. Supreme Court of Judicature Act (Cap. 322, R. 5, 2014 Rev. Ed.) Rules of Court, O 57 r 9A(2).
1662. Supreme Court of Judicature Act (Cap. 322, R. 5, 2014 Rev. Ed.) Rules of Court, O 57 rr 9(2), (2A), 9A; Supreme Court Practice Directions 2013 (Part XI). Notably, the appellant's case and the respondent's case in civil matters before the Court of Appeal cannot exceed fifty pages unless leave of the Court of Appeal is obtained. The appellant's reply, if any, cannot exceed thirty pages unless leave of the Court of Appeal is obtained.
1663. Supreme Court of Judicature Act (Cap. 322, R. 5, 2014 Rev. Ed.) Rules of Court, O 57 r 9A(5A), introduced by way of Supreme Court of Judicature Act (Cap. 322) Rules of Court (Amendment) Rules 2013 (S265/2013).
1664. Supreme Court of Judicature Act (Cap. 322, R. 5, 2014 Rev. Ed.) Rules of Court, O 57 r 9A(5B).
1665. Supreme Court of Judicature Act (Cap. 322, R. 5, 2014 Rev. Ed.) Rules of Court, O 57 r 9A(5C).
1666. *See also* P. Tan, *New Emphases in Appellate Advocacy before the Singapore Court of Appeal*, Sing. L. Gaz. (May 2013).

served.[1667] The 'Appeals Information Sheet' requires parties to state details such as the subject matter of the appeal, questions of law on appeal, estimated time required for the appeal hearing, whether there are any applications to be made in the appeal, whether some form of alternative dispute resolution has been considered, and estimated costs of the appeal.[1668] The parties or their solicitors may be asked to attend in person to take directions on the conduct of the appeal where appropriate.[1669] On Monday, three weeks before the week of the Court of Appeal sitting for the appeal hearing, parties are required to submit skeletal arguments (which are abbreviated notes of the arguments that will be presented), the contents and form of which are prescribed by the Supreme Court Practice Directions.[1670] Generally, appeals before a Court of Appeal of three Judges of Appeal will be fixed for hearing within nineteen weeks from the date of notification by the Registrar to collect the record of proceedings, and those before two Judges of Appeal will be fixed for hearing within fifteen weeks of the same.[1671] An appeal does not operate as a stay of execution or of proceedings and does not invalidate any intermediate act or proceeding unless otherwise directed by the Court of Appeal.[1672]

III. Approach Towards Matters Not Raised in the Court Below

482. In relation to the approach of the Court of Appeal towards new matters, as a starting point, the Rules of Court permit the Court of Appeal to admit a new point or argument not taken at trial.[1673] However, the Court of Appeal is only likely to exercise this discretion if:[1674] first, the court is satisfied beyond all doubt 'it has before it all the facts bearing upon the new contention, as completely as would have been the case if the controversy had arisen at the trial';[1675] second, 'no satisfactory explanation could have been offered by those whose conduct is impugned if an

1667. Supreme Court Practice Directions 2013 (Part XI), introduced by way of Supreme Court Practice Directions (Amendment No 1) 2013.

1668. Supreme Court Practice Directions 2013 (Appendix A).

1669. Supreme Court Practice Directions 2013 (Part XI).

1670. Supreme Court Practice Directions 2013 (Part XI). Notably, there is a 20 page limit on skeletal arguments for civil matters before the Court of Appeal.

1671. Supreme Court Practice Directions 2013 (Appendix B).

1672. Supreme Court of Judicature Act (Cap. 322, R. 5, 2014 Rev. Ed.) Rules of Court, O 57 r 15.

1673. Supreme Court of Judicature Act (Cap. 322, R. 5, 2014 Rev. Ed.) Rules of Court, O 57 r 13(4). *See also Ang Sin Hock v. Khoo Eng Lim*, [2010] 3 SLR 179, [55]–[63]; *Chai Cher Watt (trading as Chuang Aik Engineering Works) v. SDL Technologies Pte Ltd*, [2012] 1 SLR 152, [17]; *Attorney-General v. . Aljunied-Hougang-Punggol East Town Council*, [2016] 1 SLR 915, [29]; C. Bull & J. Pinsler, *Civil Procedure: Annual Review of Singapore Cases* [8.19] (Sing. Acad. L. 2010).

1674. *See also North Staffordshire Railway Company v. Edge*, [1920] AC 254, 263; cited in *Susilawati v. American Express Bank Ltd*, [2009] 2 SLR(R) 737, [48].

1675. *The Owners of the Ship 'Tasmania' and the Owners of the Freight v. Smith, The Owners of the Ship 'City of Corinth', The Tasmania* (1890) 15 LR App Cas 223, 225; cited in *Panwah Steel Pte Ltd v. Koh Brothers Building & Civil Engineering Contractor (Pte) Ltd*, [2006] 4 SLR(R) 571, [15]. *See also Riduan bin Yusof v. Khng Thian Huat*, [2005] 4 SLR(R) 234, [35]; *Susilawati v. American Express Bank Ltd*, [2009] 2 SLR(R) 737, [52].

opportunity for explanation had been afforded them when in the witness box';[1676] third, the respondent would not be unduly prejudiced as a result and costs may form a proper remedy for the respondent;[1677] and fourth, it is very clear that it is in the interests of justice to allow the appellant to raise a new point or argument, notwithstanding the subversion of all legitimate expectations of the respondent to also receive justice (such as expecting finality and not be subject to further delays and expenses).[1678]

A question may arise as to whether the court – as opposed to the parties – may introduce new issues on its own accord independently of the parties' submissions.[1679] Generally, the principles which restrict the parties from raising new points on appeal, particularly where the facts have not been investigated at trial, apply equally where it is the court which seeks to introduce the new legal issue(s).[1680] This notion that new points or arguments[1681] should generally be restricted from being made at the appellate stage[1682] dovetails with the related notion that the main arena for the resolution of evidential disputes (i.e., the trial court) should not be allowed to be shifted to the appellate court, as to do so would fundamentally alter the limited role of appellate review.[1683] Thus, under the traditional English approach – which continues to be adopted in Singapore – fresh evidence (i.e., as opposed to a fresh point or argument, though they can of course converge) at an appeal can only be admitted if three conditions are met:

> To justify the reception of fresh evidence … three conditions must be fulfilled: first, it must be shown that the evidence could not have been obtained

---

1676. *The Owners of the Ship 'Tasmania' and the Owners of the Freight v. Smith, The Owners of the Ship 'City of Corinth', The Tasmania* (1890) 15 LR App Cas 223, 225; cited in *Panwah Steel Pte Ltd v. Koh Brothers Building & Civil Engineering Contractor (Pte) Ltd*, [2006] 4 SLR(R) 571, [15]. *See also Riduan bin Yusof v. Khng Thian Huat*, [2005] 4 SLR(R) 234, [35].

1677. *North Staffordshire Railway Company v. Edge*, [1920] AC 254, 263; cited in *Susilawati v. American Express Bank Ltd*, [2009] 2 SLR(R) 737, [48]. *See also Feoso (Singapore) Pte Ltd v. Faith Maritime Co Ltd*, [2003] 3 SLR(R) 556, [32].

1678. *Susilawati v. American Express Bank Ltd*, [2009] 2 SLR(R) 737, [50], citing *Geelong Building Society v. Encel*, [1996] 1 VR 594, 605. In other words, the situation must be very exceptional: *Susilawati v. American Express Bank Ltd*, [2009] 2 SLR(R) 737, [51], citing *Rengasamy Pillai v. Comptroller of Income Tax*, [1970] 1 MLJ 233.

1679. *See also* C. Bull & J. Pinsler, *Civil Procedure: Annual Review of Singapore Cases* [7.8]–[7.11] (Sing. Acad. L. 2007).

1680. *Townsing Henry George v. Jenton Overseas Investment Pte Ltd (in liquidation)*, [2007] 2 SLR(R) 597, [85]–[89], citing *Panwah Steel Pte Ltd v. Koh Brother Building & Civil Engineering Contractor (Pte) Ltd*, [2006] 4 SLR(R) 472.

1681. C.f. *Chua Choon Cheng v. Allgreen Properties Ltd*, [2009] 3 SLR(R) 724, [34]–[35], where the Court of Appeal allowed a new point that was not based on new evidence but instead on policy arguments; *PT Jaya Sumpiles Indonesia v. Kristle Trading Ltd*, [2009] 3 SLR(R) 689, [19], where the Court of Appeal allowed a new point of law and not of fact, and also placed weight on the fact that the application had been filed at a relatively early stage.

1682. *See also Holcombe v. Coulton*, (1988) 17 NSWLR 71, 77–78; cited in *Susilawati v. American Express Bank Ltd*, [2009] 2 SLR(R) 737, [49].

1683. *Susilawati v. American Express Bank Ltd*, [2009] 2 SLR(R) 737, [51]. In a related vein, a trial judge's finding of facts should not ordinarily be disturbed where they hinge on assessing witness credibility, but may be disturbed where the finding is plainly wrong or against the weight of the evidence (for instance where the inferences drawn are not supported by the primary or objective evidence on record): *Lim Koon Park v. Yap Jin Meng Bryan*, [2013] 4 SLR 150, [37].

> with reasonable diligence for use at the trial; second, the evidence must be such that, if given, it would probably have an important influence on the result of the case, though it need not be decisive; third, the evidence must be such as is presumably to be believed, or in other words, it must be apparently credible, though it need not be incontrovertible.[1684]

These conditions have been held to be cumulative.[1685] In addition, where a party to an appeal seeks to adduce fresh evidence relating to events that occurred after the decision of the trial judge, such evidence may only be admitted if it 'will materially alter the basis of the decision' in the sense that it will have a '*perceptible impact* on the decision such that it is in the interest of justice that it should be admitted'.[1686] Put another way, the three conditions restricting new evidence on appeal may be applied less rigidly if to do so would allow a miscarriage of justice to go uncorrected, for instance if new evidence uncovering fraud or deception of the party that goes to the root of the dispute is found.[1687]

483. Parenthetically, a distinction should also be drawn between appellate jurisdiction and confirmatory jurisdiction in this context. Specifically, when a judge in chambers hears an appeal from a decision of the registrar, he is exercising the latter and not the former; thus, because he is in effect rehearing the application and treats the matter afresh, he is entitled to exercise an unfettered discretion of his own.[1688] However, when a judge in chambers is hearing an appeal from decisions that were made in the context of something that is akin to a trial – such as the assessment of damages, where oral evidence in addition to affidavit evidence is presented – the three conditions restricting new evidence on appeal are applied, albeit less rigidly

1684. *Ladd v. Marshall*, [1954] 1 WLR 1489, 1491; cited in *Mykytowych, Pamela Jane v. V I P Hotel* [2016] SGCA 44; [47]; *ACU v. ACR*, [2011] 1 SLR 1235, [12]. However, the rule in this case is not necessarily applicable in all contexts. For instance, it is usually applied with some modifications for patent disputes: *Martek Biosciences Corp v. Cargill International Trading Pte Ltd*, [2011] 1 SLR 1287, [8]–[17]. At some point, it was also assumed that the rule is not applicable for interlocutory appeals: C. Bull & J. Pinsler, *Civil Procedure: Annual Review of Singapore Cases* [6.4] (Sing. Acad. L. 2004) citing *Jurong Town Corp v. Wishing Star Ltd*, [2004] 2 SLR(R) 427, [27]. *See also Cheng-Wong Mei Ling Theresa v. Oei Hong Leong*, [2006] 2 SLR(R) 637, [39] and [45]; C. Bull & J. Pinsler, *Civil Procedure: Annual Review of Singapore Cases* [8.14]–[8.20] (Sing. Acad. L. 2012).

1685. *Sim Cheng Soon v. BT Engineering Pte Ltd*, [2006] 3 SLR(R) 551, [7] and [9]. *See also Anan Group (Singapore) Pte Ltd v. VTB Bank (Public Joint Stock Co)*, [2019] 2 SLR 341, which provided a modified two-stage analysis when determining if it is in the interests of justice to relax the rule.

1686. *Yeo Chong Lin v. Tay Ang Choo*, [2011] 2 SLR 1157, [13] (emphasis in original). *See also* C. Bull & J. Pinsler, *Civil Procedure: Annual Review of Singapore Cases* [8.4]–[8.6] (Sing. Acad. L. 2011).

1687. *Su Sh-Hsyu v. Wee Yue Chew*, [2007] 3 SLR 673, [36]. *See also* C. Bull & J. Pinsler, *Civil Procedure: Annual Review of Singapore Cases* [7.12]–[7.15] (Sing. Acad. L. 2007).

1688. *Lassiter Ann Masters v. To Keng Lam (alias Toh Jeanette)*, [2004] 2 SLR(R) 392, [10], citing *Herbs and Spices Trading Post Pte Ltd v. Deo Silver (Pte) Ltd*, [1990] 2 SLR(R) 685, [12]. *See also Lipkin International Ltd v. Swiber Holdings Ltd*, [2015] 5 SLR 962, [14]–[15].

with respect to the first condition.[1689] To return to the earlier point: notably, the principles applicable to an application for leave to adduce further evidence at an appeal have been found to be conceptually similar to those applicable to an application for a new trial.[1690] In this connection, it should be noted that a new trial can be ordered on the basis of improper admission or rejection of evidence even if such admission or rejection has not resulted in some substantial wrong or miscarriage of justice, especially if there is new evidence which has a real prospect of making a significant difference to the outcome of the dispute.[1691] Similar principles apply mutatis mutandis to appeals before the High Court and will not be repeated below.[1692]

IV. Inherent Jurisdiction

484. Points have been made earlier about inherent jurisdiction and inherent powers and will not be rehashed here.[1693] In a narrower context, the Court of Appeal has decided that it has the inherent jurisdiction to reopen and rehear an earlier decision if any issue was decided in breach of the rules of natural justice, and in turn, set aside the whole or part of its earlier decision that was founded on any such issue(s).[1694] This is because if there was a breach of natural justice, the court cannot be said to have 'fully apprised or informed at the material time of all the relevant considerations pertaining to that issue' and thus it 'would not have exercised its jurisdiction properly vis-à-vis that issue, and, therefore, it cannot to be said to be functus officio in the sense of having exhausted its power to adjudicate on that issue'.[1695] Nonetheless, while a breach of natural justice is 'basically a procedural wrong because it denies the aggrieved party a full, fair and impartial hearing … not every breach of natural justice is equally serious'.[1696] Indeed, if a decision is made in breach of the bias rule (whether apparent or actual), that decision must be set aside and the matters reheard as the decision has been corrupted by a conflict of interest; conversely, if a decision is made in breach of the hearing rule, it does not entail that the tainted decision must be set aside:[1697]

1689. *Lassiter Ann Masters v. To Keng Lam (alias Toh Jeanette)*, [2004] 2 SLR(R) 392, [24]–[25]; *WBG Networks (S) Pte Ltd v. Sunny Daisy Ltd*, [2007] 1 SLR(R) 1133, [14]–[15]; *Bounty Resources Armenia Ltd v. Li Haidong*, [2015] SGHC 188, [17]–[18]. C.f. *Tan Sia Boo v. Ong Chiang Kwong*, [2007] 4 SLR(R) 298, [3].
1690. *Susilawati v. American Express Bank Ltd*, [2009] 2 SLR(R) 737, [23]–[24].
1691. *Basil Anthony Herman v. Premier Security Co-operative Ltd*, [2010] 3 SLR 110.
1692. *See also* Supreme Court of Judicature Act (Cap. 322, R. 5, 2014 Rev. Ed.) Rules of Court, O 55D and O 57.
1693. *See* the General Introduction.
1694. *MCST Plan No 301 v. Lee Tat Development Pte Ltd*, [2011] 1 SLR 998, [55].
1695. *MCST Plan No 301 v. Lee Tat Development Pte Ltd*, [2011] 1 SLR 998, [55]. *See also Ong Chai Hong v. Chiang Shirley*, [2016] SGHC 91, [12].
1696. *MCST Plan No 301 v. Lee Tat Development Pte Ltd*, [2011] 1 SLR 998, [56].
1697. *MCST Plan No 301 v. Lee Tat Development Pte Ltd*, [2011] 1 SLR 998, [57]–[59]. It should be noted that a judge who has previously criticised the conduct of a party in the course of his judgment on a matter, which he considers relevant to his decision, is not precluded from hearing a subsequent dispute involving the same party as the judge is simply exercising his judicial function; however, if the views were expressed in outspoken, extreme, or unbalanced terms as to cast doubt

> Instead, it merely requires that: (a) the aggrieved party be given, in appropriate cases, the opportunity to be heard on the issues on which he was not heard; and (b) the court thereafter considers whether its previous decision was correct and, if it finds that that decision was not correct, either sets aside or rectifies (depending on what the circumstances of the case require) that decision … In other words, where the hearing rule is breached, the aggrieved party has a prima facie right to be heard on the matters on which he has not been heard, but only on those matters and not on any other matters in respect of which no allegation of breach of the hearing rule has been made. Natural justice does not require that the aggrieved party be over-compensated by being given more than what he claims he has been denied … However, if a hearing on those matters will not change the ultimate outcome of the case … then the hearing would be in vain and an exercise in futility. In such a situation, the court would be entitled to exercise its discretion not to grant the aggrieved party a hearing on the matters on which he was not heard.[1698]

§3. Appeals to the High Court

485. Apart from matters over which it has original jurisdiction, the High Court also has appellate jurisdiction as well as supervisory and revisionary jurisdiction. Supervisory jurisdiction refers to the 'inherent power of the superior court to review the proceedings and decisions of inferior courts and tribunals or other public bodies discharging public functions'.[1699] The High Court is the only court that has supervisory jurisdiction.[1700] This is evident both by the express wording of section 27(1) of the Supreme Court of Judicature Act as well as case law that recognizes the High Court's inherent supervisory jurisdiction over inferior tribunals.[1701] Such supervisory jurisdiction is primarily exercised by the High Court through the making of prerogative orders, namely mandatory orders, prohibiting orders, quashing orders and orders for review of detention pursuant to Order 53 of the Rules of Court.[1702] The High Court's supervisory jurisdiction over inferior tribunals and its original jurisdiction, which is broadly defined to refer to the court's power to hear a matter

---

on the judge's ability to approach the subsequent case with an open mind should he recuse himself: *Ong Wui Teck v. Ong Wui Swoon*, [2016] 2 SLR 1067, [25].

1698. *MCST Plan No 301 v. Lee Tat Development Pte Ltd*, [2011] 1 SLR 998, [59] (emphasis in original).

1699. *Citiwall Safety Glass Pte Ltd v. Mansource Interior Pte Ltd*, [2015] 1 SLR 797, [42], citing *Haron bin Mundir v. Singapore Amateur Athletic Association*, [1991] 2 SLR(R) 494, [18]–[19].

1700. *Citiwall Safety Glass Pte Ltd v. Mansource Interior Pte Ltd*, [2015] 1 SLR 797, [52].

1701. *Citiwall Safety Glass Pte Ltd v. Mansource Interior Pte Ltd*, [2015] 1 SLR 797, [54]; *Muhammad Ridzuan bin Md Ali v. Public Prosecutor*, [2014] 3 SLR 721, [94]–[95]; *Ng Chye Huey v. PP*, [2007] 2 SLR(R) 106, [55]; *R v. Northumberland Compensation Appeal Tribunal; ex parte Shaw*, [1952] 1 KB 338, 346–347.

1702. *See Citiwall Safety Glass Pte Ltd v. Mansource Interior Pte Ltd*, [2015] 1 SLR 797, [50]; *Muhammad Ridzuan bin Md Ali v. Public Prosecutor*, [2014] 3 SLR 721, [102]; *Ng Chye Huey v. PP*, [2007] 2 SLR(R) 106, [55].

at first instance before any other court can consider it,[1703] are not mutually exclusive. Rather, the former is part of the latter.[1704] While the High Court's supervisory jurisdiction and revisionary jurisdiction overlap to a considerable degree, there remains sufficient areas of differences to warrant their treatment as 'different bases of jurisdiction'.[1705]

486. The High Court may hear appeals from the District Courts, Magistrates' Courts, and other tribunals as prescribed by written law.[1706] The High Court has general supervisory and revisionary jurisdiction over all State courts.[1707] In this capacity, it may 'call for and examine the record of any civil proceedings before any state court for the purpose of satisfying itself as to the correctness, legality or propriety of any decision recorded or passed, and as to the regularity of any proceedings of any such state court'[1708] as well as 'give such orders thereon, either by directing a new trial or otherwise, as seem necessary to secure that substantial justice is done'.[1709] Where an 'appeal lies from any decision in any civil matter, and no appeal is brought, no proceeding by way of revision shall be entertained at the instance of a party who could have appealed'.[1710] If a case has been the subject of an appeal, the High Court in the exercise of its supervisory and revisionary jurisdiction will 'have regard to whether that matter was, or could reasonably have been, raised in that appeal'.[1711] This section will focus on the key substantive and procedural aspects of appeals to the High Court.

I. The Right to Appeal

487. An appeal is available to a High Court Judge in chambers from any judgment, order, or decision of a registrar.[1712] However, it has been noted that although referred to as an 'appeal', the High Court judge in such a situation is actually exercising a confirmatory jurisdiction rather than an appellate function.[1713] An appeal lies to the High Court from the decision of a District or Magistrate's Court in the following circumstances:

1703. *Citiwall Safety Glass Pte Ltd v. Mansource Interior Pte Ltd*, [2015] 1 SLR 797, [68].
1704. *Citiwall Safety Glass Pte Ltd v. Mansource Interior Pte Ltd*, [2015] 1 SLR 797, [60], citing *Ng Chye Huey v. PP*, [2007] 2 SLR(R) 106, [52]–[53] and *State of Uttar Pradesh v. Dr Vijay Anand Maharaj*, [1963] 1 SCR 1. *See also Citiwall Safety Glass Pte Ltd v. Mansource Interior Pte Ltd*, [2015] 1 SLR 797, [77]–[79].
1705. *Ng Chye Huey v. PP*, [2007] 2 SLR(R) 106, [46]. *See also Citiwall Safety Glass Pte Ltd v. Mansource Interior Pte Ltd*, [2015] 1 SLR 797, [44].
1706. Supreme Court of Judicature Act (Cap. 322, 2007 Rev. Ed.), s 20.
1707. Supreme Court of Judicature Act (Cap. 322, 2007 Rev. Ed.), s 27(1).
1708. Supreme Court of Judicature Act (Cap. 322, 2007 Rev. Ed.), s 24.
1709. Supreme Court of Judicature Act (Cap. 322, 2007 Rev. Ed.), s 25.
1710. Supreme Court of Judicature Act (Cap. 322, 2007 Rev. Ed.), s 26.
1711. Supreme Court of Judicature Act (Cap. 322, 2007 Rev. Ed.), s 27(4).
1712. Supreme Court of Judicature Act (Cap. 322, R. 5, 2014 Rev. Ed.) Rules of Court, O 56 r 1(1).
1713. *See* J. Pinsler, *Principles of Civil Procedure* 924 (Acad. Publg. 2013) citing *Augustine Zacharia Norman v. Goh Sian Yong*, [1992] 1 SLR(R) 746, [11]; *Herbs and Spices Trading Post Pte Ltd v. Deo Silver (Pte) Ltd*, [1990] 2 SLR(R) 685, [11]–[12].

(a) in any case where the amount in dispute, or the value of the subject matter, at the hearing before that District Court or Magistrate's Court (excluding interest and costs) exceeds SGD 50,000 … or;
(b) with the leave of that District Court or Magistrate's Court or the High Court, in any other case.[1714]

488. Where a case involves a claim for unliquidated damages which have yet to be assessed or where quantum has not been determined due to a bifurcation order, the High Court has clarified that leave would not be necessary if the maximum possible amount which could be assessed is 'not clearly below SGD 50,000'.[1715] Both parties must assist the court to come to an appropriate determination, and it would be for the party claiming that the SGD 50,000 threshold had been crossed to substantiate that claim.[1716] An order of the High Court refusing or granting leave to appeal is final.[1717] The principles governing leave to appeal to the Court of Appeal also apply to leave applications to the State Courts or the High Court. Thus, leave will be granted if 'an appellate investigation is necessary in the interests of justice or if a denial of leave could result in a miscarriage of justice'.[1718] There are also circumstances where no appeal may be brought to the High Court against orders made by a District Court or Magistrate's Court, and these are specified in the Third Schedule to the Supreme Court of Judicature Act as follows:

(a) where a District Court or Magistrate's Court makes an order giving unconditional leave to defend any proceedings;
(b) where a District Court or Magistrate's Court makes an order giving leave to defend any proceedings on condition that the party defending those proceedings pays into court or gives security for the sum claimed, except if the appellant is that party;
(c) where a District Court or Magistrate's Court makes an order setting aside unconditionally a default judgment, regardless of how the default judgment was obtained (including whether by reason of a breach of an order of court or otherwise);
(d) where a District Court or Magistrate's Court makes an order setting aside a default judgment on condition that the party against whom the judgment had been entered pays into court or gives security for the sum claimed, regardless of how the default judgment was obtained (including whether by reason of a breach of an order of court or otherwise), except if the appellant is that party.

1714. Supreme Court of Judicature Act (Cap. 322, 2007 Rev. Ed.), s 21(1).
1715. J. Pinsler, *Principles of Civil Procedure* 940–941 (Acad. Publg. 2013) citing *Ong Wah Chuan v. Seow Hwa Chuan*, [2011] 3 SLR 1150; *Hailisen Shipping Co Ltd v. Pan-United Shipyard Pte Ltd*, [2004] 1 SLR(R) 148.
1716. J. Pinsler, *Principles of Civil Procedure* 940–941 (Acad. Publg. 2013) citing *Ong Wah Chuan v. Seow Hwa Chuan*, [2011] 3 SLR 1150, [35]–[38].
1717. Supreme Court of Judicature Act (Cap. 322, 2007 Rev. Ed.), s 21(2A).
1718. J. Pinsler, *Principles of Civil Procedure* 941 (Acad. Publg. 2013) citing *Anthony s/o Savarimuthu v. So Chuan Tin*, [1989] 1 SLR(R) 588; *Lee Kuan Yew v. Tang Liang Hong*, [1997] 2 SLR(R) 862; *Lam Seng Hang Co Pte Ltd v. The Insurance Corp of Singapore Ltd*, [2001] 1 SLR(R) 320; *Eng Poh Su v. Yap Ah Ho*, [2001] 1 SLR(R) 546.

489. Save for the situations specified in the Third Schedule, an appeal shall lie to a Judge of the High Court in chambers from: any judgment, order, or decision of a District Judge in chambers (not given or made in his capacity as a registrar), including a judgment given, or an order or a decision made, on appeal from a registrar; and any judgment, order or decision of a Magistrate in chambers (not given or made in his capacity as a registrar).[1719] The Chief Justice may, from time to time, direct that such class or classes or description of proceedings be heard in chambers, and any such proceedings, whether in fact heard in open court or in chambers, shall be deemed to have been heard in chambers for the purpose of determining the right to appeal.[1720] The High Court may also hear appeals from any court, tribunal or person as stipulated by legislation. Some examples include an appeal from the decision of a disciplinary tribunal under the Medical Registration Act,[1721] an appeal from the decision of the Maintenance of Parents Tribunal,[1722] and an appeal from the decision of the Commissioner under the Employment Act.[1723] The right to appeal in such situations will be governed by the legislation in question and any relevant provisions of the Rules of Court. All appeals to the High Court in the exercise of its appellate civil jurisdiction shall be by way of rehearing, and the High Court has the powers and jurisdiction on the hearing of such appeals as the Court of Appeal has on hearing of appeals from the High Court.[1724]

II. The Process of Appealing

490. Where leave to appeal is required under section 21(1) of the Supreme Court of Judicature Act to appeal against any judgment, order or decision of a District Judge or magistrate in chambers, the party must file his application to the District Judge or magistrate in chambers within seven days from the date of the judgment, order, or decision.[1725] If such leave is refused, then the party must apply to the High Court within seven days from the date of the refusal.[1726] An appeal is brought to a Judge of the High Court against any judgment, order or decision of a registrar of the High Court, District Judge in chambers or magistrate in chambers, by serving on every other party to the proceedings a notice of appeal to attend before the judge on a day specified in the notice.[1727] This notice must be issued within fourteen days after the judgment, order or decision appealed against was given and served on all parties within seven days of it being issued, unless the court otherwise orders.[1728]

1719. Supreme Court of Judicature Act (Cap. 322, R. 5, 2014 Rev. Ed.) Rules of Court, O 55C r 1(1).
1720. Supreme Court of Judicature Act (Cap. 322, R. 5, 2014 Rev. Ed.) Rules of Court, O 55C r 1(2).
1721. Medical Registration Act (Cap. 174, 2004 Rev. Ed.), s 55.
1722. Maintenance of Parents Act (Cap. 167B, 1996 Rev. Ed.), s 18.
1723. Employment Act (Cap. 91, 2009 Rev. Ed.), s 117.
1724. Supreme Court of Judicature Act (Cap. 322, 2007 Rev. Ed.), s 22.
1725. Supreme Court of Judicature Act (Cap. 322, R. 5, 2014 Rev. Ed.) Rules of Court, O 55C r 2(1).
1726. Supreme Court of Judicature Act (Cap. 322, R. 5, 2014 Rev. Ed.) Rules of Court, O 55C r 2(1).
1727. Supreme Court of Judicature Act (Cap. 322, R. 5, 2014 Rev. Ed.) Rules of Court, O 55C r 1(3) and O 56 r 1(2).
1728. Supreme Court of Judicature Act (Cap. 322, R. 5, 2014 Rev. Ed.) Rules of Court, O 55C r 1(4); O 56 r 1(3).

491. Where leave to appeal is required under section 21(1) of the Supreme Court of Judicature Act and is obtained, the notice of appeal must be filed within fourteen days from the date leave was given.[1729] An application for extension of time for filing a notice of appeal to the High Court after expiry of the fourteen-day timeline should be made to the High Court.[1730] This is to ensure parity of treatment between appeals under O 55C and O 55D.[1731] Similarly, in respect of all other appeals to the High Court from the State Courts, an appeal is brought by way of filing and service of a notice of appeal.[1732] The notice of appeal must state whether the whole or part (and if so what part) of the judgment or order is complained of, contain an address for service, and be signed by the appellant or his solicitor.[1733] At the time of filing the notice of appeal, the appellant must deposit in the registry the required fee for making copies of the record of proceedings as well as provide security for the respondent's costs of the appeal in the sum of SGD 2,000 for Magistrate's Court actions and SGD 3,000 for District Court actions.[1734]

492. As with appeals to the Court of Appeal, appeals to the High Court from the State Courts other than those from a District Judge or magistrate in chambers follow a similar process after the notice of appeal is filed, including the judge certifying the grounds of the judgment or order, the preparation of a copy of the copy of record of proceedings and notification of its availability to the appellant, and the preparation of the record of appeal, appellant's case and respondent's case.[1735] There is, however, no appellant's reply or appeals information sheet for appeals to the High Court. The required documents are filed in the State Courts and then transmitted to the High Court.[1736] The appeals are usually heard before one Judge of the High Court, although the judge may, if he thinks fit, reserve any appeal for the decision of a court consisting of three judges.[1737]

493. Generally, registrar's appeals to a High Court Judge in chambers will be fixed for hearing within three weeks from the date of filing of the appeal, save for appeals involving assessment of damages, which will be fixed for hearing within four weeks from the date of filing of the appeal.[1738] Appeals to the High Court from the State Courts will usually be fixed for hearing within four weeks from the date

1729. Supreme Court of Judicature Act (Cap. 322, R. 5, 2014 Rev. Ed.) Rules of Court, O 55C r 2(2).
1730. *Lioncity Construction Company Pte Ltd v. JFC Builders Pte Ltd*, [2015] 3 SLR 141, [33]–[34]. *See also* C. Bull & C. Voon Jiet, *Civil Procedure: Annual Review of Singapore Cases* [8.1] (Sing. Acad. L. 2015).
1731. *Lioncity Construction Company Pte Ltd v. JFC Builders Pte Ltd*, [2015] 3 SLR 141, [37], [39]–[40].
1732. Supreme Court of Judicature Act (Cap. 322, R. 5, 2014 Rev. Ed.) Rules of Court, O 55D rr 3(1) and 3(8). The notice of appeal should be served at the time of filing on parties to the proceedings in the court below who are directly affected by the appeal or their solicitors.
1733. Supreme Court of Judicature Act (Cap. 322, R. 5, 2014 Rev. Ed.) Rules of Court, O 55D r 3(2).
1734. Supreme Court of Judicature Act (Cap. 322, R. 5, 2014 Rev. Ed.) Rules of Court, O 55D rr 3(4)–(5).
1735. Supreme Court of Judicature Act (Cap. 322, R. 5, 2014 Rev. Ed.) Rules of Court, O 55D rr 5–7.
1736. Supreme Court of Judicature Act (Cap. 322, R. 5, 2014 Rev. Ed.) Rules of Court, O 55D r 8.
1737. Supreme Court of Judicature Act (Cap. 322, 2007 Rev. Ed.), s 21(2).
1738. Supreme Court Practice Directions 2013 (Appendix B).

of receipt of the record of proceedings from the State Courts.[1739] An appeal does not operate as a stay of execution or of proceedings and does not invalidate any intermediate act or proceeding unless otherwise directed by the High Court.[1740]

494. The process for appeals to the High Court from a court, tribunal, or person pursuant to legislation is different from other appeals from ordinary courts of law. Such appeals are brought by way of originating summons, which must state the grounds of the appeal and, if the appeal is against a judgment, order or other decision of a court, must state whether the appeal is against the whole or a part of that decision and, if against a part only, must specify the part.[1741] Where the appeal is against a judgment, order or decision of a court, the originating summons must be served on the registrar or clerk of the court and any party to the proceedings directly affected by the appeal, within twenty-eight days from the date of the judgment or order or the date on which the decision was given.[1742] Where the appeal is against an order, determination, award, or other decision of a tribunal, Minister, Government department or other person, the originating summons must be served on the Minister or Government department or person, as the case may be, and every party to the proceedings in which the decision appealed against was given, within twenty-eight days from the date on which notice of the decision was given.[1743] The hearing date of the appeal cannot be sooner than twenty-one days after service of the originating summons by which the appeal is brought.[1744] The originating summons may be amended by the appellant, without leave, by serving an amended originating summons not less than seven days before the hearing of the appeal, on each of the persons on whom the originating summons to be amended was served.[1745] Subject to the court's powers of amendment, the appellant cannot rely on grounds of appeal not stated in the originating summons.[1746]

§4. Appeals to a District Judge in Chambers

495. Similar to an appeal from decisions of a registrar of the High Court to a judge in chambers, an appeal from decisions of a registrar of the State Courts to a District Judge in chambers is styled as an 'appeal' but is in actuality the District Judge exercising confirmatory jurisdiction – the rationale being that the jurisdiction

1739. Supreme Court Practice Directions 2013 (Appendix B).
1740. Supreme Court of Judicature Act (Cap. 322, R. 5, 2014 Rev. Ed.) Rules of Court, O 55D r 13.
1741. Supreme Court of Judicature Act (Cap. 322, R. 5, 2014 Rev. Ed.) Rules of Court, O 55 r 2.
1742. Supreme Court of Judicature Act (Cap. 322, R. 5, 2014 Rev. Ed.) Rules of Court, O 55 rr 3(1)–(3).
1743. Supreme Court of Judicature Act (Cap. 322, R. 5, 2014 Rev. Ed.) Rules of Court, O 55 rr 3(1), (2), and (4). Where an appeal is brought against an order, determination or decision of a Minister of government department, the Minister or department is entitled to appear and be heard in the appeal proceedings. Supreme Court of Judicature Act (Cap. 322, R. 5, 2014 Rev. Ed.) Rules of Court, O 55 r 7.
1744. Supreme Court of Judicature Act (Cap. 322, R. 5, 2014 Rev. Ed.) Rules of Court, O 55 r 4.
1745. Supreme Court of Judicature Act (Cap. 322, R. 5, 2014 Rev. Ed.) Rules of Court, O 55 r 5(1).
1746. Supreme Court of Judicature Act (Cap. 322, R. 5, 2014 Rev. Ed.) Rules of Court, O 55 rr 5(3)–(4).

of the District Court is being exercised in two stages.[1747] Such an appeal is brought by serving on every other party to the proceedings a notice of appeal in the prescribed form to attend before the District Judge in chambers on a day specified in the notice.[1748] Unless otherwise ordered by the court, the notice of appeal 'must be issued within 14 days after the judgment, order or decision appealed against was given or made and served on all other parties within seven days of it being issued'.[1749] Similar to a registrar's appeal, the proceedings before the District Judge are by way of rehearing although appropriate weight may be given to the registrar's decision. The State Courts Practice Directions require parties in inter partes registrar's appeals to a District Judge in chambers to file and serve written submissions no later than three working days prior to the hearing of the appeal.[1750]

§5. Further Arguments Procedure

496. The further arguments procedure enables parties to offer additional arguments after the court has decided an interlocutory matter.[1751] The purpose of the procedure 'is basically to give the judge another opportunity to review his decision'[1752] and is appropriate when the case involves issues which were not fully considered at the original hearing in chambers due to a lack of time.[1753] In the State Courts, the process of further arguments does not affect the right of parties to appeal decisions from registrars to a District Judge in chambers. However, it may affect the right of parties to appeal decisions of District Judges or Magistrates in chambers to the High Court, which has since 2012 been aligned with the practice in respect of further arguments before the High Court.[1754] There is no requirement for an application for further arguments to be made. However, where the application is made, a notice of appeal cannot be filed until the court affirms, varies or sets aside the judgment, order or decision after hearing the further arguments, or certifies that no further arguments are required.[1755] The time for filing of the notice of appeal will begin to run from the date the court affirms, varies or sets aside the judgment, order or decision after hearing the further arguments, or certifies (or is deemed to certify) that no further arguments are required.[1756] The court will be deemed to have certified that it requires no further arguments where the party making the application for further

1747. *See* J. Pinsler, *Principles of Civil Procedure* 924 (Acad. Publg. 2013) citing *Augustine Zacharia Norman v. Goh Sian Yong*, [1992] 1 SLR(R) 746, [11]; *Herbs and Spices Trading Post Pte Ltd v. Deo Silver (Pte) Ltd*, [1990] 2 SLR(R) 685, [11]–[12].
1748. Supreme Court of Judicature Act (Cap. 322, R. 5, 2014 Rev. Ed.) Rules of Court, O 55B r 1(3).
1749. Supreme Court of Judicature Act (Cap. 322, R. 5, 2014 Rev. Ed.) Rules of Court, O 55B r 1(4).
1750. State Courts Practice Directions (Part III).
1751. J. Pinsler, *Principles of Civil Procedure* 930 (Acad. Publg. 2013).
1752. *Aberdeen Asset Management Asia Ltd v. Fraser & Neave Ltd*, [2001] 3 SLR(R) 355, [23].
1753. J. Pinsler, *Principles of Civil Procedure* 930 (Acad. Publg. 2013).
1754. *See* Supreme Court of Judicature Act (Cap. 322) Rules of Court (Amendment No. 2) Rules 2012 (S241/2012), which were introduced after the decision of *Lim Kok Boon (Lin Guowen) v. Lee Poh King Melissa*, [2012] 2 SLR 1082.
1755. Supreme Court of Judicature Act (Cap. 322, R. 5, 2014 Rev. Ed.) Rules of Court, O 55C r 1(6).
1756. Supreme Court of Judicature Act (Cap. 322, R. 5, 2014 Rev. Ed.) Rules of Court, O 55C r 1(6).

arguments does not receive information from the registrar within fourteen days of the receipt of the application that the court requires further arguments.[1757]

497. A party wishing to seek further arguments in the State Courts should do so by way of letter addressed to the registrar of the State Courts. The letter should state: the party making request; identify the judge or registrar who heard the matter in question; specify when the order concerned was made; state the provision of law under which the request is made; set out the proposed further arguments briefly, together with any authorities; and include a copy of the authorities cited.[1758] A copy of the request for further arguments should also be furnished to all parties concerned.[1759] In the High Court, there is similarly no requirement to request for further arguments before a notice of appeal is filed in respect of any judgment or order made by a judge in exercising the civil jurisdiction of the High Court after any hearing other than a trial of the action.[1760] However, the High Court may hear further arguments on request by any party before the earlier of: the time the judgment or order is extracted; or the expiration of fourteen days after the date the judgment or order is made.[1761] Where such a request is made, no notice of appeal shall be filed as described above in relation to the State Courts.[1762] The same conditions apply for when a judge is deemed to have certified that no further arguments are required.[1763] On hearing the further arguments, the judge may affirm, vary or set aside the judgment or order.[1764] The process of making further arguments to the High Court is governed by Practice Directions[1765] and is similar to the process in the State Courts save that the mode of making the request is specified to be through the Electronic Filing System.[1766] Unlike the position in respect of the State Courts and the High Court, further arguments should not be requested before the Court of Appeal because 'all relevant arguments should have been presented at the hearing proper'.[1767] Accordingly, the Chief Justice has directed that 'as a general rule, unless asked for by the Court of Appeal itself, the Court of Appeal will not receive further arguments after the conclusion of the hearing of the appeal'.[1768] The 'general rule will be relaxed in only very exceptional circumstances', for example, if an authority not available at the hearing would be decisive, and counsel seeking to submit further arguments are expected to satisfy themselves as to the existence of such 'very exceptional circumstances' and, if so, to seek the consent of the other parties to their request.[1769] The procedure for requesting further arguments before the Court of Appeal is the same as that before the High Court.

1757. Supreme Court of Judicature Act (Cap. 322, R. 5, 2014 Rev. Ed.) Rules of Court, O 55C r 1(7).
1758. State Courts Practice Directions (Part XII).
1759. State Courts Practice Directions (Part XII).
1760. Supreme Court of Judicature Act (Cap. 322, 2007 Rev. Ed.), s 28B(4).
1761. Supreme Court of Judicature Act (Cap. 322, 2007 Rev. Ed.), s 28B(1).
1762. Supreme Court of Judicature Act (Cap. 322, 2007 Rev. Ed.), s 28B(3).
1763. Supreme Court of Judicature Act (Cap. 322, R. 5, 2014 Rev. Ed.) Rules of Court, O 56 r 2(2).
1764. Supreme Court of Judicature Act (Cap. 322, 2007 Rev. Ed.), s 28B(2).
1765. Supreme Court of Judicature Act (Cap. 322, R. 5, 2014 Rev. Ed.) Rules of Court, O 56 r 2(1).
1766. Supreme Court Practice Directions 2013 (Part XI).
1767. Supreme Court Practice Directions 2013 (Part XI).
1768. Supreme Court Practice Directions 2013 (Part XI).
1769. Supreme Court Practice Directions 2013 (Part XI).

§6. Alternatives to the Appellate Process

498. An appeal is not the only available mechanism to challenge an unsatisfactory decision. Some examples have been summarized as follows:

> if an order was made in ex parte proceedings, the party concerned may be entitled to apply to [set it aside]. If he was not present during a hearing which resulted in a decision against him, he may be entitled to have the matter reheard if he can justify his absence. Likewise, if the court dismisses the proceedings in the absence of one or more parties, the same court has the discretion to reinstate the suit on application by a party. Where a judgement or order grants a party … 'liberty to apply' for further orders, it may be sufficient for him to make an application to this court rather than appeal its decision … Occasionally, the parties may agree not to appeal or enter into a consent judgment which would preclude the right of appeal.[1770]

499. The test for setting aside a consent judgment or order on the basis that the trial judge had pressurized a party into settlement is whether a reasonably minded person, having read the remarks by the trial judge, would consider that there was at least an appearance that the order was brought about by such pressure.[1771] A judgment cannot be set aside if the defendant delays in making the application and if he is unable to persuade the court that such an outcome would be in the interests of justice.[1772] An appeal may also not be provided by legislation against orders, determinations, or decisions of certain courts, tribunals or persons and in such situations, judicial review (where not precluded) would be the appropriate avenue.[1773] There is a further mechanism under Order 55A of the Rules of Court which permits an application to be made for 'an order directing a Minister, tribunal or other person to state a case for determination by the Court or to refer a question of law to the Court by way of case stated'.[1774] This mechanism supplements the appeal process from any court, tribunal or person to the High Court under Order 55 of the Rules of Court.[1775]

1770. J. Pinsler, *Principles of Civil Procedure* 919–920 (Acad. Publg. 2013) citing Supreme Court of Judicature Act (Cap. 322, R. 5, 2014 Rev. Ed.) Rules of Court, O 32 r 6, O 35 r 2, and O 25 r 5; Supreme Court of Judicature Act (Cap. 322, 2007 Rev. Ed.), s 34(1)(d); State Courts Act (Cap. 321, 2007 Rev. Ed.), s 48.

1771. *Nim Minimaart (a firm) v. MCST Plan No 1079*, [2010] 2 SLR 1. *See also Bakery Mart Pte Ltd v. Ng Wei Teck Michael*, [2005] 1 SLR(R) 28, [13]; *Poh Heng Huat Corp Pte Ltd v. Hafizul Islam Kofil Uddin*, [2012] 3 SLR 1003, [18]; *Sentosa Building Construction Pte Ltd v. DJ Builders & Contractors Pte Ltd*, [2015] SGHCR 18, [21]–[27].

1772. *Lee Ngiap Peng Tony v. Cheong Ming Kiat*, [2010] 4 SLR 831. C.f. *Su Sh-Hsyu v. Wee Yue Chew*, [2007] 3 SLR(R) 673.

1773. Supreme Court of Judicature Act (Cap. 322, R. 5, 2014 Rev. Ed.) Rules of Court, O 53.

1774. Supreme Court of Judicature Act (Cap. 322, R. 5, 2014 Rev. Ed.) Rules of Court, O 55A r 2.

1775. J. Pinsler, *Principles of Civil Procedure* 982 (Acad. Publg. 2013).

Part V. Incidents

Chapter 1. Interim Measures

§1. Introduction

500. 'Interim measures' will be defined broadly here to encompass four types of interlocutory or interim measures that can be applied for by the parties. Specifically, prohibitory and mandatory injunctions, anti-suit injunctions, Mareva injunctions (otherwise known as freezing orders), Anton Piller orders (otherwise known as search orders), and interim payments. These measures or injunctions may be applied for before or at the commencement of the action (including the pre-trial process); though of course some of these measures may also be sought as a form of final relief granted only at the conclusion of the trial.[1776] All the aforementioned interim measures, with the exception of interim payments, have a number of features in common.[1777] First, because most of these measures are granted before the conclusion of the trial, they will, unless otherwise ordered, usually lapse after a period of time (for instance, just before the trial commences) as fixed by the court.[1778] In addition, the practice is not to set a return date for a hearing (i.e., the injunction will be allowed to lapse without any subsequent hearing, unless the injunction is challenged).[1779] Second, as these measures constitute invasive relief (bearing in mind that the full evidentiary record will not have been established before the trial), they will only be granted under stringent conditions, with the court paying particularly close attention to the facts and justice of each case.[1780] Perhaps as a result of this, applications seeking such interim relief are usually heard by a judge, rather than a registrar, albeit in chambers rather than open court.[1781] Third, also because of the invasive nature of the relief, these measures may be granted with conditions attached, such as an undertaking to indemnify the respondent if the applicant is later shown to have asked for the injunction unjustifiably. Fourth, these measures are usually sought because damages (which will usually follow if the applicant wins the claim) may not be adequate or appropriate compensation for the harm that is sought to be prevented at the interlocutory stage. Fifth, these measures presuppose that there is an

1776. J. Pinsler, *Principles of Civil Procedure* 395–399 (Acad. Publg. 2013).
1777. J. Pinsler, *Principles of Civil Procedure* 396 (Acad. Publg. 2013).
1778. *See also* J. Pinsler, *Principles of Civil Procedure* 400 (Acad. Publg. 2013).
1779. *Singapore Civil Procedure 2015 Volume 1* at 633 (G.P. Selvam ed., Sweet & Maxwell Asia 2014).
1780. In particular, in an *ex parte* application for injunctions and search orders, the Supreme Court Practice Directions 2013 (Part IV) requires various information to be provided.
1781. Supreme Court Practice Directions 2013 (Part IV).

underlying cause of action to begin with; accordingly, they cannot be granted in the abstract without an obvious connection to a justiciable dispute, and by extension are much less likely to be granted when an originating process has not yet been served.[1782] However, it is not necessary for the injunctive relief to have been pleaded in the statement of claim. Sixth, it is of paramount importance for parties to respect and obey orders of court, as at the core of this principle is 'the public interest in the administration of justice, including the dispatch of litigation as expeditiously as justice in the case requires'.[1783] Seventh, in terms of costs, it is normal practice for a successful applicant to be awarded costs in the cause and for a successful respondent to be awarded costs in the cause.[1784]

501. The jurisdiction of a court to grant interim relief can be found in section 4(10) of the Civil Law Act,[1785] which states that: 'A Mandatory Order or an injunction may be granted or a receiver appointed by an interlocutory order of the court, either unconditionally or upon such terms and conditions as the court thinks just, in all cases in which it appears to the court to be just or convenient that such order should be made.' In addition to this, paragraph 5 of the First Schedule of the Supreme Court of Judicature Act[1786] states that the court has the power:

> before or after any proceedings are commenced to provide for … the interim preservation of property which is the subject-matter of the proceedings by sale or by injunction or the appointment of receiver or the registration of a caveat or a lis pendens or in any manner whatsoever; … the preservation of evidence by seizure, detention, inspection, photographing, the taking of samples, the conduct of experiments or in any manner; and … the preservation of assets for the satisfaction of any judgment which has been or may be made.[1787]

502. Paragraph 15 of the First Schedule then states that the court has the power 'to order a party in a pending proceeding to make interim payments to another party or to a stakeholder or into court on account of any damages, debt or other sum, excluding costs, which he may subsequently in the proceeding be adjudged to be liable to pay'.[1788] As will be seen, the law on interim measures or injunctions has

1782. *See* Supreme Court of Judicature Act (Cap. 322, R. 5, 2014 Rev. Ed.) Rules of Court, O 29 r 1(3).
1783. *Lee Shieh-Peen Clement v. Ho Chin Nguang*, [2010] 4 SLR 801, [15].
1784. *Singapore Civil Procedure 2015 Volume 1*, at 633 (G.P. Selvam ed., Sweet & Maxwell Asia 2014).
1785. (Cap. 43, 1999 Rev. Ed.).
1786. (Cap. 322, 2007 Rev. Ed.). *See also* State Courts Act (Cap. 321, 2007 Rev. Ed.), s 31 for a District Judge's powers; Supreme Court of Judicature Act (Cap. 322, R. 5, 2014 Rev. Ed.) Rules of Court, O 32 r 9, which confers on registrars the same powers as a judge in chambers.
1787. Certain statutes also empower a court to grant injunctions, such as the Companies Act (Cap. 50, 1994 Rev. Ed.); conversely, a court's power to grant injunctions can be curtailed, as seen for instance in the Government of Proceedings Act (Cap. 121, 1985 Rev. Ed.). *See also Singapore Civil Procedure 2015 Volume 1*, at 622 (G.P. Selvam ed., Sweet & Maxwell Asia 2014): 'Occasionally, judicial pronouncements have been made suggesting that the court has a very broad inherent jurisdiction upon which it may rely for the purpose of granting interlocutory relief.'
1788. *See also* Supreme Court of Judicature Act (Cap. 322, R. 5, 2014 Rev. Ed.) Rules of Court, O 29 rr 9–15. O 29 also provides for the detention and preservation of subject matter (r 2), power to

largely been shaped by case law (as opposed to the Rules of Court),[1789] much of which has been adopted from English developments.

§2. Procedural Aspects and General Principles

503. An application for an interim injunction (interim payment is considered separately) should be made promptly, that is, after the applicant becomes aware of the facts which he seeks protection; if there is a delay, then it is less likely that he will obtain the injunction, 'because his failure to move with real expedition is taken by the court as an indication of the lack of any urgent need to grant relief'.[1790] An application for interim injunction is made by summons supported by an affidavit that sets out the grounds for the application (there are also prescribed forms for the various orders, which provide for, inter alia, the terms, the duration of the injunction, as well as any undertakings made).[1791] The starting point is that the application should be made inter partes,[1792] but because most injunctions are applied for on an urgent basis, they may alternatively be applied for ex parte, that is, for the hearing to take place in the absence of the other party[1793] (the nature of the Anton Piller order (which will be elaborated upon below), however, means that it will always be justifiably be applied for ex parte).[1794] In such a situation, notwithstanding the ex parte nature of the hearing, 'an opponent to an ex parte application, especially where the application seeks injunctive relief, should be invited to attend at the hearing of the application'.[1795] Indeed, the practice is that:

---

order samples to be taken (r 3), sale of perishable property (r 4), recovery of movable property subject to lien (r 6), and allowance of income of property pending trial (r 8).

1789. Supreme Court of Judicature Act (Cap. 322, R. 5, 2014 Rev. Ed.) Rules of Court.

1790. *Singapore Civil Procedure 2015 Volume 1*, at 632 (G.P. Selvam ed., Sweet & Maxwell Asia 2014), citing *Bates v. Lord Hailsham of St Marylebone*, [1972] 1 WLR 1373, 1379. *See also Meespierson NV v. Industrial and Commercial Bank of Vietnam*, [1998] 1 SLR(R) 287, [29]–[30].

1791. Supreme Court of Judicature Act (Cap. 322, R. 5, 2014 Rev. Ed.) Rules of Court, O 29 r 1(4). In *Astro Nusantara International BV v. PT Ayunda Prima Mitra*, [2016] 2 SLR 737, [23]–[41], the court first noted that it retained the discretion as to whether the undertaking as to damages should be enforced or not. Generally, this discretion would be exercised based on whether the injunction was wrongly asked for (by considering for instance the unnecessary oppressiveness of the injunction) and whether there were any special circumstances (by considering for instance whether it would inequitable to enforce the undertaking). With respect to Mareva injunctions in particular, however, the court noted that because a plaintiff who obtains a Mareva injunction is making no claim to the assets covered by the injunction, any compensation is for the loss arising from interfering with the defendant's substantive rights.

1792. Supreme Court of Judicature Act (Cap. 322, R. 5, 2014 Rev. Ed.) Rules of Court, O 29 r 1(2). The originating process should also be brought along for the hearing.

1793. Supreme Court of Judicature Act (Cap. 322, R. 5, 2014 Rev. Ed.) Rules of Court, O 29 r 1(2).

1794. *Computerland Corp v. Yew Seng Computers Pte Ltd*, [1991] 2 SLR(R) 379, [17]–[23].

1795. Supreme Court Practice Directions 2013 (Part IV), citing *Castle Fitness Consultancy Pte Ltd v. Manz*, [1989] 2 SLR(R) 308, [7]; *The 'Nagasaki Spirit'*, [1993] 3 SLR(R) 878, [39]–[40]. If the opposing party attends the hearing without the intention of challenging the application, this will be known as an 'opposed ex parte application', where the opposing party will simply be present to assist the court in ascertaining all relevant aspects of the dispute: J. Pinsler, *Principles of Civil Procedure* 403–404 (Acad. Publg. 2013).

> any party applying ex parte for an injunction … must give notice of the application to the other concerned parties … The notice may be given by way of facsimile transmission or telex, or, in cases of extreme urgency, orally by telephone. The notice should inform the other parties of the date, time and place fixed for the hearing of the application and the nature of the relief sought. If possible, a copy of the ex parte summons should be given to each of the other parties. At the hearing … the applicant's solicitors should inform the Court of: … the attempts that were made to notify the other parties or their solicitors of the making of the application; and … whether the other parties or their solicitors consent to the application being heard without their presence.[1796]

504. Further, even though an ex parte application may be urgent, the summons must still be served on the respondent at least two clear days before the hearing.[1797] The rationale for these requirements for notice is that 'natural justice and the adversarial system ordinarily require all interested parties to be heard in a proceeding … as the applicant is the only party present … the court is deprived of the opportunity to consider any challenges which the opposing party might make if present … The potential for abuse by the applicant in such a proceeding is very real'.[1798] Having said all of the above, the notice requirements can be dispensed with 'if the giving of the notice to the other parties, or some of them, would or might defeat the purpose of the ex parte application. However, in such cases, the reasons for not following the directions should be clearly set out in the affidavit prepared in support of the ex parte application.'[1799]

505. The purpose of the application may be defeated:

> where there is a compelling and urgent need for secrecy and/or immediate relief (e.g., to secure property or evidence which is in imminent danger of being dissipated or removed or to prevent a current activity which is causing significant harm), so that notice to the other party would very likely jeopardise the applicant's position.[1800]

506. But regardless of whether the notice requirements apply, there is an obligation on the applicant to make full and frank disclosure of all material facts during an ex parte hearing for injunctive relief. In this regard, there are at least twelve modern principles that have emerged from the case law to govern this obligation. First, 'the judge hearing an inter partes application to discharge an ex parte injunction on the ground that the plaintiff has failed to make full and frank disclosure would not

---

1796. Supreme Court Practice Directions 2013 (Part IV).
1797. Supreme Court of Judicature Act (Cap. 322, R. 5, 2014 Rev. Ed.) Rules of Court, O 32 r 3.
1798. J. Pinsler, *Principles of Civil Procedure* 401 (Acad. Publg. 2013).
1799. Supreme Court Practice Directions 2013 (Part IV).
1800. J. Pinsler, *Principles of Civil Procedure* 400 (Acad. Publg. 2013) citing *Tay Long Kee Impex Pte Ltd v. Tan Beng Huwah*, [2000] 1 SLR(R) 786, [20]; *Multi-Code Electronics Industries (M) Bhd v. Toh Chun Toh Gordon*, [2009] 1 SLR(R) 1000, [122]. *See also Singapore Civil Procedure 2015 Volume 1*, at 652 (G.P. Selvam ed., Sweet & Maxwell Asia 2014), citing *Expanded Metal Manufacturing Pte Ltd v. Expanded Metal Co Ltd*, [1995] 1 SLR 673.

be sitting in appeal over the decision of the first judge who granted the injunction at the ex parte hearing'.[1801] Second, 'the plaintiff in an ex parte application is under a clear duty to make full and frank disclosure of all material facts in his possession at the time of application, even if they are prejudicial to his claim'.[1802] Third, 'this duty is to disclose all material facts … materiality is to be decided by the court and not by the applicant or their advisers'.[1803] Fourth, material facts 'cover both factual and legal matters, which may be advantageous or prejudicial to the applicant's application. It extends to facts which the applicant has knowledge of and facts which he ought to know or could have discovered had he made proper inquiries.'[1804] Fifth, 'even if the plaintiff has made a disclosure of material facts, mere disclosure without more or devoid of the proper context is in itself insufficient to constitute full and frank disclosure'.[1805] Sixth, 'where the court finds that the plaintiff has not made a full and frank disclosure, it does not necessarily follow that the court must discharge the … injunction. There is discretion in the matter. The court may continue the injunction notwithstanding non-disclosure … or deal with the non-disclosure by discharging the original injunction and granting a fresh injunction.'[1806] Seventh, 'whether or not the court would exercise its discretion depends on factors such as the particular relief sought, how serious the material non-disclosure is or how important the undisclosed facts are, and the overall merits of the plaintiff's case'.[1807] Eighth, 'where the information suppressed is sufficiently material, the court would then have to consider whether the material non-disclosure was inadvertent or innocent … or whether it was deliberate and intended to mislead the court into granting the injunction'.[1808] Ninth, 'courts tend to take a stricter view of any material non-disclosure in respect of Mareva injunctions as compared with other orders because the grant of the former will confer on the applicant an advantage over the party restrained'.[1809] Tenth, 'the court is less likely to exercise its discretion to set aside the … injunction where the plaintiff did not have any deliberate intention to suppress those material facts from the court … [but] this

1801. *Bahtera Offshore (M) Sdn Bhd v. Sim Kok Beng*, [2009] 4 SLR(R) 365, [19], citing *Tay Long Kee Impex Pte Ltd v. Tan Beng Huwah*, [2000] 1 SLR(R) 786, [18].
1802. *Bahtera Offshore (M) Sdn Bhd v. Sim Kok Beng*, [2009] 4 SLR(R) 365, [20], citing *Poon Kng Siang v. Tan Ah Keng* [1991] 2 SLR(R) 621, [40].
1803. *Bahtera Offshore (M) Sdn Bhd v. Sim Kok Beng*, [2009] 4 SLR(R) 365, [21], citing *The King v. The General Commissioners for the Purposes of the Income Tax Acts for the District of Kensington; Ex parte Princess Edmond de Polignac*, [1917] 1 KB 486, 504; *The 'Vasiliy Golovnin'*, [2008] 4 SLR(R) 994, [85].
1804. *Bahtera Offshore (M) Sdn Bhd v. Sim Kok Beng*, [2009] 4 SLR(R) 365, [22], citing *Multi-Code Electronics Industries (M) Bhd v. Toh Chun Toh Gordon*, [2009] 1 SLR(R) 1000, [124].
1805. *Bahtera Offshore (M) Sdn Bhd v. Sim Kok Beng*, [2009] 4 SLR(R) 365, [24], citing *The 'Vasiliy Golovnin'*, [2008] 4 SLR(R) 994, [91].
1806. *Bahtera Offshore (M) Sdn Bhd v. Sim Kok Beng*, [2009] 4 SLR(R) 365, [25], citing *Mohamed Said bin Ali v. Ka Wah Bank*, [1989] 1 SLR(R) 689; *Lee Hung Khoon v. Yeo Tang Mui*, [1990] 1 SLR(R) 459.
1807. *Bahtera Offshore (M) Sdn Bhd v. Sim Kok Beng*, [2009] 4 SLR(R) 365, [26].
1808. *Bahtera Offshore (M) Sdn Bhd v. Sim Kok Beng*, [2009] 4 SLR(R) 365, [27], citing *Multi-Code Electronics Industries (M) Bhd v. Toh Chun Toh Gordon*, [2009] 1 SLR(R) 1000, [129].
1809. *Bahtera Offshore (M) Sdn Bhd v. Sim Kok Beng*, [2009] 4 SLR(R) 365, [28], citing *Brink's Mat Ltd v. Elcombe*, [1988] 1 WLR 1350, 1358.

does not mean that all innocent non-disclosures are excused'.[1810] Eleventh, 'where the plaintiff did intend to suppress material facts from the court … The court would have to balance, amongst other factors, the degree of the plaintiff's culpability and the burden of the injunction against the defendants should the injunction be upheld, against the adverse impact on the plaintiff should the injunction be discharged.'[1811] Twelfth, 'where there has been culpable non-disclosure, the court would be more inclined towards exercising its discretion to discharge the injunction for abuse of process, unless there are very extenuating circumstances for which the court would be prepared to excuse the plaintiff'.[1812] If the respondent wishes to challenge the injunction, he will make an application by summons, which will be heard inter partes.[1813] Finally, it should be noted that it is possible that only parts of the order requested for may be granted by the court.

§3. PROHIBITORY AND MANDATORY INJUNCTIONS

507. To obtain an interlocutory (prohibitory) injunction to restrain the respondent from continuing with a certain conduct pending trial or a further order from the court, the applicant must show that first, there is a serious question to be tried with a real prospect of success, and second, that the balance of convenience lies in favour of granting the injunction.[1814] With respect to the first (and threshold) requirement, the court must be satisfied, without looking at the merits of the case but only at the evidence, that the applicant's claim is neither frivolous nor vexatious (i.e., there is a valid cause of action), and that the applicant has a realistic prospect

1810. *Bahtera Offshore (M) Sdn Bhd v. Sim Kok Beng*, [2009] 4 SLR(R) 365, [29], citing *Lloyds Bowmaker Ltd v. Britannia Arrow Holdings Plc*, [1988] 1 WLR 1337, 1343–1344.

1811. *Bahtera Offshore (M) Sdn Bhd v. Sim Kok Beng*, [2009] 4 SLR(R) 365, [30].

1812. *Bahtera Offshore (M) Sdn Bhd v. Sim Kok Beng*, [2009] 4 SLR(R) 365, [33] (emphasis in original).

1813. *Tay Long Kee Impex Pte Ltd v. Tan Beng Huwah*, [2000] 1 SLR(R) 786, [49]. *See also* Supreme Court of Judicature Act (Cap. 322, R. 5, 2014 Rev. Ed.) Rules of Court, O 32 r 6.

1814. *RGA Holdings International Inc v. Loh Choon Phing Robin*, [2017] SGCA 55, [28]; *American Cyanamid Co v. Ethicon Ltd*, [1975] AC 396, 407–408; cited in *ANB v. ANC*, [2014] 4 SLR 747, [54]; *UDL Marine (Singapore) Pte Ltd v. Jurong Town Corp*, [2011] SGHC 153, [13]; *Astrata (Singapore) Pte Ltd v. Tridex Technologies Pte Ltd*, [2011] 1 SLR 449, [17]. For the granting of an overseas injunction (and against a foreign sovereign state specifically), *see Maldives Airports Co Ltd v. GMR Malé International Airport Pte Ltd*, [2013] 2 SLR 449. For the granting of a 'springboard' injunction which restrains a person who had obtained information in confidence to use it as a springboard for activities detrimental to the person who made the confidential communication, even if such information had already become available publicly, *see Jardine Lloyd Thopson Pte Ltd v. Howden Insurance Brokers (S) Pte Ltd*, [2015] 5 SLR 258, [21]. There, the court held that a court considering if a springboard injunction should be granted had to consider beyond the usual principles governing an interim injunction and assess the relative strengths of the arguments of the parties at the interlocutory stage; this evaluation was also necessary to determine the appropriate length of the injunction if a court decided such an injunction is warranted. *See also Goh Seng Heng v. RSP Investments*, [2016] SGHC 275, [67]. For other types of prohibitory injunctions – such as 'Erinford orders' – *see Sin Herh Construction Pte Ltd v. Hyundai Engineering & Construction Co Ltd*, [2017] SGHC 3.

of obtaining a permanent injunction subsequently at the trial.[1815] This is a low threshold and the prospects of the plaintiff's success are to be investigated only to a limited extent.[1816] With respect to the second requirement, a number of factors are considered:

> the court should first consider whether, if the plaintiff were to succeed at the trial in establishing his right to a permanent injunction, he would be adequately compensated by an award of damages for the loss he would have sustained as a result of the defendant's continuing to do what was sought to be enjoined between the time of the application and the time of the trial. If damages in the measure recoverable at common law would be adequate remedy and the defendant would be in a financial position to pay them, no interlocutory injunction should normally be granted, however strong the plaintiff's claim appeared to be at that stage. If, on the other hand, damages would not provide an adequate remedy for the plaintiff in the event of his succeeding at the trial, the court should then consider whether, on the contrary hypothesis that the defendant were to succeed at the trial in establishing his right to do that which was sought to be enjoined, he would be adequately compensated under the plaintiff's undertaking as to damages for the loss he would have sustained by being prevented from doing so between the time of the application and the time of the trial. If damages in the measure recoverable under such an undertaking would be an adequate remedy and the plaintiff would be in a financial position to pay them, there would be no reason upon this ground to refuse an interlocutory injunction.
>
> It is where there is doubt as to the adequacy of the respective remedies in damages available to either party or to both, that the question of balance of convenience arises. It would be unwise to attempt even to list all the various matters which may need to be taken into consideration in deciding where the balance lies, let alone to suggest the relative weight to be attached to them. These will vary from case to case.
>
> Where other factors appear to be evenly balanced it is a counsel of prudence to take such measures as are calculated to preserve the status quo. If the defendant is enjoined temporarily from doing something that he has not done before, the only effect of the interlocutory injunction in the event of his succeeding at the trial is to postpone the date at which he is able to embark upon a course of action which he has not previously found it necessary to undertake; whereas to interrupt him in the conduct of an established enterprise would cause much greater inconvenience to him since he would have to start again to establish it in the event of his succeeding at the trial.

1815. *New Civilbuild Pte Ltd v. Guobena Sdn Bhd*, [1998] 2 SLR(R) 732, [20]–[22]; *Mothercare Ltd v. Robson Brooks Ltd*, [1979] FSR 466, 474; *Alfred Dunhill Ltd v. Sunoptic SA*, [1979] FSR 337, 373. In *ANB v. ANC*, [2015] 5 SLR 522, the applicant claimed that there was a breach of confidence and sought an injunction. However, the claim also involved elements of privacy, and there was no developed tort of privacy in Singapore. The court held that this fact pointed not only towards the first limb of the test but the second one as well.

1816. *Challenger Technologies Limited v. Courts (Singapore) Pte Ltd*, [2015] 5 SLR 679, [17].

> Save in the simplest cases, the decision to grant or to refuse an interlocutory injunction will cause to whichever party is unsuccessful on the application some disadvantages which his ultimate success at the trial may show he ought to have been spared and the disadvantages may be such that the recovery of damages to which he would then be entitled either in the action or under the plaintiff's undertaking would not be sufficient to compensate him fully for all of them … if the extent of the uncompensatable disadvantage to each party would not differ widely, it may not be improper to take into account in tipping the balance the relative strength of each party's case as revealed by the affidavit evidence adduced on the hearing of the application.[1817]

508. In other words, the court will first hypothesize and assume: if the interlocutory injunction is refused, and the applicant succeeds at trial in establishing his right to a permanent junction, the interlocutory injunction will usually not be granted if he can be adequately compensated by damages; conversely, if the interlocutory injunction is granted, and the respondent succeeds in resisting the applicant's request at trial for a permanent injunction, the interlocutory injunction will usually be granted if the defendant can be adequately compensated by damages undertaken to be paid by the applicant during the hearing for the interlocutory injunction.[1818] It is only when there is still an impasse after this stage that the court will decide where the balance of convenience lies by considering various factors alluded to above. However, there may be situations where a different analysis is warranted and the merits of the case – specifically, a prima facie case needs to be established – are considered instead. Thus, where the respondent has no arguable defence such that there is no dispute[1819] or where the grant of the injunction would effectively conclude all proceedings,[1820] the balance of convenience analysis will be superseded by the prima facie case analysis (provided, of course, that the applicant also comes to the court with clean hands since he is seeking an equitable remedy).[1821] As a final point, it should be noted that if there are arbitration proceedings that are pending, 'the courts should generally decline to exercise their jurisdiction to grant interim injunctions pending arbitration where an arbitral tribunal has concurrent jurisdiction to make such orders and there are no special circumstances to justify the application being made to the court instead of to the tribunal'.[1822] Indeed, a party seeking

---

1817. *American Cyanamid Co v. Ethicon Ltd*, [1975] AC 396, 408–409; cited in *Brown Noel Trading Pte Ltd v. Singapore Press Holdings Ltd*, [1993] 2 SLR(R) 840, [3]; *Bengawan Solo Pte Ltd v. Season Confectionary Co (Pte) Ltd*, [1994] 1 SLR(R) 448, [19]. *Cf RGA Holdings International Inc v. Loh Choon Phing Robin*, [2017] SGCA 55, [42]; *Tan Choon Wee v. Pine Capital Group Ltd*, [2019] SGHC 201.

1818. *See also Fellows & Son v. Fisher*, [1976] QB 122, 137; *Millennium Pharmaceuticals, Inc v. Drug Houses of Australia Pte Ltd*, [2018] SGHC 149 at [59]–[63].

1819. *Official Custodian for Charities v. Mackey*, [1985] Ch 168, 187; cited in *Société Générale v. City Holdings (Pte) Ltd*, [1990] 2 SLR(R) 582, [135].

1820. *NWL Ltd v. Woods*, [1979] 1 WLR 1294, 1307. *See also Federal Computer Services Sdn Bhd v. Ang Jee Hai Eric*, [1991] 2 SLR(R) 427, [26].

1821. *See also Smith v. Inner London Education Authority*, [1978] 1 All ER 411, 422–423.

1822. *NCC International AB v. Alliance Concrete Singapore Pte Ltd*, [2008] 2 SLR(R) 565, [61] (emphasis in original).

interim relief from the Court, especially one that is governed by the International Arbitration Act,[1823] must satisfy the strict conditions set out in sections 12A(3) to (6) of International Arbitration Act.[1824]

509. Whereas prohibitory injunctions restrain conduct, mandatory injunctions compel parties to perform certain positive acts.[1825] In that sense, mandatory injunctions present an even more invasive remedy than prohibitory injunctions; thus, they have been described as highly exceptional remedies that can only be justified by special circumstances,[1826] especially since they often have the effect of granting the applicant the entire or major part of the relief sought.[1827] Moreover, the nature of a mandatory injunction is that if granted, it will definitely alter the status quo (as the respondent has to expend time and money to comply with the positive obligation imposed by the injunction), leading to a greater likelihood of injustice if it is subsequently determined that it should not have been granted.[1828] As a result, courts are likely to be more reluctant to grant mandatory injunctions (as compared to prohibitory injunctions). However, there is as yet no conclusive case law that affirms this unequivocally. The traditional test was to ask if the court would feel 'a high degree of assurance that at the trial it will appear that the injunction was rightly granted'.[1829] Subsequently, however, case law has recharacterized this requirement as a mere guideline:

> [The test of high degree of assurance] was plainly intended as a guideline rather than an independent principle. It is another way of saying that the features which justify describing an injunction as 'mandatory' will usually also have the consequence of creating a greater risk of injustice if it is granted rather than withheld … If it appears to the court that, exceptionally, the case is one in which withholding a mandatory interlocutory injunction would in fact carry a greater risk of injustice than granting it even though the court does not feel a 'high degree of assurance' about the plaintiff's chances of establishing his right, there cannot be any rational basis for withholding the injunction.[1830]

1823. (Cap. 143A, 2002 Rev. Ed.).

1824. For an analysis of the conditions, *see Maldives Airports Co Ltd and another v. GMR Male International Airport Pte Ltd* [2013] 2 SLR 449, [33]–[80].

1825. *Singapore Civil Procedure 2015 Volume 1*, at 621 (G.P. Selvam ed., Sweet & Maxwell Asia 2014).

1826. *Rivkin Consultancy Pte Ltd v. Pardeep Singh Boparai*, [2010] SGHC 191, [12], citing *NCC International AB v. Alliance Concrete Singapore Ptd Ltd*, [2008] 2 SLR(R) 565, [75]–[76]. *See also RGA Holdings International Inc v. Loh Choon Phing Robin*, [2017] SGCA 55, [31]; *ANB v. ANC*, [2014] 4 SLR 747, [56].

1827. *Films Rover International Ltd v. Cannon Film Sales Ltd*, [1987] 1 WLR 670, 681; *Swiss Singapore Overseas Enterprises Pte Ltd v. Navalmar UK Ltd*, [2003] 1 SLR(R) 587, [35].

1828. *Chuan Hong Petrol Station Pte Ltd v. Shell Singapore (Pte) Ltd*, [1992] 2 SLR(R) 1, [80]–[89].

1829. *Shepherd Homes Ltd v. Sandham*, [1971] Ch 340, 351.

1830. *Films Rover International Ltd v. Cannon Film Sales Ltd*, [1987] 1 WLR 670, 680–681; cited in *Heysek v. Boyden World Corp*, [1988] 2 SLR(R) 298, [20]; *NCC International AB v. Alliance Concrete Singapore Pte Ltd*, [2007] SGHC 64, [21]. *See also National Commercial Bank Jamaica Ltd v. Olint Corpn Ltd*, [2009] 1 WLR 1405, 1409.

510. Be that as it may, 'the plaintiff will usually have to show that he has an unusually strong and clear case' when applying for mandatory injunctions.[1831]

511. It has been held that a cross-undertaking in damages will be implied whenever an interlocutory injunction or voluntary undertaking is given, unless the contrary is expressed.[1832]

§4. Anti-suit Injunction

512. An anti-suit injunction serves to restrain proceedings in another country, but is distinct from an application to stay proceedings on the basis of forum non conveniens.[1833] The fundamental principles relating to anti-suit injunctions are that:[1834] first, the jurisdiction is to be exercised when the 'ends of justice' require it; second, where the court decides to grant an injunction restraining proceedings in a foreign court, its order is directed not against the foreign court but against the parties so proceeding or threatening to proceed; third, an injunction will only be issued to restrain a party who is amenable to the jurisdiction of the court, against whom an injunction will be an effective remedy; and fourth, since such an order indirectly affects the foreign court, the jurisdiction is one which must be exercised with caution.

513. In determining where the balance of the justice of the case lies, the following factors can be considered:[1835] first, whether the defendants are amenable to the jurisdiction of the Singapore court;[1836] second, the natural forum for resolution of

1831. *Singapore Civil Procedure 2015 Volume 1*, at 628 (G.P. Selvam ed., Sweet & Maxwell Asia 2014).

1832. *Neptune Capital Group and others v. Sunmax Global Capital Fund 1 Pte Ltd and another* [2016] 4 SLR 1177, [44].

1833. J. Pinsler, *Principles of Civil Procedure* 422 (Acad. Publg. 2013). For anti-arbitration injunctions, *see* N. Poon, *The Use and Abuse of Anti-Arbitration Injunctions: A Way Forward for Singapore*, 25 Sing. Acad. L.J. 244 (2013). As to whether the right to apply for an anti-suit injunction is itself the cause of action or merely ancillary proceedings, *see PT Sandipala Arthaputra v. STMicroelectronics Asia Pacific Pte Ltd*, [2015] 5 SLR 873.

1834. *Hai Jiang 1401 Pte Ltd v. Singapore Technologies Marine Ltd*, [2020] SGHC 20, [20]; *Lakshmi Anial Salgaocar v. Jhaveri Darsan Jitendra*, [2019] SGCA 42, [49]; *John Reginald Stott Kirkham v. Trane US Inc*, [2009] 4 SLR(R) 428, [25], citing *Société Nationale Industrielle Aerospatiale v. Lee Kui Jak*, [1987] AC 871, 892. *See also Bank of America National Trust and Savings Association v. Djoni Widjaja*, [1994] 2 SLR(R) 898, [10]–[14]; C. Bull & J. Pinsler, *Civil Procedure: Annual Review of Singapore Cases* [7.40]–[7.44] (Sing. Acad. L. 2008); *Hong Hin Kay Albert v. AAHG, LLC*, [2014] SGHC 206, [29]; *BC Andaman Co Ltd v. Xie Ning Yun*, [2017] SGHC 64, [52]–[54].

1835. *John Reginald Stott Kirkham v. Trane US Inc*, [2009] 4 SLR(R) 428, [28]–[29], citing *Evergreen International SA v. Volkswagen Group Singapore Pte Ltd*, [2004] 2 SLR(R) 457, [16]; *South Carolina Insurance Co v. Assurantie Maatschappij 'De Zeven Provincien' NV*, [1987] AC 24. *See also BC Andaman Co Ltd v. Xie Ning Yun*, [2017] SGHC 64, [56]; *BC Andaman Co Ltd v. Xie Ning Yun*, [2017] 4 SLR 1332, [56]; *Lakshmi Anial Salgaocar v. Jhaveri Darsan Jitendra*, [2019] SGCA 42, [49].

1836. *See also Koh Kay Yew v. Inno-Pacific Holdings Ltd*, [1997] 2 SLR(R) 148, [17].

the dispute between the parties;[1837] third, the alleged vexation or oppression to the plaintiffs if the foreign proceedings are to continue;[1838] fourth, the alleged injustice to the defendants as an injunction would deprive the defendants of the advantages sought in the foreign proceedings; and fifth, whether the institution of the foreign proceedings is in breach of any agreement between the parties. While considerations of international comity will ultimately weigh heavily in the court's consideration, if public policy demands the restraint of the foreign suit, the court would act accordingly even if this is perceived as being antithetical to promoting international comity.[1839]

514. It should be noted that anti-suit injunctions may also apply to enforce breaches of arbitration agreements.[1840] Generally, an anti-suit injunction should be granted in aid of arbitration proceedings if it can be shown that there is a valid and binding arbitration agreement and there is evidence that a contracting party has breached the agreement.[1841]

§5. Mareva Injunction

515. The Mareva injunction – named after the English case *Mareva Compania Naviera SA v. International Bulk Carriers SA*[1842] – is 'designed to prevent a defendant from removing from the jurisdiction assets that may in due course be attached for the purposes of satisfying the plaintiff's judgment. It is a special kind of injunction, quite different from another.'[1843] Further, unlike prohibitory or mandatory injunctions which can be the actual remedy sought at trial, Mareva injunctions will always be collateral to the main action (but like prohibitory or mandatory injunctions can be granted before, during, or after the trial); also, Mareva injunction hearings will usually be ex parte (so that the opponent cannot act preemptively), so any injunction granted is usually only challenged after it has come into operation. It should be noted at the outset, however, that third-party rights are not affected by the grant of a Mareva injunction, since no proprietary interests are created by the

1837. *See also John Reginald Stott Kirkham v. Trane US Inc*, [2009] 4 SLR(R) 428, [33]–[34].

1838. *Hong Hin Kay Albert v. AAHG, LLC*, [2014] SGHC 206, [48]: '[w]hat amount to vexation or oppression has never been conclusively defined in the numerous case authorities dealing with the grant of anti-suit injunctions'. *See also McHenry v. Lewis*, (1882) 22 Ch D 397, 407–408; *John Reginald Stott Kirkham v. Trane US Inc*, [2009] 4 SLR(R) 428, [47].

1839. C. Bull & J. Pinsler, *Civil Procedure: Annual Review of Singapore Cases* [8.95] (Sing. Acad. L. 2010) citing *Q&M Enterprises Sdn Bhd v. Poh Kiat*, [2005] 4 SLR(R) 494, [25].

1840. *WSG Nimbus Pte Ltd v. Board of Control for Cricket in Sri Lanka*, [2002] 1 SLR(R) 1088; *R 1 International Pte Ltd v. Lonstroff AG*, [2015] 1 SLR 521.

1841. *Maldives Airports Co Ltd v. GMR Male International Airport Pte Ltd*, [2013] 2 SLR 449. *See also* Nicholas Poon, "Enforcing the Negative Promise in an Arbitration Agreement". [2013] LMCLQ 432.

1842. [1980] 1 All ER 213.

1843. *Singapore Civil Procedure 2015 Volume 1* 636 (G.P. Selvam ed., Sweet & Maxwell Asia 2014) citing *Heng Holdings SEA (Pte) Ltd v. Tomongo Shipping Co Ltd*, [1997] 2 SLR(R) 669, [31]. *See also Parakou Shipping Pte Ltd (in liquidation) v. Liu Cheng Chan*, [2015] SGHC 96, [6].

injunction; in other words, the injunction takes effect against the defendant in personam and gives the plaintiff no advantage over other creditors of the defendant.[1844] In addition, the injunction is not granted to punish the defendant or to enable the plaintiff to exert pressure on the defendant to come to a settlement – it is simply an enforcement mechanism.[1845] In this respect, Mareva injunctions are different from proprietary injunctions.[1846] Practical problems that have arisen vis-à-vis the granting of a Mareva injunction include:

> how to frame an order which, one the one hand protects the claimant against the manipulations of a defendant who may prove to be unscrupulous, without strangling the working capital of a defendant at the instance of a claimant who may prove to be unscrupulous; how to form the necessary judgment at a time when every fact is hotly controverted; how to choose ancillary orders which are effective without oppressive.[1847]

516. Perhaps because of all of the aforementioned challenges that accompany a Mareva injunction, four stringent requirements must be satisfied by the plaintiff for a Mareva injunction application to succeed: first, there is a valid cause of action over which the court has jurisdiction; second, the plaintiff has a good arguable case; third, the defendant has assets within or outside the jurisdiction; and fourth, there is a real risk that those assets may be disposed of or dissipated so that any judgment which the plaintiff may obtain cannot be enforced.[1848]

1844. *Sumifru Singapore Pte Ltd v. Felix Santos Ishizuka*, [2020] SGHC 7, [1]; *Allied Marine Services Ltd v. LMJ International Ltd*, [2006] 1 SLR(R) 261, [5]; *Tribune Investment Trust Inc v. Dalzavod Joint Stock Co*, [1998] 1 SLR 1003; *The 'Nagasaki Spirit'*, [1993] 3 SLR(R) 878; *Singapore Civil Procedure 2015 Volume 1*, at 637 (G.P. Selvam ed., Sweet & Maxwell Asia 2014). *See also* C. Bull & J. Pinsler, *Civil Procedure: Annual Review of Singapore Cases* [6.68] (Sing. Acad. L. 2005).

1845. *Mercedes-Benz AG v. Leiduck*, [1995] 3 All ER 929, 941. In *Chung Khin Chun K (by her deputy Mok Chiu Ling Hedy) v. Yang Yin*, [2015] 5 SLR 467, [24] the court noted the distinction between a 'normal' Mareva injunction and one that not only preserved assets so as to ensure a defendant could meet a judgment, but was also put in place to protect the applicant from having his property used by the defendant for his own benefit. *See also Tang Ying v. Chen Mingliang*, [2018] SGHC 226.

1846. *See Bouvier, Yves Charles Edgar v. Accent Delight International Ltd*, [2015] 5 SLR 558, [144]: 'An interlocutory proprietary injunction … is granted in support of a claim for proprietary relief. It is a prohibitory injunction that fastens on the specific asset in which the plaintiff asserts a proprietary interest. It prevents the defendant, pending the resolution of the dispute, from dealing with that asset and its traceable proceeds. An interlocutory proprietary injunction is governed by the *American Cyanamid* principles.' *See also TYV Investment Group Pte Ltd v. ERC Holdings Pte Ltd*, [2020] SGHC 157.

1847. On the court's power to vary Mareva injunctions already granted, *see Sea Trucks Offshore Ltd v. Roomans, Jacobus Johannes*, [2019] 3 SLR 836, [55]; *Sumifru Singapore Pte Ltd v. Felix Santos Ishizuka*, [2020] SGHC 7, [19]–[22].

1848. *Bahtera Offshore (M) Sdn Bhd v. Sim Kok Beng*, [2009] 4 SLR(R) 365, [13]; *Liberty Sky Investments Ltd v. Goh Seng Heng*, [2017] SGHC 182, [8]. Even if a good arguable case can be established, the presence of a collateral or ulterior purpose in seeking relief can militate against the grant of the injunction: *JTrust Asia Pte Ltd v. Group Lease Holdings Pte Ltd*, [2018] SGCA 27, [102]. Whether aiding of foreign proceedings is a factor, *see Bi Xiaoqing v. China Medical Technologies, Inc*, [2019] 2 SLR 595.

517. With respect to the first requirement, jurisdiction is typically asserted over the defendant via service of the originating process on the defendant.[1849] As regards arbitration proceedings, the Court of Appeal has held that the Singapore court has the power to grant a Mareva injunctions to assist arbitration proceedings in Singapore, provided the Singapore court has the jurisdiction to hear the substantial dispute.[1850] However, the court does not have the power or jurisdiction to grant a Mareva injunction against the assets of a defendant in Singapore on the basis of the existence of the assets alone if the plaintiff does not have an accrued cause of action (against that defendant) that is justiciable in a Singapore court;[1851] thus, if adjudication (including arbitration) of the main dispute is to take place in another jurisdiction, the injunction would not be awarded.[1852] The court also does not have the power or jurisdiction to grant a Mareva injunction for anticipated claims.[1853]

518. Nonetheless, the court does have residual jurisdiction to grant or allow the continuation of a Mareva injunction even if there is a stay of local proceedings in favour of a foreign jurisdiction. But this is only if: the plaintiff demonstrates that a reasonable accrued cause of action is recognisable or justiciable in a Singapore court; the court has ordinary domestic or in personam jurisdiction over the Singapore defendant duly served in Singapore with the writ; there are assets within Singapore that can be subject to a Mareva injunction; and substantive proceedings have been brought in Singapore against the defendant(s), although these proceedings have been stayed either as a result of an arbitration clause or forum non conveniens.[1854] If the defendant is restrained from disposing assets that belong to a company, the court has jurisdiction to join the company as another defendant and to grant a Mareva injunction against it even if there is no cause of action against the company.[1855]

519. With respect to the second requirement, a good arguable case is one which is more than barely capable of serious argument, but not necessarily one which the judge would consider to have more than 50% chance of success.[1856] This test is thus different from the one used for prohibitory injunctions, which requires 'a serious question to be tried'.

1849. *The Siskina,* [1979] AC 210.
1850. *Swift-Fortune Ltd v. Magnifica Marine SA*, [2007] 1 SLR(R) 629.
1851. *Karaha Bodas Co LLC v. Pertamina Energy Trading Ltd*, [2006] 1 SLR(R) 112, [35]–[44].
1852. *Petroval SA v. Stainby Overseas Ltd*, [2008] 3 SLR(R) 856, [13]. *See also The Siskina*, [1979] AC 210, 363; *Wu Yang Construction Group Ltd v. Mao Yong Hui*, [2008] 2 SLR 350, [28].
1853. *Veracruz Transportation Inc. v. V. C. Shipping Co Inc*, [1992] 1 Lloyd's Rep 353.
1854. *Multi-Code Electronics Industries (M) Bhd v. Toh Chun Toh Gordon*, [2009] 1 SLR(R) 1000, [116]; *Front Carriers Ltd v. Atlantic & Orient Shipping Corp*, [2006] 3 SLR(R) 854, [52]–[53]. C.f. *Petroval SA v. Stainby Overseas Ltd*, [2008] 3 SLR(R) 856, [13]–[18].
1855. *Singapore Civil Procedure 2015 Volume 1*, at 638 (G.P. Selvam ed., Sweet & Maxwell Asia 2014).
1856. *Amixco Asia Pte Ltd v. Bank Negara Indonesia 1946*, [1991] 2 SLR(R) 713, [16], citing *Ninemia Maritime Corporation v. Trave Schiffahrtsgesellschaft mbH und Co KG*, [1983] 1 WLR 1412, 1471.

520. With respect to the third requirement, if the value of the assets sought to be attached is minimal relative to the claim or if the value of the claim is small, an injunction may not be granted.[1857] In addition, the plaintiff must provide a specific evidential basis for the existence of the assets, and while the court has the power to grant relief in respect of a broad range of assets, the coverage should not be unduly general or wide.[1858] It is therefore important for the plaintiff to identify the specific assets and explain why he thinks those assets are within jurisdiction. A Mareva injunction must be distinguished from an injunction to preserve assets which belong to the plaintiff in equity, where such assets would not be subject to a Mareva injunction.[1859] If there is a dispute as to ownership of assets that are subject to a Mareva injunction, the following factors should be taken into consideration: third-party assets should not be included, though the defendant cannot merely assert third-party ownership; the court should do what is just and convenient between all concerned; where appropriate the court may direct an issue to be tried either before or after the main action as to the question of ownership.[1860]

521. With respect to the fourth requirement, the plaintiff must furnish some grounds for his belief in the real risk of dissipation, since a mere possibility or unsupported fear is insufficient:[1861]

> It is not enough for the plaintiff to assert a risk that the assets will be dissipated. He must demonstrate this by solid evidence. This evidence may take a number of different forms. It may consist of direct evidence that the defendant has previously acted in a way which shows that his probity is not to be relied on. Or the plaintiff may show what type of company the defendant is (where it is incorporated, what are its corporate structure and assets, and so on) so as to raise an inference that the company is not to be relied on. Or, again, the

---

1857. *Sions v. Price*, The Independent (19 Dec. 1988). It should be noted that the maximum value to be subject to a Mareva injunction should be level with the plaintiff's *prima facie* claim; further, if the defendant's assets are insufficient to cover the plaintiff's claim, the order may extend to assets acquired in the future by the defendant.

1858. *Teo Siew Har v. Lee Kuan Yew*, [1999] 3 SLR(R) 410, [40].

1859. *Parakou Shipping Pte Ltd (in liquidation) v. Liu Cheng Chan*, [2015] SGHC 96, [8].

1860. *Singapore Civil Procedure 2015 Volume 1*, at 640 (G.P. Selvam ed., Sweet & Maxwell Asia 2014) citing *SCF Finance Co Ltd v. Masri*, [1985] 2 All ER 747, 753.

1861. *Art Trend Ltd v. Blue Dolphin Ltd*, [1981–1982] SLR(R) 633, [30]; *O'Regan v. Iambic Productions Ltd*, (1989) 139 NLJ 1378, 1379. *See also Bouvier, Yves Charles Edgar v. Accent Delight International Ltd*, [2015] 5 SLR 558, [93]–[94]: 'if there is a unifying principle that can adequately rationalise and explain the circumstances in which a court may legitimately infer a real risk of dissipation from nothing more than a good arguable case of dishonesty, it is this – the alleged dishonesty must be of such a nature that it has a real and material bearing on the risk of dissipation … a well-substantiated allegation that a defendant has acted dishonestly can … be relevant to whether there is a real risk that the defendant may dissipate his assets. But … it is incumbent on the court to examine the precise nature of the dishonesty that is alleged and the strength of the evidence relied on in support of the allegation, keeping fully in mind that the proceedings are only at an interlocutory stage and assessing, in that light, whether there is sufficient basis to find a real risk of dissipation. That alone is the justification which lies at the heart of the court's jurisdiction to grant Mareva injunctions. An allegation of dishonesty does not in itself form a substitute for an examination of the degree of risk of dissipation unless … that allegation is of a nature or characteristic that sufficiently bears upon the risk of dissipation.'

plaintiff may be able to found his case on the fact that inquiries about the characteristics of the defendant have led to a blank wall. Precisely what form the evidence may take will depend on the particular circumstances of the case. But the evidence must always be there.[1862]

522. In this regard, evidence of dishonesty on the part of the defendant is relevant in that if there is a good arguable case that the defendant has acted dishonestly or unconscionably, this per se may suffice to justify a Mareva injunction.[1863] However, while there must be some evidence for risk of dissipation, it is not necessary to show that the defendant has the intention to dissipate assets.[1864] Another possible factor for the court's consideration in this regard is the nature of the assets that are sought to be injuncted, in that the easier it is to liquidate, realize, transfer, or move the assets, the higher its risk of dissipation.[1865]

523. Once a Mareva injunction has been granted, the court will likely order the defendant to disclose his assets. Where necessary, orders to give discovery and answer interrogatories may also be made. The party against whom a Mareva injunction operates must obey both the letter and the spirit of the terms of the injunction.[1866] For instance, where a party's disclosed assets are insufficient to secure the claim, and the Mareva injunction is not limited to the disclosed assets, the injunction extends to assets acquired subsequent to the date of the injunction to the extent necessary to meet the claim.[1867] A Court of Appeal decision has thus described the consequence of a party obstructing the operation of a Mareva injunction in the following terms:[1868]

1862. *The Niedersachsen; Ninemia Maritime Corp v. Trave Schiffahrtsgesellschaft mbH & Co KG*, [1984] 1 All ER 398, 406; cited in *Choy Chee Keen Collin v. Public Utilities Board*, [1996] 3 SLR(R) 812, [20]–[21]; *Petromar Energy Resources Pte Ltd v. Glencore International AG*, [1999] 1 SLR(R) 1152, [6]. *See also Guan Chong Cocoa Manufacturer Sdn Bhd v. Pratiwi Shipping SA*, [2003] 1 SLR(R) 157, [19].

1863. *Spectramed Pte Ltd v. Lek Puay Puay*, [2010] SGHC 112, [18]. C.f. *PT Sariwiguna Binasentosa v. Sindo Damai Shipping Ltd*, [2015] 5 SLR 45, [8]–[13]. There, the court also held that a court would be more ready to draw an inference that there was a real risk from evidence of dishonesty in cases where a defendant was well-versed in intricate, sophisticated and international financial transactions and had been shown to use his expertise for dishonest purposes, as opposed to cases where the defendant lied in the course of his business dealings with the plaintiff.

1864. *Solvadis Commodity Chemicals GmbH v. Affert Resources Pte Ltd*, [2014] 1 SLR 174, [16].

1865. *Spectramed Pte Ltd v. Lek Puay Puay*, [2010] SGHC 112, [18].

1866. *Lee Shieh-Peen Clement v. Ho Chin Nguang*, [2010] 4 SLR 801, [15]. *See also Sun Electric Pte Ltd v. Menrva Solutions Pte Ltd*, [2020] SGHC 18, [65]–[73].

1867. C. Bull & J. Pinsler, *Civil Procedure: Annual Review of Singapore Cases* [8.61] (Sing. Acad. L. 2010). *See also Sea Trucks Offshore Ltd v. Roomans, Jacobus Johannes*, [2018] SGHC 248, [46]: 'Even in a situation where the defendant has disclosed assets sufficient to meet the sums restrained by the Mareva injunction, there is still utility in requiring the defendant to disclose information pertaining to the defendant's other assets.'

1868. *Pertamina Energy Trading Ltd v. Karaha Bodas Co LLC*, [2007] 2 SLR(R) 518, [97] (emphasis in original).

> The Mareva injunction is an important remedy, whose terms cannot – and ought not to – be thwarted … such conduct would … also herald the commencement of possible legal anarchy across jurisdictions. Respect for court orders in any and every jurisdiction is a given. Any contravention of such orders cannot be excused on the ground that it was effected in aid of possibly legitimate legal proceedings elsewhere. Indeed, such contravention could not, in our view, be excused even on the ground that it was effected in clearly legitimate legal proceedings elsewhere. How the courts in other jurisdictions decide on legal proceedings as well as issues brought before them is wholly within their purview. What is within this court's purview, however, is the need to ensure that its orders are not contravened or thwarted. We cannot overemphasise the importance of this fundamental proposition, and trust that nothing akin to the conduct in the present proceedings will ever come before this court again. If, in the unfortunate event it does, more stringent sanctions will be meted out accordingly.

524. On the other hand, if a Mareva injunction is awarded and the claim is not prosecuted any further, the plaintiff may be found to have abused the process of the court, even if he applies to have the injunction discharged later on.[1869] Indeed, a frivolous application for a Mareva injunction itself may be an abuse of the process of the court.[1870]

525. The principles stated above pertain to domestic Mareva injunctions – it is also possible to apply for worldwide Mareva injunctions, but there are some additional conditions to fulfil. First, the plaintiff will have to show that there are either no or insufficient assets within jurisdiction to satisfy the claim. Second, the plaintiff will have to show that there are assets outside the jurisdiction. Third, because a worldwide Mareva is an assertion of extraterritorial jurisdiction, any order made has to consider if it will offend principles of international comity.[1871] Fourth, the plaintiff should ordinarily undertake to the court that it shall not, without the court's leave, enforce the injunction or seek an order of a similar nature in any jurisdiction

1869. *Singapore Civil Procedure 2015 Volume 1*, at 638 (G.P. Selvam ed., Sweet & Maxwell Asia 2014). For post-judgments Mareva injunctions (and disclosure orders), *see Sun Electric Pte Ltd v. Menrva Solutions Pte Ltd*, [2020] SGHC 18, [75]–[81].

1870. In *Bouvier, Yves Charles Edgar v. Accent Delight International Ltd*, [2015] 5 SLR 558, [108]–[134], the court pointed to four facts in holding there was an abuse of process: the applicant had provided no good reason for the delay in seeking the application; the applicant had failed to comply with the practice directions in giving notice; the multiple injunctions were unjustifiably wide in their scope; and information was disseminated in a misleading manner.

1871. On the other hand, the propriety of a worldwide Mareva may be justified on the basis that it only operates in personam against the defendant. At any rate, it is common for provisos to be built into the order, such as the non-binding nature of the order on foreign parties until it is declared enforceable by the foreign court in question. *See also PT Gunung Madu Plantations v. Muhammad Jimmy Goh Mashun*, [2018] SGHC 64; *China Medical Technologies, Inc (in liquidation) v. Wu Xiaodong*, [2018] SGHC 178; *The Micro Tellers Network Ltd v. Cheng Yi Han*, [2020] SGHC 130.

outside Singapore; this undertaking is important because it protects a defendant from the risk of oppression which may arise from a multiplicity of suits.[1872]

§6. Anton Piller Order

526. A search order or Anton Piller order – named after the English case *Anton Piller KG v. Manufacturing Processes Ltd*[1873] – authorizes[1874] the applicant to enter the respondent's premises to inspect, seize, and remove into safe custody any documents relating to the dispute that may be destroyed by the respondent to avoid liability or paying on a finding of liability.[1875] Like a Mareva injunction, an Anton Piller order is a form of collateral relief sought to protect the applicant's potential rights. Also like a Mareva injunction, the applicant is usually required to give a number of undertakings to safeguard the respondent's rights, such as those relating to damages (if the application turns out to be unjustified), informing the respondent of the contents of the order and his rights, and the prescribed times in which the order will be executed. Four questions must be answered in determining whether an Anton Piller order would be granted:[1876] first, whether the plaintiff has shown an extremely strong prima facie case; second, whether the damage suffered by the plaintiff would be very serious; third, whether there is a real possibility that the defendants would destroy relevant documents; and fourth, whether the effect of the order would be disproportionate to the legitimate object of the order.

527. With respect to the first question, notably, the standard required is higher than the 'good arguable case' test for Mareva injunctions; indeed, cases have suggested that an Anton Piller order should only be granted when it is 'essential' to do so.[1877] This is because a search order 'involves a serious interference with the defendant's privacy' and 'in the case of business premises, the seizure of records and stock may effectively put an end to the defendant's livelihood'.[1878] With respect to the second question, it has been suggested that 'damage' can refer to either actual or potential damage, but ultimately, the seriousness of the damage would depend on the impact of the infringement on the respondent's personal situation or business.[1879] With respect to the third question, as is the case with Mareva injunctions,

1872. *Bouvier, Yves Charles Edgar v. Accent Delight International Ltd*, [2015] 5 SLR 558, [131]. *See also TYV Investment Group Pte Ltd v. ERC Holdings Pte Ltd*, [2020] SGHC 157.

1873. [1976] 1 All ER 779.

1874. *See* J. Pinsler, *Principles of Civil Procedure* 490 (Acad. Publg. 2013).

1875. *Singapore Civil Procedure 2015 Volume 1*, at 623 (G.P. Selvam ed., Sweet & Maxwell Asia 2014). C.f. Supreme Court of Judicature Act (Cap. 322, R. 5, 2014 Rev. Ed.) Rules of Court, O 29 r 2(1).

1876. *Inphosoft Pte Ltd v. Ho Jin Kiat*, [2009] SGHC 152, [6], citing *Asian Corporate Services (SEA) Pte Ltd v. Eastwest Management Ltd (Singapore Branch)*, [2006] 1 SLR(R) 901, [14]. *See also BP Singapore Pte Ltd v. Quek Chin Thean* [2011] 2 SLR541 at [21]; *Peh Yeng Yok v. Tembusus Systems Pte Ltd (formerly known as Tembusu Terminals Pte Ltd)*, [2016] 2 SLR 781, [14]–[15]; *Werner Samuel Vuillemin v. Overseas-Chinese Banking Corp Ltd* [2018] SGHC 92 at [71].

1877. *Computerland Corp v. Yew Seng Computers Pte Ltd*, [1991] 2 SLR(R) 379, [6], citing *Yousif v. Salama*, [1980] 1 WLR 1540.

1878. J. Pinsler, *Principles of Civil Procedure* 493 (Acad. Publg. 2013).

1879. J. Pinsler, *Principles of Civil Procedure* 492–493 (Acad. Publg. 2013).

'there must be "solid evidence" of a risk that the defendant might destroy or conceal evidence relevant to the case'.[1880] The evidence may be direct or circumstantial, as long as it is generally internally consistent and persuasive enough.[1881] However, 'where the alleged infringer is operating his business openly, and there is nothing to indicate that it is being conducted in a surreptitious or underhanded manner, the court is not likely to accept the argument (without more) that there is an imminent danger that the evidence will be compromised'.[1882] Indeed, a 'real possibility' must be distinguished from 'extravagant fears which seem to afflict all plaintiffs who have complaints of breach of confidence, breach of copyright or passing-off'.[1883] With respect to the fourth question, the viability of alternative measures such as a prohibitive injunction or simpler court order for documents to be handed over, as well as the scope of the terms of the search order must be considered.[1884] At bottom, the court will have to balance the plaintiff's need for the order against the risk of injustice to the respondent in making the order ex parte, inasmuch as *audi alteram partem* is a rule of natural justice.[1885] Accordingly, there must be 'a paramount need to prevent of denial of justice to the plaintiff'.[1886] In very rare cases, the court may also consider any threat to the safety of the defendant and his family.[1887] For instance, there was a case of overzealous executors of a search order who led themselves to believe that they were investigation officers with broader powers to ask harsh questions and make threats of criminal proceedings.[1888]

528. Those rare instances aside, if a defendant refuses to comply with a search order, he may be subject to committal proceedings.[1889] However, there are various procedural requirements that should be complied with in the execution of the search

1880. *Petromar Energy Resources Pte Ltd v. Glencore International AG*, [1999] 1 SLR(R) 1152, [6]. *See also National Scientific (S) Pte Ltd v. Ho Wai Ming*, [2002] 1 SLR(R) 660, [5], which uses the language of 'high likelihood'; *Werner Samuel Vuillemin v. Overseas-Chinese Banking Corp Ltd*, [2018] SGHC 92.
1881. *Nikkomann Co Pte Ltd v. Yulean Trading Pte Ltd*, [1992] 2 SLR(R) 328, [69]; *Asian Corporate Services (SEA) Pte Ltd v. Eastwest Management Ltd (Singapore Branch)*, [2006] 1 SLR(R) 901, [14] and [27]; C. Bull & J. Pinsler, *Civil Procedure: Annual Review of Singapore Cases* [6.74] (Sing. Acad. L. 2005).
1882. J. Pinsler, *Principles of Civil Procedure* 496 (Acad. Publg. 2013) citing *Bengawan Solo Pte Ltd v. Season Confectionary Co (Pte) Ltd*, [1994] 1 SLR(R) 448, [16]. *See also Lock International Plc v. Beswick*, [1989] 1 WLR 1268, 1281.
1883. *Booker McConnell v. Plascow plc*, [1985] RPC 425, 441.
1884. J. Pinsler, *Principles of Civil Procedure* 496 (Acad. Publg. 2013).
1885. *Asian Corporate Services (SEA) Pte Ltd v. Eastwest Management Ltd (Singapore Branch)*, [2006] 1 SLR(R) 901, [35]–[36]. *See also* C. Siyuan & L. Leo, *Natural Justice: A Case for Uniform Rigour*, 20 Sing. Acad. L.J. 820 (2009).
1886. J. Pinsler, *Principles of Civil Procedure* 498 (Acad. Publg. 2013) citing *Lock International plc v. Beswick*, [1989] 1 WLR 1268, 1279; *Computerland Corp v. Yew Seng Computers Pte Ltd*, [1991] 2 SLR(R) 379, [21]–[23].
1887. *Singapore Civil Procedure 2013 Volume 1*, at 580 (G.P. Selvam ed., Sweet & Maxwell Asia 2012) citing *Coca Cola Co v. Gilbey*, [1995] 4 All ER 471.
1888. *Fong Wai Lyn Carolyn v. Airtrust (Singapore) Pte Ltd*, [2011] 3 SLR 980, [96]–[97].
1889. *Singapore Civil Procedure 2013 Volume 1*, at 579 (G.P. Selvam ed., Sweet & Maxwell Asia 2012).

order. These are:[1890] the restrictions as to the times in which the order may be served, as well as the number of persons permitted to execute the order (both would have been set out in the order); not carrying out the order at the same time as a search warrant; the defendant being entitled to require the lawyer serving the order to explain the terms of the order; the defendant being entitled to require the lawyer serving the order to explain his rights (such as that against self-incrimination)[1891] and the evidence on which the order was made, so that he can decide if he wants to challenge the order immediately; the defendant being entitled to seek legal advice (but the lawyer is still permitted to enter the premises (without starting the search yet)); the provision to the defendant a list of items, and if copies are made, the prompt return of the originals.

529. It is possible that an Anton Piller Order is being executed at several places simultaneously and some of those addresses are vacant at the time. In such a situation, it should be 'made clear to the defendant that he is expected to make arrangements to enable the search to commence at each of those places immediately'.[1892] Failure to comply with these procedural requirements can be a ground for the defendant to challenge the order and may also amount to contempt of court. An Anton Piller order is not breached if the defendant provides an inaccurate answer, provided that 'the inaccurate answer is given in good faith, and if the inaccurate answer is given after investigating the matter in a way which is reasonable in all circumstances'.[1893]

§7. Interim Payment

530. As the name suggests, a plaintiff may be entitled to a payment of money before the trial. Per the Rules of Court, an interim payment, 'in relation to a defendant, means a payment on account of any damages, debt or other sum (excluding costs) which he may be held liable to pay to or for the benefit of the plaintiff'.[1894] The rationale for this interim is relief is that 'it may not be just to withhold the monetary remedy until the conclusion of the proceedings' as it 'has the potential to counter the effects of delay in the proceedings and may protect the plaintiff's position to a certain extent should the defendant attempt to dissipate or remove his assets in order to defeat a potential judgment'.[1895]

1890. *Singapore Civil Procedure 2015 Volume 1*, at 652 (G.P. Selvam ed., Sweet & Maxwell Asia 2014). *See also* Supreme Court Practice Directions 2013 (Part IV); *Maruti Shipping Pte Ltd v. Tay Sien Djim*, [2014] SGHC 227.
1891. *See Hung Ka Ho v. A-1 Office System Pte Ltd*, [1992] 1 SLR(R) 550, [10]–[11].
1892. *Maruti Shipping Pte Ltd v. Tay Sien Djim*, [2014] SGHC 227, [72].
1893. *Maruti Shipping Pte Ltd v. Tay Sien Djim*, [2014] SGHC 227, [101], citing *Bird v. Hadkinson*, [2000] CP Rep 21.
1894. Supreme Court of Judicature Act (Cap. 322, R. 5, 2014 Rev. Ed.) Rules of Court, O 29 r 9. *See also HRA Corp (SG) Pte Ltd v. Cheng Mun Yip Marcus*, [2018] SGHCR 7.
1895. J. Pinsler, *Principles of Civil Procedure* 428 (Acad. Publg. 2013).

531. An application for interim payment is made 'at any time after the writ has been served on a defendant and the time limited for him to enter appearance has expired'.[1896] The application is by summons, supported by an affidavit which: verifies the amount of the sum claimed; sets out the grounds of the application; and exhibits any documentary evidence in support of the application.[1897] The 'summons and the supporting affidavit or affidavits must be filed at the same time, and must be served on the defendant against whom the order is sought within three days from the date of filing'.[1898] If the interim payment is for damages, and the court is satisfied:

> that the defendant against whom the order is sought has admitted liability for the plaintiff's damages; … that the plaintiff has obtained judgment against the defendant for damages to be assessed; or … that, if the action proceeded to trial, the plaintiff would obtain judgment for substantial damages against the defendant or, where there are 2 or more defendants, against any one or more of them, the Court may, if it thinks fit … order the defendant to make an interim payment of such amount as it thinks just, not exceeding a reasonable proportion of the damages which in the opinion of the Court are likely to be recovered by the plaintiff after taking into account any relevant contributory negligence and any set-off, cross-claim or counterclaim on which the defendant may be entitled to rely.[1899]

532. The appropriate standard of proof here is the civil standard of balance of probabilities, rather than beyond a reasonable doubt.[1900] In addition, the phrase 'if it thinks fit' suggests an element of discretion; hence, the court will consider if it is just in the circumstances of the case to make the order, and factor in (inter alia) the stage of the proceedings and the parties' financial circumstances.[1901] In this connection, it should further be noted that an interim payment for damages shall not be made in an action for personal injuries if the defendant is insured in respect of the plaintiff's claim or a defendant does not have the means and resources to make an interim payment.[1902] If the interim payment is for sums other than damages (such as for a debt), and the court is satisfied:

> that the plaintiff has obtained an order for an account to be taken as between himself and the defendant and for any amount certified due on taking the account to be paid; … that the plaintiff's action includes a claim for possession of land and, if the action proceeded to trial, the defendant would be held liable to pay to the plaintiff a sum of money in respect of the defendant's use

1896. Supreme Court of Judicature Act (Cap. 322, R. 5, 2014 Rev. Ed.) Rules of Court, O 29 r 10(1).
1897. Supreme Court of Judicature Act (Cap. 322, R. 5, 2014 Rev. Ed.) Rules of Court, O 29 rr 10(2) and 10(3).
1898. Supreme Court of Judicature Act (Cap. 322, R. 5, 2014 Rev. Ed.) Rules of Court, O 29 r 10(4).
1899. Supreme Court of Judicature Act (Cap. 322, R. 5, 2014 Rev. Ed.) Rules of Court, O 29 r 11(1).
1900. *Singapore Civil Procedure 2015 Volume 1*, at 658 (G.P. Selvam ed., Sweet & Maxwell Asia 2014) citing *Shearson Lehman Bros Inc v. Maclaine Watson & Co Ltd*, [1987] 1 WLR 480, 489.
1901. J. Pinsler, *Principles of Civil Procedure* 430 (Acad. Publg. 2013).
1902. Supreme Court of Judicature Act (Cap. 322, R. 5, 2014 Rev. Ed.) Rules of Court, O 29 r 11(2).

> and occupation of the land during the pendency of the action, even if a final judgment or order were given or made in favour of the defendant; or … that, if the action proceeded to trial, the plaintiff would obtain judgment against the defendant for a substantial sum of money apart from any damages or costs, the Court may, if it thinks fit, and without prejudice to any contentions of the parties as to the nature or character of the sum to be paid by the defendant, order the defendant to make an interim payment of such amount as it thinks just, after taking into account any set-off, cross-claim or counterclaim on which the defendant may be entitled to rely.[1903]

533. Any interim payment ordered to be made: 'shall be paid to the plaintiff unless the order provides for it to be paid into Court, and where the amount is paid into Court, the Court may, on the application of the plaintiff, order the whole or any part of it to be paid out to him at such time or times as the Court thinks fit'[1904] and may also be ordered 'to be made in one sum or by such instalments as the Court thinks fit'.[1905] Finally, the fact that an interim payment has been ordered:

> shall not be pleaded and, unless the defendant consents or the Court so directs, no communication of that fact or of the fact that an interim payment has been made, whether voluntarily or pursuant to an order, shall be made to the Court at the trial, or hearing, of any question or issue as to liability or damages until all questions of liability and amount have been determined.[1906]

§8. Possibility of Appeal

534. Section 34 of the Supreme Court of Judicature Act,[1907] read together with the Fourth and Fifth Schedules of the statute, determines whether any given order of civil procedure is appealable to the Court of Appeal[1908] or not.[1909] However, both the Fourth (orders made by a judge that are non-appealable) and Fifth Schedules (orders made by a judge that are appealable only with leave) are silent on injunctions – be it prohibitory, mandatory, anti-suit, Mareva, or Anton Piller (both Schedules are silent on interim payments as well). Accordingly, pursuant to section

---

1903. Supreme Court of Judicature Act (Cap. 322, R. 5, 2014 Rev. Ed.) Rules of Court, O 29 r 12.
1904. Supreme Court of Judicature Act (Cap. 322, R. 5, 2014 Rev. Ed.) Rules of Court, O 29 r 13(1).
1905. Supreme Court of Judicature Act (Cap. 322, R. 5, 2014 Rev. Ed.) Rules of Court, O 29 r 13(3). *See also id.*, O 29 r 17, which allows the court to make adjustments (repayment, variation, discharge, and contribution) if the action is discontinued; *Main-Line Corporate Holdings Ltd v. United Overseas Bank Ltd*, [2010] 2 SLR 986, which states that the mere fact that the sums of money in issue cannot be precisely ascertained should not be a reason for depriving a party of an interim payment against the interests of justice.
1906. Supreme Court of Judicature Act (Cap. 322, R. 5, 2014 Rev. Ed.) Rules of Court, O 29 r 15.
1907. (Cap. 322, 2007 Rev. Ed.).
1908. Below it is the High Court, followed by the District and Magistrates' Courts. For appeals arising from the lower courts, *see* Supreme Court of Judicature Act (Cap. 322, R. 5, 2014 Rev. Ed.) Rules of Court, O 55B, 55C, and 55D. There is a right of appeal from a registrar in chambers to a judge in chambers (District Judge if it is the State Courts), but not necessarily after that stage.
1909. The statute was amended in 2010 and 2014.

29A(1) of the Supreme Court of Judicature Act, it would seem that an appeal against any decision relating to injunctions and interim payments (including attempts to set them aside) may be brought as of right to the Court of Appeal, since the Fourth Schedule does not declare it to be non-appealable and the Fifth Schedule does not require leave to be sought.

535. Due to recent amendments to the Supreme Court of Judicature Act, the law on this is currently in flux and while it has been suggested that the 'default' position is that all interlocutory applications, unless provided for statutorily, are appealable with leave,[1910] it may also be possible to argue that for interlocutory applications not expressly addressed by the Fourth and Fifth Schedules, 'an appeal to the Court of Appeal will remain as of right for orders made at interlocutory applications which will finally dispose of the substantive rights of the parties'.[1911] It is suggested that applications for interim injunctions and interim payments should not be considered 'interlocutory' in nature as the very relief sought formed the entire and sole purpose of the application and 'once the application for such relief has been considered and ruled upon by the court, that matter ends'.[1912] If this argument is accepted, then the provisions of section 34, including the Fourth and Fifth Schedules do not apply to limit the right of appeal for applications for interim injunctions and interim payments, and an appeal may accordingly be brought to the Court of Appeal. However, it should be noted that it is also possible for the court to regard such applications as 'interlocutory' in nature because they are brought by way of summons and are made and heard 'between the time a party files a civil case in court and when that case is finally heard for disposal'.[1913] If so, then an application for leave to appeal would be required before an appeal may be brought to the Court of Appeal. Nevertheless, assuming that an appeal in respect of an order refusing or granting an interim injunction or interim payment is before the Court of Appeal, it should be noted that the:

> Court of Appeal will generally be slow to interfere with the decision of a judge on an application for an interlocutory injunction [and, it is suggested, an application for an interim payment], in view of the wide discretion given to the judge … It defers to the judge's exercise of his discretion. It may set aside the

1910. *See* E. Chua, *Defining an 'Interlocutory Application*, Sing. L. Watch Commentaries (4/2013); D. Chi, *Clarification on Leave to Appeal Regime in Respect of Interlocutory Matters: OpenNet Pte Ltd v. Info-Communications Development Authority of Singapore*, [2013] 2 SLR 880, Sing. L. Watch Commentaries (4/2013); C. Siyuan & E. Chua, *The Right to Appeal Against a Decision Made on an Interlocutory Application: The Immediate Aftermath of the 2010 Amendments*, 25 Sing. Acad. L.J. 424 (2013).

1911. *OpenNet Pte Ltd v. Info-Communications Development Authority of Singapore*, [2013] 2 SLR 8802 SLR 880, [29]. *See also Dorsey James Michael v. World Sport Group Pte Ltd*, [2013] 3 SLR 354, [98]. On the other hand, where the statute has made it clear that there is no appeal as of right, one is precluded from arguing that substantive rights have been engaged: *Kosui Singapore Pte Ltd v. Thangavelu*, [2016] 2 SLR 105, [28]–[29].

1912. *Dorsey James Michael v. World Sport Group Pte Ltd*, [2013] 3 SLR 354, [60].

1913. *Dorsey James Michael v. World Sport Group Pte Ltd*, [2013] 3 SLR 354, [60] (emphasis in original).

judge's exercise of his discretion on the ground that it was based upon a misunderstanding of the law or of the evidence before him or upon an inference that particular facts existed or did not exist … or upon the ground that there has been a change of circumstances.[1914]

1914. *Singapore Civil Procedure 2015 Volume 1*, at 635 (G.P. Selvam ed., Sweet & Maxwell Asia 2014).

Chapter 2. Withdrawal and Discontinuance

§1. Introduction

536. A full trial may be obviated if a party to the litigation wishes to discontinue or withdraw from the proceedings. This may take several forms, such as the discontinuance of the entire action, or the withdrawal of a claim, summons, appearance, or defence.[1915] In certain circumstances, discontinuance may be presumed. Exceptionally, it may be possible for discontinued proceedings to be reinstated upon application.[1916] The rules and procedures for withdrawal and discontinuance are primarily found in O 21 of the Rules of Court,[1917] part of which has been shaped by English law.[1918]

§2. Procedural Aspects

537. O 21 r 1 of the Rules of Court states that a party 'who has entered an appearance in an action may withdraw the appearance at any time with the leave of the Court'. This application for leave is made by ex parte summons.[1919] O 21 r 2 addresses discontinuance of action without leave: a plaintiff in an action begun by writ may, without leave of the court, discontinue the action or withdraw any claim made as against all or any of the defendants at any time no later than fourteen days after service of the last defence on him by serving a notice in the prescribed form;[1920] while a defendant may, without leave of the court, withdraw his defence (or any part of it) at any time or discontinue a counterclaim against any of the parties at any time no later than fourteen days after service on him of a defence to counterclaim by serving a notice in the prescribed form.[1921] However, if 'all the parties to an action consent, the action may be withdrawn without the leave of the Court at any time before trial by producing … a written consent to the action being withdrawn signed by all the parties'.[1922] O 21 r 2 also addresses deemed discontinuance. Specifically, an action begun by writ is:

> deemed to be discontinued against a defendant if the memorandum of service … is not filed in respect of the service of the writ on the defendant within 12 months after the validity of the writ for the purpose of service has expired, and,

1915. J. Pinsler, *Principles of Civil Procedure* 368 (Acad. Publg. 2013). Withdrawal and discontinuance should be differentiated from a situation where a lawyer discharges himself from the case.
1916. *See also Moguntia-Est Epices SA v. Sea-Hawk Freight Pte Ltd*, [2003] 4 SLR(R) 429, [21].
1917. Supreme Court of Judicature Act (Cap. 322, R. 5, 2014 Rev. Ed.) Rules of Court.
1918. J. Pinsler, *Principles of Civil Procedure* 374–375 (Acad. Publg. 2013).
1919. *Singapore Civil Procedure 2015 Volume 1*, at 432 (G.P. Selvam ed., Sweet & Maxwell Asia 2014). *See also* Supreme Court of Judicature Act (Cap. 322, R. 5, 2014 Rev. Ed.) Rules of Court, O 2 rr 1(1)–(3).
1920. Supreme Court of Judicature Act (Cap. 322, R. 5, 2014 Rev. Ed.) Rules of Court, O 21 r 2(1).
1921. Supreme Court of Judicature Act (Cap. 322, R. 5, 2014 Rev. Ed.) Rules of Court, O 21 r 2(2). *See also* J. Pinsler, *Principles of Civil Procedure* 380 (Acad. Publg. 2013).
1922. Supreme Court of Judicature Act (Cap. 322, R. 5, 2014 Rev. Ed.) Rules of Court, O 21 r 2(4).

> within that time … a memorandum of appearance has not been filed in the action by that defendant; and … judgment has not been obtained in the action against that defendant in respect of the whole or any part of the relief claimed.[1923]

538. In addition, 'if no party to an action or a cause of matter has, for more than one year … taken any step or proceeding in the action, cause or matter that appears from records maintained by the Court, the action, cause or matter is deemed to have been discontinued'.[1924] However, this does not apply if 'the action, cause or matter has been stayed pursuant to an order of court'.[1925] It should also be noted that where 'an action, a cause or a matter has been discontinued under [O 21 rr 2(5) and 2(6)], the Court may, on application, reinstate the action, cause or matter, and allow it to proceed on such terms as it thinks just'.[1926]

539. O 21 r 3 addresses discontinuance of action with leave:

> a party may not discontinue an action (whether begun by writ or otherwise) or counterclaim, or withdraw any particular claim made by him therein, without the leave of the Court and the Court hearing an application for the grant of such leave may order the action or counterclaim to be discontinued, or any particular claim made therein to be struck out, as against all or any of the parties against whom it is brought or made on such terms as to costs, the bringing of a subsequent action or otherwise as it thinks just.

540. This application for leave may be made by summons.[1927] Finally, O 21 r 6 provides (similar to O 21 r 1) that a 'party who has taken out a summons in a cause or matter may not withdraw it without the leave of the Court'.

1923. Supreme Court of Judicature Act (Cap. 322, R. 5, 2014 Rev. Ed.) Rules of Court, O 21 r 2(5).
1924. Supreme Court of Judicature Act (Cap. 322, R. 5, 2014 Rev. Ed.) Rules of Court, O 21 r 2(6). Sub-rule 2(6B) further states that 'The Court may, on an application by any party made before the one year … has elapsed, extend the time to such extent as it may think fit.' In this regard, the court would consider why no step was taken for so long; the conduct of the parties; and whether the plaintiff has an arguable case to go trial: J. Pinsler, *Principles of Civil Procedure* 371 (Acad. Publg. 2013). It should further be noted that even if an interlocutory judgment has been entered, further steps are required before the action can be completed; accordingly, O 21 r 2(6) applies even after interlocutory judgment is entered: *Tan Kim Seng v. Ibrahim Victor Adam*, [2004] 1 SLR(R) 181, [15] and [26]. For an elaboration of what constitutes a 'step' and what does not, *see Singapore Civil Procedure 2015 Volume 1*, at 436 (G.P. Selvam ed., Sweet & Maxwell Asia 2014); J. Pinsler, *Principles of Civil Procedure* 371–373 (Acad. Publg. 2013). *See also Chua Peng Ho v. Saravanan a/l Subramaniam (dependent of the estate of Lingaswari a/p Koushanan (deceased)) and others*, [2017] SGCA 35; *Jagbir Singh s/o Baldhiraj Singh v. Lim Keh Thye*, [2009] 4 SLR(R) 305, [16]–[25]. C.f. *Chellaiya Chandra v. Cheng Song Thiam*, (Suit No 600011 of 2001); *James Lee Chong Hwa v. Phang Yen Hoong*, (Magistrate's Court Suit No 3456 of 2002).
1925. Supreme Court of Judicature Act (Cap. 322, R. 5, 2014 Rev. Ed.) Rules of Court, O 21 r 2(6A).
1926. Supreme Court of Judicature Act (Cap. 322, R. 5, 2014 Rev. Ed.) Rules of Court, O 21 r 2(8).
1927. Supreme Court of Judicature Act (Cap. 322, R. 5, 2014 Rev. Ed.) Rules of Court, O 21 r 3(2).

§3. SUBSTANTIVE ASPECTS

541. Generally, 'the fact that a party has discontinued or is deemed to have discontinued an action or counterclaim or withdrawn a particular claim made by him therein shall not be a defence to a subsequent action for the same, or substantially the same, cause of action'.[1928] However, this is assuming that the limitation period has not expired.[1929] Where a party has an action that is discontinued or that is deemed to be discontinued or any claim that is withdrawn and 'he is liable to pay any other party's costs of the action or counterclaim or the costs occasioned to any other party by the claim withdrawn, then, if before payment of those costs, he subsequently brings an action for the same, or substantially the same, cause of action, the Court may order the proceedings in that action to be stayed until those costs are paid'.[1930] An application for an order under this is made by summons or by notice.[1931]

542. For withdrawal of appearance, the court will examine the circumstances of the case and 'weigh the balance between the faults of the parties and the prejudice which will or may be occasioned to each of them' before deciding whether to exercise its discretion to grant a party leave to withdraw.[1932] Leave has been granted in instances such as where a lawyer had entered an appearance without authority and where some mistake had been made such that it was only just to allow the appearance to be withdrawn.[1933] Leave has been denied in instances such as where there had been unreasonable delay by the defendant in making the application but yet in the same period or so he had made several other interlocutory applications.[1934]

543. For discontinuance of action without leave:

> although the plaintiff has the unqualified right under r 2(1) to discontinue his action without the leave of the court … the court may intervene and set aside a purported discontinuance or withdrawal if it amounts to an abuse of process

1928. Supreme Court of Judicature Act (Cap. 322, R. 5, 2014 Rev. Ed.) Rules of Court, O 21 r 4. *See also* Lim H.M., *Automatic Discontinuance under Order 21 Rule 2 – First Dormant, Then Dead …*, 13 Sing. Acad. L.J. 150, 185 (2001).
1929. *Singapore Civil Procedure 2015 Volume 1*, at 441 (G.P. Selvam ed., Sweet & Maxwell Asia 2014). *See also* J. Pinsler, *Principles of Civil Procedure* 376 (Acad. Publg. 2013).
1930. Supreme Court of Judicature Act (Cap. 322, R. 5, 2014 Rev. Ed.) Rules of Court, O 21 r 5(1). *See also* J. Pinsler, *Principles of Civil Procedure* 385–387 (Acad. Publg. 2013).
1931. Supreme Court of Judicature Act (Cap. 322, R. 5, 2014 Rev. Ed.) Rules of Court, O 21 r 5(2).
1932. *Singapore Civil Procedure 2015 Volume 1*, at 432 (G.P. Selvam ed., Sweet & Maxwell Asia 2014). *See also* J. Pinsler, *Principles of Civil Procedure* 370 (Acad. Publg. 2013).
1933. *Singapore Civil Procedure 2015 Volume 1*, at 432 (G.P. Selvam ed., Sweet & Maxwell Asia 2014) citing *Somportex Ltd v. Philadelphia Chewing Gum Corp*, [1968] 3 All ER 26; *Firth v. John Mowlem & Co Ltd*, [1978] 3 All ER 331.
1934. *Singapore Civil Procedure 2015 Volume 1*, at 433 (G.P. Selvam ed., Sweet & Maxwell Asia 2014) citing *EG Tan & Co (Pte) (in liquidation) v. Tan Chong San* [1993] 1 MLJ 256.

> ... For instance, if the plaintiff abuses such right by serving a notice of discontinuance after obtaining substantial advantages in the action to the prejudice of the defendant ... by securing substantial interim payments and an admission of liability or otherwise.[1935]

544. For discontinuance of action with leave, 'the general principle is that the court will not compel a plaintiff to continue his action against the defendant ... if he does not wish to do so, provided that no injustice is caused to the other party'.[1936] In addition, the court 'will be cautious in protecting the defendant so that the latter is not deprived of some advantage which he has already gained in the litigation. Furthermore, it will impose conditions if these are necessary either for the protection of the other party or in the public interest.'[1937] Thus, the mere fact that an action has been discontinued does not preclude the institution of new legal proceedings unless the terms on which the original action was discontinued prohibit this.[1938]

545. For deemed discontinuance of action, a plaintiff can either 'apply for reinstatement of the discontinued action and face the stringent criteria governing reinstatement ... [or] avoid the stringent criteria for reinstatement and start a fresh action ... [or] take no further action and accept that his action has been discontinued'.[1939] The applicable guidelines governing reinstatement of a discontinued action are 'whether the plaintiff is innocent of any significant failure to conduct the case with expedition prior to the trigger date ... whether his failure to take any step in the action since the trigger date is excusable; or ... whether the balance of justice indicates that the action should be reinstated. If the answer to any of the above questions is in the negative, then reinstatement will most likely be refused.'[1940]

546. In terms of costs implications, the party which has been significantly more blameworthy will likely have to incur some costs. The court will consider the reasons for the withdrawal or discontinuance as well as whether the withdrawal or discontinuance is indicative of an acknowledgement of defeat or likely defeat.[1941]

1935. *Singapore Civil Procedure 2015 Volume 1*, 435 (G.P. Selvam ed., Sweet & Maxwell Asia 2014).
1936. J. Pinsler, *Principles of Civil Procedure* 383 (Acad. Publg. 2013).
1937. J. Pinsler, *Principles of Civil Procedure* 383 (Acad. Publg. 2013) citing *Rhode & Liesenfeld Pte Ltd v. Jorg Geselle*, [1998] 3 SLR(R) 335, [11]–[13].
1938. *Tong Guan Food Products v. Teo Cheow Ngoh*, [2004] SGHC 261, [50].
1939. *Woon Tek Seng v. v. Jayaraman a/l v. A Vellasamy*, [2008] 3 SLR(R) 43, [11], citing *Moguntia-Est Epices SA v. Sea-Hawk Freight Pte Ltd*, [2003] 4 SLR(R) 429. *See also Lai Swee Lin Linda v. Attorney-General*, [2008] 2 SLR(R) 794, [8].
1940. *Woon Tek Seng v. v. Jayaraman a/l v. A Vellasamy*, [2008] 3 SLR(R) 43, [13]–[14].
1941. *Karaha Bodas Co LLC v. Perusahaan Pertambangan Minyak dan Gas Bumi Negara*, [2006] SGHC 195, [11]; *Ong Chai Hong v. Chiang Shirley*, [2016] SGHC 91, [31].

§4. Possibility of Appeal

547. Section 34 of the Supreme Court of Judicature Act,[1942] read together with the Fourth and Fifth Schedules of the statute, determines whether any given order of civil procedure is appealable to the Court of Appeal[1943] or not.[1944] However, withdrawal, discontinuance, and reinstatement are all not explicitly covered by the Fourth (orders made by a judge that are non-appealable) and Fifth (orders made by a judge that are only appealable with leave) Schedules. Presumably, as regards withdrawal or discontinuance, this is because leave is almost certain to be granted, while the opposing party will not possibly try to appeal against the decision either. But as regards reinstatement of the action after discontinuance, it would seem an appeal from which is either as of right or requires leave from the court, since the Fourth Schedule does not declare it to be non-appealable and the Fifth Schedule does not require leave to be sought.

548. Due to recent amendments to the Supreme Court of Judicature Act, the law on this is currently in flux and while it has been suggested that the 'default' position is that all interlocutory applications, unless provided for statutorily, are appealable with leave,[1945] it may also be possible to argue that for interlocutory applications not expressly addressed by the Fourth and Fifth Schedules, 'an appeal to the Court of Appeal will remain as of right for orders made at interlocutory applications which will finally dispose of the substantive rights of the parties'.[1946]

1942. (Cap. 322, 2007 Rev. Ed.).

1943. Below it is the High Court, followed by the District and Magistrates' Courts. For appeals arising from the lower courts, *see* Supreme Court of Judicature Act (Cap. 322, R. 5, 2014 Rev. Ed.) Rules of Court, O 55B, 55C, and 55D. There is a right of appeal from a registrar in chambers to a judge in chambers (District Judge if it is the State Courts), but not necessarily after that stage.

1944. The statute was amended in 2010 and 2014.

1945. *See* E. Chua, *Defining an 'Interlocutory Application*, Sing. L. Watch Commentaries (4/2013); D. Chi, *Clarification on Leave to Appeal Regime in Respect of Interlocutory Matters: OpenNet Pte Ltd v. Info-Communications Development Authority of Singapore [2013] SGCA 24*, Sing. L. Watch Commentaries (4/2013); C. Siyuan & E. Chua, *The Right to Appeal Against a Decision Made on an Interlocutory Application: The Immediate Aftermath of the 2010 Amendments*, 25 Sing. Acad. L.J. 424 (2013).

1946. *OpenNet Pte Ltd v. Info-Communications Development Authority of Singapore*, [2013] 2 SLR 880, [29]. *See also Dorsey James Michael v. World Sport Group Pte Ltd*, [2013] 3 SLR 354, [98]. On the other hand, where the statute has made it clear that there is no appeal as of right, one is precluded from arguing that substantive rights have been engaged: *Kosui Singapore Pte Ltd v. Thangavelu*, [2016] 2 SLR 105, [28]–[29].

Chapter 3. Offer to Settle

§1. Introduction

549. Parties may avoid going to a full trial by agreeing to an offer to settle. This option is distinct from options such as summary judgment, striking out, and default judgment and setting aside, which are adversarial and combative by nature and definition, and so perhaps an offer to settle may be more appropriately described as an alternative dispute resolution option.[1947] Nonetheless, the offer to settle mechanism is similarly provided for in the Rules of Court.[1948] It is provided for in O 22A, one of the rare provisions in the Rules of Court that was not adopted from English law but instead was drawn from certain state laws in jurisdictions such as Canada and Australia.[1949] O 22A was introduced as a more flexible alternative to payment into court (under O 22),[1950] which only applies to cases where there is a monetary claim (thus excluding things like injunctions);[1951] is only available to the plaintiff(s) and defendant(s) in a claim (and counterclaim as the case may be) and thus not to third parties; and does not allow the plaintiff to take the initiative.[1952] Furthermore, O 22 A is considered more attractive for three other reasons. Specifically:

> if the party who makes the offer to settle gets an order or a judgment that is no more favourable than what is set out in his offer, the other party will be penalised with costs on an indemnity basis … the party making the offer to settle does not have to have the money immediately ready as he would have to when he makes payment into court … [the offer to settle procedure] is less complicated. The procedures for withdrawing money that has been paid in are not so simple. The party making the offer to settle is also free to formulate the offer and is not confined solely to an offer for payment alone.[1953]

550. Ultimately, the 'whole object of O 22A is to spur the parties to bring litigation to an expeditious end without judgment and thus to save costs and judicial

1947. The most common forms of 'alternative' dispute resolution would include negotiation, mediation, conciliatory proceedings, and lay adjudication.
1948. Supreme Court of Judicature Act (Cap. 322, R. 5, 2014 Rev. Ed.) Rules of Court.
1949. *Singapore Civil Procedure 2015 Volume 1* (G.P. Selvam ed., Sweet & Maxwell Asia 2014), 472–473, citing *The Endurance 1*, [1998] 3 SLR(R) 970, [40]. *See also Fairview Developments Pte Ltd v. Ong & Ong Pte Ltd*, [2015] 2 SLR 470, [15] for other common law jurisdictions with similar regimes.
1950. O 22 is still used, however, 'where the court imposes terms to set aside judgments, grants conditional leave to defend, interpleaders, providing security for costs. and in appeals and where there are statutory provisions providing for such payment': *Singapore Civil Procedure 2015 Volume 1*, at 472 (G.P. Selvam ed., Sweet & Maxwell Asia 2014). *See also* J. Pinsler, *Principles of Civil Procedure* 63–65 (Acad. Publg. 2013); *The Endurance 1*, [1998] 3 SLR(R) 970, [48].
1951. *See also Calderbank v. Calderbank*, [1975] 3 All ER 333; *Shi Fang v. Koh Pee Huat*, [1996] 1 SLR(R) 906.
1952. *Singapore Civil Procedure 2015 Volume 1*, at 472 (G.P. Selvam ed., Sweet & Maxwell Asia 2014).
1953. *Singapore Civil Procedure 2015 Volume 1*, at 472 (G.P. Selvam ed., Sweet & Maxwell Asia 2014).

time'.[1954] An offer to settle under O 22A is also 'deemed to be an offer of compromise made without prejudice save as to costs'.[1955]

§2. Procedural Aspects

551. A 'party to any proceedings[1956] may serve on any other party an offer to settle any one or more of the claims in the proceedings on the terms specified in the offer to settle'.[1957] There is a prescribed form to be used,[1958] though the failure to use the prescribed form does not necessarily mean that the court is precluded from taking it into account.[1959] The offer is only considered made when it is properly served.[1960] More than one offer can be made; counter-offers can also be made, using the same prescribed form.[1961]

552. However, an offer to settle under O 22A must be 'made at any time before the Court disposes of the matter in respect of which it is made'.[1962] In terms of when it may be accepted, if there is no time specified in the offer, 'it may be accepted at any time before the Court disposes of the matter in respect of which it is made'.[1963] A complication may arise in the situation of a bifurcated trial,[1964] where there is a

1954. *Singapore Airlines Ltd v. Tan Shwu Leng*, [2001] 3 SLR(R) 439, [37]. *See also id.*, [38]; *Fairview Developments Pte Ltd v. Ong & Ong Pte Ltd*, [2015] 2 SLR 470, [16]; *The Endurance 1*, [1998] 3 SLR(R) 970, [41], citing *Data General (Canada) Ltd v. Molnar Systems Group Inc*, (1991) 85 DLR (4th) 392.
1955. Supreme Court of Judicature Act (Cap. 322, R. 5, 2014 Rev. Ed.) Rules of Court, O 22A r 4. *See also* C. Bull & J. Pinsler, *Civil Procedure: Annual Review of Singapore Cases* [6.112] (Sing. Acad. L. 2005) citing *Yip Jenn Yeuan v. Ng Ah Chen*, [2005] SGHC 21, [18].
1956. An offer to settle under O 22A has to be made after, and not before the commencement of proceedings: *Singapore Civil Procedure 2015 Volume 1*, at 473 (G.P. Selvam ed., Sweet & Maxwell Asia 2014) citing *Bodenhamer v. Bodenhamer*, [1991] 2 OR (3d) 767. While, it would appear that O 22A does not apply to appeals: *Singapore Civil Procedure 2015 Volume 1*, at 473 (G.P. Selvam ed., Sweet & Maxwell Asia 2014) citing *Meadowfield Ventures v. Kennedy*, (1990) 75 OR (2d) 760. O 22A r 9(3) was held to be applicable in *Ram Das v. N P v. SIA Engineering Co Ltd*, [2015] 3 SLR 267, [73]–[74] on work done in relation to a High Court appeal.
1957. Supreme Court of Judicature Act (Cap. 322, R. 5, 2014 Rev. Ed.) Rules of Court, O 22A r 1.
1958. Supreme Court of Judicature Act (Cap. 322, R. 5, 2014 Rev. Ed.) Rules of Court, O 22A r 1. *See also id.*, O 2 rr 1(1)–(3).
1959. *Sie Choon Poh v. Amara Hotel Properties Pte Ltd*, [2008] 2 SLR(R) 1076, [19].
1960. *Singapore Civil Procedure 2015 Volume 1*, at 474 (G.P. Selvam ed., Sweet & Maxwell Asia 2014).
1961. *Singapore Civil Procedure 2015 Volume 1*, at 474 (G.P. Selvam ed., Sweet & Maxwell Asia 2014).
1962. Supreme Court of Judicature Act (Cap. 322, R. 5, 2014 Rev. Ed.) Rules of Court, O 22A r 2. However, as will be elaborated upon below, the reasonableness of the timing of the offer is a factor for the court to consider when deciding costs implications under O 22A: *Singapore Civil Procedure 2015 Volume 1*, at 476 (G.P. Selvam ed., Sweet & Maxwell Asia 2014), citing *Denis Matthew Harte v. Dr Tan Hun Hoe*, [2001] SGHC 19. In addition, the effective date when computing the costs will be with reference to the date of any last amended offer: *Teo An Nyah v. Tan Jenny*, [1998] SGHC 276, [92].
1963. Supreme Court of Judicature Act (Cap. 322, R. 5, 2014 Rev. Ed.) Rules of Court, O 22A r 3(5).
1964. D. Wong, *Clarification on the Offer to Settle Regime in Order 22A of the Rules of Court*, http://www.singaporelawblog.sg/blog/article/93, 30 Apr. 2015.

global offer to settle (drafted to include both the claim and counterclaim) and the counterclaim is resolved before the main claim.[1965] Adopting a purposive approach, the Court of Appeal in *Fairview Developments Pte Ltd v. Ong & Ong Pte Ltd* interpreted O 22A r 3(5) to mean 'that so long as there is an outstanding matter not disposed of which is within the scope of the offer to settle, the offer to settle remains open for acceptance'.[1966] In other words, since the main claim has yet to be resolved and/or damages have yet to be assessed, the global offer to settle remains open for acceptance.[1967] Any concern that such an interpretation of O 22A r 3(5) will be unfair to the offeror can be mitigated in two ways. First, the offeror can withdraw his offer in accordance with the procedure stated in O 22A.[1968] Second, if the offeree accepts the offer before the offeror properly withdraws the offer, it does not follow that the offer to settle will be binding on the offeror. The court still has discretion to determine if it is fair and just in the circumstances for the offer to settle to be enforced against the offeror.[1969] In addition, an offer to settle 'shall be open for acceptance for a period of not less than 14 days after it is served. If an offer to settle is made less than 14 days before the hearing of the matter, it shall remain open for a period of not less than 14 days unless in the meanwhile the matter is disposed of'.[1970] If an offer is accepted, an acceptance of offer using the prescribed form has to be served on the offeror.[1971] If the offeree 'rejects the offer or responds with a counter-offer that is not accepted, the [offeree] may thereafter accept the original offer to settle, unless it has been withdrawn or the Court has disposed of the matter in respect of which it was made'.[1972]

553. As regards withdrawal:

> an offer to settle which is expressed to be limited as to the time within which it is open for acceptance shall not be withdrawn within that time without the leave of the Court. An offer to settle which does not specify a time for acceptance may be withdrawn at any time after the expiry of 14 days from the date

---

1965. D. Wong, *Clarification on the Offer to Settle Regime in Order 22A of the Rules of Court:*, http://www.singaporelawblog.sg/blog/article/93, 30 Apr. 2015.
1966. *Fairview Developments Pte Ltd v. Ong & Ong Pte Ltd*, [2015] 2 SLR 470, [55], cited in *Ram Das v. N P v. SIA Engineering Co Ltd*, [2015] 3 SLR 267, [73]–[74]. *See also NTUC Foodfare Co-operative Ltd v. SIA Engineering Co Ltd*, [2018] SGCA 56.
1967. *See also* C. Siyuan & E. Chua, *Recent Developments in the Offer to Settle Regime in Singapore – Accepting an Offer to Settle before Damages are Assessed and the Contra Proferentem Rule: Ong & Ong Pte Ltd v. Fairview Developments Pte Ltd [2014] 2 SLR 1285*, 26 Sing. Acad. L.J. 687 (2014).
1968. *Fairview Developments Pte Ltd v. Ong & Ong Pte Ltd*, [2015] 2 SLR 470, [56].
1969. *Fairview Developments Pte Ltd v. Ong & Ong Pte Ltd*, [2015] 2 SLR 470, [56].
1970. Supreme Court of Judicature Act (Cap. 322, R. 5, 2014 Rev. Ed.) Rules of Court, O 22A r 3(1). *See also S & E Tech Pte Ltd v. Western Electric Pacific*, [2006] 2 SLR(R) 7, [16]: *Chia Kim Huay (litigation representative of the estate of Chua Chye Hee, deceased) v. Saw Shu Mawa Min Min*, [2012] 4 SLR 1096, [31].
1971. Supreme Court of Judicature Act (Cap. 322, R. 5, 2014 Rev. Ed.) Rules of Court, O 22A r 6(1). *See also Chia Kim Huay (litigation representative of the estate of Chua Chye Hee, deceased) v. Saw Shu Mawa Min Min*, [2012] 4 SLR 1096, [34] and [44].
1972. Supreme Court of Judicature Act (Cap. 322, R. 5, 2014 Rev. Ed.) Rules of Court, O 22A r 6(2).

of service of the offer on the other party provided that at least one day's prior notice of the intention to withdraw the offer is given.[1973]

554. There is a prescribed form to be used for withdrawal of the offer to settle.[1974] Although the form is titled 'Notice of Withdrawal of Offer', it is effective as a withdrawal of the offer to settle and the offer cannot be accepted once it is validly served.[1975] There is no prescribed form for the notice of the intention to withdraw the offer and 'a clearly worded letter evincing such intention will suffice'.[1976] If an offer to settle is not accepted or withdrawn within the specified time for acceptance, 'it shall be deemed to have been withdrawn when the time expires'.[1977] A complication may arise when an offeror's offer is retracted immediately after a change of circumstances that would substantially affect the quantum offered but the offeree has already accepted the offer. For instance, if an offer is predicated on loss of amenities and medical care, it would be considered an over-offer by the offeror if the offeree passes away. In such a situation, '[w]hat is fair and just will be decided by the parties within the time limited for the offer to be accepted. The court is only required to adjudge whether the offer was fair and just when the offer has lapsed and the issues goes back before the court'.[1978]

555. An offer to settle under O 22A 'shall not be filed and no statement of the fact that such an offer has been made shall be contained in any pleading or affidavit'.[1979] Likewise, where 'an offer to settle is not accepted, no communication respecting the offer shall be made to the Court at the hearing of the proceeding until all questions of liability and the relief to be granted, other than costs, have been determined'.[1980]

§3. Substantive Aspects

556. An offer to settle under O 22A should be clear and unequivocal,[1981] with the precise scope of the offer (such as the extent of the claim and the party to which it is addressed) stated as well.[1982] It should be genuine and serious in that it should contain in it an element which would induce settlement.[1983] An offer also cannot be

1973. Supreme Court of Judicature Act (Cap. 322, R. 5, 2014 Rev. Ed.) Rules of Court, O 22A r 3(2).
1974. Supreme Court of Judicature Act (Cap. 322, R. 5, 2014 Rev. Ed.) Rules of Court, O 22A r 3(3).
1975. *Tanner Sheridan Wayne v. NRG Engineering Pte Ltd*, [2014] 1 SLR 475, [21], [24].
1976. *Tanner Sheridan Wayne v. NRG Engineering Pte Ltd*, [2014] 1 SLR 475, [21].
1977. Supreme Court of Judicature Act (Cap. 322, R. 5, 2014 Rev. Ed.) Rules of Court, O 22A r 3(4).
1978. *Teo Gim Tiong v. Krishnasamy Pushpavathi*, [2013] SGHC 178, [6].
1979. Supreme Court of Judicature Act (Cap. 322, R. 5, 2014 Rev. Ed.) Rules of Court, O 22A r 5(1).
1980. Supreme Court of Judicature Act (Cap. 322, R. 5, 2014 Rev. Ed.) Rules of Court, O 22A r 5(2). *See also Zalco Marine Services Pte Ltd v. Humboldt Shipping Company Ltd*, [1998] SGCA 36.
1981. *Denis Matthew Harte v. Dr Tan Hun Hoe*, [2001] SGHC 19, [47]. *See also* Supreme Court of Judicature Act (Cap. 322, R. 5, 2014 Rev. Ed.) Rules of Court, O 22A r 8(2).
1982. J. Pinsler, *Principles of Civil Procedure* 66–67 (Acad. Publg. 2013). *See also SBS Transit Ltd v. Teo Chye Seng Douglas*, [2005] SGHC 15, [22].
1983. *Singapore Airlines Ltd v. Fujitsu Microelectronics (Malaysia) Sdn Bhd*, [2001] 1 SLR(R) 38, [5] and [10], citing *The Endurance 1*, [1998] 3 SLR(R) 970, [44]–[47]. *See also MCST Plan No 3563*

made just to attract payment of costs on an indemnity basis;[1984] cannot be qualified as a non-admission of liability, and cannot be an ex gratia lump sum.[1985] If an offer has been made by mistake, or if there is, say, a mistake in the terms of the offer, the doctrine of mistake will apply; accordingly, no valid settlement can arise from the offeree's acceptance of such an offer to settle.[1986]

557. As regards acceptance of the offer, rules on offer and acceptance under the O 22A regime have to be interpreted according to their own terms and not according to general contractual principles.[1987] Instead, general contractual principles are relevant for decisions concerning the enforcement of offers to settle. In exercising its discretion in determining if the offer to settle should be enforced, the court should have regard to general contractual principles as well as general principles of fairness and justice.[1988] Specifically, the factors of consideration are: (a) whether there was a sufficient change of circumstances after the offer was made such that the offeror should be given an opportunity to withdraw or modify his offer without being held to it; (b) whether the offeree engaged in any unfair conduct; and (c) whether the enforcement of the offer would cause any injustice.[1989] If an offer is accepted, 'the Court may incorporate any of its terms into a judgment'.[1990] Such a judgment is often referred to as a consent judgment.[1991] A party to an accepted offer to settle has to comply with the terms of the offer, or the other party may either 'make an application to a judge for judgment in the terms of the accepted offer, and the judge may grant judgment accordingly' or 'continue the proceeding as if there had been no accepted offer to settle'.[1992]

---

v. Wintree Investment Pte Ltd, [2018] SGHC 111, [39]–[43]; *Lim Geok Lin Andy v. Yap Jin Meng Bryan*, [2017] SGCA 45, [69]; *Peter Gontha v. Bdo Binder*, [1997] SGHC 85, [32]–[33]; *Colliers International (Singapore) Pte Ltd v. Senkee Logistics Pte Ltd*, [2007] 2 SLR(R) 230, [111]; *Chia Kok Kee v. HX Investment Pte Ltd (So Lai Har (alias Chia Choon), third party in issue (Tan Wah, third party in counterclaim)*, [2007] SGHC 164, [89]–[90]; *Wyno Marine Pte Ltd (in liquidation) v. Lim Teck Cheng*, [1998] SGHC 340, [9].

1984. *Singapore Airlines Ltd v. Fujitsu Microelectronics (Malaysia) Sdn Bhd*, [2001] 1 SLR(R) 38, [5], citing *Man B&W Diesel S E Asia Pte Ltd v. PT Bumi International Tankers*, [2004] 3 SLR(R) 267, [7].
1985. *Colliers International (Singapore) Pte Ltd v. Senkee Logistics Pte Ltd*, [2007] 2 SLR(R) 230, [119]. *Cf Goh Kok Liang v. GYP Properties Ltd*, [2020] SGHC 53, [25].
1986. *Singapore Civil Procedure 2015 Volume 1*, at 477 (G.P. Selvam ed., Sweet & Maxwell Asia 2014) citing *S & E Tech Pte Ltd v. Western Electric Pacific*, [2006] 2 SLR(R) 7, [19].
1987. *See also Fairview Developments Pte Ltd v. Ong & Ong Pte Ltd*, [2015] 2 SLR 470, [41], [44]–[53].
1988. *Fairview Developments Pte Ltd v. Ong & Ong Pte Ltd*, [2015] 2 SLR 470, [69].
1989. *Fairview Developments Pte Ltd v. Ong & Ong Pte Ltd*, [2015] 2 SLR 470, [70].
1990. Supreme Court of Judicature Act (Cap. 322, R. 5, 2014 Rev. Ed.) Rules of Court, O 22A r 6(3).
1991. J. Pinsler, *Principles of Civil Procedure* 70 (Acad. Publg. 2013). C.f. *Airtrust (Singapore) Pte Ltd v. Kao Chai-Chau Linda*, [2014] 2 SLR 693, [22]–[23]; *Sentosa Building Construction Pte Ltd v. DJ Builders & Contractors Pte Ltd*, [2015] SGHCR 18, [25]–[27].
1992. Supreme Court of Judicature Act (Cap. 322, R. 5, 2014 Rev. Ed.) Rules of Court, O 22A r 8(1).

558. O 22A induces parties to settle via its costs implications in three ways,[1993] though 'where an offer to settle has been made, and notwithstanding anything in the offer to settle, the Court shall have full power to determine by whom and to what extent any costs are to be paid, and the Court may make such a determination upon the application of a party or of its own motion'.[1994] First, where an offer to settle made by a plaintiff:

> is not withdrawn and has not expired before the disposal of the claim in respect of which the offer to settle is made; and … is not accepted by the defendant, and the plaintiff obtains a judgment not less favourable than the terms of the offer to settle, the plaintiff is entitled to costs on the standard basis to the date an offer to settle was served and costs on the indemnity basis from that date, unless the Court orders otherwise.[1995]

559. However, if the plaintiff obtains a judgment less favourable than his offer, O 22A does not apply; rather, the general rules concerning costs would apply.[1996] Second, where an accepted offer to settle does not provide for costs:

> where the offer was made by the plaintiff, he will be entitled to his costs assessed to the date that the notice of acceptance was served … where the offer was made by the defendant, the plaintiff will be entitled to his costs assessed to the date he was served with the offer, and the defendant will be entitled to his costs from the date 14 days after the date of the service of the offer assessed up to the date that the notice of acceptance was served.[1997]

560. Third, where an offer to settle made by a defendant:

> is not withdrawn and has not expired before the disposal of the claim in respect of which the offer to settle is made; and … is not accepted by the plaintiff, and the plaintiff obtains judgment not more favourable than the terms of the

1993. This applies even if a plaintiff's action is dismissed: *Heng Chyu Kee v. Far East Square Pte Ltd*, [2001] 3 SLR(R) 651, [17]; *Merchant Industries (S) Pte Ltd v. X-Media Communications Pte Ltd*, [2001] SGHC 338, [149]. *See also MCST Plan No 3563 v. Wintree Investment Pte Ltd*, [2018] SGHC 111, [50].

1994. Supreme Court of Judicature Act (Cap. 322, R. 5, 2014 Rev. Ed.) Rules of Court, O 22A r 9(5). *See also Seraya Energy Pte Ltd v. Denka Advantech Pte Ltd (YTL PowerSeraya Pte Ltd, third party)*, [2019] SGHC 100. *CCM Industrial Pte Ltd v. Uniquetech Pte Ltd*, [2009] 2 SLR(R) 20, [45]; *Man B&W Diesel S E Asia Pte Ltd v. PT Bumi International Tankers*, [2004] 3 SLR(R) 267, [7]; Supreme Court of Judicature Act (Cap. 322, R. 5, 2014 Rev. Ed.) Rules of Court, O 22A r 12. In this connection it should be noted that O 22A r 12 is not an empowering rule; rather, O 22A r 9 is the empowering rule and if it does not apply, O 22A r 12 cannot apply in its place: *CCM Industrial Pte Ltd v. Uniquetech Pte Ltd*, [2009] 2 SLR(R) 20, [27].

1995. Supreme Court of Judicature Act (Cap. 322, R. 5, 2014 Rev. Ed.) Rules of Court, O 22A r 9(1). *See also Mopi Pte Ltd v. Central Mercantile Corp (S) Ltd*, [2005] SGHC 183, [13].

1996. J. Pinsler, *Principles of Civil Procedure* 72 (Acad. Publg. 2013). As to what counts as a judgment, such as a striking out order, *see MCSTA Plan No 3563 v. Wintree Investment Pte Ltd*, [2018] SGHC 111, [34].

1997. Supreme Court of Judicature Act (Cap. 322, R. 5, 2014 Rev. Ed.) Rules of Court, O 22A r 9(2). *See also Vita Life Sciences Ltd v. Arthur Andersen*, [2008] SGHC 85, [33]–[44].

offer to settle, the plaintiff is entitled to costs on the standard basis to the date the offer was served and the defendant is entitled to costs on the indemnity basis from that date, unless the Court orders otherwise.[1998]

561. If the plaintiff obtains judgment more favourable than the defendant's offer, the general rules concerning costs would apply,[1999] rather than the costs consequences under the offer to settle process.[2000] However, if the plaintiff does not obtain judgment at all, 'he would suffer the same cost consequences as if he rejected an offer which is more favourable than a judgment'.[2001] Whether a judgment obtained is more or less 'favourable' than the terms in the offer to settle depends on the dollar value of what has been awarded.[2002] However, the terms need not always be monetary in nature; the length of a license, for instance, is a possible term.[2003]

562. Where there are two or more defendants:

> the plaintiff may offer to settle with any defendant and any defendant may offer to settle with the plaintiff, but where the defendants are alleged to be jointly or jointly and severally liable to the plaintiff in respect of a claim and rights of contribution or indemnity may exist between the defendants, the cost consequences prescribed by [O 22A r 9] do not apply to an offer to settle.[2004]

563. The exceptions to this are if:

> in the case of an offer made by the plaintiff, the offer is made to all the defendants, and is an offer to settle the claim against all the defendants; or … in the case of an offer made to the plaintiff … the offer is an offer to settle the plaintiff's claim against all the defendants and to pay the costs of any defendant who does not join in making the offer; or the offer is made by all the defendants and is an offer to settle the claim against all the defendants, and, by the terms of the offer, they are made jointly and severally liable to the plaintiff for the whole of the offer.[2005]

1998. Supreme Court of Judicature Act (Cap. 322, R. 5, 2014 Rev. Ed.) Rules of Court, O 22A r 9(3). *See also L K Ang Construction Pte Ltd v. Chubb Singapore Pte Ltd (judgment on costs)*, [2004] 1 SLR(R) 134, [15]; *Main-line Corporation v. United Overseas Bank Ltd*, [2017] SGHC 27, [14]–[16]; *NTUC Foodfare Co-operative Ltd v. SIA Engineering Co Ltd*, [2018] SGCA 56; *Resorts World at Sentosa Pte Ltd v. Goel Adesh Kumar*, [2018] SGCA 58.
1999. J. Pinsler, *Principles of Civil Procedure* 72–73 (Acad. Publg. 2013).
2000. *CCM Industrial Pte Ltd v. Uniquetech Pte Ltd*, [2009] 2 SLR(R) 20, [32]–[34].
2001. J. Pinsler, *Principles of Civil Procedure* 72–73 (Acad. Publg. 2013).
2002. *Tan Shwu Leng v. Singapore Airlines Limited*, [2001] SGHC 51, [96]. C.f. *CCM Industrial Pte Ltd v. Uniquetech Pte Ltd*, [2009] 2 SLR(R) 20, [24]–[26]. *See also* Supreme Court of Judicature Act (Cap. 322, R. 5, 2014 Rev. Ed.) Rules of Court, O 22A r 9(4).
2003. *LK Ang Construction Pte Ltd v. Chubb Singapore Pte Ltd*, [2003] 1 SLR(R) 635, [21]. *See also Ram Das v. N P v. SIA Engineering Co Ltd*, [2015] 3 SLR 267, [42]–[45].
2004. Supreme Court of Judicature Act (Cap. 322, R. 5, 2014 Rev. Ed.) Rules of Court, O 22A r 10. *See also Noor Azlin bte Abdul Rahman v. Changi General Hospital Pte Ltd*, [2018] SGHC 146.
2005. Supreme Court of Judicature Act (Cap. 322, R. 5, 2014 Rev. Ed.) Rules of Court, O 22A r 10. *See also MCST Plan No 3563 v. Wintree Investment Pte Ltd*, [2018] SGHC 111, [45].

564. Also where there are two or more defendants (who are alleged to be jointly and severally liable to the plaintiff), any defendant may make to any other defendant an offer to contribute towards a settlement of the claim, using the prescribed form.[2006] When this happens, the court 'may take into account an offer to contribute in determining whether another defendant should be ordered … to pay the costs of the defendant who made the offer; or … to indemnify the defendant who made the offer for any costs he is liable to pay to the plaintiff, or to do both'.[2007]

§4. Possibility of Appeal

565. Section 34 of the Supreme Court of Judicature Act,[2008] read together with the Fourth and Fifth Schedules of the statute, determines whether any given order of civil procedure is appealable to the Court of Appeal[2009] or not.[2010] The Fourth and Fifth Schedules are silent on appealing against the costs implications triggered by O 34A, but section 34(2) of the Supreme Court of Judicature Act makes it clear that: 'Except with the leave of a Judge, no appeal shall be brought to the Court of Appeal … where the only issue in the appeal relates to costs or fees for hearing dates.'[2011] In this respect, an order of a judge refusing or granting leave is final.[2012] If the costs order is made in the context of a taxation by the registrar, the order of costs is subject to review by a High Court Judge in chambers. The appellate court's approach towards an appeal against a decision made on review is different from that of the judge conducting the taxation review. When an appeal is lodged against a judicial decision that has been made in the exercise of a judicial officer's discretion, it must be shown that the judicial officer had erred in principle or had reached a conclusion that is plainly wrong before the appellate court will overrule that decision.[2013]

2006. Supreme Court of Judicature Act (Cap. 322, R. 5, 2014 Rev. Ed.) Rules of Court, O 22A r 11(1).
2007. Supreme Court of Judicature Act (Cap. 322, R. 5, 2014 Rev. Ed.) Rules of Court, O 22A r 11(2).
2008. (Cap. 322, 2007 Rev. Ed.).
2009. Below it is the High Court, followed by the District and Magistrates' Courts. For appeals arising from the lower courts, *see* Supreme Court of Judicature Act (Cap. 322, R. 5, 2014 Rev. Ed.) Rules of Court, O 55B, 55C, and 55D. There is a right of appeal from a registrar in chambers to a judge in chambers (District Judge if it is the State Courts), but not necessarily after that stage.
2010. The statute was amended in 2010 and 2014.
2011. Supreme Court of Judicature Act (Cap. 322, 2007 Rev. Ed.), s 34(2)(b). If a party does not obtain leave to appeal against the High Court's order as to costs, the Court of Appeal has no jurisdiction to hear the appeal and the notice of appeal would be struck out: *Kosui Singapore Pte Ltd v. Thangavelu*, [2016] 2 SLR 105, [3]–[4] and [33]. *See also Clearlab SG Pte Ltd v. Ma Zhi and another* [2016] SGCA 31, [12]–[13].
2012. Supreme Court of Judicature Act (Cap. 322, 2007 Rev. Ed.), s 34(2B).
2013. *Nim Minimaart (a firm) v. MCST Plan No 1079*, [2013] 2 SLR 1025, [12].

Chapter 4. Committal for Contempt of Court

§1. INTRODUCTION

566. The doctrine of contempt of court 'is intended to preserve and protect the authority of the courts so that they are able to perform their critical functions effectively in the public interest'.[2014] It 'is not intended, in any manner or fashion whatsoever, to protect the dignity of the judges as such; its purpose is more objective and is (more importantly) rooted in the public interest'.[2015] Contempt of court may arise in more general circumstances, such as scandalizing the court and making derogatory comments about the judicial process, or upon failure to comply with a judgment or order.[2016] This chapter will focus on the former and the failure of comply with a court order as a later chapter relating to enforcement of judgments will deal with the latter (committal specifically). It should also be noted that the Penal Code[2017] also contains punishment for contempt; for example, section 288 states:

> Whoever intentionally offers any insult or causes any interruption to any public servant, while such public servant is sitting in any stage of a judicial proceeding shall be punished with imprisonment for a term which may extend to one year, or with fine which may extend to SGD 5,000, or with both.[2018]

567. It has been said that the utility of the traditional classification into civil and criminal contempt, whilst serving its purpose in the past, is of questionable utility today and tends to mislead given the singular standard of proof for both types of contempt, and a mixed approach to sanctions (punitive and remedial) in both categories of contempt.[2019] However, a distinction between civil and criminal contempt can still be drawn:

> An action for civil contempt is directed at a party who is bound by an order of court but is alleged to have breached the terms of that order. Such an action is directed at securing compliance with the order in question. An action for criminal contempt on the other hand need not be confined to parties who are directly bound by the order. Any person, even one not directly bound by the order, can act so as to deliberately frustrate or undermine its purpose but if he does that, then he commits criminal contempt.[2020]

2014. J. Pinsler, *Principles of Civil Procedure* 862 (Acad. Publg. 2013).
2015. *Pertamina Energy Trading Ltd v. Karaha Bodas Co LLC*, [2007] 2 SLR(R) 518, [22], citing *Attorney-General v. Times Newspapers Ltd*, [1974] AC 273, 302.
2016. J. Pinsler, *Principles of Civil Procedure* 862–863 (Acad. Publg. 2013). It should be noted that in 2016, the Administration of Justice (Protection) Act was passed. It codifies various types of contempt (including contempt by disobedience of court orders or undertakings), the jurisdiction and punishment for contempt, and defences to contempt. The legislation, however, was not intended to replace the law developed by case law, but to clarify it.
2017. Penal Code (Cap. 224, 2008 Rev. Ed.).
2018. J. Pinsler, *Principles of Civil Procedure* 864 (Acad. Publg. 2013).
2019. *Sembcorp Marine Ltd v. Aurol Anthony Sabastian*, [2012] 2 SLR 645, [28]–[29].
2020. *Aurol Anthony Sabastian v. Sembcorp Marine Ltd*, [2013] 2 SLR 246, [29].

568. The distinction between civil and criminal contempt also lies in the type of sentencing options that are meted out. O 52 rr 1(1) and 8 provide that the High Court may make an order for the defendant to stand committed to prison for a time, pay a fine or give security for his good behaviour. However, the sentencing options under the Criminal Procedure Code for criminal contempt are more varied, and include a community sentence. In a recent High Court case concerning civil contempt, the judge was reluctant to extend the sentencing options under the Criminal Procedure Code on the basis that '[d]espite its quasi-criminal nature, a civil contempt does not amount to a criminal offence'.[2021]

569. It is suggested that the difference between civil and criminal contempt is largely procedural. Accordingly, the reader may find reference to cases on both civil and criminal contempt in the section on the substantive aspects of committal for contempt of court.

§2. Procedural Aspects

570. The court's jurisdiction to issue an order of committal for contempt of court may be found in the Supreme Court of Judicature Act[2022] as well as the State Courts Act.[2023] The power of the court to punish for contempt of court may be exercised by an order of committal,[2024] and this enables 'justice to be administered in a regular and orderly way'.[2025] Where contempt of court is committed in connection with proceedings in the High Court or in the State Courts, then an order of committal may be made by the High Court or State Courts, as the case may be.[2026] However, where contempt of court is not committed in connection with any proceedings, an order of committal may only be made by the High Court.[2027] The High Court may also make an order of committal in respect of any person charged with having done anything in relation to a court, tribunal or person which would, if it had been done in relation to the High Court, have been a contempt of the High Court.[2028] Where contempt of the Court of Appeal is committed, the order of committal may be made by the High Court or the Court of Appeal.[2029]

571. An order of committal may be made on the court's own motion,[2030] or upon application.[2031] The court may make an order of committal on its own motion, for

2021. *Maruti Shipping Pte Ltd v. Tay Sien Djim*, [2014] SGHC 227, [134], citing *Tan Beow Hiong v. Tan Boon Aik*, [2010] 4 SLR 870 [24]–[25].
2022. Supreme Court of Judicature Act (Cap. 322, 2007 Rev. Ed.), s 7(1).
2023. State Courts Act (Cap. 321, 2007 Rev. Ed.), s 8(1).
2024. Supreme Court of Judicature Act (Cap. 322, R. 5, 2014 Rev. Ed.) Rules of Court, O 52 r 1(1).
2025. *Lee Hsien Loong v. Singapore Democratic Party*, [2009] 1 SLR(R) 642, [176].
2026. Supreme Court of Judicature Act (Cap. 322, R. 5, 2014 Rev. Ed.) Rules of Court, O 52 r 1(2).
2027. Supreme Court of Judicature Act (Cap. 322, R. 5, 2014 Rev. Ed.) Rules of Court, O 52 r 1(3). *See also Au Wai Pang v. Attorney-General*, [2014] 3 SLR 357 [38]–[39].
2028. Supreme Court of Judicature Act (Cap. 322, R. 5, 2014 Rev. Ed.) Rules of Court, O 52 r 1(5).
2029. Supreme Court of Judicature Act (Cap. 322, R. 5, 2014 Rev. Ed.) Rules of Court, O 52 r 1(4).
2030. Supreme Court of Judicature Act (Cap. 322, R. 5, 2014 Rev. Ed.) Rules of Court, O 52 r 4.
2031. Supreme Court of Judicature Act (Cap. 322, R. 5, 2014 Rev. Ed.) Rules of Court, O 52 r 2.

example, in response to contempt in the face of the court.[2032] Contempt in the face of the court has been described as conduct 'aimed at interfering with the authority of the Judiciary and proper functioning of the court, and at impairing the public's respect and confidence in the Judiciary'.[2033] In such a situation, the power to punish for contempt may be exercised summarily, but this power will not be exercised lightly.[2034] Where the alleged act of contempt occurs in the course of a trial, it will be in the discretion of the presiding judge whether to deal with the alleged contempt immediately or whether the matter can be deferred until after the trial.[2035]

572. The following procedural safeguards will generally be adhered to in order to ensure that any perception of 'rough justice' will be minimized: maintenance of a proper record of the acts of contempt; informing the alleged contemnor of the court's desire to pursue contempt proceedings; imposition of a 'cooling-off period' before commencement of contempt proceedings; giving the alleged contemnor an opportunity to apologize; informing the alleged contemnor of formal commencement of contempt proceedings; observance of the rules of natural justice; and giving the alleged contemnor an opportunity to be heard in mitigation.[2036]

573. Before an application for an order of committal is made, leave must first be obtained by ex parte originating summons or by summons in the proceedings, as the case may be, and the application for leave must be supported by a statement setting out the name and description of the applicant, the name, description and address of the person sought to be committed and the grounds on which his committal is sought, and by an affidavit, verifying the facts relied on.[2037] The statement must set out clearly and distinctly the ground on which committal is sought so that the respondent is aware of the allegations against him and be in a position to respond to them.[2038] The threshold for the grant of leave is that of a prima facie case of contempt while for the respondent to succeed in opposing he must show exceptional circumstances directly impinging on the applicant's entitlement to apply for leave; the court must be mindful not to venture into or purport to decide the substantive merits of the application, for it is only at the second phase of proceedings where the

---

2032. *See Attorney-General v. Chee Soon Juan*, [2006] 2 SLR(R) 650; *Lee Hsien Loong v. Singapore Democratic Party*, [2009] 1 SLR(R) 642.

2033. *Attorney-General v. Chee Soon Juan*, [2006] 2 SLR(R) 650, [17].

2034. *Lee Hsien Loong v. Singapore Democratic Party*, [2009] 1 SLR(R) 642, [177]–[178], citing *Morris v. Crown Office*, [1970] 2 QB 114, 122; *You Xin v. Public Prosecutor*, [2007] 4 SLR(R) 17, [165].

2035. *Lee Hsien Loong v. Singapore Democratic Party*, [2009] 1 SLR(R) 642, [175] and [185]–[194].

2036. *You Xin v. Public Prosecutor*, [2007] 4 SLR(R) 17, [46]–[77].

2037. Supreme Court of Judicature Act (Cap. 322, R. 5, 2014 Rev. Ed.) Rules of Court, O 52 r 2.

2038. J. Pinsler, *Principles of Civil Procedure* 868 (Acad. Publg. 2013) citing *Summit Holdings Ltd v. Business Software Alliance*, [1999] 2 SLR(R) 592. As stated in *Mok Kah Hong v. Zheng Zhuan Yao*, [2016] SGCA 8, [62]: 'the test is whether the O 52 r 2(2) statement is of sufficient particularity such that it gives the respondent adequate information to enable him to meet the charges against him ... The test is to be applied with reference to and from the perspective of a reasonable person in the position of the alleged contemnor reading the O 52 r 2(2) statement in a fair and sensible manner.' *See also Technigroup Far East Pte Ltd v. Jaswinderpal Singh s/o Bachint Singh*, [2017] SGHC 68, [21].

substantive allegations are contested.[2039] When leave is granted, the application for an order of committal must be made by summons in the proceedings in which leave was obtained, and, unless the judge granting leave has otherwise directed, there must be at least eight clear days between the service of the application and the day for the hearing.[2040] If the application for an order of committal is not made within fourteen days after leave was granted, the leave lapses.[2041] Generally, the application for leave and the accompanying statement and affidavit, as well as the application for the order of committal, must be served personally on the person sought to be committed.[2042] However, the court may dispense with service of the documents if it thinks it just to do so, without prejudice to the rules on substituted service contained in O 62 r 5 of the Rules of Court.[2043]

574. The hearing of the application for an order of committal will take place in open court, subject to the following exceptions:

(a) where the application arises out of proceedings relating to the wardship or adoption of an infant or wholly or mainly to the guardianship, custody, maintenance or upbringing of an infant, or rights of access to an infant;
(b) where the application arises out of proceedings relating to a person who lacks capacity within the meaning of the Mental Capacity Act (Cap. 177A) in relation to matters concerning his property and affairs;
(c) where the application arises out of proceedings in which a secret process, discovery or invention was in issue; and
(d) where it appears to the Court that in the interests of the administration of justice or for reasons of national security the application should be heard in private.[2044]

575. Nevertheless, if the court hearing the application for an order of committal does sit in private and decides to make an order of committal, it will still have to state in open court: the name of the person to be committed; in general terms the nature of the contempt of court in respect of which the order of committal is being made; and, if the person is to be committed for a fixed period, the length of that period.[2045] During the hearing, an applicant cannot rely on grounds for an order of committal except for those stated in the statement accompanying the application for leave.[2046] Although the court may grant leave for the statement to be amended, it is unlikely to do so unless it would be in the interest of justice.[2047] The person sought

2039. *BMP v. BMQ*, [2014] 1 SLR 1140, [13]–[19]; *Mok Kah Hong v. Zheng Zhuan Yao*, [2016] SGCA 8, [57]–[59]. Examples of such exceptional circumstances include the order of court being complied with and the plaintiffs having undertaken not to take out committal proceedings: *Ang Boon Chye v. Ang Tin Yong*, [2011] SGHC 124, [12].
2040. Supreme Court of Judicature Act (Cap. 322, R. 5, 2014 Rev. Ed.) Rules of Court, O 52 r 3(1).
2041. Supreme Court of Judicature Act (Cap. 322, R. 5, 2014 Rev. Ed.) Rules of Court, O 52 r 3(3).
2042. Supreme Court of Judicature Act (Cap. 322, R. 5, 2014 Rev. Ed.) Rules of Court, O 52 r 3(4).
2043. Supreme Court of Judicature Act (Cap. 322, R. 5, 2014 Rev. Ed.) Rules of Court, O 52 r 3(5).
2044. Supreme Court of Judicature Act (Cap. 322, R. 5, 2014 Rev. Ed.) Rules of Court, O 52 r 5(1).
2045. Supreme Court of Judicature Act (Cap. 322, R. 5, 2014 Rev. Ed.) Rules of Court, O 52 r 5(2).
2046. Supreme Court of Judicature Act (Cap. 322, R. 5, 2014 Rev. Ed.) Rules of Court, O 52 r 5(3).
2047. J. Pinsler, *Principles of Civil Procedure* 868 (Acad. Publg. 2013).

to be committed is entitled to give oral evidence on his own behalf at the hearing if he wishes to do so.[2048] In granting an order of committal, the court may direct that the execution of the order be suspended for such period or on such terms or conditions as it may specify.[2049]

576. A procedure was introduced in 2011 to allow an applicant for an order of committal to allow for a suspension of a committal order to be lifted in any of the terms of the suspension have been breached.[2050] Such an application must be made by way of summons supported by an affidavit and, unless the court directs otherwise, the application and supporting affidavit must be served on the person against whom the order of committal had been granted.[2051] Where a suspended order for committal is made, and the contemnor breached the terms and conditions on which the order was suspended, the court is not obligated to impose the suspended sentence, but retains a discretion to do what was just in the circumstances.[2052] The court may, on the application of any person committed to prison for any contempt of court, discharge him where the circumstances justify his release prior to the expiry of the sentence.[2053]

§3. Substantive Aspects

577. As alluded to earlier, contempt of court 'is based upon the broadest of principles, namely, that the courts cannot and will not permit interference with the due administration of justice'.[2054] Although contempt may take a myriad of forms, it has been noted that contempt can be divided into two broad categories – contempt by interference and contempt by disobedience:

> The former category comprises a wide range of matters such as disrupting the court process itself (contempt in the face of the court), publications or other acts which risk prejudicing or interfering with particular legal proceedings, and publications or other acts which interfere with the course of justice as a continuing process (for example, publications which 'scandalise' the court and retaliation against witnesses for having given evidence in proceedings which

---

2048. Supreme Court of Judicature Act (Cap. 322, R. 5, 2014 Rev. Ed.) Rules of Court, O 52 r 5(4).
2049. Supreme Court of Judicature Act (Cap. 322, R. 5, 2014 Rev. Ed.) Rules of Court, O 52 r 6(1).
2050. Supreme Court of Judicature Act (Cap. 322, R. 5, 2014 Rev. Ed.) Rules of Court, O 52 r 6(3)–(5), introduced by way of Supreme Court of Judicature Act (Cap. 322) Rules of Court (Amendment No. 4) Rules 2010 (S708/2010).
2051. Supreme Court of Judicature Act (Cap. 322, R. 5, 2014 Rev. Ed.) Rules of Court, O 52 r 6(4)–(5).
2052. *Tan Beow Hiong v. Tan Boon Aik*, [2010] 4 SLR 870, [68].
2053. Supreme Court of Judicature Act (Cap. 322, R. 5, 2014 Rev. Ed.) Rules of Court, O 52 r 7(1); J. Pinsler, *Principles of Civil Procedure* 872 (Acad. Publg. 2013).
2054. *Attorney-General v. Newspaper Publishing Plc*, [1988] Ch 333, 368; cited in *You Xin v. Public Prosecutor*, [2007] 4 SLR(R) 17, [14]; *Lee Hsien Loong v. Singapore Democratic Party*, [2009] 1 SLR(R) 642, [165].

are concluded). The second category comprises disobeying court orders and breaching undertakings given to the court.[2055]

578. The first category of contempt concerns contempt in the face of the court and scandalizing the court or a judge. The courts have generally eschewed any precise definition of contempt in the face of the court.[2056] However, the rationale for such a principle is that '[a] court of law must be able to maintain within its confines an atmosphere conducive to orderly proceedings so that justice is seen to be conducted in a meticulous and structured manner, and, most crucially, fairly and impartially to all who appear before it'.[2057] The High Court has commented that insulting or disrespectful behaviour even though it falls short of being physically obstructive will amount to contempt of court.[2058] Examples of acts that have been held to be contempt in the face of the court include a debtor refusing to answer any questions posed by an assistant registrar at a bankruptcy hearing and then reading in court the bankruptcy statement that contained passages which scandalized the judiciary;[2059] and accused persons chanting with their backs to the court.[2060] In relation to scandalizing the court or a judge, the test for liability is the 'real risk' test, that is, whether there is 'a real risk that the impugned statement has undermined – or might undermine – public confidence in the administration of justice'.[2061] The Court of Appeal has stated as follows in relation to the 'real risk' test:

> In applying this test, the court must avoid either extreme on the legal spectrum, viz, of either finding that contempt has been established where there is only a remote or fanciful possibility that public confidence in the administration of justice is (or might be) undermined or finding that contempt has been established only in the most serious situations (which is, as we shall see in the next section of this judgment, embodied within the 'clear and present danger' test). In undertaking such an analysis, the court must not substitute its own subjective view for the view of the average reasonable person as it is clear that the inquiry must necessarily be an objective one. Much would depend, in the final analysis, on the precise facts and context in which the impugned statement is made.[2062]

2055. *You Xin v. Public Prosecutor*, [2007] 4 SLR(R) 17, [16], citing N. Lowe & B. Sufrin, *The Law of Contempt* 2 (3d ed., Butterworths 1996). *See also Shadrake Alan v. Attorney-General*, [2011] 3 SLR 778, [19]; *Tahir v. Tay Kar Oon*, [2016] SGHC 60, [43].
2056. *You Xin v. Public Prosecutor*, [2007] 4 SLR(R) 17, [17]–[18].
2057. *You Xin v. Public Prosecutor*, [2007] 4 SLR(R) 17, [19].
2058. *Attorney-General v. Chee Soon Juan*, [2006] 2 SLR(R) 650, [16].
2059. *Attorney-General v. Chee Soon Juan*, [2006] 2 SLR(R) 650.
2060. *You Xin v. Public Prosecutor*, [2007] 4 SLR(R) 17.
2061. *Shadrake Alan v. Attorney-General*, [2011] 3 SLR 778, [36] and [57].
2062. *Shadrake Alan v. Attorney-General*, [2011] 3 SLR 778, [36] (emphasis in original). *See also Au Wai Pang v. Attorney-General*, [2016] 1 SLR 992, [17]–[18].

579. On the issue as to who constituted 'the public' for the purposes of the law relating to scandalizing contempt, the Court of Appeal has stated that the 'court concerned had to make an objective decision as to whether or not the allegedly contemptuous statement would undermine public confidence in the administration of justice, as assessed by the effect of the impugned statement on the average reasonable person'.[2063] Absent any statutory guidance, the Court of Appeal has also held that the concept of fair criticism goes towards liability for contempt of court.[2064] In applying the concept of fair criticism, a court should bear in mind the following non-exhaustive factors: the extent to which the allegedly fair criticism is supported by argument and evidence; the manner in which the alleged criticism is made; the party's attitude in court; the number of instances of contemning conduct; and all other circumstances of the case which may go towards showing bad faith.[2065]

580. The second category of contempt on disobedience with court orders encompasses the following three main types of civil contempt: first, disobedience of an order requiring an act to be done (for example, a mandatory injunction); second, disobedience of an order prohibiting the doing of an act (for example, a prohibitive or restrictive injunction); and third, breach of an undertaking given to the court.[2066] The standard of proof is the criminal standard of proof beyond a reasonable doubt.[2067] However, the threshold to establish the guilty intent necessary for a finding of civil contempt is a low one.[2068] Specifically, the alleged contemnor just needs to intend to do acts which are in breach of a coercive court order; there is no need to show his specific intention.[2069] Further, it must be shown that the alleged contemnor was aware of his obligations to the court.[2070] However, it is not necessary for a defendant to have a total understanding of the court order before he can

2063. *Shadrake Alan v. Attorney-General*, [2011] 3 SLR 778, [34] (emphasis in original).

2064. *Shadrake Alan v. Attorney-General*, [2011] 3 SLR 778, [79]–[80].

2065. *Shadrake Alan v. Attorney-General*, [2011] 3 SLR 778, [81]–[82], citing *Attorney-General v. Tan Liang Joo John*, [2009] 2 SLR(R) 1132, [15]–[23]. *See also Au Wai Pang v. Attorney-General*, [2016] 1 SLR 992, [49]–[53],

2066. *Singapore Civil Procedure 2015 Volume 1*, at 886 (G.P. Selvam ed., Sweet & Maxwell Asia 2014). *See also STX Corp v. Jason Surjana Tanuwidjaja*, [2014] 2 SLR 1261, [7], cited in *Maruti Shipping Pte Ltd v. Tay Sien Djim*, [2014] SGHC 227, [17]; *Technigroup Far East Pte Ltd v. Jaswinderpal Singh s/o Bachint Singh*, [2017] SGHC 68, [25]; *PT Sandipala Arthaputra v. STMicroelectronics Asia Pacific Pte Ltd*, [2018] SGHC 20.

2067. *Tan Beow Hiong v. Tan Boon Aik*, [2010] 4 SLR(R) 870, [47]; *STX Corp v. Jason Surjana Tanuwidjaja*, [2014] 2 SLR 1261, [8]; *Maruti Shipping Pte Ltd v. Tay Sien Djim*, [2014] SGHC 227, [17]; *Tahir v. Tay Kar Oon*, [2016] SGHC 60, [35].

2068. *Tan Beow Hiong v. Tan Boon Aik*, [2010] 4 SLR(R) 870, [47], cited in *STX Corp v. Jason Surjana Tanuwidjaja*, [2014] 2 SLR 1261, [8]. *See also Maruti Shipping Pte Ltd v. Tay Sien Djim*, [2014] SGHC 227, [17].

2069. *Tan Beow Hiong v. Tan Boon Aik*, [2010] 4 SLR(R) 870, [47], cited in *STX Corp v. Jason Surjana Tanuwidjaja*, [2014] 2 SLR 1261, [8]. *See also Maruti Shipping Pte Ltd v. Tay Sien Djim*, [2014] SGHC 227, [17].

2070. *Pertamina Energy Trading Ltd v. Karaha Bodas Co LLC*, [2007] 2 SLR(R) 518, [51], cited in *Maruti Shipping Pte Ltd v. Tay Sien Djim*, [2014] SGHC 227, [18].

be held liable for contempt, so long he understands what he must not do and that he will be in trouble if he disobeys the court order.[2071]

581. In situations where a body corporate disobeys an order, the order for committal may be issued against a director of the corporation[2072] if he knowingly participated, aided, or abetted in the breach of the order.[2073] A director is under a duty to take reasonable steps to ensure that the corporation complies with the court order.[2074] Therefore, any failure by the director to supervise or investigate or wilful blindness on the part of the director may be regarded as wilful conduct.[2075] The director may then be liable for contempt of court, unless he can show that he reasonably believed that some other director or officer was taking such steps.[2076]

582. As long as there is a deliberate breach of the court order, the reasons for disobedience are irrelevant in establishing liability, and are only relevant for sentencing.[2077] It is no defence for the defendant to dispute that the court order should not have been made or discharged.[2078] While a defendant may plead that he is mentally unwell to negate the mens rea for contempt of court and hence should not be liable for contempt of court on this basis if he does not appear in court, the court is wary of such defendants who may use this as a tactic to delay court proceedings.[2079]

583. The penalty for contempt of court may take the form of a term of imprisonment, a fine, or the provision of security for good behaviour.[2080] The penalties that may be imposed for contempt by the State Courts for contempt in the face of the court and contempt in connection with proceedings in the State Courts are limited by the State Courts Act to imprisonment for a term not exceeding six months or a

---

2071. *Maruti Shipping Pte Ltd v. Tay Sien Djim*, [2014] SGHC 227, [43], citing *P v. P (Contempt of Court: Mental Capacity)*, [1999] 2 FLR 897, 902.

2072. Supreme Court of Judicature Act (Cap. 322, R. 5, 2014 Rev. Ed.) Rules of Court, O 45 r 5.

2073. *Singapore Civil Procedure 2015 Volume 1*, at 890 (G.P. Selvam ed., Sweet & Maxwell Asia 2014), citing *Re Galvanised Tank Manufacturers' Association Agreement*, [1965] 2 All ER 1003.

2074. *Singapore Civil Procedure 2015 Volume 1*, at 890 (G.P. Selvam ed., Sweet & Maxwell Asia 2014).

2075. *Maruti Shipping Pte Ltd v. Tay Sien Djim*, [2014] SGHC 227, [117], citing *Attorney General of Tuvalu v. Philatelic Distribution Corp Ltd*, [1990] 1 WLR 926, 938.

2076. *Singapore Civil Procedure 2015 Volume 1*, at 890 (G.P. Selvam ed., Sweet & Maxwell Asia 2014)., citing *Attorney General of Tuvalu v. Philatelic Distribution Corp Ltd*, [1990] 1 WLR 926, 938.

2077. *Global Distressed Alpha Fund I Ltd Partnership v. PT Bakrie Investindo*, [2013] SGHC 105, [33], cited in *STX Corp v. Jason Surjana Tanuwidjaja*, [2014] 2 SLR 1261, [9]. *See also Maruti Shipping Pte Ltd v. Tay Sien Djim*, [2014] SGHC 227, [17].

2078. *Maruti Shipping Pte Ltd v. Tay Sien Djim*, [2014] SGHC 227, [90]: An order of the court must be obeyed while it stands, and a breach is still contempt even if, at a later stage, the order is in fact discharged. The same principle applies if the original order was wrongly made; the defendant's remedy is to apply for its immediate discharge while keeping to its terms.

2079. *Maruti Shipping Pte Ltd v. Tay Sien Djim*, [2014] SGHC 227, [34]–[35], citing *Forresters Ketley v. Brent*, [2012] EWCA Civ 324, [25].

2080. *Lee Hsien Loong v. Singapore Democratic Party*, [2009] 1 SLR(R) 642, [179]; Supreme Court of Judicature Act (Cap. 322, R. 5, 2014 Rev. Ed.) Rules of Court, O 52 r 8.

fine not exceeding SGD 2,000 or both.[2081] In deciding the appropriate punishment, the court will consider the following: the culpability of the contemnor; the nature and gravity of the contempt; the seriousness of the occasion on which the contempt was committed; the number of contemptuous statements made; the type and extent of dissemination of the contemptuous statements; the importance of deterring would be contemnors from following suit; whether the contemnor was a repeat offender; and whether or not the contemnor was remorseful (this particular factor being embodied paradigmatically in a sincere apology).[2082] The court's power to imprison should only be imposed in the most serious cases.[2083] It has been noted that conduct clearly calculated to interrupt court proceedings commonly attract terms of imprisonment.[2084] However, there was no starting point of imprisonment for the offence of scandalizing contempt.[2085]

§4. POSSIBILITY OF APPEAL

584. An appellate court has the power to hear and adjudicate an appeal against an order for committal and sentence and, if necessary, quash the order for committal and sentence, notwithstanding that the sentence had already been fully served.[2086] The traditional grounds for appellate intervention apply to reverse findings of contempt of court and have been summarized as follows:

> where the lower court has erred in applying legal rules to the facts before it (… where it has no discretion, such as making a finding of contempt) are well-known: an appellate court will intervene where the lower court has misdirected itself as to the law, or where the lower court has made findings of fact which are plainly wrong or against the weight of the evidence … Where a lower court has made a decision in the exercise of judicial discretion, e.g., the sentence to be imposed in respect of a proven contempt, an appellate court will not intervene unless' … it is clearly wrong, as when the judge was mistaken

2081. State Courts Act (Cap. 321, 2007 Rev. Ed.), s 8(2).

2082. *Maruti Shipping Pte Ltd v. Tay Sien Djim*, [2014] SGHC 227, [114], citing *Sembcorp Marine Ltd v. Aurol Anthony Sabastian*, [2013] 1 SLR 245, [68]. *See also Regina v. Thomson Newspapers Ltd, Ex Parte Attorney-General*, [1968] 1 WLR 1, 4; *Attorney-General v. Zimmerman Fred*, [1985–1986] SLR(R) 476, [51]; *Lee Hsien Loong v. Singapore Democratic Party*, [2009] 1 SLR(R) 642, [179], citing *Attorney-General v. Chee Soon Juan*, [2006] 2 SLR(R) 650, [57]; *Attorney-General v. Hertzberg Daniel*, [2009] 1 SLR(R) 1103, [59]; *Shadrake Alan v. Attorney-General*, [2011] 3 SLR 778, [146] citing *Attorney-General v. Tan Liang Joo John*, [2009] 2 SLR(R) 1132, [31], [39]. C.f. *Tahir v. Tay Kar Oon*, [2016] SGHC 60, [43]–[46].

2083. *You Xin v. Public Prosecutor*, [2007] 4 SLR(R) 17, [78].

2084. *You Xin v. Public Prosecutor*, [2007] 4 SLR(R) 17, [78]–[79], citing *R v. Thomson Newspapers Ltd, Ex parte Attorney-General* [1968] 1 WLR 1, 4; *Attorney-General v. Chee Soon Juan*, [2006] 2 SLR(R) 650, [58]; *Re Tan Khee Eng John* [1997] 1 SLR(R) 870, [14].

2085. *Tay Kar Oon v. Tahir*, [2017] SGCA 31, [58]; *Shadrake Alan v. Attorney-General*, [2011] 3 SLR 778, [148].

2086. *Tan Beow Hiong v. Tan Boon Aik*, [2010] 4 SLR 870, [30].

in law or disregarded or misapplied a significant principle or failed to appreciate the true facts or took into account irrelevant considerations or exceeded the discretion vested in him or failed to exercise any discretion at all'.[2087]

585. In respect of an order refusing or granting leave for an application for an order of committal to be brought, it is not quite clear whether an appeal is available to the Court of Appeal. Section 34 of the Supreme Court of Judicature Act,[2088] read together with the Fourth and Fifth Schedules of the statute, determines whether any given order of civil procedure is appealable to the Court of Appeal[2089] or not.[2090] Due to recent amendments to the Supreme Court of Judicature Act, the law on this is currently in flux and while it has been suggested that the 'default' position is that all interlocutory applications, unless provided for statutorily, are appealable with leave,[2091] it may also be possible to argue that for interlocutory applications not expressly addressed by the Fourth and Fifth Schedules, 'an appeal to the Court of Appeal will remain as of right for orders made at interlocutory applications which will finally dispose of the substantive rights of the parties'.[2092]

586. It is suggested that an analogy may be drawn between an order refusing or granting leave for an application for an order of committal to be brought and an order refusing or granting leave in an application for leave to administer pre-action interrogatories, which the Court of Appeal has held to be appealable as of right to the Court of Appeal.[2093] This is because, similar to an application for leave to administer pre-action interrogatories, an application for leave to apply for an order of committal should not be regarded as an interlocutory application within the meaning of the Fifth Schedule of the Supreme Court of Judicature Act. Although it may be sought by way of originating summons or summons, it has as its only end

---

2087. *Tan Beow Hiong v. Tan Boon Aik*, [2010] 4 SLR 870, [45]–[46], citing J. Pinsler, *Singapore Court Practice 2009* (Singapore: LexisNexis, 2009), [57/1/12]–[57/1/15]; *Re Bramblevale Ltd*, [1970] Ch 128; *Banton v. Banton*, [1990] 2 FLR 465.
2088. (Cap. 322, 2007 Rev. Ed.).
2089. Below it is the High Court, followed by the District and Magistrates' Courts. For appeals arising from the lower courts, *see* Supreme Court of Judicature Act (Cap. 322, R. 5, 2014 Rev. Ed.) Rules of Court, O 55B, 55C, and 55D. There is a right of appeal from a registrar in chambers to a judge in chambers (District Judge if it is the State Courts), but not necessarily after that stage.
2090. The statute was amended in 2010 and 2014.
2091. *See* E. Chua, *Defining an 'Interlocutory Application'*, Sing. L. Watch Commentaries (4/2013); D. Chi, '*Clarification on Leave to Appeal Regime in Respect of Interlocutory Matters: OpenNet Pte Ltd v. Info-Communications Development Authority of Singapore [2013] SGCA 24*, Sing. L. Watch Commentaries (4/2013); C. Siyuan & E. Chua, *The Right to Appeal Against a Decision Made on an Interlocutory Application: The Immediate Aftermath of the 2010 Amendments*, 25 Sing. Acad. L.J. 424 (2013).
2092. *OpenNet Pte Ltd v. Info-Communications Development Authority of Singapore*, [2013] 2 SLR 8802 SLR 880, [29]. *See also Dorsey James Michael v. World Sport Group Pte Ltd*, [2013] 3 SLR 354, [98]. On the other hand, where the statute has made it clear that there is no appeal as of right, one is precluded from arguing that substantive rights have been engaged: *Kosui Singapore Pte Ltd v. Thangavelu*, [2016] 2 SLR 105, [28]–[29].
2093. *Dorsey James Michael v. World Sport Group Pte Ltd*, [2013] 3 SLR 354.

the particular relief sought and 'once the application for such relief has been considered and ruled upon by the court, that matter ends'.[2094] If this argument is accepted, then the provisions of section 34, including the Fourth and Fifth Schedule do not apply to limit the right of appeal for an application for leave to apply for an order of committal, and an appeal may accordingly be brought to the Court of Appeal. However, it should be noted that this position is far from certain given that it is also possible for the court to regard such an application as 'interlocutory' in nature when it is brought by way of summons and is made and heard 'between the time a party files a civil case in court and when that case is finally heard for disposal'.[2095] If so, then an application for leave to appeal would be required before an appeal may be brought to the Court of Appeal.

2094. *Dorsey James Michael v. World Sport Group Pte Ltd*, [2013] 3 SLR 354, [60].
2095. *Dorsey James Michael v. World Sport Group Pte Ltd*, [2013] 3 SLR 354, [60] (emphasis in original).

Chapter 5. Stay of Proceedings

§1. Introduction

587. A stay of proceedings refers to the postponement, halting, or suspension of legal proceedings; it may be permanent or limited in nature and may be granted for a variety of reasons.[2096] This chapter will discuss in detail not only the two most common types of stay applications – a stay on the basis of forum non conveniens and a stay in favour of arbitration proceedings – but will also briefly examine other situations in which a stay of proceedings may be granted. A stay of proceedings ought to be distinguished from a stay of execution – the former relates to the entire legal proceedings, whereas the latter relates to the execution of a judgment resulting from legal proceedings. A stay of execution will be discussed separately in a subsequent Part, but suffice to say for now it is usually sought with a view to lodging an appeal. The power of the court to stay of proceedings may be found in paragraph 9 of the First Schedule of the Supreme Court of Judicature Act,[2097] which states that the court has the power 'to dismiss or stay proceedings where the matter in question is res judicata between the parties, or where by reason of multiplicity of proceedings in any court or courts or by reason of a court in Singapore not being the appropriate forum the proceedings ought not to be continued'. This power also allows the court to grant a limited stay of its proceedings pending the determination of foreign proceedings. This limited stay will be ordered when there is a multiplicity of proceedings; and in exercising these powers, the court is entitled to consider all the circumstances of the case. The underlying concern is the need to ensure the efficient and fair resolution of the dispute as a whole.[2098]

§2. Forum Non Conveniens

588. A 'defendant who wishes to contend that the Court should not assume jurisdiction over the action on the ground that Singapore is not the proper forum for the dispute shall enter an appearance and, within the time limited for serving a defence, apply to Court for an order staying the proceedings'.[2099] Such an application should be made by way of 'summons supported by an affidavit verifying the facts on which the application is based and a copy of the affidavit must be served with the summons'.[2100] At the hearing of the application, the court may make orders it thinks fit and 'give such directions for its disposal as may be appropriate, including directions for the trial thereof as a preliminary issue'.[2101] An order to stay the Singapore

2096. *Black's Law Dictionary* (B.A. Garner ed., Thomson Reuters 2009), 'stay'.
2097. (Cap. 322, 2007 Rev. Ed.).
2098. *BNP Paribas Wealth Management v. Jacob Agam and another* [2017] 3 SLR 27, [35].
2099. Supreme Court of Judicature Act (Cap. 322, R. 5, 2014 Rev. Ed.) Rules of Court, O 12 r 7(2), O 28 r 2A(2).
2100. Supreme Court of Judicature Act (Cap. 322, R. 5, 2014 Rev. Ed.) Rules of Court, O 12 r 7(3), O 28 r 2A(3).
2101. Supreme Court of Judicature Act (Cap. 322, R. 5, 2014 Rev. Ed.) Rules of Court, O 12 r 7(4), O 28 r 2A(4).

court proceedings is only suspensory. The court remains seised of proceedings and may, in principle, lift the stay if, for example, the premise upon which the stay was granted turns out to be mistaken.[2102]

I. Matters to Be Considered

589. The principles governing the determination of the proper forum for a dispute in Singapore are largely derived from the House of Lords decision of *Spiliada Maritime v. Cansulex Ltd.*[2103] First, the court has to consider whether there is prima facie some other available forum having competent jurisdiction that is more appropriate for the trial of the dispute in question; and, second, whether, although there is prima facie another forum which is the more appropriate forum for trial based on the first stage of the test, there are circumstances by reason of which justice requires that a stay of proceedings should nevertheless be refused.[2104] In the first stage of the Spiliada test, the court considers the relevant connecting factors including the locations of the parties, relevant witnesses,[2105] facts, and evidence, and the applicable law to the issues in dispute.[2106] The list of connecting factors is not closed and will depend on the factual matrix of each case.[2107] They may be categorized as follows: personal connections; connections to events and transactions; governing law; other parallel proceedings;[2108] and shape of the litigation.[2109] The merits of the claim or

---

2102. *Rotary Engineering Ltd and others v. Kioumji & Eslim Law Firm and another and another appeal* [2017] 1 SLR 907, [24].

2103. [1987] AC 460. *See also JIO Minerals FZC v. Mineral Enterprises Ltd*, [2011] 1 SLR 391, [38].

2104. *Sun Jin Engineering Pte Ltd v. Hwang Jae Woo*, [2011] 2 SLR 196, [11] and [13]; *Abdul Rashid bin Abdul Manaf v. Hii Yii Ann*, [2016] SGHCR 1, [10].

2105. In considering the location of witnesses as a factor, the court must bear in mind the issues in the action. Only witnesses whose evidence is potentially material and relevant to the issues in the action should be reckoned. Moreover, location of witnesses is only really significant in relation to third-party witnesses who are not in the employ of the party as it could give rise to issues of compellability: *see CIMB Bank Bhd v. Dresdner Kleinwort Ltd* [2008] 4 SLR(R) 543, [69]; *Trung Nguyen Group Corp v. Trung Nguyen International Pte Ltd and others* [2016] SGHC 256, [34].

2106. *JIO Minerals FZC v. Mineral Enterprises Ltd*, [2011] 1 SLR 391, [41], citing Yeo T.M., *Halsbury's Laws of Singapore*, vol. 6(2), [75.090] (LexisNexis 2009). *See also UBS AG v. Telesto Investments Ltd*, [2011] 4 SLR 503, [52]; *Rickshaw Investments Ltd v. Nicolai Baron von Uexkull*, [2007] 1 SLR(R) 377, [15].

2107. For example, in the family law context, where the main question before the court was whether divorce proceedings should be heard in Singapore or England, the factors taken into account by the court included the intended relocation of the wife and the children to England (pointing towards England as the English courts could better determine the best interests of the children in the light of the wife's lifestyle and children's new schooling schedule), the no fault basis for divorce in both England and Singapore (making the location of evidence and witnesses a neutral point as both parties acknowledged that the marriage had broken down irretrievably) and the location of assets (pointing to the English courts being more able to anticipate the future conduct and circumstances of the parties taking into account the standard of living in England and the potential earning capacity of parties in their respective contexts). *See also AQD v. AQE*, [2011] SGHC 92; J. Lee, *Conflict of Laws: Annual Review of Singapore Cases* [10.4] (Sing. Acad. L. 2008).

2108. *Virsagi Management (S) Pte Ltd v. Welltech Construction Pte Ltd and another appeal* [2013] 4 SLR 1097, [39]. In this regard, the risk of conflicting judgments is not decisive, and must be weighed against the other factors: *see Trisuryo Garuda Nusa Pte Ltd v. SKP Pradiksi (North) Sdn Bhd and another and another appeal* [2017] SGCA 49, [64].

defence are irrelevant.[2110] In any particular case, it is essential to identify those factors that are likely to be material to the fair determination of the dispute, and to ascribe greater weight to such factors over others.[2111] In the second stage of the Spiliada test, all the circumstances of the case, including the factors in the first stage of the Spiliada test,[2112] may be considered but 'the court is primarily concerned with the question whether there are circumstances by reason of justice why it should exercise its jurisdiction even if it is not the prima facie natural forum'.[2113] In doing so:

> The court of the forum needs to tread a fine balance between justice to the parties and international comity. In considering this question, the court will not pass judgment on the competence or independence of the judiciary of another country, all the more so of a friendly foreign country, and will assiduously avoid comparing the quality of justice obtainable under its own legal system and the foreign legal system. It is not true that the quality of foreign judiciary will never be questioned, but the court of the forum will take a very cautious approach. The mere fact that the plaintiff has a legitimate or juridical advantage in proceedings in Singapore will not be decisive. The plaintiff must establish with cogent evidence that he will be denied substantial justice if the case is not heard in the forum.[2114]

590. In the final analysis, it is the quality of the connecting factors that is crucial in determining whether a particular forum is more appropriate than another for the determination of a dispute. The search is for the connections that are most relevant to the dispute so as to enable it to be tried in the jurisdiction that is most suitable for the interests of the parties and the ends of justice.[2115] It is worth noting that with the establishment of the SICC, the fact that a matter in the High Court is appropriate for transfer to the SICC is a relevant consideration when determining whether there is a more appropriate forum.[2116]

591. In terms of the burden of proof,[2117] at the first stage of the Spiliada test, the defendant has the legal burden of proving the facts which establish that another

---

2109. *JIO Minerals FZC v. Mineral Enterprises Ltd*, [2011] 1 SLR 391, [41]–[42], citing Yeo T.M., *Halsbury's Laws of Singapore*, vol. 6(2), [75.091]–[75.095] (LexisNexis 2009). *See also Abdul Rashid bin Abdul Manaf v. Hii Yii Ann*, [2016] SGHCR 1, [27]–[34].

2110. *The 'Rainbow Joy'*, [2005] 3 SLR(R) 719, [27]. *C.f. Abdul Rashid bin Abdul Manaf v. Hii Yii Ann*, [2016] SGHCR 1, [15]–[20].

2111. *Trisuryo Garuda Nusa Pte Ltd v. SKP Pradiksi (North) Sdn Bhd and another and another appeal* [2017] SGCA 49, [39].

2112. The court can also consider whether the applicable rules of evidence in the foreign jurisdiction would in fact give rise to a risk of injustice: *see Rotary Engineering Ltd and others v. Kioumji & Eslim Law Firm and another and another appeal* [2017] 1 SLR 907, [23].

2113. Yeo T.M., *Halsbury's Laws of Singapore*, vol. 6(2), [75.096] (LexisNexis 2009).

2114. Yeo T.M., *Halsbury's Laws of Singapore*, vol. 6(2), [75.096] (LexisNexis 2009).

2115. *Rappo, Tania v. Accent Delight International Ltd and another and another appeal* [2017] SGCA 27, [70].

2116. *Rappo, Tania v. Accent Delight International Ltd and another and another appeal* [2017] SGCA 27, [120]–[124].

2117. *See* J. Pinsler, *Evidence and the Litigation Process* 401–434 (3rd ed., LexisNexis 2010).

jurisdiction is 'clearly or distinctly more appropriate than Singapore'.[2118] The plaintiff would have the evidential burden of adducing evidence of facts supporting his contention that Singapore is the proper forum.[2119] An action would not be stayed if it is merely shown that connecting factors are interspersed across various jurisdictions other than Singapore.[2120] If the inquiry proceeds to the second stage of the Spiliada test when the first stage is answered in the affirmative, then the plaintiff would have the legal burden of establishing the facts which would persuade the court why the stay should be denied in the interests of justice.[2121] As an illustration of how the Spiliada test applies in Singapore, the following summary is helpful:

> the appellant company brought an action against its employee for breaches of certain duties under his contract of employment (by making unauthorised payments to third parties), in the course of his work in the Maldives, resulting in losses sustained by the appellant. The respondent applied to stay the Singapore proceedings. The Court of Appeal affirmed the High Court's finding that the Maldives was the proper forum for the adjudication of the dispute. The factors which justified this conclusion included the respondent's performance of his contract of employment in the Maldives at the material time, the alleged breaches of duty occurred in that country, the probability that Maldivian law governed the dispute, and (more importantly in the circumstances of the case) the fact that the relevant witnesses could only be compelled to testify in the Maldives, and were not willing to come to Singapore for this purpose. As for the second stage of the Spiliada test, both the High Court and Court of Appeal concluded that there were no circumstances which would justify a refusal of that stay. The Court of Appeal also confirmed the High Court's determination that the Singapore judiciary would not pass judgment on the competence or independence of a foreign court even if such a factor would ultimately affect its decision.[2122]

II. Effect of a Step in the Proceedings

592. A court has two distinct jurisdictions – the first jurisdiction is to determine if it has jurisdiction to hear a case and the second is to hear the merits of the case.[2123] Submission to the court's jurisdiction is an important issue to be determined since it represents an independent basis for the court to assume jurisdiction over the defendant.[2124] It is a question of fact in each case whether there has been

2118. *JIO Minerals FZC v. Mineral Enterprises Ltd*, [2011] 1 SLR 391, [38].
2119. *JIO Minerals FZC v. Mineral Enterprises Ltd*, [2011] 1 SLR 391, [38].
2120. *Orchard Capital I Ltd v. Ravindra Kumar Jhunjhunwala*, [2012] 2 SLR 519, [34]; *Abdul Rashid bin Abdul Manaf v. Hii Yii Ann*, [2016] SGHCR 1, [12].
2121. J. Pinsler, *Principles of Civil Procedure* 204–205 (Acad. Publg. 2013).
2122. J. Pinsler, *Principles of Civil Procedure* 205–206 (Acad. Publg. 2013).
2123. *Williams & Glyn's Bank plc v. Astro Dinamico Compania Naviera SA*, [1984] 1WLR 438.
2124. Supreme Court of Judicature Act (Cap. 322, R. 5, 2014 Rev. Ed.), s 16(1)(b).

a submission.[2125] The key consideration is that 'so long as the foreign defendant has not done anything which, considered in the context and circumstances of the case, is meaningful only if he has waived any objection to the existence of the local court's jurisdiction, he should not be treated as having submitted to jurisdiction'.[2126] Specifically, an application to challenge service out of jurisdiction, coupled with a fall-back application to stay on the grounds of forum non conveniens, does not constitute submission to a Singapore court.[2127]

593. In an application under O 12 r 7(1) of the Rules of Court, a step in the proceedings, such as the service of the defence or other acts involving the merits of the case, could constitute a submission to the jurisdiction of the court which would be wholly inconsistent with an application to challenge the court's jurisdiction.[2128] If the foreign defendant has been validly served with an originating process out of jurisdiction, he should enter an appearance and challenge the existence of Singapore courts' jurisdiction by applying for an order to 'set aside the writ or service of the writ'.[2129] However, a step in the proceedings will not have the same significance in an application for a stay of proceedings under O 12 r 7(2) of the Rules of Court because the defendant in this situation accepts the jurisdiction of the court and is merely asking the court not to exercise it on the basis that Singapore is not the proper forum.[2130]

594. Although applications under O 12 rr 7(1) and 7(2), taken separately, are inconsistent courses of conduct,[2131] a foreign defendant:

> who disputes the existence of the Singapore courts' jurisdiction under O 12 r 7(1) and also applies for a stay of proceedings on improper forum grounds

2125. *Zoom Communications Ltd v. Broadcast Solutions Pte Ltd*, [2014] 4 SLR 500, [32]; *International SOS Pte Ltd v. Overton Mark Harold George*, [2001] 2 SLR(R) 777, [5].
2126. *Zoom Communications Ltd v. Broadcast Solutions Pte Ltd*, [2014] 4 SLR 500, [33]. As a matter of principle, a party should only be taken to have waived a legal right if his conduct is unequivocal: *id.*, [44], citing *Advent Capital plc v. G N Ellinas Imports-Exports Ltd,* [2005] EWHC 1242 (Comm), [78].
2127. *Zoom Communications Ltd v. Broadcast Solutions Pte Ltd*, [2014] 4 SLR 500, [56].
2128. J. Pinsler, *Principles of Civil Procedure* 208 (Acad. Publg. 2013) citing *Chan Chin Cheung v. Chan Fatt Cheung*, [2010] 1 SLR 1192; *Sun Jin Engineering Pte Ltd v. Hwang Jae Woo*, [2011] 2 SLR 196. *See also Zoom Communications Ltd v. Broadcast Solutions Pte Ltd*, [2014] 4 SLR 500, [1].
2129. Supreme Court of Judicature Act (Cap. 322, R. 5, 2014 Rev. Ed.) Rules of Court, O 12 r 7(1)(a).
2130. For example, in *Sim Hok Hkun @ Hadi Gunawan v. Henry Budi Harsono @ Sim Hok Kiong* [2012] SGHCR 1, the defendant's application for extension of time to file his defence did not preclude an application for a stay of proceedings on the basis of *forum non conveniens.*
2131. The inconsistency arises because a prayer challenging the existence of the Singapore court's jurisdiction denies that the Singapore courts have jurisdiction over the foreign defendant, while a prayer for a stay of proceedings on improper forum grounds admits that the Singapore courts have jurisdiction but pleads that it should not be exercised: *Zoom Communications Ltd v. Broadcast Solutions Pte Ltd*, [2014] 4 SLR 500, [45] *See also* Yeo T.M., *Halsbury's Laws of Singapore*, vol. 6(2), [75.095] (LexisNexis 2009).

under O 12 r 7(2) will generally not be taken to have submitted to the jurisdiction of the Singapore courts provided the latter application for a stay is made as a fall-back to the jurisdictional challenge.[2132]

595. In other words, when the prayer for stay of proceedings on improper forum grounds is framed as a fall-back to a prayer challenging existence of the Singapore courts' jurisdiction), the foreign defendant's conduct would not constitute a waiver of its objection to the existence of the Singapore court's jurisdiction.[2133] This is because the foreign defendant has not waived any objection to the existence of the Singapore courts' jurisdiction.[2134] A foreign defendant who applies to stay proceedings in a local court pending the outcome of proceedings in a foreign jurisdiction would also not amount to submission to the local court, if the outcome of the foreign proceedings had to be known before the question of the local court's jurisdiction can be determined.[2135] On the other hand, a foreign defendant who applies for a stay of proceedings on improper forum grounds without also contesting the existence of the Singapore court's jurisdiction will ordinarily be taken to have submitted to the jurisdiction.[2136]

III. Effect of Expiry of Time Limit for Making an Application

596. The Rules of Court provide that an application for a stay of proceedings on the basis of forum non conveniens is to be made 'within the time limited for serving a defence'.[2137] In other words, the application must be made 'before the expiration of 14 days after the time limited for appearing or after the statement of claim is served on [the defendant], whichever is the later'.[2138] Nevertheless, the court has

2132. *Zoom Communications Ltd v. Broadcast Solutions Pte Ltd*, [2014] 4 SLR 500, [56]. *See also* D. Tay, *When Does One Cross the Rubicon of Submission?*,26 Sing. Acad. L.J. 738 (2014).

2133. While it seem advantageous to adopt such a strategy since the timelines in O 12 rr 7(1) and 7(2) are the same, it is not advisable for a foreign defendant to do so based on the same material: *Zoom Communications Ltd v. Broadcast Solutions Pte Ltd*, [2014] 4 SLR 500, [30], [47] and [78] to [80]. *See also* D. Tay, *When Does One Cross the Rubicon of Submission?*,26 Sing. Acad. L.J. 738 (2014).

2134. *Zoom Communications Ltd v. Broadcast Solutions Pte Ltd*, [2014] 4 SLR 500, [65], citing *Williams & Glyn's Bank plc v. Astro Dinamico Compania Naviera SA*, [1984] 1WLR 438, [22]; *In re Dulles' Settlement (No 2)*, [1951] Ch 842, 850.

2135. *Williams & Glyn's Bank plc v. Astro Dinamico Compania Naviera SA*, [1984] 1WLR 438, 442. However, the Court of Appeal in *Zoom Communications Ltd v. Broadcast Solutions Pte Ltd*, [2014] 4 SLR 500, [54] cautioned that unlike English procedural rules, it is not clear if Singapore procedural rules or the High Court's inherent powers provide Singapore courts the power to stay proceedings without first assuming jurisdiction.

2136. *Chan Chin Cheung v. Chan Fatt Cheung*, [2010] 1 SLR 1192, [22]; *The Jian He*, [1999] 3 SLR(R) 432, [44], cited in *Broadcast Solutions Pte Ltd v. Zoom Communications Ltd*, [2014] 1 SLR 1324, [56].

2137. Supreme Court of Judicature Act (Cap. 322, R. 5, 2014 Rev. Ed.) Rules of Court, O 12 r 7(2) and O 28 r 2A(2).

2138. Supreme Court of Judicature Act (Cap. 322, R. 5, 2014 Rev. Ed.) Rules of Court, O 18 r 2(1).

the discretion to extend time,[2139] and the parties may also by consent (given in writing) extend time without an order of court.[2140] In exercising its discretion whether or not to grant an extension of time, the court has to balance the competing interests of the parties concerned, and the factual matrix of the case at hand will be paramount.[2141] The following factors will be relevant to the court's exercise of discretion: the length of the delay; the reasons for the delay; the chances of the defaulting party succeeding in its application if the time for filing it was extended; and the degree of prejudice to the other party if the extension of time were granted.[2142] An application for an extension of time does not in itself amount to an unequivocal submission to jurisdiction.[2143]

597. Although this is not a point that has been addressed by the Singapore courts in detail, it is possible that a lengthy delay in making a stay application may be treated as a waiver of one's right to make such an application.[2144] One commentator has argued that the applicant 'may be regarded as having waived his right where the delay is inexcusably long and he could have reasonably applied for a stay at an earlier point in time'.[2145]

§3. Stay in Favour of Arbitration Proceedings

598. A party to an arbitration agreement may, if any other party to the agreement commences court proceedings, apply for a stay of proceedings pursuant to the Arbitration Act[2146] or the International Arbitration Act.[2147] Whether or not the application is to be made under the Arbitration Act or the International Arbitration Act will depend on the nature of the arbitration. The International Arbitration Act will apply to any arbitration which is international[2148] or where parties have agreed in writing that the International Arbitration Act shall apply to the arbitration.[2149] For example, where parties to a domestic arbitration have agreed to adopt the rules of the Singapore International Arbitration Centre, these may provide that the law of the arbitration should be the International Arbitration Act.[2150] The Arbitration Act will

---

2139. Supreme Court of Judicature Act (Cap. 322, R. 5, 2014 Rev. Ed.) Rules of Court, O 3 r 4(1).
2140. Supreme Court of Judicature Act (Cap. 322, R. 5, 2014 Rev. Ed.) Rules of Court, O 3 r 4(3).
2141. *Sun Jin Engineering Pte Ltd v. Hwang Jae Woo*, [2011] 2 SLR 196, [30].
2142. *Sun Jin Engineering Pte Ltd v. Hwang Jae Woo*, [2011] 2 SLR 196, [29]–[30].
2143. *Broadcast Solutions Pte Ltd v, Zoom Communications Ltd*, [2014] 1 SLR 1324, [16].
2144. *Sun Jin Engineering Pte Ltd v. Hwang Jae Woo*, [2011] 2 SLR 196, [46], citing J. Pinsler, *Singapore Court Practice 2009* (Singapore: LexisNexis, 2009), [12/7/6].
2145. J. Pinsler, *Principles of Civil Procedure* 212 (Acad. Publg. 2013) citing *Caribbean Gold Ltd v. Alga Shipping Co Ltd*, [1993] 1 WLR 1100; *Lawson v. Midland Travellers Ltd*, [1993] 1 WLR 735.
2146. (Cap. 10, 2002 Rev. Ed.), s 6(1).
2147. (Cap. 143A, 2002 Rev. Ed.), s 6(1).
2148. *See* International Arbitration Act (Cap. 143A, 2002 Rev. Ed.), s 5(2).
2149. International Arbitration Act (Cap. 143A, 2002 Rev. Ed.), s 5.
2150. *See Cars & Cars Pte Ltd v. Volkswagen AG*, [2010] 1 SLR 625; *Navigator Investment Services Ltd v. Acclaim Insurance Brokers Pte Ltd*, [2010] 1 SLR 25.

apply to any arbitration where the place of arbitration is Singapore and where the International Arbitration Act does not apply to that arbitration.[2151]

599. In ordering a stay of proceedings, the court may impose such terms as it thinks fit.[2152] For example, the court has ordered a stay of proceedings on the condition that the applicants waive the defence of time bar.[2153] The discretion of the court to impose terms and conditions upon a stay in favour of arbitration is unfettered although it must be exercised judiciously.[2154] Where after a stay is ordered, no party to the proceedings takes any further step in the proceedings for a period of not less than two years after the stay order, the court may, on its own motion, make an order discontinuing the proceedings without prejudice to the right of any of the parties to apply for the discontinued proceedings to be reinstated.[2155]

I. Matters to Be Considered

600. In applications for a stay in favour of arbitration proceedings, it is important to bear in mind the overarching 'unequivocal judicial policy of facilitating and promoting arbitration' in Singapore.[2156] It has been said that '[i]n essence, a court ought to give effect to the parties' contractual choice as to the manner of dispute resolution unless it offends the law'.[2157] In respect of a stay application under the Arbitration Act, the court has some discretion as to whether or not to order a stay. The test is whether it is satisfied that 'there is no sufficient reason why the matter should not be referred in accordance with the arbitration agreement; and … the applicant was, at the time when the proceedings were commenced, and still remains, ready and willing to do all things necessary to the proper conduct of the arbitration'.[2158] However, in respect of a stay application under the International Arbitration Act, the court 'shall' order a stay 'unless it is satisfied that the arbitration agreement is null and void, inoperative or incapable of being performed'.[2159] This means that under the Arbitration Act, 'the court may determine if there is in fact a

2151. Arbitration Act (Cap. 10, 2002 Rev. Ed.), s 3.

2152. Arbitration Act (Cap. 10, 2002 Rev. Ed.), s 6(2); International Arbitration Act (Cap. 143A, 2002 Rev. Ed.), s 6(2).

2153. *See The Xanadu*, [1997] 3 SLR(R) 360; *The Duden*, [2008] 4 SLR(R) 984.

2154. *BAF v. BAG and others* [2016] SGHC 251, [42].

2155. Arbitration Act (Cap. 10, 2002 Rev. Ed.), s 6(4); International Arbitration Act (Cap. 143A, 2002 Rev. Ed.), s 6(4).

2156. *Tjong Very Sumito v. Antig Investments Pte Ltd*, [2009] 4 SLR(R) 732, [28].

2157. *Tjong Very Sumito v. Antig Investments Pte Ltd*, [2009] 4 SLR(R) 732, [28].

2158. Arbitration Act (Cap. 10, 2002 Rev. Ed.), s 6(2).

2159. International Arbitration Act (Cap. 143A, 2002 Rev. Ed.), s 6(2). Where there are remaining claims in the court proceedings not subject to the mandatory stay under the International Arbitration Act, the court in considering whether or not to grant a "case management stay" and the extent of the stay will, as final arbiter, take the lead in ensuring the efficient and fair resolution of the dispute as a whole and that this would turn on the facts of each individual case. *Tomolugen Holdings Ltd v. Silica Investors Ltd*, [2015] SGCA 57, [186]. The court will strike a balance between: first, a plaintiff's right to choose whom he wants to sue and where; second, the court's desire to prevent a plaintiff from circumventing the operation of an arbitration clause; and third, the court's inherent power to manage its processes to prevent an abuse of process and ensure the

dispute before deciding to order a stay, although the court should not examine the validity of the dispute as though the stay application is an application for summary judgment'.[2160] In contrast, the position under the International Arbitration Act is that once there is a dispute, and the arbitration agreement is not 'null and void, inoperative or incapable of being performed' a stay order is mandatory; the 'court is not to consider if there is in fact a dispute or whether there is a genuine dispute'.[2161] The standard to be applied in determining whether there is an arbitration agreement is a prima facie standard.[2162] The approach to determining whether a dispute exists has been summarized as follows:

> The common form arbitration agreement provides for disputes to be decided by arbitrators. In such a case the court should, save in obvious cases, adopt a holistic and commonsense approach to see if there is a dispute. The justification for this approach is that it is important to hold a party to his agreement and avoid double and split hearing of matters.[2163]

601. It has also been held that where the defendant makes a positive assertion that he is disputing the claim, then there is a dispute even though it can be easily demonstrated that the defendant is wrong.[2164] However, 'an admission by a defendant will, generally speaking, be contrary to a dispute but not every admission will necessarily avoid a stay order'.[2165] In short, all the defendant has to do is to make out a prima facie case of the existence of a dispute referable to arbitration. Once this is done, the burden will be on the plaintiff to show that there was no defence to the claim, the claim was so unanswerable that there was nothing to arbitrate,[2166] or that the arbitration agreement is null and void, inoperative or incapable of being performed.[2167] In other respects, the court's powers on granting a stay of proceedings under the Arbitration Act and the International Arbitration Act are similar.[2168]

---

efficient and fair resolution of disputes. *Tomolugen Holdings Ltd and another v. Silica Investors Ltd*, [2015] SGCA 57, [188]. *See also Epoch Minerals Pte Ltd v. Raffles Asset Management (S) Pte Ltd*, [2018] SGHC 223.

2160. *Dalian Hualiang Enterprise Group Co Ltd v. Louis Dreyfus Asia Pte Ltd*, [2005] 4 SLR(R) 646, [74].

2161. *Dalian Hualiang Enterprise Group Co Ltd v. Louis Dreyfus Asia Pte Ltd*, [2005] 4 SLR(R) 646, [75].

2162. *Malini Ventura v. Knight Capital Pte Ltd and others* [2015] SGHC 225; cited in *Tomolugen Holdings Ltd and another v. Silica Investors Ltd and other* appeals [2015] SGCA 57, [59]–[62].

2163. *Uni-Navigation Pte Ltd v. Wei Loong Shipping Pte Ltd*, [1992] 3 SLR(R) 595, [16]; cited in *Kwan Im Tong Chinese Temple v. Fong Choon Hung Construction Pte Ltd*, [1998] 1 SLR(R) 401, [14].

2164. *Tjong Very Sumito v. Antig Investments Pte Ltd*, [2009] 1 SLR(R) 861, [7]–[8]; *Dalian Hualiang Enterprise Group Co Ltd v. Louis Dreyfus Asia Pte Ltd*, [2005] 4 SLR(R) 646, [75].

2165. *Dalian Hualiang Enterprise Group Co Ltd v. Louis Dreyfus Asia Pte Ltd*, [2005] 4 SLR(R) 646, [75].

2166. *Kwan Im Tong Chinese Temple v. Fong Choon Hung Construction Pte Ltd*, [1998] 1 SLR(R) 401, [14]–[15].

2167. For an analysis of whether an arbitration agreement is null and void, inoperative or incapable of being performed, *see Dyna-Jet Pte Ltd v. Wilson Taylor Asia Pacific Pte Ltd* [2016] SGHC 238, [140]–[178].

2168. *See* Arbitration Act (Cap. 10, 2002 Rev. Ed.), s 7; International Arbitration Act (Cap. 143A, 2002 Rev. Ed.), s 7.

II. Effect of a Step in the Proceedings

602. The application for a stay of proceedings under both the Arbitration Act and the International Arbitration Act is to be made 'at any time after appearance and before delivering any pleading or taking any other step in the proceedings'.[2169] In other words, the earliest time at which a stay application in favour of arbitration can be made was when a substantive claim had already crystallized.[2170] The Court of Appeal has held that a 'step in the proceedings' referred to a step taken where the defendant had, first, evinced its intention to submit to the court's jurisdiction rather than seek recourse via arbitration; and, second, advanced the hearing of the matter in court.[2171] Applications which would amount to a step in the proceedings include an application for leave to defend, an application for discovery and an application for directions.[2172] A 'step in the proceedings' has also been judicially interpreted to exclude a defendant's application for an extension of time to serve the defence or to set aside a default judgment when such applications were filed bona fide in order to protect the defendant's position pending the determination of the stay application and were not intended to contest the merits of the case.[2173]

603. An act of the applicant in which he specifically states that he intends to seek a stay of proceedings or expressly reserves his right to do so, may also be excluded from being a 'step in the proceedings'.[2174] However, this is 'subject to the caveat that it is of course conceptually possible for an earlier reservation to be subsequently waived by clearly inconsistent conduct'.[2175] For example, where after filing an application for a stay of proceedings together with a defence and counterclaim stating that it was filed without prejudice to the defendant's right to stay proceedings, the defendant subsequently served a forty-eight hour notice on the plaintiff to file and serve a defence to counterclaim, the Singapore court has held that the serving of the forty-eight-hour notice constituted a 'step in the proceedings' which nullified the defendant's right to apply for a stay.[2176]

2169. Arbitration Act (Cap. 10, 2002 Rev. Ed.), s 6(1); International Arbitration Act (Cap. 143A, 2002 Rev. Ed.), s 6(1).

2170. *Navigator Investment Services Ltd v. Acclaim Insurance Brokers Pte Ltd*, [2010] 1 SLR 25, [53] and [68]. Therefore, an application for pre-action discovery and/or pre-action interrogatories would, by its very nature, not fall within the scope of s 6 of the Arbitration Act or the International Arbitration Act.

2171. *Carona Holdings Pte Ltd v. Go Go Delicacy Pte Ltd*, [2008] 4 SLR(R) 460, [52], [55], [93], [100].

2172. *Carona Holdings Pte Ltd v. Go Go Delicacy Pte Ltd*, [2008] 4 SLR(R) 460, [52]–[55].

2173. J. Pinsler, *Principles of Civil Procedure* 212–213 (Acad. Publg. 2013).

2174. J. Pinsler, *Principles of Civil Procedure* 213 (Acad. Publg. 2013) citing *Australian Timber Products Pte Ltd v. Koh Brothers Building and Civil Engineering Contractor (Pte) Ltd*, [2005] 1 SLR(R) 168; *Carona Holdings Pte Ltd v. Go Go Delicacy Pte Ltd*, [2008] 4 SLR(R) 460, [29]; *Chong Long Hack Kee Construction Trading Co v. IEC Global Pte Ltd*, [2003] 4 SLR(R) 499. *See also* J. Pinsler, *Singapore Court Practice 2009* (Singapore: LexisNexis, 2009), [69/2/8].

2175. *Carona Holdings Pte Ltd v. Go Go Delicacy Pte Ltd*, [2008] 4 SLR(R) 460, [101].

2176. *Chong Long Hak Kee Construction Trading Co v. IEC Global Pte Ltd*, [2003] 4 SLR(R) 499.

§4. Other Situations in Which a Stay of Proceedings May Be Granted

604. Apart from forum non conveniens, under paragraph 9 of the First Schedule of the Supreme Court of Judicature Act, the court may grant a stay of proceedings where the matter in question is res judicata between the parties,[2177] or by reason of multiplicity of proceedings in any court or courts.[2178] Under the Rules of Court, the court may order a stay of proceedings in, inter alia, the following situations: where two or more causes or matters are pending and it appears to the court that some common question of law or fact arises in both or all of them, that the rights to relief claimed therein are in respect of or arise out of the same transaction or series of transactions, or that for some other reason it is desirable to make an order;[2179] where relief is claimed against some but not all persons that are jointly but not severally liable under a contract, on application of any defendant, until the other persons so liable are added as defendants;[2180] where a defendant applies for interpleader relief;[2181] where a plaintiff in an action for personal injuries fails to serve a medical report and a statement of the special damages claimed with the statement of claim;[2182] when the court orders any pleading or the endorsement of any writ in the action or anything in any pleading or the endorsement to be struck out or amended;[2183] when the court makes an order for the production of documents in an action relating to a marine insurance policy;[2184] where a party who has discontinued or withdrawn a claim and is liable to pay the other party's costs, brings an action for the same or substantially the same cause of action, that action may be stayed pending the payment of outstanding costs;[2185] if it appears to the court that there is undue delay in the prosecution of any accounts or inquiries, or in any other proceedings under any judgment or order;[2186] when leave is granted to apply for a prohibiting order or a quashing order, pending the determination of the application;[2187] pending the provision of security in collision actions;[2188] in an action brought by partners in the name of a firm, when a notice to disclose the names and places of

---

2177. *See also* Supreme Court of Judicature Act (Cap. 322, R. 5, 2014 Rev. Ed.) Rules of Court, O 18 r 19(1).
2178. *See Chan Chin Cheung v. Chan Fatt Cheu*, [2010] 1 SLR 1192, [47]. A stay on the basis of multiplicity of proceedings may be permanent or limited and each would be treated differently: *RBS Coutts Bank Ltd v. Brunner Hans-Peter*, [2010] SGHC 342, [23]–[28]. In respect of the former, *see Multi-Code Electronics Industries (M) Bhd v. Toh Chun Toh Gordon*, [2009] 1 SLR(R) 1000; *Golden Shore Transportation Pte Ltd v. UCO Bank*, [2004] 1 SLR(R) 6. In respect of the latter, *see Chan Chin Cheung v. Chan Fatt Cheung*, [2010] 1 SLR 1192; *RBS Coutts Bank Ltd v. Brunner Hans-Peter*, [2010] SGHC 342.
2179. Supreme Court of Judicature Act (Cap. 322, R. 5, 2014 Rev. Ed.) Rules of Court, O 4 r 1(1).
2180. Supreme Court of Judicature Act (Cap. 322, R. 5, 2014 Rev. Ed.) Rules of Court, O 15 r 4(3).
2181. Supreme Court of Judicature Act (Cap. 322, R. 5, 2014 Rev. Ed.) Rules of Court, O 17 r 7.
2182. Supreme Court of Judicature Act (Cap. 322, R. 5, 2014 Rev. Ed.) Rules of Court, O 18 r 12(1).
2183. Supreme Court of Judicature Act (Cap. 322, R. 5, 2014 Rev. Ed.) Rules of Court, O 18 r 19(1).
2184. Supreme Court of Judicature Act (Cap. 322, R. 5, 2014 Rev. Ed.) Rules of Court, O 24 r 18.
2185. Supreme Court of Judicature Act (Cap. 322, R. 5, 2014 Rev. Ed.) Rules of Court, O 21 r 5.
2186. Supreme Court of Judicature Act (Cap. 322, R. 5, 2014 Rev. Ed.) Rules of Court, O 43 r 7.
2187. Supreme Court of Judicature Act (Cap. 322, R. 5, 2014 Rev. Ed.) Rules of Court, O 53 r 1(5).
2188. *See* Supreme Court of Judicature Act (Cap. 322, R. 5, 2014 Rev. Ed.) Rules of Court, O 70 r 27.

residence of all partners in the firm has not been complied with;[2189] in administration actions, when the plaintiff alleges that no or insufficient accounts have been furnished by the personal representatives, pending the furnishing of proper accounts.[2190] A stay of proceedings will automatically be in place under the Rules of Court on acceptance of money paid into court.[2191]

605. There are also other pieces of legislation which provide for a stay of proceedings in various contexts and situations.[2192] Further, a stay of proceedings may also be granted under the inherent jurisdiction of the court although no specific provision is made for it in primary or subsidiary legislation. For example, the High Court has granted a temporary stay of proceedings in exercise of its inherent jurisdiction on the ground that there was an arbitration which was intended to take place and the outcome of that arbitration would effectively determine the issues in dispute in the court proceedings.[2193] This was so even when there was no arbitration agreement between the immediate parties to those proceedings.[2194] The Court of Appeal has also granted a stay of court proceedings to allow arbitration proceedings which were related to the court proceedings to reach a conclusion,[2195] and where a dispute involves parties who are not bound by any arbitration agreement, if to do so was necessary to serve the ends of justice.[2196]

606. However, it must be borne in mind that the court will very rarely exercise its inherent jurisdiction to grant such a stay on case management grounds.[2197] The essential touchstone for the court to exercise its inherent jurisdiction is that of 'need'.[2198] Where the relevant arbitration agreement is governed by the Arbitration Act, pursuant to section 6 of the aforesaid Act, instead of imposing a stay on case management grounds, the court has the discretion to allow all claims, including those governed by the arbitration agreement, to proceed in the courts. That being

2189. Supreme Court of Judicature Act (Cap. 322, R. 5, 2014 Rev. Ed.) Rules of Court, O 77 r 2(1).

2190. Supreme Court of Judicature Act (Cap. 322, R. 5, 2014 Rev. Ed.) Rules of Court, O 80 r 5(2).

2191. Supreme Court of Judicature Act (Cap. 322, R. 5, 2014 Rev. Ed.) Rules of Court, O 22 r 3 and O78 r 4.

2192. *See* Bankruptcy Act (Cap. 20, 2009 Rev. Ed.), ss 64 and 74; Companies Act (Cap. 50, 2006 Rev. Ed.), ss 258, 279, 353.

2193. *Shanghai Construction (Group) General Co. Singapore Branch v. Tan Poo Seng*, [2012] SGHCR 10. *See also Borneo Ventures Pte Ltd v. Ong Han Nam*, [2017] SGHC 320; *Chan Chin Cgheung v. Chan Fatt Cheung*, [2010] 1 SLR 1192.

2194. *See Shanghai Construction (Group) General Co. Singapore Branch v. Tan Poo Seng*, [2012] SGHCR 10.

2195. *Tomolugen Holdings Ltd v. Silica Investors Ltd and other* appeals [2015] SGCA 57.

2196. *Gulf Hibiscus Ltd v. Rex International Holding Ltd and another* [2017] SGHC 210, [54]–[60].

2197. *Koh Kow Tee Michael v. Lee Ewe Ming Edward*, [2015] SGHC 60, [12]–[14], citing *Shanghai Construction (Group) General Co. Singapore Branch v. Tan Poo Seng*, [2012] SGHCR 10. *See also* D. Dubey, *Case Comment: Koh Kow Tee Michael v. Lee Ewe Ming Edward [2015] SGHC 60*, http://www.singaporelawblog.sg/blog/article/99, 30 Sep. 2017.

2198. *Koh Kow Tee Michael v. Lee Ewe Ming Edward*, [2015] SGHC 60, [15], citing *Wee Soon Kim Anthony v. Law Society of Singapore*, [2001] 2 SLR(R) 821. *See also Heng Joo See v. Ho Pol Ling*, [1993] 2 SLR(R) 763, [24]-[25], cited in *Eleven Gesellschaft Zur Entwicklung Und Vermarktung Von Netzwerktechonologien MBH v. Boxsentry Pte Ltd*, [2014] SGHC 210, [61].

said, the court will be slow to adopt that action as it was out of line with the desirability of holding the parties to their agreement, as well as Singapore's strong policy in favour of arbitration. Certainly, the fact that there were related actions, some governed by arbitration agreements and some not, was not in itself a sufficient reason for the court to adopt this option.[2199]

§5. Possibility of Appeal

607. An application for a stay of proceedings is usually heard by a registrar, against whose decision there is an automatic right of appeal to a High Court Judge. Section 34 of the Supreme Court of Judicature Act,[2200] read together with the Fourth and Fifth Schedules of the statute, determines whether any given order of civil procedure is appealable to the Court of Appeal[2201] or not.[2202] The Fourth Schedule makes no specific reference to an order relating to a stay of proceedings. The Fifth Schedule states that: 'Except with the leave of a Judge, no appeal shall be brought to the Court of Appeal … where a Judge makes an order refusing a stay of proceedings.' In other words, an appeal may be brought to the Court of Appeal against a decision refusing a stay of proceedings with the leave of a judge. In this respect, an order of a judge giving or refusing leave is final.[2203] However, where a High Court Judge makes an order granting a stay of proceedings, such an order will in all likelihood be appealable to the Court of Appeal as of right because no specific provision in the Supreme Court of Judicature Act and any other written law specify otherwise.[2204] Further, given that such an order will finally dispose of a party's substantive rights, it would be consistent with parliamentary intention for the matter to be appealable as of right to the Court of Appeal.[2205]

2199. *Maybank Kim Eng Securities Pte Ltd v. Lim Keng Yong and another* [2016] 3 SLR 431, [22], [23]. A similar approach was adopted in *BDC v. BDD and another* [2016] SGHC 202.
2200. (Cap. 322, 2007 Rev. Ed.).
2201. Below it is the High Court, followed by the District and Magistrates' Courts. For appeals arising from the lower courts, *see* Supreme Court of Judicature Act (Cap. 322, R. 5, 2014 Rev. Ed.) Rules of Court, O 55B, 55C, and 55D. There is a right of appeal from a registrar in chambers to a judge in chambers (District Judge if it is the State Courts), but not necessarily after that stage.
2202. The statute was amended in 2010 and 2014.
2203. Supreme Court of Judicature Act (Cap. 322, 2007 Rev. Ed.), s 34(2B).
2204. Supreme Court of Judicature Act (Cap. 322, 2007 Rev. Ed.), s 29A(1).
2205. *See* E. Chua, *Defining an 'Interlocutory Application*, Sing. L. Watch Commentaries (4/2013); D. Chi, *Clarification on Leave to Appeal Regime in Respect of Interlocutory Matters: OpenNet Pte Ltd v. Info-Communications Development Authority of Singapore [2013] SGCA 24*, Sing. L. Watch Commentaries (4/2013); C. Siyuan & E. Chua, *The Right to Appeal Against a Decision Made on an Interlocutory Application: The Immediate Aftermath of the 2010 Amendments*, 25 Sing. Acad. L.J. 424 (2013); *OpenNet Pte Ltd v. Info-Communications Development Authority of Singapore*, [2013] 2 SLR 8802 SLR 880; *Dorsey James Michael v. World Sport Group Pte Ltd*, [2013] 3 SLR 354.

Part VI. Legal Aid, Legal Costs, and Damages

Chapter 1. Legal Aid

608. The culture and infrastructure supporting legal aid in Singapore is probably only moderate in level. There is as yet no mandatory pro bono requirement for Singapore lawyers (though there is 'pro bono pledge' of twenty-four hours per lawyer), but there is generally no shortage of legal aid options. The Law Society of Singapore is responsible for legal aid in indirect and direct ways. First, it has the responsibility to protect and assist the public in Singapore in all matters relating to the law. This general responsibility is translated into programmes such as the Community Legal Clinic Scheme, Community Organisation Clinic, Law Awareness, Project Law Help, and the Ad Hoc Pro Bono Referral Scheme, of which many rely on student volunteers. Most of these services are rendered by the Pro Bono Services Office of the society, and is dependent on donations for sustainability. Second, it makes provision for or assists in the promotion of the Criminal Legal Aid Scheme whereby impecunious persons on non-capital charges have legal representation; for capital charges, the Supreme Court runs the Legal Assistance Scheme for Capital Offences.[2206] Third, it provides legal education in the form of literature, seminars, and conferences.

609. Then there is the Legal Aid Bureau, which is one of the departments run by the Ministry of Law. The Legal Aid Bureau, while providing services on a wide range of civil matters, does not handle criminal matters. To qualify for legal aid, an applicant must be a Singapore citizen or permanent resident. An applicant must also satisfy the means test (annual disposable income cannot exceed SGD 10,000 and

2206. In 2015, the Singapore government said that it would pledge up to SGD 3.5 million a year to fund the Criminal Legal Aid Scheme – up until that point, the scheme was not funded by the government at all. With this financial injection, the scheme is expected to serve up to 6,000 accused persons yearly, up from 400 now (there are more than 1,000 applications a year). Lawyers who do pro bono work for the scheme will also be given an honorarium of between SGD 500 and SGD 2,500, though many lawyers involved in pro bono work now are either attracted by the possibility of providing aid or the litigation exposure afforded to young lawyers. To ensure greater sustainability, a fellowship program will be created, in which five lawyers will be hired by the Law Society to do criminal legal aid work on a full-time basis; this will be developed in tandem with a structured mentorship program for young volunteer lawyers.

disposal capital cannot exceed SGD 10,000) and the merits test. The total contribution by an applicant usually does not exceed SGD 1,000. Assigned solicitors are drawn from a pool of volunteer lawyers.

610. The State Courts have a general help centre that explains court processes, procedures, and practices but does not provide legal advice. There is also a Family Court Legal Clinic, but the eligibility requirements are similar to that of the Legal Aid Bureau. There are walk-in pro bono centres run by the law schools; these centres are largely manned by students, but with some faculty oversight. Pro bono became compulsory for local law students matriculating from 2013 onwards. These students would need to clock at least twenty hours of pro bono work over the course of their undergraduate studies. Various private organizations such as religious groups and special interest associations also provide informal legal advice from time to time, usually in the form of workshops and knowledge dissemination.

611. In 2015, as part of his vision of increasing access to justice, Chief Justice Menon announced three initiatives: first, the Guidance for Plea scheme will be expanded so that pro bono lawyers are assigned to certain cases where accused persons intend to plead guilty and judges will identify the types of suitable cases to the Community Justice Centre so that suitable lawyers can be assigned to assist on matters such as bail, mental impairment, and multiple charges; second, to provide legal aid in suitable cases where the prosecution and accused person are exploring ways to resolve the matter without a trial; and third, the Primary Justice Project will be launched to offer basic legal advice for a fixed fee to parties in divorce cases and low-value civil cases. Also in 2015 it was announced that the processes in the State Courts would be made simpler and more expedient. For instance, fines and fees can be paid using self-service kiosks instead of counters, and more information booklets will be made available to help litigants navigate through the various court processes. In the Coroner's Court, iPads and still photographs will be used in deceased identification in lieu of identification in-person. Finally, together with the paradigm shift in the family court justice process, the State Courts will also be considering the feasibility of a more judge-lead approach in simple civil cases involving litigants-in-person.

Chapter 2. Security for Costs

§1. Introduction

612. When a defendant is sued, he is bound to incur costs as he is likely to engage the services of a lawyer and in addition there will be fees that need to be paid for the various applications that follow. In certain situations, it may be just and fair to require that if the event that the defendant either succeeds in defending the claim or is awarded costs in his favour.[2207] In other words, 'provision of security for costs ensures that a successful defendant (or a plaintiff who is defending a counterclaim) will have a fund, guarantee or other security available within the jurisdiction against which he can enforce the judgment for costs'.[2208] In the same vein, 'while it is up to the plaintiff to decide on whether to run the risk of suing a party who may not be good for costs, a defendant has no comparable choice and consequently, the law regards him more favourably, but only slightly'.[2209] However, security for costs will not be provided in all proceedings irrespective of the circumstances. Such 'an undiscriminating rule may undermine the fundamental principle of access to justice if the plaintiff is unable to put up security and is consequently prevented from proceeding with his action. The law strikes a balance between the plaintiff and defendant's interests.'[2210] The rules and procedures for security for costs are primarily found in O 23 of the Rules of Court,[2211] a large part of which continues to rely, but increasingly less so, on old English case law for its interpretation.[2212]

§2. Procedural Aspects

613. The Rules of Court do not provide for when security for costs should be sought and indeed the court can order it at any point of the proceedings,[2213] but there should not be any unnecessary delay on the part of the defendant to bring such an application. This is because unnecessary delay: may raise questions about the defendant's bona fides; may be impractical as the longer the delay, the more likely the plaintiff may preemptively dissipate funds in avoidance of any obligation to furnish security; and may cause the plaintiff to be unduly prejudiced if he had proceeded deep into the proceedings on the assumption that no security would be furnished

2207. Naturally, the defendant will return the security for costs to the plaintiff if the plaintiff prevails to the extent of costs awarded in his favour.

2208. J. Pinsler, *Principles of Civil Procedure* 1064 (Acad. Publg. 2013).

2209. *Singapore Civil Procedure 2015 Volume 1*, at 489 (G.P. Selvam ed., Sweet & Maxwell Asia 2014).

2210. J. Pinsler, *Principles of Civil Procedure* 1065 (Acad. Publg. 2013).

2211. Supreme Court of Judicature Act (Cap. 322, R. 5, 2014 Rev. Ed.) Rules of Court. *See also id.*, O 57 r 3(3).

2212. *Singapore Civil Procedure 2015 Volume 1*, at 489–506 (G.P. Selvam ed., Sweet & Maxwell Asia 2014). One particular difference with the English position is Supreme Court of Judicature Act (Cap. 322, R. 5, 2014 Rev. Ed.) Rules of Court, O 23 r 1(3), which gives the court the power to order a non-party to the proceedings to provide security for costs.

2213. *See also* Supreme Court of Judicature Act (Cap. 322, 2007 Rev. Ed.), s 36(1).

since there was no early indication.[2214] A defendant is at liberty to, and should on his own initiative attempt to obtain security from the plaintiff via a written request before making an application to court.[2215] Once that attempt has been exhausted, the defendant may apply to court by summons supported by an affidavit which states the grounds of the application.[2216]

§3. Substantive Aspects

614. The court must be satisfied that two requirements are met before granting the application.[2217]

I. Establishing a Ground

615. For the first requirement, the defendant must show that:

> that the plaintiff is ordinarily resident out of the jurisdiction; … that the plaintiff (not being a plaintiff who is suing in a representative capacity) is a nominal plaintiff who is suing for the benefit of some other person and that there is reason to believe that he will be unable to pay the costs of the defendant if ordered to do so; … that the plaintiff's address is not stated in the writ or other originating process or is incorrectly stated therein; or … that the plaintiff has changed his address during the course of the proceedings with a view to evading the consequences of the litigation.[2218]

616. It should be noted at this point that if the plaintiff is a corporation, section 388(1) of the Companies Act[2219] would apply.[2220] Likewise, if the plaintiff is a registered society of an officer acting on behalf of a registered society, section 36(1) of the Societies Act[2221] would apply.[2222]

2214. J. Pinsler, *Principles of Civil Procedure* 1067 (Acad. Publg. 2013) citing *Janred Properties v. Ente Nazionale Italiano per il Turismo*, (1986) TLR 1.
2215. J. Pinsler, *Principles of Civil Procedure* 1067 (Acad. Publg. 2013).
2216. J. Pinsler, *Principles of Civil Procedure* 1067 (Acad. Publg. 2013). *See also* Supreme Court of Judicature Act (Cap. 322, R. 5, 2014 Rev. Ed.) Rules of Court, O 23 r 1(4).
2217. *Elbow Holdings Pte Ltd v. Marina Bay Sands Pte Ltd*, [2014] SGHC 219, [6]; *Creative Elegance (M) Sdn Bhd v. Puay Kim Seng*, [1999] 1 SLR(R) 112, [13].
2218. Supreme Court of Judicature Act (Cap. 322, R. 5, 2014 Rev. Ed.) Rules of Court, O 23 r 1(1). It should be noted that if the plaintiff is a company, residence will be determined with reference to the *situs* of its central control or management.
2219. (Cap. 50, 2006 Rev. Ed.).
2220. *See also Ho Wing On Christopher v. ECRC Land Pte Ltd (in liquidation)*, [2006] 4 SLR(R) 817, [72]; *Siva Industries and Holdings Ltd v. Foreguard Shipping I Singapore Pte Ltd*, [2017] SGHCR 5, [3].
2221. (Cap. 311, 1985 Rev. Ed.).
2222. For a discussion on whether security of costs can be ordered against a not-for-profit society, *see Diamond Exchange of Singapore v. Singapore Diamond Exchange Pte Ltd*, [2013] SGHCR 10. It should also be noted that the power to order security for costs also arises in non-judicial settings,

617. With respect to the ground of the plaintiff being ordinarily out of jurisdiction, this can be said to be the most commonly invoked ground, and it stands to reason that if the plaintiff has no assets within the jurisdiction, he can easily avoid paying up should the defendant be awarded costs.[2223] This ground, however, sometimes requires a holistic examination of the facts. For instance, the mere fact that a plaintiff has been granted the status of permanent resident in Singapore is by no means conclusive in and of itself.[2224] In addition, a plaintiff who is abroad in an official capacity of a public servant will not be required to give security.[2225] Instead, ordinary residence 'is to be determined not only by his or her physical presence in a place, but also his mental attitude and purpose in relation to that place. In other words, the test for "ordinary residence" depends to a significant degree upon the state of mind of the person. It also connotes residence in a place with some degree of continuity apart from accidental or temporary absences';[2226] accordingly, it is possible that a plaintiff is found to be ordinarily resident out of, as well as within, the jurisdiction.[2227] Nonetheless, ordinary residence can be construed literally, in that it is usually sufficient if the foreign jurisdiction is the plaintiff's normal and habitual residence even if he is not domiciled there and has a permanent home elsewhere.[2228]

618. With respect to the ground of the plaintiff being a nominal plaintiff,[2229] examples include: where the plaintiff has assigned the benefit of an action;[2230] and where the plaintiff is insolvent and he assigns to a trustee for the benefit of his creditors all his estate and covenants to prosecute.[2231] However, it should be noted that an administrator, who is suing in a representative capacity, will not be considered a nominal plaintiff,[2232] and neither will a litigation representative.[2233] In addition, trustees in bankruptcy cannot be ordered to give security.[2234]

---

such as in domestic arbitration (Arbitration Act (Cap. 10, 2002 Rev. Ed.), s 28(2)) and international arbitration (International Arbitration Act (Cap. 143A, 2002 Rev. Ed.), s 12(1)). For a discussion on whether security of costs can be ordered against a foreign sovereign state (or its organs), *see Ministry of Rural Development, Fishery, Craft Industry and Environment of the Union of Comoros v. Chan Leng Leng*, [2013] 3 SLR 214.

2223. J. Pinsler, *Principles of Civil Procedure* 1068 (Acad. Publg. 2013).

2224. *Lek Swee Hua v. American Express International Inc*, [1990] 2 SLR(R) 514, [11].

2225. *Singapore Civil Procedure 2013 Volume 1*, at 442 (G.P. Selvam ed., Sweet & Maxwell Asia 2012) citing *Hugh Cecil Rabbetts v. Tatting Co (HK) Ltd*, [1950] 1 HKLR 31.

2226. *Tjong Very Sumito v. Chan Sing En*, [2011] 4 SLR 580, [22], citing *Akbarali v. Brent London Borough Council*, [1983] 2 AC 309, 343; *Levene v. Commissioners of Inland Revenue*, [1928] AC 217, 225. *See also Sin Tiong Wah International Pte Ltd v. Pee Wee Liang* [2019] SGHC 124.

2227. C. Bull & J. Pinsler, *Civil Procedure: Annual Review of Singapore Cases* [8.45] (Sing. Acad. L. 2010).

2228. J. Pinsler, *Principles of Civil Procedure* 1068 (Acad. Publg. 2013). C.f. *Tjong Very Sumito v. Chan Sing En*, [2011] 4 SLR 580, [51].

2229. *See also* J. Pinsler, *Principles of Civil Procedure* 1072 (Acad. Publg. 2013).

2230. *Semler v. Murphy*, [1968] 1 Ch 183, 189.

2231. *Lloyd v. Hathern Station Brick Co Ltd*, (1901) 85 LT 158.

2232. *Rainbow v. Kittoe*, [1916] 1 Ch 313, 315. *See also Envis v. Thakkar*, The Times (1995).

2233. *Fellows v. Barrett*, (1836) 48 ER 252.

2234. *Cowell v. Taylor*, (1885) 31 Ch D 34.

619. With respect to the ground of the plaintiff's address being incorrectly stated, the court will not require a plaintiff to give security if the plaintiff 'satisfies the Court that the failure to state his address or the mis-statement thereof was made innocently and without intention to deceive'.[2235] It is, of course, open to the defendant to present evidence to the court to show that the plaintiff actually lacks good faith.

620. With respect to the ground of the plaintiff changing his address during proceedings to evade the consequences of litigation, the court will not require a plaintiff to give security if he has endorsed a sufficient address on his writ and has afterwards removed that address, but is prevented by poverty and adversity from acquiring a fresh permanent address.[2236] However, it is open to the defendant to present evidence to the court that the plaintiff in any other situation has an intention to evade.

II. Whether It Is Just in All the Circumstances of the Case

621. For the second requirement (and this is regardless of whether the Rules of Court, Companies Act, or Societies Act applies),[2237] 'having regard to all the circumstances of the case, the Court thinks it just to do so, it may order the plaintiff to give such security for the defendant's costs of the action or other proceeding as it thinks just'.[2238] The second requirement is ultimately a weighing exercise for the court between different competing factors, as no objective criteria can ever be established as to the weight any particular factor should be accorded; moreover, the court has complete discretion in deciding the matter and will consider all the circumstances of the case to determine where the justice lies.[2239] In addition, there 'is no presumption in favour of, or against, a grant of security'.[2240] If anything, a court hearing a security for costs application should invariably adopt a more conservative approach so as to balance the interests of all the parties.[2241] The court may or may not investigate the merits of the case at this juncture as this security of costs hearing is a hearing of an interlocutory application and not a full trial, so all the relevant

---

2235. Supreme Court of Judicature Act (Cap. 322, R. 5, 2014 Rev. Ed.) Rules of Court, O 23 r 1(2). *See also Chellew v. Brown*, [1923] 2 KB 844, 847; *Pittsburgh Crushed Steel Co v. Jacob Marx & Co*, [1897] WN 36; *Knight v. Ponsonby*, [1925] 1 KB 545.

2236. *Knight v. Ponsonby*, [1925] 1 KB 545, 553.

2237. Supreme Court of Judicature Act (Cap. 322, R. 5, 2014 Rev. Ed.) Rules of Court, O 23 r 3: '[O 23] is without prejudice to the provisions of any written law which empowers the Court to require security to be given for the costs of any proceedings.' *See also Creative Elegance (M) Sdn Bhd v. Puay Kim Seng*, [1999] 1 SLR(R) 112, [13]; cited in *Wonda Kitchareon Ltd v. Greenlam Asia Pacific Pte Ltd*, [2010] SGHC 355, [10].

2238. Supreme Court of Judicature Act (Cap. 322, R. 5, 2014 Rev. Ed.) Rules of Court, O 23 r 1(1).

2239. *Jurong Town Corp v. Wishing Star Ltd*, [2004] 2 SLR(R) 427, [14], citing *Keary Developments Ltd v. Tarmac Construction Ltd*, [1995] 3 All ER 534.

2240. *Ong Jane Rebecca v. Pricewaterhousecoopers*, [2009] 2 SLR(R) 796, [21], citing *Jurong Town Corp v. Wishing Star Ltd*, [2004] 2 SLR(R) 427, [14].

2241. *Ong Jane Rebecca v. Pricewaterhousecoopers*, [2009] 2 SLR(R) 796, [34]. *See also Elbow Holdings Pte Ltd v. Marina Bay Sands Pte Ltd*, [2014] SGHC 219, [13].

evidence is unlikely to be at hand and all the issues may not be entirely clear.[2242] Be that as it may, the court will also consider the relative strengths and weaknesses of the parties' respective cases.[2243] Security for costs is unlikely to be awarded if the plaintiff demonstrates a very high probability of succeeding in the main trial.[2244] Likewise, if there is a strong prima facie presumption that the defendant will fail in his defence to the claim, the court will refuse to award any security for costs.[2245] In principle, one may presume the converse to be true as well: if the defendant can demonstrate a very high probability of defending the claim, the court would be minded to award security for costs.[2246]

622. Some other possible factors (some of which are related to the merits of the case) that the court may take into consideration when deciding whether an order will be just are: whether the plaintiff's claim is bona fide and not a sham; whether there is an admission to liability by the defendant in the pleadings or elsewhere; whether the application for security for costs is being used oppressively; whether the plaintiff's want of means has been brought about by the defendant; and whether the application was taken out in a timely manner.[2247] In addition, the court may also consider the complexity of the claim and the defence, since that would affect the quantum of legal cost;[2248] whether the order can be enforced or whether it will be unduly difficult to enforce it;[2249] whether the plaintiff has property in jurisdiction or out of jurisdiction;[2250] the reasonableness of the conduct of the parties,[2251] including whether the application is taken out in bad faith[2252] and whether the plaintiff is unduly placing obstacles in the path of the defendant to financially cripple him;[2253]

2242. *Frantonios Marine Services Pte Ltd v. Kay Swee Tuan*, [2008] 4 SLR(R) 224, [50]–[51], citing *Porzelack KG v. Porzelack (UK) Ltd*, [1987] 1 WLR 420, 423.

2243. *Elbow Holdings Pte Ltd v. Marina Bay Sands Pte Ltd*, [2014] SGHC 219, [17] citing *Creative Elegance (M) Sdn Bhd v. Puay Kim Seng*, [1999] 1 SLR(R) 112.

2244. That the test is significantly different (if different at all) for companies (the test being the plaintiff company need only show a bona fide claim with a reasonable prospect of success) was rejected in *Creative Elegance (M) Sdn Bhd v. Puay Kim Seng*, [1999] 1 SLR(R) 112, [25].

2245. *Crozat v. Brodgen*, [1894] 2 QB 30, 45; *Sir Lindsay Parkinson & Co Ltd v. Triplan Ltd*, [1973] QB 609, 626–627; *Porzelack KG v. Porzelack (UK) Ltd*, [1987] 1 WLR 420, 423. *See also Amar Hoseen Mohammed Revai v. Singapore Airlines Ltd*, [1994] 3 SLR(R) 290, [50]–[54]; *Tjong Very Sumito v. Chan Sing En*, [2011] 2 SLR 360, [10]. C.f. *Frantonios Marine Services Pte Ltd v. Kay Swee Tuan*, [2008] 4 SLR(R) 224, [49].

2246. J. Pinsler, *Principles of Civil Procedure* 1077 (Acad. Publg. 2013) citing *Thune v. London Properties Ltd*, [1990] 1 WLR 562.

2247. *L&M Concrete Specialists Pte Ltd v. United Eng Contractors Pte Ltd*, [2001] 3 SLR(R) 208, [10].

2248. *Frantonios Marine Services Pte Ltd v. Kay Swee Tuan*, [2008] 4 SLR(R) 224, [47]. That is to say, if the complexity of the issues is such that the defendant has to incur higher costs in responding to the plaintiff's claim, this will be a factor in favour of the defendant.

2249. *See also Frantonios Marine Services Pte Ltd v. Kay Swee Tuan*, [2008] 4 SLR(R) 224, [34].

2250. J. Pinsler, *Principles of Civil Procedure* 1077 (Acad. Publg. 2013) citing *De Bry v. Fitzgerald*, [1990] 1 WLR 552. *See also* J. Pinsler, *Principles of Civil Procedure* 1081 (Acad. Publg. 2013).

2251. *Omar Ali bin Mohd v. Syed Jafaralsadeg bin Abdulkadir Alhadad*, [1995] 2 SLR(R) 407, [33]–[36]. *See also Abdul Salam Asanaru Pillai v. Nomanbhoy & Sons Pte Ltd*, [2008] SGHC 48, [6].

2252. *Peng Ann Realty Pte Ltd v. Liu Cho Chit*, [1992] 3 SLR(R) 178, [16].

2253. *Abdul Salam Asanaru Pillai v. Nomanbhoy & Sons Pte Ltd*, [2008] SGHC 48, [6]. *See also Ooi Ching Ling Stanley v. Just Gems Inc*, [2002] 2 SLR(R) 738, [22].

whether a genuine claim from a small company against a big company may be stifled as a result of the security;[2254] whether there has been negotiations for a settlement and/or payment into court made by the defendant;[2255] whether the litigant is a natural person (since public policy leans favourably towards encouraging access to the courts);[2256] whether there are parallel international arbitration proceedings;[2257] and the commonality of the issues in both the main claim and counterclaim.[2258] The wide range of factors and factual scenarios listed above only serve to confirm that the court has a broad discretion when deciding whether the ordering of security for costs will be just.[2259] However, it should be noted that the fact that the defendant has been insured for legal costs is not considered a relevant factor.[2260] The impecuniousness of the plaintiff would also generally not preclude an order for security for costs either,[2261] even if the plaintiff is on legal aid.[2262]

III. Mode of Security

623. Once an order for security for costs is made, 'the security shall be given in such manner, at such time, and on such terms (if any), as the Court may direct'.[2263] Parties can agree as to the particular mode of security, but common modes include furnishing a banker's guarantee to the satisfaction of the defendant;[2264] payment into court;[2265] security by bond or charge;[2266] and providing a solicitor's undertaking.[2267] These will typically be facilitated within two to four weeks of the order being made, and it is also possible for the payments to be made in instalments. The order may also include peremptory consequences upon default, such as the staying of the action or dismissal of the action.[2268]

2254. *See Sembawang Engineering Pte Ltd v. Priser Asia Engineering Pte Ltd*, [1992] 2 SLR(R) 358, [19], citing *Pearson v. Naydler*, [1977] 3 All ER 531, 536.
2255. J. Pinsler, *Principles of Civil Procedure* 1077 (Acad. Publg. 2013).
2256. *Ong Jane Rebecca v. Pricewaterhousecoopers*, [2009] 2 SLR(R) 796, [30].
2257. *Zhong Da Chemical Development Co Ltd v. Lanco Industries Ltd*, [2009] 3 SLR(R) 1017, [11]–[13].
2258. *Ong Jane Rebecca v. Pricewaterhousecoopers*, [2009] 2 SLR(R) 796, [26]; *SIC College of Business and Technology Pte Ltd v. Yeo Poh Siah*, [2016] 2 SLR 118, [77] and [83]; *Siva Industries and Holdings Ltd v. Foreguard Shipping I Singapore Pte Ltd*, [2017] SGHCR 5, [25].
2259. *See also Pandian Marimuthu v. Guan Leong Construction Pte Ltd*, [2001] 2 SLR(R) 18; C. Bull & J. Pinsler, *Civil Procedure: Annual Review of Singapore Cases* [8.27]–[8.28] (Sing. Acad. L. 2009).
2260. *Ong Jane Rebecca v. Pricewaterhousecoopers*, [2009] 2 SLR(R) 796, [25].
2261. *Ong Jane Rebecca v. Pricewaterhousecoopers*, [2009] 2 SLR(R) 796, [28]–[30].
2262. *Singapore Civil Procedure 2015 Volume 1*, at 503 (G.P. Selvam ed., Sweet & Maxwell Asia 2014).
2263. Supreme Court of Judicature Act (Cap. 322, R. 5, 2014 Rev. Ed.) Rules of Court, O 23 r 2.
2264. J. Pinsler, *Principles of Civil Procedure* 1082–1083 (Acad. Publg. 2013).
2265. *See* Supreme Court of Judicature Act (Cap. 322, R. 5, 2014 Rev. Ed.) Rules of Court, O 22.
2266. *Singapore Civil Procedure 2015 Volume 1*, at 503 (G.P. Selvam ed., Sweet & Maxwell Asia 2014).
2267. *PT Bumi International Tankers v. Man B&W Diesel S E Asia Pte Ltd*, [2004] 3 SLR(R) 69, [1]–[5].
2268. *See* e.g., *Palaniappan v. Ramanathan*, [1972] 1 MLJ 227, 229.

624. While the court can order security for the entire costs of the action (i.e., costs already incurred and prospective costs),[2269] 'it often reduces the amount estimated and put forward by the defendant ... so that it is still meaningful to the defendant and the plaintiff is not unjustly burdened. The key concern is to balance the interests and rights of the parties ... the court may increase the amount of security on a subsequent application if the circumstances have changed.'[2270] Indeed, a plaintiff can seek to vary or discharge an order for security for costs if circumstances have worked against his favour.[2271] Finally, a defaulting plaintiff can always apply for an extension of time to furnish security,[2272] though this may be financially even more detrimental if costs penalties result.

§4. Possibility of Appeal

625. Section 34 of the Supreme Court of Judicature Act,[2273] read together with the Fourth and Fifth Schedules of the statute, determines whether any given order of civil procedure is appealable to the Court of Appeal[2274] or not.[2275] The Fourth Schedule states that: 'No appeal shall be brought to the Court of Appeal ... where a Judge makes an order refusing security for costs.'[2276] The Fifth Schedule states that: 'Except with the leave of a Judge, no appeal shall be brought to the Court of Appeal ... where a Judge makes an order giving security for costs.' In other words, if a defendant fails to get an order for security for costs, he cannot appeal against the decision at all. As for the plaintiff, if he has security for costs awarded against him, he cannot appeal unless leave is given to do so.

2269. *Singapore Civil Procedure 2015 Volume 1*, at 504–505 (G.P. Selvam ed., Sweet & Maxwell Asia 2014).
2270. J. Pinsler, *Principles of Civil Procedure* 1082 (Acad. Publg. 2013).
2271. *Singapore Civil Procedure 2015 Volume 1*, at 506 (G.P. Selvam ed., Sweet & Maxwell Asia 2014).
2272. Supreme Court of Judicature Act (Cap. 322, R. 5, 2014 Rev. Ed.) Rules of Court, O 3 rr 4(1)–(2).
2273. (Cap. 322, 2007 Rev. Ed.).
2274. Below it is the High Court, followed by the District and Magistrates' Courts. For appeals arising from the lower courts, *see* Supreme Court of Judicature Act (Cap. 322, R. 5, 2014 Rev. Ed.) Rules of Court, O 55B, 55C, and 55D. There is a right of appeal from a registrar in chambers to a judge in chambers (District Judge if it is the State Courts), but not necessarily after that stage. It should also be noted that for such appeals from first instance, the cases are heard de novo.
2275. The statute was amended in 2010 and 2014.
2276. *See also* Supreme Court of Judicature Act (Cap. 322, 2007 Rev. Ed.), s 34(2)(b): 'Except with the leave of a Judge, no appeal shall be brought to the Court of Appeal ... where the only issue in the appeal relates to costs or fees for hearing dates.' Presumably, however, the reference to 'costs' here does not include security for costs.

Chapter 3. Possible Costs Orders

§1. Introduction

626. A party's entitlement to costs can only be a result of legislation, a contract, or an order of court;[2277] for present purposes, the focus is on costs arising out of orders of court. With the rapid evolution of civil litigation, there can be no exhaustive definition of 'costs', but under the Rules of Court,[2278] 'costs' include 'fees, charges, disbursements, expenses and remuneration'.[2279] The fundamental importance attached to costs has been described in the following terms:

> While access to justice is often touted as being a fundamental right, in reality the ability of a person to pursue or defend a claim or interest is very much determined by his financial standing … litigants who are sufficiently impecunious to benefit from legal aid may be denied justice because they are compelled to capitulate or, if they do commence proceedings, to limit or forgo potential litigation initiatives because of the expense involved … The client must be informed of the cost consequences of litigation from the outset of the retainer … As the case progresses, he will need to be advised about the pecuniary effect of particular initiatives or steps which he decides to take. The lawyer's role is underscored by his ethical and procedural duties to act in the best interests of his client and assist in the administration of justice.[2280]

627. The incidence of costs in civil litigation is governed by the indemnity principle, i.e. that an unsuccessful party would generally be ordered to pay the successful party's reasonable litigation costs.[2281]

628. O 59, the principal provision in the Rules of Court that pertains to costs, comprises 37 rules and two appendices (divided into seven parts). O 59 is based on the English rules of civil procedure, but these rules have been substantially reformed and recast since 1986.[2282] O 59 is primarily concerned with 'contentious

---

2277. *See Telemedia Pacific Group Ltd v. Credit Agricole (Suisse) SA (Yeh Mao-Yuan, third party)*, [2015] 4 SLR 1019, [24].

2278. Supreme Court of Judicature Act (Cap. 322, R. 5, 2014 Rev. Ed.) Rules of Court, O 59 r 1(1). It should be noted that contingency fees are prohibited in Singapore.

2279. Costs may even include the expenses involved in engaging a private investigator to obtain evidence: *Singapore Civil Procedure 2015 Volume 1*, at 1033 (G.P. Selvam ed., Sweet & Maxwell Asia 2014). As for travel expenses (of the litigant) being claimed as disbursements, *see Lam Hwa Engineering & Trading Pte Ltd v. Yang Qiang*, [2014] 2 SLR 191 (for the travel expenses of the witness, *see* Supreme Court of Judicature Act (Cap. 322, R. 5, 2014 Rev. Ed.) Rules of Court, O 38 r 22); c.f. *Rajabali Jumabhoy v. Ameerali R Jumabhoy*, [1998] 2 SLR(R) 576.

2280. J. Pinsler, *Principles of Civil Procedure* 1020–1021 (Acad. Publg. 2013).

2281. *Deepak Sharma v. Law Society of Singapore*, [2017] SGCA 43, [40]–[42]; *Ng Eng Ghee v. Mamata Kapildev Dave (Horizon Partners Pte Ltd, intervener)*, [2009] 4 SLR(R) 155, [6]; *Then Khek Koon v. Arjun Permanand Samtani*, [2014] 1 SLR 245, [153]–[154].

2282. *Singapore Civil Procedure 2015 Volume 1*, at 1031 (G.P. Selvam ed., Sweet & Maxwell Asia 2014).

business',[2283] which is defined as 'business done in or for the purposes of proceedings begun before a court of justice or before an arbitrator',[2284] and includes work done before proceedings for the purpose of those proceedings.[2285] In certain circumstances, costs may also carry interest.[2286]

629. There are essentially two types of costs. The first type pertains to costs (not to be confused with damages) that are claimable from an opponent (usually when the party wins the case or application). This is otherwise known as party and party costs, and is usually determined on a standard basis. The second type pertains to costs payable to the lawyer (regardless of whether a party has won or lost the case). This is otherwise known as solicitor and client costs, and is usually determined on an indemnity basis, which is more generous than costs on a standard basis. This Chapter is concerned with party and party costs. Generally, two recurring themes in costs are that first, the party which has behaved in a more blameworthy manner is likely to be penalized with costs, be it for the purposes of interlocutory applications or at the end of the trial and second, the more (justifiably) complex an application or matter is, the more justifiable the request for higher costs to be awarded.

§2. Powers of the Court

630. As a starting point, 'the costs of and incidental to proceedings in the Supreme Court or the State Courts, including the administration of estates and trusts, shall be in the discretion of the Court, and the Court shall have full power to determine by whom and to what extent the costs are to be paid'.[2287] This gives the court complete and very broad control over matters of costs; indeed, generally, 'no party shall be entitled to recover any costs of or incidental to any proceedings from any other party to the proceedings except under an order of the Court'.[2288] Any question relating to costs 'may be dealt with by the Court at any stage of the proceedings or after the conclusion of the proceedings; and any costs ordered shall be paid forthwith notwithstanding that the proceedings have not been concluded, unless the Court otherwise orders'.[2289] This means that the court may award costs upon the hearing of interlocutory proceedings, after the trial, after the appeal and

2283. Supreme Court of Judicature Act (Cap. 322, R. 5, 2014 Rev. Ed.) Rules of Court, O 59 r 1(1). For contentious business agreements (and their statutory bases), *see Chancery Law Corp v. MCST Plan No 1024*. [2016] SGHC 121.

2284. Legal Profession Act (Cap. 161, 2009 Rev. Ed.), s 2(1).

2285. *Re Simpkin Marshall Ltd*, [1959] 1 Ch 229, 235–236. *See also* Supreme Court of Judicature Act (Cap. 322, R. 5, 2014 Rev. Ed.) Rules of Court, O 59, Appendix 1.

2286. Supreme Court of Judicature Act (Cap. 322, R. 5, 2014 Rev. Ed.) Rules of Court, O 59 r 37. For interest on judgments, *see id.*, O 42 r 12.

2287. Supreme Court of Judicature Act (Cap. 322, R. 5, 2014 Rev. Ed.) Rules of Court, O 59 r 2(2). C.f. *id.*, O 59 r 10. For criminal proceedings, *see Arun Kaliamurthy v. Public Prosecutor*, [2014] 3 SLR 1023, [35]; *Huang Liping v. Public Prosecutor*, [2016] SGCA 43, [15]–[18].

2288. Supreme Court of Judicature Act (Cap. 322, R. 5, 2014 Rev. Ed.) Rules of Court, O 59 r 3(1). *See also Ganesan Carlose & Partners v. Lee Siew Chun*, [1995] 1 SLR(R) 358, [18]; *The Century Dawn*, [1997] 2 SLR(R) 876, [21].

2289. Supreme Court of Judicature Act (Cap. 322, R. 5, 2014 Rev. Ed.) Rules of Court, O 59 r 4(1).

even post-adjudication (such as for the purposes of taxation or enforcement of judgments),[2290] but for interlocutory applications, costs are usually payable forthwith.

631. Questions of costs will always have two aspects: liability and quantum; quantum will be briefly considered here. There are a number of ways in which the quantum of costs may be determined. First, parties may agree beforehand to 'the allocation and assessment of costs should a dispute occur, in which case the court's discretion and the rules concerning automatic mechanisms ... may be circumscribed or excluded by the pertinent term of a binding contract'.[2291] It should be noted, however, that even if there is such an agreement, the court may disregard it if a party has acted unconscionably and engaged in misconduct.[2292] Second, parties may agree at a hearing on the costs to be paid. Third, costs (for certain applications such as summary judgment and default judgment) may be fixed by the Rules of Court; these are known as fixed costs or scaled costs.[2293] Fourth, the court may assess the quantum after a hearing (of an interlocutory application or the main matter itself), and even award a lump sum where appropriate.[2294] Fifth, the court may order the costs to be taxed.[2295]

§3. Types of Orders

632. We turn then to the other aspect of costs: liability. In this regard, as mentioned above, the court may make different orders at different times. When an order for 'costs' is made in interlocutory proceedings, 'the party in whose favour it is made shall be entitled to his costs in respect of those proceedings whatever the outcome of the cause or matter in which the proceedings arise'.[2296] This should be distinguished from 'costs to follow the event', which means that costs are awarded to the party that has won the application or suit; 'costs' can theoretically be (and often is) awarded to the losing party of an application or suit (for instance, if the winning party had behaved in a significantly blameworthy manner). An order for 'costs in any event' has the same effect as costs, 'except that the costs shall be taxed only after the conclusion of the cause or matter in which the proceedings arise'.[2297] When an order for 'costs reserved' is made, the party 'in whose favour an order for costs is made at the conclusion of the cause or matter in which the proceedings arise shall be entitled to his costs of the proceedings in respect of which this order is made

2290. *See also* Supreme Court of Judicature Act (Cap. 322, R. 5, 2014 Rev. Ed.) Rules of Court, O 59 r 4(2).
2291. J. Pinsler, *Principles of Civil Procedure* 1022 (Acad. Publg. 2013) citing *United Overseas Bank Ltd v. Sin Leong Ironbed & Furniture Manufacturing Co (Pte) Ltd*, [1988] 1 SLR(R) 76, [16].
2292. *Hong Leong Finance Ltd v. Lee Siang Wah*, [1993] 2 SLR(R) 577, [76].
2293. Supreme Court of Judicature Act (Cap. 322, R. 5, 2014 Rev. Ed.) Rules of Court, O 59, Appendix 2.
2294. Supreme Court of Judicature Act (Cap. 322, R. 5, 2014 Rev. Ed.) Rules of Court, O 59 r 9(4).
2295. *See also* Supreme Court of Judicature Act (Cap. 322, R. 5, 2014 Rev. Ed.) Rules of Court, O 59 r 9(1).
2296. Supreme Court of Judicature Act (Cap. 322, R. 5, 2014 Rev. Ed.) Rules of Court, O 59 r 1(3).
2297. Supreme Court of Judicature Act (Cap. 322, R. 5, 2014 Rev. Ed.) Rules of Court, O 59 r 1(3). *See also Long Well Group Ltd v. Commerzbank AG*, [2018] SGHC 164.

unless the Court orders otherwise'.[2298] In certain interlocutory applications, the court may not wish to make any decision as to entitlement of costs as it may either be doubtful of the likely final outcome of the substantive action or the reasonableness of the interlocutory application. In such circumstances, an order for 'costs reserved' postpones the question of costs to a later date, and if no subsequent order as to costs is made, the default is that 'costs in the cause' will apply (see below). When an order for 'costs here and below' is made, the party 'in whose favour this order is made shall be entitled not only to his costs in respect of the proceedings in which it is made but also to his costs of the same proceedings in any lower court, tribunal or other body constituted under any written law or in arbitral proceedings'.[2299] Thus, if an appeal is dismissed, the respondent would be awarded the costs of the appeal and also the costs which have already been awarded to him in the trial; if the appeal succeeds, the appellant would be awarded the costs of the appeal; and if the order for costs of the trial is reversed by the appeal court, the appellant would be entitled to those costs.[2300] When an order for 'costs in the cause' or 'costs in the application' is made, the party 'in whose favour an order for costs is made at the conclusion of the cause or matter in which the proceedings arise shall be entitled to his costs of the proceedings in respect of which such an order is made'.[2301] This is usually made when an application is required to be made by the Rules of Court, or when an application is justified by the circumstances and not particularly occasioned by a party's improper action.[2302] An order for costs in the cause may also be awarded when a plaintiff applies to join more parties as defendants and the application is allowed.[2303] Indeed, on one view, it has been said that for many interlocutory applications, 'the usual order for costs should be costs in the cause. This is because an interlocutory application does not purport to decide a matter on its merits. The decision of the trial judge will determine whether the interim relief ought to have been granted.'[2304] However, it should be noted that an order for 'plaintiff's costs in the cause' or 'defendant's costs in the cause' has a different effect from 'costs in the cause'. For these orders, the 'plaintiff or defendant, as the case may be, shall be entitled to his costs of the proceedings in respect of which such an order is made if judgment is given in his favour in the cause or matter in which the proceedings arise, but he shall not be liable to pay the costs of any other party in respect of those proceedings if judgment is given in favour of any other party or parties in the cause or matter in question'.[2305]

2298. Supreme Court of Judicature Act (Cap. 322, R. 5, 2014 Rev. Ed.) Rules of Court, O 59 r 1(3).
2299. Supreme Court of Judicature Act (Cap. 322, R. 5, 2014 Rev. Ed.) Rules of Court, O 59 r 1(3).
2300. J. Pinsler, *Principles of Civil Procedure* 1029 (Acad. Publg. 2013).
2301. Supreme Court of Judicature Act (Cap. 322, R. 5, 2014 Rev. Ed.) Rules of Court, O 59 r 1(3).
2302. J. Pinsler, *Principles of Civil Procedure* 1028 (Acad. Publg. 2013). *See also Chiarapurk Jack v. Haw Par Brothers International Ltd*, [1993] 2 SLR(R) 620, [55]; *Ng Chong Ping v. Ng Chih-Ming Daren (Richwood Design Pte Ltd, third party; Archideas Design Inc, fourth party)*, [2015] 3 SLR 292, [7]–[8].
2303. *Ng Chong Ping v. Ng Chih-Ming Daren (Richwood Design Pte Ltd, third party; Archideas Design Inc, fourth party)*, [2015] 3 SLR 292, [11].
2304. *Singapore Civil Procedure 2015 Volume 1*, at 1033 (G.P. Selvam ed., Sweet & Maxwell Asia 2014).
2305. Supreme Court of Judicature Act (Cap. 322, R. 5, 2014 Rev. Ed.) Rules of Court, O 59 r 1(3).

633. An order for 'costs thrown away' refers to the situation where 'proceedings or any part thereof have been ineffective or have been subsequently set aside, the party in whose favour this order is made shall be entitled to his costs of those proceedings or that part in respect of which it is made'.[2306] This may occur when a defendant applies to set aside a regular default judgment (obtained as a result of the defendant's procedural lapse); however, if the judgment set aside is irregular, the plaintiff may have to bear the costs thrown away.[2307] Another example is when (in an action begun by writ) a plaintiff amends his statement of claim to the point that the defendant needs to draft a substantially different defence. Where a court orders that no order as to costs will be made, it means that the parties are to bear their own costs. Such an order is usually made when there is no clearly blameworthy party (or that both parties are equally blameworthy).[2308] Complementing the costs orders set out in the Rules of Court are two orders developed in the common law that address the situation when a plaintiff sues more than one defendant. The first is known as a Bullock order (named after the case *Bullock v. London General Omnibus Co*),[2309] which may be awarded when the plaintiff is liable to pay the costs of a successful defendant but is entitled to recover those costs as well as his own costs from an unsuccessful defendant.[2310] The second is known as a Sanderson order (named after the case *Sanderson v. Blyth Theatre Co*),[2311] which may be awarded when the plaintiff is seeking to recover his own costs from an unsuccessful defendant who will also have to pay the plaintiff's costs payable to a successful defendant.[2312] The main purpose of either order is to avoid the unjust situation of a successful claimant who has been awarded damages but would have them eroded by an order to pay costs to the successful defendants whom it was reasonable for him to sue, but he did not know which of them to sue.[2313] In deciding whether either order is appropriate, the court will ask whether it would be fair and reasonable for the unsuccessful defendant to bear the costs of the successful co-defendant(s) (for instance, did the unsuccessful defendant attempt to pin the blame on the successful co-defendant(s) such that it was reasonable for the plaintiff to have also sued the co-defendant(s))[2314] and to ask if the unsuccessful defendant is solvent or not.[2315] However, if the plaintiff had included an additional defendant because of his uncertainty of the law rather than the facts, it will not be appropriate to make either order.[2316]

2306. Supreme Court of Judicature Act (Cap. 322, R. 5, 2014 Rev. Ed.) Rules of Court, O 59 r 1(3).
2307. J. Pinsler, *Principles of Civil Procedure* 1029 (Acad. Publg. 2013).
2308. *See also Sabani Kan v. Lachmandas Ramesh*, [1994] 2 SLR(R) 474; *Gimpex Ltd v. Unity Holdings Business Ltd*, [2015] SGCA 17; C. Bull & C. Voon Jiet, *Civil Procedure: Annual Review of Singapore Cases* [8.20]–[8.23] (Sing. Acad. L. 2015).
2309. [1907] 1 KB 264.
2310. *Ma HongFei v. U-Hin Manufacturing Pte Ltd*, [2009] 4 SLR(R) 336, [55].
2311. [1903] 2 KB 533.
2312. *Ma HongFei v. U-Hin Manufacturing Pte Ltd*, [2009] 4 SLR(R) 336, [55].
2313. *Chua Teck Chew Robert v. Goh Eng Wah*, [2009] 4 SLR(R) 716, [40].
2314. *Chua Teck Chew Robert v. Goh Eng Wah*, [2009] 4 SLR(R) 716, [40]–[44].
2315. *DBS Vickers Securities (Singapore) Pte Ltd v. Chin Pang Joo*, [2009] SGHC 248, [39].
2316. *Mohd bin Sapri v. Soil-Build (Pte) Ltd*, [1996] 2 SLR(R) 223, [65].

§4. MAIN CONSIDERATIONS

634. Notwithstanding the courts' broad powers as regards the awarding of costs, as a starting point, when making any order as to costs, the court will 'order the costs to follow the event, except when it appears to the Court that in the circumstances of the case some other order should be made as to the whole or any part of the costs'.[2317] Indeed, the principles on which costs are to be awarded have been summarized as follows:

> The principles on which costs were to be awarded were (i) that costs were in the discretion of the court, (ii) that costs should follow the event except when it appeared to the court that in the circumstances of the case some other order should be made, (iii) that the general rule did not cease to apply simply because the successful party raised issues or made allegations that failed, but that he could be deprived of his costs in whole or in part where he had caused a significant increase in the length of the proceedings, and (iv) that where the successful party raised issues or made allegations improperly or unreasonably the court could not only deprive him of his costs but could also order him to pay the whole or part of the unsuccessful party's costs. The fourth principle implied, moreover, that a successful party who neither improperly nor unreasonably raised issues or made allegations which failed ought not to be ordered to pay any part of the unsuccessful party's costs.[2318]

635. These principles are also confirmed in varying degrees by the Rules of Court. The court may also take into account the conduct of the winning party in the proceedings. Thus, where the conduct of the winning party is clearly dishonest and reprehensive,[2319] or where the court has awarded an order of committal against the winning party for contempt of court, that party will not be awarded his costs.[2320]

636. O 59 r 6A states that:

> where a party has failed to establish any claim or issue which he has raised in any proceedings, and has thereby unnecessarily or unreasonably protracted, or added to the costs or complexity of those proceedings, the Court may order that

2317. Supreme Court of Judicature Act (Cap. 322, R. 5, 2014 Rev. Ed.) Rules of Court, O 59 r 3(2). For examples of specific departures from this starting point (notwithstanding the court's unfettered discretion) in the Rules of Court, *see id.*, O 20 r 5 (amendment of pleadings), O 22A r 9 (offer to settle), O 24 r 6(9) (discovery against other person), O 59 r 3(4) (extension of time), O 59 r (7) (discontinuance), and O 13 r 8 and O 19 r 9 (setting aside regular judgment). For matrimonial proceedings under the newly constituted Family Justice Courts, *see JBB v. JBA*, [2015] 5 SLR 153, [27]–[32]. For criminal proceedings, *see Arun Kaliamurthy v. Public Prosecutor*, [2014] 3 SLR 1023, [35]; *Huang Liping v. Public Prosecutor*, [2016] SGCA 43, [15]–[18].

2318. *Tullio Planeta v. Maoro Andrea G*, [1994] 2 SLR(R) 501, [24], citing the headnote of *Re Elgindata Ltd (No 2)*, [1993] 1 All ER 232; cited in *Low Leong Meng v. Koh Pong Seng*, [2012] 1 SLR 1076, [29]. *See also Harte Denis Matthew v. Tan Hun Hoe*, [2001] SGHC 19, [42]; C. Bull & J. Pinsler, *Civil Procedure: Annual Review of Singapore Cases* [8.21] (Sing. Acad. L. 2012).

2319. *Ng Kek Wee v. Sim City Technology Ltd*, [2014] 4 SLR 723, [73].

2320. *Aurol Anthony Sabastian v. Sembcorp Marine Ltd*, [2013] 2 SLR 246, [115].

the costs of that party shall not be allowed in whole or in part, or that any costs occasioned by that claim or issue to any other party shall be paid by him to that other party, regardless of the outcome of the cause or matter.[2321]

637. The factors in O 59 6A, however, are not exhaustive.[2322]

638. O 59 r 7(1) then states that:

Where it appears to the Court in any proceedings that any thing has been done, or that any omission has been made, unreasonably or improperly by or on behalf of any party, the Court may order that the costs of that party in respect of the act or omission, as the case may be, shall not be allowed and that any costs occasioned by it to any other party shall be paid by him to that other party.[2323]

639. In this regard, 'the Court shall … have regard in particular to the following matters … the omission to do any thing the doing of which would have been calculated to save costs; … the doing of any thing calculated to occasion, or in a manner or at a time calculated to occasion unnecessary costs; and … any unnecessary delay in the proceedings'.[2324] Thus, the raising of irrelevant issues or claims (and not merely issues or claims that were not very strong on the merits), adducing of unnecessary evidence, making of immaterial submissions, failure to put the case properly, failure to raise matters in a timely fashion (for instance, at appeal rather than at trial), or any other form of unreasonable, oppressive, or unethical conduct is likely to result in a successful party receiving less costs or a losing party being made to pay additional costs.[2325] It should be borne in mind, however, that if a court is not presented with any evidence that a successful party should be deprived of his costs, it should be slow to exercise its discretion to go against the starting point of

2321. *See also Jet Holding Ltd v. Cooper Cameron (Singapore) Pte Ltd*, [2006] SGHC 20, [8]–[13]; *Khng Thuan Huat v. Riduan bin Yusof*, [2005] 1 SLR(R) 130, [21].
2322. *Lim Lie Hoa v. Ong Jane Rebecca*, [2005] 3 SLR(R) 116, [61]–[63].
2323. *See also* Supreme Court of Judicature Act (Cap. 322, R. 5, 2014 Rev. Ed.) Rules of Court, O 59 r 8(1); *Tan Kin Hiang v. United Engineers (Singapore) Pte Ltd*, [2005] 3 SLR(R) 529, [21]; *Ong Eng Kae v. Rupesh Kumar*, [2015] SGHC 163, [17].
2324. Supreme Court of Judicature Act (Cap. 322, R. 5, 2014 Rev. Ed.) Rules of Court, O 59 r 7(2). *See also* C. Bull & J. Pinsler, *Civil Procedure: Annual Review of Singapore Cases* [6.14] (Sing. Acad. L. 2005).
2325. *Ng Sing King v. PSA International Pte Ltd*, [2005] 2 SLR(R) 56, [177]–[180]; *Bank Nationale de Paris v. Tan Nancy*, [2001] 3 SLR(R) 726, [75]–[77]; *Chan Choy Ling v. Chua Che Teck*, [1995] 3 SLR(R) 310, [22]; *Swee Hong Investment Pte Ltd v. Swee Hong Exim Pte Ltd (Kiaw Aik Hang Land Pte Ltd)*, [1994] 3 SLR(R) 259, [43]; *L&M Airconditioning & Refrigeration (Pte) Ltd v. S A Shee & Co (Pte) Ltd*, [1993] 2 SLR(R) 346, [19]–[20]; *Re Kumagai-Zenecon Construction Pte Ltd; Kumagai Gumi Co Ltd v. Kumagai-Zenecon Construction Pte Ltd*, [1994] 2 SLR(R) 970, [127]; *Brink's Inc v. Singapore Airlines Ltd*, [1998] 2 SLR(R) 372, [21]; *Mohamed Amin bin Taib v. Lim Choon Thye*, [2011] 2 SLR 343, [32]. *See also Bank of China v. First National Bank of Boston*, [1992] 1 SLR(R) 72, [34]; *Lee Seng Choon Ronnie v. Singapore Island Country Club*, [1991] 1 SLR(R) 557, [32]; *Jurong Town Corporation v. Wishing Star (No 2)*, [2005] 3 SLR(R) 283, [204]; *VI v. VH*, [2008] 1 SLR(R) 742, [51]–[53].

'costs to follow the event'.[2326] Where a successful plaintiff is only awarded nominal damages, he may be treated as having lost the case and accordingly, costs may be awarded against him.[2327] However, a plaintiff need not succeed on all the issues that were argued as full costs may be awarded as long as he substantially succeeded in his claim; this marks a departure from the English approach.[2328] In addition, even if a plaintiff had grossly overstated the value of his claim, he should still be entitled to some or all of his costs, unless there is some ground of reproachable conduct.[2329] If a plaintiff succeeds in his claim and the defendant succeeds in his counterclaim, the default position is that the plaintiff will be awarded the costs of his claim and the defendant will be awarded the costs of his counterclaim.[2330] Finally, it should be noted that the conduct of the parties before litigation commenced may also be taken into account, especially if a party has unreasonably caused the litigation to commence,[2331] or has acted improperly or vexatiously against the other party.[2332] At bottom, the overarching concern for the court is to achieve the fairest allocation of costs between the parties.[2333]

§5. Involvement of Unique or Multiple Parties

640. Costs would generally not be ordered against a person who brings an action on behalf of another party, unless the litigation was not properly incurred.[2334] Costs would also generally not be awarded against a party that is a public body that was carrying out its duties pursuant to a public interest, unless it has acted in bad faith or is guilty of gross dereliction in its duties.[2335] Costs may be awarded in favour of or against non-parties to the action,[2336] but as regards the latter, the non-party must

2326. *Singapore Civil Procedure 2015 Volume 1*, at 1040 (G.P. Selvam ed., Sweet & Maxwell Asia 2014) citing *Civil Service Co-Operative Society General Steam Navigation Co*, [1903] 2 KB 756.

2327. *Mahtani v. Kiaw Aik Hang Land Pte Ltd*, [1994] 2 SLR(R) 996, [57]–[59]; *Ng Kian Huan Edmund v. Suying Metropolitan Studio Pte Ltd*, [2019] SGHC 234.

2328. *Parno v. SC Marine Pte Ltd*, [1999] 3 SLR(R) 377, [72]–[74]. *See also* C. Bull & J. Pinsler, *Civil Procedure: Annual Review of Singapore Cases* [6.53] (Sing. Acad. L. 2004).

2329. *Zaiton Bee Bee bte Abdul Majeed v. Chan Poh Teong*, [2010] 3 SLR 697, [73].

2330. *Medway Oil and Storage Company Limited v. Continental Contractors Limited*, [1929] 1 AC 88, 98; cited in *Mok Kwong Yue v. Ding Leng Kong*, [2012] 1 SLR 737, [28].

2331. *Paul Tsakok & Associates v. Engineering & Marine Services (Pte) Ltd*, [1990] 2 SLR(R) 278, [24].

2332. *Chew Kia Ngee v. Singapore Society of Accountants*, [1988] 2 SLR(R) 597, [24].

2333. *Aurol Anthony Sabastian v. Sembcorp Marine Ltd*, [2013] 2 SLR 246, [103].

2334. *Hsu Ann Mei Amy (personal representative of the estate of Hwang Cheng Tsu Hsu deceased) v. Oversea-Chinese Banking Corp Ltd*, [2011] 2 SLR 178, [41]. C.f. *Wong Meng Cheong v. Ling Ai Wah*, [2012] 1 SLR 549, [193].

2335. *Law Society of Singapore v. Top Ten Entertainment Pte Ltd*, [2011] 2 SLR 1279, [24]–[33], citing *Baxendale-Walker v. Law Society*, [2008] 1 WLR 426, 436–437. C.f. *Lim Teng Eee Joyce v. Singapore Medical Council*, [2005] 3 SLR(R) 709.

2336. *Centre for Laser and Aesthetic Medicine Pte Ltd v. GPK Clinic (Orchard) Pte Ltd*, [2017] SGCA 68, [99]. *See also Singapore Civil Procedure 2015 Volume 1*, at 1037 (G.P. Selvam ed., Sweet & Maxwell Asia 2014) citing *Symphony Group plc v. Hodgson*, [1994] QB 179.

be afforded due process and have his views adequately considered first.[2337] In addition, it must be just in all the circumstances to award costs against the non-party, with particular consideration placed on the close connection between the non-party and the proceedings and a causal link between the non-party and the incurring of costs.[2338] Similarly, a plaintiff can be made to bear the costs of third-party proceedings when the defendant can show that those proceedings were inevitable as a direct result of the plaintiff's claim.[2339] Costs may be awarded to a non-appealing party, provided that it had expended money and/or effort in contributing to the final success of the appeal.[2340]

641. If a successful litigant was represented pro bono, he may not be entitled to any costs as this may be tantamount to a court endorsing a champertous agreement; further, a party with the benefit of pro bono services does not need to be indemnified for any costs and a litigant should not get to enjoy any windfall by virtue of costs awards.[2341] On the other hand, costs remain largely a matter of the court's discretion and it is possible, depending on the circumstances of the case, for costs to be awarded to a successful litigant who was represented pro bono, especially if greater access to justice is achieved.[2342]

642. Where there are more than two lawyers for a party, 'costs for getting up the case by and for attendance in Court … shall not be allowed unless the Court so certifies at the hearing or upon an application made by that party within one month from the date of the judgment or order';[2343] such costs 'may be allowed notwithstanding that the solicitors are members of the same firm of solicitors'.[2344] There are two possible approaches to this rule: the first, the 'headcount approach', requires

2337. *DB Trustees (Hong Kong) Ltd v. Consult Asia Pte Ltd*, [2010] 3 SLR 542, [47]–[48]; *Ng Kian Huan Edmund v. Suying Metropolitan Studio Pte Ltd*, [2019] SGHC 234. *See also* C. Bull & J. Pinsler, *Civil Procedure: Annual Review of Singapore Cases* [8.24]–[8.25] (Sing. Acad. L. 2012).

2338. *Raffles Town Club Pte Ltd v. Lim Eng Hock Peter*, [2011] 1 SLR 582, [22]–[24]; *South East Enterprises (Singapore) Pte Ltd v. Hean Nerng Holdings Pte Ltd*, [2012] 3 SLR 864; *SIC College of Business and Technology Pte Ltd v. Yeo Poh Siah*, [2016] 2 SLR 118, [89]. *See also Resorts World at Sentosa Pte Ltd v. Goel Adesh Kumar*, [2018] SGCA 58.

2339. Inevitability could be demonstrated if the real issue at the heart of the action is one that ought to be properly litigated between the plaintiff and the third party, rather than the plaintiff and the defendant. Another scenario was where the plaintiff's claim against the defendant was clearly against the wrong party and there was clearly another party that the plaintiff should have sued. The touchstone was whether the plaintiff's conduct justified a costs order that exceptionally made the plaintiff bear the costs of proceedings instituted by the defendant: *Telemedia Pacific Group Ltd v. Credit Agricole (Suisse) SA (Yeh Mao-Yuan, third party)*, [2015] 4 SLR 1019, [89]. *See also* C. Bull & C. Voon Jiet, *Civil Procedure: Annual Review of Singapore Cases* [8.13]–[8.15] (Sing. Acad. L. 2015).

2340. *Ng Eng Ghee v. Mamata Kapildev Dave*, [2009] 4 SLR(R) 155, [17]–[19].

2341. *SATS Construction Pte Ltd v. Islam Md Ohidul*, [2016] SGHC 99, [2] and [6].

2342. *SATS Construction Pte Ltd v. Islam Md Ohidul*, [2016] SGHC 99, [8]–[19].

2343. Supreme Court of Judicature Act (Cap. 322, R. 5, 2014 Rev. Ed.) Rules of Court, O 59 r 19(1). Certification is only awarded in exceptional circumstances, such as when the case involves a high degree of complexity of facts and/or law: *Parakou Shipping Pte Ltd v. Liu Cheng Chan*, [2017] SGHC 91, [14].

2344. Supreme Court of Judicature Act (Cap. 322, R. 5, 2014 Rev. Ed.) Rules of Court, O 59 r 19(2).

the applicant to elect two named counsel for which costs are to be claimed; the second, the 'notional approach', assumes the court might award costs for the work that would reasonably have been done by a notional two-counsel team.[2345] It appears the latter approach is preferred by the courts because: first, factoring in the work done by the legal team as a whole better assists the court in having a full picture of the magnitude of the legal task at hand; second, the 'headcount approach' rewards law practices where counsel, regardless of seniority, specialize on a particular file and penalizes law practices where counsel of varying seniority work on different files; third, greater proportionality in costs is likely to be achieved; and finally, the 'notional approach' would not render O 59 r 19 nugatory.[2346]

643. Where there are two (or more) co-defendants, only one set of costs will normally be payable to them if both (or all) of them succeed, even if they were separately represented.[2347] However, the court may allow separate costs where reasonable grounds have been shown for the severance of defences.[2348] In addition, the court will balance the right to separate counsel against the possibility of unduly penalizing the losing party with costs that were not reasonably incurred.[2349] In this regard, the court will consider these factors: whether there is community of interests between the parties; the size of or importance of the interest that is the subject of the dispute; and the degree of overlap in the preparations and conduct of proceedings.[2350]

644. Counsel may be personally liable for costs if they fail to conduct proceedings with reasonable competence and expedition.[2351]

§6. Recent Innovations

645. In 2015, the Supreme Court announced at the Opening of the Legal Year a slew of measures designed to reduce the cost of litigation. First, following amendments to the Practice Directions, parties would be required to furnish their costs estimates before the outcome in each case is known. This enables the court to obtain a reasonable picture of the level of costs claimed, and also discourages satellite litigation over the issue of costs. Second, in tandem with the docket system that was introduced for the hearing of cases, judges assigned to each docket would help

2345. *Trans Eurokars Pte Ltd v. Koh Wee Meng*, [2015] SGHCR 6.
2346. C. Bull & C. Voon Jiet, *Civil Procedure: Annual Review of Singapore Cases* [8.25] (Sing. Acad. L. 2015).
2347. *Wing Joo Loong Ginseng Hong (Singapore) Co Pte Ltd v. Qinghai Xinyuan Foreign Trade Co Ltd*, [2009] 2 SLR(R) 814, [200].
2348. *Wing Joo Loong Ginseng Hong (Singapore) Co Pte Ltd v. Qinghai Xinyuan Foreign Trade Co Ltd*, [2009] 2 SLR(R) 814, [200].
2349. *Ng Eng Ghee v. Mamata Kapildev Dave*, [2009] 4 SLR(R) 155, [22]; cited in *Raffles Town Club Pte Ltd v. Lim Eng Hock Peter*, [2011] 1 SLR 582, [50].
2350. *Ng Eng Ghee v. Mamata Kapildev Dave*, [2009] 4 SLR(R) 155, [24]–[26]; cited in *Raffles Town Club Pte Ltd v. Lim Eng Hock Peter*, [2011] 1 SLR 582, [50].
2351. *See Tan King Hiang v. United Engineers (Singapore) Pte Ltd*, [2005] 3 SLR(R) 529; *Ong Eng Kae v. Rupesh Kumar*, [2015] SGHC 163.

ensure that cases are being managed within a sensible and proportionate budget; judges would be trained and briefings would be conducted for lawyers to this end. Third, costs guidelines will be published in the Practice Directions and Supreme Court website. Although the issue of costs will always remain at the full discretion of the court, these guidelines are meant to signpost to the parties the level of costs they can expect at various stages of litigation. These developments are likely to be welcomed by the legal fraternity, as there has been an increasing divergence between the courts and the practitioners as to what constitutes justified billing – costs taxations often result in figures wildly different from what lawyers (and their clients) expect. The publication of guidelines will not only help clients manage their finances, but also help firms plan in work allocation.

Chapter 4. Taxation Process

§1. Introduction

646. Taxation of costs is a process where a registrar will determine the costs a party is entitled to after assessing the items claimed in the bill of costs. Unless otherwise ordered or directed, a party who has been awarded costs is entitled to have his costs taxed.[2352] The need for taxation may be obviated in the following situations: where recovery of costs from the party ordered to pay is unlikely; where the difference between the assessed amount and the amount to be determined is unlikely to be significant; where the judge or registrar is in a better position than the taxing registrar to assess costs; where parties mutually agree to the amount of costs; or where the Rules of Court provide for fixed or scaled costs.[2353] However, the mere fact that there is an agreement for payment of costs between the client and his lawyer does not make the agreement immune from an investigation by the court as to whether it is reasonable and fair.[2354]

§2. Bases of Taxation

647. As mentioned, the default position is that party, and party costs are taxed on a standard basis while solicitor and client costs are taxed on an indemnity basis. Where costs are taxed on a standard basis, 'there shall be allowed a reasonable amount in respect of all costs reasonably incurred and any doubts which the Registrar may have as to whether the costs were reasonably incurred or were reasonable in amount shall be resolved in favour of the paying party'.[2355] Where costs are taxed on an indemnity basis, 'all costs shall be allowed except in so far as they are of an unreasonable amount or have been unreasonably incurred and any doubts which the Registrar may have as to whether the costs were reasonably incurred or were reasonable in amount shall be resolved in favour of the receiving party'.[2356] An order of costs on the indemnity basis is the exception rather than the norm and requires exceptional justification.[2357] It should be noted that where the court 'makes

2352. Supreme Court of Judicature Act (Cap. 322, R. 5, 2014 Rev. Ed.) Rules of Court, O 59 rr 9(1)–(3). *See also id.*, O 59 r 9(4).

2353. J. Pinsler, *Principles of Civil Procedure* 1046–1047 (Acad. Publg. 2013).

2354. *Wong Foong Chai v. Lin Kuo Hao*, [2005] 3 SLR 74, [29]–[31]; *Pang Giap Oon v. Harmesh Singh s/o Ram Singh*, [2016] SGHC 149, [9].

2355. Supreme Court of Judicature Act (Cap. 322, R. 5, 2014 Rev. Ed.) Rules of Court, O 59 r 27(2); *Airtrust (Hong Kong) Ltd v. PH Hydraulics & Engineering Pte Ltd*, [2016] SGHC 167, [17].

2356. Supreme Court of Judicature Act (Cap. 322, R. 5, 2014 Rev. Ed.) Rules of Court, O 59 r 27(3); *Airtrust (Hong Kong) Ltd v. PH Hydraulics & Engineering Pte Ltd*, [2016] SGHC 167, [17]. *See also id.*, O 59 r 27(1).

2357. *CCM Industrial Pte Ltd v. Uniquetech Pte Ltd*, [2009] 2 SLR(R) 20, [32]; *Airtrust (Hong Kong) Ltd v. PH Hydraulics & Engineering Pte Ltd*, [2016] SGHC 167, [17]; *Lim Geok Lin Andy v. Yap Jin Meng Bryan*, [2016] SGHC 261, [3].

an order for costs without indicating the basis of taxation or an order that costs be taxed on any basis other than the standard basis or the indemnity basis, the costs shall be taxed on the standard basis'.[2358]

648. There are two main differences between the standard basis and the indemnity basis. First, the standard basis does not indemnify the party as the indemnity basis does for the lawyer, as the rationale behind party and party costs is neither to enrich nor fully compensate the party, but simply to ensure that the party is able to pay (albeit only for a portion of) for his legal representation.[2359] In this regard, while there 'appears to be a general practice whereby costs assessed on an indemnity basis are taken to be usually one-third more than that assessed on a standard basis … this is not a hard and fast rule which applies invariably each time costs are ordered to be taxed on an indemnity basis'.[2360] Be that as it may, party and party costs should never exceed the receiving party's solicitor and client costs.[2361]

649. The Court of Appeal has also clarified that the general rule on recovery of legal costs of previous proceedings as damages in subsequent proceedings which disallows such a claim for damages applies to both same-party and third-party cases.[2362] The former refers to situations where the defendant in the later proceedings was a party to the earlier proceedings; the latter refers to situations where the defendant in the later proceedings was not a party to the earlier proceedings. However, the Court of Appeal also recognized a possible caveat to this general rule – situations where the measure of damages awarded by the court might consist of the full costs (i.e. costs that go beyond the measure awardable pursuant to the indemnity principle), although acknowledging that such a situation would be exceptionally rare.[2363]

650. Second, although both the standard basis and indemnity basis are founded on the concept of reasonableness, another difference, as seen in the Rules of Court provisions set out above, lies in how any doubts about the reasonableness of the costs should be resolved in favour of one party or the other.[2364]

2358. Supreme Court of Judicature Act (Cap. 322, R. 5, 2014 Rev. Ed.) Rules of Court, O 59 r 27(4).
2359. *See Basil Anthony Herman v. Premier Security Co-operative Ltd*, [2012] 2 SLR 616, [5]: 'The important purpose of the exercise of assessing costs is to ensure that the receiving party is given a fair amount of money towards compensating the costs he expended in pursuit of his cause. It is not to compensate him for every cent he expended even if they were reasonably expended. It is in the public interest to keep costs within reasonable limits.' *See also Maryani Sadeli v. Arjun Permanand Samtani*, [2015] 1 SLR 496: [24]–[33].
2360. *Lin Jian Wei v. Lim Eng Hock Peter*, [2011] 3 SLR 1052, [83].
2361. *Gundry v. Sainsbury*, [1910] 1 KB 645, 651.
2362. *Maryani Sadeli v. Arjun Permanand Samtani*, [2015] 1 SLR 496, [20] and [46]. C.f. *Li Siu Lun v. Looi Kok Poh*, [2015] SGHC 149, [124].
2363. *Maryani Sadeli v. Arjun Permanand Satanic*, [2015] 1 SLR 496, [53].
2364. *See also* Supreme Court of Judicature Act (Cap. 322, R. 5, 2014 Rev. Ed.) Rules of Court, O 59 r 28(2).

651. An order for (party and party) costs to be made on an indemnity basis may be made when there is an agreement between the parties,[2365] when there have been exceptional or special circumstances (such as when a party had acted unreasonably and wasted everybody's time and resources, and the extent of such unreasonableness and whether any prejudice is caused),[2366] when a party had pursued a completely unmeritorious appeal,[2367] or when a party to an arbitration agreement or jurisdiction agreement breaches that agreement and causes the other party to incur legal costs.[2368] While the circumstances in which the court will depart from the standard basis default position are certainly not exhaustive – O 59 r 5 also provides a non-exhaustive list of factors – a possible test is to see if there is 'a degree of dishonesty, impropriety or abuse of judicial process to warrant a departure from the usual basis of costs'.[2369] To ascertain this, the court must conduct a rigorous review;[2370] the burden on a party who seeks an order for indemnity costs as a matter of discretion is a high one.[2371]

652. Finally, it should be mentioned that though the standard and indemnity bases are the most commonly encountered, there are also other (and not frequently invoked) bases of taxation,[2372] such as for litigants-in-person. Specifically, for 'a taxation of the costs of a litigant in person, there may be allowed such costs as would reasonably compensate the litigant for the time expended by him, together with all expenses reasonably incurred'.[2373]

§3. Procedural Aspects

653. A party 'entitled to require any costs to be taxed must begin proceedings for the taxation of those costs by filing the bill of costs at the Registry within 12 months from the date on which the entire cause or matter is finally disposed of,

2365. *United Overseas Bank Ltd v. Sin Leong Ironbed & Furniture Manufacturing Co (Pte) Ltd*, [1988] 1 SLR(R) 76, [16]–[17]. C.f. *Gomba Holdings (UK) Ltd v. Minories Finance Ltd (No 2)*, [1993] 1 Ch 171, 175; *Susilawati v. American Express Bank Ltd*, [2008] 1 SLR(R) 237, [100]–[101].
2366. *Lee Kuan Yew v. Vino cur John*, [1996] 1 SLR(R) 840, [30]; *Teo Siew Peng v. Neo Hock Pheng*, [1998] 3 SLR(R) 472, [34]; *Tan Chin Yew Joseph v. Saxo Capital Markets Pte Ltd*, [2013] SGHC 274, [97]; *PT Sandipala Arthaputra v. STMicroelectronics Asia Pacific Pte Ltd*, [2016] 1 SLR 748, [12]; *Airtrust (Hong Kong) Ltd v. PH Hydraulics & Engineering Pte Ltd*, [2016] SGHC 167, [32] and [51]. *See also Colliers International (Singapore) Pte Ltd v. Senkee Logistics Pte Ltd*, [2007] 2 SLR(R) 230, [111]–[127]; C. Bull & C. Voon Jiet, *Civil Procedure: Annual Review of Singapore Cases* [8.12] (Sing. Acad. L. 2015).
2367. *Tjong Very Sumito v. Antig Investments Pte Ltd*, [2009] 4 SLR(R) 732, [71]. C.f. *Raffles Town Club Pte Ltd v. Lim Eng Hock Peter*, [2011] 1 SLR 582, [32].
2368. *Tjong Very Sumito v. Antig Investments Pte Ltd*, [2009] 4 SLR(R) 732, [71].
2369. *Raffles Town Club Pte Ltd v. Lim Eng Hock Peter*, [2011] 1 SLR 582, [32]. *See also Airtrust (Hong Kong) Ltd v. PH Hydraulics & Engineering Pte Ltd*, [2016] SGHC 167, [18] and [23].
2370. *Lin Jian Wei v. Lim Eng Hock Peter*, [2011] 3 SLR 1052, [65].
2371. *Tan Chin Yew Joseph v. Saxo Capital Markets Pte Ltd*, [2013] SGHC 274, [97]; *PT Sandipala Arthaputra v. STMicroelectronics Asia Pacific Pte Ltd*, [2016] 1 SLR 748, [8]. *See also Beckkett Pte Ltd v. Deutsche Bank AG*, [2011] 2 SLR 96, [26].
2372. *See* e.g. Singapore Academy of Law Act (Cap. 294A, 1997 Rev. Ed.), s 25.
2373. Supreme Court of Judicature Act (Cap. 322, R. 5, 2014 Rev. Ed.) Rules of Court, O 59 r 18A.

including any appeals therefrom, unless the Court otherwise orders'.[2374] Once this has been done, 'the Registrar shall give to the party beginning the proceedings not less than 14 days notice of the date and time appointed for taxation'.[2375] Within two days after receiving this notice, a party whose costs are to be taxed must send a copy of his bill of costs to every other party entitled to be heard in the taxation proceedings.[2376] Every bill of costs must set out three separate sections: work done in the cause or matter, except for taxation of costs; work done for and in the taxation of costs; and all disbursements made in the cause or matter.[2377] For the first two sections, they shall be indicated 'as one global sum for each section', while the costs claimed in the third section 'must set out the sum claimed for each item of disbursement'.[2378] Every bill of costs must:

> be headed in the cause or matter to which the bill relates, with the name of the party whose bill it is, and the judgment, direction or order under which the bill is to be taxed, the basis of taxation and whether the bill is to be taxed between party and party or solicitor and client ... [and] be endorsed with the name or firm and business address of the solicitor whose bill it is.[2379]

654. Every bill of costs must set out sufficient information that will enable the registrar to determine the amount of costs to be awarded.[2380] Where 'attendances, telephone conversations and correspondence are concerned, it shall be sufficient to state only the number of such attendances, telephone calls and correspondence, and, where possible, the total number of hours of such attendances and telephone calls'[2381] and where 'costs have already been awarded for any of the events set out, this fact and the amount awarded must be indicated'.[2382] Every bill of costs 'must also contain a succinct narrative of the legal and factual issues involved'[2383] and 'may also contain the lists of authorities cited, indicating, where possible, those

2374. Supreme Court of Judicature Act (Cap. 322, R. 5, 2014 Rev. Ed.) Rules of Court, O 59 r 20. *See also* Legal Profession Act (Cap. 161, 2009 Rev. Ed.), ss 120(1) and 120(3).
2375. Supreme Court of Judicature Act (Cap. 322, R. 5, 2014 Rev. Ed.) Rules of Court, O 59 r 21.
2376. Supreme Court of Judicature Act (Cap. 322, R. 5, 2014 Rev. Ed.) Rules of Court, O 59 r 22(1). *See also id.*, O 59 r 22(2); Legal Profession Act (Cap. 161, 2009 Rev. Ed.), s 125.
2377. Supreme Court of Judicature Act (Cap. 322, R. 5, 2014 Rev. Ed.) Rules of Court, O 59 r 24(1).
2378. Supreme Court of Judicature Act (Cap. 322, R. 5, 2014 Rev. Ed.) Rules of Court, O 59 r 24(2).
2379. Supreme Court of Judicature Act (Cap. 322, R. 5, 2014 Rev. Ed.) Rules of Court, O 59 rr 24(3)–(4).
2380. Supreme Court of Judicature Act (Cap. 322, R. 5, 2014 Rev. Ed.) Rules of Court, O 59, Appendix 1. *See also Nim Minimaart (a firm) v. MCST Plan No 1079*, [2013] 2 SLR 1025, [15]–[23] (samples of bill of costs (such as one found in the Practice Directions) need not be followed slavishly; moreover, a bill of costs does not have to account for how every hour of work was spent); *Shorvon Simon v. Singapore Medical Council*, [2006] 1 SLR(R) 182, [40].
2381. Supreme Court of Judicature Act (Cap. 322, R. 5, 2014 Rev. Ed.) Rules of Court, O 59, Appendix 1.
2382. Supreme Court of Judicature Act (Cap. 322, R. 5, 2014 Rev. Ed.) Rules of Court, O 59, Appendix 1.
2383. Supreme Court of Judicature Act (Cap. 322, R. 5, 2014 Rev. Ed.) Rules of Court, O 59, Appendix 1.

cited in the judgment of the Court'.[2384] If there are any objections in principle or as to quantum of the items claimed in a bill of costs, they must be indicated by the filling and service of a notice of dispute (using the prescribed form) at least seven days before the date fixed for the taxation.[2385]

655. If 'any party entitled to be heard in any taxation proceedings does not attend within a reasonable time after the time appointed for the taxation, the Registrar, if satisfied by affidavit or otherwise that the party had due notice of the date and time appointed, may proceed with the taxation'.[2386] If necessary, the registrar may also adjourn the taxation proceedings from time to time.[2387] Once the bill of costs has been taxed, 'the solicitor shall cast up the deductions therefrom, which, with the casting of the bill, shall be checked by the Registrar, and the Registrar shall proceed to make his certificate for the amount of such costs less the deductions'.[2388] This certificate, 'unless set aside, shall be conclusive as to the amount thereof, and, where the order contains a submission to pay, the solicitor may after 48 hours, if there is no application for review, issue execution in respect thereof'.[2389]

656. For solicitor and client costs, 'no solicitor shall, except by leave of the court, commence or maintain any action for the recovery of any costs due for any business done by him until the expiration of one month after he has delivered to the party to be charged therewith, or sent by post to, or left with him at his office or place of business, dwelling-house or last known place of residence, a bill of those costs'.[2390] If the twelve-month period for commencement of taxation proceedings has expired, 'no order shall be made for taxation of a solicitor's bill of costs, except upon notice to the solicitor and under special circumstances to be proved to the satisfaction of the court'.[2391] Special circumstances in any given case cannot be asserted in a vacuum but have to, in some rational way, demonstrate how the conduct should be excused, since the requirement that the client apply to tax the bill before paying it served to discourage the client from approbating and reprobating and upheld the solicitor's interest in security of receipt for his fees.[2392] There is no exhaustive list of what constitutes special circumstances, but possible examples

---

2384. Supreme Court of Judicature Act (Cap. 322, R. 5, 2014 Rev. Ed.) Rules of Court, O 59, Appendix 1.
2385. State Courts Practice Directions (Part XIV); Supreme Court Practice Directions 2013 (Part XII). The former also contains directions with regard to the lawyers conferring before the date of taxation to resolve, limit, or clarify any items in dispute.
2386. Supreme Court of Judicature Act (Cap. 322, R. 5, 2014 Rev. Ed.) Rules of Court, O 59 r 25(1). *See also id.*, O 59 r 14(1).
2387. Supreme Court of Judicature Act (Cap. 322, R. 5, 2014 Rev. Ed.) Rules of Court, O 59 r 25(2). *See also id.*, O 59 r 8(6).
2388. Supreme Court of Judicature Act (Cap. 322, R. 5, 2014 Rev. Ed.) Rules of Court, O 59 r 32.
2389. Supreme Court of Judicature Act (Cap. 322, R. 5, 2014 Rev. Ed.) Rules of Court, O 59 r 33.
2390. Legal Profession Act (Cap. 161, 2009 Rev. Ed.), s 118(1). *See also id.*, s 119.
2391. Legal Profession Act (Cap. 161, 2009 Rev. Ed.), s 122.
2392. *Kosui Singapore Pte Ltd v. Thangavelu*, [2015] 5 SLR 722, [62]–[65]. For instance, if a bill lacks particularisation, the lack of necessary detail could have left the applicant unable to take an informed decision on whether to apply for taxation as a result of which the client let the 12-month period expire, or the lack of detail could lead the client to pay the bill in ignorance of what work it actually covered.

include prolong negotiations over the quantum of fees, coercion, overcharging, and fraud.[2393] In addition, the 'delivery of a bill of costs by a solicitor to his client shall not preclude the solicitor from presenting a bill for a larger amount or otherwise for taxation, if taxation is ordered by the Court or is consented to by the solicitor and his client'[2394] and upon such taxation 'the solicitor shall be entitled to such amount as is allowed by the Registrar, notwithstanding that such amount may be more than that claimed in any previous bill of costs delivered to his client'.[2395]

§4. Substantive Aspects

657. A registrar of the Supreme Court shall have power to tax 'the costs of or arising out of any cause or matter in the Supreme Court; … the costs directed by an award made on a reference to arbitration under any written law or pursuant to an arbitration agreement to be paid; … any other costs the taxation of which is directed by an order of the Court; and … any costs directed to be taxed or settled by or under any written law'.[2396] A taxation registrar also has the power to:

> take an account of any dealings in money made in connection with the payment of the costs being taxed, if the Court so directs; … require any party represented jointly with any other party in any proceedings before him to be separately represented; … examine any witness in those proceedings; and … direct the production of any document which may be relevant in connection with those proceedings.[2397]

658. Ultimately, the amount of costs to be allowed at taxation shall 'be in the discretion of the Registrar',[2398] though such discretion must be exercised judiciously in accordance with established rules and principles.[2399] In exercising his discretion, he shall 'have regard to the principle of proportionality and all the relevant circumstances'.[2400] In particular, O 59, Appendix 1[2401] requires him to have regard to the following:

2393. *Sports Connection Pte Ltd v. Asia Law Corp*, [2010] 4 SLR 590, [35]–[43]; *Kosui Singapore Pte Ltd v. Thangavelu*, [2015] 5 SLR 722, [78] and [97].
2394. Supreme Court of Judicature Act (Cap. 322, R. 5, 2014 Rev. Ed.) Rules of Court, O 59 r 28(4).
2395. Supreme Court of Judicature Act (Cap. 322, R. 5, 2014 Rev. Ed.) Rules of Court, O 59 r 28(5).
2396. Supreme Court of Judicature Act (Cap. 322, R. 5, 2014 Rev. Ed.) Rules of Court, O 59 r 12(1). The taxation powers of a registrar of the Subordinate Courts are largely similar.
2397. Supreme Court of Judicature Act (Cap. 322, R. 5, 2014 Rev. Ed.) Rules of Court, O 59 r 13. *See also Mok Kwong Yue v. Ding Leng Kong*, [2012] 1 SLR 737, [22]–[28].
2398. Supreme Court of Judicature Act (Cap. 322, R. 5, 2014 Rev. Ed.) Rules of Court, O 59, Appendix 1. C.f. Legal Profession Act (Cap. 161, 2009 Rev. Ed.), ss 109(1), 111(1), 112(1), and 113(1).
2399. *Tan Guek Ngor Engelin nee Tan v. Chia Ee Lin Evelyn*, [2005] 3 SLR(R) 22, [25].
2400. Supreme Court of Judicature Act (Cap. 322, R. 5, 2014 Rev. Ed.) Rules of Court, O 59, Appendix 1. *See also* J. Pinsler, *Proportionality in Costs*, 23 Sing. Acad. L.J. 125, 143–144 (2011).
2401. *See also Basil Anthony Herman v. Premier Security Co-operative Ltd*, [2012] 2 SLR 616, [5].

> the complexity of the item or of the cause or matter in which it arises and the difficulty or novelty of the questions involved; … the skill, specialised knowledge and responsibility required of, and the time and labour expended by, the solicitor; … the number and importance of the documents (however brief) prepared or perused; … the place and circumstances in which the business involved is transacted; … the urgency and importance of the cause or matter to the client; and … where money or property is involved, its amount or value.[2402]

659. As was held recently by the Court of Appeal, it is important for taxing registrar to be properly apprised of the complexity of the case:

> the Court should first assess the relative complexity of the matter, the work supposedly done against what was reasonably required in the prevailing circumstances, the reasonableness and proportionality of the amounts claimed on an item by item basis and thereafter, assess the proportionality of the resulting aggregate costs. In this exercise, all the [O 59, Appendix 1] considerations are relevant. In the general scheme of things, no single consideration ordinarily ought to take precedence. In every matter, this calls for careful judgment by reference to existing precedents and guidelines. A taxing officer should consider the complexity of the issues of fact and law which arose in the matter against the backdrop of the statements as to the amount of time spent by the solicitors and also the seniority of the counsel involved in order to determine whether the costs claimed for the amount of time spent is reasonable and proportionate.[2403]

660. The Court of Appeal added, however, that it is not realistic to expect the taxation process to be mathematically unassailable:

> The Court has to ensure that a fair balance is struck in every assessment of costs. We accept that timesheets, an important management tool for law firms, have a role to play in an assessment but they should not be given the status of a decisive costing mechanism … Taxing officers should also note that costs taxed on an indemnity basis are the equivalent of the solicitor and client costs under the old regime. Ordinarily, under the old regime, solicitor and client costs were about one third more than party and party costs (which were awarded on a stricter basis than the former common fund basis which the current standard basis is modelled on) and only 'necessary or proper' costs were allowed … there now appears to be a general practice whereby costs assessed

---

2402. It is further stated in O 59, Appendix 1 that: 'Work done in the cause or matter includes work done in connection with the negotiation of a settlement.' *See also Francis v. Francis and Dickerson*, [1955] 3 WLR 973, 980.

2403. *Lin Jian Wei v. Lim Eng Hock Peter*, [2011] 3 SLR 1052, [78]. *See also id.*, [56]; *Turf Club Auto Emporium Pte Ltd v. Yeo Boong Hua*, [2018] SGCA 79; *Yeo Boong Hua v. Turf Club Auto Emporium Pte Ltd*, [2019] SGHC 73. C.f. *Lownds v. Home Office*, [2002] 1 WLR 2450, [31].

on an indemnity basis are taken to be usually one third more than that assessed on a standard basis. It should be noted, however, that this is not a hard and fast rule … [2404]

§5. One-Sixth and One-Half Rules

661. Apart from possible disciplinary proceedings,[2405] there are certain significant implications for the lawyer if he is found (through the taxation process) to have overcharged. Section 128(1) of the Legal Profession Act[2406] states that if:

> any order for taxation is made upon the application of the party chargeable or liable, or of the solicitor, the costs of the order and taxation, except when the order has been made after the expiration of 12 months, shall be paid according to the event of the taxation … if the bill when taxed is less by a sixth part than the bill delivered, then the solicitor shall pay the costs; or … if the bill when taxed is not less by a sixth part, then the party chargeable or liable, if the application is made by him, or if he attends the taxation, shall pay the costs.

662. This is otherwise known as the one-sixth rule. In the taxation of any bill of costs, if one-half or more of the total amount of the bill is taxed off, the Registrar has the power to make one or both of the following orders: first, 'that the solicitor who presented the bill be disallowed the costs for the work done for and in the taxation of costs', and second, that the solicitor who presented the bill:

> stamp the bill with the whole of the amount of fees which would be payable if the bill was allowed by the Registrar at the full amount thereof; … be entitled to be reimbursed by the paying party (in the case of a bill between party and party) or his client (in the case of a bill between the solicitor and his client) only the amount of fees payable on the amount allowed on taxation; … pay personally the difference between the amounts of fees mentioned … above; and … pay personally the fee payable for the Registrar's Certificate.[2407]

663. This is otherwise known as the one-half rule. There are some important differences as to the operation of these two rules. First, unlike the one-sixth rule, the one-half rule is not mandatory in its operation but is discretionary. Second, the one-sixth rule only applies to solicitor and client costs, while the one-half rule applies to all bills of costs. Third, the one-sixth rule affects the incidence of the liability to pay the costs of the taxation and the costs of obtaining the order for taxation, while the first limb of the one-half rule affects the right to recover the costs of the taxation only. Fourth, under the one-sixth rule, if one-sixth or more of the costs claimed in

---

2404. *Lin Jian Wei v. Lim Eng Hock Peter*, [2011] 3 SLR 1052, [83]. *See also Diversey (Far East) Pte Ltd v. Chai Chung Ching Chester (No 2)*, [1992] 3 SLR(R) 420, [39].

2405. *See* e.g., *Law Society of Singapore v. Low Yong Sen*, [2009] 1 SLR(R) 802.

2406. (Cap. 161, 2009 Rev. Ed.). *See also Atlantis Engineering & Construction Pte Ltd v. Chong Yeo & Partners*, [1996] SGHC 1.

2407. Supreme Court of Judicature Act (Cap. 322, R. 5, 2014 Rev. Ed.) Rules of Court, O 59 r 8(7).

a bill is taxed off, the solicitor will be actually liable to pay the client the costs the client incurred for the taxation and obtaining the order for taxation; under the first limb of one-half rule, the solicitor can only be disallowed his own costs of the taxation; he cannot be ordered to pay costs to another person.

Chapter 5. Review of Taxation

§1. Introduction

664. A party 'to any taxation proceedings who is dissatisfied with the allowance or disallowance in whole or in part of any item by the Registrar, or with the amount allowed by the Registrar in respect of any item, may apply to a Judge to review the taxation as to that item or part of an item, as the case may be'.[2408] Although there is a difference in the procedures between an appeal from the decision of a registrar on a matter heard before him and an application to review an item or sum allowed or disallowed by a registrar on taxation, it has been held by the High Court that an appeal and a review are the same in that they essentially involved an appeal from the decision of the registrar.[2409]

§2. Procedural Aspects

665. An application for review of taxation 'may be made at any time within 14 days after that decision, or such longer time as the Registrar or the Court at any time may allow'.[2410] Further, such an application 'shall be made by summons and shall, except where the Judge thinks fit to adjourn into Court, be heard in Chambers'.[2411] When the judge reviews the decision, unless he otherwise directs, 'no further evidence shall be received on the hearing of the review of the Registrar's decision by the Judge, but … on the hearing of the review, the Judge may exercise all such powers and discretion as are vested in the Registrar in relation to the subject-matter of the application'.[2412] Nonetheless, the review is heard de novo, and the judge is not fettered by the decision exercised by the registrar in determining the quantum of any item in the bill of costs.[2413] In other words, 'the judge is entitled to exercise the powers and discretion vested in him by the rules and make a completely fresh decision, among other things, substituting his own discretion for that of the Registrar and awarding a different figure altogether in place of that awarded by the Registrar'.[2414] However, 'de novo' does not mean that that the taxation proceedings begin afresh before the judge because '[t]he power to decide afresh and conducting

2408. Supreme Court of Judicature Act (Cap. 322, R. 5, 2014 Rev. Ed.) Rules of Court, O 59 r 34(1).
2409. *Tan Boon Hai v. Lee Ah Fong*, [2001] 3 SLR(R) 693, [34].
2410. Supreme Court of Judicature Act (Cap. 322, R. 5, 2014 Rev. Ed.) Rules of Court, O 59 r 34(2). An earlier version of this provision stated that the request for review 'must be made within 14 days after the review or such other period as may be fixed by the Registrar'. This caused some confusion as to whether the 14-day period ran from the date of a registrar's decision or the date of delivery of the registrar's grounds of decision: *Sumitomo Bank Ltd v. Kartika Ratna Thahir*, [1996] 3 SLR(R) 165, [5]. However, the present formulation of O 59 r 34(2) makes clear that it is 14 days from the date of the registrar's decision.
2411. Supreme Court of Judicature Act (Cap. 322, R. 5, 2014 Rev. Ed.) Rules of Court, O 59 r 34(3).
2412. Supreme Court of Judicature Act (Cap. 322, R. 5, 2014 Rev. Ed.) Rules of Court, O 59 r 35(1).
2413. *Tan Boon Hai v. Lee Ah Fong*, [2001] 3 SLR(R) 693, [31]; cited in *Shorvon Simon v. Singapore Medical Council*, [2006] 1 SLR(R) 182; *Nim Minimaart (a firm) v. MCST Plan No 1079*, [2013] 2 SLR 1025, [11].
2414. *Tan Boon Hai v. Lee Ah Fong*, [2001] 3 SLR(R) 693, [31].

the proceedings afresh are not the same thing'.[2415] Accordingly, a judge reviewing a registrar's taxation of costs will usually consider only the areas where the registrar is alleged to have erred; there is no necessity to begin the taxation process completely afresh.

§3. Substantive Aspects

666. As for the approach that should be taken by the reviewing judge, it has been said that:

> So long as the registrar taxing the bill of costs has taken all these factors as well as any other unusual or special circumstances into account, his decision will not be easily disturbed. The discretion of a court cannot be displaced by any specific finding in the way one might say a principle of law was misapplied or a fact was found against the weight of the evidence. It can only be displaced by another discretionary decision … The lower court's discretion should not be held to be wrong just because the reviewing court would have exercised its discretion differently …[2416]

667. The reviewing judge will not interfere with the functions of the trial judge by, for example, varying the proportion of the costs to be allowed in view of certain failed defences.[2417] After the review, 'the Judge may make such order as the circumstances require, and in particular may order the Registrar's certificate to be amended or, except where the dispute as to the item under review is as to amount only, order the item to be remitted to the Registrar for taxation'.[2418]

§4. Possibility of Appeal

668. The High Court's decision on costs[2419] is appealable to the Court of Appealable only with the leave of a judge.[2420] In this respect, an order of a judge refusing or granting leave is final.[2421] The appellate court's approach towards an appeal against a decision made on review is different from that of the judge conducting the taxation review. When an appeal is lodged against a judicial decision that has been made in the exercise of a judicial officer's discretion, it must be shown

2415. *Lau Liat Meng & Co v. Lum Kai Keng*, [2002] 2 SLR(R) 593, [10]; *Wong Foong Chai v. Lin Kuo Hao*, [2005] 3 SLR(R) 74, [17].
2416. *Basil Anthony Herman v. Premier Security Co-operative Ltd*, [2012] 2 SLR 616, [7].
2417. *Tan Yeow Hiang Kenneth v. Tan Chor Chuan*, [2006] 1 SLR(R) 557, [8]–[9].
2418. Supreme Court of Judicature Act (Cap. 322, R. 5, 2014 Rev. Ed.) Rules of Court, O 59 r 35(2).
2419. 'Costs' refer to both solicitor-and-client and party-and-party costs, and is also not limited to the issue of quantum of costs: *Kosui Singapore Pte Ltd v. Thangavelu*, [2016] 2 SLR 105, [31]–[33].
2420. Supreme Court of Judicature Act (Cap. 322, 2007 Rev. Ed.), s 34(2)(b). If a party does not obtain leave to appeal against the High Court's order as to costs, the Court of Appeal has no jurisdiction to hear the appeal and the notice of appeal would be struck out: *Kosui Singapore Pte Ltd v. Thangavelu*, [2016] 2 SLR 105, [3]–[4].
2421. Supreme Court of Judicature Act (Cap. 322, 2007 Rev. Ed.), s 34(2B).

that the judicial officer had erred in principle or had reached a conclusion that is plainly wrong before the appellate court will overrule that decision.[2422]

2422. *Nim Minimaart (a firm) v. MCST Plan No 1079*, [2013] 2 SLR 1025, [12].

Chapter 6. Assessment of Damages

§1. INTRODUCTION

669. Damages refers to the '[m]oney claimed by, or ordered to be paid to, a person as compensation for loss or injury'.[2423] Apart from his or her entitlement to costs, a successful litigant will usually be most concerned with his or her entitlement to damages. It is important to understand recognize that there are two concepts – proof of damage and proof of quantum. For the former, the court can still award damages even if there is no appropriate measure of damages.[2424] The latter requires some proof of the quantum of damage suffered, albeit not a precise quantification.

670. Where a claim is liquidated, an assessment of damages is usually not necessary. A successful litigant may receive an award of damages on termination of the litigation, whether after a trial or not. Where a claim is unliquidated and an assessment of damages is necessary, the court may pronounce judgment on the issue of liability and either assess damages itself or order that the assessment be conducted by a registrar.[2425] Where no provision is made in the judgment for how damages are to be assessed, the damages will generally be assessed by a registrar and the party entitled to benefit has to apply for directions within one month from the date of judgment.[2426] In the case of a default judgment against some but not all of the defendants, the damages under the judgment shall be assessed at the trial unless the court otherwise orders.[2427] It would be preferable for the assessment of damages to be conducted by the trial judge (as opposed to a registrar) where there is a link between determination of liability and the nature of the damages, or where the nature of the assessment is factually or legally complex.[2428] The rules for assessment of damages are primarily found in O 37 of the Rules of Court.[2429]

§2. PROCEDURAL ASPECTS

671. Where damages are to be assessed separately from the trial on liability, pretrial conferences will generally be fixed for the registrar to give directions relating to discovery, the filing and exchange of affidavit evidence, the filing of a notice of appointment for assessment of damages, and the fixing of dates for the assessment

2423. *Black's Law Dictionary* (B.A. Garner ed., Thomson Reuters 2009), 'damages'. *See also Marco Polo Shipping Co Pte Ltd v. Fairmacs Shipping & Transport Services Pte Ltd*, [2015] 5 SLR 541, [28]: 'at the broadest level of abstraction, the object of an award of damages is to compensate the plaintiff for the damage it has suffered'.
2424. *Li Siu Lun v. Looi Kok Poh*, [2015] SGHC 149, [43]–[48].
2425. J. Pinsler, *Principles of Civil Procedure* 819 (Acad. Publg. 2013); Supreme Court of Judicature Act (Cap. 322, R. 5, 2014 Rev. Ed.) Rules of Court, O 37 r 4.
2426. Supreme Court of Judicature Act (Cap. 322, R. 5, 2014 Rev. Ed.) Rules of Court, O 37 r 1(1).
2427. Supreme Court of Judicature Act (Cap. 322, R. 5, 2014 Rev. Ed.) Rules of Court, O 37 r 3.
2428. J. Pinsler, *Principles of Civil Procedure* 820 (Acad. Publg. 2013).
2429. Supreme Court of Judicature Act (Cap. 322, R. 5, 2014 Rev. Ed.) Rules of Court.

of damages.[2430] Where the assessment is to be heard by the registrar, the hearing will be conducted in chambers following a similar order of proceedings used in trials before judges.[2431] The attendance of witnesses and the production of documents may be compelled by subpoena.[2432] The registrar will hear evidence from the relevant witnesses, including factual and any expert witnesses, to determine the appropriate quantum of damages to be awarded.[2433] After the assessment, the registrar will certify the amount of damages.[2434] The registrar will also usually award interest on the judgment sum[2435] and make the appropriate costs orders.[2436]

§3. General Considerations During the Hearing

672. The court will consider all the items of a claim during the assessment hearing and is not entitled to dismiss an item unless an application is made for that purpose and is successful or the parties agree to dispense with a particular item.[2437] In practice, the plaintiff would typically propose an appropriate measure of damages to be used as a yardstick to arrive at a monetary figure to award damages. Even though damages cannot be assessed with certainty, this does not relieve the wrongdoer from paying damages.[2438] While the plaintiff does not need to plead general damage, he is required to plead damage which is not the necessary and immediate consequence of the wrongful act in question so as to give notice to the defendant(s).[2439] However, the court will not usually disallow a claim merely because of a technical error of pleading but will consider the entire factual matrix and the 'paramount rationale of dispensing even handed justice'.[2440] In the event of a continuing cause of action, damages are assessed down to the time of the assessment.[2441] When a party's liability has been fixed at a certain percentage (either by mutual agreement

2430. Supreme Court of Judicature Act (Cap. 322, R. 5, 2014 Rev. Ed.) Rules of Court, O 25 r 3 and O 37 r 1.
2431. Supreme Court of Judicature Act (Cap. 322, R. 5, 2014 Rev. Ed.) Rules of Court, O 35 and O 37 r 1(4).
2432. Supreme Court of Judicature Act (Cap. 322, R. 5, 2014 Rev. Ed.) Rules of Court, O 37 r 1(4).
2433. Evidence-in-chief of the witnesses is generally given by way of affidavit and the bulk of the evidence before the court will comprise cross-examination and re-examination: Supreme Court of Judicature Act (Cap. 322, R. 5, 2014 Rev. Ed.) Rules of Court, O 38 r 3.
2434. Supreme Court of Judicature Act (Cap. 322, R. 5, 2014 Rev. Ed.) Rules of Court, O 37 r 2.
2435. Supreme Court Practice Directions 2013 (Part IX). The present default post-judgment interest rate is 5.33% per annum.
2436. *See* Supreme Court of Judicature Act (Cap. 322, R. 5, 2014 Rev. Ed.) Rules of Court, O 59 r 4(1).
2437. J. Pinsler, *Principles of Civil Procedure* 821 (Acad. Publg. 2013) citing *Triangle Auto Pte Ltd v. Zheng Zi Construction Pte Ltd*, [2000] 3 SLR(R) 594.
2438. *Li Siu Lun v. Looi Kok Poh*, [2015] SGHC 149, [41]; *Robertson Quay Investment Pte Ltd v. Steen Consultants Pte Ltd*, [2008] 2 SLR(R) 623, [30].
2439. C. Bull & J. Pinsler, *Civil Procedure: Annual Review of Singapore Cases* [7.67] (Sing. Acad. L. 2007) citing *Lee Chee Wei v. Tan Hor Peow Victor*, [2007] 3 SLR(R) 537, [61]. *See also Perestrello E Companhia Limitada v. United Paint Co Ltd*, [1969] 1 WLR 570.
2440. *Lee Chee Wei v. Tan Hor Peow Victor*, [2007] 3 SLR(R) 537, [80]–[82].
2441. Supreme Court of Judicature Act (Cap. 322, R. 5, 2014 Rev. Ed.) Rules of Court, O 37 r 6.

or by the court) and damages have been ordered to be assessed, the fixed percentage applies to the amount of damages assessed and not the pecuniary limit of the court in question.[2442]

§4. Personal Injury

673. It is trite law that a plaintiff has the burden of proving his or her claim in damages.[2443] However, proof is not required where both parties are able to agree on the quantification of damages.[2444] In personal injury claims, general damages will usually include pain and suffering, loss of amenities, future medical expenses, future transport expenses, loss of future earnings, and/or loss of earning capacity.[2445] Special damages will usually include pre-trial medical expenses, pre-trial transport expenses and pre-trial loss of earnings.[2446] Damages for loss of expectation of life have been abolished by the Civil Law Act, which provides quite unequivocally that:

> No damages shall be recoverable in respect of any loss of expectation of life caused to the injured person by the injuries, except that if the injured person's expectation of life has been reduced by the injuries, the court, in assessing damages in respect of pain and suffering caused by the injuries, shall take into account any suffering caused or likely to be caused to him by awareness that his expectation of life has been so reduced.[2447]

674. It is important to bear in mind that the overarching objective of awarding damages is to 'compensate the injured victim by restoring him or her to the position that he or she would have been (in a monetary sense) had the accident not happened'.[2448] Damages are assessed on a once and for all basis (including pre-trial loss and prospective loss) at the time of the trial or the assessment of damages, although there is an exception for provisional damages to be assessed in two stages if there

---

2442. C. Bull & J. Pinsler, *Civil Procedure: Annual Review of Singapore Cases* [7.19] (Sing. Acad. L. 2007) citing *Ng Chan Teng v. Keppel Singmarine Dockyard Pte Ltd*, [2007] 4 SLR(R) 633, [3].

2443. *Chai Kang Wei Samuel v. Shaw Linda Gillian*, [2010] 3 SLR 587, [19], citing *Bonham-Carter v. Hyde Park Hotel, Limited* [1948] 64 TLR 177, 178.

2444. Audrey Lim et al., *Assessment of Damages: Personal Injuries and Fatal Accidents* 6 (2d ed., LexisNexis, 2005).

2445. *See Poh Huat Heng Corp Pte Ltd v. Hafizul Islam Kofil Uddin*, [2012] 3 SLR 1003, [8]; *Ng Chee Wee v. Tan Chin Seng*, [2013] SGHC 54, [6]. *See also Rahman Lutfar v. Scanpile Contractors Pte Ltd*, [2016] SGHC 41, [60].

2446. *See Liu Haixiang v. China Construction (South Pacific) Development Co Pte Ltd*, [2009] SGHC 21, [20]; *Poh Huat Heng Corp Pte Ltd v. Hafizul Islam Kofil Uddin*, [2012] 3 SLR 1003, [8]; *Ng Chee Wee v. Tan Chin Seng*, [2013] SGHC 54, [7]; *Wang Jianbin v. Hong De Development Pte Ltd*, [2015] SGHC 242, [11].

2447. Civil Law Act (Cap. 43, 1999 Rev. Ed.), s 11(1).

2448. *Chai Kang Wei Samuel v. Shaw Linda Gillian*, [2010] 3 SLR 587, [29].

is a risk that the plaintiff would develop a serious disease or deterioration in condition.[2449] In what follows we will examine the approach towards assessing damages for pain and suffering and loss of amenities, the relationship between loss of future earnings and loss of earning capacity, the approach towards assessing special damages, and dependency claims.

I. Pain and Suffering and Loss of Amenities

675. The phrase 'pain and suffering' refers to 'the physical pain, emotional and intellectual suffering arising from the injury'.[2450] Shock is included as are anxiety, fear, as well as feelings of frustration and anguish for the loss.[2451] Loss of amenities is the 'loss of the ability to enjoy life to its fullest' and in determining the extent of the loss, the restriction to the plaintiff's activities, his sex life, the ability to have children and marriage prospects are some matters to consider.[2452] As a matter of practice, the courts in Singapore have often lumped the claim for 'pain and suffering' together with that of 'loss of amenities'.[2453] However, they are not the same.[2454]

676. Where the plaintiff has been reduced to a persistent vegetative state, his unconsciousness as to his surroundings may result in the claim for pain and suffering being negated, but substantial damages may still be awarded for loss of amenities.[2455] Whether or not there is loss of amenities is an objective fact that does not depend on an appreciation of the loss by the victim.[2456] It should be noted that the pain and suffering and loss of amenities in a person not in a vegetative state need not always be for less than the amount awarded to an unconscious victim as each

2449. Audrey Lim et al., *Assessment of Damages: Personal Injuries and Fatal Accidents* 3–6 (2d ed., LexisNexis 2005) citing *British Transport Commission v. Gourley*, [1956] AC 185, 213. *See also* Supreme Court of Judicature Act (Cap. 322, R. 5, 2014 Rev. Ed.), First Schedule; *Pritchard v. JH Cobden Ltd*, [1987] 2 WLR 627.

2450. Audrey Lim et al., *Assessment of Damages: Personal Injuries and Fatal Accidents* 42 (2d ed., LexisNexis 2005); *Au Yeong Wing Loong v. Chew Hai Ban*, [1993] 2 SLR(R) 209, [11].

2451. *Au Yeong Wing Loong v. Chew Hai Ban*, [1993] 2 SLR(R) 209, [11]; *Tan Kok Lam (next friend to Teng Eng) v. Hong Choon Peng*, [2001] 1 SLR(R) 786, [30].

2452. Audrey Lim et al., *Assessment of Damages: Personal Injuries and Fatal Accidents* 53 (2d ed., LexisNexis 2005) citing *Manley v. Rugby Portland Cement Co Ltd*, (1951) CA No 286.

2453. *See Tan Juay Mui (by his next friend Chew Chwee Kim) v. Sher Kuan Hock (Liberty Insurance Pte Ltd, codefendant; Liberty Insurance Pte Ltd and another, third parties)*, [2012] 3 SLR 496; *Chai Kang Wei Samuel v. Shaw Linda Gillian*, [2010] 3 SLR 587; *Tan Siew Bin Ronnie v. Chin Wee Keong*, [2008] 1 SLR(R) 178; *Mei Yue Lan Margaret v. Raffles City (Pte) Ltd*, [2005] 4 SLR(R) 740.

2454. *Tan Kok Lam (next friend to Teng Eng) v. Hong Choon Peng*, [2001] 1 SLR(R) 786, [25].

2455. *Tan Kok Lam (next friend to Teng Eng) v. Hong Choon Peng*, [2001] 1 SLR(R) 786, [28] and [33], citing *Wise v. Kaye*, [1962] 1 QB 638; *H West & Son Ltd v. Shephard*, [1964] AC 326.

2456. *Tan Kok Lam (next friend to Teng Eng) v. Hong Choon Peng*, [2001] 1 SLR(R) 786, [28].

case will depend on its particular facts.[2457] The starting point for evaluating pain and suffering is the injury itself, including fright at the time of the injury and fright reaction.[2458]

677. The quantum of the award for pain and suffering will 'take into consideration the plaintiff's awareness of the pain, his capacity for suffering, the extent of the pain, whether it was continuous or intermittent, and whether it was permanent or temporary'.[2459] Where there are specific injuries, the courts' approach for awarding damages for each injury is to compare the injury with the same or similar injury in previous cases, and award the appropriate damages; hence, precedent cases for previous injuries are highly relevant although the court may, where appropriate, consider the increase in the value of money over the years.[2460] Where there are multiple injuries, the court may take a 'component approach', meaning that the injuries suffered are classified into separate domains, such as 'structural' injury; 'psychological' injury; and 'cognitive' impairment.[2461] The court will then quantify the loss for each of the different types of injuries.[2462] It has been observed that, properly applied, the component approach could prevent overcompensation as it enabled the court to address the different aspects of pain, suffering and loss of amenities arising out of an injury systematically; however, the courts should always be mindful that the 'overall quantum must be a reasonable sum reflective of the totality of the injury'.[2463] The court may also, where appropriate, take a 'global approach' towards assessing damages for multiple injuries, meaning that discrete injuries will be considered, but a single award will be made for all the damages.[2464] It has also been pointed out that both approaches need not be viewed as 'functionally distinct' as the 'global approach arrives at a global figure after taking into account the component figures, and the component approach starts by adding up the component figures and ends by ensuring that the aggregate amount is reflective of the "totality of the injury"'.[2465]

2457. *Tan Juay Mui (by his next friend Chew Chwee Kim) v. Sher Kuan Hock (Liberty Insurance Pte Ltd, codefendant; Liberty Insurance Pte Ltd and another, third parties)*, [2012] 3 SLR 496, [30].

2458. *Au Yeong Wing Loong v. Chew Hai Ban*, [1993] 2 SLR(R) 209, [11], citing *Thompson v. Royal Mail Lines Ltd*, [1957] 1 Lloyds Rep 99.

2459. Audrey Lim et al., *Assessment of Damages: Personal Injuries and Fatal Accidents* 42 (2d ed., LexisNexis 2005) citing *Lim Poh Choo v. Camden and Islington Area Health Authority*, [1980] AC 174.

2460. Audrey Lim et al., *Assessment of Damages: Personal Injuries and Fatal Accidents* 43–44 (2d ed., LexisNexis 2005) citing *TV Media Pte Ltd v. De Cruz Andrea Heidi*, [2004] 3 SLR(R) 543.

2461. *Tan Yu Min Winston v. Uni-Fruitveg Pte Ltd*, [2008] 4 SLR(R) 825, [25].

2462. *Tan Yu Min Winston v. Uni-Fruitveg Pte Ltd*, [2008] 4 SLR(R) 825, [26].

2463. *Chai Kang Wei Samuel v. Shaw Linda Gillian*, [2010] 3 SLR 587, [49].

2464. *Tan Yu Min Winston v. Uni-Fruitveg Pte Ltd*, [2008] 4 SLR(R) 825, [15]; *Lee Wei Kong (by his litigation representative Lee Swee Chit) v. Ng Siok Tong*, [2010] SGHC 371, [13].

2465. *Lee Wei Kong (by his litigation representative Lee Swee Chit) v. Ng Siok Tong*, [2010] SGHC 371, [15].

678. To facilitate reference to precedent, a set of guidelines derived from precedents has been published in Singapore.[2466] The guidelines may be used as follows: first, identifying a category of injury;[2467] second, understanding the severity of the injury;[2468] third, looking up range values in the guidelines; and finally, considering the effect of multiple injuries to take into account any overlap.[2469] To aid the courts in making an appropriate award for loss of amenities, particularly where a separate award is claimed,[2470] evidence should be adduced 'from friends or relatives of the plaintiff comparing his pre- and post-accident situation in respect of his hobbies and leisure activities, as well as any significant personality changes'.[2471]

II. Loss of Future Earnings and Loss of Earning Capacity

679. Loss of future earnings and loss of earning capacity compensate for different losses, and hence there is nothing in principle which bars a plaintiff from being entitled to claim for both provided that the necessary evidence is present.[2472] Loss of future earnings is awarded for real assessable loss proved by evidence – this is a loss arising from a situation where a victim of an accident finds that he or she can no longer, as a result of the accident, earn his or her pre-accident rate of earnings.[2473] In other words, loss of future earnings 'refers to the difference between

2466. *See Guidelines for the Assessment of General Damages in Personal Injury Cases* (Acad. Publg. 2010). These guidelines provide a range of awards for pain and suffering for a list of different types of personal injuries and are based on actual awards in local cases or, where these were unavailable, the guidelines contained in *Assessment of General Damages in Personal Injury Cases* (8th ed., Oxford U. Press 2006).

2467. For instance, injuries to the head, neck, spine and back, upper limbs, lower limbs, psychological injuries, and internal organ injuries: *Guidelines for the Assessment of General Damages in Personal Injury Cases* 2 (Acad. Publg. 2010). *See also Wang Jianbin v. Hong De Development Pte Ltd*, [2015] SGHC 242, [4].

2468. These range from severe, moderately severe, moderate, to minor, and are based on the degree of disruption to lifestyle, pain, and permanency: *Guidelines for the Assessment of General Damages in Personal Injury Cases* 2 (Acad. Publg. 2010).

2469. *Guidelines for the Assessment of General Damages in Personal Injury Cases* 2 (Acad. Publg. 2010).

2470. Examples of cases where loss of amenities were awarded include *Mohamed Repin v. Lim Yu Kee*, [1969] 1 MLJ 64; *Lai Wee Lian v. Singapore Bus Service (1978) Ltd*, [1983–1984] SLR(R) 388; *Au Yeong Wing Loong v. Chew Hai Ban*, [1993] 2 SLR(R) 209. *See also* Audrey Lim et al., *Assessment of Damages: Personal Injuries and Fatal Accidents* 55–56 (2d ed., LexisNexis 2005).

2471. Audrey Lim et al., *Assessment of Damages: Personal Injuries and Fatal Accidents* 54 (2d ed., LexisNexis 2005).

2472. *Chai Kang Wei Samuel v. Shaw Linda Gillian,* [2010] 3 SLR 587, [24], citing *Moeliker v. A Reyrolle and Co Ltd*, [1977] 1 WLR 132.

2473. *Sun Delong v. Teo Poh Soon and another* [2016] SGHC 129; *Chai Kang Wei Samuel v. Shaw Linda Gillian,* [2010] 3 SLR 587, [12]–[14], citing *Fairley v. John Thompson (Design and Contracting Division) Ltd*, [1973] 2 Lloyd's Rep 40, 42; *Smith v. Manchester Corporation*, (1974) 17 KIR 1, 7–8. *See also* Audrey Lim et al., *Assessment of Damages: Personal Injuries and Fatal Accidents* 30 (2d ed., LexisNexis 2005).

post-accident and pre-accident income or rate of income'.[2474] Loss of earning capacity, on the other hand, addresses the loss arising from the weakening of the plaintiff's competitive position in the open labour market.[2475]

680. An award for loss of earning capacity, as opposed to an award for loss of future earnings, is generally made in the following cases: where, at the time of trial, the plaintiff is in employment and has suffered no loss of earnings, but there is a risk that he may lose that employment at some time in the future, and may then, as a result of his injury, be at a disadvantage in getting another job or an equally well paid job; or where there is no available evidence of the plaintiff's earnings to enable the court to properly calculate future earnings, for example, young children who have no earnings on which to base an assessment for loss of future earnings.[2476] Calculation of loss future earnings should be based on the use of multipliers, and parties should not rely entirely on present value calculations.[2477] The method of assessing of loss of future earnings has been described in the following terms:

> the difference between [the plaintiff's] pre-accident income and his present income is assessed and calculated on an annual basis, and after making the necessary deductions for income tax, the multiplicand is derived. The number of years for which the plaintiff would suffer this reduction in earnings is assessed as a round figure, thus giving the multiplier. Multiplying the multiplier with the multiplicand, assessed as [the plaintiff's] annual loss per year, will therefore give the total sum for the loss of future earnings.[2478]

681. The underlying objective in fixing the multiplier is 'to derive a final award that provides the plaintiff with full compensation to the nearest extent possible'.[2479] The Court of Appeal has recently clarified that multipliers under the conventional approach need not be revised upwards even though there has been an increase in the retirement age over the years since this is already a factor that the court will take into account under the conventional approach.[2480] Similarly, the multipliers need not be revised upwards to determine the discount for accelerated receipt even though the real rate of return of fixed deposits under the current economic circumstances are not as high as before. This is because it was not reasonable for a plaintiff to invest his entire lump sum award in fixed deposits (especially if the damage award was meant to compensate the plaintiff for decades of lost earnings) and there was

---

2474. *Chai Kang Wei Samuel v. Shaw Linda Gillian,* [2010] 3 SLR 587, [14].
2475. *Chai Kang Wei Samuel v. Shaw Linda Gillian,* [2010] 3 SLR 587, [14]–[15], citing *Smith v. Manchester Corporation*, [1974] 1 KIR 1, 8; *Moeliker v. A Reyrolle and Co Ltd*, [1977] 1 WLR 132. *See also Seow Hwa Chuan v. Ong Wah Chuan*, [2016] SGHC 146, [12].
2476. *Teo Sing Keng v. Sim Ban Kiat*, [1994] 1 SLR(R) 240, [40]; *Chai Kang Wei Samuel v. Shaw Linda Gillian,* [2010] 3 SLR 587, [16].
2477. *Lai Wai Keong Eugene v. Loo Wei Yen*, [2014] 3 SLR 702, [20].
2478. Audrey Lim et al., *Assessment of Damages: Personal Injuries and Fatal Accidents* 30–31 (2d ed., LexisNexis 2005). *See also Koh Chai Kwang v. Teo Ai Ling*, [2011] 3 SLR 610, [37].
2479. *Poh Huat Heng Corp Pte Ltd v. Hafizul Islam Kofil Uddin*, [2012] 3 SLR 1003, [46], citing *Lai Wee Lian v. Singapore Bus Service (1978) Ltd*, [1983–1984] SLR(R) 388, [20] (emphasis in original).
2480. *Lai Wai Keong Eugene v. Loo Wei Yen*, [2014] 3 SLR 702, [26].

also no guarantee that the present low rates of return would persist.[2481] Nonetheless, the Court of Appeal acknowledged that the present state of affairs was not ideal and there was indeed scope for review of the multipliers used. However, the Court of Appeal opined that this was a matter that fell within the institutional competence of the Legislature after it has undertaken a careful study with input from the relevant experts and stakeholders.[2482]

682. In assessing the multiplier, the courts will consider the plaintiff's age at the time of assessment and the prevailing retirement age.[2483] However, the duration for which the plaintiff would have been expected to earn an income if not for the accident must be discounted for three contingent factors so the plaintiff will not be overcompensated: first, the plaintiff may have stopped working for reasons other than the accident; second, the plaintiff will be receiving a lump sum award in advance of the dates when he would actually have received his future income but for the accident; and third, the plaintiff should be protected against the effects of future inflation.[2484] Although the use of actuarial tables based on projections of the mortality rate of the general population may 'provide a more scientific basis for discounting a lump sum award to account for premature death', in the absence of such actuarial tables in Singapore, the following approaches would be 'the next most appropriate':[2485] first, to fix the multiplier by looking at the multipliers used in comparable cases;[2486] and second, by discounting the plaintiff's stream of income over his expected working life by an appropriate rate.[2487]

683. Determining an appropriate multiplicand will depend on the evidence of the plaintiff's difference in earnings per year, but may be more difficult in cases involving injured plaintiffs who were young at the time of the accident and had not yet commenced work at the time of trial.[2488] In such situations, the courts may adopt a particular occupation as an appropriate career model where: the plaintiff had indicated a clear intention to enter that particular occupation; there was a strong probability that he would be able to enter that occupation; and that occupation provided a sufficiently certain career model for the estimation of loss of future earnings.[2489] Where these conditions are not satisfied, the courts may use alternative bases, such as the national wage average for a young man or woman as the case may be (where

2481. *Lai Wai Keong Eugene v. Loo Wei Yen*, [2014] 3 SLR 702, [32]–[36].
2482. *Lai Wai Keong Eugene v. Loo Wei Yen*, [2014] 3 SLR 702, [37].
2483. Audrey Lim et al., *Assessment of Damages: Personal Injuries and Fatal Accidents* 31 (2d ed., LexisNexis 2005).
2484. *Poh Huat Heng Corp Pte Ltd v. Hafizul Islam Kofil Uddin*, [2012] 3 SLR 1003, [47], citing *Wells v. Wells*, [1999] 1 AC 345, 364–364 and 372.
2485. *Poh Huat Heng Corp Pte Ltd v. Hafizul Islam Kofil Uddin*, [2012] 3 SLR 1003, [53]–[54].
2486. *Poh Huat Heng Corp Pte Ltd v. Hafizul Islam Kofil Uddin*, [2012] 3 SLR 1003, [48(a)], citing *Loh Chia Mei v. Koh Kok Han*, [2009] SGHC 181, [41].
2487. *Poh Huat Heng Corp Pte Ltd v. Hafizul Islam Kofil Uddin*, [2012] 3 SLR 1003, [48(b)], citing *Shaw Linda Gillian v. Chai Kang Wei Samuel*, [2009] SGHC 187.
2488. *Lee Wei Kong (by his litigation representative Lee Swee Chit) v. Ng Siok Tong*, [2012] 2 SLR 85, [29] and [33].
2489. *Koh Chai Kwang v. Teo Ai Ling*, [2011] 3 SLR 610, [35]. *See also Quek Yen Fei Kenneth v. Yeo Chye Huat*, [2016] SGHC 96, [84].

the plaintiff was fourteen years old on the date of the accident and in secondary school),[2490] the civil service pay scale for polytechnic diploma holders (where the plaintiff was a polytechnic student with a broad range of career opportunities and it was unclear which career path she would eventually take),[2491] and the median earnings of a university graduate over a period of years (where the plaintiff was a junior college student).[2492] Depending on the facts of each case, it may be possible to split the multiplier, with a different multiplicand applied to each multiplier period.[2493]

684. The method of assessing a loss of earning capacity involves the courts taking into account numerous factors, including: the age and sex of the plaintiff, his skills and training, the nature of his disabilities, the kind of job he was holding before the accident, the degree of the risk of him losing his job, the time when loss of employment might occur, the general employment situation for his type of job, the kind of jobs he could hold at present or in future, and the earnings he is likely to command.[2494] The courts will usually assess the plaintiff's weakness 'in the round' and award a lump sum,[2495] but in certain circumstances it may apply the multiplier and multiplicand approach.[2496]

685. In certain cases, the court may also award damages for loss of future earning capacity.[2497] An award of loss of future earning capacity is given as part of general damages to compensate a plaintiff for the weakening of his competitive position

2490. *Peh Diana v. Tan Miang Lee*, [1991] 1 SLR(R) 22, [28]. However, due to the absence of such evidence in that particular case, the High Court based the multiplicand on the mean starting wage of stenographic secretaries and rounded it upwards.

2491. *Koh Chai Kwang v. Teo Ai Ling*, [2011] 3 SLR 610, [24].

2492. *See Lee Wei Kong (by his litigation representative Lee Swee Chit) v. Ng Siok Tong*, [2012] 2 SLR 85, [39]–[41].

2493. Audrey Lim et al., *Assessment of Damages: Personal Injuries and Fatal Accidents* 32 (2d ed., LexisNexis 2005) citing *Ho Yiu v. Lim Peng Seng*, [2004] SGHC 218 (multiplier of fifteen split into three equal periods of five years each with a different multiplicand applied to each tranche on the basis that the plaintiff would obtain an increase in salary over those period had the plaintiff not been injured); *Tan Shwu Leng v. Singapore Airlines Ltd*, [2001] SGHC 51 (multiplier of six was split into a one-year period and a subsequent five-year period to reflect the different term contracts the plaintiff would have signed with the defendant had the plaintiff not been injured).

2494. Audrey Lim et al., *Assessment of Damages: Personal Injuries and Fatal Accidents* 33–34 (2d ed., LexisNexis 2005) citing *Moeliker v. A Reyrolle & Co Ltd*, [1977] 1 All ER 9, 16–17. *See also Tan Yu Min Winston (by his next friend Tan Cheng Tong) v. Uni-Fruitveg Pte Ltd*, [2008] 4 SLR(R) 825, [44].

2495. In *Tan Yu Min Winston (by his next friend Tan Cheng Tong) v. Uni-Fruitveg Pte Ltd*, [2008] 4 SLR(R) 825, [45], although the High Court accepted that the loss of earning capacity should be assessed 'in the round' in that case, it stated that a useful parameter to make a very rough check on whether or not the assessment of the lump sum was overly excessive or manifestly inadequate was to compute 'what that lump sum amount to be awarded would have in effect produced, if it was distributed as a stream of income per month in the future over the period of the working life of the plaintiff, assuming a certain rate of interest to be used as a discount rate for the computation'.

2496. Audrey Lim et al., *Assessment of Damages: Personal Injuries and Fatal Accidents* 34 –35 (2d ed., LexisNexis 2005) citing *Smith v. Manchester Corporation*, (1974) 17 KIR 1; *Chang Ah Lek v. Lim Ah Koon*, [1998] 3 SLR(R) 551, [31]; *Ang Leng Hock v. Leo Ee Ah*, [2004] 2 SLR(R) 361.

2497. *Mykytowych, Pamela Jane v. V I P Hotel* [2016] SGCA 44; [139]; *Ng Chee Wee v. Tan Ching Seng* [2013] SGHC 54, [68].

in the open labour market.[2498] The test to be applied is therefore whether there is a real risk that the plaintiff will be at a disadvantage in the open employment market because of the injury sustained in the accident.

III. Special Damages

686. The general rule is that 'a plaintiff is entitled to recover damages in respect of all reasonable expenses incurred as a result of the injuries he suffered, and these special damages have to be strictly proved, otherwise they are not recoverable'.[2499] The rule against double recovery applies and will require the court to deduct expenses incurred in the course of earning revenue from any award for loss of earnings.[2500] In assessing pre-trial loss of earnings, the multiplier and multiplicand approach may also be applied.[2501]

IV. Dependency Claims

687. The Civil Law Act provides for a right of action for any wrongful act, neglect or default that causes death.[2502] An action under this section may include a claim for damages for bereavement, which is presently fixed at the sum of SGD 15,000 to be divided equally between the persons entitled to claim such damages.[2503] Damages for bereavement may only be claimed by persons specified in the Civil Law Act and do not survive to benefit those persons' estates;[2504] according to section 21(2), they are:

> (a) the wife or husband of the deceased; (b) where there is no spouse by or for whom a claim can be made under paragraph (a), the children of the deceased; (c) where there is no person by or for whom a claim can be made under paragraph (a) or (b), the parents of the deceased or, if the deceased was illegitimate, his mother; (d) where there is no person by or for whom a claim can be made under paragraph (a), (b) or (c), but the deceased was at the date of his

2498. *Mykytowych, Pamela Jane v. V I P Hotel* [2016] SGCA 44; [140]; *Chai Kang Wei Samuel v. Shaw Linda Gillian* [2010] 3 SLR 587, [17]–[22].
2499. Audrey Lim et al., *Assessment of Damages: Personal Injuries and Fatal Accidents* 12 (2d ed., LexisNexis 2005) citing *Bocotra Construction Pte Ltd v. Thorkildsen*, [1994] 2 SLR(R) 387; *Wee Sia Tian v. Long Thik Boon*, [1996] 2 SLR(R) 420, [12]. In the context of personal injury cases, *see Lee Mui Yeng v. Ng Tong Yoo*, [2016] SGHC 46, [63]–[66].
2500. Audrey Lim et al., *Assessment of Damages: Personal Injuries and Fatal Accidents* 12 (2d ed., LexisNexis 2005) citing *Hunt v. Severs*, [1994] 2 AC 350; *Gul Chandiram Mahtani (administrators of the estate of Harbajan Kaur, deceased) v. Chain Singh*, [1998] 2 SLR(R) 801, [25]; *Lim Poh Choo v. Camden & Islington Area Health Authority*, [1980] AC 174.
2501. *See also Ng Chee Wee v. Tan Chin Seng* [2013] SGHC 54.
2502. Civil Law Act (Cap. 43, 1999 Rev. Ed.), s 20. *See also Law Kin Ying v. Lim Hong Hock*, [2015] SGHCR 14, [9].
2503. Civil Law Act (Cap. 43, 1999 Rev. Ed.), s 21(1) and 21(4)–(5). The sum of SGD 15,000 may be varied by the Minister by order published in the Gazette: *id.*, s 21(6).
2504. Civil Law Act (Cap. 43, 1999 Rev. Ed.), s 21(2)–(3).

death a minor, any person who during any marriage to which that person was a party treated the deceased as a child of the family in relation to that marriage; or (e) where there is no other person by or for whom a claim can be made under this subsection, any brother or sister of the deceased.

688. In assessing damages for an action for wrongful death, 'the court may award such damages as are proportioned to the losses resulting from the death to the dependants respectively', except that the following shall not be taken into account: 'any sum paid or payable on the death of the deceased under any contract of assurance or insurance; … any sum payable as a result of the death under the Central Provident Fund Act … or … any pension or gratuity which has been or will or may be paid as a result of the death'.[2505] The court assessing damages is required to 'take into account any moneys or other benefits which the deceased would be likely to have given to the dependants by way of maintenance, gift, bequest or devise or which the dependants would likely to have received by way of succession from the deceased had [he] lived beyond the date of the wrongful death'.[2506] Where damages are payable to a widow in respect of the death of her husband, the remarriage of the widow or her prospect of remarriage shall not be taken into account by the court assessing damages.[2507] Where damages are payable to a former wife, these 'shall only be in respect of a subsisting maintenance order against the deceased at the time of his death'.[2508]

689. It is axiomatic that the objective of calculating loss of dependency is to make an assessment of the value of the reasonable expectation of pecuniary benefit from the continuance of the life.[2509] It is also axiomatic that the longer the period of dependency, the greater would be the percentage reduction to take into account the vicissitudes of life and the investment value of receiving a lump sum payment in an award.[2510] In situations where an application is claiming damages on the basis of loss of inheritance claim, the appropriate method of calculation is the amount of wealth the deceased would have accumulated but for his death.[2511] Funeral expenses

2505. Civil Law Act (Cap. 43, 1999 Rev. Ed.), s 22(1).
2506. Civil Law Act (Cap. 43, 1999 Rev. Ed.), s 22(1A).
2507. Civil Law Act (Cap. 43, 1999 Rev. Ed.), s 22(3).
2508. Civil Law Act (Cap. 43, 1999 Rev. Ed.), s 22(3A).
2509. *Zhu Xiu Chun (alias Myint Myint Kyi) v. Rockwills Trustee (administrators of the estate of and on behalf of the dependants of Heng Ang Tee Franklin, deceased) and other appeals* [2016] SGCA 52, [91]; *Gul Chandiram Mahtani v. Chain Singh*, [1999] 1 SLR(R) 154, [17]; *Law Kin Ying v. Lim Hong Hock*, [2015] SGHCR 14, [11]. This is done by way of the multiplier-multiplicand approach, where the multiplicand is determined either by adding the value of the benefits received by the dependants or by deducting a percentage from the deceased's income which forms the deceased's personal expenditure; the balance is then assumed to be for the benefit of the dependants: *Hanson Ingrid Christina v. Tan Puey Tze*, [2008] 1 SLR(R) 409, [26]; *Sulastri bte Achmad v. Tan Hee Hang*, [2017] SGHC 7, [32].
2510. *Rockwills Trustee Ltd (administrators of the estate of and on behalf of the dependants of Heng Ang Tee Franklin, deceased) v. Wong Meng Hang*, [2015] SGHC 138, [21]; *Balanalagirisamy Gowri Rajeswari (administrators of the estate of Radhakrishnan Hari Babu, deceased) v. Wong Si Wah*, [2009] 1 SLR(R) 819, [10].
2511. *Rockwills Trustee Ltd (administrators of the estate of and on behalf of the dependants of Heng Ang Tee Franklin, deceased) v. Wong Meng Hang*, [2015] SGHC 138, [27].

in respect of the deceased incurred by the dependants may be recoverable in damages.[2512] If there are costs not recovered from the defendant, these costs are deductible from the damages assessed, and those damages will be divided among the dependants in the proportions determined by the court.[2513]

§5. Contractual Damages

690. As with other claims for damages in different contexts, it is trite law that a plaintiff in the contractual context must prove his damage.[2514] The process of proving damage is 'intensely factual' and what constitutes adequate proof of damage will depend on the particular factual circumstances.[2515] The plaintiff is not required to prove 'with complete certainty the exact amount of damage that he has suffered', and accordingly the court has to adopt a flexible approach: 'where precise evidence is obtainable, the court naturally expects to have it. Where it is not, the court must do the best it can.'[2516] Contractual damages will generally be assessed on a compensatory basis. Therefore, the innocent party must be put in the same position as if the breach of contract had not occurred.[2517]

691. It has recently been observed that the law on punitive damages or the award of damages pursuant to the principles laid down in *Attorney General v. Blake (Jonathan Cape ltd Third Party)*[2518] are still 'in a state of flux'.[2519] A plaintiff will have to adduce evidence to prove the losses caused by any breach of contract, that the damages were not too remote, and the quantum of the damage. In determining factual causation, the 'but-for' test is used.[2520] The law on remoteness of damage is governed by the principles in *Hadley v. Baxendale*[2521] and the Singapore courts have not followed the approach advocated by Lord Hoffman in *Transfield Shipping Inc v.*

2512. Civil Law Act (Cap. 43, 1999 Rev. Ed.), s 22(4).
2513. Civil Law Act (Cap. 43, 1999 Rev. Ed.), s 22(2).
2514. *Robertson Quay Investment Pte Ltd v. Steen Consultants Pte Ltd*, [2008] 2 SLR(R) 623, [27].
2515. *Robertson Quay Investment Pte Ltd v. Steen Consultants Pte Ltd*, [2008] 2 SLR(R) 623, [27]. In the context of goods, *see Marco Polo Shipping Co Pte Ltd v. Fairmacs Shipping & Transport Services Pte Ltd*, [2015] 5 SLR 541, [29]–[30]: 'there is, understandably, no universal rule for the assessment of damages … The typical approach, however, is to equate damages with the value of the goods … There may be cases where the plaintiff is also allowed to recover consequential losses such as loss of profits and losses incurred by being deprived of the use of the goods … How, then, is the value of the goods determined? Typically, curts look to the market value … the best approximate of the loss suffered by the plaintiff who has been deprived of his goods … The market price is typically determined as at the date of conversion … or … at the date of expected delivery.' The court in that case also went on to define (at [30]–[32]) what constitutes a relevant market.
2516. *Robertson Quay Investment Pte Ltd v. Steen Consultants Pte Ltd*, [2008] 2 SLR(R) 623, [28]–[30], citing H. McGregor, *McGregor on Damages*, 17th ed. (Sweet & Maxwell, 2003), [8002]; *Biggin & Co Ld v. Permanite, Ld*, [1951] 1 KB 422, 438.
2517. *Gimpex Ltd v. Unity Holdings Business Ltd*, [2015] 2 SLR 686, [211]–[213].
2518. [2001] 1 AC 268.
2519. *MFM Restaurants Pte Ltd v. Fish & Co Restaurants Pte Ltd*, [2011] 1 SLR 150, [32]–[36].
2520. *See Sunny Metal & Engineering Pte Ltd v. Ng Khim Ming Eric*, [2007] 3 SLR(R) 782, [63]; *Anti-Corrosion Pte Ltd v. Berger Paints Singapore Pte Ltd*, [2012] 1 SLR 427, [39].
2521. (1854) 9 Exch 341.

Mercator Shipping Inc,[2522] save to the extent that it was already incorporated or embodied in the two limbs of *Hadley v. Baxendale*.[2523] If evidence of damages has not been adequately adduced, the court will only award nominal damages.[2524] Mitigation of damages as a defence must be properly pleaded and proved.[2525] It involves an inquiry as to the reasonableness of the innocent party's action or inaction after the breach, and ordinarily it is the defendant's burden of proving that the innocent party had failed to take reasonable steps to mitigate its loss.[2526]

§6. Damages for Tortious Claims

692. One of the judicial remedies for tortious claims is an award for damages, with the most common type being compensatory damages. This section will examine compensatory damages, nominal damages, and aggravated damages. Compensatory damages aim to put the victim in the same position as if the tort had not occurred.[2527] Nominal damages are awarded in torts which are actionable per se. This means that nominal damages may be awarded where the plaintiff's rights have been infringed by the defendant's tortious conduct, but the plaintiff suffers no loss.[2528] Nominal damages may also be awarded if the plaintiff is unable to adduce sufficient evidence to prove the loss.[2529]

693. It is a question of fact whether the plaintiff has proven the amount of his loss with sufficient clarity.[2530] The plaintiff may do so by providing evidence of the existence of the damage.[2531] However, where such evidence is limited or unavailable, it is also possible to adopt the reasonable man yardstick to determine a sum that is reasonable having regard to all circumstances of the case.[2532] This is

2522. [2009] 1 AC 61.
2523. *MFM Restaurants Pte Ltd v. Fish & Co Restaurants Pte Ltd*, [2011] 1 SLR 150, [72]–[113], [140]. An analytical framework for questions of remoteness of damage was set out by the Court of Appeal in *Out of the Box Pte Ltd v. Wanin Industries Pte Ltd*, [2013] 2 SLR 363, [47].
2524. *Lee Chee Wei v. Tan Hor Peow Victor*, [2007] 3 SLR(R) 537, [64], citing H. McGregor, *McGregor on Damages* [10-003]–[10-005] (17th ed., Sweet & Maxwell, 2003).
2525. *Yip Holdings Pte Ltd v. Asia Link Marine Industries Pte Ltd,* [2012] 1 SLR 131, [23], citing *Jia Min Building Construction Pte Ltd v. Ann Lee Pte Ltd*, [2004] 3 SLR(R) 288, [71]. *See also Geest plc v. Lansiquot*, [2002] 1 WLR 3111, [16]; *The 'Rainbow Star'*, [2011] 3 SLR 1, [56].
2526. *The 'Asia Star'*, [2010] 2 SLR 1154, [24].
2527. *See Livingstone v. Rawyards Coal Co*, (1880) 5 App Cas 25, 239.
2528. G. Chan, *The Law of Tors in Singapore* 736 (Acad. Publg. 2011).
2529. G. Chan, *The Law of Tors in Singapore* 736 (Acad. Publg. 2011). *See also Li Siu Lun v. Looi Kok Poh,* [2015] SGHC 149, [40]: Generally, substantial damages will not be awarded where the plaintiff adduces no evidence to support the amount of his claim, and nominal damages may be awarded instead.
2530. *Li Siu Lun v. Looi Kok Poh,* [2015] SGHC 149, [40].
2531. *R+V Versicherung AG v. Risk Insurance and Reinsurance Solutions SA,* [2006] EWHC 42, [60]: the court is not over-concerned to require the plaintiff to prove precise quantification of its losses.
2532. *Li Siu Lun v. Looi Kok Poh,* [2015] SGHC 149, [51]–[53]. *See id.*, [57]–[59]: one recognized measure of damages is the expenses incurred in investigations.

especially so in a claim for damages for economic torts, where damage as a constituent of the cause of action had been established.[2533]

694. Aggravated damages may be awarded for the additional injury suffered by the plaintiff arising from the manner and motives of the defendant's commission of the tort or his subsequent conduct.[2534] The purpose of aggravated damages is to compensate the victim for the injury suffered, and not to punish the wrongdoer.[2535] The principle of proportionality applies to the assessment of aggravated damages.[2536] Aggravated damages are not awarded to companies.[2537] In the context of aggravated damages for economic torts, the High Court has held that while the award of such damages are justifiable since these torts are intentionally committed,[2538] a principled approach is still needed.[2539] Therefore, the plaintiff needs to show that there is contumelious or exceptional conduct or motive on the part of the defendant and that the plaintiff suffered an intangible loss, injury to personality or mental distress, as the case may be.[2540] Factors that the court will take into consideration in an award of aggravated damages include the vulnerability of the plaintiff (e.g. if the defendant is a dental surgeon and the plaintiff is his patient); the conduct of the defendant given the trust reposed in him by virtue of his position as a medical professional; the defendant's calculated plan to deter the plaintiff from proceedings; and the degree of mental anguish suffered by the plaintiff.[2541] Since aggravated damages are parasitic on compensatory damages,[2542] aggravated damages should not be an independent measure of damages.[2543] At the same time, the plaintiff has to specifically plead for aggravated damages and the amount of aggravated damages to be identified separately in the court's final award of damages.[2544]

2533. *Li Siu Lun v. Looi Kok Poh,* [2015] SGHC 149, [60].
2534. G. Chan, *The Law of Tors in Singapore* 726 (Acad. Publg. 2011).
2535. *Thompson v. Commissioner of Police of the Metropolis*, [1998] QB 498.
2536. *Li Siu Lun v. Looi Kok Poh,* [2015] SGHC 149, [161]. *See also Koh Sin Chong Freddie v. Chan Cheng Wah Bernard*, [2013] 4 SLR 629, [74]–[77].
2537. *Li Siu Lun v. Looi Kok Poh,* [2015] SGHC 149, [149].
2538. *Li Siu Lun v. Looi Kok Poh,* [2015] SGHC 149, [150]: as a matter of Singapore law, aggravated damages may be awarded in an action for conspiracy by unlawful means.
2539. *Li Siu Lun v. Looi Kok Poh,* [2015] SGHC 149, [147]–[148].
2540. *Tan Harry v. Teo Chee Yeow Aloysius*, [2004] 1 SLR(R) 513, [82]. *See also Ramesh s/o Krishnan v. AXA Life Insurance Singapore Pte Ltd*, [2017] SGHC 197, [130]; *Li Siu Lun v. Looi Kok Poh,* [2015] SGHC 149, [138].
2541. *Li Siu Lun v. Looi Kok Poh,* [2015] SGHC 149, [166]–[172].
2542. *Li Siu Lun v. Looi Kok Poh,* [2015] SGHC 149, [156]: This is because aggravated damages exist to augment the amount of general damages available so as to adequately compensate the plaintiff for the aggravation of the injury. *See also Koh Sin Chong Freddie v. Chan Cheng Wah Bernard,* [2013] 4 SLR 629, [152]; *Thompson & Hsu v. Commissioner of Police of the Metropolis*, [1998] QB 498, 516; *Lamb v. Cotogno*, [1987] 164 CLR 1, 8; *Taylor v. Beere*, [1982] 1 NZLR 81, 93–94.
2543. *Li Siu Lun v. Looi Kok Poh,* [2015] SGHC 149, [158].
2544. *Li Siu Lun v. Looi Kok Poh,* [2015] SGHC 149, [163].

§7. POSSIBILITY OF APPEAL

695. In an appeal against a registrar's decision on the assessment of damages, a question may arise as to whether the court has less discretion to admit new evidence since a registrar's decision in this context would have involved the reception of not merely affidavit evidence but oral evidence as well; moreover, most other types of registrars' appeals are heard de novo, but an appeal against a registrar's assessment of damages may be considered differently.[2545] In this regard, it has been said that:

> We recognise that the very raison d'etre of having an assessment of damages being carried out by the Registrar, instead of before the court, is to save the time of the judge. This object would be lost, or substantially diminished, if the applicable principle is that either party is freely entitled to adduce new evidence at the hearing before the judge or that the judge should, as a rule, exercise his discretion liberally to admit such fresh evidence, including the viva voce examination of witnesses. This approach would mean that everything could be re-opened or further clarified. We do not see how such a rule could serve the interest of justice. It would only protract the assessment process and could lead to abuse. It is our opinion that the parties should, as a rule, present their entire evidence at the assessment …
>
> …
>
> … The discretion rests with the judge. Reasonable conditions must be set … it must be shown that the new evidence could not have been obtained with reasonable diligence at the trial. Any sort of judgmental error would not be sufficient to meet this condition … Sufficiently strong reasons must be shown why the new evidence was not adduced at the assessment before the Registrar.
>
> The next question to ask is whether … the evidence must be such that, if given, it would probably have an important influence on the result of the case and that it must be apparently credible though it need not be incontrovertible, are in any way relevant. To our mind, these two conditions are eminently reasonable ones. If the new evidence sought to be admitted cannot satisfy the two conditions, what would be the point of admitting the evidence? It would be meaningless to do so.[2546]

696. Accordingly, fresh evidence may be adduced on an appeal from a registrar's assessment of damages if: the evidence could not have been obtained with reasonable diligence for use at the trial; the evidence, if given, would probably have an important influence on the result of the case; and the evidence must be apparently

2545. *Tan Sia Boo v. Ong Chiang Kwong*, [2007] 4 SLR(R) 298, [5]. *See also* C. Bull & J. Pinsler, *Civil Procedure: Annual Review of Singapore Cases* [7.20] (Sing. Acad. L. 2007).

2546. *Lassiter Ann Masters v. To Keng Lam (alias Toh Jeanette)*, [2004] 2 SLR(R) 392, [20] and [24]–[25]. *See also WBG Network (S) Pte Ltd v. Sunny Daisy Ltd*, [2007] 1 SLR(R) 1133.

credible.[2547] At the hearing, a plaintiff may be permitted to file supplementary affidavits of evidence-in-chief if it is in the interest of justice and does not cause prejudice to the other parties that cannot be compensated with costs.[2548] The High Court may even recall witnesses.[2549] On the other hand, it has also been said that such an appeal is not treated as an appellate court hearing an appeal from a decision of a trial judge, as the review is as though the matter came before him the first time and so the assessment on appeal is heard de novo.[2550] As for an appeal against a High Court's decision on an appeal from a registrar's award of damages, it has been declared that as the registrar is the original finder of fact (and therefore has the benefit of seeing and hearing the witnesses first hand as they give evidence), the High Court is in no better position than the Court of Appeal when it comes to evaluating the evidence.[2551] In any event, the standard of review of a registrar's finding of fact on oral evidence is the same as that applied to a trial judge's findings on appeal to an appellate court – which means that these findings may only be overturned if they are plainly wrong or against the weight of the evidence.[2552] However, a judge in chambers is in as good a position as the registrar to assess the veracity of the witness' evidence if the registrar's assessment was based on inferences drawn from the internal consistency in the contents of the witness' testimony or the external consistency between the contents of the witness' evidence and the extrinsic evidence.[2553] An appellate court may vary the quantum of damages awarded by the trial judge. However, it must be shown that the trial judge had: acted on the wrong principles; misapprehended the facts; or had for these or other reasons made a whole erroneous estimate of the damages.[2554]

2547. *Singapore Civil Procedure 2015 Volume 1*, at 730 (G.P. Selvam ed., Sweet & Maxwell Asia 2014).
2548. *Singapore Civil Procedure 2015 Volume 1*, at 730 (G.P. Selvam ed., Sweet & Maxwell Asia 2014) citing *Malayan Banking Bhd v. United Arab Shipping Co (SAG) and Another (Agrizala Co (Pte) Ltd, Third Party)*, [2008] SGHC 214; *Chua Jia Yan Emily (by her next friend Chua Kiaw Swan) v. See Mun Li*, [2009] SGHC 26.
2549. *AOD (a minor suing by his litigation representative) v. AOE* [2015] SGHC 272, [21]; *Swiss Butchery Pte Ltd v. Huber Ernst and others and another suit* [2013] 4 SLR 381; *Lassiter Ann Masters v. To Keng Lam (alias Toh Jeanette)* [2004] 2 SLR(R) 392, [10].
2550. *AOD (a minor suing by his litigation representative) v. AOE* [2015] SGHC 272, [19]; *Tan Boon Heng v. Lau Pang Cheng David* [2013] 4 SLR 718, [16]; *Teo Ai Ling v. Koh Chai Kwang*, [2010] 2 SLR 1037, [46], *Chang Ah Lek v. Lim Ah Koon*, [1998] 3 SLR(R) 551; *Ho Yeow Kim v. Lai Hai Kuen*, [1999] 1 SLR(R) 1068.
2551. *The 'Asia Star'*, [2010] 2 SLR 1154, [21].
2552. *Tan Boon Heng v. Lau Pang Cheng David*, [2013] 4 SLR 718, [43].
2553. *Tan Boon Heng v. Lau Pang Cheng David*, [2013] 4 SLR 718, [43].
2554. *Singapore Airlines Ltd v. Tan Shwu Leng*, [2001] 3 SLR(R) 439, [11]–[13]; *Tan Boon Heng v. Lau Pang Cheng David*, [2013] 4 SLR 718, [7]. These principles are similar to those that apply in situations where an appellate court intervenes in the exercise of a trial judge's discretion (judge was misguided with regard to the principles under which his discretion was to be exercised; judge took into account matters which he ought not to have or failed to take into account matters which he ought to have; or judge's decision was plainly wrong): *Hong Leong Bank Bhd v. Soh Seow Poh*, [2009] 4 SLR(R) 525, [45].

§8. PROVISIONAL DAMAGES

697. In actions for personal injuries, an award of provisional damages may be made, under which: '(a) damages are assessed on the assumption that a contingency will not happen; and (b) the injured person is entitled to apply for further damages at a future date if the contingency happens'.[2555] The court's power to make such an award is found in the Supreme Court of Judicature Act.[2556] A claim for provisional damages must be pleaded and specify the contingency or contingencies in respect of which an application may be made at a future date as well as the period within which the application(s) may be made.[2557] The court may, on application within the period specified, extend that period 'if it thinks it just to do so'.[2558] An application for a further award of damages may also be made by the plaintiff within the period specified or the extended period.

698. The plaintiff must give not less than three months written notice to the defendant and to the defendant's insurers (where the plaintiff knows the defendant is insured in respect of the plaintiff's claim) of the intention to apply for further damages.[2559] The plaintiff must then within twenty-one days after the expiry of the period specified or the extended period take out a summons for directions as to the future conduct of the action.[2560] On the hearing of the summons for directions, the court will give the appropriate directions, including disclosure of medical reports and fixing the time and place of the hearing of the application for further damages.[2561] It is important to note that only one application for further damages may be made in respect of each contingency specified in the award of provisional damages.[2562]

699. Where an application is made for an award of provisional damages, the defendant may at any time make a written offer to the plaintiff: to tender a sum of money (which may include an amount to be specified, in respect of interest) in satisfaction of the plaintiff's claim for damages assessed on the assumption that the injured person will not develop the contingency and identifying the contingency in question; and to agree to the making of an award of provisional damages.[2563] If such an offer is made, the plaintiff has twenty-one days after receipt of the offer to accept the offer by giving written notice; thereafter, the plaintiff shall make an application

2555. Supreme Court of Judicature Act (Cap. 322, R. 5, 2014 Rev. Ed.) Rules of Court, O 37 r 7.
2556. Supreme Court of Judicature Act (Cap. 322, R. 5, 2014 Rev. Ed.), First Schedule.
2557. Supreme Court of Judicature Act (Cap. 322, R. 5, 2014 Rev. Ed.) Rules of Court, O 37 rr 8(1)–(4).
2558. Supreme Court of Judicature Act (Cap. 322, R. 5, 2014 Rev. Ed.) Rules of Court, O 37 r 8(3).
2559. Supreme Court of Judicature Act (Cap. 322, R. 5, 2014 Rev. Ed.) Rules of Court, O 37 r 10(1)–(3).
2560. Supreme Court of Judicature Act (Cap. 322, R. 5, 2014 Rev. Ed.) Rules of Court, O 37 r 10(4).
2561. Supreme Court of Judicature Act (Cap. 322, R. 5, 2014 Rev. Ed.) Rules of Court, O 37 r 10(5).
2562. Supreme Court of Judicature Act (Cap. 322, R. 5, 2014 Rev. Ed.) Rules of Court, O 37 r 10(6).
2563. Supreme Court of Judicature Act (Cap. 322, R. 5, 2014 Rev. Ed.) Rules of Court, O 37 r 9(1).

to the Court for an order of provisional damages.[2564] Any offer made by the defendant shall not be brought to the attention of the Court until after the Court has determined the claim for an award of provisional damages.[2565]

700. Case law has clarified that the contingency specified in an award of provisional damages is not limited to the injured plaintiff developing some serious disease or suffering some serious deterioration in his or her physical or mental condition, but may 'relate to some other future fact or circumstance, so long as the occurrence of that fact or circumstance is something which can be objectively determined'.[2566] For example, the contingency may be that that the plaintiff's employment prospects can be shown to be more severely prejudiced than assessed by the trial judge; or where the plaintiff was pursuing a polytechnic course, the contingency may be failing to obtain a diploma in the course.[2567] Regardless of the nature of the contingency, it must also be serious and precisely defined.[2568] Where the contingency related to business or employment, there should be a prescribed minimum period of time that had to elapse before an application for further assessment might be made.[2569] It would also be necessary for the court to fix a time period beyond which no application for further damages could be made.

2564. Supreme Court of Judicature Act (Cap. 322, R. 5, 2014 Rev. Ed.) Rules of Court, O 37 r 9(3).
2565. Supreme Court of Judicature Act (Cap. 322, R. 5, 2014 Rev. Ed.) Rules of Court, O 37 r 9(2).
2566. *Koh Chai Kwang v. Teo Ai Ling*, [2011] 3 SLR 610, [51].
2567. *Tan Yu Min Winston v. Uni-Fruitveg Pte Ltd* (Civil Appeal No 94 of 2008) (unreported); *Koh Chai Kwang v. Teo Ai Ling*, [2011] 3 SLR 610, [51].
2568. The contingencies of 'arthritic changes' and 'functional decline' have been rejected by the High Court on the basis that the former was not reasonably likely to occur in the near future and the latter was not a precise event: *Tan Juay Mui (by his next friend Chew Chwee Kim) v. Sher Kuan Hock and another (Liberty Insurance Pte Ltd, codefendant; Liberty Insurance Pte Ltd and another, third parties)*, [2012] 3 SLR 496, [82]–[84], citing *ACD (by her next friend B) v. See Mun Li*, [2009] SGHC 217; *Koh Chai Kwang v. Teo Ai Ling*, [2011] 3 SLR 610.
2569. *Koh Chai Kwang v. Teo Ai Ling*, [2011] 3 SLR 610, [55].

Part VII. Evidence

Chapter 1. Burden of Proof

701. All matters of evidence are theoretically governed by the Evidence Act,[2570] which in turn is theoretically the paramount source of evidence law in Singapore. The Evidence Act was largely modelled after Sir James Fitzjames Stephen's iconic Indian Evidence Act of 1872, and despite its many antiquated provisions and principles and lack of any meaningful amendment over the years, the statute remains on the statutory books. Perhaps for this reason alone the law of evidence barely features with any degree of prominence in Singapore jurisprudence as the courts have taken a largely non-legalistic approach in the regulation of many aspects of evidence, preferring, inter alia, counsel objections inherent in an adversarial system of litigation to run their course – though to be clear, notwithstanding the previously mentioned inapplicability of common law that is inconsistent with the Evidence Act, the common law of evidence, even with its injections of modernity, is seldom dispositive of cases in Singapore as well. This is certainly the situation in civil proceedings even if not in criminal proceedings, given that parties in civil proceedings are presumed to be equal and party autonomy is allowed to flourish and manifest as much as possible, and less grave interests are at stake. This is even truer in pre-trial proceedings – or where the rules of civil procedure feature the most – as evidence at this stage is largely confined to affidavit assertions usually without the benefit of relevancy objection and cross-examination, though there is some containment through the likes of the discovery (mainly on the grounds of privilege) process.

702. Technical and adjectival law – that is, evidence law – unlike procedural law, is simply subordinate to so-called common sense and commercial pragmatism (i.e., the more evidence admitted, the better for everyone) in Singapore, and unless the evidence in question is of critical importance upon which the resolution of the dispute turns and also has some critical flaws to it, it will be considered part of the evidential record, with less weight given to it if the doubt as to its reliability or relevance persists. Such an approach of flexibility dovetails with the community belief that ever since the abolition of trial-by-jury several decades ago, trial judges – who have long-standing professional legal expertise – are well-placed to analyse and weigh the voluminous evidence that frequently pervades many modern trials, especially civil ones, without going through the time-consuming and tedious process of formally admitting or not admitting evidence. The general philosophy to not have

2570. (Cap. 97, 1997 Rev. Ed.).

evidence be overly shackled by rules is reflected in the Rules of Court[2571] as well, as there are only a few perfunctory provisions on affidavit evidence, expert evidence, hearsay evidence, and general presentation of trial and appellate evidence – though one could argue that the Rules of Court are meant to be an embodiment of a distinct purpose (i.e., procedure rather than evidence), one could equally argue that procedure and evidence should reflect the same amount of rigour.

703. Nevertheless, turning to the specific question of burden of proof, as mentioned, sections 103, 104, 105, and 108 of the Evidence Act[2572] are the relevant provisions that establish the burden of proof in civil cases. Whereas section 103 concerns the proof of facts in issue, section 105 governs the proof of relevant facts by providing that the party who wishes to rely on a particular fact must prove it.[2573] Section 108 provides that if a fact is especially within the knowledge of a person, that person has the burden of proving that fact. Section 104 provides that the burden of proof in a suit or proceeding lies on the person who would fail if no evidence at all were given by either side; this means that if neither party adduces evidence, the party who assets the fact would fail to prove it.[2574] These provisions are generally consistent with the positions adopted in other common law jurisdictions. Since the party who asserts a fact must adduce sufficient evidence to prove that fact, it is apposite at this juncture to consider the burden of proof[2575] that is required. The burden of proof as defined by the Evidence Act applies in practice to both pre-trial proceedings that involve the furnishing of proof (such as summary judgment) and trial proceedings (despite the technical inapplicability of the Evidence Act to pre-trial proceedings).

704. It must be noted that the legal burden of proof and evidential burden of proof are two distinct concepts. The former refers to the burden of proving a fact to the requisite standard of proof, while the legal burden of proof does not shift and will always remain on the party who seeks to prove that fact.[2576] The latter refers to the burden of adducing evidence to meet the standard of proof or to prevent the other party from meeting the required standard of proof. The evidential burden of proof may be on either party depending on the circumstances of the case.[2577] Essentially, the party making the allegation or raising the cause of action bears the burden

2571. Supreme Court of Judicature Act (Cap. 322, R. 5, 2014 Rev. Ed.).
2572. (Cap. 97, 1997 Rev. Ed.).
2573. 'Facts in issue' are primary facts concerning liability and non-liability, whereas 'relevant facts' are the related circumstances from which the facts in issue may be inferred: J. Pinsler, *Evidence and the Litigation Process* 47 (4th ed., LexisNexis 2013).
2574. J. Pinsler, *Evidence and the Litigation Process* 429 (4th ed., LexisNexis 2013).
2575. *See Lim Andy v. Tea Yeok Kian Terence*, [2015] SGHC 92, [12] citing *Britestone Pte Ltd v. Smith & Associates Far East, Ltd*, [2007] 4 SLR(R) 855, [58].
2576. C. Siyuan and L. Leo, *The Law of Evidence in Singapore* 160–164 (Sweet & Maxwell 2016). *See also Lim Andy v. Tea Yeok Kian Terence*, [2015] SGHC 92, [12] citing *Cooperatieve Centrale Raiffeisen-BA (trading as Rabobank International), Singapore Branch v. Motorola Electronics Pte Ltd*, [2011] 2 SLR 63, [30].
2577. C. Siyuan and L. Leo, *The Law of Evidence in Singapore* 160–164 (Sweet & Maxwell 2016). The evidential burden of proof has also been referred to the 'tactical onus to contradict, weaken or

of proving his case,[2578] and this is established as early on as during the pleadings process. This applies as well to defendants raising counterclaims (thus assuming the role of plaintiffs) and defendants vis-à-vis third parties (the former also assuming the role of plaintiffs). To determine which party bears the burden of proving a pleaded defence, the court will examine the substance of the pleadings, and not just the grammatical form.[2579] This is because the assignment of the legal burden, as discussed, should take into account who is positively asserting a particular fact and who would likely and generally have the relevant evidence to prove that fact.[2580] This principle also applies to third-party claims. For example, the High Court had to determine the burden of proof in the context of a garnishee proceeding involving third-party claims to the money sought to be garnished.[2581] Although the judgment debtor and the third parties were all defendants in the garnishee proceeding, the court held that since the third parties were essentially asserting an ownership claim over the debt, they had to bear the legal burden of proof that they had beneficial ownership over the funds. To make the judgment creditor (who was also the plaintiff) bear the burden of proof in this instance would be tantamount to making the judgment creditor prove a negative.[2582]

705. Despite the ambiguity of the language of the Evidence Act, the uncontroverted standard of proof required in all civil proceedings is that of balance of probabilities; in mathematical terms, if the judge, after considering evidence from both sides, is more than 50% convinced by the plaintiff, the plaintiff will get judgment in his favour. Conversely, if a judge is more than 50% convinced by the defendant (whether he has a defence or otherwise), then the defendant will not be found liable. Where it comes to allegations of fraud or other serious allegations that have shades of criminality, more cogent evidence is usually required (but the standard of proof is supposed to remain the same) from the plaintiff. A fact is disproved if a court does not believe it to exist; a fact which is not proved is neither proved nor disproved (i.e., it may still exist, subject to proof). The mere fact that a defendant does not raise a defence does not automatically result in the plaintiff proving his case successfully; evidence of the requisite standard is still required, though if the defendant admits unequivocally to the allegations this may well be obviated.[2583] Naturally, this applies to counterclaims and third-party claims as well.

---

explain away evidence that has been led': *Nava Bharat (Singapore) Pte Ltd v. Straits Law Practice LLC*, [2015] SGHC 146, [369], citing *Cooperatieve Centrale Raiffeisen-Boerenleenbank BA (trading as Rabobank International), Singapore Branch v. Motorola Electronics Pte Ltd*, [2011] 2 SLR 63, [30].

2578. Evidence Act (Cap. 97, 1997 Rev. Ed.), s 103.

2579. *SCT Technologies Pte Ltd v. Western Copper Co Ltd*, [2015] SGHC 135, [13], citing *Cooperatieve Centrale Raiffeisen-BA (trading as Rabobank International), Singapore Branch v. Motorola Electronics Pte Ltd*, [2011] 2 SLR 63, [32].

2580. *SCT Technologies Pte Ltd v. Western Copper Co Ltd*, [2015] SGHC 135, [15].

2581. *Westacre Investments Inc v. The State-Owned Company Yugoimport SDPR (also known as Jugoimport-SDPR)*, [2015] SGHC 143.

2582. *Westacre Investments Inc v. The State-Owned Company Yugoimport SDPR (also known as Jugoimport-SDPR)*, [2015] SGHC 143, [27]. *See also id.*, [28].

2583. If either party does not turn up at pre-trial adjudications or at trial itself, the court may order an adjournment (and probably impose costs) or simply award judgment.

706. As mentioned, the legal burden of proof (i.e., to prove a fact) should not be confused with the evidential burden (i.e., to adduce the evidence to meet the standard of proof). That is to say, once a plaintiff has adduced his evidence in court to prove his case, the evidential burden shifts to the defendant to adduce evidence to prove his defence (either can only succeed on a balance of probabilities). The evidential burden may shift more than once during the trial, depending on how and when the evidence is being presented in court. To better understand the interplay between the legal and evidential burden of proof, it is helpful to consider the illustration provided by the Court of Appeal in *Britestone Pte Ltd v. Smith & Associates Far East, Ltd*:

> To contextualise the above principles, at the start of the plaintiff's case, the legal burden of proving the existence of any relevant fact that the plaintiff must prove and the evidential burden of adducing some (not inherently incredible) evidence of the existence of such fact coincide. Upon adduction of that evidence, the evidential burden shifts to the defendant, as the case may be, to adduce some evidence in rebuttal. If no evidence in rebuttal is adduced, the court may conclude from the evidence of the plaintiff that the legal burden is also discharged and making a finding on the fact against the defendant. If, on the other hand, evidence in rebuttal is adduced, the evidential burden shifts back to the plaintiff. If, ultimately, the evidential burden comes to rest on the defendant, the legal burden of proof of that relevant fact would have been discharged by the plaintiff. The legal burden of proof – a permanent and enduring burden – does not shift. A party who has the legal burden of proof on any issue must discharge it throughout.[2584]

707. Nor should the standard of proof be confused with the various legal thresholds in proceeding with certain interlocutory claims (such as default judgment). The latter only requires the court to consider the (limited) evidence on its face, without subjecting it to any real interrogation as to its veracity; as a safeguard, interlocutory applications that resolve liability will almost certainly be appealable as of right. A party may be estopped from proving facts in certain limited situations – for instance, if a person by his conduct intentionally causes another person to believe a fact is true and that party acts on that belief, the representor will not be able to deny the fact in question or be allowed to adduce proof to contradict the fact. There are also statutory reversals of burden of proof in Singapore,[2585] but these have largely nothing to do with civil litigation and civil procedure in Singapore as these are usually used to combat crimes (such as drug trafficking) in which it is easier for accused persons to dispute the evidence and/or there is some policy consideration to facilitate prosecution and conviction. The same can be said for corroboration, which have virtually no application in the civil realm; in contrast, for criminal matters, issues may be raised as regards the quality of evidence of say, child witnesses and victims of certain types of offences. In other words, the only controversies in burdens and standards of proof lie in criminal law and not in civil proceedings.

2584. *Britestone Pte Ltd v. Smith & Associates Far East, Ltd,* [2007] 4 SLR(R) 855, [60].
2585. These should not be confused with (rebuttable) presumptions in law or presumptions of fact.

708. There may be proceedings that involve the use of foreign law. For such proceedings, the content of foreign law is a question of fact that must be pleaded and proved, although parties are not obligated to do so, particularly where an application of foreign law will lead to the same result as an application of the law of the forum.[2586] A party who has pleaded and wishes to prove foreign law can do so by either directly adducing raw sources of foreign law as evidence; and/or adducing the opinion of an expert on foreign law.[2587] If foreign law is not proved, the content of foreign law will be presumed to be the same as the law of the forum.[2588] In this regard, where documents in foreign languages are used in court proceedings, only a court interpreter or a person qualified to translate may offer a translation of that document. The court is not in a position, and not entitled, to translate the foreign text, including foreign law. A fortiori, the court is not permitted to offer a translation that differs from the opinion of the experts of that foreign law.[2589]

2586. *Westacre Investments Inc v. The State-Owned Company Yugoimport SDPR (also known as Jugoimport-SDPR)*, [2015] SGHC 143, [157].

2587. *Westacre Investments Inc v. The State-Owned Company Yugoimport SDPR (also known as Jugoimport-SDPR)*, [2015] SGHC 143, [158], citing *Pacific Recreation Pte Ltd v. S Y Technology Inc*, [2008] 2 SLR(R) 49, [54].

2588. *Westacre Investments Inc v. The State-Owned Company Yugoimport SDPR (also known as Jugoimport-SDPR)*, [2015] SGHC 143, [159], citing *Goh Chok Tong v. Tang Liang Hong*, [1997] 1 SLR(R) 811, [84].

2589. *Shi Wen Yue v. Shi Minjiu and another*, [2016] 4 SLR 911, [7]–[9].

Chapter 2. Admissibility of Evidence

§1. Introduction

709. The admissibility (or relevancy) of evidence is, again, theoretically governed by the Evidence Act,[2590] which theoretically, cannot be displaced by developments in the common law unless expressly amended to reflect this. In practice, however – particularly in civil proceedings – unless the evidence in question very clearly contravenes some sense of fairness and/or cannot be said to have any relevance at all, the evidence will almost always be admitted without objection from either the adversary or the court and be considered together with the rest of the evidence (with weight being a controlling mechanism). The Evidence Act comprises several parts, with Part I being the most important as it defines the meaning of relevance over some 40 provisions. Of these provisions, they are divided into general relevancy and specific relevancy provisions, with the latter meant to be a codification of exceptions to common law exclusionary rules (hearsay, similar fact/ character, and opinion). Part I was perhaps the most groundbreaking aspect of Stephen's work, as it was an attempt to present the common law position on admissibility (as it stood in the late-1800s) in the most direct and coherent way possible. Specifically, there was (and still is) only one question to be answered when determining if a piece of evidence is admissible under the Evidence Act: is the evidence relevant as defined by the relevant relevancy provisions? This approach can be contrasted with the modern common law position, which seeks to answer the question of admissibility in several parts. First, is the evidence logically relevant? Second, is the evidence caught by a legal (exclusionary) rule? Third, is the evidence nonetheless admissible by virtue of an exception? Fourth, is the evidence nonetheless excludable on the basis of, inter alia, its undue prejudicial effect? The Evidence Act, in reducing the inquiry into just one step, thus obviated the need to differentiate between logical and legal relevance, and between admissibility and exclusion: once the evidence has been deemed admissible by the relevant relevancy provision, the court must admit the evidence, and there is no discretion to exclude it or not admit it on whatever other basis. If there is some doubt about the reliability of the evidence – reliability being the key principle that undergirds Part I of the Evidence Act – the judge (bearing in mind that jury trial was abolished decades ago) can assign the appropriate weight, after consideration of the entire evidential record. Conversely, if the evidence was neither relevant nor reliable (or relevant but not reliable or reliable but not relevant), the evidence would not be admissible ab initio.

710. Parenthetically, it ought to be made clear that the difference between not admitting evidence ab initio and excluding it later is not an academic one. If a piece of evidence is not part of the evidentiary record at all, the option of weight-assignment is completely foreclosed. Further, an appellate court has much less, if not virtually no room to interfere with what is not part of the evidentiary record, as fact-finding is not its province. It is therefore imperative to determine if there is

2590. (Cap. 97, 1997 Rev. Ed.).

actually such a concept as exclusion (under the Evidence Act), and if a piece of evidence is even going to be part of the record in the first place (for it will not be if it is inadmissible ab initio). Stephen's conceptualization of relevance and admissibility did have at least a couple of unanswered questions, however. First, it was and still is unclear if all manner of evidence had to satisfy the relevancy provisions in the statute; in modern litigation where there is voluminous evidence (especially in civil litigation), it is simply impractical to subject all the evidence to the relevancy provisions – in this light the common law position of a de facto presumption of admissibility is more attractive. At the same time, however, if one (as is often done) prefers to determine admissibility based on whether the opposing counsel objects, should there not be some clear limits and exceptions to this approach even though it is an adversarial system? Second, it was and still is unclear if a piece of evidence has to satisfy either, or both of the relevancy provisions before it can be admitted; two subsidiary problems are embedded in this, in that the general relevancy provisions were drafted so widely that the specific relevancy provisions can be subsumed, and a piece of evidence that does not pass muster under a specific relevancy provision may be recharacterized can simply be relabelled and admitted under a general relevancy provision instead.

§2. 2012 Amendments to the Evidence Act

711. The Evidence Act was amended in 2012 to broaden the scope of admissibility for hearsay and expert opinion evidence, the two most commonly invoked evidence (as far as 'exclusionary' rules are concerned) in commercial disputes. These amendments upended the admissibility paradigm of the Evidence Act in many ways. In the main, although the admissibility of certain types of evidence was broadened, two subsections to exclude these evidence were introduced, purportedly to prevent abuse. The primary driving force behind these particular amendments was twofold: to allow (and trust) the judges to be able to sift through a greater amount of (hearsay and expert opinion) evidence, and to better match commercial expectations in civil disputes.

§3. Admissibility of Hearsay Evidence

712. The hearsay rule provides that out-of-court statements are not to be admitted as proof of their content, unless the maker of those statements is present in court.[2591] Section 32 of the Evidence Act was amended in 2012 to introduce more flexible exceptions to the hearsay rule.[2592] Notable amendments to section 32 include extensions to the business record exception in section 32(1)(b); moving existing exceptions of the Criminal Procedure Code 2010 to the Evidence Act so that they apply to both criminal and civil proceedings; and granting the court a

2591. J. Pinsler, *Evidence and the Litigation Process* 115–116 (4th ed., LexisNexis 2013).
2592. Second Reading of the Evidence (Amendment) Bill (*Singapore Parliamentary Debates, Official Report* (14 Feb. 2012), vol. 88.

residual discretion to exclude hearsay evidence in the name of justice.[2593] As regards section 32(1)(b), the business record exception, that refers to statements made in the course of a trade, business, profession or other occupation, now expressly includes even such statements 'based on information supplied by other persons'. Section 32(1)(b)(iv) is also new and refers to composite business records. It provides that the hearsay exception applies to documents constituting or forming part of the records of a trade, business, profession or other occupation. It has been suggested that the effect of section 32(1)(b)(iv), which does not expressly require the compiler and the persons who supplied the information in the report to have personal knowledge of that information, is such that it may permit multiple hearsay (hearsay upon hearsay) to an unlimited degree to be admitted without safeguards concerning the knowledge of the persons involved in transmitting the information. However, this sub-provision only prima facie admits such hearsay evidence. Section 32(1)(b)(iv) must be considered in the wider context of section 32 (specifically section 32(3)), which also supposedly provides the court residual discretion to exclude hearsay evidence in the interest of justice.[2594] When exercising its supposed residual discretion, the court will consider whether there are other countervailing factors, such as a lack of a minimal degree of reliability of the evidence,[2595] that outweigh the benefit of admitting the piece of hearsay evidence. Specifically, if the hearsay evidence is of limited probative value, such evidence can supposedly be excluded.[2596] Should the supposed prejudicial effect of the evidence outweigh its probative value, it has been suggested that the court's exclusionary discretion ought to be exercised differently in civil, as opposed to criminal proceedings.[2597]

713. In civil proceedings, the hearsay rule in practice assumes a lighter weight and role, as opposed to criminal proceedings where the presumption of innocence is paramount, when put in the balance against the probative value component; in most instances, it boils down to a matter of weight in civil proceedings.[2598] Therefore, even if the court ultimately admits the evidence because it was not as deficit so that it should be excluded pursuant to section 32(3), the court may still assign that piece of evidence less weight.[2599] Another significant addition to section 32 is section 32(1)(j) that concerns statements made by persons who are unable to act as witnesses. One possible reason is because the person is outside Singapore and it is not

---

2593. Second Reading of the Evidence (Amendment) Bill (*Singapore Parliamentary Debates, Official Report* (14 Feb. 2012), vol. 88. *See also* J. Pinsler, *Evidence and the Litigation Process* 218–239 (4th ed., LexisNexis 2013).
2594. *Gimpex Ltd v. Unity Holdings Business Ltd*, [2015] 2 SLR 686, [105]–[110].
2595. *Gimpex Ltd v. Unity Holdings Business Ltd*, [2015] 2 SLR 686, [120]. *See also SIC College of Business and Technology Pte Ltd v. Yeo Poh Siah*, [2015] SGHC 133, [20].
2596. *Gimpex Ltd v. Unity Holdings Business Ltd*, [2015] 2 SLR 686, [109]. a minimal degree of reliability. 30 Sep. 2017
2597. *ANB v. ANC*, [2014] 4 SLR 747, [50]–[52].
2598. *ANB v. ANC*, [2014] 4 SLR 747, [52].
2599. Evidence Act (Cap. 97, 1997 Rev. Ed.), s 32(5). *See also Gimpex Ltd v. Unity Holdings Business Ltd*, [2015] 2 SLR 686, [130]–[131].

practicable to secure his attendance in court.[2600] The Court of Appeal has recognized that the impracticality requirement would depend on the circumstances,[2601] hence a helpful guide would be to:

> [assess] the likely effectiveness of taking normal steps to secure the attendance of the witness, and considering in relation to such a judgment the importance of the evidence, the degree of prejudice if it is admitted, and the expense and inconvenience involved in securing attendance.[2602]

714. The 2012 amendments also extended the hearsay exception rule to implied assertions in statements.[2603] However, a similar extension of the exception rule was not provided for implied assertions by conduct.

§4. Analysis of the 2012 Amendments to the Evidence Act

715. Quite apart from the aim of the amendments to the Evidence Act being a questionable premise, the subsections introducing the exclusionary discretion are problematic not only because the Evidence Act previously did not allow relevant (and reliable) evidence to be excluded, but also the basis upon which the evidence can be excluded is that of 'in the interests of justice'.[2604] This test is so broad that it is meaningless, and is not modelled after any established statute in particular: does one use the 'traditional' balancing test of probative value versus prejudicial effect and if so does one define prejudice to include more than just distortive evidence; and if one does not use the 'traditional' test, it is absolutely unclear what the new test entails.[2605] Further and more fundamentally, the normative justification for this test is unclear; during the parliamentary debates some references were made to

2600. Evidence Act (Cap. 97, 1997 Rev. Ed.), s 32(1)(j)(iii).

2601. *Gimpex Ltd v. Unity Holdings Business Ltd*, [2015] 2 SLR 686, [98].

2602. C. Tapper, *Cross and Tapper on Evidence* 607 (12th ed., LexisNexis 2010).

2603. Evidence Act (Cap. 97, 1997 Rev. Ed.), s 32A.

2604. *See also* C. Siyuan, *The 2012 Amendments to Singapore's Evidence Act: More Questions than Answers as Regards Expert Opinion Evidence?* 34 Stat. L. Rev. 262 (2013).

2605. *See also ANB v. ANC*, [2015] 5 SLR 522, [29]–[30]: 'different societal and policy reasons as well as arguments may apply *vis-à-vis* the inherent discretion of the court to exclude evidence as between criminal and civil proceedings, we do not … think that this *necessarily* leads to the conclusion … that the exclusionary discretion would be exercised with less rigidity such that most evidence would not be excluded in civil proceedings. First, it may simply be the case that the probative value/prejudicial effect balancing exercise … cannot be applied to civil proceedings and that a different balancing exercise should be conducted in that respect. Secondly, [previous case law] related to fact situations which concerned the propriety of the conduct of law enforcement officers and private investigators with regard to the obtaining of the evidence and the effect of that conduct on the quality of the evidence … Thirdly … the exclusion of the evidence [in those cases] … deprived the prosecuting parties in both cases of certain evidence which could have been used to convict the defendants … [All of this] illustrate the fact that too sharp a distinction should not be drawn between criminal and civil proceedings without further analysis of the *precise type* of impropriety or illegality behind the evidence attempted to be adduced … ' (emphasis in original).

inherent jurisdiction,[2606] but this cannot be the case as inherent jurisdiction is not as expansive as the broad notion of 'interests of justice' and has always been relied upon only in highly exceptional situations. Alternative normative justifications for the test (assuming it is the 'traditional' one), that of fairness of trial and the disciplining of enforcement agencies, have already been thoroughly discredited by the courts. All of this is without first mentioning that by limiting the exclusionary discretion to just certain types of hearsay and opinion evidence, the fate of the similar fact and character provisions – the other 'exclusionary' rules captured in Part I – becomes uncertain, as there is no reason in logic or principle to treat hearsay and opinion evidence differently, not least because one of the other 'exclusionary' rules (similar fact) uses the 'traditional' balancing test under the common law (albeit in clear contravention of the similar fact provisions of the Evidence Act). At bottom, the 2012 amendments reflect a manifest misunderstanding of how relevancy in the Evidence Act operates and the structures and principles of the statute. This should not be surprising, since as mentioned earlier the Evidence Act has for the larger part of Singapore jurisprudence been ignored and/or misapplied.[2607] If this done even for criminal proceedings[2608] where greater things are at stake, a fortiori it was done in a far greater extent for civil proceedings. In short, the Evidence Act simply has little or no bearing in an overwhelming number of civil proceedings (particularly at the pre-trial stage) in Singapore.

2606. Even further confusion arose when at one point it was said that irrelevant and/or unreliable evidence should not be admitted *ab initio*, and another point it was said that judges have always had a residual discretion to exclude prejudicial evidence.

2607. Perhaps the only 'useful' provisions in the Evidence Act are those pertaining to privilege (no surprises given that it is fundamental to civil litigation), but those are not relevancy provisions.

2608. In other jurisdictions, they have created separate evidence statutes for criminal proceedings and ironically, many jurisdictions that had previously relied on the common law are now attempting to have attempted to codify their law of evidence.

Chapter 3. Administration of Evidence

§1. Forced Production of Documents

716. Subpoenas are applied for so that the witnesses and documents of a party (usually the opposing party) are compelled to be produced in court.[2609] In other words, it is only if there is some unwillingness of the witness to come to court that a subpoena should be sought.[2610] There are essentially three types of subpoenas: one for persons to testify in court; two for the production of documents; and three a combined type to testify and produce documents.[2611] There is a prescribed form to be used for subpoenas.[2612] In a subpoena for persons to testify, the names of two or more persons can be included in just one subpoena.[2613] However, a subpoena to produce documents must contain the name of one person only.[2614] Any party dissatisfied with any decision regarding subpoenas may apply for a review of the decision; this is done by summons supported by an affidavit, within fourteen days of that decision.[2615] A subpoena to produce documents 'need not, before it is actually issued, specify the documents to be brought: it is sufficient if they are inserted afterwards with reasonable distinctiveness … But if a witness, served with a subpoena in a general form, admits that he has in his possession the documents thereby referred to, he must produce them.'[2616]

717. The issue of the subpoena takes place 'upon its being sealed by an officer of the Registry'.[2617] Unless the court otherwise orders, 'a subpoena must be served personally and the service shall not be valid unless effected within twelve weeks after the date of issue of the subpoena'.[2618] However, a subpoena shall not be served on any person outside the jurisdiction, and there are no exceptions provided for this.[2619] If there is a mistake in a subpoena (such as in the person's name or address),

---

2609. C.f. Supreme Court of Judicature Act (Cap. 322, R. 5, 2014 Rev. Ed.) Rules of Court, O 38 r 13(1).The subpoena mechanism is also found in arbitration: *see* Arbitration Act (Cap. 10, 2002 Rev. Ed.), s 30(1); International Arbitration Act (Cap. 143A, 2002 Rev. Ed.), s 13(1).

2610. J. Pinsler, *Principles of Civil Procedure* 733–734 (Acad. Publg. 2013) citing *Macmillan Inc v. Bishopsgate Investment Trust plc*, [1993] 1 WLR 1372, 1378.

2611. *See also* Supreme Court of Judicature Act (Cap. 322, R. 5, 2014 Rev. Ed.) Rules of Court, O 38 r 16(2); *Civil Procedure 2015 Volume 1*, at 751 (G.P. Selvam ed., Sweet & Maxwell Asia 2014) citing *Burchard v. McFarlane, ex p Tindall*, [1891] 2 QB 241, 247–248.

2612. Supreme Court of Judicature Act (Cap. 322, R. 5, 2014 Rev. Ed.) Rules of Court, O 38 r 14(1).

2613. Supreme Court of Judicature Act (Cap. 322, R. 5, 2014 Rev. Ed.) Rules of Court, O 38 r 15.

2614. Supreme Court of Judicature Act (Cap. 322, R. 5, 2014 Rev. Ed.) Rules of Court, O 38 r 16(1). For subpoenas against companies, *see Singapore Civil Procedure 2015 Volume 1*, at 753 (G.P. Selvam ed., Sweet & Maxwell Asia 2014) citing *Penn-Texas Corp v. Murat Anstalt (No 2)*, [1964] 2 QB 647.

2615. Supreme Court of Judicature Act (Cap. 322, R. 5, 2014 Rev. Ed.) Rules of Court, O 38 r 14(6).

2616. *Singapore Civil Procedure 2015 Volume 1*, at 752 (G.P. Selvam ed., Sweet & Maxwell Asia 2014) citing *Soul v. Inland Revenue Commissioners*, [1963] 1 WLR 112; *Lee v. Angus*, (1866) LR 2 Eq 59. *See also* Evidence Act (Cap. 97, 1997 Rev. Ed.), s 3 for the various definitions for 'document'.

2617. Supreme Court of Judicature Act (Cap. 322, R. 5, 2014 Rev. Ed.) Rules of Court, O 38 r 14(2).

2618. Supreme Court of Judicature Act (Cap. 322, R. 5, 2014 Rev. Ed.) Rules of Court, O 38 r 18(1).

2619. Supreme Court of Judicature Act (Cap. 322, R. 5, 2014 Rev. Ed.) Rules of Court, O 38 r 18(2).

it may be amended if it has not been served.[2620] An amended subpoena has to be filed and resealed in the correct form, and then served.[2621]

718. For subpoenas to produce documents, there are three stages in the process: first, the witness has to bring the documents to the court and hand them to the judge so as to determine whether there are any objections of the witness to the subpoena;[2622] second, the judge will decide on the preliminary use of the documents, such as whether permissions should be given to a party to inspect the documents; and third, the judge will decide if the document, whether in whole or part, should be admitted into the evidential record.[2623] If a witness denies that he has in his possession any of the documents listed in the subpoena, the court may direct that he be cross-examined on this, though the evidence emerging from such cross-examination will not form part of the evidential record.[2624]

719. If a witness disobeys a subpoena, the court has jurisdiction to enforce obedience by committal, regardless of whether such disobedience is wilful or not.[2625] In an extreme scenario, the unreasonable resistance against subpoenas may lead to a retrial.[2626] A subpoena 'continues to have effect until the conclusion of the trial at which the attendance of the witness is required'.[2627] A party who is dissatisfied with any decision made regarding subpoenas (usually by registrars) may apply to a judge or District Judge (as the case may be) for a review of the decision.[2628] In addition, the court may revoke a subpoena upon application by any person or on its own motion.[2629] Whether a subpoena should be set aside would largely depend on the purpose for which it was sought. For instance, the subpoena should not be used to fish for evidence, or 'used indiscriminately without any basis or reason so as to embarrass or inconvenience the person subpoenaed'.[2630] Indeed, any ulterior motive can be construed as an abuse of the court's process. Likewise, if the discovery process should be used instead to obtain the documents sought, a subpoena should not be resorted to.[2631] On the other hand, the mere fact that a witness has no knowledge

2620. Supreme Court of Judicature Act (Cap. 322, R. 5, 2014 Rev. Ed.) Rules of Court, O 38 r 17.
2621. Supreme Court of Judicature Act (Cap. 322, R. 5, 2014 Rev. Ed.) Rules of Court, O 38 r 17.
2622. *See also* Evidence Act (Cap. 97, 1997 Rev. Ed.), s 164(1).
2623. *Singapore Civil Procedure 2015 Volume 1*, at 751 (G.P. Selvam ed., Sweet & Maxwell Asia 2014) citing *National Employers' Mutual General Association v. Waind and Hill*, [1978] 1 NSWLR 372, 381.
2624. *Singapore Civil Procedure 2015 Volume 1*, at 752 (G.P. Selvam ed., Sweet & Maxwell Asia 2014) citing *Trade Practices Commission and Arnotts Ltd; Arnott's Biscuits Ltd; Feldspac Pty Ltd and the Dickens Corp Pty Ltd*, (1989) 87 ALR 73.
2625. *Singapore Civil Procedure 2015 Volume 1*, 752 (G.P. Selvam ed., Sweet & Maxwell Asia 2014) citing *R v. Daye*, [1908] 2 KB 333.
2626. *Basil Anthony Herman v. Premier Security Co-operative Ltd*, [2010] 3 SLR 110, [85].
2627. Supreme Court of Judicature Act (Cap. 322, R. 5, 2014 Rev. Ed.) Rules of Court, O 38 r 19.
2628. Supreme Court of Judicature Act (Cap. 322, R. 5, 2014 Rev. Ed.) Rules of Court, O 38 r 14(5).
2629. Supreme Court of Judicature Act (Cap. 322, R. 5, 2014 Rev. Ed.) Rules of Court, O 38 r 14(4).
2630. *Ong Jane Rebecca v. Lim Lie Hoa*, [2003] 1 SLR(R) 457, [6].
2631. C.f. *Basil Anthony Herman v. Premier Security Co-operative Ltd*, [2010] 3 SLR 110, [21]–[23].

of the material sought by subpoena is unlikely to be a valid ground to set a subpoena aside.[2632] Ultimately, a subpoena is likely to be justified if it is critical to establishing relevant aspects of a litigant's evidential base, as this is one of the manifestations of his right to present his case.[2633] Finally, it ought to be borne in mind that whether a witness or a document can be compelled to be produced must be subject to the provisions in the Evidence Act.[2634]

§2. Deposition by Witnesses

720. This is not applicable in Singapore.

§3. Deposition by the Parties Themselves

721. This is not applicable in Singapore.

§4. Expert Evidence

722. The purpose of expert opinion evidence is to objectively assist the court in deciding issues beyond the court's knowledge regardless of the positions taken by parties.[2635] The 2012 amendments to the Evidence Act broadened the criteria for admissibility of expert opinion to 'scientific, technical or other specialized knowledge'[2636] (when previously only specific categories of topics were specified), which also include 'matters of common knowledge'.[2637] Additionally, the basis of admissibility of expert opinion evidence has changed from necessity to that of assistance.[2638] Similar to the admissibility of the hearsay evidence, the 2012 amendments also expressly grant the court a supposed discretion not to admit expert opinion evidence in the interests of justice, which is purportedly in addition to the court's inherent jurisdiction to exclude prejudicial evidence; the supposed rationale is to counter the potential increase of evidence likely to be adduced as a consequence of expanding the scope of admissibility of expert opinion evidence.[2639] In assisting the court, the expert has a legal duty not to express any opinion on what he thinks he would have done had he been placed, hypothetically and without the benefit of hindsight,

2632. *National Employers' Mutual General Association Ltd v. Waind and Hill*, [1978], 1 NSWLR 378, 382.
2633. J. Pinsler, *Principles of Civil Procedure* 734–735 (Acad. Publg. 2013) citing *Basil Anthony Herman v. Premier Security Co-operative Ltd*, [2010] 3 SLR 110, [23]–[26].
2634. (Cap. 97, 1997 Rev. Ed.). The most obvious rules that may apply are those relating to privilege. In the main, there is ss 128(1), 128A(1), and 131.
2635. J. Pinsler., *Expert Evidence and Adversarial Compromise*, 27 Sing. Acad. L.J. 155, 57 (2015).
2636. Evidence Act (Cap. 97, 1997 Rev. Ed.), s 47(1).
2637. Evidence Act (Cap. 97, 1997 Rev. Ed.), s 47(3).
2638. J. Pinsler, *Evidence and the Litigation Process* 300 (4th ed., LexisNexis 2013).
2639. *Singapore Parliamentary Debates, Official Report* (14 Feb. 2012) vol. 88 (The Minister for Law, Mr K Shanmugam).

in the position of the party, so as not to unduly influence or usurp the court's function to decide the very question.[2640] This is also known as the ultimate issue rule.[2641] Therefore, it is mandatory that expert witnesses comply with the requirement under O 40A r 3(2) and contain a statement setting out the issues they were asked to consider and the basis upon which the evidence was given.[2642] Consistent with the objective of providing objective assistance to the court, expert witnesses must also be impartial and independent.[2643] Examples of partiality displayed by expert witnesses include sweeping generalizations redolent of a predisposition to shore up the respondent's stance, baseless conclusions adverse to the other party, and leaving out crucial portions of a quotation which cast an entirely different light on the materials the expert produces.[2644]

§5. Affidavit

723. In civil cases, the evidence of a witness is normally adduced at trial by an affidavit of the evidence-in-chief (usually prepared by the lawyers),[2645] before the witness is turned over to be cross-examined by the opposing lawyer. These affidavits contain the witnesses' written testimonies,[2646] and will have been filed and exchanged by the parties before the trial.[2647] The affidavits should be drafted in a succinct, precise, and clear manner, and ambiguities, unsubstantiable claims, and inconsistences should be avoided as these would present ammunition for the opponents during cross-examination.[2648] If there are any objections to the contents of the

2640. *Nava Bharat (Singapore) Pte Ltd v. Straits Law Practice LLC*, [2015] SGHC 146, [165]–[168], citing *Su Ah Tee v. Allister Lim and Thrumurgan (sued as a firm) (William Cheng and others, third parties)*, [2014] SGHC 159; *Fong Maun Yee v. Yoong Weng Ho Robert*, [1997] 1 SLR(R) 751; *Midland Bank Trust Co Ltd v. Hett, Stubbs & Kemp (a firm)*, [1979] Ch 384. C.f. J. Pinsler, *Evidence and the Litigation Process* 317–318 (4th ed., LexisNexis 2013).

2641. J. Pinsler, *Evidence and the Litigation Process* 317 (4th ed., LexisNexis 2013).

2642. *Nava Bharat (Singapore) Pte Ltd v. Straits Law Practice LLC*, [2015] SGHC 146, [190], citing *Pacific Recreation Pte Ltd v. S Y Technology Inc*, [2008] 2 SLR(R) 491, [74]–[75].

2643. *See Pacific Recreation Pte Ltd v. S Y Technology Inc*, [2008] 2 SLR(R) 491, [70]; *Vita Health Laboratories Pte Ltd v. Pang Seng Meng*, [2004] 4 SLR(R) 162, [82]. *See also* J. Pinsler, *Expert Evidence and Adversarial Compromise,* 27 Sing. Acad. L.J. 55 (2015).

2644. *JSI Shipping (S) Pte Ltd v. Teofoongwonglcloong (a firm)*, [2007] 4 SLR(R) 460, [71]. *See also Nava Bharat (Singapore) Pte Ltd v. Straits Law Practice LLC*, [2015] SGHC 146, [202]; *Wong Meng Cheong v. Ling Ai Wah*, [2012] 1 SLR 549, [63].

2645. Supreme Court of Judicature Act (Cap. 322, R. 5, 2014 Rev. Ed.) Rules of Court, O 38 r 2(1). C.f. *id.*, O 38 r 2(4): 'the Court may, if it thinks just, order that evidence of a party or any witness or any part of such evidence be given orally at the trial or hearing of any cause or matter.'

2646. *See also* Supreme Court of Judicature Act (Cap. 322, R. 5, 2014 Rev. Ed.) Rules of Court, O 41 r 5(1). The court also has the power to permit supplemental affidavits to be filed, provided they are related to the initial affidavits: *Singapore Civil Procedure 2013 Volume 1*, at 660 (G.P. Selvam ed., Sweet & Maxwell Asia 2012).

2647. For the formal and substantive requirements of affidavits, *see* Court of Judicature Act (Cap. 322, R. 5, 2014 Rev. Ed.) Rules of Court, O 41; State Courts Practice Directions (Part VII); Supreme Court Practice Directions 2013 (Part VIII).

2648. J. Pinsler, *Evidence and the Litigation Process* 767–768 (4th ed., LexisNexis 2013). *See also Compact Metal Industries Ltd v. PPG Industries (Singapore) Ltd*, [2006] SGHC 242, [5].

affidavits, these should be raised within the period fixed by the court at the summons for directions.[2649] The main restrictions[2650] on the evidence that may be contained in the affidavits are the hearsay rule[2651] and the requirement for relevance.[2652] The witness is also not obligated to disclose any evidence that is protected by the rules of privilege.[2653] The affidavit evidence is then sworn or affirmed in court and stands as the testimony of the witness as if it had been adduced through examination-in-chief at trial (see below).[2654] Unless the court otherwise orders or the parties agree, witnesses who have given testimony by affidavit 'shall attend trial for cross-examination and, in default of his attendance, his affidavit shall not be received in evidence except with the leave of the Court'.[2655]

§6. INSPECTION BY JUDGE

724. This is not applicable in Singapore.

2649. Supreme Court of Judicature Act (Cap. 322, R. 5, 2014 Rev. Ed.) Rules of Court, O 25 r 3(1).
2650. Other possible restrictions, but perhaps not enforced with as high a degree of consistency, are the similar fact rule (including character evidence) and the rule against opinion evidence.
2651. Supreme Court of Judicature Act (Cap. 322, R. 5, 2014 Rev. Ed.) Rules of Court, O 38 r 2(5): 'Nothing in this Rule shall make admissible evidence which if given orally would be inadmissible.' C.f. Evidence Act (Cap. 97, 1997 Rev. Ed.), ss 32(1) and 32(2).
2652. Supreme Court of Judicature Act (Cap. 322, R. 5, 2014 Rev. Ed.) Rules of Court, O 41 r 6: 'The Court may order to be struck out of any affidavit any matter which is scandalous, irrelevant or otherwise oppressive.'
2653. *See* Evidence Act (Cap. 97, 1997 Rev. Ed.), ss 128 and 131.
2654. J. Pinsler, *Evidence and the Litigation Process* 762 (4th ed., LexisNexis 2013).
2655. Supreme Court of Judicature Act (Cap. 322, R. 5, 2014 Rev. Ed.) Rules of Court, O 38 r 2(1).

Part VIII. Particular Proceedings

Chapter 1. Summons for Directions

§1. Introduction

725. Summons for directions provides the court an occasion to consider, for the purposes of preparing for the full trial, two main things. The first is for the court to consider 'all matters which must or can be dealt with on interlocutory applications and have not already been dealt with may so far as possible be dealt with'.[2656] The second is for the court to consider 'such directions may be given as to the future course of the action as appear best adapted to secure the just, expeditious and economical disposal thereof'.[2657] In other words, the main purpose of the process is for 'a thorough stocktaking relating to issues in an action and the manner in which the evidence should be presented at trial with a view to shortening the length of the trial and saving costs generally'.[2658] Parenthetically, it ought to be noted briefly at this point that while the hearings for summons for directions provide the main occasion(s) on which the court gives the parties the appropriate orders or directions, this process is supplemented by the pre-trial conference mechanism, which allows the court to further manage the expediency of the dispute. The summons for directions and pre-trial conference mechanisms work together and are a reflection of the court's broad powers and prerogatives to manage the case effectively. The rules and procedures for summons for directions are primarily found in O 25 of the Rules of Court.[2659] A related phase of the proceedings – that of setting down for trial – is also addressed in this chapter. The rules and procedures for setting down are primarily found in O 34 of the Rules of Court.

2656. Supreme Court of Judicature Act (Cap. 322, R. 5, 2014 Rev. Ed.) Rules of Court, O 25 r 1(1).
2657. Supreme Court of Judicature Act (Cap. 322, R. 5, 2014 Rev. Ed.) Rules of Court, O 25 r 1(1).
2658. *Singapore Civil Procedure 2015 Volume 1*, at 563 (G.P. Selvam ed., Sweet & Maxwell Asia 2014).
2659. Supreme Court of Judicature Act (Cap. 322, R. 5, 2014 Rev. Ed.) Rules of Court.

§2. Procedural Aspects

726. The plaintiff 'must, within one month after the pleadings in the action are deemed to be closed,[2660] take out a summons in [the prescribed form] returnable in not less than 14 days'.[2661] It does not matter that discovery has not taken place.[2662] This timeline applies to all actions begun by writ, although a number of exceptions are provided for.[2663] If the plaintiff fails to take out a summons for directions within the stipulated time, the defendant or any defendant may do so, or apply for an order to dismiss the action.[2664] With regard to the latter, the court 'may either dismiss the action on such terms as may be just or deal with the application as if it were a summons for directions'.[2665] It should also be noted that any party:

> to whom the summons for directions is addressed must so far as practicable apply at the hearing of the summons for any order or directions which he may desire as to any matter capable of being dealt with on an interlocutory application in the action and must, not less than 7 days before the hearing of the summons, serve on the other parties a summons for directions specifying those orders and directions in so far as they differ from the orders and directions asked for by the summons.[2666]

727. In addition, if:

> the hearing of the summons for directions is adjourned and any party to the proceedings desires to apply at the resumed hearing for any order or directions not asked for by the summons, he must, not less than 7 days before the resumed hearing of the summons, serve on the other parties a summons for directions

2660. *See* Supreme Court of Judicature Act (Cap. 322, R. 5, 2014 Rev. Ed.) Rules of Court, O 18 r 20(1). It should be noted that court orders granting leave to amend pleadings do not affect close of pleadings: *United Engineers (Singapore) Pte Ltd v. Lee Lip Hiong*, [2004] 4 SLR(R) 305, [42]. In addition, if there are several parties, separate timelines may apply to each party and separate directions may be given instead: *Singapore Civil Procedure 2015 Volume 1*, at 565 (G.P. Selvam ed., Sweet & Maxwell Asia 2014).
2661. Supreme Court of Judicature Act (Cap. 322, R. 5, 2014 Rev. Ed.) Rules of Court, O 25 r 1(1). However, if good cause is shown, the court may abridge the time and make the summons returnable in less than 14 days: *Singapore Civil Procedure 2015 Volume 1*, at 565 (G.P. Selvam ed., Sweet & Maxwell Asia 2014).
2662. *Singapore Civil Procedure 2015 Volume 1*, at 565 (G.P. Selvam ed., Sweet & Maxwell Asia 2014).
2663. Supreme Court of Judicature Act (Cap. 322, R. 5, 2014 Rev. Ed.) Rules of Court, O 25 r 1(2). The exceptions are where summary judgment has been applied for (O 14); where trial without pleadings has been applied for or further pleadings and directions have been given pursuant to that (O18 r 22); where an order has been made for the trial of the issue or question before discovery (O 24 r 2); where directions have been given under interlocutory injunctions (O 29 r 7); where an order for the taking of an account has been made (O 43 r 1); where the action has been referred to the Registrar for trial; where automatic directions are provided (O 25 r 8); and for certain types of non-injury motor accident actions filed in the Subordinate Courts (O 59, Appendix 2). *See also* Supreme Court of Judicature Act (Cap. 322, R. 5, 2014 Rev. Ed.) Rules of Court, O 25 r 1A(1).
2664. Supreme Court of Judicature Act (Cap. 322, R. 5, 2014 Rev. Ed.) Rules of Court, O 25 r 1(4).
2665. Supreme Court of Judicature Act (Cap. 322, R. 5, 2014 Rev. Ed.) Rules of Court, O 25 r 1(5).
2666. Supreme Court of Judicature Act (Cap. 322, R. 5, 2014 Rev. Ed.) Rules of Court, O 25 r 7(1).

specifying those orders and directions in so far as they differ from the orders and directions asked for by the summons.[2667]

§3. SUBSTANTIVE ASPECTS

I. Matters to Be Considered

728. At the first hearing for summons for directions, the court shall consider whether it is possible to deal forthwith with all of the following matters, or consider whether it is expedient to instead adjourn the consideration of all or any of these matters until a later stage:[2668] when parties have to exchange affidavits of the evidence-in-chief of all witnesses named in the summons for directions who may give evidence at the trial;[2669] whether the number of witnesses and number of affidavits of evidence-in-chief should be limited;[2670] the mode in which the evidence-in-chief should be given by any witness;[2671] whether the number of expert witnesses should be limited;[2672] whether the number of affidavits of evidence-in-chief of the expert witnesses should be limited;[2673] whether to specify the issues which the expert witnesses are to discuss and whether they should prepare a joint statement;[2674] the period when objections to affidavits and other evidence of a witness must be taken;[2675] whether any orders should be made with regard to amendments to the writ, evidence in general, and expert witnesses in general;[2676] all admissions and agreements as to the conduct of the proceedings;[2677] and any limitation of the right to appeal.[2678] As can be seen, many of the matters relate to witnesses and their evidence.

729. Also at the first hearing for summons for directions, the court 'shall endeavour to secure that all other matters which must or can be dealt with on interlocutory applications and have not already been dealt with are also then dealt with'.[2679] Such

2667. Supreme Court of Judicature Act (Cap. 322, R. 5, 2014 Rev. Ed.) Rules of Court, O 25 r 7(2).
2668. Supreme Court of Judicature Act (Cap. 322, R. 5, 2014 Rev. Ed.) Rules of Court, O 25 r 2(1). *See also Singapore Civil Procedure 2015 Volume 1*, at 568 (G.P. Selvam ed., Sweet & Maxwell Asia 2014) citing *Pepperell v. Hird*, [1902] 1 Ch 477.
2669. Supreme Court of Judicature Act (Cap. 322, R. 5, 2014 Rev. Ed.) Rules of Court, O 25 r 3(1). *See also id.*, O 34 r 3A and O 38 r 2.
2670. Supreme Court of Judicature Act (Cap. 322, R. 5, 2014 Rev. Ed.) Rules of Court, O 25 r 3(1).
2671. Supreme Court of Judicature Act (Cap. 322, R. 5, 2014 Rev. Ed.) Rules of Court, O 25 r 3(1).
2672. Supreme Court of Judicature Act (Cap. 322, R. 5, 2014 Rev. Ed.) Rules of Court, O 25 r 3(1).
2673. Supreme Court of Judicature Act (Cap. 322, R. 5, 2014 Rev. Ed.) Rules of Court, O 25 r 3(1).
2674. Supreme Court of Judicature Act (Cap. 322, R. 5, 2014 Rev. Ed.) Rules of Court, O 25 r 3(1).
2675. Supreme Court of Judicature Act (Cap. 322, R. 5, 2014 Rev. Ed.) Rules of Court, O 25 r 3(1).
2676. Supreme Court of Judicature Act (Cap. 322, R. 5, 2014 Rev. Ed.) Rules of Court, O 25 r 3(1).
2677. Supreme Court of Judicature Act (Cap. 322, R. 5, 2014 Rev. Ed.) Rules of Court, O 25 r 4.
2678. Supreme Court of Judicature Act (Cap. 322, R. 5, 2014 Rev. Ed.) Rules of Court, O 25 r 5. *See also Singapore Civil Procedure 2015 Volume 1*, at 570 (G.P. Selvam ed., Sweet & Maxwell Asia 2014) citing *Re Hull & County Bank, Trotter's Claim*, (1880) 13 Ch D 261.
2679. Supreme Court of Judicature Act (Cap. 322, R. 5, 2014 Rev. Ed.) Rules of Court, O 25 r 2(2).

matters and applications would probably include (but are not limited to) amendments to the pleadings and the furnishing of further and better particulars; discovery and interrogatories; extensions of time; consent orders;[2680] and maybe even unless orders. It is also possible that alternative dispute resolution options (including settlement) are explored at the summons for directions stage. However, the court will only go as far as to raise awareness of the possibilities, and will not seek to impose on the parties.

730. At any given hearing for summons for directions:

> no affidavit shall be used on the hearing of the summons for directions except by the leave or direction of the Court, but … it shall be the duty of the parties to the action and their solicitors to give all such information and produce all such documents on any hearing of the summons as the Court may reasonably require for the purposes of enabling it properly to deal with the summons. The Court may, if it appears proper to do so in the circumstances, authorise any such information or documents to be given or produced to the Court without being disclosed to the other parties but, in the absence of such authority, any information or document given or produced under this paragraph shall be given or produced to all the parties present or represented on the hearing of the summons as well as to the Court.[2681]

731. If the aforementioned information is not forthcoming, the court may, unless such information is privileged,[2682] 'cause the facts to be recorded in the order with a view to such special order, if any, as to costs as may be just being made at the trial; or … if it appears to the Court to be just to do so, order the whole or any part of the pleadings of the party concerned to be struck out, or, if the party is plaintiff or the claimant under a counterclaim, order the action or counterclaim to be dismissed on such terms as may be just'.[2683] If the hearing of any given summons for directions is adjourned without a day being fixed for the resumed hearing, any party may restore it to the list on two days' notice to the other parties.[2684] If 'on the summons for directions, the action or any question or issue therein is ordered to be tried before the Registrar, the Court may, without giving any further directions, adjourn the summons so that it can be heard by the Registrar, and the party required to apply to the Registrar for directions may do so by taking out a fresh summons for directions'.[2685]

2680. In relation to extending time for consent orders, because such orders represent a contract, the court would only interfere in exceptional or unusual circumstances: *Yeo Boong Hua v. Turf City Pte Ltd*, [2008] 4 SLR(R) 425; *Rosemawati bte Rafdi v. Buang bin Ani*, [2016] SGHC 223, [23]. This also relates to whether the court should exercise its inherent power to amend or vary a consent judgment so as to prevent injustice: *Airtrust (Singapore) Pte Ltd v. Kao Chai-Chau Linda*, [2014] 2 SLR 693.
2681. Supreme Court of Judicature Act (Cap. 322, R. 5, 2014 Rev. Ed.) Rules of Court, O 25 r 6(1).
2682. Supreme Court of Judicature Act (Cap. 322, R. 5, 2014 Rev. Ed.) Rules of Court, O 25 r 6(4).
2683. Supreme Court of Judicature Act (Cap. 322, R. 5, 2014 Rev. Ed.) Rules of Court, O 25 r 6(3).
2684. Supreme Court of Judicature Act (Cap. 322, R. 5, 2014 Rev. Ed.) Rules of Court, O 25 r 2(6).
2685. Supreme Court of Judicature Act (Cap. 322, R. 5, 2014 Rev. Ed.) Rules of Court, O 25 r 2(5).

732. For the purposes of the hearing, there is a prescribed form:

> which lists out 34 paragraphs covering a variety of interlocutory matters which may be addressed. The plaintiff is required to 'strike out the number' corresponding to the particular matter. The defendant is also entitled to raise any of the matters … for the court's consideration … in [another prescribed form] … The prescribed form, which sets out the commonly occurring interlocutory issues arising for consideration at this stage of the proceedings, does not prevent the parties from addressing the court on unlisted issues.[2686]

II. Subsequent Orders, Directions, and Applications

733. As a preliminary point, if an action needs to be transferred to the State Courts, the court is not required to (but it can) make any further order on the summons.[2687] This is so that the State Courts can have the opportunity to consider the interlocutory matters raised by the parties.[2688] For the matters (as listed above and some of which will be addressed specifically below) that are considered by the court during the first hearing for summons for directions, if 'any party fails to comply with the Court's directions for the filing and exchange of affidavits, an application may be made by summons at any time after the default for an order to enter judgment or to dismiss the action, as the case may be, or for such other order as to costs or otherwise that the Court thinks just in the circumstances'.[2689] In terms of general evidential matters, the default rule is that affidavits of evidence-in-chief will first be adduced at trial, and this is then followed by cross-examination of the witnesses.[2690] Thus, during the hearing for the first summons for directions, the court will make an order for the period of exchange of affidavits of evidence-in-chief for witnesses testifying at trial. The judge has the discretion to determine the period of exchange based on the circumstances of the case, but four months is commonly ordered.[2691] The parties may also extend the time by consent in writing without an order of the court being made for that purpose, unless the court has specified otherwise.[2692] Generally, parties are expected to exchange the affidavits simultaneously, so that neither side gains an unfair advantage.[2693] In certain cases, however, the court will order sequential exchange(s) if it is of the view that it will be fairer

2686. J. Pinsler, *Principles of Civil Procedure* 705 (Acad. Publg. 2013).
2687. Supreme Court of Judicature Act (Cap. 322, R. 5, 2014 Rev. Ed.) Rules of Court, O 25 r 2(4).
2688. J. Pinsler, *Principles of Civil Procedure* 704 (Acad. Publg. 2013).
2689. Supreme Court of Judicature Act (Cap. 322, R. 5, 2014 Rev. Ed.) Rules of Court, O 25 r 3(2).
2690. The court can direct that the witness give evidence by some other mode if there is sufficient cause: Supreme Court of Judicature Act (Cap. 322, R. 5, 2014 Rev. Ed.) Rules of Court, O 25 r 3(1).
2691. J. Pinsler, *Principles of Civil Procedure* 707 (Acad. Publg. 2013). For automatic directions for certain types of claims, *see* Supreme Court of Judicature Act (Cap. 322, R. 5, 2014 Rev. Ed.) Rules of Court, O 25 r 8(1).
2692. Supreme Court of Judicature Act (Cap. 322, R. 5, 2014 Rev. Ed.) Rules of Court, O 3 r 4(3).
2693. J. Pinsler, *Principles of Civil Procedure* 711 (Acad. Publg. 2013) citing *Mercer v. Chief Constable of the Lancashire Constabulary*, [1991] 1 WLR 367, 376.

in the circumstances – for instance, if it is near-impossible for a defendant witness to come up with an affidavit until and unless he has sight of a plaintiff witness's affidavit.[2694]

734. Within seven days after the exchange has taken place, 'the plaintiff shall file a certificate in [the prescribed form], signed by all parties to the action or their solicitors, to the effect that all affidavits of the evidence-in-chief of witnesses ordered or required to be exchanged … have been so exchanged'.[2695] After the exchange of affidavits, parties will be given time to object to the contents of the affidavits of evidence-in-chief or other evidence of the witnesses.[2696] While the objections are usually determined at the full trial, the objections themselves are normally taken one month after the exchange of affidavits, after which objections may not be accepted by the court.[2697] Parties may request for more time to object, and the court has the discretion to extend the period based on the circumstances of the case.[2698] At the hearing for summons for directions, the court will also decide if the number of witnesses should be limited, and whether each witness shall be limited to one affidavit of evidence-in-chief. It may be said that for most matters relating to witnesses and their evidence that are considered at the various hearings of the summons for direction, the governing principle is:

> the court must always be conscious of the fact that circumstances may and do arise which result in parties being unable to name all their witnesses at the stage of the summons for directions and, consequently, leave should be given to allow the parties to introduce new witnesses subsequent to the directions that have been given. There are multiple reasons for this, such as the failure of parties in giving proper or adequate instructions to their solicitors at the initial stage, failure of the parties and those advising them in properly weighing or assessing the evidence, subsequent amendments to pleadings, discovery of evidence relevant to the claim or defence or some other new development arising … the courts should not adopt an unduly rigid or restrictive approach in considering the directions to be given concerning matters pertaining to the trial or hearing. Instead, a balance should be struck between the need to comply with the rules and the parties' right to call witnesses whom they deem necessary to establish their case. It may well be that the additional evidence to be adduced by the parties may assist in illuminating the issues before the court or result in the expeditious disposal of the proceedings … the trial judge is in full control and is in a position to deal with the party adducing such evidence in an appropriate way, such as by disallowing the evidence which is being elicited from

2694. J. Pinsler, *Principles of Civil Procedure* 711–712 (Acad. Publg. 2013) citing *Kirkup v. British Rail Engineering Ltd*, [1983] 1 WLR 1165.
2695. Supreme Court of Judicature Act (Cap. 322, R. 5, 2014 Rev. Ed.) Rules of Court, O 25 r 3(3).
2696. *See* e.g. Supreme Court of Judicature Act (Cap. 322, R. 5, 2014 Rev. Ed.) Rules of Court, O 38 r 2(5), which prohibits hearsay evidence generally.
2697. Supreme Court Practice Directions 2013 (Part VI); State Courts Practice Directions (Part IV).
2698. *Hua Khian Co (Pte) Ltd v. Lee Eng Kiat*, [1996] 2 SLR(R) 562, [19]–[22].

> the witness and/or by an order as to costs … the duty of the court is to examine all the evidence put forward by the parties which is material and relevant to the dispute between the parties … [2699]

735. Then there is the process of securing all the necessary admissions and agreements at the hearing for the summons for directions so that the issues in dispute are further streamlined and delay and costs are minimized as a result. In this regard, the court is supposed to take a proactive role, a role which is 'backed up by the very real possibility that an uncooperative party may be penalised in costs at the trial'.[2700] In terms of matters relating to expert evidence (if any), the court should consider at the first hearing of the summons for directions if it is required, based on two sources of law. First, the main Evidence Act provision on expert evidence, which was amended only in 2012, sets out certain criteria that must be met before the expert evidence can be considered relevant and admissible.[2701] Second, the Rules of Court also establishes the rules and requirements regarding the limitation of the amount of expert evidence;[2702] the expert's duty to the court (an overriding duty to assist the court); the requirements of expert's evidence (such as qualifications of the expert, the material being relied on in the report, the issues being considered, and summary of the conclusions); the written questions to the opponent's expert witness (which must be answered so as to clarify any doubts about the report); the discussions between the experts (including identification of points of agreement and resolution of disagreements between the experts); and concurrent expert evidence.[2703]

III. Setting Down for Trial

736. The hearing for the summons for direction is also an occasion for the court to provide directions concerning:[2704] the period within which the plaintiff must set down the action for trial;[2705] the estimated duration of the trial and the number of witnesses to be called;[2706] and subsequently, the dates for trial.[2707] A number of

---

2699. *Auto Clean 'N' Shine Services (a firm) v. Eastern Publishing Associates Pte Ltd*, [1997] 2 SLR(R) 427, [17]. *See also Basil Anthony Herman v. Premier Security Co-operative Ltd*, [2010] 3 SLR 110, [24]–[26].

2700. J. Pinsler, *Principles of Civil Procedure* 713 (Acad. Publg. 2013); Supreme Court of Judicature Act (Cap. 322, R. 5, 2014 Rev. Ed.) Rules of Court, O 25 r 4.

2701. Evidence Act (Cap. 97, 1997 Rev. Ed.), s 47. C.f. C. Siyuan, *The 2012 Amendments to Singapore's Evidence Act: More Questions than Answers as Regards Expert Opinion Evidence?* 34 Stat. L. Rev. 262 (2013); C. Siyuan, *The Future of the Similar Fact Rule in an Indian Evidence Act Jurisdiction*, 6 Nat. U. Jur. Sci. L. Rev. 361 (2014); C. Siyuan, *Redefining Relevancy and Exclusionary Discretion in Sir James Fitzjames Stephen's Indian Evidence Act of 1872: The Singapore Experiment and Lessons for Other Indian Evidence Act Jurisdictions*, 10 Intl. Comm. Evid. 1 (2014).

2702. *See also* Supreme Court of Judicature Act (Cap. 322, R. 5, 2014 Rev. Ed.) Rules of Court, O 40A.

2703. *See* J. Pinsler, *Principles of Civil Procedure* 720–721 (Acad. Publg. 2013). *See also Teo Ai Ling v. Koh Chai Kwang*, [2010] 2 SLR 1037, [20]–[22].

2704. J. Pinsler, *Principles of Civil Procedure* 725 (Acad. Publg. 2013).

2705. *See* Supreme Court of Judicature Act (Cap. 322, R. 5, 2014 Rev. Ed.) Rules of Court, O 34 r 2.

2706. *See* Supreme Court of Judicature Act (Cap. 322, R. 5, 2014 Rev. Ed.) Rules of Court, O 34 r 5.

things must be done in this respect. First, the party setting down for trial 'must file with the Registrar a notice for setting down an action for trial in [the prescribed form] together with a bundle for the use of the Judge consisting of one copy of each of the following documents … the writ; … the pleadings … all orders made on the summons for directions'.[2708] Second, the said bundle 'must be bound up in the proper chronological order and have endorsed thereon the names, addresses and telephone numbers of the solicitors for the parties or, in the case of a party who has no solicitor, of the party himself'.[2709] Third, certain documents must be filed no less than five days before the trial:

> the originals of the affidavit of the evidence-in-chief of all witnesses; … a bundle of all documents that will be relied on or referred to in the course of the trial by any party, including any documents that are exhibited to the affidavits of the evidence-in-chief of all witnesses; and … where the trial is in the High Court, opening statements of all parties as may be prescribed in any practice directions for the time being issued by the Registrar.[2710]

737. Fourth, the contents of the said documents 'shall be agreed on between all parties as far as possible and this bundle of agreed documents shall be filed by the plaintiff'.[2711] Fifth, each party 'shall file the affidavits of the evidence-in-chief of that party's witnesses'.[2712] Sixth, if the parties 'are unable to agree on the inclusion of certain documents, those documents on which agreement cannot be reached shall be included in separate bundles, and each such bundle shall be filed by the party that intends to rely on or refer to the documents in that bundle at the same time as the bundle of documents referred to in [O 34 r 3A(1)]'.[2713] Seventh, the 'documents contained in bundles must be arranged chronologically or in some logical order and must be paginated'.[2714] Eighth, care must be taken to avoid duplication within the same bundle.[2715] Ninth, the 'contents and format of every bundle of documents filed in pursuance of this Rule shall comply with the requirements laid down in any practice directions for the time being issued by the Registrar'.[2716] Finally, any party 'may apply at any time to the Registrar for directions as to the filing, bundling and organization of documents intended to be used at the trial of the action, and, on such

2707. *See* Supreme Court of Judicature Act (Cap. 322, R. 5, 2014 Rev. Ed.) Rules of Court, O 34 r 4.
2708. Supreme Court of Judicature Act (Cap. 322, R. 5, 2014 Rev. Ed.) Rules of Court, O 34 r 3(1).
2709. Supreme Court of Judicature Act (Cap. 322, R. 5, 2014 Rev. Ed.) Rules of Court, O 34 r 3(2).
2710. Supreme Court of Judicature Act (Cap. 322, R. 5, 2014 Rev. Ed.) Rules of Court, O 34 r 3A(1).
2711. Supreme Court of Judicature Act (Cap. 322, R. 5, 2014 Rev. Ed.) Rules of Court, O 34 r 3A(3). *See also* Supreme Court Practice Directions 2013 (Part VI); State Courts Practice Directions (Part IV).
2712. Supreme Court of Judicature Act (Cap. 322, R. 5, 2014 Rev. Ed.) Rules of Court, O 34 r 3A(2).
2713. Supreme Court of Judicature Act (Cap. 322, R. 5, 2014 Rev. Ed.) Rules of Court, O 34 r 3A(4).
2714. Supreme Court of Judicature Act (Cap. 322, R. 5, 2014 Rev. Ed.) Rules of Court, O 34 r 3A(5).
2715. Supreme Court of Judicature Act (Cap. 322, R. 5, 2014 Rev. Ed.) Rules of Court, O 34 r 3A(6).
2716. Supreme Court of Judicature Act (Cap. 322, R. 5, 2014 Rev. Ed.) Rules of Court, O 34 r 3A(7).

application, the Registrar may make such order or give such direction as he thinks is necessary to achieve the just, expeditious and economical conduct of the trial of the action'.[2717]

§4. Possibility of Appeal

738. Section 34 of the Supreme Court of Judicature Act,[2718] read together with the Fourth and Fifth Schedules of the statute, determines whether any given order of civil procedure is appealable to the Court of Appeal[2719] or not.[2720] Of the various scenarios discussed solely in this Chapter,[2721] where appeals may arise (though not necessarily legitimately) would be when the plaintiff fails to apply for summons for directions and his action is dismissed; when extensions of time (with regard to evidence, witnesses, and/or other dates) are granted/denied; when subpoenas are granted/denied; and upon the court giving any order direction that a party may be dissatisfied with. Because 'any judgment, order or decision' of a registrar is appealable to a High Court Judge in chambers,[2722] a party will at least have one tier of appeal.

739. However, whether or not there is a further avenue of appeal to the Court of Appeal will depend on the order appealed against. Where an order is made by consent of the parties or if it is listed in under the Fourth Schedule, no appeal shall be brought to the Court of Appeal.[2723] Where an order is 'interlocutory' in nature, leave to appeal is generally required unless the order falls within one of the exceptions in paragraph (e) of the Fifth Schedule. Due to recent amendments to the Supreme Court of Judicature Act, the law on this is currently in flux and while it has been suggested that the 'default' position is that all interlocutory applications, unless provided for statutorily, are appealable with leave,[2724] it may also be possible to argue that for interlocutory applications not expressly addressed by the Fourth and Fifth

2717. Supreme Court of Judicature Act (Cap. 322, R. 5, 2014 Rev. Ed.) Rules of Court, O 34 r 3A(8). *See also id.*, O 38 r 5.
2718. (Cap. 322, 2007 Rev. Ed.).
2719. Below it is the High Court, followed by the District and Magistrates' Courts. For appeals arising from the lower courts, *see* Supreme Court of Judicature Act (Cap. 322, R. 5, 2014 Rev. Ed.) Rules of Court, O 55B, 55C, and 55D. There is a right of appeal from a registrar in chambers to a judge in chambers (District Judge if it is the State Courts), but not necessarily after that stage.
2720. The statute was amended in 2010 and 2014.
2721. The possibility for appeal for applications discussed at greater length in other Parts and Chapters will be discussed there instead.
2722. Supreme Court of Judicature Act (Cap. 322, R. 5, 2014 Rev. Ed.) Rules of Court, O 56 r 1.
2723. Supreme Court of Judicature Act (Cap. 322, 2007 Rev. Ed.), s 34(1) and Fourth Schedule.
2724. *See* E. Chua, *Defining an 'Interlocutory Application*, Sing. L. Watch Commentaries (4/2013); D. Chi, *Clarification on Leave to Appeal Regime in Respect of Interlocutory Matters: OpenNet Pte Ltd v. Info-Communications Development Authority of Singapore [2013] SGCA 24*, Sing. L. Watch Commentaries (4/2013); C. Siyuan & E. Chua, *The Right to Appeal Against a Decision Made on an Interlocutory Application: The Immediate Aftermath of the 2010 Amendments*, 25 Sing. Acad. L.J. 424 (2013).

Schedules, 'an appeal to the Court of Appeal will remain as of right for orders made at interlocutory applications which will finally dispose of the substantive rights of the parties'.[2725]

2725. *OpenNet Pte Ltd v. Info-Communications Development Authority of Singapore*, [2013] 2 SLR 880, [29]. *See also Dorsey James Michael v. World Sport Group Pte Ltd*, [2013] SLR 354, [98]. On the other hand, where the statute has made it clear that there is no appeal as of right, one is precluded from arguing that substantive rights have been engaged: *Kosui Singapore Pte Ltd v. Thangavelu*, [2016] 2 SLR 105, [28]–[29].

Chapter 2. Pre-trial Conferences and Unless Orders

§1. Introduction

740. As stated earlier, the summons for directions process is the main occasion whereby the court meets the parties to make the necessary orders and directions. Pre-trial conferences present a parallel mechanism for the courts to manage the cases,[2726] but whereas the summons for directions is initiated by the parties, pre-trial conferences are initiated by the court[2727] and furthermore, pre-trial conferences can take place any time as the court sees fit.[2728] One of the most important orders that can be made at pre-trial conferences, unless orders, will be considered in greater detail here. Other important matters that usually arise at pre-trial conferences will also be considered.

§2. Pre-trial Conference

741. The rules and procedures for pre-trial conferences are primarily found in O 34A of the Rules of Court.[2729] The court may 'at any time before any action or proceedings are tried … direct parties to attend a pre-trial conference relating to the matters arising in the action or proceedings'.[2730] The parties 'shall be informed of the date and time appointed for the holding of the pre-trial conference by way of a notice in accordance with [the prescribed form], and each party shall comply with any directions contained in such notice'.[2731] Where appropriate, a pre-trial conference may be adjourned, either generally or to a particular date.[2732] If a party fails to attend a pre-trial conference, the Court 'may, if it thinks fit, adjourn the conference'[2733] or it 'may dismiss the action or proceedings or strike out the defence or counterclaim or enter judgment or make such other order as the Court thinks fit'.[2734] However, any such order made 'may be set aside by the Court, on the application of that party, on such terms as it thinks just'.[2735] During the pre-trial conference, the court:

2726. *See also Singapore Civil Procedure 2015 Volume 1*, at 703 (G.P. Selvam ed., Sweet & Maxwell Asia 2014) citing *Lea Tool & Moulding Industries Pte Ltd (in liquidation) v. CGU International Insurance plc (formerly known as Commercial Union Assurance Co plc)*, [2000] 3 SLR(R) 745, [15].

2727. It is possible for parties to request for a pre-trial conference: *Lin Securities (Pte) (in liquidation) v. Official Assignee of the Property of Tan Koon Swan*, [1992] 2 SLR(R) 519, [17].

2728. *Singapore Civil Procedure 2015 Volume 1*, at 703 (G.P. Selvam ed., Sweet & Maxwell Asia 2014).

2729. Supreme Court of Judicature Act (Cap. 322, R. 5, 2014 Rev. Ed.) Rules of Court.

2730. Supreme Court of Judicature Act (Cap. 322, R. 5, 2014 Rev. Ed.) Rules of Court, O 34A r 2(1).

2731. Supreme Court of Judicature Act (Cap. 322, R. 5, 2014 Rev. Ed.) Rules of Court, O 34A r 3. *See also id.*, O 34A r 4.

2732. Supreme Court of Judicature Act (Cap. 322, R. 5, 2014 Rev. Ed.) Rules of Court, O 34A r 5.

2733. Supreme Court of Judicature Act (Cap. 322, R. 5, 2014 Rev. Ed.) Rules of Court, O 34A r 6(3).

2734. Supreme Court of Judicature Act (Cap. 322, R. 5, 2014 Rev. Ed.) Rules of Court, O 34A r 6(1). *See also id.*, O 35 r 1.

2735. Supreme Court of Judicature Act (Cap. 322, R. 5, 2014 Rev. Ed.) Rules of Court, O 34A r 6(2).

may consider any matter including the possibility of settlement of all or any of the issues in the action or proceedings and require the parties to furnish the Court with any such information as it thinks fit, and may also give all such directions as appear to be necessary or desirable for securing the just, expeditious and economical disposal of the action or proceedings.[2736]

742. If the court has made directions during a pre-trial conference, it 'may either on its own motion or upon the application of any party, if any party defaults in complying with any such directions, dismiss such action or proceedings or strike out the defence or counterclaim or enter judgment or make such order as it thinks fit'.[2737] However, any such judgment made 'may be set aside by the Court, on the application of the party, on such terms, if any, as it thinks just'.[2738] The pre-trial conference also presents an opportunity for parties to settle; at any time during the conference, 'where the parties are agreeable to a settlement of some or all of the matters in dispute in the action or proceedings, the Court may enter judgment in the action or proceedings or make such order to give effect to the settlement'.[2739] Indeed, where the prospects of settlement appear to be good and neither party has acted unreasonably with regard to the court process, the court should, notwithstanding its broad powers to manage the case, refrain from issuing any unless order during the pre-trial conference.[2740] If the settlement agreement was mediated by the court, there is no need for a separate process to convert the settlement agreement into a judgment.[2741]

743. In conjunction with its powers exercisable during pre-trial conferences,[2742] the court 'may, at any time after the commencement of any proceedings, of its own motion direct any party or parties to those proceedings to appear before it, in order that the Court may make such order or give such direction as it thinks fit, for the just, expeditious and economical disposal of the cause or matter'.[2743] In furtherance of the aforementioned broad powers, the court 'may take into account whether or not a party has complied with any relevant pre-action protocol or practice direction for the time being issued by the Registrar',[2744] 'dismiss the action, strike out the defence or counterclaim or make such other order as it thinks fit',[2745] and 'make such order as to costs as it thinks fit'.[2746] However, any 'judgment, order or direction given or made against any party who does not appear before the Court when directed to do so under [O 34A r 1(1)] may be set aside or varied by the Court on

2736. Supreme Court of Judicature Act (Cap. 322, R. 5, 2014 Rev. Ed.) Rules of Court, O 34A r 2(2).
2737. Supreme Court of Judicature Act (Cap. 322, R. 5, 2014 Rev. Ed.) Rules of Court, O 34A r 2(3).
2738. Supreme Court of Judicature Act (Cap. 322, R. 5, 2014 Rev. Ed.) Rules of Court, O 34A r 2(4).
2739. Supreme Court of Judicature Act (Cap. 322, R. 5, 2014 Rev. Ed.) Rules of Court, O 34A r 2(6). *See also id.*, O 34A r 7.
2740. *The Bonito*, [2001] 1 SLR(R) 828, [13].
2741. *Lock Han Chng Jonathan (Jonathan Luo Hancheng) v. Goh Jessiline*, [2008] 2 SLR(R) 455, [37].
2742. *See also* J. Pinsler, *Principles of Civil Procedure* 723 (Acad. Publg. 2013).
2743. Supreme Court of Judicature Act (Cap. 322, R. 5, 2014 Rev. Ed.) Rules of Court, O 34A r 1(1).
2744. Supreme Court of Judicature Act (Cap. 322, R. 5, 2014 Rev. Ed.) Rules of Court, O 34A r 1(1A).
2745. Supreme Court of Judicature Act (Cap. 322, R. 5, 2014 Rev. Ed.) Rules of Court, O 34A r 1(2).
2746. Supreme Court of Judicature Act (Cap. 322, R. 5, 2014 Rev. Ed.) Rules of Court, O 34A r 1(3).

such terms as it thinks just'.[2747] An application to set aside a judgment entered pursuant to an O 34A r 1 or O 34A r 2 order made at a pre-trial conference should be made within a reasonable period.[2748]

§3. UNLESS ORDER

744. The unless order is a powerful tool to ensure and enforce compliance with court orders in order to secure the 'efficient and prompt administration of justice' and realisation of the rule of law.[2749] In essence, it is an order 'which directs the defendant to comply with the terms failing which … he will have to face certain automatic consequences'.[2750] An unless order may be made on the court's own motion[2751] or on application by one of the parties.[2752] Where a party applies for an unless order, it should raise all its arguments at the earliest opportunity as the late employment of a new objection will leave the other party without an opportunity to rectify the breach or prove its bona fides.[2753] Although an unless order is generally self-executing and takes effect without any further order, the unless order has to be perfected in the absence of specific rules relating to perfection.[2754] It has been held that a party in whose favour an unless order is made can take one of two actions where there has been a default on the unless order: he may file a letter accompanied by a draft order of court for judgment or the dismissal of the action as the case may be and when the draft order is approved and extracted, the unless order is perfected; or he may file a general application to perfect the unless order, for example, an application to strike out or dismiss the claim.[2755]

745. Because of its potentially draconian consequences, an unless order is one of last resort and is not made unless there is a history of failure to comply with other orders.[2756] The Court of Appeal has suggested the following guidelines for the 'more scrupulous use' of unless orders:

2747. Supreme Court of Judicature Act (Cap. 322, R. 5, 2014 Rev. Ed.) Rules of Court, O 34A r 1(4).

2748. *Lea Tool & Moulding Industries Pte Ltd (in liquidation) v. CGU International Insurance plc (formerly known as Commercial Union Assurance Co plc)*, [2000] 3 SLR(R) 745, [17].

2749. *Mitora Pte Ltd v. Agritrade International (Pte) Ltd*, [2013] 3 SLR 11793 SLR 1179, [42], citing *Hytec Information Systems Ltd v. Coventry City Council*, [1997] 1 WLR 1666, 1674–1675.

2750. J. Pinsler, *Principles of Civil Procedure* 35 (Acad. Publg. 2013).

2751. *See Giorgio Ferrari Pte Ltd v. Lifebrandz Ltd*, [2013] 1 SLR 358; *Vijayalakshmi Sivaprakasapillai v. Mrinalini Ponnambalam*, [2009] SGHC 183.

2752. *See The 'MMM Diana' ex 'Able Director'*, [2004] 3 SLR(R) 611; *Changhe International Investments Pte Ltd (formerly known as Druidstone Pte Ltd) v. Dexia BIL Asia Singapore Ltd (formerly known as Banque Internationale A Luxembourg BIL (Asia) Ltd)*, [2005] 3 SLR(R) 344.

2753. *Mitora Pte Ltd v. Agritrade International (Pte) Ltd*, [2013] 3 SLR 11793 SLR 1179, [29].

2754. *Changhe International Investments Pte Ltd (formerly known as Druidstone Pte Ltd) v. Banque International A Luxembourg Bil (Asia) Ltd*, [2000] 2 SLR(R) 798, [6].

2755. *Changhe International Investments Pte Ltd (formerly known as Druidstone Pte Ltd) v. Banque International A Luxembourg Bil (Asia) Ltd*, [2000] 2 SLR(R) 798, [6].

2756. *Syed Mohamed Abdul Muthaliff v. Arjan Bhisham Chotram*, [1999] 1 SLR(R) 361, [15], citing *Hytec Information Systems Ltd v. Coventry City Council*, [1997] 1 WLR 1666, 1674.

a. 'unless orders' stipulating the consequence of dismissal should not be given as a matter of course but as a last resort when the defaulter's conduct is inexcusable;
b. the conditions appended to 'unless orders' should as far as possible be tailored to the prejudice which would be suffered should there be non-compliance; and
c. other means of penalising contumelious or persistent breaches are available, including but not limited to:
   1. awarding costs on an indemnity basis;
   2. ordering the payment of the plaintiff's claim or part thereof into court where the defaulting party is a defendant … ;
   3. striking out relevant portions of the defaulting party's Statement of Claim or Defence rather than the whole;
   4. barring the defaulting party from adducing certain classes of evidence or calling related witnesses; and
   5. raising adverse inferences against the defaulting party at trial.[2757]

746. While the failure to adhere to the terms of an unless order may result in the striking out of the offending party's claim (or defence and counterclaim as the case may be), much depends on whether there is a good reason for the failure to adhere (for instance, a justifiable delay), and whether the other party has suffered any undue prejudice.[2758] The court has residual discretion to determine the appropriate sanction, which must be commensurate with the prejudice suffered by the other party as a result of the breach of the unless order; in the final analysis, the court must be guided by the consideration of proportionality.[2759] Thus, a court order to strike out can be justified if there is more than a reasonable suspicion that certain documents exist but there has been contumacious and continuous failure to comply with orders for further discovery.[2760]

747. It should be noted that the court has the discretion to extend the time for compliance with the unless order, even if the application for extension of time is made after the dateline for compliance.[2761] However, this power is to be 'exercised cautiously' and the onus will be on the defaulter to demonstrate that he had in fact

2757. *Mitora Pte Ltd v. Agritrade International (Pte) Ltd*, [2013] 3 SLR 1179, [45].
2758. C. Bull & J. Pinsler, *Civil Procedure: Annual Review of Singapore Cases* [6.62]–[6.64] (Sing. Acad. L. 2001), citing *S3 Building Services Pte Ltd v. Sky Technology Pte Ltd*, [2001] 3 SLR(R) 213. *See also Kraze Entertainment (S) Pte Ltd v. Marina Bay Sands Pte Ltd*, [2014] 1 SLR 78, [55]. It has been suggested that implicit in the Court of Appeal's observations in *Mitora Pte Ltd v. Agritrade International (Pte) Ltd*, [2013] 3 SLR 1179, [48] is that a court has the discretion to strike out when it was in the public interest to do so: *Ramindo Sukses Perkasa Pte Ltd v. Sim Kwang Oo*, [2015] 3 SLR 403, [84].
2759. Bull & J. Pinsler, *Civil Procedure: Annual Review of Singapore Cases* [8.50] (Sing. Acad. L. 2013).
2760. Bull & J. Pinsler, *Civil Procedure: Annual Review of Singapore Cases* [6.37] (Sing. Acad. L. 2002), citing *Soh Lup Chee v. Seow Boon Cheng*, [2002] 1 SLR(R) 604. *See also Giorgio Ferrari Pte Ltd v. Lifebrandz Ltd*, [2013] 1 SLR 358.
2761. Supreme Court of Judicature Act (Cap. 322, R. 5, 2014 Rev. Ed.) Rules of Court, O 3 r 4; *Syed Mohamed Abdul Muthaliff v. Arjan Bhisham Chotram*, [1999] 1 SLR(R) 361.

made positive efforts to comply, and that he was not intentionally ignoring or flouting the order but was constrained by extraneous circumstances.[2762] Nevertheless, the above are guidelines and not fixed rules of law; the court will consider all the circumstances of the case, including the prejudice caused to the other party and the proportionality of depriving the offending party of a determination on the merits, to determine if its refusal to extend time for compliance with the unless order would be in the interests of justice.[2763]

748. It has been suggested that the court, when exercising its discretion, particularly if the consequence of non-adherence to the unless order is a striking out of the offending party's claim, should draw a distinction between true unless orders and peremptory orders of a 'housekeeping' nature.[2764] More broadly, in every case, a careful balance must be struck between furthering case management objectives on one hand, while at the same time ensuring that a deserving claimant is able to use the civil justice process to ventilate his or her claim.[2765] Even where the contumelious conduct is that of the litigant's solicitor rather than that of the litigant himself, the litigant has to bear the consequences of such contumely.[2766] There may be instances where a consent unless order is made pursuant to the consent of both parties. This situation normally arises 'when the defaulting party faces sanctions and agrees to the unless order so that he has a final opportunity to comply before the consequences of his default kick in'.[2767] It has been held that the court still retains the discretion to interfere with the contract between the parties and prevent the consequences that would normally follow from the consent unless order for the following reasons:

> It must be borne in mind that a consent unless order, whilst technically a contract between the parties, is one that allows one party to wholly deprive the other of its legal rights in the context of litigation. Even though such an order has been agreed upon between the parties, there may, in my view, arise certain

---

2762. *Kraze Entertainment (S) Pte Ltd v. Marina Bay Sands Pte Ltd*, [2013] SGHC 39, [7]; *Changhe International Investments Pte Ltd (formerly known as Druidstone Pte Ltd) v. Dexia BIL Asia Singapore Ltd (formerly known as Banque Internationale A Luxembourg BIL (Asia) Ltd)*, [2005] 3 SLR(R) 344, [10]; *Syed Mohamed Abdul Muthaliff v. Arjan Bhisham Chotram*, [1999] 1 SLR(R) 361, [10]; *The 'Tokai Maru'*, [1998] 2 SLR(R) 646, [11]; *Tang Liang Hong v. Lee Kuan Yew*, [1997] 3 SLR(R) 576, [101], citing *Tolley v. Morris*, [1979] 1 WLR 592, 603.

2763. J. Pinsler, *Principles of Civil Procedure* 38–39 (Acad. Publg. 2013) citing *Syed Mohamed Abdul Muthaliff v. Arjan Bhisham Chotram*, [1999] 1 SLR(R) 361; *Teeni Enterprise Ptd Ltd v. Singco Pte Ltd*, [2008] SGHC 115. *See also Mitora Pte Ltd v. Agritrade International (Pte) Ltd*, [2013] 3 SLR 1179, [35]–[40].

2764. A. Zuckerman, *Zuckerman on Civil Procedure: Principles of Practice* [10.144] (Sweet & Maxwell. 2006), cited in D. Wong, *Sanctions: Where Law and Justice Collide*, 33(1) Civ. J. Q. 24 (2014). *See also Keen Philips (A Firm) v. Field*, [2006] EWCA Civ 1524; *JTrust Asia Pte Ltd v. Group Lease Holdings Pte Ltd* [2019] SGHC 21 at [8]–[9].

2765. D. Wong, *Sanctions: Where Law and Justice Collide*, 33(1) Civ. J. Q. 24 (2014).

2766. *Changhe International Investments Pte Ltd (formerly known as Druidstone Pte Ltd) v. Dexia BIL Asia Singapore Ltd (formerly known as Banque Internationale A Luxembourg BIL (Asia) Ltd)*, [2005] 3 SLR(R) 344, [12], citing *Hytec Information Systems Ltd v. Coventry City Council*, [1997] 1 WLR 1666, 1675–1676.

2767. J. Pinsler, *Principles of Civil Procedure* 39 (Acad. Publg. 2013).

> special circumstances where it would nevertheless be unjust for the party in whose favour the consent order operates to insist on its enforcement in the absence of a high degree of intentionally contumacious or contumelious conduct.
>
> Such a discretion is, in the final analysis, merely an aspect of the court's power to have ultimate control over its own procedure. This is not at all unreasonable, in my view, and does, on balance, conduce to justice and fairness. The focus is still on procedure, rather than substance. It might be argued that the substantive rights of the plaintiff would be adversely affected. This is arguably the case but it must never be forgotten that an unless order is part of the procedural armoury and is not based on the substantive merits of the case as such. Thus, an unless order (whether by consent or otherwise) deals, in the final analysis, with the litigation process and, on this score, the courts ought to have the final say.[2768]

749. In summary, it bears repeating that unless orders are not intended to punish misconduct but to secure a fair trial; accordingly, they should be drafted with due care and consideration.[2769] The striking out of litigant's claim or defence in its entirety ought not to be the default consequence of an unless order as it would effectively deprive the litigant of its substantive rights on account of a procedural fault.[2770] Nevertheless, litigants should be aware that the court's power to strike out an action may be properly invoked in cases involving an inexcusable breach of a significant procedural obligation, even where there might still be a reasonable prospect of a fair trial.[2771]

§4. OTHER MATTERS

750. Although it is common for parties to propose agreed timelines and directions to the court during pre-trial conferences, it is ultimately within the discretion of the court whether to make the consent orders as requested, or to give other directions 'it thinks fit, for the just, expeditious and economical disposal of the cause or matter'.[2772] As a guide to solicitors, the Practice Directions contain average waiting times between the filing of certain processes or other steps in the proceedings and the date for the hearing or pre-trial conference of the matter.[2773] Solicitors should

2768. *Wellmix Organics (International) Pte Ltd v. Lau Yu Man*, [2006] 2 SLR(R) 117, [90]–[91] (emphasis in original).
2769. *Mitora Pte Ltd v. Agritrade International (Pte) Ltd*, [2013] 3 SLR 11793 SLR 1179, [45].
2770. *Mitora Pte Ltd v. Agritrade International (Pte) Ltd*, [2013] 3 SLR 11793 SLR 1179, [46].
2771. *Mitora Pte Ltd v. Agritrade International (Pte) Ltd*, [2013] 3 SLR 11793 SLR 1179, [47]–[48], citing *Manilal and Sons (Pte) Ltd v. Bhupendra K J Shan (trading as JB International)*, [1989] 2 SLR(R) 603; *Tan Kok Ing v. Ang Boon Aik*, [2002] SGHC 215; *Lee Chang-Rung v. Standard Chartered Bank*, [2011] 1 SLR 337; *Singapore Civil Procedure 2015 Volume 1*, at 559–560 (G.P. Selvam ed., Sweet & Maxwell Asia 2014).
2772. Supreme Court of Judicature Act (Cap. 322, R. 5, 2014 Rev. Ed.) Rules of Court, O 34A r 1(1).
2773. Supreme Court Practice Directions 2013 (Appendix B); State Courts Practice Directions (Appendix D).

accordingly be ready to proceed at the end of the relevant period.[2774] In the Supreme Court, it is possible for solicitors to request a hearing date for the following classes of applications: interlocutory applications heard by registrars; bankruptcy applications; and winding up applications.[2775] In both the Supreme Court and the State Courts, Practice Directions exhort solicitors to 'provide updated information as to the current status of the cause or matter, including the prospects of settlement and any other developments which are likely to affect the length of the trial' in order to assist the registrar at the fixing of hearing dates.[2776] To facilitate a more realistic assessment of the time required for the hearing, solicitors are also required to inform the registrar of the number of witnesses they intend to call, the estimated amount of time required for each party to cross-examine all the opposing party's witnesses and the estimated total length of hearing.[2777] It has been observed that the courts have a 'religious and punctilious observance of hearing dates and minimal tolerance for unmeritorious adjournments' and that 'strong compelling grounds must prevail before the court would exercise its discretion to vacate trial dates'.[2778] Indeed, the:

> administration of justice would be impaired if counsel were to be allowed to coerce the court into granting an adjournment by simply stating that he is unable to argue the matter or proceed with the hearing as a result of his utter failure to be ready for the hearing. Such irresponsible conduct should not be countenanced by the court and it could well invite personal cost orders against the counsel concerned.[2779]

§5. Possibility of Appeal

751. Section 34 of the Supreme Court of Judicature Act,[2780] read together with the Fourth and Fifth Schedules of the statute, determines whether any given order of civil procedure is appealable to the Court of Appeal[2781] or not.[2782] The Fourth

---

2774. Supreme Court Practice Directions 2013 (Part VII); State Courts Practice Directions (Part V).
2775. Supreme Court Practice Directions 2013 (Part VII).
2776. Supreme Court Practice Directions 2013 (Part VII); State Courts Practice Directions (Part V).
2777. Supreme Court Practice Directions 2013 (Part VII); State Courts Practice Directions (Part V).
2778. C. Bull & J. Pinsler, *Civil Procedure: Annual Review of Singapore Cases* [7.86], (Sing. Acad. L. 2007), citing *Su Sh-Hsyu v. Wee Yue Chew*, [2007] 3 SLR(R) 673; *Chan Kern Miang v. Kea Resources Pte Ltd*, [1998] 2 SLR(R) 85. *See also* Supreme Court Practice Directions 2013 (Part VII); State Courts Practice Directions 2012 (Part V); *PT Humpuss Intermoda Transportasi v. Humpuss Sea Transport Pte Ltd (in compulsory liquidation)*, [2019] SGCA 8.
2779. *Singapore Investments (Pte) Ltd v. Golden Asia International (Singapore) Pte Ltd*, [2009] 4 SLR(R) 291, [3].
2780. (Cap. 322, 2007 Rev. Ed.).
2781. Below it is the High Court, followed by the District and Magistrates' Courts. For appeals arising from the lower courts, *see* Supreme Court of Judicature Act (Cap. 322, R. 5, 2014 Rev. Ed.) Rules of Court, O 55B, 55C, and 55D. There is a right of appeal from a registrar in chambers to a judge in chambers (District Judge if it is the State Courts), but not necessarily after that stage. It should also be noted that for such appeals from first instance, the cases are heard de novo and the judge may therefore choose to admit fresh evidence if appropriate.
2782. The statute was amended in 2010 and 2014.

and Fifth Schedules are silent as regards pre-trial conferences and unless orders specifically, but they do address matters pursuant to unless orders. The Fourth Schedule states that: 'No appeal shall be brought to the Court of Appeal … where a Judge makes an order refusing to strike out … an action or a matter commenced by a writ of summons or by any other originating process; or … a pleading or a part of a pleading.' The Fifth Schedule then states that:

> Except with the leave of a Judge, no appeal shall be brought to the Court of Appeal … where a Judge makes an order at the hearing of any interlocutory application other than an application … to strike out an action or a matter commenced by a writ of summons or by any other originating process, a pleading or a part of a pleading … to dismiss an action or a matter commenced by a writ of summons or by any other originating process.

752. In other words, whether or not there is a further avenue of appeal to the Court of Appeal will depend on the order appealed against. Where an order is made by consent of the parties or if it is listed in under the Fourth Schedule, no appeal shall be brought to the Court of Appeal.[2783] Where an order is 'interlocutory' in nature, it has been suggested that leave to appeal is generally required unless the order falls within one of the exceptions in paragraph (e) of the Fifth Schedule.[2784] An example of an order falling within one of the exceptions in paragraph (e) of the Fifth Schedule is if the court dismisses or strikes out the action during a pre-trial conference. In such a situation, an appeal will probably lie to the Court of Appeal as of right.[2785] However, due to recent amendments to the Supreme Court of Judicature Act, the law on this is currently in flux, and it may also be possible to argue that for interlocutory applications not expressly addressed by the Fourth and Fifth Schedules, 'an appeal to the Court of Appeal will remain as of right for orders made at interlocutory applications which will finally dispose of the substantive rights of the parties'.[2786] It should be noted that because 'any judgment, order or decision' of a registrar is appealable to a High Court Judge in chambers,[2787] a party will at least have one tier of appeal in respect of any order made at a pre-trial conference.

2783. Supreme Court of Judicature Act (Cap. 322, 2007 Rev. Ed.), s 34(1) and Fourth Schedule.

2784. *See* E. Chua, *Defining an 'Interlocutory Application*, Sing. L. Watch Commentaries (4/2013); D. Chi, *Clarification on Leave to Appeal Regime in Respect of Interlocutory Matters: OpenNet Pte Ltd v. Info-Communications Development Authority of Singapore [2013] SGCA 24*, Sing. L. Watch Commentaries (4/2013); C. Siyuan & E. Chua, *The Right to Appeal Against a Decision Made on an Interlocutory Application: The Immediate Aftermath of the 2010 Amendments*, 25 Sing. Acad. L.J. 424 (2013).

2785. Supreme Court of Judicature Act (Cap. 322, 2007 Rev. Ed.), s 29A(1).

2786. *OpenNet Pte Ltd v. Info-Communications Development Authority of Singapore*, [2013] 2 SLR 880, [29]. *See also Dorsey James Michael v. World Sport Group Pte Ltd*, [2013] 3 SLR 354, [98].

2787. Supreme Court of Judicature Act (Cap. 322, R. 5, 2014 Rev. Ed.) Rules of Court, O 56 r 1.

Part IX. Seizure for Security and Enforcement of Judgments

Chapter 1. Seizure for Security

753. This is not applicable in Singapore.

Chapter 2. Enforcement of Domestic Judgments

§1. Introduction

754. When a court grants judgment, the losing party is known as the judgment debtor and the winning party the judgment creditor. In most cases, the judgment debtor would abide by the ruling (for instance, by making the necessary payment) without further action on the part of the judgment creditor.[2788] However, the law provides for various enforcement measures for the judgment creditor[2789] that can be taken out against the judgment debtor[2790] if he refuses to abide by the ruling.[2791] The enforcement process has been described in the following terms:

> This is a critical area of civil litigation as the ultimate purpose of the claimant in allocating his resources to the pursuit of civil litigation is the remedy or relief which he hopes to obtain. Therefore, he will give considerable thought to the likelihood of satisfaction of the judgment even before he commences proceedings, and may even monitor the financial position of a defendant whose circumstances may change in the course of the action. The power to compel satisfaction of a judgment must be balanced against the broader social consequences of enforcement on the judgment debtor, his family and other persons who may be affected by a particular process of execution … legislation offers a variety of methods for the enforcement of a judgment after trial, the applicability of which depend on the nature of the judgment, the intention of the judgment creditor and/or the assets of the judgment debtor.[2792]

755. Although various statutes provide for enforcement mechanisms,[2793] the focus here will be the ones found in the Rules of Court. The primary enforcement mechanisms (writ of seizure and sale, writ of possession, and writ of delivery (these three fall under writs of execution),[2794] garnishee proceedings, equitable execution, and order of committal) will now be examined in turn.

2788. Supreme Court of Judicature Act (Cap. 322, R. 5, 2014 Rev. Ed.) Rules of Court, O 42 r 6(1).

2789. It is also possible for a non-party to enforce a judgment if he obtains an order or in whose favour an order is made: Supreme Court of Judicature Act (Cap. 322, R. 5, 2014 Rev. Ed.) Rules of Court, O 45 r 9(1).

2790. Generally, enforcement measures under the Rules of Court do not apply against the government: Supreme Court of Judicature Act (Cap. 322, R. 5, 2014 Rev. Ed.) Rules of Court, O 73 r 12(1).

2791. It should be noted that a judgment creditor is entitled to use more than one enforcement measure. *See also* Supreme Court of Judicature Act (Cap. 322, R. 5, 2014 Rev. Ed.) Rules of Court, O 45 r 10.

2792. J. Pinsler, *Principles of Civil Procedure* 827–828 (Acad. Publg. 2013). *See also* Court of Judicature Act (Cap. 322, R. 5, 2014 Rev. Ed.) Rules of Court, O 45 r 11A.

2793. *See* e.g., Bankruptcy Act (Cap. 20, 2009 Rev. Ed.); Companies Act (Cap. 50, 2006 Rev. Ed.); Debtors Act (Cap. 73, 1985 Rev. Ed.).

2794. Supreme Court of Judicature Act (Cap. 322, R. 5, 2014 Rev. Ed.) Rules of Court, O 46 r 1.

§2. Enforcement Mechanisms

I. Writ of Seizure and Sale

756. A writ of seizure and sale is usually appropriate[2795] for judgments for payment and/or recovery of money (including costs and arrears)[2796] and property (movable and immovable,[2797] as well as securities).[2798] It also enables a court official to seize and sell property to satisfy a judgment or order.[2799] A writ of seizure and sale will only be issued with the leave of the court where:

> 6 years or more have lapsed since the date of the judgment or order; … any change has taken place, whether by death or otherwise, in the parties entitled or liable to execution under the judgment or order; … the judgment or order is against the assets of a deceased person coming into the hands of his executors or administrators after the date of the judgment or order, and it is sought to issue execution against such assets; … under the judgment or order any person is entitled to relief subject to the fulfilment of any condition which it is alleged has been fulfilled; and … any movable property sought to be seized under a writ of execution is in the hands of a receiver appointed by the Court.[2800]

757. An application for leave to issue a writ of seizure and sale should be made by ex parte summons using the prescribed form.[2801] Such an application must be supported by affidavit, giving information as is necessary to satisfy the court that the applicant is entitled to proceed to execution on the judgment or order in question and that the person against whom it is sought to issue execution is liable to execution.[2802] The court may then 'grant leave in accordance with the application or may order that any issue or question, a decision on which is necessary to determine the rights of the parties, be tried in any manner in which any question of fact

2795. J. Pinsler, *Principles of Civil Procedure* 829–830 (Acad. Publg. 2013).
2796. Supreme Court of Judicature Act (Cap. 322, R. 5, 2014 Rev. Ed.) Rules of Court, O 47.
2797. Supreme Court of Judicature Act (Cap. 322, 2007 Rev. Ed.), s 13.
See also Supreme Court of Judicature Act (Cap. 322, R. 5, 2014 Rev. Ed.) Rules of Court, O 47 rr 4 and 5 for the procedures on how to seize and sell immovable property. It should be noted that previously, charging orders were used: J. Pinsler, *Principles of Civil Procedure* 847–848 (Acad. Publg. 2013). As to whether a property held in joint tenancy (as opposed tenancy-in-common) needs to be severed before a writ of seizure and sale can be issued, *see Chan Shwe Ching v. Leong Lai Yee*, [2015] 5 SLR 295, [11]–[23]; *Chan Yat Chun v. Sng Jin Chye*, [2016] SGHCR 4, [4]–[12].
2798. *See* Supreme Court of Judicature Act (Cap. 322, R. 5, 2014 Rev. Ed.) Rules of Court, O 47 rr 6 and 7 for the procedures on how to seize and sell securities. It should be noted that previously, charging orders were used: J. Pinsler, *Principles of Civil Procedure* 849 (Acad. Publg. 2013).
2799. *See also* Supreme Court of Judicature Act (Cap. 322, R. 5, 2014 Rev. Ed.) Rules of Court, O 47 r 3(1).
2800. Supreme Court of Judicature Act (Cap. 322, R. 5, 2014 Rev. Ed.) Rules of Court, O 46 r 2(1). *See also id.*, O 46 r 2(2).
2801. Supreme Court of Judicature Act (Cap. 322, R. 5, 2014 Rev. Ed.) Rules of Court, O 46 r 3(1).
2802. Supreme Court of Judicature Act (Cap. 322, R. 5, 2014 Rev. Ed.) Rules of Court, O 46 r 3(2). The grounds that need to be stated depend on what is argued under *id.*, O 46 r 2(1).

or law arising in an action may be tried and, in either case, may impose such terms as to costs or otherwise as it thinks just'.[2803]

758. O 46 r 4 sets out the other formal requirements for a writ of seizure and sale, such as the prescribed form, when it is deemed to be issued, and the conditions for it to be sealed.[2804] In addition, a writ of seizure and sale on immovable property requires the obtaining of the order and registration with the relevant authorities (Registry of Deeds, Land Titles Registry, or Singapore Land Authority).[2805] The priority of a writ of seizure and sale 'shall be determined by reference to the date on which it was originally issued',[2806] and this would apply as between writs issued in the High Court and State Courts as well.[2807] A writ of execution (including a writ of seizure and sale) is issued when it was sealed after stamping.[2808] If the court grants leave 'for the issue of a writ of execution and the writ is not issued within one year after the date of the order granting such leave, the order shall cease to have effect, without prejudice, however, to the making of a fresh order'.[2809] An execution creditor can request the court to withdraw any seizure, and if so he shall be deemed to have abandoned the execution.[2810] However, if this is done, a writ of seizure and sale 'shall not be reissued but the execution creditor may apply by summons supported by affidavit stating the grounds of the application for a fresh writ of seizure and sale to be issued, and such writ shall take priority according to its date of issue'.[2811] Finally, it should be noted that if a judgment creditor has a beneficial interest in securities in which he has an enforceable judgment against, he may require notice of any attempts to transfer or otherwise deal with them (these are known as stop notices).[2812] But to restrain any transfer or payment, he will need to apply for an order to prohibit such activity under O 50 r 5.

II. Writ of Possession

759. A writ of possession is usually appropriate for judgments for possession of land and recovery of land (or immovable property).[2813] The circumstances in which leave of court is required before a writ of possession will be issued are the same as

2803. Supreme Court of Judicature Act (Cap. 322, R. 5, 2014 Rev. Ed.) Rules of Court, O 46 r 3(3).
2804. For a discussion on whether there can be excessive seizure (on the part of the bailiff) and whether the bailiff can be sued (either under common law or statutory law) for wrongful execution, *see South East Enterprises (Singapore) Pte Ltd v. Hean Nerng Holdings Pte Ltd*, [2013] 2 SLR 908.
2805. Supreme Court of Judicature Act (Cap. 322, R. 5, 2014 Rev. Ed.) Rules of Court, O 47 r 4(1)(d).
2806. Supreme Court of Judicature Act (Cap. 322, R. 5, 2014 Rev. Ed.) Rules of Court, O 46 r 6(4). *See also* Supreme Court of Judicature Act (Cap. 322, R. 5, 2014 Rev. Ed.) Rules of Court, O 46 r 17(3)(f).
2807. *Singapore Civil Procedure 2015 Volume 1*, at 835 (G.P. Selvam ed., Sweet & Maxwell Asia 2014). *See also Emjay Enterprises Pte Ltd v. Thakral Brothers (Pte) Ltd*, [2000] 2 SLR(R) 729.
2808. *Singapore Civil Procedure 2015 Volume 1*, at 834 (G.P. Selvam ed., Sweet & Maxwell Asia 2014), citing *Emjay Enterprises Pte Ltd v. Thakral Brothers (Pte) Ltd*, [2000] 2 SLR(R) 729, [44]–[45].
2809. Supreme Court of Judicature Act (Cap. 322, R. 5, 2014 Rev. Ed.) Rules of Court, O 46 r 2(3).
2810. Supreme Court of Judicature Act (Cap. 322, R. 5, 2014 Rev. Ed.) Rules of Court, O 47 r 9(1).
2811. Supreme Court of Judicature Act (Cap. 322, R. 5, 2014 Rev. Ed.) Rules of Court, O 47 r 9(2).
2812. Supreme Court of Judicature Act (Cap. 322, R. 5, 2014 Rev. Ed.) Rules of Court, O 50 r 1(1).
2813. J. Pinsler, *Principles of Civil Procedure* 829–830 (Acad. Publg. 2013).

those of a writ of seizure and sale set out above.[2814] The formal requirements for an application for leave to issue a writ of possession are the same as those of a writ of seizure and sale set out above.[2815] In addition, a writ of possession 'to enforce a judgment or order for the giving of possession of any immovable property shall not be issued without the leave of the Court except where the judgment or order was given or made in a mortgage action to which [O 83] applies',[2816] and such leave 'shall not be granted unless it is shown that every person in actual possession of the whole or any part of the immovable property has received such notice of the proceedings as appears to the Court sufficient to enable him to apply to the Court for any relief to which he may be entitled'.[2817] O 46 r 4 sets out the other formal requirements for a writ of possession, such as the prescribed form, when it is deemed to be issued, and the conditions for it to be sealed. The priority of a writ of possession 'shall be determined by reference to the date on which it was originally issued'.[2818]

III. Writ of Delivery

760. A writ of delivery is usually appropriate for judgments for delivery of goods and return of movable property.[2819] Specifically:

> a judgment or order for the delivery of any movable property which does not give a person against whom the judgment is given or order made the alternative of paying the assessed value of the property may be enforced by … writ of delivery to recover the property without alternative provision for recovery of the assessed value thereof.[2820]

761. In addition, 'a judgment or order for the delivery of any movable property or payment of their assessed value may be enforced by … writ of delivery to recover the property or its assessed value; … [or] with the leave of the Court, writ of specific delivery'.[2821] A 'judgment or order for the payment of the assessed value of any movable property may be enforced by the same means as any other judgment or order for the payment of money'.[2822] The circumstances in which leave of court is required before a writ of delivery will be issued are the same as those of a writ of seizure and sale set out above.[2823] The formal requirements for an application for leave to issue a writ of delivery are the same as those of a writ of seizure

2814. Supreme Court of Judicature Act (Cap. 322, R. 5, 2014 Rev. Ed.) Rules of Court, O 46 r 2.
2815. Supreme Court of Judicature Act (Cap. 322, R. 5, 2014 Rev. Ed.) Rules of Court, O 46 r 3.
2816. Supreme Court of Judicature Act (Cap. 322, R. 5, 2014 Rev. Ed.) Rules of Court, O 45 r 3(2). O 83 deals with mortgage actions.
2817. Supreme Court of Judicature Act (Cap. 322, R. 5, 2014 Rev. Ed.) Rules of Court, O 45 r 3(3).
2818. Supreme Court of Judicature Act (Cap. 322, R. 5, 2014 Rev. Ed.) Rules of Court, O 46 r 6(4).
2819. J. Pinsler, *Principles of Civil Procedure* 829–830 (Acad. Publg. 2013).
2820. Supreme Court of Judicature Act (Cap. 322, R. 5, 2014 Rev. Ed.) Rules of Court, O 45 r 4(1).
2821. Supreme Court of Judicature Act (Cap. 322, R. 5, 2014 Rev. Ed.) Rules of Court, O 45 r 4(2).
2822. Supreme Court of Judicature Act (Cap. 322, R. 5, 2014 Rev. Ed.) Rules of Court, O 45 r 4(4).
2823. Supreme Court of Judicature Act (Cap. 322, R. 5, 2014 Rev. Ed.) Rules of Court, O 46 r 2. *See also id.*, O 37 r 5 (assessment of value of goods).

and sale set out above.[2824] O 46 r 4 sets out the other formal requirements for a writ of delivery, such as the prescribed form, when it is deemed to be issued, and the conditions for it to be sealed. The priority of a writ of delivery 'shall be determined by reference to the date on which it was originally issued'.[2825]

IV. Garnishee Proceedings

762. Garnishee proceedings are usually appropriate for judgments for payment of money and recovery of money.[2826] A garnishee order is in substance the same as a writ of seizure and sale as it is the court's direction to the garnishee to pay the judgment creditor. Both modes of execution involve attachment and transfer of the judgment debtor's interest in property to the judgment creditor, whether by the proceeds of sale or by payment to the judgment creditor.[2827] Specifically, the process – an equitable remedy – is appropriate when the judgment creditor intends to recover the money owed to him by the judgment debtor from a third party (i.e., the garnishee) who is indebted to the judgment debtor; the debt owed by the garnishee is attached for the benefit of the judgment creditor.[2828] If the garnishee fails to comply with an order, for instance, by disposing of money which he knows has been attached by the court, he may be held in contempt of court.[2829] Procedurally, there are two parts to the application. First, there must be an order (using the prescribed form and made by ex parte summons supported by an affidavit) 'to show cause, specifying the time and place for further consideration of the matter, and in the meantime attaching such debt … or so much thereof as may be specified in the order, to answer the judgment or order mentioned in that paragraph and the costs of the garnishee proceedings'.[2830] This order 'must, at least 7 days before the time appointed thereby for the further consideration of the matter, be served … on the garnishee personally; and … unless the Court otherwise directs, on the judgment debtor'.[2831] Second, if the garnishee does not attend the hearing (which may be heard summarily)[2832] or is unsuccessful in disputing his liability, the provisional

2824. Supreme Court of Judicature Act (Cap. 322, R. 5, 2014 Rev. Ed.) Rules of Court, O 46 r 3.
2825. Supreme Court of Judicature Act (Cap. 322, R. 5, 2014 Rev. Ed.) Rules of Court, O 46 r 6(4).
2826. J. Pinsler, *Principles of Civil Procedure* 829–830 (Acad. Publg. 2013).
2827. *Singapore Civil Procedure 2015 Volume 1*, at 831 (G.P. Selvam ed., Sweet & Maxwell Asia 2014), citing *American Express Bank Ltd v. Abdul Manaff bin Ahmad*, [2003] 4 SLR(R) 780, [27].
2828. J. Pinsler, *Principles of Civil Procedure* 854 (Acad. Publg. 2013).
2829. Supreme Court of Judicature Act (Cap. 322, 2007 Rev. Ed.), ss 7(2) and 7(3). *See also Singapore Civil Procedure 2015 Volume 1*, at 857 (G.P. Selvam ed., Sweet & Maxwell Asia 2014).
2830. Supreme Court of Judicature Act (Cap. 322, R. 5, 2014 Rev. Ed.) Rules of Court, O 49 r 1(2).
2831. Supreme Court of Judicature Act (Cap. 322, R. 5, 2014 Rev. Ed.) Rules of Court, O 49 r 3(1).
2832. Supreme Court of Judicature Act (Cap. 322, R. 5, 2014 Rev. Ed.) Rules of Court, O 49 r 5. As to on whom the burden of proof lies in garnishee show cause proceedings and what that burden entails, *see The State-Owned Company Yugoimport SDPR (also known as Jugoimport-SDPR) v. Westacre Investments and other appeals* [2016] SGCA 51, [85]; *Telecom Credit Inc v. Star Commerce Pte Ltd*, [2017] SGHCR 3.

order would be converted into a final order (using the prescribed form),[2833] and this final order may be enforced in the same manner as any other order for the payment of money.[2834]

763. However, if 'it is brought to the notice of the Court that some person other than the judgment debtor is or claims to be entitled to the debt sought to be attached or has or claims to have a charge or lien upon it, the Court may order that person to attend before the Court and state the nature of the claim with particulars thereof'.[2835] Third parties asserting ownership claims over the debt bear the legal burden of proof to prove that they had beneficial ownership over the funds. Although the garnishee process does not involve seizure and sale, transfer of possession, or delivery, a court may 'order the garnishee to pay the judgment creditor the amount of any debt due or accruing due to the judgment debtor from the garnishee, or so much thereof as is sufficient to satisfy that judgment or order and the costs of the garnishee proceedings'.[2836] The court will take into account the interests of other creditors affected by the order, especially if the debtor is insolvent.[2837] The scope of the garnishee process is further qualified in a number of ways. First, it does not apply to any judgment or order that is for the payment of money into court.[2838] Second, the garnishee cannot be out of jurisdiction.[2839] Third, wages and salary are exempted from garnishee proceedings.[2840] Fourth, a court should not summarily determine an application for a garnishee order when there are outstanding issues between parties that need to be fully resolved (for instance, who the judgment debt belongs to).[2841] Any payment made by a garnishee in compliance with a final order 'and any execution levied against him in pursuance of such an order, shall be a valid discharge of his liability to the judgment debtor to the extent of the amount paid or levied notwithstanding that the garnishee proceedings are subsequently set aside or the judgment or order from which they arose reversed'.[2842]

2833. Supreme Court of Judicature Act (Cap. 322, R. 5, 2014 Rev. Ed.) Rules of Court, O 49 r 4(1).
2834. Supreme Court of Judicature Act (Cap. 322, R. 5, 2014 Rev. Ed.) Rules of Court, O 49 r 4(2).
2835. Supreme Court of Judicature Act (Cap. 322, R. 5, 2014 Rev. Ed.) Rules of Court, O 49 r 6(1).
2836. Supreme Court of Judicature Act (Cap. 322, R. 5, 2014 Rev. Ed.) Rules of Court, O 49 r 1(1). *See id.*, O 49 r 1(3). *See also Singapore Civil Procedure 2015 Volume 1*, at 858 (G.P. Selvam ed., Sweet & Maxwell Asia 2014).
2837. *Asia Commercial Finance Ltd v. Udai*, [1991] 2 SLR(R) 372, [13]–[17].
2838. Supreme Court of Judicature Act (Cap. 322, R. 5, 2014 Rev. Ed.) Rules of Court, O 49 r 9(1).
2839. J. Pinsler, *Principles of Civil Procedure* 855 (Acad. Publg. 2013); *Singapore Civil Procedure 2015 Volume 1*, at 859–860 (G.P. Selvam ed., Sweet & Maxwell Asia 2014): temporary physical presence within the jurisdiction at the time of the making of the provisional order may suffice; and, if the garnishee has agreed to submit to the jurisdiction for the purposes of the garnishee proceedings, that will suffice even though he has left the jurisdiction before the provisional order is made.
2840. *American Express Bank Ltd v. Abdul Manaff bin Ahmad*, [2003] 4 SLR(R) 780, [30]–[31]. *See also* Supreme Court of Judicature Act (Cap. 322, 2007 Rev. Ed.), s 13(c). C.f. J. Pinsler, *Section 13 of the Supreme Court of Judicature Act and Enforcement Against the Judgment Debtor's Earnings*, 16 Sing. Acad. L.J. 27 (2004).
2841. *Teleoptik-Zirovskopi v. Westacre Investments Inc*, [2012] 2 SLR 177.
2842. Supreme Court of Judicature Act (Cap. 322, R. 5, 2014 Rev. Ed.) Rules of Court, O 49 r 8. For the setting aside of final garnishee orders, *see Harmonious Coretrades Pte Ltd v. United Integrated Services Pte Ltd*, [2019] 1 SLR 206.

V. Equitable Execution

764. Equitable execution is usually appropriate for judgments for payment of money, payment of money into court, and recovery of money.[2843] It is considered a less invasive form of enforcement as it does not transfer or attach to any property in favour of the judgment creditor; what happens instead is that a receiver is appointed to receive the money, and he holds it for the benefit of the judgment creditor and also preserves the judgment creditor's priority as against subsequent judgment creditors.[2844] An application for the appointment of a receiver by way of equitable execution has to be made in accordance with O 30 (the order governing receivers), and the summons for the appointment of a receiver and the order for the appointment of a receiver by way of equitable execution must be made with the prescribed forms.[2845] When an application is made for the appointment of a receiver, 'the Court in determining whether it is just or convenient that the appointment should be made shall have regard to the amount claimed by the judgment creditor, to the amount likely to be obtained by the receiver and to the probable costs of his appointment and may direct an inquiry on any of these matters or any other matter before making the appointment'.[2846] Where necessary, the court has the power 'to grant an injunction if, and only so far as, the injunction is ancillary or incidental to such an order'.[2847]

VI. Committal

765. Committal as a form of enforcing compliance with a judgment or order is a very serious matter as it may lead to a fine or even imprisonment.[2848] Accordingly, the court will only make an order of committal in such situations of contempt as a measure of last resort; other forms of enforcement should be attempted first.[2849] The rationale and procedure for obtaining an order of committal have earlier been set out and apply in respect of non-compliance with judgments and orders of court as they do to other forms of contempt. An order of committal is usually

2843. J. Pinsler, *Principles of Civil Procedure* 829–830 (Acad. Publg. 2013).
2844. J. Pinsler, *Principles of Civil Procedure* 852–853 (Acad. Publg. 2013).
2845. Supreme Court of Judicature Act (Cap. 322, R. 5, 2014 Rev. Ed.) Rules of Court, O 51 r 3.
2846. Supreme Court of Judicature Act (Cap. 322, R. 5, 2014 Rev. Ed.) Rules of Court, O 51 r 1(1).
2847. Supreme Court of Judicature Act (Cap. 322, R. 5, 2014 Rev. Ed.) Rules of Court, O 51 r 2.
2848. J. Pinsler, *Principles of Civil Procedure* 864 (Acad. Publg. 2013). Factors such as the attitude behind the contemptuous behaviour, the motive for committing the contemptuous act, the adequacy of the deterrent, the reversibility of the breach, the standard of care expected of the individual, the nature of the contemptuous act, the remorse of the contemnor, and whether others were procured to commit the contemptuous act are relevant: *Sembcorp Marine Ltd v. Aurol Anthony Sabastian*, [2013] 1 SLR 245, [68]; *Ho Seow Wan v. Ho Poey Wee*, [2015] SGHC 304, [10]. Committal to prison is also normally a measure of last resort, as a fine is often regarded as an appropriate remedy in cases where the disobedience is of a less serious nature, or where the contempt is technical in nature and did not cause substantial prejudice to either the opposing party or the due administration of justice: *Lee Shieh-Peen Clement v. Ho Chin Nguang*, [2010] 4 SLR 801, [45]; *Mok Kah Hong v. Zheng Zhuan Yao*, [2016] SGCA 8, [50].
2849. *P J Holdings Inc v. Ariel Singapore Pte Ltd*, [2009] 3 SLR(R) 582, [5], citing *Danchevsky v. Danchevsky*, [1975] 1 Fam 17, 21–22 and 24.

appropriate for judgments for payment of money, payment of money into court, possession of land, and the requirement of an act to be done or abstention of an act.[2850] However, it has been said that the 'logical ending point' where there has been non-payment of money due to impecuniosity is a winding up or bankruptcy order, as the case may be, and not an order of committal.[2851] This is because O 45 r 5(1) of the Rules of Court applies only when 'a person required by a judgment or order to do an act within a time specified in the judgment or order refuses or neglects to do it', suggesting the requirement of some element of conscious volition or fault.[2852] Where 'a party has obtained a judgment or order of court requiring a person to perform an act, and no time for its performance is fixed by the judgment or order, a further application would be necessary to set a period of time if eventual committal proceedings are contemplated'.[2853] It should be noted that the court may extend time for performing the act in question.[2854]

766. To establish committal, it is sufficient for a plaintiff to show that a defendant had committed a deliberate act that was intentionally in breach of an order of court.[2855] Although there has to be an element of culpability for a committal order to be appropriate, bad faith or deliberate disregard of the judgment or court order is not required.[2856] The reasons for non-compliance would, however, be relevant at the sentencing stage.[2857] In the case of a body corporate, an order of committal may be

---

2850. J. Pinsler, *Principles of Civil Procedure* 829–830 (Acad. Publg. 2013).

2851. *P J Holdings Inc v. Ariel Singapore Pte Ltd*, [2009] 3 SLR(R) 582, [7].

2852. *P J Holdings Inc v. Ariel Singapore Pte Ltd*, [2009] 3 SLR(R) 582, [7], citing *Re Quintin Dick*, [1926] Ch 992; *Ng Tai Tuan v. Chng Gim Huat Pte Ltd*, [1990] 2 SLR(R) 23; *In re London and Paris Banking Corporation*, (1874) LR 19 Eq 444; *DP Vijandran v. Majlis Peguam*, [1995] 2 MLJ 391; *Lowson v. Percy Main & District Social Club & Institute Ltd*, [1979] ICR 568.

2853. C. Bull & J. Pinsler, *Civil Procedure: Annual Review of Singapore Cases* [7.51] (Sing. Acad. L. 2008) citing *QU v. QV*, [2008] 2 SLR(R) 702, [19]; J. Pinsler, *Principles of Civil Procedure* 865 (Acad. Publg. 2013). The court's power to subsequently make an order requiring an act to be done within a specific time is contained in Supreme Court of Judicature Act (Cap. 322, R. 5, 2014 Rev. Ed.) Rules of Court, O 45 r 6(2). *See also Mok Kah Hong v. Zheng Zhuan Yao*, [2016] SGCA 8, [41]–[47].

2854. Supreme Court of Judicature Act (Cap. 322, R. 5, 2014 Rev. Ed.) Rules of Court, O 45 r 6(1). The procedure for such an application may be found in O 45 r 6(3).

2855. *Summit Holdings Ltd v. Business Software Alliance*, [1999] 2 SLR(R) 592, [52]–[53]; *OCM Opportunities Fund II, LP v. Burhan Uray (alias Wong Ming Kiong)*, [2005] 3 SLR(R) 60, [27]; *Ho Seow Wan v. Ho Poey Wee*, [2015] SGHC 235, [23].

2856. J. Pinsler, *Principles of Civil Procedure* 866 (Acad. Publg. 2013).

2857. *Global Distressed Alpha Fund I Ltd Partnership v. PT Bakrie Investindo*, [2013] SGHC 105, [33], citing *OCM Opportunities Fund II, LP v. Burhan Uray*, [2005] 3 SLR(R) 60, [27]; *Summit Holdings Ltd v. Business Software Alliance*, [1999] 2 SLR(R) 592, [52]–[53]. *See also Mok Kah Hong v. Zheng Zhuan Yao*, [2016] SGCA 8, [92]: 'in addressing the argument whether committal proceedings can be brought against "impecunious judgment debtors", it is crucial to bear in mind, *inter alia*, the distinction between a case where no finding has been made on the defendant's financial means and a case where a specific finding on the defendant's financial means has been determined in the course of the substantive hearing.'

enforced against 'any director or officer of the body'.[2858] Any 'director or officer' does not include a solicitor or a firm of solicitors acting in their professional capacity.[2859]

767. An order of committal may only be enforced if the following two conditions are satisfied. First: 'a copy of the order has been served personally on the person required to do or abstain from doing the act in question'; and 'in the case of an order requiring a person to do an act, the copy has been so served before the expiration of the time within which he was required to do the act'.[2860] This applies similarly to bodies corporate, in which case the service must be on the officer against whom the order of committal is sought.[2861] Second, the copy of the order must be endorsed with a penal notice that informs the person served that 'if he neglects to obey the order within the time specified therein, or, if the order is to abstain from doing an act, that if he disobeys the order, he is liable to process of execution to compel him to obey it'.[2862] An order extending or abridging time for doing an act as well as an order requiring the person to do an act if made under O 45 r 5(3) or O 45 r 6 of the Rules of Court must, where relevant, also be served.[2863] However, the court may still enforce the order requiring someone to abstain from doing an act notwithstanding that service of a copy of the order has not been properly effected if the court is satisfied that the person against whom or against whose property it is sought to enforce the order has had notice of the order either: 'by being present when the order was made'; or 'by being notified of the terms of the order, whether by telephone, telegram or otherwise'.[2864]

§3. Stay of Execution

768. Circumstances may arise after a judgment or order has been given that may justify the suspension of its execution – this is known as a stay of execution.[2865] Under the Rules of Court, 'a party against whom a judgment has been given or an order made may apply to the Court for a stay of execution of the judgment or order or other relief on the ground of matters which have occurred since the date of the judgment or order, and the Court may by order grant such relief, and on such terms,

2858. Supreme Court of Judicature Act (Cap. 322, R. 5, 2014 Rev. Ed.) Rules of Court, O 45 r 5.

2859. *Karaha Bodas Co LLC v. Pertamina Energy Trading Ltd*, [2006] 3 SLR(R) 721, [26]–[28].

2860. J. Pinsler, *Principles of Civil Procedure* 869 (Acad. Publg. 2013) citing *Sabah Gas Industries Sdn Bhd v. Trans Samudera Lines (S) Sdn Bhd*, [1993] 2 MLJ 396; *Tiu Shi Kian v. Red Rose Restaurant Sdn Bhd*, [1984] 2 MLJ 313; *Leow Seng Huat v. Low Mui Yein*, [1996] 5 MLJ 381.

2861. J. Pinsler, *Principles of Civil Procedure* 869 (Acad. Publg. 2013) citing *OCM Opportunities Fund II, LP v. Burhan Uray*, [2005] 3 SLR(R) 60.

2862. Supreme Court of Judicature Act (Cap. 322, R. 5, 2014 Rev. Ed.) Rules of Court, O 45 r 7(4).

2863. Supreme Court of Judicature Act (Cap. 322, R. 5, 2014 Rev. Ed.) Rules of Court, O 45 r 7(5).

2864. Supreme Court of Judicature Act (Cap. 322, R. 5, 2014 Rev. Ed.) Rules of Court, O 45 r 7(6). *See also Allport Alfred James v. Wong Soon Lan*, [1992] 2 SLR(R) 100.

2865. This should not be confused with stay of proceedings.

as it thinks fit'.[2866] With regard to staying an execution of a summary judgment, the court will consider the following factors: first, the degree of connection between the claim and counterclaim; second, the merits of the counterclaim; third, the financial ability of the plaintiff to satisfy any judgment on the counterclaim; and fourth, whether a stay of execution will effectively require a successfully plaintiff to wait for his money.[2867] With regard to staying an execution of a writ of seizure and sale specifically, if:

> the Court is satisfied, on an application made at the time of the judgment or order, or at any time thereafter, by the judgment debtor or other party liable to execution … that there are special circumstances which render it inexpedient to enforce the judgment or order; or … that the applicant is unable from any cause to pay the money, then … the Court may by order stay the execution of the judgment or order by writ of seizure and sale either absolutely or for such period and subject to such conditions as the Court thinks fit.[2868]

769. If such an application is not made at the time the judgment or order is given, it 'must be made by summons and may be so made notwithstanding that the party liable to execution did not enter an appearance in the action'[2869] and 'must be supported by an affidavit made by or on behalf of the applicant stating the grounds of the application and the evidence necessary to substantiate them and, in particular, where such application is made on the grounds of the applicant's inability to pay, disclosing his income, the nature and value of any property of his and the amount of any other liabilities of his'.[2870] In addition, the summons and a copy of the supporting affidavit must, 'not less than four clear days before the return day, be served on the party entitled to enforce the judgment or order'.[2871]

770. With regard to staying an execution of lump sum or instalment payments specifically, if a judgment or order is given by a District Court and 'it appears to the satisfaction of a District Court that any party to any proceedings is unable from any cause to pay any sum recovered against him (whether by way of satisfaction of the claim or counterclaim in the proceedings or by way of costs or otherwise) or any instalment thereof, the Court may, in its discretion, suspend or stay any judgment or order given or made in the proceedings for such time and on such terms as the Court

---

2866. Supreme Court of Judicature Act (Cap. 322, R. 5, 2014 Rev. Ed.) Rules of Court, O 45 r 11. *See also SAL Leasing (Pte) Ltd v. Hendmaylex Pte Ltd* [1987] SLR(R) 303, [6]; cited in *Re Shaw, ex parte Banque Indosuez*, [1989] 2 SLR(R) 668, [4].

2867. *Australian and New Zealand Banking Group Ltd v. Joseph Shihara Rukshan De Saram*, [2015] 1 SLR 625, [84]. *See also PT Sariwiguna Binasentosa v. Sindo Damai Shipping Pte Ltd*, [2015] SGHCR 20, [8]; *NK Mulisan Co Ltd v. INTL Asia Pte Ltd*, [2018] SGHC 242. In the context of an appeal, while strong grounds for an appeal would not by itself be a reason for granting a stay, little merit in the appeal is a relevant circumstance: *Standore Invest A/S v. Soh Kim Wat*, [2010] SGHC 174, [10].

2868. Supreme Court of Judicature Act (Cap. 322, R. 5, 2014 Rev. Ed.) Rules of Court, O 47 r 1(1). Such an order may be varied or revoked by a subsequent order: *id.*, O 47 r 1(5).

2869. Supreme Court of Judicature Act (Cap. 322, R. 5, 2014 Rev. Ed.) Rules of Court, O 47 r 1(2).

2870. Supreme Court of Judicature Act (Cap. 322, R. 5, 2014 Rev. Ed.) Rules of Court, O 47 r 1(3).

2871. Supreme Court of Judicature Act (Cap. 322, R. 5, 2014 Rev. Ed.) Rules of Court, O 47 r 1(4).

thinks fit, and so from time to time until it appears that the cause of inability has ceased'.[2872] In addition, for payment by instalments, 'the payment shall be made into court and no execution shall issue, except with the leave of the District Court'.[2873] Finally, it should be noted that an appeal does not operate as a stay of execution, unless the court orders a stay.[2874]

§4. Examination of Judgment Debtor

771. A person who has obtained a judgment or order for the payment of money may apply to the court for an order that the judgment debtor attend before the registrar 'and be orally examined on whatever property the judgment debtor has and wheresoever situated', and the court may also order the judgment debtor 'to produce any books or documents the possession of the judgment debtor relevant to the questions aforesaid'.[2875] Where the judgment debtor is a body corporate, an officer of the body corporate may be subject to oral examination or be ordered to produce any relevant books or documents.[2876] If a writ of seizure and sale has been issued, it is not necessary to wait for a return of the writ to be made before applying for an examination under O 48.[2877]

772. Where the judgment or order is not for money, an application may be made to the court for an order requiring the party liable to satisfy the judgment or order to attend for examination on the questions specified in the order.[2878] It has been said that the policy underlying the process of examination 'is to prevent a defendant from denying a successful plaintiff the fruits of his judgment' and can only be given effect 'if a defendant provides information about the nature and whereabouts of his assets and produces documentary evidence that are relevant on which he may be examined'.[2879] The examination of judgment debtor is not, in and of itself, a mode of execution of a judgment. It is to aid the judgment creditor in garnering additional information that might or might not result in the implementation of actual execution of the judgment concerned.[2880] Applications for examination are made by ex

---

2872. State Courts Act (Cap. 321, 2007 Rev. Ed.), s 43(2).
2873. State Courts Act (Cap. 321, 2007 Rev. Ed.), s 43(3). *See* Supreme Court of Judicature Act (Cap. 322, R. 5, 2014 Rev. Ed.) Rules of Court, O 47 rr 1A and 1B for the other procedural requirements.
2874. Supreme Court of Judicature Act (Cap. 322, 2007 Rev. Ed.), s 41; *Lian Soon Construction Pte Ltd v. Guan Qian Realty Pte Ltd*, [1999] 1 SLR(R) 1053, [13]. *See also HSBC Institutional Trust Services (Singapore) Ltd v. Picket & Rail Asia Pacific Pte Ltd*, [2010] 4 SLR 326, [7].
2875. Supreme Court of Judicature Act (Cap. 322, R. 5, 2014 Rev. Ed.) Rules of Court, O 48 r 1(1). As to whether the term 'execution' includes examination of judgment debtor, *see PT Bakrie Investindo v. Global Distressed Alpha Fund 1 Ltd Partnership*, [2013] 4 SLR 1116.
2876. Supreme Court of Judicature Act (Cap. 322, R. 5, 2014 Rev. Ed.) Rules of Court, O 48 r 1(1).
2877. *Singapore Civil Procedure 2015 Volume 1*, at 854 (G.P. Selvam ed., Sweet & Maxwell Asia 2014).
2878. Supreme Court of Judicature Act (Cap. 322, R. 5, 2014 Rev. Ed.) Rules of Court, O 48 r 2.
2879. *United Overseas Bank Ltd v. Thye Nam Loong (S) Pte Ltd*, [1994] SGHC 262.
2880. *Singapore Civil Procedure 2015 Volume 1*, at 854 (G.P. Selvam ed., Sweet & Maxwell Asia 2014) citing *PT Bakrie Investindo v. Global Distressed Alpha Fund 1 Ltd Partnership*, [2013] 4 SLR

parte summons supported by affidavit[2881] and are usually dealt with by the duty registrar.[2882] The affidavit in support must, inter alia, identify the judgment to be enforced, state that the purpose of the examination is to enable the judgment creditor to 'decide upon the methods to employ to enforce the said judgment', and state whether the judgment debtor is to produce any books or documents at the time and place appointed for examination.[2883] Once an order for examination is made, it must be served personally on the judgment debtor and on any officer of a body corporate ordered to attend for examination.[2884] In practice, a questionnaire is annexed to the copy of the order that is served, and solicitors should attempt to resolve any disputes as to the reasonableness of any question before the examination hearing.[2885]

773. If before the examination the judgment debtor is able to provide his answers to the questionnaire by way of an affidavit or a statutory declaration and counsel for the judgment creditor agrees to discharge the order for examination at the examination hearing, the judgment debtor need not attend the examination.[2886] At the examination hearing, the answered questionnaire is to be produced and received as evidence on the judgment debtor's confirmation on oath that his answers are true and correct; the judgment debtor may then be discharged or subject to further examination.[2887] In the course of the examination, any difficulty arising, including any dispute relating to the obligation of the person examined to answer any question put to him, may be determined by the court, or the court may give such directions for determining it as it thinks fit.[2888] The registrar conducting the examination will record the statements made by the judgment debtor or other person at the examination and such record shall serve as an official record of the hearing.[2889] The nature of the examination is that of the 'severest kind' of cross-examination in order to establish the judgment debtor's means and assets and the appropriate methods to enforce the judgment.[2890]

774. Under O 48 r 1, the judgment debtor will be 'orally examined on whatever property the judgment debtor has and wheresoever situated'.[2891] Since oral examination of the judgment debtor only pertains to property that the judgment debtor has,

---

1116, [16]. As to the extent to which a judgment creditor may ask questions on the historical aspect of a judgment debtor's estate, *see Pacific Harbor Advisors Pte Ltd v. Tiny Tantono*, [2015] SGHCR 3.

2881. Supreme Court of Judicature Act (Cap. 322, R. 5, 2014 Rev. Ed.) Rules of Court, O 48 r 1(1).
2882. Supreme Court Practice Directions 2013 (Part II).
2883. Supreme Court of Judicature Act (Cap. 322, R. 5, 2014 Rev. Ed.) Rules of Court, Appendix A.
2884. Supreme Court of Judicature Act (Cap. 322, R. 5, 2014 Rev. Ed.) Rules of Court, O 48 r 1(2).
2885. *Singapore Civil Procedure 2015 Volume 1*, at 854 (G.P. Selvam ed., Sweet & Maxwell Asia 2014) citing State Courts Practice Directions (Part XIII).
2886. State Courts Practice Directions (Part XIII).
2887. State Courts Practice Directions (Part XIII).
2888. Supreme Court of Judicature Act (Cap. 322, R. 5, 2014 Rev. Ed.) Rules of Court, O 48 r 1(3).
2889. Supreme Court of Judicature Act (Cap. 322, R. 5, 2014 Rev. Ed.) Rules of Court, O 38A r 1(1) and O 48 r 3.
2890. *United Overseas Bank Ltd v. Thye Nam Loong (S) Pte Ltd*, [1994] SGHC 262.
2891. Supreme Court of Judicature Act (Cap. 322, R. 5, 2014 Rev. Ed.) Rules of Court, O 38A r 1(1). *See also Sun Travels & Tours Pvt Ltd v. Hilton International Manage (Maldives) Pvt Ltd*, [2019] SGHC 291.

the judgment debtor may not be asked questions on the historical aspects of his property, i.e. prior to the date of final judgment.[2892] Oral examination of the judgment debtor may also extend to assets which are situated outside Singapore; however, the court has no jurisdiction in relation to the enforcement of proceedings in any other countries in which those assets may be situated.[2893] In a situation where an examination of judgment debtor is sought against a foreign officer of a company,[2894] whether local or foreign, the examination of judgment debtor order could be served out of jurisdiction on the foreign officer with the leave of the court.[2895] In deciding whether to grant leave, the fundamental question was whether the foreign officer was so closely connected to the substantive claim that the Singapore court was justified in taking jurisdiction over him.[2896] Costs are usually at the discretion of the examining registrar but are not usually allowed unless the judgment creditor can show that the examination was justified in the sense that it produced some fruitful information or the disclosure of some income, property or assets on which enforcement may be issued.[2897]

§5. Possibility of Appeal

775. Because 'any judgment, order or decision' of a registrar is appealable to a High Court Judge in chambers,[2898] a party will at least have one tier of appeal in respect of an order refusing leave to issue a writ of execution or an order refusing or granting an application to set aside a writ of execution. However, section 34 of the Supreme Court of Judicature Act,[2899] read together with the Fourth and Fifth Schedules of the statute, will determine whether any given order of civil procedure is appealable to the Court of Appeal or not.[2900] Due to recent amendments to the Supreme Court of Judicature Act, the law on this is currently in flux and while it has been suggested that the 'default' position is that all interlocutory applications, unless provided for statutorily, are appealable with leave,[2901] it may also be possible to argue that for interlocutory applications not expressly addressed by the Fourth and Fifth Schedules, 'an appeal to the Court of Appeal will remain as of right for

2892. *Pacific Harbor Advisors Pte Ltd v. Tiny Tantono (representative of the estate of Lim Susanto, deceased)*, [2015] SGHCR 3, [31].
2893. *Singapore Civil Procedure 2015 Volume 1*, at 855 (G.P. Selvam ed., Sweet & Maxwell Asia 2014), citing *Interpol Ltd v. Galani*, [1987] 2 All ER 981.
2894. *Burgundy Global Exploration Corp v. Transocean Offshore International*, [2014] 3 SLR 381, [82].
2895. *Burgundy Global Exploration Corp v. Transocean Offshore International*, [2014] 3 SLR 381, [88]–[92].
2896. *Burgundy Global Exploration Corp v. Transocean Offshore International*, [2014] 3 SLR 381, [112].
2897. *Singapore Civil Procedure 2015 Volume 1*, at 856 (G.P. Selvam ed., Sweet & Maxwell Asia 2014).
2898. Supreme Court of Judicature Act (Cap. 322, R. 5, 2014 Rev. Ed.) Rules of Court, O 56 r 1.
2899. (Cap. 322, 2007 Rev. Ed.).
2900. The statute was amended in 2010 and 2014.
2901. *See* E. Chua, *Defining an 'Interlocutory Application'*, Sing. L. Watch Commentaries (4/2013); D. Chi, *Clarification on Leave to Appeal Regime in Respect of Interlocutory Matters: OpenNet Pte Ltd v. Info-Communications Development Authority of Singapore [2013] SGCA 24*, Sing. L.

orders made at interlocutory applications which will finally dispose of the substantive rights of the parties'.[2902] An application for leave to issue a writ of execution or an application to set aside a writ of execution is not specifically referred to in the Fourth and Fifth Schedules. Accordingly, it is suggested that these applications should accordingly be appealable to the Court of Appeal as of right unless they may be regarded as 'interlocutory' in nature and hence falling within paragraph (e) of the Fifth Schedule.

776. Based on the indicia outlined in two recent Court of Appeal cases, it is suggested that such applications ought not to be regarded as 'interlocutory' because they are not 'made between the time a party files a civil case in court and when that case is finally heard for disposal',[2903] and more importantly they have as their only end the particular relief sought and 'once the application for such relief has been considered and ruled upon by the court, that matter ends'.[2904] In other words, an order refusing leave to issue a writ of execution or an order refusing or granting an application to set aside a writ of execution finally disposes of the substantive rights of the parties[2905] in respect of enforcement. If such an argument is not accepted, then leave may be required before an appeal is brought to the Court of Appeal.

Watch Commentaries (4/2013); C. Siyuan & E. Chua, *The Right to Appeal Against a Decision Made on an Interlocutory Application: The Immediate Aftermath of the 2010 Amendments*, 25 Sing. Acad. L.J. 424 (2013).

2902. *OpenNet Pte Ltd v. Info-Communications Development Authority of Singapore*, [2013] 2 SLR 880, [29]. *See also Dorsey James Michael v. World Sport Group Pte Ltd*, [2013] 3 SLR 354, [98].

2903. *Dorsey James Michael v. World Sport Group Pte Ltd*, [2013] 3 SLR 354, [60] (emphasis in original).

2904. *Dorsey James Michael v. World Sport Group Pte Ltd*, [2013] 3 SLR 354, [60].

2905. *OpenNet Pte Ltd v. Info-Communications Development Authority of Singapore*, [2013] 2 SLR 880, [29]. *See also Wellmix Organics (International) Pte Ltd v. Lau Yu Man*, [2006] 2 SLR(R) 525, [14].

Chapter 3. Enforcement of Foreign Judgments Locally and Domestic Judgments Abroad

§1. Introduction

777. A foreign judgment[2906] may be registered and enforced locally under the Reciprocal Enforcement of Commonwealth Judgments Act[2907] or the Reciprocal Enforcement of Foreign Judgments Act,[2908] depending on whether the foreign judgment is obtained from a country gazetted under either of these legislation. A judgment from a gazetted country would, upon successful registration, be enforceable in the forum with the same legal force as if it had been a judgment from the court of the forum. In other words, the Reciprocal Enforcement of Commonwealth Judgments Act and the Reciprocal Enforcement of Foreign Judgments Act obviate the need to commence proceedings to sue on the foreign judgment.[2909] If a foreign judgment is obtained from a country that is not gazetted under the Reciprocal Enforcement of Commonwealth Judgments Act or the Reciprocal Enforcement of Foreign Judgments Act, then one may commence a writ action in Singapore to enforce the foreign judgment under common law.[2910]

§2. Enforcement under the Reciprocal Enforcement of Commonwealth Judgments Act

778. A 'judgment' for the purposes of the Reciprocal Enforcement of Commonwealth Judgments Act is:

> any judgment or order given or made by a court in any civil proceedings … whereby any sum of money is made payable, and includes an award in proceedings on an arbitration if the award has, in pursuance of the law in force in the place where it was made, become enforceable in the same manner as a judgment given by a court in that place.[2911]

779. Where a judgment is obtained in 'a superior court of the United Kingdom of Great Britain and Northern Ireland', the judgment may be registered within twelve months after the date of judgment, or such longer time as may be allowed by the court, on application by the judgment creditor to the High Court and the application may be allowed if the court thinks it is just and convenient bearing in mind all the circumstances of the case.[2912] This has been extended to other Commonwealth jurisdictions based on reciprocity by way of notification in the gazette by the

2906. Strictly speaking, a foreign judgment cannot be enforced in Singapore. A party, in essence, is enforcing a local judgment to pay a foreign debt that has been recognized by the Singapore court.
2907. Reciprocal Enforcement of Commonwealth Judgments Act (Cap. 264, 1985 Rev. Ed.).
2908. Reciprocal Enforcement of Foreign Judgments Act (Cap. 265, 2001 Rev. Ed.).
2909. Yeo T.M., *Halsbury's Laws of Singapore*, vol. 6(2) (Singapore: LexisNexis, 2009), [75.151].
2910. *Hong Pian Tee v. Les Placements Germain Gauthier Inc*, [2002] 1 SLR(R) 515, [7].
2911. Reciprocal Enforcement of Commonwealth Judgments Act (Cap. 264, 1985 Rev. Ed.), s 2(1).
2912. Reciprocal Enforcement of Commonwealth Judgments Act (Cap. 264, 1985 Rev. Ed.), s 3(1).

minister[2913] to include the superior courts of the Commonwealth, States and Territories of Australia;[2914] Hong Kong;[2915] New Zealand; Sri Lanka; Malaysia; Wind ward Islands; Pakistan; Brunei Darussalam; Papua New Guinea; and India (except Jammu and Kashmir).[2916] Because the purpose of the Reciprocal Enforcement of Commonwealth Judgments Act is to facilitate the enforcement of Commonwealth judgments and does not state a definitive time period for registration of a judgment (the court has the discretion to permit registration after the twelve-month period from the date of judgment has lapsed), it cannot be said that a foreign judgment sought to be registered in Singapore is an implied contract and is therefore subject to Singapore rules on limitation.[2917]

780. In considering whether it is just and convenient that the judgment should be enforced in Singapore,[2918] the factors that the court will consider are: whether the delay will cause prejudice to the judgment debtor; whether the judgment creditor is able to give a reasonable explanation for its delay in applying to register the Commonwealth judgment; whether the judgment creditor has been reasonably diligent in seeking to enforce the Commonwealth judgment; and whether the judgment debtor has been obstructive.[2919] However, the threshold requirement for registering a Commonwealth judgment in Singapore is that the Commonwealth judgment must have been enforceable in its own jurisdiction.[2920] There are also restrictions to registration, for example, if the plaintiff had procured the judgment by fraud, the enforcement of the judgment would be contrary to public policy, or the proceedings leading up to the judgment breached the rules of natural justice.[2921] In respect of the exception of fraud, it should be noted that when the allegation of fraud had been considered and adjudicated upon by a competent foreign court, the foreign judgment might be challenged on the ground of fraud only where fresh evidence had come to light which reasonable diligence on the part of the defendant would not have uncovered and the fresh evidence would have been likely to make a difference

---

2913. Reciprocal Enforcement of Commonwealth Judgments Act (Cap. 264, 1985 Rev. Ed.), s 5(1).

2914. Reciprocal Enforcement of Commonwealth Judgments Act (Cap. 264, 1 Dec. 1999 Rev. Ed.), Declaration Under Section 5.

2915. For judgments obtained on or before 30 Sep. 1997. Reciprocal Enforcement of Commonwealth Judgments Act (Cap. 264, N. 1, 1999 Rev. Ed.), Reciprocal Enforcement of Commonwealth Judgments (Extension) (Consolidation) Notification, Schedule.

2916. Reciprocal Enforcement of Commonwealth Judgments Act (Cap. 264, N. 1, 1999 Rev. Ed.), Reciprocal Enforcement of Commonwealth Judgments (Extension) (Consolidation) Notification.

2917. *Westacre Investments Inc v. The State-Owned Company Yugoimport SDPR*, [2009] 2 SLR(R) 166, [4]–[5].

2918. *Westacre Investments Inc v. The State-Owned Company Yugoimport SDPR*, [2009] 2 SLR(R) 166, [21].

2919. *Westacre Investments Inc v. The State-Owned Company Yugoimport SDPR*, [2009] 2 SLR(R) 166, [24]. *See also id.*, [28].

2920. *Westacre Investments Inc v. The State-Owned Company Yugoimport SDPR*, [2009] 2 SLR(R) 166, [9].

2921. *Bellezza Club Japan Co Ltd v. Matsumura Akihiko*, [2010] 3 SLR 342, [10]–[11], citing *Hong Pian Tee v. Les Placements Germain Gauthier Inc*, [2002] 1 SLR(R) 515, [12]. *See also Poh Soon Kiat v. Desert Palace Inc (trading as Caesars Palace)*, [2010] 1 SLR 1129, [13]–[15], citing L. Collins (ed.), *Dicey, Morris and Collins on The Conflict of Laws*, 14th ed. (UK: Sweet & Maxwell, 2006), [14-202].

in the eventual result of the case.[2922] An example of a judgment contrary to public policy is a judgment whose underlying cause of action was a gambling debt.[2923] Other exceptions are as follows: the original court acted without jurisdiction; the judgment debtor neither carried on business nor was ordinarily resident within the jurisdiction of the original court and did not voluntarily appear or otherwise submit or agree to submit to the jurisdiction of that court; the judgment debtor, being the defendant in the proceedings, was not duly served with the process of the original court and did not appear, notwithstanding that he was ordinarily resident or was carrying on business within the jurisdiction of that court or agreed to submit to the jurisdiction of that court; and the judgment debtor satisfies the registering court either that an appeal is pending, or that he is entitled and intends to appeal, against the judgment.[2924]

781. The effect of registration of a Commonwealth judgment locally is that: it has the same force and effect from the date of registration as a judgment of the registering court; the registering court has the same control and jurisdiction over the judgment as it has over similar judgments given by itself in relation to execution; and the reasonable costs of and incidental to the registration of the judgment becomes recoverable as if they were sums payable under the judgment.[2925] Registration of a Commonwealth judgment may be open to challenge and being set aside if the judgment comes within any of the circumstances in which a judgment may not be registered (in accordance with the statutory requirements) or if it is not 'just or convenient' that the judgment should be enforced in Singapore.[2926] In setting aside the registration, the court may impose such terms as it thinks fit.[2927]

§3. ENFORCEMENT UNDER THE RECIPROCAL ENFORCEMENT OF FOREIGN JUDGMENTS ACT

782. As mentioned, there is also the Reciprocal Enforcement of Foreign Judgments Act.[2928] A 'judgment' under this statute means 'a judgment or order given or made by a court in any civil proceedings, or a judgment or order given or made by a court in any criminal proceedings for the payment of a sum of money in respect

---

2922. *Hong Pian Tee v. Les Placements Germain Gauthier Inc*, [2002] 1 SLR(R) 515, [30].
2923. *Poh Soon Kiat v. Desert Palace Inc (trading as Caesars Palace)*, [2010] 1 SLR 1129, [120]; Civil Law Act (Cap. 43, 1999 Rev. Ed.), s 5(2). The Court of Appeal held that insofar as the earlier decisions of *Star City Pty Ltd v. Tan Hong Woon*, [2002] 1 SLR(R) 306 and *Liao Eng Kiat v. Burswood Nominees Ltd*, [2004] 4 SLR(R) 690 suggested that gambling per se was no longer contrary to the public interest of Singapore because the legislature had allowed for various types of legalized gambling, this could not be supported as it only meant that regulated gambling was not contrary to public policy, and there had been nothing to indicate a detraction from the general policy encapsulated in Civil Law Act (Cap. 43, 1999 Rev. Ed.), s 5.
2924. Reciprocal Enforcement of Commonwealth Judgments Act (Cap. 264, 1985 Rev. Ed.), s 3(2).
2925. Reciprocal Enforcement of Commonwealth Judgments Act (Cap. 264, 1985 Rev. Ed.), s 3(3).
2926. J. Pinsler, *Principles of Civil Procedure* 898 (Acad. Publg. 2013); Reciprocal Enforcement of Commonwealth Judgments Act (Cap. 264, 1985 Rev. Ed.), s 3(2).
2927. Supreme Court of Judicature Act (Cap. 322, R. 5, 2014 Rev. Ed.) Rules of Court, O 67 r 9(3).
2928. (Cap. 265, 2001 Rev. Ed.).

of compensation or damages to an injured party'.[2929] This definition differs from that under the Reciprocal Enforcement of Commonwealth Judgments Act in that it is not limited only to judgments or orders in civil proceedings, and it does not include a reference to an arbitration award.[2930] The foreign judgments of a superior court may be enforced in Singapore by the order of minister if he is satisfied that 'substantial reciprocity of treatment will be assured', with such order being published in the gazette.[2931] Thus far, there is only one jurisdiction gazetted – the Hong Kong Special Administrative Region of the People's Republic of China, and its Court of Final Appeal and High Court have been deemed superior courts for the purposes of the Reciprocal Enforcement of Foreign Judgments Act.[2932] To be registered, the foreign judgment in question must satisfy the following threshold criteria: it is not a judgment of a superior court given on appeal from a court which is not a superior court; it is final and conclusive as between the parties; a sum of money is payable under the judgment which is not in respect of taxes or other charges of a like nature or in respect of a fine or other penalty; and it is given after the coming into operation of the order extending registration to that foreign country.[2933]

783. Unlike under the Reciprocal Enforcement of Commonwealth Judgments Act, a judgment under the Reciprocal Enforcement of Foreign Judgments Act 'shall be deemed to be final and conclusive notwithstanding that an appeal may be pending against it, or that it may still be subject to appeal, in the courts of the country of the original court'.[2934] Nevertheless, it should be noted that where it is just to do so, a court may set aside the registration of a foreign judgment where it is satisfied that an appeal is pending or that a judgment debtor is entitled to appeal and intends to do so.[2935] The conditions for applying for registration under the Reciprocal Enforcement of Foreign Judgments Act also differ from those under the Reciprocal Enforcement of Commonwealth Judgments Act in that there is a fixed time period within which the application must be brought – within six years after the date of judgment, or where there have been proceedings by way of appeal against the judgment, after the date of the last judgment given in those proceedings.[2936] Similar to the Reciprocal Enforcement of Commonwealth Judgments Act, a judgment to be registered under the Reciprocal Enforcement of Foreign Judgments Act must also be enforceable by execution in the country of the original court.[2937] In addition, it cannot have been wholly satisfied.[2938] Where it has been partly satisfied, the judgment can only be registered in respect of the balance remaining payable at the date

2929. Reciprocal Enforcement of Foreign Judgments Act (Cap. 265, 2001 Rev. Ed.), s 2(1).
2930. It does, however, encompass judgments based on arbitration awards. J. Pinsler, *Principles of Civil Procedure* 885 (Acad. Publg. 2013).
2931. Reciprocal Enforcement of Foreign Judgments Act (Cap. 265, 2001 Rev. Ed.), s 3(1).
2932. Reciprocal Enforcement of Foreign Judgments Act (Cap. 265, O. 1, 2001 Rev. Ed.), Reciprocal Enforcement of Foreign Judgments (Hong Kong Special Administrative Region of the People's Republic of China) Order.
2933. Reciprocal Enforcement of Foreign Judgments Act (Cap. 265, 2001 Rev. Ed.), s 3(2).
2934. Reciprocal Enforcement of Foreign Judgments Act (Cap. 265, 2001 Rev. Ed.), s 3(3).
2935. Reciprocal Enforcement of Foreign Judgments Act (Cap. 265, 2001 Rev. Ed.), s 6(1).
2936. Reciprocal Enforcement of Foreign Judgments Act (Cap. 265, 2001 Rev. Ed.), s 4(1).
2937. Reciprocal Enforcement of Foreign Judgments Act (Cap. 265, 2001 Rev. Ed.), s 4(3).
2938. Reciprocal Enforcement of Foreign Judgments Act (Cap. 265, 2001 Rev. Ed.), s 4(3).

of the application for registration.[2939] If it is registered for the whole sum despite having been partly satisfied as at the date of the registration application, then the registration is liable to be set aside; however, the registering court shall, on the application of the judgment creditor, order judgment to be registered for the balance remaining payable at that date.[2940]

784. The effect of registering a judgment is as follows:[2941]

(a) a registered judgment shall, for the purposes of execution, be of the same force and effect;
(b) proceedings may be taken on a registered judgment;
(c) the sum for which a judgment is registered shall carry interest; and
(d) the registering court shall have the same control over the execution of a registered judgment, as if the judgment had been a judgment originally given in the registering court and entered on the date of registration.

785. In this regard, the term 'proceedings' has been interpreted to include the initiation of bankruptcy proceedings.[2942] Notably, the Reciprocal Enforcement of Foreign Judgments Act may be extended to a Commonwealth country and where this is so, some of its provisions are modified.[2943] Another feature of the Reciprocal Enforcement of Foreign Judgments Act not present in the Reciprocal Enforcement of Commonwealth Judgments Act is that it provides for recognition of a foreign judgment even if it cannot be registered. This means that the foreign judgment is treated by the Singapore courts as conclusive between the parties for proceedings founded on the same cause of action and may be relied on by way of defence or counterclaim.[2944] However, recognition will not be extended in certain situations:

(a) where the judgment has been registered and the registration thereof has been set aside on some ground other than:
   (1) that a sum of money was not payable under the judgment;
   (2) that the judgment had been wholly or partly satisfied; or
   (3) that at the date of the application the judgment could not be enforced by execution in the country of the original court; or
(a) where the judgment has not been registered, it is shown (whether it could have been registered or not) that if it had been registered the registration thereof would have been set aside on an application for that purpose on some ground other than one of the grounds specified in paragraph(a).[2945]

2939. Reciprocal Enforcement of Foreign Judgments Act (Cap. 265, 2001 Rev. Ed.), s 4(6).
2940. Reciprocal Enforcement of Foreign Judgments Act (Cap. 265, 2001 Rev. Ed.), s 6(3).
2941. Reciprocal Enforcement of Foreign Judgments Act (Cap. 265, 2001 Rev. Ed.), s 4(4).
2942. J. Pinsler, *Principles of Civil Procedure* 896 (Acad. Publg. 2013) citing *Re Tan Patrick, ex parte Walter Peak Resorts Ltd*, [1994] 2 SLR(R) 379; *Re A Judgment Debtor*, [1939] 1 All ER 1.
2943. Reciprocal Enforcement of Foreign Judgments Act (Cap. 265, 2001 Rev. Ed.), s 10.
2944. Reciprocal Enforcement of Foreign Judgments Act (Cap. 265, 2001 Rev. Ed.), s 11(1).
2945. Reciprocal Enforcement of Foreign Judgments Act (Cap. 265, 2001 Rev. Ed.), s 11(2).

786. As alluded to earlier, registration of a foreign judgment is liable to be set aside under the Reciprocal Enforcement of Foreign Judgments Act as it is under the Reciprocal Enforcement of Commonwealth Judgments Act. However, the former takes a different approach from the latter by providing for categories of circumstances in which registration must be set aside and others in which the court has discretion to set aside.[2946] The circumstances in which a foreign judgment must be set aside are as follows: the judgment is not a 'judgment' within the meaning of the Reciprocal Enforcement of Foreign Judgments Act or contravened the registration provisions;[2947] the courts of the country of the original court had no jurisdiction in the circumstances of the case; the judgment debtor did not receive notice of the original proceedings in sufficient time to enable him to defend them and did not appear; the judgment was obtained by fraud; the enforcement of the judgment would be contrary to public policy in the country of the registering court; or the rights under the judgment are not vested in the person by whom the application for registration was made.[2948]

787. In respect of when the courts of the country of the original court may be deemed as having jurisdiction or not, the Reciprocal Enforcement of Foreign Judgments Act contains detailed stipulations distinguishing between judgments given in an action in personam and one in rem.[2949] There are two circumstances in which the court has discretion as to whether it wants to set aside registration. First, 'the registering court is satisfied that the matter in dispute in the proceedings in the original court had before the date of the judgment in the original court been the subject of a final and conclusive judgment by a court having jurisdiction in the matter'.[2950] Second and in the alternative, 'the applicant satisfies the registering court either that an appeal is pending, or that he is entitled and intends to appeal, against the judgment'.[2951] Where the second basis is made out, the court may set aside the registration or adjourn it until 'after the expiration of such period as appears to the court to be reasonably sufficient to enable the applicant to take the necessary steps to have the appeal disposed of by the competent tribunal'.[2952] Where a foreign judgment is set aside on this second basis or solely for the reason that the judgment was not at the date of the application for registration enforceable by execution in the country of the original court, a further application to register the judgment may be made in future when the appeal has been disposed of or if and when the judgment becomes enforceable by execution in that country, as the case may be.[2953] Although the Reciprocal Enforcement of Foreign Judgments Act specify in detail the circumstances in which registration may be set aside, it has been observed that these

2946. J. Pinsler, *Principles of Civil Procedure* 905 (Acad. Publg. 2013).
2947. *See* Reciprocal Enforcement of Foreign Judgments Act (Cap. 265, 2001 Rev. Ed.), ss 3–4.
2948. Reciprocal Enforcement of Foreign Judgments Act (Cap. 265, 2001 Rev. Ed.), s 5(1).
2949. Reciprocal Enforcement of Foreign Judgments Act (Cap. 265, 2001 Rev. Ed.), ss 5(2)–(3).
2950. Reciprocal Enforcement of Foreign Judgments Act (Cap. 265, 2001 Rev. Ed.), s 5(1).
2951. Reciprocal Enforcement of Foreign Judgments Act (Cap. 265, 2001 Rev. Ed.), s 6(1).
2952. Reciprocal Enforcement of Foreign Judgments Act (Cap. 265, 2001 Rev. Ed.), s 6(1).
2953. Reciprocal Enforcement of Foreign Judgments Act (Cap. 265, 2001 Rev. Ed.), s 6(2).

'should not be regarded as excluding the court's discretion to set aside a registration in the interest of justice or on the basis of a serious procedural irregularity'.[2954]

§4. Enforcement under Common Law

788. A foreign judgment may also be enforced under common law; such enforcement creates a 'fresh obligation to pay the judgment debt which is an independent obligation, distinct from the cause of action underlying the foreign judgment'.[2955] A foreign judgment (in personam) from a foreign court of law, which is final and conclusive on the merits of the case for a fixed or ascertainable sum of money may be enforced by action under common law, provided the foreign court was internally competent, had international jurisdiction over the party sought to be bound, and there are no relevant defences available.[2956]

789. First, a judgment must be pronounced by a court of law. While 'court of law' has not been defined, it has been suggested that what matters is not the labels attached to the tribunal, but the tribunal's competence.[2957] Second, a judgment must be regarded as final and conclusive under the laws of the originating jurisdiction. This means that the judgment must be res judicata between the parties under the law through the final determination of rights between the parties.[2958] Therefore, a judgment is not final and conclusive if it can be reopened by the same tribunal, or if the tribunal can abrogate or alter its terms,[2959] or if there is another body (not being an appellate court or supervisory body) that can override the tribunal's decision.[2960] Whether the judgment was intended to be final and conclusive is critical.[2961] Third, the judgment has to be a decision on the merits of the case. This is satisfied if the foreign court had held that it had jurisdiction on the cause of action and its judgment on that cause of action is one that cannot be varied, reopened, or set aside by the court (although it may be subject to appeal).[2962] A foreign judgment on the merits is distinguishable from a foreign judgment on the rules of procedure; at the same

2954. J. Pinsler, *Principles of Civil Procedure* 907 (Acad. Publg. 2013). These may include, for example, non-compliance with the Reciprocal Enforcement of Foreign Judgments Act (Cap. 265, 2001 Rev. Ed.), s 4, that are not apparent at the time of the application for registration or a breach of the applicant's obligation to make full and frank disclosure.
2955. *Alberto Justo Rodriguez Licea v. Curacao Drydock Co, Inc*, [2015] SGHC 136, [21] citing *Ralli v. Angullia*, [1917] SSLR 33. *See also Hong Pian Tee v. Les Placements Germain Gauthier Inc*, [2002] 1 SLR(R) 515, [30].
2956. Yeo T.M., *Halsbury's Laws of Singapore*, vol. 6(2) (Singapore: LexisNexis, 2009), [75.146] citing *Poh Soon Kiat v. Desert Palace Inc (trading as Caesars Palace)*, [2010] 1 SLR 1129.
2957. Yeo T.M., *Halsbury's Laws of Singapore*, vol. 6(2) (Singapore: LexisNexis, 2009), [75.155] citing *The Rainbow Joy*, [2005] 3 SLR 719, [18]; *Muttiah v. Cheng Kiam Ho*, [1933] SSLR 392, 393.
2958. *Murakami Takako (executrix of the estate of Takashi Murakami Suroso, deceased) v. Wiryadi Louise Maria*, [2007] 4 SLR(R) 565, [51].
2959. *Humpuss Sea Transport Pte Ltd (in compulsory liquidation) v. PT Humpuss Intermoda Transportasi TBK and another* [2016] 5 SLR 1322, [78].
2960. Yeo T.M., *Halsbury's Laws of Singapore*, vol. 6(2) (Singapore: LexisNexis, 2009), [75.157].
2961. *Humpuss Sea Transport Pte Ltd (in compulsory liquidation) v. PT Humpuss Intermoda Transportasi TBK and another* [2016] 5 SLR 1322, [77].
2962. *The Sennar (No 2)*, [1985] 1 WLR 490, 494 and 499.

time, while a decision on procedure alone is not a decision on the merits, a judgement is still on the merits of the case even if the plaintiff won the case as a result of the defendant's failure to appear or enter a defence or to discharge the burden of proving a point.[2963] Fourth, the judgment must be for a fixed or ascertainable sum of money. As regards as to the quantum, a foreign judgment that is objectionable in part, may be severed and the unobjectionable parts enforced, if the unobjectionable part could be clearly identified and separated from the objectionable part.[2964] Fifth, the foreign court must be internally competent. This means that it must have the jurisdiction to make a decision that is binding on the party sought to be bound and it must have subject matter jurisdiction over the dispute in question.[2965] Finally, the foreign court must have international jurisdiction over the party sought to be bound. In general, a foreign court may establish international jurisdiction through one of the three following ways: (a) if the party sought to be bound was a resident; (b) or present, in the foreign country at the time of proceedings commenced; (c) or if that party had voluntarily submitted to the jurisdiction of the foreign court.[2966]

§5. Procedural Aspects of Reciprocal Enforcement of Judgments Pursuant to Legislation

790. The procedural rules applicable to the enforcement of judgments whether under the Reciprocal Enforcement of Commonwealth Judgments Act or under the Reciprocal Enforcement of Foreign Judgments Act are the same. The application for registration in the High Court must be made by ex parte originating summons.[2967] The summons must be supported by an affidavit: exhibiting the judgment or an authenticated copy of it;[2968] stating the name, trade or business and the usual or last known place of abode or business of the judgment creditor and the judgment debtor respectively;[2969] stating to the best of the information or belief of the deponent that the judgment creditor is entitled to enforce the judgment, and that the judgment has not been satisfied or the amount in respect of which it remains unsatisfied.[2970] Additionally, where the judgment is sought to be registered under the Reciprocal Enforcement of Commonwealth Judgments Act, the affidavit must also state to the best of the information or belief of the deponent that the judgment does not fall within any of the cases in which a judgment may not be registered.[2971] Where the application is made under the Reciprocal Enforcement of Foreign Judgments Act, then the affidavit must also state that to the best of the information or belief of the

2963. Yeo T.M., *Halsbury's Laws of Singapore*, vol. 6(2) (Singapore: LexisNexis, 2009), [75.162].
2964. *Alberto Justo Rodriguez Licea v. Curacao Drydock Co, Inc*, [2015] SGHC 136, [28].
2965. Yeo T.M., *Halsbury's Laws of Singapore*, vol. 6(2) (Singapore: LexisNexis, 2009), [75.196].
2966. Yeo T.M., *Halsbury's Laws of Singapore*, vol. 6(2) (Singapore: LexisNexis, 2009), [75.170]–[75.188].
2967. Supreme Court of Judicature Act (Cap. 322, R. 5, 2014 Rev. Ed.) Rules of Court, O 67 r 2.
2968. *See also* Supreme Court of Judicature Act (Cap. 322, R. 5, 2014 Rev. Ed.) Rules of Court, O 67 r 3(1).
2969. *See also* Supreme Court of Judicature Act (Cap. 322, R. 5, 2014 Rev. Ed.) Rules of Court, O 67 r 3(1).
2970. Supreme Court of Judicature Act (Cap. 322, R. 5, 2014 Rev. Ed.) Rules of Court, O 67 r 3(1).
2971. Supreme Court of Judicature Act (Cap. 322, R. 5, 2014 Rev. Ed.) Rules of Court, O 67 r 3(1).

deponent, at the date of the application the judgment can be enforced by execution in the country of the original court and that, if it were registered, the registration would not be, or be liable to be, set aside; as well as specify the amount of interest, if any, which under the law of the country of the original court has become due under the judgment up to the time of registration.[2972] Further, where a judgment sought to be enforced under the Reciprocal Enforcement of Foreign Judgments Act is in respect of different matters, and some, but not all, of the provisions of the judgment are such that if those provisions had been contained in separate judgments, those judgments could properly have been registered, the affidavit must state the provisions in respect of which it is sought to register the judgment.[2973] Finally, the affidavit in support of an application under the Reciprocal Enforcement of Foreign Judgments Act must be accompanied by 'such other evidence with respect to the enforceability of the judgment by execution in the country of the original court, and of the law of that country under which any interest has become due under the judgment, as may be required' by the order of the Minister made under the Reciprocal Enforcement of Foreign Judgments Act.[2974]

791. It should be noted that the court has the discretion to order the judgment creditor to give security for costs of the application for registration and of any proceedings which may be brought to set aside the registration.[2975] If the court gives leave for the registration of the foreign judgment, an order must be drawn up by, or on behalf of, the judgment creditor and served on the judgment debtor.[2976] The order must state the period within which an application may be made to set aside the registration and contain a notification that execution on the judgment will not issue until after the expiration of that period.[2977] After the foreign judgment is registered, a notice of registration is required to be served on the judgment debtor personally unless the court otherwise orders.[2978] Where the judgment debtor is out of the jurisdiction, service may be effected out of jurisdiction without leave of court through the means stipulated in the Rules of Court.[2979] The notice of registration must contain the following information: 'full particulars of the judgment registered and the order for registration'; 'the name and address of the judgment creditor or of his solicitor on whom, and at which, any summons issued by the judgment debtor may be served'; 'the right of the judgment debtor to apply to have the registration set

2972. Supreme Court of Judicature Act (Cap. 322, R. 5, 2014 Rev. Ed.) Rules of Court, O 67 r 3(1).
2973. Supreme Court of Judicature Act (Cap. 322, R. 5, 2014 Rev. Ed.) Rules of Court, O 67 r 3(3).
2974. Supreme Court of Judicature Act (Cap. 322, R. 5, 2014 Rev. Ed.) Rules of Court, O 67 r 3(4).
2975. Supreme Court of Judicature Act (Cap. 322, R. 5, 2014 Rev. Ed.) Rules of Court, O 67 r 4. This is, however, subject to any notification or order made under the Reciprocal Enforcement of Commonwealth Judgments Act and Reciprocal Enforcement of Foreign Judgments Act, respectively.
2976. Supreme Court of Judicature Act (Cap. 322, R. 5, 2014 Rev. Ed.) Rules of Court, O 67 r 5(1) and Appendix A.
2977. Supreme Court of Judicature Act (Cap. 322, R. 5, 2014 Rev. Ed.) Rules of Court, O 67 r 5(2). The court may, on application before the expiration of the time period for setting aside the registration, extend the period within which the setting aside application may be made: Supreme Court of Judicature Act (Cap. 322, R. 5, 2014 Rev. Ed.) Rules of Court, O 67 r 5(3).
2978. Supreme Court of Judicature Act (Cap. 322, R. 5, 2014 Rev. Ed.) Rules of Court, O 67 r 7(1).
2979. Supreme Court of Judicature Act (Cap. 322, R. 5, 2014 Rev. Ed.) Rules of Court, O 67 r 7(1)–(2). *See also id.*, O 11 rr 3–4 and 6.

aside'; and 'the period within which an application to set aside the registration may be made'.[2980] Within three days after service of the notice of registration, or such longer period as the court may 'in special circumstances' allow, the notice or a copy of it must be 'endorsed by the person who served it with the day of the week and date on which it was served', failing which, the judgment creditor may not issue execution on that judgment without the leave of court.[2981]

792. An application to set aside registration of a foreign judgment must be made by summons supported by an affidavit.[2982] On hearing the setting aside application, the court may order any issue between the judgment creditor and the judgment debtor to be tried, and in respect of a judgment registered under the Reciprocal Enforcement of Commonwealth Judgments Act, it may set aside the registration on such terms as it thinks fit where it: 'is satisfied that the judgment falls within any of the cases in which a judgment may not be ordered to be registered … or that it is not just or convenient that the judgment should be enforced in Singapore or that there is some other sufficient reason for setting aside the registration'.[2983] Execution on the registered foreign judgment may only be issued after the expiration of the time period (or extended time period allowed by the court) for a setting aside application to be made has passed; and where a setting aside application is made, not until the setting aside application is 'finally determined'.[2984] The process for issuing execution on a registered foreign judgment involves producing to the Sheriff an affidavit of service of the notice of registration of the judgment and any order made by the court in relation to the judgment.[2985]

§6. Action on a Foreign Judgment Debt

793. Ordinarily, registration of a foreign judgment offers the judgment creditor 'a more practical, swifter and less expensive mechanism for effectuating his remedy relative to a fresh action brought on the basis of a judgment debt'.[2986] However, registration may not be available and where this is so, the judgment creditor would have to sue on the judgment debt under common law by filing the appropriate originating process in the appropriate Singapore court. Such an action is an action on an implied debt and will be subject to a limitation period of six years.[2987] It should be noted that the right to bring a common law action for a judgment debt is not always available. Such a right does not arise where the judgment falls within the ambit of

2980. Supreme Court of Judicature Act (Cap. 322, R. 5, 2014 Rev. Ed.) Rules of Court, O 67 r 7(3).
2981. Supreme Court of Judicature Act (Cap. 322, R. 5, 2014 Rev. Ed.) Rules of Court, O 67 r 8.
2982. Supreme Court of Judicature Act (Cap. 322, R. 5, 2014 Rev. Ed.) Rules of Court, O 67 r 9(1).
2983. Supreme Court of Judicature Act (Cap. 322, R. 5, 2014 Rev. Ed.) Rules of Court, O 67 r 9(2)–(3).
2984. Supreme Court of Judicature Act (Cap. 322, R. 5, 2014 Rev. Ed.) Rules of Court, O 67 r 10(1)–(2).
2985. Supreme Court of Judicature Act (Cap. 322, R. 5, 2014 Rev. Ed.) Rules of Court, O 67 r 10(3).
2986. J. Pinsler, *Principles of Civil Procedure* 885 (Acad. Publg. 2013).
2987. Limitation Act (Cap. 163, 1996 Rev. Ed.), s 6(1) *Poh Soon Kiat v. Desert Palace Inc (trading as Caesars Palace)*, [2010] 1 SLR 1129, [54].

the Reciprocal Enforcement of Foreign Judgments Act – where this is so, only registration will be entertained by any court in Singapore.[2988]

§7. Enforcement of Local Judgments Abroad

794. On the basis of the Reciprocal Enforcement of Commonwealth Judgments Act and the Reciprocal Enforcement of Foreign Judgments Act, a foreign court in a country with which Singapore has a reciprocal arrangement will also permit registration and enforcement of Singapore judgments abroad. Accordingly, both pieces of legislation prescribe a process by which a judgment creditor may obtain a certified copy of the judgment from the Singapore High Court.[2989] The process is similar to the extent that the application for the certified copy of the Singapore judgment must be made by ex parte summons to the Registrar supported by an affidavit,[2990] and that the certified copy of the Singapore judgment is sealed with the seal of the Supreme Court.[2991] However, there are some differences. The first difference is in respect of the supporting affidavit to the application for the certified copy of the judgment. Under the Reciprocal Enforcement of Commonwealth Judgments Act, the affidavit must give particulars of the judgment, show that the judgment debtor is resident in the territory to which the Act extends and state the name, trade or business and the usual or last known place of abode of the judgment creditor and the judgment debtor respectively, so far as known to the deponent.[2992] Under the Reciprocal Enforcement of Foreign Judgments Act, the affidavit must:

(a) give particulars of the proceedings in which the judgment was obtained;
(b) have annexed to it a copy of the writ or originating summons by which the proceedings were begun, the evidence of service thereof on, or appearance by, the defendant, copies of the pleadings, if any, and a statement of the grounds on which the judgment was based;
(c) state whether the defendant did or did not object to the jurisdiction, and, if so, on what grounds;
(d) show that the judgment is not subject to any stay of execution;
(e) state that the time for appealing has expired or, as the case may be, the date on which it will expire and in either case whether notice of appeal against the judgment has been entered; and
(f) state the rate at which the judgment carries interest.[2993]

795. The second difference is in respect of the documents accompanying the certified copy of the judgment. Under the Reciprocal Enforcement of Commonwealth

2988. Reciprocal Enforcement of Foreign Judgments Act (Cap. 265, 2001 Rev. Ed.), s 7(1).
2989. Reciprocal Enforcement of Commonwealth Judgments Act (Cap. 264, 1985 Rev. Ed.), s 4; Reciprocal Enforcement of Foreign Judgments Act (Cap. 265, 2001 Rev. Ed.), s 13.
2990. Supreme Court of Judicature Act (Cap. 322, R. 5, 2014 Rev. Ed.) Rules of Court, O 67 r 13(1).
2991. Supreme Court of Judicature Act (Cap. 322, R. 5, 2014 Rev. Ed.) Rules of Court, O 67 rr 13(4)–(5).
2992. Supreme Court of Judicature Act (Cap. 322, R. 5, 2014 Rev. Ed.) Rules of Court, O 67 r 13(2).
2993. Supreme Court of Judicature Act (Cap. 322, R. 5, 2014 Rev. Ed.) Rules of Court, O 67 r 13(3).

Judgments Act, the certified copy of a judgment is accompanied by a certificate signed by the Registrar certifying that the copy is a true copy of a judgment obtained in the High Court in Singapore and stating the rate at which the judgment carries interest.[2994] Under the Reciprocal Enforcement of Foreign Judgments Act, the certified copy of a judgment is annexed with a copy of the originating process, and accompanied by a certificate signed by the Registrar certifying that the judgment is a true copy of a judgment obtained in the High Court in Singapore and stating:

(a) the manner in which the writ or such summons was served on the defendant or that the defendant appeared thereto;
(b) what objections, if any, were made to the jurisdiction;
(c) what pleadings, if any, were served;
(d) the grounds on which the judgment was based;
(e) that the time for appealing has expired or, as the case may be, the date on which it will expire;
(f) whether notice of appeal against the judgment has been entered;
(g) such other particulars as it may be necessary to give to the court in the foreign country in which it is sought to obtain execution of the judgment; and
(h) the rate at which the judgment carries interest.

796. It has been observed that the requirements under the Reciprocal Enforcement of Foreign Judgments Act are more extensive than those applicable to the Reciprocal Enforcement of Commonwealth Judgments Act.[2995] Further, it is legislatively prescribed that where execution of a judgment is stayed for any period pending an appeal or for any other reason, an application shall not be made for the issue of a certified copy of a judgment under the Reciprocal Enforcement of Foreign Judgments Act until the expiration of that period.[2996] There is no similar restriction under the Reciprocal Enforcement of Commonwealth Judgments Act. Nonetheless, it has been argued that it may be possible for the court to refuse certification on the basis that the judgment is not ready for enforcement or to set aside the certificate on the basis of the court's inherent jurisdiction to prevent injustice.[2997] However, this is an untested proposition. Upon obtaining the certified copy of the local judgment, the judgment creditor will then have to comply with all the procedural requirements in the foreign jurisdiction. Otherwise, he has to risk a stay of execution being granted in respect of the order for registration.[2998]

2994. Supreme Court of Judicature Act (Cap. 322, R. 5, 2014 Rev. Ed.) Rules of Court, O 67 r 13(4).
2995. J. Pinsler, *Principles of Civil Procedure* 911 (Acad. Publg. 2013).
2996. Reciprocal Enforcement of Foreign Judgments Act (Cap. 265, 2001 Rev. Ed.), s 13(2).
2997. J. Pinsler, *Principles of Civil Procedure* 911–912 (Acad. Publg. 2013).
2998. J. Pinsler, *Principles of Civil Procedure* 912 (Acad. Publg. 2013) citing *Ngan Chin Wen v. Panin International Credit (S) Pte Ltd*, [2003] MLJ 279.

§8. POSSIBILITY OF APPEAL

797. Because 'any judgment, order or decision' of a registrar is appealable to a High Court Judge in chambers,[2999] a party will at least have one tier of appeal in respect of an application to register a foreign judgment in the High Court or to set aside such registration. However, section 34 of the Supreme Court of Judicature Act,[3000] read together with the Fourth and Fifth Schedules of the statute, will determine whether any given order of civil procedure is appealable to the Court of Appeal or not.[3001] Due to recent amendments to the Supreme Court of Judicature Act, the law on this is currently in flux and while it has been suggested that the 'default' position is that all interlocutory applications, unless provided for statutorily, are appealable with leave,[3002] it may also be possible to argue that for interlocutory applications not expressly addressed by the Fourth and Fifth Schedules, 'an appeal to the Court of Appeal will remain as of right for orders made at interlocutory applications which will finally dispose of the substantive rights of the parties'.[3003] It is suggested that an analogy may be drawn between an order refusing or granting leave to register a foreign judgment and an order refusing or granting leave in an application for leave to administer pre-action interrogatories, which the Court of Appeal has held to be appealable as of right to the Court of Appeal.[3004] This is because, similar to an application for leave to administer pre-action interrogatories, an application for leave to register a foreign judgment should not be regarded as an interlocutory application within the meaning of the Fifth Schedule of the Supreme Court of Judicature Act. It is brought by originating summons and 'is not an application made between the time a party files a civil case in court and when that case is finally heard for disposal'.[3005] Additionally, it has as its only end the particular relief sought and 'once the application for such relief has been considered and ruled upon by the court, that matter ends'.[3006] Accordingly, a High Court's order refusing or giving leave to register a foreign judgment should be appealable as of right to the Court of Appeal. In respect of a High Court's order refusing or agreeing to set aside a registration, although it is brought by way of summons rather than originating

2999. Supreme Court of Judicature Act (Cap. 322, R. 5, 2014 Rev. Ed.) Rules of Court, O 56 r 1.
3000. (Cap. 322, 2007 Rev. Ed.).
3001. The statute was amended in 2010 and 2014.
3002. *See* E. Chua, *Defining an 'Interlocutory Application'*, Sing. L. Watch Commentaries (4/2013); D. Chi, *Clarification on Leave to Appeal Regime in Respect of Interlocutory Matters: OpenNet Pte Ltd v. Info-Communications Development Authority of Singapore [2013] SGCA 24*, Sing. L. Watch Commentaries (4/2013); C. Siyuan & E. Chua, *The Right to Appeal Against a Decision Made on an Interlocutory Application: The Immediate Aftermath of the 2010 Amendments*, 25 Sing. Acad. L.J. 424 (2013).
3003. *OpenNet Pte Ltd v. Info-Communications Development Authority of Singapore*, [2013] 2 SLR 880, [29]. *See also Dorsey James Michael v. World Sport Group Pte Ltd*, [2013] 3 SLR 354, [98]. On the other hand, where the statute has made it clear that there is no appeal as of right, one is precluded from arguing that substantive rights have been engaged: *Kosui Singapore Pte Ltd v. Thangavelu*, [2016] 2 SLR 105, [28]–[29].
3004. *Dorsey James Michael v. World Sport Group Pte Ltd*, [2013] 3 SLR 354.
3005. *Dorsey James Michael v. World Sport Group Pte Ltd*, [2013] 3 SLR 354, [60] (emphasis in original).
3006. *Dorsey James Michael v. World Sport Group Pte Ltd*, [2013] 3 SLR 354, [60].

summons, it may similarly be argued that it should not be regarded as 'interlocutory' in nature because the High Court's order will finally dispose of the matter. If such an argument is not accepted, then leave may be required before an appeal is brought to the Court of Appeal.

Part X. Arbitration

Chapter 1. Arbitrability

798. Any dispute which the parties have agreed to submit to arbitration under an arbitration agreement can be determined by arbitration, unless it is contrary to public policy to do so. This principle is enshrined in the International Arbitration Act,[3007] and is likely to also apply to arbitrations governed by the domestic Arbitration Act. It has been held by the Singapore Court of Appeal that claims pursuant to section 216 of the Companies Act of oppressive or unfairly prejudicial treatment of a minority shareholder are arbitrable as section 216 is concerned with protecting the commercial expectations of parties and not with furthering any public interest.[3008]

3007. International Arbitration Act (Cap. 143A, 2002 Rev. Ed.), s 11.

3008. *See Tomolugen Holdings Ltd v. Silica Investors Ltd*, [2016] 1 SLR 373, [88]. Although the Singapore High Court in *Maniach Pte Ltd v. L Capital Jones Ltd*, [2016] SGHC 65 appears to have come to a different conclusion in a later decision, the judgment of the court cites the lower court's decision in *Silica Investors Ltd v. Tomolugen Holdings Ltd*, [2014] 3 SLR 815 instead of the Court of Appeal decision of *Tomolugen Holdings Ltd*, as the latter was not published at the time the High Court in *Maniach* gave its decision.

Chapter 2. Arbitration Agreement and Party Autonomy

799. The concept of separability is well established under Singapore law. Thus, an arbitration clause that forms part of a contract shall be treated as an agreement independent of the other terms of the contract (or an arbitration agreement may simply take the form of a separate agreement).[3009] This doctrine serves to give effect to the parties' expectation that their arbitration clause – embodying their chosen method of dispute resolution – remains effective even if the main contract is alleged or found to be invalid, and therefore takes on significance principally when the validity of the arbitration agreement itself is challenged.[3010] So too is the concept of kompetenz-kompetenz,[3011] but while the tribunal can rule on its own jurisdiction, such a decision is (with certain procedural conditions) reviewable by the courts.[3012] Any party may, within thirty days after having received notice of the tribunal's ruling on its jurisdiction, apply to the High Court to decide the matter, and if leave is granted, appeal to the Court of Appeal after the High Court has made a decision.[3013] The arbitration proceedings may continue even if the tribunal's ruling is being challenged, albeit the court has the discretion to stay the arbitration proceedings if there were special circumstances which warranted the suspension of the arbitration proceedings.[3014]

800. In construing an arbitration agreement, the general assumption that the parties, as rational businessmen, are likely to have intended any dispute arising out of the relationship into which they have entered or purported to enter to be decided by the same tribunal, is not a rule of construction to be applied irrespective of the context in which the underlying agreement was entered into, or the plain meaning of the words. Where there are compelling reasons, commercial or otherwise, that may displace any assumed intention of the parties that claims of a particular kind are to fall within the scope of an arbitration clause, the court should be slow to conduct

3009. Arbitration Act (Cap. 10, 2002 Rev. Ed.), ss 4 and 21.

3010. *BCY v. BCZ*, [2016] SGHC 249, [16].

3011. On the nature of the doctrine of *kompetenz-kompetenz*, *see* Nicholas Poon, "The Use and Abuse of Anti-Arbitration Injunctions" (2013) 25 SAcLJ 244, [12]–[17].

3012. Arbitration Act (Cap. 10, 2002 Rev. Ed.), ss 21 and 21A. *See also Sim Chay Koon v. NTUC Income Insurance Co-operative Ltd*, [2015] SGCA 46, [5]–[6]: 'where a party seeks to avoid its obligation to arbitrate its dispute, the court should undertake a restrained review of the facts and circumstances before it in order to determine whether it appears on a *prima facie* basis that there is an arbitration clause and that the dispute is caught by that clause … we should hold the parties to their duty to arbitrate and allow them to raise any relevant objections such as those in relation to jurisdiction, the validity of the arbitration agreement, or subject matter arbitrability before the tribunal … If the appellants should consider that the tribunal was wrong in the view it may eventually take on any of these matters, they can then seek relief from the court.'

3013. International Arbitration Act (Cap. 143A, 2002 Rev. Ed.), s 10. An Assistant Registrar of the High Court has held that a stay of arbitration will generally be ordered under s 10(9) if "an applicant is able to demonstrate with reasonable and credible substantiation that a refusal of stay would result in detriment in respect of which the applicant could not later be adequately restituted." *AYY v. AYZ*, [2015] SGHCR 22, [7].

3014. *See* generally *BLY v. BLZ and another* [2017] 4 SLR 410.

the exercise of contractual construction from the general rule.[3015] In the final analysis, the court will give effect to what the parties bargained for. The plain words in the parties' arbitration agreement will only be overridden if their meaning is absurd.[3016]

801. The law governing the arbitration agreement is to be determined by Singapore's conflict of laws rules. Generally, where parties have expressly chosen a law to govern the arbitration agreement, their choice will be given effect. The difficulty which arises when there is no express choice has been settled by the courts in the form of a rebuttable presumption that the express choice of law to govern the substantive contract is the implied choice of law governing the arbitration agreement.[3017]

802. The rules of arbitration adopted by the parties will be given effect to the extent that they are not inconsistent with or derogate from provisions in the Model Law.[3018] The International Arbitration Act stipulates a document in writing for an arbitration agreement to be formed.[3019] This writing requirement is met if one party to the agreement unilaterally recorded it in writing; it does not matter that the written version of the agreement is neither signed nor confirmed by all the parties involved.[3020] Where a party institutes any proceedings in any court against another party in respect of any matter which is the subject of the arbitration agreement, and party may at any time after appearance and before delivering any pleading or taking any other step in the proceedings, apply to that court to stay the proceedings insofar as the proceedings relate to that matter.[3021]

803. When considering a stay application, the court must be satisfied that there is a valid arbitration agreement which covers the scope of the dispute and is not null and void, inoperative or incapable of being performed. Consistent with the principle of kompetenz-kompetenz, the standard of review for this test is a prima facie standard, not a balance of probability standard.[3022] The party resisting the stay bears the burden of showing that no arguable case can be made against the proposition that the arbitration agreement is null and void, inoperative or incapable of being performed.[3023] An arbitration agreement which conferred on only one (or a specific)

3015. *BNP v. BNR* [2017] SGHC 269, [4]; *Rals International Pte Ltd v. Cassa di Risparmio di Parma e Piacenza SpA* [2016] 5 SLR 455, [34].
3016. *TMT Co Ltd v. The Royal Bank of Scotland plc (trading as RBS Greenwich Futures) and others* [2017] SGHC 21, [67].
3017. *BCY v. BCZ* [2016] SGHC 249, [49]–[65]; *BMO v. BMP* [2017] SGHC 127, [39].
3018. International Arbitration Act (Cap. 143A, 2002 Rev. Ed.), s 15A.
3019. International Arbitration Act (Cap. 143A, 2002 Rev. Ed.), s 2A.
3020. *AQZ v. ARA*, [2015] 2 SLR 972, [110]–[119].
3021. International Arbitration Act (Cap. 143A, 2002 Rev. Ed.), s 6.
3022. *See Tomolugen Holdings Ltd v. Silica Investors Ltd*, [2016] 1 SLR 373, [70]; citing *The Titan Unity* [2013] SGHCR 28; *Malini Ventura v. Knight Capital Pte Ltd* [2015] SGHC 225; *Sim Chay Koon v. NTUC Income Insurance Co-operative Limited*, [2015] SGCA 46.
3023. *Dyna-Jet Pte Ltd v. Wilson Taylor Asia Pacific Pte Ltd* [2016] SGHC 238, [180].

party the right to elect to arbitrate a future dispute is enforceable. However, a stay will only be granted if the party with the right to elect arbitration has exercised that right.[3024]

3024. *Wilson Taylor Asia Pacific Pte Ltd v. Dyna-Jet Pte Ltd* [2017] 2 SLR 362, [15], [16], [23], [24].

Chapter 3. Composition of Arbitral Tribunal

804. The default number of arbitrators is just one under the Arbitration Act.[3025] For arbitrations caught by the International Arbitration Act, if the number of arbitrators is not determined by the parties, there will be a single arbitrator by default; generally, in an arbitration with three arbitrators, each party shall appoint one arbitrator, and the parties shall by agreement appoint the third arbitrator.[3026] Exceptionally, it has been held that where the place or seat of arbitration was unclear or undetermined, and there is a deadlock between the parties in relation to the appointment of the tribunal which is unregulated by the arbitration agreement, the President of the Singapore International Arbitration Centre is empowered to determine the issue.[3027] The High Court may even step in as a "last resort" to directly appoint the arbitrator.[3028]

805. The grounds for challenging the appointment of an arbitrator are justifiable doubts as to his impartiality or independence (i.e., apparent or actual bias), or if he does not possess the qualifications as agreed to by the parties.[3029] The grounds for removing an arbitrator are (physical or mental) incapability and substantial injustice by failing to properly conduct the proceedings or failing to use all reasonable dispatch in conducting the proceedings or making an award; the previous ground of misconduct is no longer available.[3030] Arbitrators are not liable for negligence for anything done or omitted to be done in the capacity of an arbitrator, or for any mistake of law, fact, or procedure in the course of arbitral proceedings or in the making of an award.[3031]

3025. Arbitration Act (Cap. 10, 2002 Rev. Ed.), s 12.
3026. International Arbitration Act (Cap. 143A, 2002 Rev. Ed.), ss 9 and 9A.
3027. *KVC Rice Intertrade Co Ltd v. Asian Mineral Resources Pte Ltd and another suit* [2017] 4 SLR 182, [34], [35], [44].
3028. *KVC Rice Intertrade Co Ltd v. Asian Mineral Resources Pte Ltd and another suit* [2017] 4 SLR 182, [71]–[73].
3029. Arbitration Act (Cap. 10, 2002 Rev. Ed.), ss 14 and 22; International Arbitration Act (Cap. 143A, 2002 Rev. Ed.), First Schedule, Model Law, Article 12.
3030. Arbitration Act (Cap. 10, 2002 Rev. Ed.), s 16. *See also* International Arbitration Act (Cap. 143A, 2002 Rev. Ed.), First Schedule, Model Law, Article 14. However, where the misconduct amounts to a breach of natural justice this will still amount to a ground under which an award may be challenged: *AUF v. AUG*, [2016] 1 SLR 859.
3031. Arbitration Act (Cap. 10, 2002 Rev. Ed.), s 20.

Chapter 4. Interim Measures and Preliminary Awards

806. Parties may agree on the powers that may be exercised by the tribunal in relation to the arbitral proceedings, though generally the tribunal has the power to make orders or give directions to any party for basic procedural and evidential matters such as security for costs, discovery and interrogatories, giving of affidavit evidence, and cross-examination.[3032] Whether the tribunal can order interim injunctions in relation to arbitrations governed by the Arbitration Act, however, is doubtful, given that such provision is only made in the International Arbitration Act and not the Arbitration Act.[3033] Parties may agree on the powers exercisable by the tribunal as regards remedies, though generally the tribunal may award any remedy that could have been ordered by the High Court as though the dispute had been the subject of civil proceedings in court.[3034] Parties can apply to the court for subpoenas of witnesses to testify or produce documents, but this is only if the witness is within Singapore.[3035] If without showing cause the claimant fails to properly communicate his statement of claim or if the respondent fails to properly communicate his defence, the tribunal may terminate the proceedings and continue with the proceedings respectively.[3036] The tribunal decides the dispute in accordance with the law chosen by the parties as applicable to the substance of the dispute; if the choice is unclear or not made, the tribunal will apply the law as determined by the conflict of laws rules.[3037]

807. For arbitration under the International Arbitration Act, the tribunal has the power to make orders or give directions to any party for, inter alia: security for costs; discovery and interrogatories; giving of evidence by affidavit; the preservation, interim custody, or sale of any property that is part of the subject matter of the dispute; securing the amount in dispute; ensuring that any award made is not rendered ineffectual by dissipation of assets; and interim measures or injunctions.[3038] The court has certain powers to urgently order interim measures in aid of international arbitration, which may apply to assets and evidence situated in Singapore and in aid of arbitrations seated in Singapore and overseas.[3039] Parties can apply to the court for subpoenas of witnesses to testify or produce documents, but this is only if the witness is within Singapore.[3040]

3032. Arbitration Act (Cap. 10, 2002 Rev. Ed.), s 28.
3033. *See also Dukkar SA v. Thailand Integrated Services Pte Ltd*, [2015] SGHC 234, [3]. *Cf.* Nicholas Poon, "Use and Abuse of Anti-Arbitration Injunction" (2013) 25 SAcLJ 244, [41]–[58].
3034. Arbitration Act (Cap. 10, 2002 Rev. Ed.), s 34.
3035. Arbitration Act (Cap. 10, 2002 Rev. Ed.), s 30.
3036. Arbitration Act (Cap. 10, 2002 Rev. Ed.), ss 24 and 29.
3037. Arbitration Act (Cap. 10, 2002 Rev. Ed.), s 32.
3038. International Arbitration Act (Cap. 143A, 2002 Rev. Ed.), s 12.
3039. International Arbitration Act (Cap. 143A, 2002 Rev. Ed.), s 12A. *See also Maldives Airports Co Ltd v. GMR Malé International Airport Pte Ltd*, [2013] 2 SLR 449. In *Five Ocean Corporation v. Cingler Ship Pte Ltd (PT Commodities & Energy Resources, intervener)*, [2016] 1 SLR 1159 the High Court granted an order for a sale of assets that were not located in Singapore but where the arbitration was seated in Singapore.
3040. International Arbitration Act (Cap. 143A, 2002 Rev. Ed.), s 13.

Chapter 5. Conduct of Arbitral Proceedings

808. Parties may agree on the procedure to be followed by the tribunal in conducting the proceedings,[3041] though by default the tribunal determines if proceedings are to be conducted by oral hearing for the presentation of evidence or oral argument or on the basis of documents and other materials.[3042] Experts may also be appointed.[3043] Any costs directed by an arbitral award to be paid shall, unless otherwise directed, be taxed by the Supreme Court.[3044] As for fees, parties are jointly and severally liable to pay the arbitrators reasonable fees and expenses as are appropriate in the circumstances, and if there is no prior agreement, any party may require that such fees be taxed by the Supreme Court.[3045] With the liberalization of third-party funding for arbitration in Singapore,[3046] the cost of third-party funding may be awarded as costs to the winning party.[3047] Separately, it should be noted that there is also the Law Society Arbitration Scheme and Pro Bono Arbitration Scheme managed by the Law Society of Singapore that help resolve general civil disputes such as employment, tenancy, and renovation works. These allow speedier resolution of disputes as the arbitrator publishes his final award no later than 120 days after the hearing, and 90 days if the arbitration is by documents-only.[3048] In matters where the disputed sum is less than SGD 60,000, arbitrations will by default be by documents-only and a scale for party and party costs applies.[3049] Where the disputed sum is less than SGD 20,000, the Pro Bono scheme applies and the sole arbitrator will waive his fees for the matter.[3050]

3041. Arbitration Act (Cap. 10, 2002 Rev. Ed.), s 23.
3042. Arbitration Act (Cap. 10, 2002 Rev. Ed.), s 25.
3043. Arbitration Act (Cap. 10, 2002 Rev. Ed.), s 27.
3044. Arbitration Act (Cap. 10, 2002 Rev. Ed.), s 39.
3045. Arbitration Act (Cap. 10, 2002 Rev. Ed.), s 40.
3046. Civil Law (Amendment) Bill, Bill No. 38/2016.
3047. *Essar Oilfields Services v. Norscot Rig Management*, [2016] EWHC 2361.
3048. *Arbitration Scheme*, http://www.lawsociety.org.sg/forMembers/ResourceCentre/ArbitrationScheme.aspx, 30 Sep. 2015.
3049. *Arbitration Scheme*, http://www.lawsociety.org.sg/forMembers/ResourceCentre/ArbitrationScheme.aspx, 30 Sep. 2015.
3050. *Arbitration Scheme*, http://www.lawsociety.org.sg/forMembers/ResourceCentre/ArbitrationScheme.aspx, 30 Sep. 2015.

Chapter 6. Arbitral Award

809. An award made by the tribunal pursuant to an arbitration agreement, including interim awards[3051] and partial awards,[3052] shall be final and binding on the parties and may be relied upon by any of the parties for a defence, set-off, or otherwise in any proceedings in any court of competent jurisdiction.[3053] The tribunal may make more than one award at different points in the proceedings on different aspects of the claim.[3054] If the parties settle the dispute during the arbitral proceedings, the tribunal will terminate the proceedings and can record the settlement in the form of an arbitral award on agreed terms.[3055] A provisional award, issued to preserve a factual or legal situation so as to safeguard rights, does not render the factual or legal situation res judicata.[3056] In the same vein, an interlocutory order by the arbitral tribunal which does not decide the substance of the dispute is not enforceable as an award and hence are not subject to the usual recourses available against an award,[3057] even though the interlocutory orders is enforceable by virtue of section 12(6) of the International Arbitration Act and 28(4) of the Arbitration Act.

810. An award made by the tribunal pursuant to an arbitration agreement caught by the International Arbitration Act shall be final and binding on the parties and may be relied upon by any of the parties for a defence, set-off, or otherwise in any proceedings in any court of competent jurisdiction.[3058] Specifically, an arbitral award has the effect of being final and binding, regardless of the stage of arbitration at which it was made.[3059] When enforcing an arbitral award, it must be noted that provisional awards fall outside the scope of 'award' in section 2 of the International Arbitration Act, and therefore are unenforceable under the International Arbitration Act.[3060] The rationale is that provisional awards do not give rise to a finding on or a determination of the substantive rights of the parties; such awards are only issued to protect a party from damages during the course of the arbitral process.[3061] The Court of Appeal recently clarified that an interim award issued by an arbitral tribunal, on the issue of prompt payment of an adjudicated sum of money by the appellant, was not a provisional award even though arbitration of the merits of the

3051. *PT First Media TBK (formerly known as PT Broadband Multimedia TBK) v. Astro Nusantara International BV*, [2014] 1 SLR 372, [138].
3052. *PT Perusahaan Gas Negara (Persero) TBK v. CRW Joint Operation*, [2015] 4 SLR 364, [46].
3053. Arbitration Act (Cap. 10, 2002 Rev. Ed.), s 44.
3054. Arbitration Act (Cap. 10, 2002 Rev. Ed.), s 33.
3055. Arbitration Act (Cap. 10, 2002 Rev. Ed.), s 37.
3056. *PT Perusahaan Gas Negara (Persero) TBK v. CRW Joint Operation*, [2015] 4 SLR 364, [46]–[50] and [105].
3057. *PT Pukuafu Indah v. Newmont Indonesia Ltd*, [2012] 4 SLR 1157, [20]–[27].
3058. International Arbitration Act (Cap. 143A, 2002 Rev. Ed.), s 19B.
3059. *PT Perusahaan Gas Negara (Persero) TBK v. CRW Joint Operation*, [2015] 4 SLR 364, [105] citing *PT First Media TBK (formerly known as PT Broadband Multimedia TBK) v. Astro Nusantara International BV*, [2014] 1 SLR 372, [133]–[142].
3060. *PT Perusahaan Gas Negara (Persero) TBK v. CRW Joint Operation*, [2015] 4 SLR 364, [50].
3061. *PT Perusahaan Gas Negara (Persero) TBK v. CRW Joint Operation*, [2015] 4 SLR 364, [50].

dispute was still ongoing.[3062] This was because the interim award was a final decision as regards the issue of prompt payment.[3063]

811. For arbitration under the International Arbitration Act, the tribunal may make more than one award at different points in the proceedings on different aspects of the claim.[3064] Therefore, section 19B of the International Arbitration Act does not have the effect of rendering the tribunal functus officio once it has made an interim, interlocutory or partial award in the sense of precluding it from deciding any further matter in the arbitration which is not covered by the award(s) already made.[3065] An arbitral award may with leave of the High Court be entered and enforced in the same manner as a judgment.[3066] If parties reach agreement in settlement of their dispute and the tribunal has recorded the terms of settlement in the form of an arbitral award on agreed terms in accordance with the Model Law, the award shall be treated as an arbitral award and with leave of the High Court be entered and enforced in the same manner as a judgment.[3067]

3062. *PT Perusahaan Gas Negara (Persero) TBK v. CRW Joint Operation*, [2015] 4 SLR 364, [105].
3063. *PT Perusahaan Gas Negara (Persero) TBK v. CRW Joint Operation*, [2015] 4 SLR 364, [109].
3064. International Arbitration Act (Cap. 143A, 2002 Rev. Ed.), s 19A.
3065. *PT Perusahaan Gas Negara (Persero) TBK v. CRW Joint Operation*, [2015] 4 SLR 364, [105].
3066. International Arbitration Act (Cap. 143A, 2002 Rev. Ed.), s 19.
3067. International Arbitration Act (Cap. 143A, 2002 Rev. Ed.), s 18.

Chapter 7. Recourse Against Arbitral Award

812. An arbitration award may be set aside by the court if: a party to the arbitration agreement was under some incapacity; the arbitration agreement is not valid under the law to which the parties have subjected it (if this is unclear then Singapore law applies); the party making the application was not given proper notice of the appointment of an arbitrator or was otherwise unable to present his case; the award dealt with a dispute not within the scope of the arbitration;[3068] the composition of the tribunal or the arbitral procedure is not in accordance with what parties had agreed; the award was induced by fraud or corruption; there was a breach of the rules of natural justice and a party suffered prejudice; the subject matter of the dispute was not capable of settlement by arbitration; or the award is contrary to public policy.[3069] An appeal to the courts – provided that there is an agreement between the parties and leave is obtained[3070] – is only possible on questions of law arising out of an award made in the proceedings, though parties may agree to exclude the jurisdiction of the courts (for instance via an agreement to dispense with reasons for the tribunal's award).[3071]

813. To set aside an arbitral award caught by the International Arbitration Act, an application must be made by originating summons.[3072] The application must be made within 3 months from the date of receipt of the award. This time limit is strict and is ordinarily not extendable by the Court.[3073] Fresh evidence not admitted in the arbitration below may be admissible in the application to set aside the award. The Court will exercise its discretion to rule on its admissibility or attach the appropriate weight to such evidence, and/or to make an adverse costs order against the

3068. The court will have to undertake a two-stage enquiry to decide: 'first, what matters were within the scope of the submission to the arbitral tribunal; and, second, whether the Award involves such matters, or whether it involves a new difference outside the scope of the submission to arbitration and, accordingly, irrelevant to the issues requiring determination'; the parties' pleaded cases and the issues of law and fact raised in the pleadings are generally looked upon as delineating the matters which are within the scope of submission to arbitration although new fact arising after submission to arbitration, which would affect the remedies recoverable in the proceedings must fall within the scope of the parties' submission to arbitration and need not be specifically pleaded: *BNX v. BOE,* [2017] SGHC 289, [56]; *AYH v. AYI* [2015] SGHC 300, citing *PT Asuransi Jasa Indonesia (Persero) .v Dexia Bank SA* [2007] 1 SLR(R) 597, [44] and *PT Prima International Development v. Kempinski Hotels SA*, [2012] 4 SLR 98, [48].

3069. Arbitration Act (Cap. 10, 2002 Rev. Ed.), s 48.

3070. The court will look at: whether the determination of the question will substantially affect the rights of at least one of the parties; whether the question is one that the tribunal was asked to determine; whether the tribunal's decision was obviously wrong based on the findings of fact; whether the question is one of general public importance and the decision of the tribunal is at least open to serious doubt; and whether it is just and proper in all the circumstances for the court to determine the question.

3071. Arbitration Act (Cap. 10, 2002 Rev. Ed.), s 49.

3072. Supreme Court of Judicature Act (Cap. 322, R. 5, 2014 Rev. Ed.) Rules of Court, O 69A r 2.

3073. *ABC Co v. XYZ Co Ltd*, [2003] 3 SLR(R) 546, [9]; *PT Pukuafu Indah v. Newmont Indonesia Ltd*, [2012] 4 SLR 1157, [30].

applicant, where appropriate, for failing to admit the evidence in the arbitration.[3074] The Court may also allow oral evidence to be admitted and cross examination of witnesses.[3075]

814. An award may be set aside by the court if the making of the award was induced by fraud or corruption; or there was a breach of the rules of natural justice and a party suffered prejudice.[3076] These grounds for setting aside an arbitral award are 'in addition to the grounds set out in Article 34(2) of the Model Law'.[3077] The High Court has recently clarified that section 10(3) of the International Arbitration Act and Article 16(3) of the Model Law that concern appeals on ruling of jurisdiction of the arbitral tribunal cannot be used to set aside an arbitral award that deals with the merits of the dispute.[3078] Singapore's pro-arbitration stance was also recently affirmed by the Court of Appeal through its narrow interpretation of what constitutes a breach of natural justice and a tribunal acting in excess of its jurisdiction in deciding if these grounds was satisfied to warrant a setting aside of an arbitral award.[3079] Specifically, the Court of Appeal affirmed the principle of minimal curial intervention in arbitral proceedings.[3080] Generally, the narrow grounds for curial intervention concern either process failures that are unfair and prejudice the parties or instances where the arbitral tribunal has made a decision that is beyond the scope of the arbitration agreement.[3081] Therefore, courts:

> do not and must not courts do not and must not interfere in the merits of an arbitral award and, in the process, bail out parties who have made choices that they might come to regret, or offer them a second chance to canvass the merits of their respective cases.[3082]

815. As regards the breach of the rules of natural justice, an arbitral award may be set aside if there was a causal nexus between the breach and the arbitral award; and the breach prejudiced the aggrieved party's rights.[3083] Examples of breaches of the rules of natural justice include the failure to consider an important issue that has been pleaded in arbitration[3084] and lack of ample notice of a notice that was only

---

3074. *Jiangsu Overseas Group Co Ltd v. Concord Energy Pte Ltd*, [2016] 4 SLR 1336, [50]–[53].
3075. *Jiangsu Overseas Group Co Ltd v. Concord Energy Pte Ltd*, [2016] 4 SLR 1336, [41]–[43].
3076. International Arbitration Act (Cap. 143A, 2002 Rev. Ed.), s 24.
3077. International Arbitration Act (Cap. 143A, 2002 Rev. Ed.), s 24.
3078. *AQZ v. ARA*, [2015] 2 SLR 972, [69]–[70].
3079. *AKN v. ALC*, [2015] 3 SLR 488, [37].
3080. *AKN v. ALC*, [2015] 3 SLR 488, [37], citing *BLC v. BLB*, [2014] 4 SLR 79, [51]–[53].
3081. *AKN v. ALC*, [2015] 3 SLR 488, [38].
3082. *AKN v. ALC*, [2015] 3 SLR 488, [37]. *See also Prometheus Marine Pte Ltd v. King, Ann Rita*, [2017] SGCA 61, [57].
3083. *BNX v. BOE*, [2017] SGHC 289, [73], citing *L W Infrastructure Pte Ltd v. Lim Chin San Contractors Pte Ltd and another appeal*, [2013] 1 SLR 125, [48]; *Mount Eastern Holdings Resources Co., Limited v. H&C S Holdings Pte Ltd*,
[2016] SGHC 1, [18], citing *Soh Beng Tee & Co Pte Ltd v. Fairmount Development Pte Ltd*, [2007] 3 SLR(R) 86, [29]; *AKN v. ALC*, [2015] 3 SLR 488, [48], citing *Soh Beng Tee & Co Pte Ltd v. Fairmount Development Pte Ltd*, [2007] 3 SLR(R) 86, [29] and *John Holland Pty Ltd v. Toyo Engineering Corp (Japan)*, [2001] 1 SLR(R) 443, [18].
3084. *AKN v. ALC*, [2015] 3 SLR 488, [46].

raised on the final day of arbitral proceedings.[3085] The threshold to establish a breach of the rules of natural justice on the former ground remains a high one since such an allegation is usually a matter of inference. It would not suffice for the applicant to barely assert in its submissions to the court that it has suffered prejudice as a result of the breach of the rules of natural justice.[3086]

816. An important distinction must be made between an arbitral tribunal's decision to reject an argument and an arbitral tribunal's failure to even consider that argument; only the latter amounts to a breach of the rules of natural justice.[3087] Therefore, if the facts relied on by the aggrieved party to prove that the arbitrator failed to consider an important issue are also consistent with the arbitrator simply having misunderstood the aggrieved party's case, or having been mistaken as to the law, or having chosen not to deal with a point pleaded by the aggrieved party because he thought it unnecessary, then the threshold is not met.[3088] The court would only consider that the tribunal had failed to consider an important issue if it was clearly and virtually inescapably the case.[3089] In this regard, the court eschews a pedantic approach, in favour of a holistic assessment, in determining the issues that were before the tribunal.[3090]

817. Apart from the examples mentioned, poor reasoning on the part of the arbitral tribunal does not constitute a breach of the rules of natural justice.[3091] If a tribunal did not express its reasoning on an issue which the parties had placed before it, the rules of natural justice would be breached only if the lack of reasoning followed from the tribunal deliberately avoiding or completely overlooking the issue. There would be no breach if the tribunal reached its decision implicitly, reached the wrong decision or failed to understand the argument.[3092]

818. As regards setting aside of an arbitral award on the grounds that the arbitral tribunal exceeded its jurisdiction, the aggrieved party must further satisfy the

3085. *AKN v. ALC,* [2015] 3 SLR 488, [75]–[79].
3086. *Zynergy Solar Projects & Services Pvt Ltd v. Phoenix Solar Pte Ltd* [2017] SGHC 223, [12].
3087. *AKN v. ALC,* [2015] 3 SLR 488, [47], citing *AQU v. AQV,* [2015] SGHC 26, [35] and *TMM Division Maritima SA de CV v. Pacific Richfield Marine Pte Ltd*, [2013] 4 SLR 972, [94].
3088. *AKN v. ALC,* [2015] 3 SLR 488, [46].
3089. *ASG v. ASH* [2016] 5 SLR 54, [61], [62]. *See also Prometheus Marine Pte Ltd v. King, Ann Rita and other matters* [2017] SGHC 36, [88], where the court noted that the "central inquiry is simply whether the award shows that the arbitrator has applied his mind to the arguments advanced by the parties".
3090. *Prometheus Marine Pte Ltd v. King, Ann Rita and other matters* [2017] SGHC 36, [60].
3091. *AKN v. ALC,* [2015] 3 SLR 488, [59].
3092. *ASG v. ASH* [2016] 5 SLR 54, [90], [91].

court that it suffered actual or real prejudice.[3093] It is well established that a tribunal's error of law, even if it were manifest, does not amount to an excess of jurisdiction.[3094]

819. Although there is the principle of minimal curial intervention in arbitral proceedings, an exception arises when the court has to determine if the arbitral tribunal acted in excess of its jurisdiction or if the arbitral tribunal lacks the jurisdiction to hear a dispute.[3095] Specifically, the court has to undertake a de novo hearing and look into the merits of the dispute. A de novo hearing does not ipso facto require a rehearing of evidence since O 69A r 2 of the Rules of Court[3096] contemplates that generally the matter will be resolved by way of affidavit evidence.[3097] Nonetheless, the court may still allow oral evidence and/or cross-examination when it considers that there is or may be a dispute as to the facts; and that to do so would secure the just, expeditious, and economical disposal of the application.[3098] Therefore, an applicant wishing to retake oral evidence should preferably at the time of filing the application, also file the affidavits of evidence of the witnesses he intends to call and make a further application to have these witnesses and the witnesses for the other side heard and cross-examined in court.[3099] An arbitral tribunal is said to exceed its jurisdiction if it issues an arbitral award that neither party requested.[3100] If the arbitral tribunal erroneously exercises an available power vested in it, that only amounts to an error of law, and does not constitute an excess of jurisdiction.[3101]

820. Once a court has set aside an arbitral award, it has no power to refer matters to arbitration before another tribunal.[3102] The court also has no power to remit – in the sense of referring certain matters arising from an arbitral award back to the very same tribunal which made the award – after setting aside;[3103] the power to remit comes exclusively from Article 34(4) of the Model Law, which is a limited

---

3093. *AKN v. ALC,* [2015] 3 SLR 488, [72], citing *CRW Joint Operation v. PT Perusahaan Gas Negara (Persero) TBK*, [2011] 4 SLR 305, [33]. *Cf.* however *GD Midea Air Conditioning Equipment Co Ltd v. Tornado Consumer Goods Ltd and another matter* [2017] SGHC 193, [60], where it was held that there it was unnecessary for the applicant to show prejudice.
3094. *Sui Southern Gas Co Ltd v. Habibullah Coastal Power Co (Pte) Ltd* [2010] 3 SLR 1, [37]. This includes errors in determining the governing law of the contract: *see Quarella SpA v. Scelta Marble Australia Pty Ltd* [2012] 4 SLR 1057; *Quanzhou Sanhong Trading Limited Liability Co Ltd v. ADM Asia-Pacific Trading Pte Ltd* [2017] SGHC 199, [14]–[19].
3095. *AKN v. ALC,* [2015] 3 SLR 488, [112], citing *AQZ v. ARA,* [2015] 2 SLR 972, [49] and *PT First Media TBK (formerly known as PT Broadband Multimedia TBK) v. Astro Nusantara International BV*, [2014] 1 SLR 372, [163].
3096. Supreme Court of Judicature Act (Cap. 322, R. 5, 2014 Rev. Ed.) Rules of Court.
3097. *AQZ v. ARA,* [2015] 2 SLR 972, [52].
3098. Supreme Court of Judicature Act (Cap. 322, R. 5, 2014 Rev. Ed.) Rules of Court, O 28 r 4(3). *See also AQZ v. ARA*, [2015] 2 SLR 972, [53]–[54].
3099. *AQZ v. ARA,* [2015] 2 SLR 972, [53].
3100. *AKN v. ALC,* [2015] 3 SLR 488, [72].
3101. *AKN v. ALC,* [2015] 3 SLR 488, [73], citing *Lesotho Highlands Development Authority v. Impregilo SpA*, [2006] 1 AC 221, [25].
3102. *AKN v. ALC,* [2016] 1 SLR 966, [10], citing *BLC v. BLB*, [2014] 4 SLR 79, [119].
3103. This includes the issue of costs. In this regard, *see Kingdom of Lesotho v. Swissbourgh Diamond Mines (Pty) Ltd and others* [2017] SGHC 195, [345].

one in that remission was an alternative to setting aside.[3104] The immediate effect of setting aside is that the award ceases to have legal effect, at least in the jurisdiction of the seat court. The mandate of the tribunal generally expires upon the issuance of a final award. However, as the arbitration agreement typically survives the setting aside of an award, it might be open for a party who has successfully obtained an award in the arbitration, and then seen that award set aside by the court, to commence a fresh arbitration.[3105]

3104. *AKN v. ALC*, [2016] 1 SLR 966, [17]–[39].

3105. *AKN v. ALC*, [2016] 1 SLR 966, [40]–[54]. Factors that may influence attempts to commence fresh arbitration proceedings following the setting aside of an award include the possibility of a limitations defence having accrued by the time the fresh set of proceedings was commenced, the possibility of objections being taken against an attempt to reappoint a member of the previous tribunal in the fresh arbitration proceedings on the grounds of a reasonable suspicion of bias, and considerations of *res judicata*.

Chapter 8. Recognition and Enforcement of Awards

821. Enforcement of international arbitral awards in Singapore is governed by the International Arbitration Act. The statute is based on the Model Law and gives effect to the New York Convention. International arbitral awards whether made in Singapore or not may, with leave of the High Court, be enforced in the same way as a High Court judgment. Where such leave is given, the High Court may enter judgment in favour of the winning party in the same terms as the award to be enforced.

Part XI. Mediation

Chapter 1. Overview and Legislation

822. Mediation can be described as a voluntary and confidential process in which the parties seek to find a practical solution to their dispute; the parties are guided in their decision-making process by a neutral third party, the mediator, who assists the parties in finding a solution to which both give their assent and which has regard to the different concerns of those involved.[3106] Mediation in the informal sense has historically been a part of Singapore's cultural landscape and Asian heritage.[3107] In the past, traditional mediation in Singapore often involved respected community leaders bringing disputing parties together to 'talk out their differences' to settle the matter amicably.[3108] For example, the Chinese community would turn to their clan associations to settle their disputes according to Chinese rules and customs;[3109] the Malay community turned to their mosques for resolution under adat and Islamic law;[3110] and the Indian community relied on the Panchayat system to provide guidance and counsel, as well as the priests in Hindu temples.[3111] However, urbanization and increased exposure to rights-based thinking led to the dispersal of traditional ethnic communities and people turning to the courts and other official tribunals in search of justice and enforcement of their rights. This led to the formation of a growing case backlog for the Singapore courts and weakening of the social fabric of the nation, prompting what is often described as the 'mediation movement' of the 1990s.[3112] The mediation movement comprised a three-pronged push to develop: (a) court-annexed mediation at the then Subordinate Courts of Singapore (now

3106. Loong S. O., *Mediation* in *Laws of Singapore*, at paragraph 3.2.1, http://www.singaporelaw.sg/sglaw/laws-of-singapore/overview/chapter-3, 30 Sep. 2017. *See also Mediation in Singapore: A Practical Guide*, at 48 (D. McFadden & G. Lim eds, Sweet & Maxwell Singapore, 2015).

3107. G. Lim & E. Chua, *Singapore* in *Asia Mediation Handbook*, at paragraph 16.04 (R. Leung ed., Thomson Reuters Hong Kong, 2015).

3108. Teh H.H., *Mediation Practices in ASEAN – the Singapore Experience*, paper presented at the 11th General Assembly of the ASEAN Law Association (2012), at 2, http://www.aseanlawassociation.org/11GAdocs/workshop5-sg.pdf, 30 Sep. 2017.

3109. L. Boulle & Teh H.H., *Mediation – Principles, Process and Practice*, at 191 (Butterworths Asia, 2000).

3110. L. Boulle & Teh H.H., *Mediation – Principles, Process and Practice*, at 191 (Butterworths Asia, 2000).

3111. L. Boulle & Teh H.H., *Mediation – Principles, Process and Practice*, at 192 (Butterworths Asia, 2000).

3112. G. Lim & E. Chua, *Singapore* in *Asia Mediation Handbook*, at paragraph 16.04 (R. Leung ed., Thomson Reuters Hong Kong, 2015).

known as the State Courts) in 1994; (b) commercial mediation through the Singapore Mediation Centre (SMC) in 1997; and (c) community mediation through Community Mediation Centres (CMCs) statutorily provided for by the Community Mediation Centres Act in 1998.[3113] There are also other agencies and tribunals such as the Industrial Arbitration Court,[3114] the Strata Titles Board,[3115] the Maintenance of Parents Tribunal,[3116] and the Intellectual Property Office[3117] which either offer mediation services (the former two) or refer cases for mediation (the latter two).

823. In terms of legislation, apart from the Community Mediation Centres Act,[3118] reference to mediation has been included in sector-specific legislation in order to encourage its use in particular contexts where mediation would generally be suitable. For example, under section 42(4)(b)(i) of the Medical Registration Act,[3119] which governs complaints against medical professionals, a Complaints Committee may refer a matter for mediation between the registered medical practitioner and the complainant when it considers that no investigation of the practitioner's conduct is required. Similarly, in the context of a failure on the part of children to maintain their parents, under section 5(6) of the Maintenance of Parents Act,[3120] the Tribunal shall, before hearing an application for maintenance orders by parents, refer the differences between the parties to a conciliation officer for mediation. A more comprehensive framework for mediation is provided for under Part IVA of the Industrial Relations Act,[3121] which makes provision for a system of tripartite mediation to resolve disputes involving executive employees and employers.[3122]

824. The mediation movement also saw mediation being provided by institutions and taking a more formal and structured process than the traditional type of mediation; now, mediators in Singapore usually undergo special training and accreditation before they practice as mediators. The success of the mediation movement is evident from the growth of the original mediation service providers (both in terms of scope of work and caseload) as well as an increase in the number of service providers to cover the whole spectrum of disputes sectors. More recently, Singapore has made more efforts to grow the space for international mediation and to

3113. *See* Teh H.H., *Mediation Practices in ASEAN – the Singapore Experience*, paper presented at the 11th General Assembly of the ASEAN Law Association (2012), at 2, http://www.aseanlawassociation.org/11GAdocs/workshop5-sg.pdf, 30 Sep. 2017.
3114. *Industrial Arbitration Court: Mediation by Registrar,* http://www.iac.gov.sg/mediation-n-arbitration/mediation-by-registrar, 30 Sep. 2017.
3115. *Strata Titles Boards: General Information,* http://www.mnd.gov.sg/stb/generalInformation.html, 30 Sep. 2017.
3116. *Maintenance of Parents: Mediation,* https://app.maintenanceofparents.gov.sg/Pages/Mediation.aspx, 30 Sep. 2017.
3117. *Intellectual Property Office: Mediation Options for Trade Marks Proceedings*, http://www.ipos.gov.sg, 30 Sep. 2017.
3118. (Cap. 49A, 1998 Rev. Ed.).
3119. (Cap. 174, 2014 Rev. Ed.).
3120. (Cap. 167B, 1996 Rev. Ed.).
3121. (Cap. 136, 2004 Rev. Ed.).
3122. *Ministry of Manpower: A Guide to Tripartite Mediation*, http://www.mom.gov.sg, 30 Sep. 2017.

position itself as an international dispute resolution hub.[3123] In early 2013, the Chief Justice of Singapore and the Ministry of Law appointed the Working Group on International Commercial Mediation. The Working Group on International Commercial Mediation report made three main recommendations in 2013: (a) establish a new mediation centre to be called the Singapore International Mediation Centre (SIMC) to provide best-of-class international commercial mediation services; (b) establish an independent professional body for mediation in Singapore to be called the Singapore International Mediation Institute (SIMI); and (c) enact legislation in the form of a Mediation Act.[3124] These recommendations were made by the government and in November 2014, both the SIMC and the SIMI were officially launched. At the launch of the SIMC, the Chief Justice announced that the Ministry of Law was working on a proposed Mediation Bill, which will include provisions for the enforceability of mediated settlements by the Singapore courts as well as the confidentiality and admissibility of communications made in the course of mediation.[3125]

3123. *Keynote speech by the Minister for Law, Mr K Shanmugam, at the 26th LAWASIA Conference 2013*, http://www.mlaw.gov.sg, 30 Sep. 2017.

3124. *Press Release by the Ministry of Law: 'Commercial Dispute Resolution Services in Singapore Set to Grow'*, https://www.mlaw.gov.sg/news/press-releases/icmwg-recommendations.html, 30 Sep. 2017.

3125. *Speech of the Honourable the Chief Justice Sundaresh Menon at the Opening of the Singapore International Mediation Centre*, http://simc.com.sg/wp-content/uploads/2014/11/Opening-of-the-Singapore-International-Mediation-Centre-on-5-November-20....pdf, 30 Sep. 2017.

Chapter 2. Rights That Can Be Subject to Mediation

825. There is presently no legislation in Singapore stipulating limits on the rights that can be subject to mediation. Generally, as the outcome of a successful mediation is a mediated settlement agreement, which has the status of a contract, any rights that are capable of being enforced as a contractual right can be subject to mediation. However, the practice of mediation in Singapore has developed beyond the mediation of commercial and civil disputes. Minor private criminal complaints known as Magistrates' Complaints as well as relational disputes under the Protection from Harassment Act 2014[3126] are mediated by the State Courts Centre for Dispute Resolution,[3127] mediation and counselling of family disputes is carried out by the Family Justice Courts,[3128] and mediation of labour and employment disputes is conducted by the Ministry of Manpower and the Industrial Arbitration Court,[3129] to name some examples. These types of mediation are conducted by the courts, government agencies, and tribunals as well as other statutory bodies and are usually supported by legislation or subsidiary legislation.

826. Although mediation is generally a voluntary process, submission to mediation may be mandated by legislation including section 42(4)(b)(i) of the Medical Registration Act,[3130] where a Complaints Committee may refer a matter for mediation between the registered medical practitioner and the complainant, and the dispute resolution provisions of the Building Maintenance and Strata Management Act,[3131] Private Education Act,[3132] and Small Claims Tribunal Act,[3133] which stipulate a mediation-arbitration process.

827. In the context of community mediation conducted pursuant to the Community Mediation Centres Act, a case concerning a family, social or community dispute that does not involve a seizable offence under any written law may be the subject of mediation.[3134] The Community Mediation Centres Act further provides that a mediation session may be commenced or continued whether the dispute is justiciable before any court, tribunal, or body and whether the dispute is the subject of any legal proceedings.[3135]

3126. (No. 17 of 2014).
3127. *Media Release: Joint Launch of the State Courts Centre for Dispute Resolution and 'Mediation in Singapore: A Practical Guide'*, a Thomson Reuters Publication, https://www.statecourts.gov.sg, 30 Sep. 2017.
3128. *Family Justice Courts: Mediation / Counselling*, https://www.familyjusticecourts.gov.sg/Common/Pages/MediationCounselling.aspx, 30 Sep. 2017.
3129. *Ministry of Manpower: Tripartite Mediation Online*, https://aceonline.mom.gov.sg/iaces/services/TMOL/TMOL_Default.aspx; Industrial Arbitration Court website, Mediation by Registrar, http://www.iac.gov.sg/mediation-n-arbitration/mediation-by-registrar, 30 Sep. 2017.
3130. (Cap. 174, 2014 Rev. Ed.).
3131. (Cap. 30C, 2008 Rev. Ed.).
3132. (Cap. 247A, 2011 Rev. Ed.).
3133. (Cap. 308, 1998 Rev. Ed.).
3134. Community Mediation Centres Act (Cap. 49A, 1998 Rev. Ed.), s 11(1).
3135. Community Mediation Centres Act (Cap. 49A, 1998 Rev. Ed.), s 11(2).

Chapter 3. Mediation Agreement

828. Unless mediation is mandated specifically by legislation or subsidiary legislation, a mediation agreement or agreement to mediate is usually required before parties enter into mediation because of the voluntary nature of mediation. The mediation service providers, both persons and institutions, are generally able to assist the parties with entering into a mediation agreement. It should be noted that mediation institutions often have prescribed forms of mediation agreements and procedures to provide a framework for mediations conducted under the auspices of their institution.[3136] However, parties may also choose to undergo mediation on an ad hoc basis and provide for their own mediation procedures. The mediation agreement may also form part of the dispute resolution clause in the contract between the parties.

829. Mediation clauses are commonly used in practice in Singapore, for example, the Attorney-General's Chambers recommends that government contracts should carry a clause referring disputes to mediation, where appropriate.[3137] Drafters of mediation clauses should be attentive to the following factors: first, mediation clauses should be clear and certain; second, they should be complete and comprehensive; third, they should specify procedures to be followed by the parties in setting up and undertaking the mediation with some reference to the identity of the mediator and procedure to be followed or incorporated by reference to the mediation agreement or mediation rules of a mediation agency; fourth, they should uphold the non-ouster principle by stipulating that the parties should first submit their dispute to mediation before they institute court proceedings; and finally the uncertainty of clauses requiring participation in good faith should be noted.[3138] In *International Research Corp PLC v. Lufthansa Systems Asia Pacific Pte Ltd*,[3139] the Cooperation Agreement between the parties contained a dispute resolution mechanism which prescribed in cl 37.2 that any dispute shall first be resolved by a specified mediation procedure, failing which, in cl 37.3, that the dispute shall be resolved by arbitration. The Court of Appeal held that where parties had clearly contracted for a specific set of dispute resolution procedures as preconditions for arbitration, then, absent any question of waiver, those preconditions had to be complied with.[3140]

3136. *The Singapore Mediation Centre's Mediation Agreement and Mediation Procedure*, http://mediation.com.sg/business-services/commercial-mediation/, 30 Sep. 2017; *The Singapore International Mediation Centre's Mediation Rules*, http://simc.com.sg/mediation-rules/, 30 Sep. 2017.

3137. Loong S. O., *Mediation* in *Laws of Singapore*, at paragraph 3.3.5, http://www.singaporelaw.sg/sglaw/laws-of-singapore/overview/chapter-3, 30 Sep. 2017.

3138. Loong S. O., *Mediation* in *Laws of Singapore*, at paragraph 3.6.8, http://www.singaporelaw.sg/sglaw/laws-of-singapore/overview/chapter-3, 30 Sep. 2017.

3139. [2014] 1 SLR 130.

3140. *International Research Corp PLC v. Lufthansa Systems Asia Pacific Pte Ltd*, [2014] 1 SLR 130, [62]. *See also PT Selecta Bestama v. Sin Huat Huat Marine Transportation Pte Ltd*, [2015] SGHC 295, [31].

Chapter 4. Persons/Institutions That Can Act as Mediators

830. This section focuses on the key domestic institutions in Singapore – the State Courts, the Family Justice Courts, the Supreme Court, the Singapore Mediation Centre and the Community Mediation Centres. It should be noted that at this time there is no legislation in Singapore specifying any requirements to be fulfilled before persons can act as mediators; individual mediators not affiliated to any institutions, however, generally possess some form of mediator training and experience before referring to themselves as mediators.

§1. Mediation in the State Courts

831. Court-based mediation first started in the State Courts when in 1994 a Court Dispute Resolution (CDR) process was implemented to assist parties to settle their civil disputes before trial. A formal Court Mediation Centre was established the following year and later became known as the Primary Dispute Resolution Centre (PDRC). Mediation in the State Courts later expanded from civil disputes to include other types of cases, namely family matters and certain criminal matters. The Family Court has offered mediation to families involved in divorce proceedings since 1995. In 2007, the Family Court established specialized Maintenance Mediation Chambers to deal with maintenance disputes. From 1996, Magistrate's Complaints, which are minor private criminal complaints concerning interpersonal relationships, such as those between relatives, friends and neighbours, were referred for mediation in the State Courts' Crime Registry.[3141] Pre-trial resolution for specific minor criminal matters were handled via Criminal Case Resolution Conferences. Court-annexed mediation at the State Courts has been consolidated under the single roof of the Centre for Dispute Resolution, which was launched in 2015.[3142] The centre adopts a holistic approach to dealing with individual disputes which may involve different aspects of the law and may cut across the civil/criminal divide.

832. The mediation in the State Courts is conducted by District Judges who are specially trained and who do not preside over trials; accredited mediators from the Singapore Mediation Centre approved by the State Courts may also mediate cases at the State Courts.[3143] As of March 2015, the Centre for Dispute Resolution has seven judge mediators and more than 100 volunteer mediators.[3144] The State Courts

3141. J. Kang & D. Quek, *Mediation of Criminal Matters in the State Courts* in *Mediation in Singapore: A Practical Guide* (D. McFadden & G. Lim eds, Sweet & Maxwell Singapore, 2015).

3142. N. Ramchandani, *New Centre for Dispute Resolution to take more holistic approach*, Business Times (5 Mar. 2015).

3143. J. Low & D. Quek, *An Overview of Court Mediation in the State Courts of Singapore* in *Mediation in Singapore: A Practical Guide*, at 216 – 220 (D. McFadden & G. Lim eds, Sweet & Maxwell Singapore, 2015).

3144. *Media Release: Joint Launch of the State Courts Centre for Dispute Resolution and 'Mediation in Singapore: A Practical Guide'*, a Thomson Reuters Publication, https://www.statecourts.gov.sg, 30 Sep. 2017.

is currently studying setting up a staff mediation scheme to recruit accredited mediators with legal training to serve as court mediators.[3145] After a restructuring exercise, pursuant to the Family Justice Act 2014 passed, new Family Justice Courts were opened in 2014 to address the needs of youth and families in distress.[3146] The Family Justice Courts offers mediation and counselling services and the new regime there will be dealt with in a separate subsection below.

§2. Mediation in the Family Justice Courts

833. The Family Justice Courts refers to the body of courts which comprise the Family Division of the High Court, the Family Courts, and the Youth Courts.[3147] These courts are administered by the Presiding Judge of the Family Justice Courts and hear all divorce and related matters, family violence cases, adoption and guardianship cases, Youth Court cases, applications for deputyship under the Mental Capacity Act,[3148] and probate and succession matters.[3149] Section 50(1) of the Women's Charter[3150] and section 26(9) of the Family Justice Act 2014[3151] empower the Family Justice Courts to direct parties or any child to undergo mediation or counselling either on its own motion or on the application of any person. A similar power is provided for by section 35(3) of the Family Justice Act 2014[3152] for parties to any proceedings in the Youth Courts. Pursuant to the Family Justice Act 2014, the First Schedule of the Supreme Court of Judicature Act has also been amended to accord to the High Court power 'to order any party to any proceedings, or any child who is a subject of those proceedings, to undergo such mediation or counselling, or to participate in such family support programme or activity (that is to say, any programme or activity carried out for the purpose of addressing or resolving any relationship issue or relationship problem between spouses or former spouses, between siblings or between parent and child), as the court may direct'.[3153]

834. As the approach to proceedings in the Family Justice Courts is judge-led rather than party-led, the courts may make the direction for parties to mediate at any time after the commencement of or at the hearing of any proceedings for the just, expeditious, and economical disposal of the cause or matter.[3154] It should be noted

3145. J. Low & D. Quek, *An Overview of Court Mediation in the State Courts of Singapore* in *Mediation in Singapore: A Practical Guide*, at 220 (D. McFadden & G. Lim eds, Sweet & Maxwell Singapore, 2015).
3146. *Speech of the Honourable the Chief Justice Sundaresh Menon at the Opening of the Family Courts,* https://www.familyjusticecourts.gov.sg, 30 Sep. 2017.
3147. *Family Justice Courts: Overview*, https://www.familyjusticecourts.gov.sg/AboutFamilyJusticeCourts/Pages/Overview.aspx, 30 Sep. 2017.
3148. (Cap. 177A, 2010 Rev. Ed.).
3149. *Family Justice Courts: Overview*, https://www.familyjusticecourts.gov.sg/AboutFamilyJusticeCourts/Pages/Overview.aspx, 30 Sep. 2017.
3150. (Cap. 353, 2009 Rev. Ed.).
3151. (No. 27 of 2014).
3152. (No. 27 of 2014).
3153. Family Justice Act 2014, (No. 27 of 2014), s 74(f).
3154. Family Justice Act 2014 (No. 27 of 2014) Family Justice Rules, rr 22(2) and (3).

that section 50(3A) of the Women's Charter[3155] makes mediation mandatory for all divorcing couples with children under 21 years of age. Working with the SMC, the Family Justice Courts requires its mediators to have attended and passed a training workshop to attain accreditation as a family mediator. The mediators may be District Judges or Registrars of the Family Justice Courts or other accredited mediators approved by the Family Justice Courts. It should, however, be noted that the Counselling and Psychological Services (CAPS), the social science arm of the Family Justice Courts is an important player in family mediations and a CAPS counsellor or psychologist may be appointed as a co-mediator together with a judge-mediator.[3156]

§3. Mediation in the Supreme Court

835. The Supreme Court of Singapore does not offer mediation services but has a practice of encouraging the appropriate use of mediation and referring domestic civil cases to the SMC. The Supreme Court does this through having in place a process where parties in all contested writs are sent a letter from the SMC explaining the benefits of mediation and inviting them to consider it as an option for dispute resolution.[3157] During pre-trial conferences, the registrars and judges managing the case will also as a matter of practice find out from counsel whether mediation or other methods of alternative dispute resolution (ADR) have been attempted and, if not, whether parties will be agreeable to make such an attempt. The Supreme Court Practice Directions contains a part on ADR which applies only to civil cases.[3158] Although this Part formally took effect in January 2014, the practice of encouraging and referring appropriate cases to mediation had been in place since the 1990s.

836. The court's general supportive attitude is evident in *HSBC Institutional Trust Services (Singapore) Ltd (trustee of Starhill Global Real Estate Investment Trust) v. Toshin Development Singapore Pte Ltd*, where the Court of Appeal observed that the parties' dispute 'ought to have been resolved by the application of commercial common sense in good faith through the mediation process, rather than through the adversarial curial process' and that regrettably, each of the parties had, in no small measure, contributed to the 'unhappy situation that has unnecessarily jeopardized a long-standing commercial relationship'.[3159] The Court of Appeal ordered that the parties bear their own costs of the proceedings both in the appeal

3155. (Cap. 353, 2009 Rev. Ed.).
3156. K. Ng, *Family Mediation – The Perspective of the Family Court* in *Mediation in Singapore: A Practical Guide*, at 304 – 305 (D. McFadden & G. Lim eds, Sweet & Maxwell Singapore, 2015).
3157. Teh H.H., *Mediation Practices in ASEAN – the Singapore Experience*, paper presented at the 11th General Assembly of the ASEAN Law Association (2012), at 14, http://www.aseanlawassociation.org/11GAdocs/workshop5-sg.pdf, 30 Sep. 2017.
3158. Supreme Court Practice Directions 2013 (Part IIIA).
3159. *HSBC Institutional Trust Services (Singapore) Ltd (trustee of Starhill Global Real Estate Investment Trust) v. Toshin Development Singapore Pte Ltd*, [2012] 4 SLR 738, [68].

and in the court below 'in the light of the questionable conduct of both of the Parties that has in turn stoked sterile litigation'.[3160]

§4. MEDIATION IN THE SINGAPORE MEDIATION CENTRE

837. The SMC[3161] is a non-profit organization guaranteed by the Singapore Academy of Law and was officially launched in 1997. The SMC provides a wide range of mediation and other ADR services, including neutral evaluation, adjudication, the Singapore Domain Name Dispute Resolution Service and collaborative family practice. It mediates all types of civil disputes, including commercial disputes as well as family and probate disputes.[3162] The SMC also runs industry-specific mediation.[3163] Over 2,300 matters have since been mediated at SMC and about 75% of the cases mediated are settled; of the cases that are settled, more than 90% are concluded within one working day.[3164] In 2017, it was reported that SMC handled 499 cases worth $775 million in 2016, a significant jump over previous years.

838. SMC maintains its own panel of mediators who have undergone formal mediation training and an evaluation process before being appointed.[3165] They comprise distinguished members of different professions and fields including Members of Parliament, former High Court Judges, Senior Counsel, lawyers, architects, doctors, engineers, psychologists, and university professors. When appointing a mediator, the SMC will consider various factors including whether a dispute requires technical knowledge, the language abilities of the mediators and disputants, and the personalities of the mediators and disputants.[3166]

839. Unlike the SIMC, which focuses on mediating international disputes, the SMC focuses on domestic disputes. Apart from offering mediation and ADR services, the SMC is also involved in promoting mediation and ADR, accrediting and qualifying mediators, and providing training and consultancy services both locally and overseas.

3160. *HSBC Institutional Trust Services (Singapore) Ltd (trustee of Starhill Global Real Estate Investment Trust) v. Toshin Development Singapore Pte Ltd*, [2012] 4 SLR 738, [72].

3161. *See* Loong S.O. & D. Koh, *The Singapore Mediation Centre (SMC)* in *Mediation in Singapore: A Practical Guide* (D. McFadden & G. Lim eds, Sweet & Maxwell Singapore, 2015).

3162. G. Lim & E. Chua, *Development of Mediation in Singapore* in *Mediation in Singapore: A Practical Guide* (D. McFadden & G. Lim eds, Sweet & Maxwell Singapore, 2015).

3163. *Mediation in Singapore: A Practical Guide* (D. McFadden & G. Lim eds, Sweet & Maxwell Singapore, 2015).

3164. *Singapore Mediation Centre: About Us, Our Statistics*, www.mediation.com.sg/about-us/#our-statistics, 30 Sep. 2017.

3165. Loong S. O., *Mediation* in *Laws of Singapore*, at paragraph 3.4.4, http://www.singaporelaw.sg/sglaw/laws-of-singapore/overview/chapter-3, 30 Sep. 2017.

3166. Loong S. O., *Mediation* in *Laws of Singapore*, at paragraph 3.4.4, http://www.singaporelaw.sg/sglaw/laws-of-singapore/overview/chapter-3, 30 Sep. 2017.

§5. Mediation in the Community Mediation Centre

840. CMCs[3167] first began operations in January 1998 with the purpose of helping 'develop a more harmonious, civil and gracious community, where social conflicts can be resolved amicably'.[3168] The Community Mediation Centres Act forms the basis for the operation of CMCs. CMCs handle relational disputes, the bulk of which involve quarrels between neighbours and also includes family conflicts, disagreements between friends, hawker or shop-owner squabbles (e.g. placement of products) and arguments between strangers (e.g. verbal abuse or insulting gestures).[3169] The CMCs have handled more than 7,000 cases and have a settlement rate of about 75%; the CMCs mediated 525 cases in 2013, 610 in 2012, and 593 in 2011.[3170] The CMC mediators are volunteer mediators appointed by the Minister of Law on the recommendation of the Director of a CMC.[3171] All candidates who have applied to be a volunteer community mediator with the CMC are required to attend a preliminary interview to assess their suitability for the role. If found suitable, they will undergo a two-day basic mediation workshop organized by the Community Mediation Unit (CMU).[3172] Upon completion of the basic mediation training, candidates will then observe a mediation session and co-mediate two cases under the guidance of an experienced mediator. At this stage, those who perform satisfactorily will be appointed by the Minister for Law as a community mediator with the CMC for a renewable three-year term.[3173] The CMC mediators are obligated to abide by the terms of a code of conduct and need to spend a minimum of twelve hours on mediation and attend at least twenty-four hours' worth of training per appointment term to be reappointed.

3167. *See* Ho P K. & G. Lim, *The Development of Mediation for Community and Social Disputes* in *Singapore* in *Mediation in Singapore: A Practical Guide* (D. McFadden & G. Lim eds, Sweet & Maxwell Singapore, 2015).

3168. G. Lim & E. Chua, *Development of Mediation in Singapore* in *Mediation in Singapore: A Practical Guide*, at 10 (D. McFadden & G. Lim eds, Sweet & Maxwell Singapore, 2015).

3169. This was 60% of the CMC's caseload in 2012. *See CMC Annual Report 2012/2013*, https://www.mlaw.gov.sg, 30 Sep. 2017.

3170. *CMC Annual Report 2013/2014*, https://www.mlaw.gov.sg, 30 Sep. 2017.

3171. Community Mediation Centres Act (Cap. 49A 1998 Rev. Ed.), s 8(1).

3172. *Community Mediation Centre: How to Become a CMC Mediator*, https://www.mlaw.gov.sg, 30 Sep. 2017.

3173. *Community Mediation Centre: How to Become a CMC Mediator*, https://www.mlaw.gov.sg, 30 Sep. 2017.

Chapter 5. Mediation Procedure

841. This section focuses on the mediation procedure and practice in the State Courts, the Family Justice Courts, the Supreme Court, the Singapore Mediation Centre, and the Community Mediation Centre.

§1. Mediation in the State Courts

842. For all civil cases save for non-injury motor accident cases, parties are required to submit an ADR Form after all the pleadings are filed. [3174] The ADR Form requires solicitors to indicate the salient characteristics of the case, including the nature and value of the claim, and the parties to certify that their lawyers have explained the different ADR options to them and their decision on the matter.[3175] The ADR Form also contains basic information about mediation and arbitration for the parties' reference. At the summons for directions stage, the judge or deputy registrar would recommend that the case proceed for: (a) mediation at the PDRC or the SMC; (b) arbitration under the Law Society Arbitration Scheme; or (c) adjudication in the trial courts. More recently, the State Courts issued Practice Directions which implemented a 'presumption of ADR' for civil claims involving SGD 20,000 or less or those involving between SGD 20,000 and SGD 60,000 which require more than three trial days.[3176] This meant that civil claims falling within the stated criteria were placed on a 'Recommended ADR track' from which parties could opt out without consequence for three reasons: (a) ADR has been attempted before; (b) the dispute involves a question of law; or (c) for other good reason.[3177] Otherwise, there may be costs consequences imposed pursuant to O 59 r 5(c) of the Rules of Court.[3178]

843. The mediation process begins with a preliminary meeting between the mediator and lawyers; there will then be a joint session with all the parties and lawyers present, as well as a private session between the mediator and each party with their lawyers.[3179] There are usually subsequent joint sessions to convey and discuss the proposals, deal with any differences, and finalize the terms of settlement or at

---

3174. *ePractice Direction No. 2 of 2010*, https://www.statecourts.gov.sg/Lawyer/Documents/ePD2of2010.pdf, 30 Sep. 2017.

3175. *The ADR Form in the Subordinate Courts: Finding the Appropriate Mode of Dispute Resolution*, http://www.lawgazette.com.sg/2010-04/feature1.htm, 30 Sep. 2017.

3176. *State Courts Practice Direction Amendment No. 2 of 2012*, https://www.statecourts.gov.sg, 30 Sep. 2017.

3177. *Introducing a 'Presumption of ADR' for Civil Matters in the Subordinate Courts*, http://www.lawgazette.com.sg/2012-05/415.htm, 30 Sep. 2017.

3178. Supreme Court of Judicature Act (Cap. 322, R. 5, 2014 Rev. Ed.) Rules of Court.

3179. *State Courts: The Mediation Process*, https://www.statecourts.gov.sg/Mediation_ADR/Pages/The-Mediation-Process.aspx, 30 Sep. 2017.

the very least narrow the issues in dispute.[3180] Court mediation sessions are usually scheduled for half a day and there are generally not more than three sessions.[3181]

844. The mediation at the State Courts is generally facilitative in nature with a focus on problem-solving; it usually involves discussions on the legal merits of the case but can be tailored to the particular circumstances of the dispute.[3182] If the parties reach settlement, the terms of settlement are recorded by the mediator, but if not, the case will proceed to trial as scheduled and be presided over by another District Judge who is not the mediator.[3183]

845. The mediation in the State Courts has been free for more than two decades, and this will continue to be offered for: (a) all civil claims falling under the Magistrate's court jurisdiction (i.e. less than USD 60,000 in value); (b) motor accident claims; (c) personal injury claims; (d) actions under the Protection from Harassment Act; and (e) Magistrate's Complaints for minor criminal offences.[3184] However, ADR fees will be introduced for District Court civil claims (excluding non-injury motor accident and personal injury claims), which are generally between USD 60,000 and USD 250,000 in value, from May 2015.[3185]

§2. Mediation in the Family Justice Courts

846. When filing a writ in the Family Justice Courts, the plaintiff is also required to file a statement of particulars stating that he is aware of, or has been informed by his solicitor about, the options of family mediation or counselling, before filing the writ.[3186] The defendant must state the same in the defence.[3187] This information is meant to ensure that the parties have been properly advised about the mediation process before commencing proceedings. However, after the commencement of proceedings, the courts may direct parties to undergo mediation or counselling on its own motion or on application.[3188]

3180. J. Low & D. Quek, '*An Overview of Court Mediation in the State Courts of Singapore*' in *Mediation in Singapore: A Practical Guide*, at 239–240 (D. McFadden & G. Lim eds, Sweet & Maxwell Singapore, 2015).
3181. *State Courts: The Mediation Process*, https://www.statecourts.gov.sg/Mediation_ADR/Pages/The-Mediation-Process.aspx, 30 Sep. 2017.
3182. J. Low & D. Quek, '*An Overview of Court Mediation in the State Courts of Singapore*' in *Mediation in Singapore: A Practical Guide*, at 233–238 (D. McFadden & G. Lim eds, Sweet & Maxwell Singapore, 2015).
3183. *See* State Courts Practice Directions, paragraph 25.30 Sep. 2017.
3184. *Media Release: Joint Launch of the State Courts Centre for Dispute Resolution and 'Mediation in Singapore: A Practical Guide'*, a Thomson Reuters Publication, https://www.statecourts.gov.sg, 30 Sep. 2017.
3185. *Media Release: Joint Launch of the State Courts Centre for Dispute Resolution and 'Mediation in Singapore: A Practical Guide'*, a Thomson Reuters Publication, https://www.statecourts.gov.sg, 30 Sep. 2017.
3186. Family Justice Act 2014 (No. 27 of 2014, No. S 813) Family Justice Rules, r 44(2)(b).
3187. Family Justice Act 2014 (No. 27 of 2014, No. S 813) Family Justice Rules, r 56(2).
3188. Family Justice Act 2014 (No. 27 of 2014), s 26(9); Women's Charter (Cap. 353 2009 Rev. Ed.), s 50(1).

847. For child-related proceedings, a Family Dispute Resolution Conference (FDR Conference) will be called to crystallize the issues of contention; all parties together with their counsel (if any) will have to attend the FDR Conference where the court may direct them to attend mediation or counselling, whichever is appropriate.[3189] For non-child related proceedings, the Registrar or the Judge may direct parties to attend mediation and/or counselling, whichever is appropriate.[3190] Counsel and parties must personally attend all mediation sessions.[3191] The appropriate attire for counsel attending such mediation sessions is the same as counsel appearing before a judge in chambers save that a single-coloured shirt or blouse or dress of neutral or subdued shades may be worn instead of white.[3192] Under section 50(3B) of the Women's Charter,[3193] the court may dispense with the attendance of the parties at mediation if it deems that it is not in the interests of the parties concerned to do so (e.g., where family violence has been committed or where Child Protection Services is involved in the case).

848. For all mediation sessions, (whether child-related or otherwise) counsel and parties are required to prepare a Summary for Mediation in the prescribed format prior to the mediation for submission and discussion during the mediation, together with all relevant documents as may be directed by the court.[3194] Mediation is conducted on a without prejudice basis and all communications made in the course of mediation will be treated in strict confidence and will not be admissible in any court unless otherwise stipulated by law.[3195] If the dispute is not resolved at the mediation session, the District Judge or Registrar will give the necessary directions to enable the case to proceed to trial, and the case will be heard by a judge other than the District Judge or Registrar who had mediated.[3196] Where there is a disagreement between the parties on the terms of the agreement which were recorded at mediation, either party may write in for a clarification before the Judge-Mediator.[3197] It should be noted that the Family Justice Courts in exercising their discretion as to costs must take into account the parties' conduct in relation to any attempt at resolving the cause or matter by mediation or any other means of dispute resolution.[3198]

§3. Mediation in the Supreme Court

849. It has been earlier noted that the Supreme Court does not offer mediation services but has a practice of encouraging and referring appropriate cases for

3189. Family Justice Courts Practice Directions, paragraph 11(2).
3190. Family Justice Courts Practice Directions, paragraph 11(3).
3191. Family Justice Courts Practice Directions, paragraph 11(4).
3192. Family Justice Courts Practice Directions, paragraph 167(5).
3193. (Cap. 353, 2009 Rev. Ed.).
3194. Family Justice Courts Practice Directions, paragraph 11(6).
3195. Family Justice Courts Practice Directions, paragraph 11(9).
3196. Family Justice Courts Practice Directions, paragraph 11(9).
3197. Family Justice Courts Practice Directions, paragraph 11(9).
3198. Family Justice Act 2014 (No. 27 of 2014, No. S 813) Family Justice Rules, r 854.

mediation. The Supreme Court Practice Directions state that alternative dispute resolution should be considered at the earliest possible stage to facilitate the just, expeditious, and economical disposal of civil cases.[3199] They also draw the attention of counsel to O 59 r 5(c) of the Rules of Court,[3200] which requires the court to take into account the parties' conduct in relation to any attempt at resolving the cause or matter by mediation or any other means of dispute resolution in exercising its discretion as to costs.[3201]

850. To provide the court the material upon which to facilitate the consideration and use of ADR, the Supreme Court Practice Directions provides for an 'ADR Offer' and 'Response to ADR Offer' procedure.[3202] Parties can register their willingness to participate in ADR by filing and serving an ADR Offer. Parties receiving the ADR Offer have fourteen days to file a Response to ADR Offer to accept the proposals in the ADR Offer, and if not, to explain why or make counterproposals. The failure to file a Response to ADR Offer within the stipulated time is taken to mean that a party is unwilling to participate in ADR without providing any reasons. These forms are to be signed by parties and their counsel and will encourage parties to seriously discuss ADR with counsel.[3203]

§4. Mediation in the Singapore Mediation Centre

851. Mediations at the SMC are governed by the provisions of the SMC Mediation Procedure.[3204] SMC Mediators are also bound to the SMC Code of Conduct pursuant to clause 4 of the SMC Mediation Procedure.[3205] The SMC Mediation Procedure directs and guides the mediator and the parties in relation to the issues of confidentiality, neutrality and impartiality, to name a few; it also requires the parties to give effect to the terms of any settlement reached.

852. The mediation process at the SMC may be initiated either by the case being referred to the SMC by the courts or through one or more of the parties contacting SMC directly with a request for mediation. If only one party makes a request, the SMC will contact all the other parties and convince them to attempt mediation.[3206] After SMC has assessed the suitability of the case for mediation and if all parties agree to mediate, the SMC will ensure that parties sign the SMC's Agreement to Mediate. The SMC will designate a date and time for the mediation and for urgent

3199. Supreme Court Practice Directions, paragraph 35B(3).
3200. Supreme Court of Judicature Act (Cap. 322, R. 5, 2014 Rev. Ed.) Rules of Court.
3201. Supreme Court Practice Directions, paragraph 35B(3).
3202. Supreme Court Practice Directions, paragraph 35C.
3203. G. Lim & E. Chua, *Singapore* in *Asia Mediation Handbook* (R. Leung ed., Thomson Reuters Hong Kong, 2015).
3204. *SMC Mediation Procedure*, http://mediation.com.sg/business-services/commercial-mediation/, 30 Sep. 2017.
3205. *Singapore Mediation Centre Mediation Service: The Mediation Procedure*, http://www.mediation.com.sg, 30 Sep. 2017.
3206. Loong S. O., *Mediation* in *Laws of Singapore*, at paragraph 3.4.9, http://www.singaporelaw.sg/sglaw/laws-of-singapore/overview/chapter-3, 30 Sep. 2017.

matters is able to do within one day. Mediation sessions are generally held at the SMC premises located in the Supreme Court, although the parties may also choose to mediate at their venue of choice. SMC will appoint suitable mediators from its panel of mediators. A party may object to the proposed mediator if it has valid reasons, but the SMC possesses the discretion in relation to accepting or rejecting the objection. SMC's mediation fees are pegged to the sum of dispute and start from SGD 963 (inclusive of tax) per party per day.[3207] However, parties may choose to appoint a mediator from SMC's principal panel of mediators who may charge their own commercial rates.

853. The parties will exchange summaries of their positions in the case and, if necessary, of important documents referred to in the summary. On the day of the mediation, the mediator will manage and facilitate the negotiation and problem-solving process between the parties. Lawyers are often involved to advise the parties. If the matter is settled, the parties will reduce in writing the terms of their settlement with the assistance of their lawyers and this settlement agreement will be signed by or on behalf of the parties.

§5. Mediation in the Community Mediation Centre

854. The Community Mediation Centres Act states that mediation sessions should be conducted with minimal formality and technicality and maximum expeditiousness.[3208] Typically, a community mediation session comprises joint session(s) involving both parties, and caucuses (or private sessions) with each party as required.[3209]A facilitative rather than evaluative approach is taken.[3210] The Community Mediation Centres Act further provides that the rules of evidence do not apply to mediation sessions, and that a dispute may not be adjudicated or arbitrated upon at a community mediation session.[3211]

855. A community mediation session is required by the Community Mediation Centres Act to be conducted in the absence of the public, but persons who are not parties to a mediation session may, with the permission of the Director and the parties, be present at or participate in a mediation session.[3212] Community mediation sessions can be conducted in various languages and can be arranged within two

---

3207. *Singapore Mediation Centre: Commercial Mediation*, http://mediation.com.sg/business-services/commercial-mediation/, 30 Sep. 2017.
3208. Community Mediation Centres Act (Cap. 49A, 1998 Rev. Ed.), s 10(2).
3209. Ho P. K. & G. Lim, *The Development of Mediation for Community and Social Disputes* in *Mediation in Singapore: A Practical Guide*, at 342 (D. McFadden & G. Lim eds, Sweet & Maxwell Singapore, 2015).
3210. Ho P. K. & G. Lim, *The Development of Mediation for Community and Social Disputes* in *Mediation in Singapore: A Practical Guide*, at 342 (D. McFadden & G. Lim eds, Sweet & Maxwell Singapore, 2015).
3211. Community Mediation Centres Act (Cap. 49A, 1998 Rev. Ed.), ss 10(3) and (4).
3212. Community Mediation Centres Act (Cap. 49A, 1998 Rev. Ed.), s 10(5).

weeks if parties can agree on the date and time of mediation.[3213] Each session is usually two hours and can be held during or after office hours on weekdays and Saturday mornings.[3214]

3213. Ho P. K. & G. Lim, *The Development of Mediation for Community and Social Disputes* in *Mediation in Singapore: A Practical Guide*, at 342 (D. McFadden & G. Lim eds, Sweet & Maxwell Singapore, 2015).
3214. Ho P. K. & G. Lim, *The Development of Mediation for Community and Social Disputes* in *Mediation in Singapore: A Practical Guide*, at 342 (D. McFadden & G. Lim eds, Sweet & Maxwell Singapore, 2015).

Chapter 6. Settlement Agreement

856. The legal status of settlement agreements will depend on the intention of the parties, the context of the mediation and the existence and nature of relevant statutory requirements.[3215] In most private mediations, parties would usually reduce the terms of their agreement in writing and sign on the document; this would then constitute a legally binding contract the enforcement of which is subject to normal contractual principles. Mediation institutions such as the SIMC and the SMC will have suggested templates for settlement agreements to assist parties. However, it will usually be the parties' lawyers who are responsible for the drafting of the settlement agreement. There may also be specific legislative requirements for sector-specific mediations. For example, to be of a binding nature, the Community Mediation Centres Act requires that settlements arrived at between parties at a mediation session be in writing with a statement of its binding effect and signed by or on behalf of the parties.[3216]

857. Where there are pending court proceedings, the settlement agreement may provide for its terms to be recorded as a consent judgment or court order. For nullity, divorce, judicial separation proceedings, where interim judgment or judgment of judicial separation has been granted, any agreement will be recorded as a consent order by the Judge-Mediator at a mediation session or any other judge sitting as a judge in chambers upon confirmation of the terms by the parties and/or counsel.[3217] Where interim judgment or judgment of judicial separation has not been granted, the agreement will be formally recorded by the judge and directions will be given for the setting down of the divorce on an uncontested basis on an expedited basis.[3218] For all other family proceedings, any agreement reached will be recorded as a consent order by the Judge-Mediator at a mediation session Mediator or any other judge sitting as a judge in chambers upon the confirmation of the terms by the parties and/or counsel. [3219]

858. It is also possible for parties to agree to have the terms of the settlement subsequently recorded as a consent arbitral award. For example, pursuant to the arbitration-mediation-arbitration service offered jointly by the SIMC and the SIAC, a mediated settlement agreement arrived at in the course of the arbitration may be recorded as a consent arbitral award.[3220]

3215. Loong S. O., *Mediation* in *Laws of Singapore*, at paragraph 3.6.1, http://www.singaporelaw.sg/sglaw/laws-of-singapore/overview/chapter-3, 30 Sep. 2017.
3216. Community Mediation Centres Act (Cap. 49A, 1998 Rev. Ed.), s 13(2).
3217. Family Justice Courts Practice Directions, paragraph 11(7).
3218. Family Justice Courts Practice Directions, paragraph 11(7).
3219. Family Justice Courts Practice Directions, paragraph 11(8).
3220. *Singapore International Mediation Centre: SIAC-SIMC Arb-Med-Arb Protocol*, http://simc.com.sg/siac-simc-arb-med-arb-protocol/, 30 Sep. 2017.

Chapter 7. Setting Aside a Settlement Agreement

859. A settlement agreement arrived at through mediation, absent any other steps taken to have it recorded as an order of court or arbitral award and assuming the mediation is not governed by any specific legislation providing otherwise, will have the status of a contract. Should a party wish to set aside a settlement agreement, he or she will have to commence an action to do so under the usual principles of contract law. Pending the enactment of a Mediation Act in Singapore and subject to written law, common law and the specific terms of the parties' agreement to mediate and mediation procedure will govern the confidentiality and privilege attaching to communications, documents and other information exchanged between the parties and third parties, and between the parties and any court or tribunal that may determine the dispute.[3221] Examples of legislation specifically providing for confidentiality and privilege of mediation proceedings include the Community Mediation Centres Act[3222] and the Family Justice Act 2014.[3223]

860. In the Family Justice Courts, the judicial officers, officers or court-appointed mediators are statutorily protected from liability for any act done by them for the purposes of any mediation or other alternative dispute resolution process conducted by them, if the act was done in good faith and did not involve any fraud or wilful misconduct.[3224] Further, all communications made in the course of mediation are not admissible in any court unless otherwise stipulated by law.[3225] In *Surindar Singh s/o Jaswant Singh v. Sita Jaswant Kaur,*[3226] the Court of Appeal upheld a settlement agreement relating to ancillary matters of a matrimonial case arrived at after a mediation process during which parties had independent legal advice and representation and the mediator was an experienced lawyer. The mediation took place from 10.00 a.m. to 5.00 p.m. during which the parties had many private sessions with the mediator. They also had the opportunity to and did in fact make amendments to the handwritten settlement agreement. The wife's lawyers sent the husband a draft consent order for the husband's endorsement; the draft consent order had reproduced the terms in the settlement agreement. The wife's lawyer later wrote a letter to the wife stating that the wife had 'confirmed the settlement arrived at during the mediation'.[3227] Although the Singapore courts have an overriding discretion in matrimonial cases and are obligated to consider the factors listed under section 112(2) of the Women's Charter,[3228] the Court of Appeal observed that 'if the mediation process is properly followed … the parties having participated in the

3221. P. Teo, *Legal Foundations of Mediation* in *Mediation in Singapore: A Practical Guide*, at 194 (D. McFadden & G. Lim eds, Sweet & Maxwell Singapore, 2015).
3222. Community Mediation Centres Act (Cap. 49A, 1998 Rev. Ed.), ss 19 and 20.
3223. (No. 27 of 2014).
3224. Family Justice Act 2014 (No. 27 of 2014), s 45(4).
3225. Family Justice Courts Practice Directions, paragraph 11(9).
3226. [2014] 3 SLR 1284.
3227. *Surindar Singh s/o Jaswant Singh v. Sita Jaswant Kaur*, [2014] 3 SLR 1284, [37].
3228. (Cap. 353, 2009 Rev. Ed.).

process and received advice thereon, and a settlement agreement results, the court will attach significant weight to the agreement unless there are good and substantial grounds for concluding that to do so would cause an injustice'.[3229]

3229. *Surindar Singh s/o Jaswant Singh v. Sita Jaswant Kaur*, [2014] 3 SLR 1284, [60].

Chapter 8. International Mediation

861. Singapore is currently regarded as the third most preferred seat of arbitration in the world, behind London and Geneva and alongside Paris and Tokyo.[3230] The SIAC has become the fourth most preferred arbitral institution behind the International Chamber of Commerce, the London Court of International Arbitration, and the American Arbitration Association/International Centre for Dispute Resolution.[3231] The caseload of the SIAC has also increased dramatically in recent years – from 99 new cases in 2008 to 259 in 2013.[3232] To leverage on the success of international arbitration in Singapore and grow Singapore into an international dispute resolution hub,[3233] the Chief Justice appointed a Working Group on International Commercial Mediation in early 2013 to propose plans to develop the international commercial mediation space. [3234] To recap, the three key recommendations, which were accepted by the government, were: (a) to establish a new mediation centre – the SIMC – to provide best-of-class international commercial mediation services; (b) to establish the SIMI to act as a professional body for mediation in Singapore; and (c) to enact a Mediation Act to strengthen the legal framework for mediation in Singapore.[3235]

§1. Singapore International Mediation Centre

862. SIMC was officially launched in November 2014. It is helmed by an international board of directors, and hosts a panel of over sixty international mediators and a panel of over sixty technical experts and specialists.[3236] SIMC is housed in Maxwell Chambers, the world's first dispute resolution complex which contains state-of-the-art facilities and key players in the ADR landscape. Consistent with the Working Group on International Commercial Mediation recommendations, SIMC provides professional case management service under the SIMC Mediation Rules

3230. *See White and Case 2010 International Arbitration Survey*, http://www.whitecase.com/, 30 Sep. 2017.
3231. *See White and Case 2010 International Arbitration Survey*, http://www.whitecase.com/, 30 Sep. 2017.
3232. Singapore International Arbitration Centre: SIAC Facts & Figures, Statistics, http://www.siac.org.sg/why-siac/facts-figures/statistics, 30 Sep. 2017.
3233. *Keynote speech by the Minister for Law, Mr K Shanmugam, at the 26th LAWASIA Conference 2013*, http://www.mlaw.gov.sg, 30 Sep. 2017.
3234. *Executive Summary: Recommendations of the Working Group to Develop Singapore into a Centre for International Commercial Mediation*, http://www.mlaw.gov.sg, 30 Sep. 2017.
3235. *Executive Summary: Recommendations of the Working Group to Develop Singapore into a Centre for International Commercial Mediation*, http://www.mlaw.gov.sg, 30 Sep. 2017.
3236. *Executive Summary: Recommendations of the Working Group to Develop Singapore into a Centre for International Commercial Mediation*, http://www.mlaw.gov.sg/content/dam/minlaw/corp/News/FINAL%20ICMWG%20Press%20Release%20-%20Annex%20A.pdf, 30 Sep. 2017.

and a flexible mediation venue of the parties' choice; a comprehensive electronic profile of its mediators; and is able to assist the parties to select the most appropriate mediator for their dispute.[3237]

863. The SIMC Mediation Rules may be modified by the agreement of the parties subject to the agreement of the mediation and SIMC, but provide a structure for the conduct of the mediation, including the commencement of mediation, agreement to mediate, appointment of mediator and fees and costs, as well as confidentiality protection. The SIMC Mediation Rules requires any party or parties wishing to mediate to file a request for mediation in the specified format.[3238] If the request for mediation is pursuant to an agreement to mediate, this document is required to be submitted to the SIMC.[3239] If not, SIMC will contact the parties regarding the proposal for mediation, and may assist the parties in considering the proposal and assist in the parties entering an agreement to mediate.[3240]

864. The parties may choose to nominate their own mediator, whether from SIMC's panel of mediators or outside of it. However, if they fail to do so within ten days, SIMC shall appoint a mediator and in doing so will consider the prospective mediator's attributes, including but not limited to nationality, language, skills, qualifications, areas of expertise, experience, and the prospective mediator's availability.[3241] Before confirmation or appointment, a prospective mediator is required to make a written declaration of his or her acceptance, availability, impartiality and independence, and is also obligated to immediately disclose to the parties any known actual or potential conflicts of interest.[3242] A process for objection for valid reasons is contemplated by the SIMC Mediation Rules and on receipt of the objection the SIMC may within ten days of receipt of notification of the objections, appoint another mediator.[3243]

865. The fees and costs for SIMC mediations are stipulated in Appendix B of the SIMC Mediation Rules and include a non-refundable filing fee, administrative fee on a scaled basis depending on the amount in dispute, and the mediator's fees.

866. The SIMC's role in the conduct of the mediation includes determining the location of the mediation in consultation with the parties, assisting parties with entering into a mediation agreement, arranging a suitable venue and date for mediation, organizing the exchange of any pertinent information and documents, providing administrative and logistical support; and providing case management

---

3237. *Executive Summary: Recommendations of the Working Group to Develop Singapore into a Centre for International Commercial Mediation*, http://www.mlaw.gov.sg/content/dam/minlaw/corp/News/FINAL%20ICMWG%20Press%20Release%20-%20Annex%20A.pdf, 30 Sep. 2017.
3238. SIMC Mediation Rules, Rule 2.1.
3239. SIMC Mediation Rules, Rule 3.1.
3240. SIMC Mediation Rules, Rule 3.3.
3241. SIMC Mediation Rules, Rules 4.1–4.4.
3242. SIMC Mediation Rules, Rule 4.5.
3243. SIMC Mediation Rules, Rule 4.7.

services.[3244] Where appropriate, SIMC may also arrange for a pre-mediation conference (whether in person or otherwise) to discuss the manner and procedure for the conduct of the mediation, including setting relevant timelines.[3245]

867. In collaboration with the SIAC, SIMC has launched an arbitration-mediation-arbitration (AMA) service that has been said to 'be tailored to [users'] needs for time- and cost-efficient dispute resolution, with a focus on finding mediated solutions to business disputes that look to the future rather than to the past'.[3246] The AMA service is governed by the SIAC-SIMC AMA Protocol, which provides that an arbitration shall be commenced according to the SIAC Arbitration Rules and then stayed for mediation at the SIMC after the filing of the notice of arbitration and response to the notice of arbitration and the appointment of the tribunal.[3247]

868. The mediation is conducted in accordance with the SIMC Mediation Rules and will terminate within eight weeks unless parties can successfully apply to the extend time. If all the issues in dispute can be settled at mediation, the parties may request the arbitral tribunal to record a consent award; if not, any remaining issues can continue with arbitration. SIMC is also in the process of implementing:

(a) deal making service to assist parties in negotiating sustainable deals;
(b) post-merger facilitation to maximize cooperation and mutual benefit from mergers;
(c) dispute process design service to assist users to develop appropriate processes to manage disputes effectively;
(d) online dispute resolution service to resolve disputes more efficiently; and
(e) e-dossier of profiles of experienced mediators that will include a feedback digest.[3248]

§2. Singapore International Mediation Institute

869. SIMI is an independent non-profit entity supported by the Ministry of Law and the National University of Singapore.[3249] SIMI serves as a professional standards body and certifies the competency of mediators, enforces world-class standards of professional ethics, delivers impartial information about mediation, and

3244. SIMC Mediation Rules, Rule 6.1.
3245. SIMC Mediation Rules, Rule 6.5.
3246. C. Boog, *The New SIAC/SIMC AMA-Protocol: A Seamless Multi-tiered Dispute Resolution Process Tailored to the User's Needs*, Asian Dispute Review 96 (Apr 2015).
3247. *Singapore International Mediation Centre: SIAC-SIMC Arb-Med-Arb Protocol*, http://simc.com.sg/siac-simc-arb-med-arb-protocol/, 30 Sep. 2017.
3248. *Executive Summary: Recommendations of the Working Group to Develop Singapore into a Centre for International Commercial Mediation*, http://www.mlaw.gov.sg/content/dam/minlaw/corp/News/FINAL%20ICMWG%20Press%20Release%20-%20Annex%20A.pdf, 30 Sep. 2017.
3249. *Executive Summary: Recommendations of the Working Group to Develop Singapore into a Centre for International Commercial Mediation*, http://www.mlaw.gov.sg/content/dam/minlaw/corp/News/FINAL%20ICMWG%20Press%20Release%20-%20Annex%20A.pdf, 30 Sep. 2017.

assists parties to make basic decisions about mediation.[3250] SIMI works with the International Mediation Institute[3251] to drive transparency and competency standards into mediation practice across all fields, worldwide.[3252]

§3. MEDIATION ACT

870. Although there is presently no Mediation Act in Singapore, the Chief Justice has announced that the Ministry of Law is working on a draft bill.[3253] The proposed Mediation Act will apply to mediations conducted in whole or part in Singapore and where parties otherwise agree for it to apply. It will provide for the enforceability of mediated settlement agreements as orders of court and contain provisions on confidentiality and the admissibility of communications made in the course of mediation as evidence in court. It will also extend exceptions under the Legal Profession Act[3254] that are currently applicable to arbitration to mediation.[3255] It is not meant to regulate mediators and mediation.[3256]

3250. *Executive Summary: Recommendations of the Working Group to Develop Singapore into a Centre for International Commercial Mediation*, http://www.mlaw.gov.sg/content/dam/minlaw/corp/News/FINAL%20ICMWG%20Press%20Release%20-%20Annex%20A.pdf, 30 Sep. 2017.

3251. *See* generally *International Mediation Institute*, www.IMImediation.org, 30 Sep. 2017.

3252. *See* generally *Singapore International Mediation Centre*, www.simi.org.sg, 30 Sep. 2017.

3253. *Speech of the Honourable the Chief Justice Sundaresh Menon at the Opening of the Singapore International Mediation Centre*, http://simc.com.sg/wp-content/uploads/2014/11/Opening-of-the-Singapore-International-Mediation-Centre-on-5-November-20....pdf, 30 Sep. 2017.

3254. (Cap. 161, 2009 Rev. Ed.).

3255. *Executive Summary: Recommendations of the Working Group to Develop Singapore into a Centre for International Commercial Mediation*, http://www.mlaw.gov.sg/content/dam/minlaw/corp/News/FINAL%20ICMWG%20Press%20Release%20-%20Annex%20A.pdf, 30 Sep. 2017.

3256. *Executive Summary: Recommendations of the Working Group to Develop Singapore into a Centre for International Commercial Mediation*, http://www.mlaw.gov.sg/content/dam/minlaw/corp/News/FINAL%20ICMWG%20Press%20Release%20-%20Annex%20A.pdf, 30 Sep. 2017.

Selected Bibliography

§1. Books and Chapters

Assessment of General Damages in Personal Injury Cases. 8th edn. Oxford: Oxford University Press, 2006.

Boulle, L. & H.H. Teh. *Mediation – Principles, Process and Practice*. Singapore: Butterworths Asia, 2000.

Bull, C. & J. Pinsler. *Civil Procedure: Annual Review of Singapore Cases*. Singapore: Singapore Academy of Law, 2000.

Bull, C. & J. Pinsler. *Civil Procedure: Annual Review of Singapore Cases*. Singapore: Singapore Academy of Law, 2001.

Bull, C. & J. Pinsler. *Civil Procedure: Annual Review of Singapore Cases*. Singapore: Singapore Academy of Law, 2002.

Bull, C. & J. Pinsler. *Civil Procedure: Annual Review of Singapore Cases*. Singapore: Singapore Academy of Law, 2003.

Bull, C. & J. Pinsler. *Civil Procedure: Annual Review of Singapore Cases*. Singapore: Singapore Academy of Law, 2004.

Bull, C. & J. Pinsler. *Civil Procedure: Annual Review of Singapore Cases*. Singapore: Singapore Academy of Law, 2005.

Bull, C. & J. Pinsler. *Civil Procedure: Annual Review of Singapore Cases*. Singapore: Singapore Academy of Law, 2006.

Bull, C. & J. Pinsler. *Civil Procedure: Annual Review of Singapore Cases*. Singapore: Singapore Academy of Law, 2007.

Bull, C. & J. Pinsler. *Civil Procedure: Annual Review of Singapore Cases*. Singapore: Singapore Academy of Law, 2008.

Bull, C. & J. Pinsler. *Civil Procedure: Annual Review of Singapore Cases*. Singapore: Singapore Academy of Law, 2009.

Bull, C. & J. Pinsler. *Civil Procedure: Annual Review of Singapore Cases*. Singapore: Singapore Academy of Law, 2010.

Bull, C. & J. Pinsler. *Civil Procedure: Annual Review of Singapore Cases*. Singapore: Singapore Academy of Law, 2011.

Bull, C. & J. Pinsler. *Civil Procedure: Annual Review of Singapore Cases*. Singapore: Singapore Academy of Law, 2012.

Chua, E. & L. Leo. 'Civil Procedure'. In *The Development of Singapore Law: 20 Years of the Application of English Law Act*, edited by Y.H. Goh & P. Tan. Singapore: Academy Publishing, 2013.

Collins, L. (ed.). *Dicey, Morris and Collins on the Conflict of Laws.* 14th edn. UK: Sweet & Maxwell, 2006.
Garner, B.A. (ed.). *Black's Law Dictionary*. United Kingdom: Thomson Reuters, 2009.
Guidelines for the Assessment of General Damages in Personal Injury Cases. Singapore: Academy Publishing, 2010.
Goh Y.H. & P. Tan (eds). *The Development of Singapore Law: 20 Years of the Application of English Law Act*. Singapore: Academy Publishing, 2013.
Lee, J. *Conflict of Laws: Annual Review of Singapore Cases.* Singapore: Singapore Academy of Law, 2008.
Lim, A., et al. *Assessment of Damages: Personal Injuries and Fatal Accidents*. 2nd edn. Singapore: LexisNexis, 2005.
Lowe, N. & B. Sufrin. *The Law of Contempt*. 3rd edn. London: Butterworths, 1996.
Marie, J. & M. Faizal (eds). *The Criminal Procedure Code of Singapore*. Singapore: Academy Publishing, 2012.
McGregor, H. *McGregor on Damages*. 17th edn. Sweet & Maxwell, 2003.
Phang, A. *From Foundation to Legacy – The Second Charter of Justice*. Singapore: Singapore Academy of Law, 2006.
Phang, A. *The Development of Singapore Law: Historical and Socio-Legal Perspectives*. Singapore: Butterworths, 1990.
Pinsler, J. *Civil Justice in Singapore*. Singapore: Butterworths, 2000.
Pinsler, J. *Ethics and Professional Responsibility*. Singapore: Academy Publishing, 2007.
Pinsler, J. *Evidence and the Litigation Process*. 3rd edn. Singapore: LexisNexis, 2010.
Pinsler, J. *Principles of Civil Procedure*. Singapore: Academy Publishing, 2013.
Pinsler, J. *Singapore Court Practice 2009*. Singapore: LexisNexis, 2009.
Siyuan, C. 'Criminal Evidence and Procedure'. In *The Development of Singapore Law: 20 Years of the Application of English Law Act*, edited by Y.H. Goh & P. Tan. Singapore: Academy Publishing, 2013.
Selvam, G.P. (ed.). *Singapore Civil Procedure 2013*. Vol. 1. Singapore: Sweet & Maxwell Asia, 2012.
Thio, S.M. *Locus Standi and Judicial Review*. Singapore: Singapore University Press, 1971.
Thian, Y.S. 'Singapore'. In *IT Support of the Judiciary*, edited by A. Oskamp, A. R. Lodder & M. Apistola. Netherlands: TMC Asser Press, 2004.
Yeo, T.M. *Halsbury's Laws of Singapore*. Vol. 6(2). Singapore: LexisNexis, 2009.

§2. Articles

Chan, S.K. 'Multiculturalism in Singapore'. *Singapore Academy of Law Journal* 25, no. 1 (2013): 84.
Chan, S.K. 'The Criminal Process – The Singapore Model'. *Singapore Law Review* 17 (1996): 431.
Chi, D. 'Clarification on Leave to Appeal Regime in Respect of Interlocutory Matters: *OpenNet Pte Ltd v Info-Communications Development Authority of Singapore* [2013] SGCA 24'. *Singapore Law Watch Commentaries* (4/2013).

Chng, M. 'Modernising the Criminal Justice Framework – The Criminal Procedure Code 2010'. *Singapore Academy of Law Journal* 23, no. 1 (2011): 23.

Chua, E. 'Defining an "Interlocutory Application"'. *Singapore Law Watch Commentaries* (4/2013).

Chung, Y.J., D. Wong & A.H. Peh. 'Recent Amendments to Order 53 of the Rules of Court'. *Singapore Law Gazette* (November 2011).

Goh, Y.H. & P. Tan. 'An Empirical Study of the Development of Singapore Law'. *Singapore Academy of Law Journal* 23, no. 1 (2011): 176.

Goh, Y.H. 'Demystifying the Inherent Jurisdiction and Inherent Powers of the Singapore Courts: Rethinking the Limits of their Exercise'. *Singapore Journal of Legal Studies* (2011): 178.

Goh, Y.H. 'Setting Aside a Default Judgment: New Developments in Singapore'. *Civil Justice Quarterly* 28, no. 2 (2009): 200.

Khng, N. 'Judicial Independence and the Singapore Judiciary'. *LAWASIA Journal* 7 (2012): 53.

Leong, S. & Z.K. Yeong. 'A Commentary on the Supreme Court Practice Directions Amendment No 1 of 2012'. *Singapore Law Gazette* (March 2012).

Lim, H.M. 'Automatic Discontinuance under Order 21 Rule 2 – First Dormant, Then Dead … '. *Singapore Academy of Law Journal* 13, no. 1 (2001): 150.

Low, J. & D. Quek. 'Introducing a "Presumption of ADR" for Civil Matters in the Subordinate Courts'. *Singapore Law Gazette* (May 2012).

Low, J. & D. Quek. 'The ADR Form in the Subordinate Courts: Finding the Appropriate Mode of Dispute Resolution'. *Singapore Law Gazette* (April 2010).

Phang, A. 'Of Generality and Specificity – A Suggested Approach Toward the Development of an Autochthonous Singapore Legal System'. *Singapore Academy of Law Journal* 1 (1989): 68.

Pinsler, J. 'Destruction of Evidence Prior to the Commencement of Civil Proceedings: How is a Court to Respond'. *Singapore Journal of Legal Studies* (2004): 20.

Pinsler, J. 'Expert's Duty to be Truthful in the Light of the Rules of Court'. *Singapore Academy of Law Journal* 16, no. 2 (2004): 407.

Pinsler, J. 'Last Flight of the Eagle: New Principles Governing the Setting Aside of Judgments in Default'. *Singapore Academy of Law Journal* 21, no. 1 (2009): 161.

Pinsler, J. 'Proportionality in Costs'. *Singapore Academy of Law Journal* 23, no. 1 (2011): 125.

Pinsler, J. 'The Court's Response to Counterclaims in Proceedings for Summary Judgment'. *Singapore Academy of Law Journal* 23, no. 2 (2011): 517.

Poon, N. 'The Use and Abuse of Anti-Arbitration Injunctions: A Way Forward for Singapore'. *Singapore Academy of Law Journal* 25, no. 1 (2013): 244.

Siyuan, C. & E. Chua. 'The Right to Appeal Against a Decision Made on an Interlocutory Application: The Immediate Aftermath of the 2010 Amendments'. *Singapore Academy of Law Journal* 25, no. 2 (2013): 424.

Siyuan, C. & E. Chua. 'Wrongful Convictions in Singapore: A General Survey of Risk Factors'. *Singapore Law Review* 28 (2010): 98.

Siyuan, C. & L. Leo. 'Natural Justice: A Case for Uniform Rigour'. *Singapore Academy of Law Journal* 20, no. 2 (2009): 820.

Siyuan, C. & L. Leo. 'Reasonable Suspicion or Real Likelihood: A Question of Semantics'. *Singapore Journal of Legal Studies* (2008): 446.

Siyuan, C. & N. Poon. 'Recent Developments in Discovery in Singapore'. *Civil Justice Quarterly* 33, no. 1 (2013): 21.

Siyuan, C. & N. Poon. 'Reliability and Relevance as the Touchstones for Admissibility of Evidence in Criminal Proceedings'. *Singapore Academy of Law Journal* 24, no. 2 (2012): 535.

Siyuan, C. 'A Preliminary Survey of the Right to Presumption of Innocence in Singapore'. *LAWASIA Journal* 7 (2012): 79.

Siyuan, C. 'Advanced Fundamentals of Oral Appellate Advocacy in a Moot Court'. *Singapore Law Review* 30 (2012): 45.

Siyuan, C. 'Is the Invocation of Inherent Jurisdiction the Same as the Exercise of Inherent Powers?'. *International Journal of Evidence & Proof* 17, no. 4 (2013): 367.

Siyuan, C. 'Jurisdiction, Power, Inherent Jurisdiction, and Inherent Power'. *Singapore Law Watch Commentaries* (4/2013).

Siyuan, C. 'The Power of the Court to Change an Order for the Division of Matrimonial Assets'. *Singapore Law Watch Commentaries* (12/2012).

Siyuan, C. 'The 2012 Amendments to Singapore's Evidence Act: More Questions than Answers as Regards Expert Opinion Evidence?'. *Statute Law Review* 34, no. 3 (2013): 262.

Siyuan, C. 'The Judicial Discretion to Exclude Relevant Evidence: Perspectives from an Indian Evidence Act Jurisdiction'. *International Journal of Evidence & Proof* 16, no. 4 (2012): 398.

Siyuan, C. 'The Limits on Prosecutorial Discretion in Singapore: Past, Present, and Future'. *International Review of Law* 2 (2013): 5.

Siyuan, C. 'The Prosecution's Duty of Disclosure in Singapore'. *Oxford University Commonwealth Law Journal* 11, no. 2 (2012): 207.

Siyuan, C. 'The Relationship between International Law and Domestic Law'. *Singapore Academy of Law Journal* 23, no. 2 (2011): 350.

Tham, L.J. '*Locus Standi* in Judicial Review: Two Roads Diverge in a Singapore Wood'. *Singapore Law Gazette* (February 2013).

Wong, D. 'Discovering the Right to Criminal Disclosure – Lessons from Civil Procedure'. *Singapore Academy of Law Journal* 25, no. 2 (2013): 548.

Yeong, Z.K. 'Recent Developments in Electronic Discovery: Discovering Electronic Documents and Discovering Documents Electronically'. *Singapore Academy of Law Journal* 19, no. 1 (2007): 101.

§3. Websites

'Attorney-General's Chambers': <www.agc.gov.sg>.
'LawNet': <www.lawnet.com.sg>.
'Law Society of Singapore': <www.lawsociety.org.sg>.
'Rules of Court Singapore': <http://app.supremecourt.gov.sg/default.aspx?pgID=97>.
'Singapore Academy of Law': <www.sal.org.sg>.
'Singapore Institute of Legal Education': <www.sile.org.sg>.
'Singapore Law': <www.singaporelaw.sg>.

'Singapore Law Watch': <www.singaporelawwatch.sg>.
'Singapore Ministry of Law': <www.minlaw.gov.sg>.
'Singapore Parliament': <www.parliament.gov.sg>.
'Singapore Statutes Online': <statutes.agc.gov.sg>.
'Statistics Singapore': <www.singstat.gov.sg>.
'Subordinate Courts of Singapore': <www.subcourts.gov.sg>.
'Supreme Court of Singapore': <www.supcourt.gov.sg>.
'Practice Directions of Subordinate Courts': <http://app.subcourts.gov.sg/subcourts/page.aspx?pageid=4433>.
'Practice Directions of Supreme Court': <http://app.supremecourt.gov.sg/default.aspx?pgID=98>.

Index

The numbers here refer to paragraph numbers.

Index

www.ingramcontent.com/pod-product-compliance
Lightning Source LLC
LaVergne TN
LVHW011102300926
849160LV00008B/256
* 9 7 8 9 4 0 3 5 3 8 2 1 1 *